BARRON'S

THE TRUSTED NAME IN TEST PREP

AP®
Spanish Language and Culture
Premium
2022-2023

Daniel Paolicchi, M.A.
Alice G. Springer, Ph.D.

Acknowledgements

For my fellow language teachers and all students of Spanish.

Published by Kaplan, Inc., d/b/a Barron's Educational Series
1515 W Cypress Creek Road
Fort Lauderdale, FL 33309
www.barronseduc.com

ISBN: 978-1-5062-7845-2

10 9 8 7 6 5 4 3 2 1

Kaplan, Inc., d/b/a Barron's Educational Series print books are available at special quantity discounts to use for sales promotions, employee premiums, or educational purposes. For more information or to purchase books, please call the Simon & Schuster special sales department at 866-506-1949.

Contents

PART ONE: INTRODUCTION

1 Preparing for the AP Spanish Language and Culture Exam 3

General Considerations 3

Description of the Exam 4

Content of the Exam 5

Scoring the Exam 9

Preparing for the Exam 16

PART TWO: READING COMPREHENSION

2 Reading Comprehension 21

General Considerations 21

Reading Strategies 22

Answering Reading Comprehension Questions 23

Understanding Meaning 34

Culture and Content Across Disciplines 39

Practice Reading Comprehension Passages 41

Reading Graphs, Tables, and Charts 42

Answer Key 108

Answers Explained 110

PART THREE: LISTENING COMPREHENSION

3 General Considerations 137

Format of the Exam 137

Types of Questions 138

Strategies for Listening Comprehension 138

Strategies for Improving Listening Comprehension 139

**4 Section I, Part B—Listening Comprehension:
Print and Audio Texts (Combined)** 141

Strategies for Reading 141

Strategies for Listening 142

Print and Audio Texts (Combined) Practice Exercises 145

Answer Key 173

Answers Explained 174

5 Section I, Part B—Listening Comprehension...185

    Strategies for Listening...185

    Listening Comprehension Practice Exercises...189

    Answer Key...213

    Answers Explained...214

PART FOUR: WRITING SKILLS

6 General Considerations...227

    Descriptions of the Writing Tasks of the Exam...227

    Scoring the Writing Tasks...227

7 Section II, Part A—Task 1: Email Reply...229

    Scoring Your Email...229

    Strategies for Task 1: Email Reply...230

    Writing your Email...230

    Sample Email Reply...232

    Email Reply Practice Exercises...235

8 Section II, Part A-Task 2: Argumentative Essay...245

    Scoring Your Argumentative Essay...245

    Strategies for Task 2: Argumentative Essay...246

    Writing Your Argumentative Essay...247

    Useful Vocabulary...248

    Sample Argumentative Essay...249

    Argumentative Essay Practice Exercises...254

PART FIVE: SPEAKING SKILLS

9 General Considerations...277

    Descriptions of the Speaking Tasks of the Exam...277

    Scoring the Speaking Tasks...277

10 Section II, Part B—Task 3: Conversation...279

    Scoring Your Conversation...279

    Strategies for Task 3: Conversation...279

    Useful Vocabulary...281

    Sample Conversation...282

    Conversation Practice Exercises...284

11 Section II, Part B—Task 4: Cultural Comparison...295

    Scoring Your Cultural Comparison Presentation...295

    Strategies for Task 4: Cultural Comparison...295

    Useful Vocabulary...296

    Sample Cultural Comparison Presentation...297

    Cultural Comparison Practice Exercises...299

PART SIX: PRACTICE TESTS

Practice Test 1..309

Section I, Part A—Interpretive Communication: Print Texts.....................309

Section I, Part B—Interpretive Communication: Print and Audio Texts
(Combined)..320

Section II—Interpersonal Writing: Email Reply...................................331

Section II—Presentational Writing: Argumentative Essay.........................333

Section II—Interpersonal Speaking: Conversation................................336

Section II—Presentational Speaking: Cultural Comparison........................337

Answer Key..338

Practice Test 2..341

Section I, Part A—Interpretive Communication: Print Texts.....................341

Section I, Part B—Interpretive Communication: Print and Audio Texts
(Combined)..351

Section II—Interpersonal Writing: Email Reply...................................361

Section II—Presentational Writing: Argumentative Essay.........................363

Section II—Interpersonal Speaking: Conversation................................366

Section II—Presentational Speaking: Cultural Comparison........................367

Answer Key..368

PART SEVEN: APPENDICES

Audioscripts..371

Grammar Review..421

PART ONE
Introduction

Preparing for the AP Spanish Language and Culture Exam

1

GENERAL CONSIDERATIONS

The AP Spanish Language and Culture exam is a rigorous test of your ability to interpret and communicate in Spanish. It challenges you in a holistic way to demonstrate a high level of proficiency in your listening, reading, writing, and speaking abilities. The exam is designed around six interrelated themes that will test your capacity to analyze and talk about a variety of issues, including practices, products, and perspectives of Spanish-speaking communities and how these compare to those of your own culture, as well as about topics that relate to other disciplines, such as science, business, art, technology, social issues, and so on.

An AP course is designed to be the equivalent of a third-year college course. At that level you should be able to understand a native speaker who speaks at a normal speed, to comprehend and analyze print materials intended for native speakers, and to be able to communicate with ease, both orally and in writing, on a variety of topics. You should be able to recognize appropriate social customs reflected in the language, in areas such as register, and also be able to notice references to traditions, customs, and values particular to Spanish-speaking societies.

Overall, the exam calls for much more sophisticated control of the language and of culture than previous exams, so it is best to prepare thoroughly. Success on the exam lies not in how much you know *about* the language, but rather in your ability to *use* the language to effectively interpret written and oral texts and to communicate at a high level on a number of different topics. This book is designed to do just that. It will prepare you for the exam by helping you develop strategies to build both your communicative and interpretive abilities. Plenty of practice exercises are included so you can gauge your readiness and prepare accordingly. The materials selected for this book include the types of selections you are likely to find on the exam, but they are, by no means, a definitive listing. You need to learn as much as you can about Spanish-speaking history, art, literature, business practices, music, humor, customs, traditions, folklore, and other social and cultural topics, and you will need to incorporate that knowledge into your responses on all parts of the exam.

DESCRIPTION OF THE EXAM

Structure

Below you will find general information regarding the structure of the exam and a brief description of each section. For more detailed information and strategies for success in each section, please refer to the section at the beginning of the chapter dedicated to that particular task.

The examination is divided into the following two sections: Interpretive Communication (Multiple-Choice) and Free Response.

STRUCTURE OF THE EXAM				
	Section	Number of questions	Percentage of total exam	Allotted time
Section I: Interpretive Communication (Multiple-Choice)				Approx. 95 mins.
Part A	Print Texts	30 questions	50%	Approx. 40 mins.
Part B	Print and Audio Texts (combined)	35 questions		Approx. 55 mins.
	Audio Texts			
Section II: Free Response				Approx. 85 mins.
Part A	Task 1: Email Reply	1 prompt	50% (12.5% each)	15 mins.
	Task 2: Argumentative Essay	1 prompt		Approx. 55 mins.
Part B	Task 3: Conversation	5 prompts		20 seconds for each response
	Task 4: Cultural Comparison	1 prompt		2 minutes to respond

Section I—Interpretive Communication

Section I is worth 50% of the total score on the examination, and is divided into three parts: Print Texts, Print and Audio Texts (combined), and Audio Texts. All questions in this section are multiple-choice, with both questions and answers printed in the text booklet. At the beginning of each printed and audio source you will be given information about that source so that you can have a contextual base before you begin your task. Section I of the examination is machine-scored, so be sure to bring several sharpened No. 2 pencils to fill out your answer sheet.

Section II—Free Response

Section II is divided into four communicative tasks: Email Reply, Argumentative Essay, Conversation, and Cultural Comparison. Each task is worth 12.5% of the total score. For the written samples, a test booklet will be provided and you must use a blue or black pen on this portion of the examination. You will be asked to submit your recordings in a digital audio file format.

Part A of Section II is the writing section, which comprises the Email Reply (Task 1) and Argumentative Essay (Task 2). For Task 1, Email Reply, your objective is to respond to a formal email that is printed in your test booklet. You will have 15 minutes to read and respond to the email. For Task 2, Argumentative Essay, you are to write an essay in which you respond to a question printed in your test booklet. In addition to the question you are to answer, you will be provided with two print texts and one audio source that present different points of view on the topic. A key component of this task is to gather information from all three texts and use it to support your own point of view on the topic.

Part B of Section II is the speaking portion of the exam, which comprises the Conversation (Task 3) and Cultural Comparison (Task 4). Task 3, Conversation, is a simulated conversation in which you are to initiate, maintain, and appropriately close a conversation. You will be provided with an outline of the flow of the conversation. You will have 5 opportunities to speak. For Task 4, Cultural Comparison, you are to give a two-minute oral presentation in which you answer a question printed in your test booklet. In your response, you have to compare a Spanish-speaking community with your own community. Unlike the previous tasks, you will not be given any additional print or audio material to use in your oral presentation.

CONTENT OF THE EXAM

Themes

The examination is designed around the following six themes:

- **Families and Communities (*Las familias y las comunidades*)**
- **Personal and Public Identities (*Las identidades personales y públicas*)**
- **Science and Technology (*La ciencia y la tecnología*)**
- **Contemporary Life (*La vida contemporánea*)**
- **Global Challenges (*Los desafíos mundiales*)**
- **Beauty and Aesthetics (*La belleza y la estética*)**

These thematic units are broad by design, allowing for multiple topics and contexts within each theme. Before each task, you will be given the overarching theme as a frame of reference. For example, a reading activity that falls under the Families and Communities thematic unit may deal with family celebrations, family structure, education, traditions and values, and so on. Although there are many topics that can fall under each thematic unit, they all will present examples of practices, products, or perspectives from the Spanish-speaking world.

It is also important to remember that these thematic units are interconnected, and one topic that appears in one thematic unit could relate to several other ones. For example, an article about a project in Bogotá, Colombia, that teaches families living in the capital how to grow their own vegetables in small spaces, such as on an apartment terrace, can help answer questions related to several of the thematic units. For example:

- **SCIENCE AND TECHNOLOGY**—How do technological innovations affect our lives and the way we live?
- **FAMILIES AND COMMUNITIES**—How do people in urban environments define quality of life?
- **GLOBAL CHALLENGES**—How do we solve some of the challenges that face world societies?

As you learn about the Spanish-speaking world through these thematic units, you will also be exposed to vocabulary, idioms, and a variety of grammatical structures that will not only reinforce your own knowledge of the language, but will also help you refine your ability to speak and write at a high level about the topic and those related to it. For example, an article on innovative cooking techniques in modern Spanish *haute cuisine* may present vocabulary that you can use to talk about food and cooking, aesthetics, and national identity. Remember, the exam tests your ability to not only interpret at a high level, but also your ability to communicate clearly on a variety of topics related to the thematic units.

Culture and Making Cultural Comparisons

A major focus of the examination is to promote a deeper awareness of culture, the interconnectedness of language and culture, and how Hispanic cultures compare to and differ from your own community. When thinking of culture, you should be thinking of the products, practices, and perspectives of that particular culture (these concepts are explained in more detail in the *Culture* section below). Learning the culture of a community also means learning more about matters that generally relate to other disciplines, such as history, geography, gastronomy, literature, music, religion, science, and so on. Language is also affected by culture, as attested by the variances in the language from country to country or even from region to region in any one country, and language is how cultural practices and perspectives are communicated. In order to effectively be able to talk about culture, you must also have the knowledge of these subject matters as well as the necessary vocabulary to appropriately articulate your ideas.

CULTURE

A common misconception is that all communities in the Spanish-speaking world are alike. Although many share common traits, such as the general language structure and religion, there are many differences within each culture that make each one unique. For example, in Spain it is common to have a three-course meal for lunch, whereas in Costa Rica you would probably be served a one-plate meal called *casado*, which includes rice, beans, a small slice of meat (chicken, beef, pork), some fresh vegetables and a plantain. Likewise, dinner in Spain is generally a smaller meal eaten around 9pm, whereas in Costa Rica it would be a normal-sized meal served between 6pm and 8pm. There are also regional differences in any given country. You might be surprised to learn that in Bogotá, Colombia, in addition to traditional Colombian fare such as *arepas* and *papa criolla*, they have a thriving pub scene, akin to those you would find in England, as well as a number of restaurants serving gourmet hamburgers. This is quite different from the coastal regions of Colombia, where seafood and coconut rice are still staples, and the food tends to be spicier than that of the Andean region of the country.

One of the biggest differences in the Spanish-speaking world is the use of vocabulary. Let's take, for example, the word "cake": in most Spanish-speaking countries, the word used is *pastel*, but in Spain it is also called *tarta*. In the Dominican Republic and Puerto Rico it is called *bizcocho*, in Costa Rica *queque*, and in Argentina, Chile, Venezuela, and Colombia it is *torta*, a word that in Mexico means "sandwich." This is not unlike some of the regional differences in the United States, where a "submarine sandwich" (a sandwich typically made with French-style bread) is also called a "hero," "hoagie," "grinder," or "po-boy," depending on what part of the country you are in. You can find more differences between English in the

United States and in England, where the rear compartment of a car is either a "trunk" (USA) or a "boot" (UK). Therefore, it is important to recognize that each country, and areas within a particular country, will have its differences. One must avoid stereotypes and learn about each culture as its own entity, identifying how it is similar and different to other cultures, and also appreciating what makes it unique.

Products, practices, and perspectives

When thinking about culture and the concept of culture in general, there are three main components to consider: products, practices, and perspectives. Here is a brief description of each:

- **PRODUCTS**—the creations of the target culture. They can be tangible (toys, food, crafts, etc.) or intangible (dances, literature, music);
- **PRACTICES**—behaviors and interactions that are common in the target culture. Examples include the number of meals eaten during the day and at what time these meals are eaten and the types of food and quantity eaten at those times; what people do in their free time; what time they wake up and go to bed; socially expected behaviors when it comes to dating and table manners; how to dress and act at certain events; holiday celebrations, and so on;
- **PERSPECTIVES**—beliefs that are valued within a culture. Examples include the importance of family, importance of quality over quantity, youth over old age, sports and education, and so on.

When learning about a particular community or culture, think about the relationship between these three components. The perspectives (beliefs) of a culture affect its practices (behaviors), and the products are created to facilitate these practices. For example, in many Hispanic communities, a common perspective is that it is important to eat a meal as a family, for this is when they have the opportunity to talk as a family, share stories, and enjoy each other's company. Another perspective is that the food should be made from scratch with fresh ingredients, and typically it is prepared by the mother as a way for her to show her love for her family. Therefore a common practice is for the mother to prepare the food while the family and guests help with other preparations, such as setting the table and prep work. The products are the dishes that are served at the meal and likely are created by following recipes that were passed from generation to generation.

You can build your awareness of culture primarily through authentic print and audio texts. The more you expose yourself to the Spanish-speaking world, the better you will understand its products, practices, and perspectives. In addition, take advantage of every opportunity to interact with Spanish speakers, for that will give you the ability to learn more about their culture and can help you clarify any doubts or questions you may have. Finally, in order to have the most complete understanding of Hispanic culture, it is important to expose yourself to as many different communities in the Spanish-speaking world as you can.

MAKING CULTURAL COMPARISONS

As you further develop your knowledge of Hispanic cultures, it is only natural to think about how they compare to and differ from your own culture. Making cultural comparisons is basically doing just that. Remember that to truly understand culture means to understand the relationship between its products, practices, and perspectives. When comparing cultures, you should think not only about *what* is similar or different, but also *why* it is similar or different. For example, our eating habits in the United States can be quite different from those in Spanish-speaking countries. The biggest meal of the day both in Spain and in Mexico is lunch, which is generally eaten between 1:00 P.M. and 3:00 P.M. (or later, in some cases). These meals tend to include three courses: an appetizer, a main course, and dessert. They also often include a *sobremesa*, or conversation afterward, that also serves as a time to relax and digest the food. In these countries, dinner tends to be considerably smaller and is usually eaten between 8:00 P.M. and 9:00 P.M. This is quite different from meals the United States, where lunches tend to be smaller and rushed and the bigger meal of the day is often dinner. Part of the reason why lunch is the biggest meal in Mexico and Spain is because it revolves around the most active part of the day. Since in the evening things tend to slow down, including one's metabolism, a lighter meal is preferred so that the food can be digested more easily overnight. Therefore, when learning about eating habits in Spain, one can clearly see that a belief, or perspective, is that the amount of food consumed should be in relation to one's activity. The resulting behavior, or practice, is to eat bigger meals during lunchtime and to have a much smaller one during dinner. The resulting product in Spain is that many restaurants serve a *menú del día* (menu of the day) during lunchtime hours that consists of one entrée, a main course, and dessert for a fixed price. In contrast, in the United States lunchtime specials generally tend to be meals that can be fixed and consumed quickly so that the downtime for a meal does not interfere too much with the most productive part of the day.

Finally, when learning about products, practices, and products, it is important to think in terms of how they are similar to or different from those of your own community rather than terms of being better or worse. Each community is proud of its culture, and although a product, practice, or perspective may seem strange to an outsider, a key part of developing better awareness and understanding of another culture is to accept the target culture as is without passing judgment.

TESTING CULTURE ON THE EXAM

Throughout the exam there will be a number of questions testing your awareness of the target cultures. In the reading and listening portions of the exam, you will have questions asking you to demonstrate understanding of a particular vocabulary word, expression, or idea presented in the print or audio text. As mentioned earlier, words may have different meanings depending on the region or country in which they are used. Even if you believe that you already know what a word means, pay attention to the context in which it is used to see if it could mean something different. In both writing sections and the conversation portions of the exam, your knowledge of culture will be demonstrated through the content of your submission. This includes your ability to use appropriate vocabulary and idiomatic expressions, your ability to recognize the correct tone to use (formal/informal), and your ability to make correct references when referring to the features of the target community. The Cultural Comparison (Task 4) of the exam is the most comprehensive test of your knowledge of culture. Here you will be asked to give a two minute presentation on a particular topic in which you are to compare the practices, perspectives, and/or products of a community of the Spanish-speaking world with those of your own community. On this section of the exam you will not be given any external aid, and your ability to answer the question and elaborate relies solely on the knowledge you already have of each culture.

SCORING THE EXAM

To keep the material fresh, new material appears on the exam every year. No matter how the material changes, however, the way your work is evaluated remains the same. Overall scores range from 1 (poor) to 5 (strong). An overall score of 3 on this exam is a passing score. In Section II, it is possible to also earn a score of zero (0) if the response is completely irrelevant to the prompt, a mere restatement of the prompt and/or language in the booklet, or written in English. A hyphen (-) is given to a non-response, meaning that the page is blank or there is no digital recording although the equipment is functioning. Most colleges and universities will award credit for scores of 4 or 5. There are a few that will also give some credit for a score of 3. To find out more information about the policy of colleges and universities when it comes to awarding credit for AP scores, visit the following site:

https://apstudent.collegeboard.org/creditandplacement/search-credit-policies

Scoring Section I

Section I is machine-scored, and the total score for each part is determined by the total number of questions answered correctly. Predicting the number of questions answered correctly and the corresponding AP score for Section I is not an exact science, as it can vary slightly from year to year. However, the following chart can give you a rough estimate of the number of questions you need to answer correctly in order to achieve a certain score.

Part A—Print Texts (30 questions)

Number of questions answered correctly	Approximate AP Score
24–30	5 (Strong)
21–23	4 (Good)
18–20	3 (Fair)
16–17	2 (Weak)
15–0	1 (Poor)

Part B—Print and Audio Texts (combined) and Audio Texts (35 questions)

Number of questions answered correctly	Approximate AP Score
29–35	5 (Strong)
25–28	4 (Good)
20–24	3 (Fair)
17–19	2 (Weak)
16–0	1 (Poor)

Scoring Section II

The scoring of each task in Section II is holistic. This means that each response is considered as a single entity, and its elements are not analyzed separately. For each of the tasks, the main considerations are what the student was able to do (appropriateness of the response within the context of the task, development of ideas), and *how* the student was able to complete the task (use of language, organization of ideas, and use of register). In order to score well on the communicative tasks, the response has to be appropriate, developed, organized, and understandable. A response that is fully understandable but off topic or inappropriate within the context of the task will likely earn a low score. The same is true for a response in which the student makes the attempt to complete the task but whose language makes the response very difficult to understand.

Below are the descriptions of the scoring guides for each task in Section II. You will notice that often the difference in the descriptors from one score to another is a single word, such as "clearly appropriate" instead of "generally appropriate".

Scoring Guildelines

TASK 1—EMAIL REPLY

5 (Strong)

- Maintains the exchange with a response that is clearly appropriate within the context of the task.
- Provides required information (responses to questions, request for details) with frequent elaboration.
- Fully understandable, with ease and clarity of expression; occasional errors do not impede comprehensibility.
- Varied and appropriate vocabulary and idiomatic language.
- Accuracy and variety in grammar, syntax, and usage, with few errors.
- Mostly consistent use of register appropriate for the situation; control of cultural conventions appropriate for formal correspondence (e.g., greeting, closing), despite occasional errors.
- Variety of simple and compound sentences, and some complex sentences.

4 (Good)

- Maintains the exchange with a response that is generally appropriate within the context of the task.
- Provides most required information (responses to questions, request for details) with some elaboration.
- Fully understandable, with some errors that do not impede comprehensibility.
- Varied and generally appropriate vocabulary and idiomatic language.
- General control of grammar, syntax, and usage.
- Generally consistent use of register appropriate for the situation, except for occasional shifts; basic control of cultural conventions appropriate for formal correspondence (e.g., greeting, closing).
- Simple, compound, and a few complex sentences.

3 (Fair)

- Maintains the exchange with a response that is somewhat appropriate but basic within the context of the task.
- Provides most required information (responses to questions, request for details).
- Generally understandable, with errors that may impede comprehensibility.
- Appropriate but basic vocabulary and idiomatic language.
- Some control of grammar, syntax, and usage.
- Use of register may be inappropriate for the situation with several shifts; partial control of conventions for formal correspondence (e.g., greeting, closing), although these may lack cultural appropriateness.
- Simple and a few compound sentences.

2 (Weak)

- Partially maintains the exchange with a response that is minimally appropriate within the context of the task.
- Provides some required information (responses to questions, request for details).
- Partially understandable with errors that force interpretation and cause confusion for the reader.
- Limited vocabulary and idiomatic language.
- Limited control of grammar, syntax, and usage.
- Use of register is generally inappropriate for the situation; includes some conventions for formal correspondence (e.g., greeting, closing) with inaccuracies.
- Simple sentences and phrases.

1 (Poor)

- Unsuccessfully attempts to maintain the exchange by providing a response that is inappropriate within the context of the task.
- Provides little required information (responses to questions, request for details).
- Barely understandable, with frequent or significant errors that impede comprehensibility.
- Very few vocabulary resources.
- Little or no control of grammar, syntax, and usage.
- Minimal or no attention to register; includes significantly inaccurate or no conventions for formal correspondence (e.g., greeting, closing).
- Very simple sentences or fragments.

TASK 2—ARGUMENTATIVE ESSAY

5 (Strong)

- Effective treatment of topic within the context of the task.
- Demonstrates a high degree of comprehension of the sources' viewpoints, with very few minor inaccuracies.
- Integrates content from all three sources in support of the essay.
- Presents and defends the student's own viewpoint on the topic with a high degree of clarity; develops a persuasive argument with coherence and detail.

- Organized essay; effective use of transitional elements or cohesive devices.
- Fully understandable, with ease and clarity of expression; occasional errors do not impede comprehensibility.
- Varied and appropriate vocabulary and idiomatic language.
- Accuracy and variety in grammar, syntax, and usage, with few errors.
- Develops paragraph-length discourse with a variety of simple and compound sentences, and some complex sentences.

4 (Good)

- Generally effective treatment of topic within the context of the task.
- Demonstrates comprehension of the sources' viewpoints; may include a few inaccuracies.
- Summarizes, with limited integration, content from all three sources in support of the essay.
- Presents and defends the student's own viewpoint on the topic with clarity; develops a persuasive argument with coherence.
- Organized essay; some effective use of transitional elements or cohesive devices.
- Fully understandable, with some errors that do not impede comprehensibility.
- Varied and generally appropriate vocabulary and idiomatic language.
- General control of grammar, syntax, and usage.
- Develops mostly paragraph-length discourse with simple, compound, and a few complex sentences.

3 (Fair)

- Suitable treatment of topic within the context of the task.
- Demonstrates a moderate degree of comprehension of the sources' viewpoints; includes some inaccuracies.
- Summarizes content from at least two sources in support of the essay.
- Presents and defends the student's own viewpoint on the topic; develops a somewhat persuasive argument with some coherence.
- Some organization; limited use of transitional elements or cohesive devices.
- Generally understandable, with errors that may impede comprehensibility.
- Appropriate but basic vocabulary and idiomatic language.
- Some control of grammar, syntax, and usage.
- Uses strings of mostly simple sentences, with a few compound sentences.

2 (Weak)

- Unsuitable treatment of topic within the context of the task.
- Demonstrates a low degree of comprehension of the sources' viewpoints; information may be limited or inaccurate.
- Summarizes content from one or two sources; may not support the essay.
- Presents, or at least suggests, the student's own viewpoint on the topic; develops an unpersuasive argument somewhat incoherently.
- Limited organization; ineffective use of transitional elements or cohesive devices.
- Partially understandable, with errors that force interpretation and cause confusion for the reader.

- Limited vocabulary and idiomatic language.
- Limited control of grammar, syntax, and usage.
- Uses strings of simple sentences and phrases.

1 (Poor)

- Almost no treatment of topic within the context of the task.
- Demonstrates poor comprehension of the sources' viewpoints; includes frequent and significant inaccuracies.
- Mostly repeats statements from sources or may not refer to any sources.
- Minimally suggests the student's own viewpoint on the topic; argument is undeveloped or incoherent.
- Little or no organization; absence of transitional elements and cohesive devices.
- Barely understandable, with frequent or significant errors that impede comprehensibility.
- Very few vocabulary resources.
- Little or no control of grammar, syntax, and usage.
- Very simple sentences or fragments.

TASK 3—CONVERSATION

5 (Strong)

- Maintains the exchange with a series of responses that is clearly appropriate within the context of the task.
- Provides required information (e.g., responses to questions, statement and support of opinion) with frequent elaboration.
- Fully understandable, with ease and clarity of expression; occasional errors do not impede comprehensibility.
- Varied and appropriate vocabulary and idiomatic language.
- Accuracy and variety in grammar, syntax, and usage, with few errors.
- Mostly consistent use of register appropriate for the conversation.
- Pronunciation, intonation, and pacing make the response comprehensible; errors do not impede comprehensibility.
- Clarification or self-correction (if present) improves comprehensibility.

4 (Good)

- Maintains the exchange with a series of responses that is generally appropriate within the context of the task.
- Provides most required information (e.g., responses to questions, statement and support of opinion) with some elaboration.
- Fully understandable, with some errors that do not impede comprehensibility.
- Varied and generally appropriate vocabulary and idiomatic language.
- General control of grammar, syntax, and usage.
- Generally consistent use of register appropriate for the conversation, except for occasional shifts.
- Pronunciation, intonation, and pacing make the response mostly comprehensible; errors do not impede comprehensibility.
- Clarification or self-correction (if present) usually improves comprehensibility.

3 (Fair)

- Maintains the exchange with a series of responses that is somewhat appropriate within the context of the task.
- Provides most required information (e.g., responses to questions, statement and support of opinion).
- Generally understandable, with errors that may impede comprehensibility.
- Appropriate but basic vocabulary and idiomatic language.
- Some control of grammar, syntax, and usage.
- Use of register may be inappropriate for the conversation with several shifts.
- Pronunciation, intonation, and pacing make the response generally comprehensible; errors occasionally impede comprehensibility.
- Clarification or self-correction (if present) sometimes improves comprehensibility.

2 (Weak)

- Partially maintains the exchange with a series of responses that is minimally appropriate within the context of the task.
- Provides some required information (e.g., responses to questions, statement and support of opinion).
- Partially understandable, with errors that force interpretation and cause confusion for the listener.
- Limited vocabulary and idiomatic language.
- Limited control of grammar, syntax, and usage.
- Use of register is generally inappropriate for the conversation.
- Pronunciation, intonation, and pacing make the response difficult to comprehend at times; errors impede comprehensibility.
- Clarification or self-correction (if present) usually does not improve comprehensibility.

1 (Poor)

- Unsuccessfully attempts to maintain the exchange by providing a series of responses that is inappropriate within the context of the task.
- Provides little required information (e.g., responses to questions, statement and support of opinion).
- Barely understandable, with frequent or significant errors that impede comprehensibility.
- Very few vocabulary resources.
- Little or no control of grammar, syntax, and usage.
- Minimal or no attention to register.
- Pronunciation, intonation, and pacing make the response difficult to comprehend; errors impede comprehensibility.
- Clarification or self-correction (if present) does not improve comprehensibility.

TASK 4—CULTURAL COMPARISON

5 (Strong)

- Effective treatment of topic within the context of the task.
- Clearly compares the student's own community with the target culture, including supporting details and relevant examples.
- Demonstrates understanding of the target culture, despite a few minor inaccuracies.
- Organized presentation; effective use of transitional elements or cohesive devices.
- Fully understandable, with ease and clarity of expression; occasional errors do not impede comprehensibility.
- Varied and appropriate vocabulary and idiomatic language.
- Accuracy and variety in grammar, syntax, and usage, with few errors.
- Mostly consistent use of register appropriate for the presentation.
- Pronunciation, intonation, and pacing make the response comprehensible; errors do not impede comprehensibility.
- Clarification or self-correction (if present) improves comprehensibility.

4 (Good)

- Generally effective treatment of topic within the context of the task.
- Compares the student's own community with the target culture, including some supporting details and mostly relevant examples.
- Demonstrates some understanding of the target culture, despite minor inaccuracies.
- Organized presentation; some effective use of transitional elements or cohesive devices.
- Fully understandable, with some errors that do not impede comprehensibility.
- Varied and generally appropriate vocabulary and idiomatic language.
- General control of grammar, syntax, and usage.
- Generally consistent use of register appropriate for the presentation, except for occasional shifts.
- Pronunciation, intonation, and pacing make the response mostly comprehensible; errors do not impede comprehensibility.
- Clarification or self-correction (if present) usually improves comprehensibility.

3 (Fair)

- Suitable treatment of topic within the context of the task.
- Compares the student's own community with the target culture, including a few supporting details and examples.
- Demonstrates a basic understanding of the target culture, despite inaccuracies.
- Some organization; limited use of transitional elements or cohesive devices.
- Generally understandable, with errors that may impede comprehensibility.
- Appropriate but basic vocabulary and idiomatic language.
- Some control of grammar, syntax, and usage.
- Use of register may be inappropriate for the presentation with several shifts.
- Pronunciation, intonation, and pacing make the response generally comprehensible; errors occasionally impede comprehensibility.
- Clarification or self-correction (if present) sometimes improves comprehensibility.

2 (Weak)

- Unsuitable treatment of topic within the context of the task.
- Presents information about the student's own community and the target culture, but may not compare them; consists mostly of statements with no development.
- Demonstrates a limited understanding of the target culture; may include several inaccuracies.
- Limited organization; ineffective use of transitional elements or cohesive devices.
- Partially understandable, with errors that force interpretation and cause confusion for the listener.
- Limited vocabulary and idiomatic language.
- Limited control of grammar, syntax, and usage.
- Use of register is generally inappropriate for the presentation.
- Pronunciation, intonation, and pacing make the response difficult to comprehend at times; errors impede comprehensibility.
- Clarification or self-correction (if present) usually does not improve comprehensibility.

1 (Poor)

- Almost no treatment of topic within the context of the task.
- Presents information only about the student's own community or only about the target culture, and may not include examples.
- Demonstrates minimal understanding of the target culture; generally inaccurate.
- Little or no organization; absence of transitional elements and cohesive devices.
- Barely understandable, with frequent or significant errors that impede comprehensibility.
- Very few vocabulary resources.
- Little or no control of grammar, syntax, and usage.
- Minimal or no attention to register.
- Pronunciation, intonation, and pacing make the response difficult to comprehend; errors impede comprehensibility.
- Clarification or self-correction (if present) does not improve comprehensibility.

PREPARING FOR THE EXAM

This book is divided into the four skill areas addressed on the exam: reading, listening, writing, and speaking. Each chapter is devoted to one single skill area but also contains information that will be useful in other skill areas. Strategies are included before each skill to help you, and some practice activities will include additional exercises not tested on the exam, but that are helpful to improving overall interpretive and communicative abilities. Also, after all reading and listening activities, as well as after communicative tasks 1 (Email Reply) and 2 (Argumentative Essay), you will find a section called "Cultural Awareness" that will highlight any products, practices, and perspectives that are present in the print and audio texts that accompany these activities. This is a good opportunity to reflect on these aspects of culture and how they are similar or different than your own community. This reflections will certainly help you better prepare for Task 4 (Cultural Comparison).

In addition to using this book as a guide, here are some suggestions that will help you prepare for this exam:

- Use Spanish as much as possible in all four skill areas (speaking, listening, writing, and reading). There is a strong correlation between different skill areas, and improvement in any one area usually affects and enhances ability in other skill areas.
- Build your vocabulary and your ability to use different grammatical structures by using new vocabulary words and repeating phrases and sentences out loud. Speaking the language out loud will help you better internalize the language. You can easily accomplish this on your own by reading your print texts out loud to yourself and by repeating sentences and phrases that you hear in your audio texts.
- When you encounter an unfamiliar word, use context clues to infer its meaning.
- Use circumlocution as much as possible.
- Identify early the skill areas that are most difficult for you and work often on developing them.
- When speaking and writing, don't be afraid to make mistakes. Look at your mistakes as opportunities to improve. After making a mistake, repeat the correct structure a few times and try again later. Many of the mistakes we routinely make are due to having internalized the language incorrectly. The only way to reverse this is by repeating the correct structure often.
- Practice speaking Spanish as much as possible. Speak with other students and with people in your community, or join a tutoring program in your community to teach English to native speakers of Spanish. Often, volunteering to teach English will put you in contact with native speakers.
- Learn as much as possible about customs, history, and current events of various Spanish-speaking countries. This will help develop better awareness of the products, practices, and perspectives of Spanish-speaking communities, and will help you on the free-response section of the exam.

Useful Websites for Additional Practice

There are many websites available to help build your proficiency in Spanish. Here are but a few that you may find helpful:

www.bbc.com/mundo (Extensive news site in Spanish with both print and audio texts)
www.muyinteresante.es (Contains many short articles on a variety of topics)
https://news.un.org/es/ (Official page of the United Nations, with print and audio texts)
www.rtve.es (Spanish online TV and radio channel with multiple shows and stories)
https://radio.garden/ (Website through which you can access any radio station in the world)
www.wordreference.com (Great reference site that can help with defining words and looking up idioms and verb conjugations)

PART TWO
Reading Comprehension

Reading Comprehension

2

GENERAL CONSIDERATIONS

Reading comprehension is one of the more important skills that you should develop over the course of your preparation. It is the one proficiency skill that is integrated throughout the examination. You will only be tested on your ability to comprehend print texts in Section I, Part A, and in the Print and Audio Texts (combined) portion of Section I, Part B, but you will also need to demonstrate good reading comprehension abilities to successfully complete Section II, Task 1 (EMail Reply), and Task 2 (Argumentative Essay).

Format of the Exam

In Section I, Part A, you will be given four reading passages and have to answer a total of 30 questions. The reading portion of the exam is usually divided in following formats:

- Advertisement, pamphlet, promotional material, or announcement (5 questions)
- Fragment of a literary text (7 questions)
- Article accompanied by a graph, table, or chart (11 questions)
- Correspondence (7 questions)

The number in parentheses indicates the typical number of questions you can expect for each reading.

Types of Questions

Reading comprehension is more than simply understanding a text. You will also be tested on your ability to think critically about the selection, infer meaning, make interdisciplinary and cultural connections, and make predictions. Although questions for each reading passage will vary, you can confidently expect them to fall into one of the following four categories:

- **UNDERSTAND CONTENT.** Identify the main idea and details.
- **THINK CRITICALLY.** Identify the purpose of the text, the target audience, point of view of its author, the tone or attitude, how the author communicates his/her ideas, and be able to separate fact from opinion, make predictions based on information presented in the text.
- **UNDERSTAND MEANING.** Infer the meaning of unfamiliar words and expressions using context clues, and comprehend a wide variety of vocabulary, idioms, and cultural expressions.
- **UNDERSTAND CULTURE AND CONTENT ACROSS DISCIPLINES.** Identify practices, products and perspectives of Hispanic cultures and information pertaining to other disciplines, such as science, geography, history, art, and so on.

Each question will have four answer choices to choose from. Out of the four options, there will be three distractors, or incorrect choices. These distractors are often not the complete opposite of the correct answer and are never nonsensical or ungrammatical. Sometimes these distractors are based on words that are false cognates or words that cause misconceptions or errors that teachers know students make. Distractors may also only be partially incorrect or correct. When selecting the correct answer, focus on the answer whose idea is correct, not the one that uses similar vocabulary or language seen in the text. You will not be penalized for incorrect answers, so if you don't know the answer, always make an educated guess.

READING STRATEGIES

The following section contains suggestions for how to better develop your reading comprehension ability and to answer the types of questions you will be asked. First is a list of strategies that you should apply when reading. This is followed by several examples of how to answer the types of questions you will be asked on the exam. After each example, there is a discussion of which answers are correct or incorrect. The logic of the answer is also explained. Pay close attention to the logic so that you can understand your errors.

Suggestions for Reading

You should follow these steps every time you approach a reading comprehension text.

Before Reading the Text

- **READ THE INTRODUCTION AND TITLE.** All reading selections will have a brief introduction about the text and its source. This information is helpful to get you thinking about what information will be presented, as well as the possible point of view of the author and intended audience.
- **SCAN THE WHOLE PASSAGE.** Scanning will help you get a general idea of the topic. Many articles are divided into subsections, and scanning beforehand will allow you to predict what information might be presented in each section.
- **SCAN THE QUESTIONS.** This will give you an idea of what information you will need to find in the passage.
- **USE VISUALS.** If the passage includes a graphic, make a note of its relation to the printed words. This will help you determine the purpose of the visual insert.

While Reading the Text

- **VISUALIZE AS YOU READ.** Imagine in your mind's eye what is being said. This will help you understand the ideas and tone of the text, and reduce the tendency to translate.
- **UNDERLINE KEY WORDS AND IDEAS.** This will allow you to quickly retrieve information from the text.
- **IDENTIFY THE MAIN IDEA.** Look for repetition of words or phrases, or look for words that are topically related.
- **IDENTIFY SETTING, ACTION, AND MAIN CHARACTERS.** When determining the setting, note the time frame and the place of the action. If there is any action, get a general idea of what happens. For more factual texts, such as a report, note when,

where, how, and why it happened. If a character has no name, identify him or her by some other characteristic, such as color of hair, personality, or clothing.

- **MAKE NOTE OF ELEMENTS RELATING TO HISPANIC CULTURE.** Remember that the examination tests both language *and* culture. It is important to identify and understand any products (food, clothing, art, etc.), the practices (customs and traditions), and perspectives (attitudes, values, and ideas) of Hispanic culture and be able to recognize how they differ from those of your own culture. Even if you are not asked a specific question about this information, it is useful to further develop your awareness of Hispanic culture and societies.
- **FOCUS ON WORDS YOU RECOGNIZE AND USE CONTEXT CLUES TO INFER THE MEANING OF UNFAMILIAR WORDS.** Unknown words are often restated with other words you do know, especially if they are important to understand the passage. There are a number of strategies that can help you infer meaning from unfamiliar vocabulary, and these are discussed more in depth in the following section.

After Reading the Text

- **REFLECT ON THE READING.** Think of the reading as a whole and synthesize the information presented. Take the information presented to you at face value, regardless of whether or not you agree with the information presented or with the author's point of view.

ANSWERING READING COMPREHENSION QUESTIONS

Always select the answer whose idea best reflects one presented in the text. Don't be distracted by answers that use the same vocabulary found in the text. The correct answer will often paraphrase the information in the text. Use the process of elimination to help answer any questions that you may have left unanswered.

The following exercises will help you better navigate the different types of questions you will find in the reading comprehension portion of the exam.

Understanding Content

Understanding content encompasses one's ability to identify the main idea of a passage and the details relating to the passage.

Identify the Main Idea

The main idea of a text is what the author wants the reader to understand is important in the entirety of the text. This is different than simply identifying what the text is about. To identify the main idea, you should scan the passage, including the title, and make a mental note of those words that are important and begin to think about what they all have in common. Pay particular attention to nouns and verbs. Do not worry about words that you do not recognize. Later you can determine which of the words are really important from among those that you do not know. Ignore words that are not needed to tell what the passage is about.

PRÁCTICA

Read the passage and select the best answer for each question that follows.

> —¡Diles que no me maten, Justino! Anda, vete a decirles eso. Que por caridad. Así diles. Diles que lo hagan por caridad.
>
> —No puedo. Hay allí un sargento que no quiere oír hablar nada de ti.
>
> *Línea*
> (5)
> —Haz que te oiga. Date tus mañas y dile que para sustos ya ha estado bueno. Dile que lo haga por caridad de Dios.
>
> —No se trata de sustos. Parece que te van a matar de a de veras. Y yo ya no quiero volver allá.
>
> —Anda otra vez. Solamente otra vez, a ver qué consigues.
>
> —No. No tengo ganas de eso, yo soy tu hijo. Y si voy mucho con ellos, acabarán
> (10) por saber quién soy y les dará por afusilarme a mí también. Es mejor dejar las cosas de este tamaño.

1. ¿Cuál es la actitud del padre de Justino?
   (A) Resignado
   (B) Impávido
   (C) Desesperado
   (D) Asustado

2. ¿Cómo caracterizaría el tipo de hijo que parece ser Justino?
   (A) Egoísta
   (B) Cruel
   (C) Cariñoso
   (D) Temeroso

RESPUESTAS

Pregunta #1: C

The lines by Justino and his father alternate between commands and refusals. The father's every line is a command for his son to go ask, tell, or beg for his life. Justino's every line communicates his desire to not become involved. Through the repetition of the command "*Diles*," the father communicates his desperation, not resignation, fear, or intrepid behavior.

Pregunta #2: D

Justino's fear for his own life overwhelms any familial love that he may have felt for his father. His constant denial and proffered "reason" are not convincing; they sound like excuses, except that there is a grain of truth to the gravity of the situation as he sees it. At the end, Justino confesses that he does not want to press too much because the sergeant apparently does not realize that Justino is the man's son, and Justino does not want the sergeant to know. Although Justino may be self-centered and cruel, his primary reaction is fear. This is indicated by the constant repetition of his denial, and after each denial, an explanation of his position in the matter.

Think Critically

In addition to understanding the passage, you must also be able to think critically about the information presented in the reading selection. The types of questions on the exam that deal with critical thinking may ask you to consider the purpose and reason of the selection, determine the tone and attitude of the author, identify the intended reader, separate fact from opinion, and make assumptions. The following steps will help you become a better critical reader:

- **READ AND SUMMARIZE.** Read the selection first so that you understand the content. Next, try to summarize the information you just read. The summary should be the main message or central idea of the passage.
- **ANALYZE.** Look at the evidence presented, draw inferences where you can, and identify the tone.
- **SYNTHESIZE.** Connect the information you read to your own prior knowledge about the theme and any personal experiences you may have on the topic. Remember that all readings somehow relate to one of the six overarching themes.
- **EVALUATE.** Assess the overall work. This is where you can determine the intended audience, the tone of the author, the validity of the argument, what evidence may be missing, and other predictions and assumptions that go beyond the text.

These steps should be implemented in order, and you should develop the habit of thinking critically with all your readings.

Questions About Purpose and Reason

There are two types of questions you are most likely going to see on the exam that deal with purpose and reason: (1) one that asks about the overall purpose of the reading selection, and (2) one that asks about the purpose, the reason, and/or the motivation of a particular event that takes place within the text. Take a look at the following samples.

PRÁCTICA #1

Read the passage and answer the questions that follow.

Para los viajes en todas las rutas TACA se permite una pieza de mano con un peso máximo de 22 libras (10 kilos) cuyas dimensiones exteriores (alto + largo + ancho) no exceda de 115 centímetros (45 pulgadas). En los módulos de los aeropuertos están los medidores de equipaje, allí puedes verificar las dimensiones de tu equipaje de mano con las normas vigentes.

Línea
(5)

Nuestros Socios LifeMiles Élite (Gold y Diamond) tienen derecho a 2 piezas de mano con un peso máximo de 22 libras (10 kilos) cada una, cuyas dimensiones exteriores (alto + largo + ancho) no exceda de 115 centímetros (45 pulgadas).*

Los Pasajeros Gold Star Alliance en clase ejecutiva tienen derecho a 2 piezas de

(10)

mano con un peso máximo de 22 libras (10 kilos) cada una, cuyas dimensiones exteriores (alto + largo + ancho) no exceda de 115 centímetros (45 pulgadas).*

*Excluye vuelos desde/hacia Estados Unidos; las regulaciones pueden variar por país y pueden ser modificadas por las autoridades de cada país en cualquier momento y sin previo aviso.

—*www.taca.com/esp/syi/bag/bagbagpol.asp?id=14*

1. ¿Cuál parece ser la función de este trozo?
   (A) Informarle a la gente de los diferentes tamaños de equipaje
   (B) Presentar la política de equipaje de mano de una compañía aérea
   (C) Mostrar los beneficios de ser socio de un club
   (D) Explicar las diferencias en regulaciones por distintos países

2. ¿Qué función tienen los *medidores de equipaje* (línea 4)?
   (A) Para medir las dimensiones de las piezas de equipaje
   (B) Para averiguar cuánto puede caber en las maletas
   (C) Para encontrar el peso del equipaje
   (D) Para asegurar que sea una pieza de mano reglamentaria

RESPUESTAS

Pregunta #1: B

This piece informs the general public about what type of carry-on luggage is permissible. It only presents one size—the maximum weight and dimensions allowed, thus eliminating (A). Choice (D) really has nothing to do with the selection, and, although the passage does include information about different membership groups, it never makes an attempt to persuade someone to try to become a member, thus eliminating (C) as an option.

Pregunta #2: D

Be careful not to be tricked by the repetition of a form of the word *medir* in the question and in the first option. The *medidor* does not measure luggage, nor does it weigh the bag. It is used to verify that the piece of luggage is small enough to be considered a carry-on according to the established *reglamento*, or regulations.

PRÁCTICA #2

Read the passage and answer the questions that follow.

> Y las manifestaciones callejeras se suceden. Pueden hacerse para la defensa del medio ambiente o contra un alcalde superviviente de la dictadura, a favor de los obreros panaderos o del Polisario, pero a juzgar por las fotografías o teledia-
> Línea rios, lo más importante para los participantes es estar allí, ser vistos y oídos. Cada
> (5) vez que una cámara de cine o fotografía les enfoca miran fijos, sonríen, levantan los brazos; en las fotos de periódicos, los de adelante aparecen satisfechos y orgullosos; los de detrás, se asoman por entre las cabezas entre los afortunados para "estar" a su vez común en esas fotografías de grupos infantiles.

1. Según el autor, ¿por qué participa la gente en las manifestaciones callejeras?
   (A) Para ser vista y reconocida
   (B) Para celebrar sus nuevas libertades
   (C) Protesta la censura del gobierno
   (D) Quiere efectuar algún cambio social

2. ¿Cómo reaccionan esas personas al ver una cámara?
   - (A) Tratan de ocultar los rostros.
   - (B) Se enorgullecen de su supuesta importancia.
   - (C) Tienen miedo de ser reconocidos.
   - (D) Se enfadan porque sacan fotografías de ellos.

RESPUESTAS

Pregunta #1: A

Don't be tricked by the reason the protests take place. The question asks you why the people choose to participate. According to the text, the author believes the people solely want to be seen and heard. No indication is given as to whether they actually support the protest itself.

Pregunta #2: B

This answer is quite straightforward. The other three all convey a similar idea—that of not wanting to be seen.

Determining Tone and Attitude

One of the more difficult aspects of reading is determining the tone of the passage. The tone or attitude of the passage refers to the author's relationship to his or her material or to the readers, or both. By changing voice or manner, a writer can create a particular tone in a work. Sometimes the writer's attitude is revealed in the use of figures of speech, such as hyperbole (exaggeration), various types of images (simile, metaphor, or metonym), humor (puns), or other devices, such as personification. In the following passages, notice the choice of words and how they are used to create a particular tone. This tone or attitude, at times, can indicate what type of writing the passage presents.

PRÁCTICA #1

Read the passage and answer the question that follows.

> El primordial objeto de la vida, para muchos millones de norteamericanos, está en "divertirse" o "troncharse de risa". "Divertirse" no es ningún asunto complicado. El cine constituye la mayor de las diversiones. Bailar, jugar a los naipes, patinar, o
> *Línea* besar y abrazar en un coche a una muchacha en cualquier momento es divertirse.
> *(5)* Mirar los grabados en una revista y beber jugo de naranja es también una gran diversión. A los norteamericanos les satisface todo y gozan de todo. Encontrarse en la calle a Peter Lorre es un gran entretenimiento; platicar con una hórrida jamona en un fonducho de mala muerte es magnífico; presenciar un buen accidente auto-movilístico en la calle es demasiado maravilloso para describirlo con palabras.

1. Ante el espectáculo de los norteamericanos tratando de divertirse en todo momento, ¿cuál de las siguientes emociones muestra el tono del narrador?
   - (A) Aburrido
   - (B) Entretenido
   - (C) No afectado
   - (D) Asombrado

RESPUESTA

Pregunta #1: B

The narrator shows a certain detached amusement for the phenomenon he is describing, as is shown in the words he chooses to name his topic: *"El primordial objeto de la vida . . . ."* Among the basic human drives, entertainment does not usually rank alongside self-preservation. The overstatement indicates that this narrator is somewhat detached. He is not commenting on what entertainment means to him, but rather on what it means to the people he is observing. He then enumerates things that he thinks North Americans find entertaining, a list that culminates with the sight of an automobile accident. Any spectacle is entertaining. Choice C is a possible answer, but not the best answer. One does not get the impression from this passage that the writer is entirely indifferent to the subject matter; if he found it entertaining enough to write about, he is not totally indifferent.

PRÁCTICA #2

Read the passage and select the best answer to the question that follows.

> Al sol, ya se sabe, hay que acercarse con las espaldas bien cubiertas. Ninguna imprudencia nos está permitida, pues este astro, que posee una memoria de elefante, puede pasarnos factura cuando menos lo esperamos. Sirve que nosotros lo
>
> *Línea*
> *(5)* tengamos en cuenta al comprar un bronceador. Vale que busquemos uno que nos ofrezca seguridad total de los efectos de rayos ultravioleta. Ahora protegernos del sol veraniego traspasa cuestiones estéticas.

1. ¿Cuál es la idea principal de esta selección?
    - (A) Lo bueno de broncearse durante el verano
    - (B) Los efectos que el sol pueden tener a la piel
    - (C) La importancia de seleccionar bien una crema protectora
    - (D) Lo que hay que hacer en caso de que uno reciba una quemadura

RESPUESTA

Pregunta #1: C

This selection informs the reader about the importance of protecting oneself from the sun. The main recommendation is to select a good sunblock. It highlights that protection is more important than aesthetics. The words that have a common connection that support the main idea are *"cubiertas," "bronceador," "seguridad total,"* and *"protegernos."*

PRÁCTICA #3

Read the passage and select the best answer to the question that follows.

> En el trayecto que se me había encomendado recorrer, hay un puente, en el que a intervalo de un minuto, debían circular por una vía única dos trenes: el que yo manejaba y un tren de mercancías. Sabiendo el peligro de estos cruces, se me
>
> *Línea* habían hecho mil recomendaciones, inútiles, por otra parte, pues es de suponer
> (5) la atención que pondría yo en las señales luminosas.
>
> Al acercarnos al puente en cuestión, divisé claramente la luz verde, que me daba libre paso, y respirando aliviado, aumenté un poco la velocidad de nuestra marcha, no mucho sin embargo, dado que había que cruzar un puente y podría resultar peligroso.
>
> (10) Segundos después se sintió una sacudida intensísima y se oyó un ruido horrible: los dos trenes chocaron, se incendiaron y se desmenuzaron. Hubo cientos de muertos y miles de heridos. Por una rara casualidad yo quedé ileso. ¡Ojalá hubiera muerto!
>
> Nunca podré olvidar un espectáculo tan espantoso. Como siempre sucede en
> (15) las catástrofes, la sensación de espanto no es simultánea con el choque; sólo al cabo de algunos minutos, cuando vi las llamas de los coches que ardían, cuando distinguí las dos locomotoras semi-erguidas como dos hombres que luchan por derribarse, cuando oí los lamentos de los heridos y vi las ambulancias que acudían a levantar las víctimas, sólo entonces me di cuenta de lo que acababa de
> (20) suceder.

1. ¿Qué se narra en este trozo?
   - (A) Un encuentro entre amigos
   - (B) Un desastre natural
   - (C) Una colisión
   - (D) La circulación de trenes

RESPUESTA

Pregunta #1: C
This selection narrates the event of a collision between two trains. The words that have a common connection are *"sacudida intensísima,"* *"ruido horrible,"* *"chocaron,"* *"muertos,"* *"heridos,"* *"espantoso,"* and *"catástrofes."*

Understand Details

After the main idea of the passage has been identified, there will be a variety of questions that ask about specific information contained in the text. These details can relate to setting or origin (where), time (when), character, definition, or identification (who or what), purpose and reason (why), or manner (how). Many times these questions can be easily recognized by focusing on a particular word or phrase, but the answer will most often be a rephrasing of a word or string of words in the text.

PRÁCTICA

Read the passage and select the best answer for each question that follows.

> Sin apenas tiempo para disfrutar de su viaje de novios, Carlos Sainz ha vuelto a tomar el volante de su Toyota Celica GT4 para afrontar una nueva prueba del Campeonato del Mundo de Rallys.
>
> *Línea*
> *(5)*
> En efecto, en la mañana del 12 de mayo Sainz y su mujer empezaron su viaje a las islas Bermudas, que duró muy poco. Después de una semana de descanso, ya estaba el piloto madrileño en Grecia junto con su copiloto Luis Moya, realizando el recorrido de entrenamiento de la 34 edición del Acrópolis, una carrera que se destaca entre las más duras del campeonato, pero que para Carlos Sainz tiene un significado muy especial, ya que allí consiguió su primera victoria en una prueba
>
> *(10)* del Mundial, concretamente hace ahora dos años.

1. ¿Quién dirigirá el equipo en la competencia?
   - (A) La señora Sainz
   - (B) Luis Moya
   - (C) Carlos Sainz
   - (D) Un entrenador griego

2. ¿Qué tipo de competencia es?
   - (A) Una carrera de caballos
   - (B) Una carrera aérea
   - (C) Una carrera de coches deportivos
   - (D) Un partido de campeonato de la Copa Mundial

3. ¿Por qué estuvo Carlos Sainz en las islas Bermudas?
   - (A) Para celebrar su primera victoria
   - (B) Es donde decidió pasar su luna de miel
   - (C) Para entrenarse para la próxima competencia
   - (D) Para recuperarse mental y físicamente

RESPUESTAS

Pregunta #1: C

Carlos, as the subject of the phrase "*ha vuelto a tomar el volante*," is identified as the driver, or "*piloto*," about which the passage speaks. Luis Moya and la señora Sainz are secondary figures, and there is no Greek trainer.

Pregunta #2: C

Toyota Celica GT4 and *Rally* both refer to car racing, to which Sainz has returned. Choices (A), (B), and (D) are based on distracting factors. "*Piloto*" is the subject of the verb in "*estaba el piloto madrileño en Grecia,*" but nowhere in the passage is any association made with anything other than cars. The word "*Mundial*" is also a distractor in choice (D), since there is a possible confusion with the World Cup in soccer competition. However, the word *Copa* never appears, nor are there any references to soccer.

Pregunta #3: B

This is a classic example of rephrasing of words or a series of words in the text. *"Luna de miel"* and *"viaje de novios"* are synonyms, and they both mean "honeymoon."

Determining the Intended Reader

The reading passages that appear on the AP Spanish Language and Culture exam represent a wide variety of sources. Most often the intended reader of a passage can be determined by the content of the reading itself. The intended reader is anyone who is interested enough to pick up the literature to read it. In some cases, the writer addresses the reader directly, and from context provided within the passage, the reader can identify him or herself. In other cases, the passage may be an essay that tries to convince a particular kind of reader to take a certain position. Read the following passage and think about the type of reader to whom it is directed.

PRÁCTICA

Quien desee comer una manzana y tenga ante si un manzano de su propiedad, cargado de manzanas maduras al alcance de la mano, no tiene problema alguno para hacerse con ellas. Coge una manzana y, con ello, ha conseguido lo que pre-

Línea tendía. Los problemas comienzan cuando las manzanas cuelgan tan altas que
(5) resulta difícil alcanzarlas. El objetivo, cogerlas, no cabe lograrlo sin dificultades. Se tropieza con un óbice en el logro de nuestro objetivo. ¿Cómo se podrá comportar uno ante esta nueva situación?

Se puede renunciar a las manzanas, si la necesidad de comerlas no es muy aciante o si se sabe por experiencia que no se halla preparado para tal situación,
(10) es decir, si no se siente uno con fuerzas suficientes para coger una manzana de un árbol elevado.

Pero también cabe la posibilidad de que comience uno a intentar conseguir su objetivo, o dicho de otro modo, de que trate de buscar, sin plan previo alguno, los medios y métodos apropiados para lograrlo. Intenta uno sacudir violentamente
(15) al árbol de un lado para otro y se da cuenta de que su tronco resulta demasiado grueso para poderlo mover. Arroja piedras a las manzanas y comprueba que para esto le falta la práctica requerida. Echa mano de un palo y trata de alcanzar con él las manzanas, pero el palo resulta demasiado corto.

Muchos intentos, muchos fracasos. Tal vez—tras largo esfuerzo—un éxito
(20) fortuito.

Pero también se puede proceder de la siguiente manera: se sienta uno y reflexiona sobre la situación.

1. ¿A quién parece estar dirigido este pasaje?
   (A) A un campesino hambriento
   (B) A un chico pequeño
   (C) A una persona perezosa
   (D) A una persona pragmática

RESPUESTA

Pregunta #1: D

The correct answer is choice (D) because the purpose of this passage is to interest the reader in learning how to solve everyday problems. This writer appeals to the reader's reason by presenting a concrete example of a problem and then offering a variety of solutions, none of which is the most efficient manner of solving the problem. This writer is addressing a reader who wants to learn how to think logically when confronted by problems and not act impulsively. A pragmatic person is one who will analyze the situation and then take the most appropriate action, which in this case is to sit and contemplate the situation.

Making Predictions

Making predictions is a skill that should be applied throughout the reading process. You can make predictions about the content of a reading selection simply by reading its title. You should continue to make predictions while you are reading as to what will happen next. Predictions are always based on prior knowledge, and, therefore, tend to be more accurate as knowledge increases. On the exam, the questions asking you to make predictions will generally present a hypothetical scenario and then ask you to make a prediction of the most probable outcome of the scenario. For example, a question might ask you to determine what the title of a book would be that you would check out if you wanted to further your understanding of the topic addressed in the reading source, or what would be an appropriate title for an essay based on the reading. In each case, there is nothing in the reading itself that will answer these questions, and you must rely on your overall understanding of the text. These types of questions will generally come at the end of the question series for any given text, and as they are presenting a hypothetical situation, the conditional mood will probably be used (*¿Cuál de las siguientes preguntas sería . . . ?, ¿Qué libro buscarías . . . , etc.*). You can expect no more than one question of this type per reading selection.

PRÁCTICA

Read the passage and answer the question that follows.

> **INGREDIENTES (para 4 personas)**
>
> 1½ litro de leche
>
> 75 gramos de arroz
>
> *Línea*   2 sobres de café soluble (o descafeinado soluble)
>
> *(5)*   50 gramos de azúcar
>
> La piel de medio limón
>
> 1 palo de canela
>
> Canela en polvo
>
>
>
> En una cazuela mezclamos un litro de leche, la piel de limón, el palo de canela
>
> *(10)* y el arroz. Removemos todo con una espátula de madera y lo cocemos a fuego suave durante 45 minutos.
>
> A media cocción, añadimos poco a poco el resto de la leche con el café soluble y el azúcar disueltos, y dejamos que siga cociendo hasta que quede cremosa la mezcla. Lo servimos en boles individuales espolvoreado con canela en polvo.
>
> *(15)*   El arroz con leche es un postre muy popular y fácil de elaborar. La leche aporta al postre proteínas y diferentes minerales como el calcio, mientras que el arroz es buen fuente de hidratos de carbono complejos. En esta receta se presenta una variante de este postre, ya que se añade un poco de café soluble, que va a dar al plato un toque de color y sabor diferente.

1. Si quisieras investigar más información a base del tema de esta lectura, ¿cuál de las siguientes publicaciones te sería más útil?
   - (A) *Postres típicos del mundo hispano*
   - (B) *Recetas sencillas, deliciosas y saludables*
   - (C) *Sea el perfecto anfitrión*
   - (D) *Por qué estudiar gastronomía*

RESPUESTA

Pregunta #1: A

The text obviously refers to cooking, and the reader should be able to identify that the dish being described is some sort of dessert. Not only does the word *postre* appear in the reading itself, but so do many ingredients associated with desserts (*azúcar, piel de limón, canela*). The theme of this particular reading is a dessert, making A the best answer. Both (B) and (D) deal with cooking, but you can eliminate (B) because of *saludable*, as most of the ingredients in this dish would not make it necessarily healthy, and choice (D) refers more to a study program, to which this text does not refer. Choice (C) is easily eliminated because it deals more with hosting a party or event but does not necessarily have anything to do with cooking.

UNDERSTAND MEANING

Besides testing how much vocabulary you already know, the examination also tests your ability to deduce the meaning of words and idioms from the context in which they appear. It is not uncommon for even the most advanced Spanish speaker to encounter unfamiliar words while reading. For most native speakers, however, unfamiliar vocabulary generally does not present a problem because they are able to extract plenty of information from context to effectively understand the passage and, in most cases, they are likely capable of giving you a probable meaning of the words they do not know. On the other hand, students of Spanish too often tend to get hung up on vocabulary they do not recognize, and some feel they cannot continue reading without knowing the meaning of the unfamiliar word. In such cases, the first reaction often is to turn to a bilingual dictionary to help learn its meaning. The use of dictionaries, however, is not permitted on the examination, and therefore it is important to learn other strategies that you can use to help you work with unfamiliar vocabulary when reading.

Inferring the Meaning of Unfamiliar Words Using Context Clues

Being able to infer the meaning of unfamiliar words or idioms using context clues is a powerful tool that can boost your interpretive ability. However, it is important to remember that you do not have to understand all words in a reading passage to be an effective reader. In many cases you won't need to worry about the words you do not recognize in order to extract all the information you will need from a text. However, there are times when unfamiliar words and idioms may play a pivotal role in your understanding of a particular sentence, and in these cases you should use the following strategies to help you make an educated guess to their meaning:

1. **READ THE ENTIRE SENTENCE OR PARAGRAPH.** You have to have a frame of reference to understand unfamiliar vocabulary.
2. **IDENTIFY THE PART OF SPEECH OF THE WORD.** Is it a noun, adjective, verb, adverb, etc.?
3. **USE CONTEXT CLUES.** To what other words does the unfamiliar word relate? If the word is an adjective, what noun is it modifying? If the word is a verb, who is the subject?
4. **DO YOU KNOW WORDS OF THE SAME FAMILY?** Often a word that may be unfamiliar is of the same family of a word you already know. For example *una docena* (a dozen) includes the number *doce* (twelve). Break up prefixes and suffixes to help you as well.
5. **IDENTIFY COGNATES AND PRONOUNCE WORDS.** For example, the Spanish verb *facilitar* is a cognate of the English *to facilitate*. Sometimes pronouncing a word can help identify its meaning.

Mastering this ability requires patience and practice, and the more you apply these strategies to your daily reading, the more comfortable you will become in your ability to read. Remember, it is not important to know the exact definition of the words; simply approximating the meaning is enough in most cases.

PRÁCTICA

Read the following text and predict the meaning of the underlined words. The entire text forms part of a story that is also an example of a product from the Spanish-speaking world.

Introducción:

El siguiente cuento es una leyenda de España. Es una adaptación de la leyenda publicada en 2008 en el boletín titulado *Materiales*, publicado por el Ministerio de Educación, Política Social y Deporte de España.

La leyenda del cuélebre

    Hace muchos, muchos, años vivía en un <u>bosque</u> verde y <u>frondoso</u> un animal fantástico que se llamaba cuélebre. Tenía el cuerpo de serpiente y las <u>alas de murciélago</u>. Su cuerpo era enorme y tenía una larga <u>cola</u>. El cuélebre vivía en el

Línea norte de España, muy cerca de las <u>orillas</u> de los ríos. Su trabajo era de proteger su

(5) precioso <u>tesoro</u>.

    Una tarde lluviosa, cuando el cuélebre se despertó, estaba tan hambriento que decidió tomar una merienda. Sabía dónde encontrarla porque, siempre cuando tenía hambre, <u>se alimentaba</u> de personas y <u>ganado</u>. Así que <u>se deslizó</u> por los árboles del bosque hasta que llegó a la orilla de un lago. Allí, al otro lado, vio a una

(10) <u>ovejita</u> que comía hierba. El cuélebre <u>se acercó</u> sigilosamente hasta alcanzar a la ovejita por detrás, abrió su boca y <u>se la tragó</u> de un solo bocado. Al haber satisfecho su hambre, decidió tomarse una siestita.

    La mañana siguiente, un niño que paseaba por allí vio al cuélebre que dormía y <u>se asustó</u> tanto que tuvo que correr para que el cuélebre no lo viera. El niño llamó

(15) a unos <u>cazadores</u>, y les llevó hasta donde estaba la bestia, todavía durmiendo junto al lago. Entonces, los cazadores abrieron su enorme boca para que la ovejita pudiera salir. Luego, recogieron unas rocas que estaban cerca y las pusieron en la boca del cuélebre.

    Unas horas después, cuando el cuélebre se despertó, se sintió tan mal que

(20) comenzó a <u>arrastrarse</u> hasta llegar al mar. Allí, por el peso de las rocas en su estómago, <u>se ahogó</u> y descansó para siempre, en el fondo del océano.

RESPUESTAS

bosque
(línea 1)

The first step is to identify that this word is a noun, as evidenced by the indefinite article. This means that it is either a person, place, thing, or idea. The next contextual clue is that the verb *vivir* and the preposition *en* indicates that the subject of the sentence, the "*cuélebre*," lived here, which gives us evidence that "bosque" is a place. When we consider that the "*cuélebre*" is an "animal fantástico," then this place is likely rural and not urban. The adjective "verde" is another clue, and when we think of a rural place that is green in which an animal might live, we likely would think of a forest, which is what this word means.

frondoso (1)	The first step again is to identify the part of speech, and this word is an adjective. We know this because it follows the conjunction "y" and, since this conjunction does not introduce a new clause, its function is to link the word "frondoso" with "verde." Since "verde" describes "bosque," and we now know that "bosque" is a forest, then "frondoso" is another adjective that is describing the forest. This information would be sufficient for general comprehension, but if we wanted to be more precise, we could think of another adjective that would describe a forest. If you thought of *leafy* or *dense*, then you would be correct.
alas de murciélago (2–3)	This is a structure in which we have two nouns, where "murciélago" is modifying "alas." When we look at the context, we can see that it too follows the conjunction "y" and, just like in the previous example, the conjunction is linking these nouns to the nouns beforehand. The previous nouns "cuerpo" and "serpiente" are describing the body of the "*cuélebre*," and therefore we can safely assume that the nouns "alas" and "murciélago" are doing the same. To be more precise, "alas" is referring to a body part just like "cuerpo" does beforehand, and since "serpiente" is a type of animal, then we can safely assume that "murciélago" is an animal as well. There is not enough context to tell us exactly *what* body part or animal these words mean, but this information is enough to establish sufficient comprehension. In case you are wondering, "alas" means *wings*, and "murciélago" means *bat*. However, this information is not vital to understand what is happening in the story.
cola (3)	We see that this word is a noun. It also follows the conjunction "y" and the conjugated verb "tenía," so it is part of a new clause, but it does relate to the clause before the conjunction. When we look at the first clause in this sentence, we see that it again describes the body of the animal. This means that the second clause is likely doing the same thing, so we can safely assume that "cola" is part of the body of the animal. When we consider the adjective "larga," it tells us that this body part is long and, when we remember that we already know this animal had a body of a serpent, then likely this word means "tail."
orillas (4)	We identify that this word is a noun. Further context clues tell us that this noun relates to the verb "vivía," so "orillas" is a place. We already know that the "*cuélebre*" lived in a forest, so this particular place must be somewhere inside the forest. Further digging tells us that "ríos" is modifying the word "orillas," and since the lack of preposition "en" rules out that it lives *in* the river, it must be somewhere nearby, which gives us words like *edge* or *shore*, which is the meaning of this word.
tesoro (5)	This word is a noun, and it is the direct object of the verb "proteger." We also know that this object is "precioso," which looks and sounds like *precious* in English. This is a clue that "tesoro" must be something of value, which makes sense because the "*cuélebre*" is protecting it. If you guessed that it means *treasure*, you are correct.
se alimentaba (8)	We easily identify that this word is a verb in the imperfect tense, and the subject is the "*cuélebre*." We also see that this verb follows the expression "*tenía hambre*," which is sufficient evidence to infer that "se alimentaba" probably means *ate*.

ganado (8)   As we begin to feel more comfortable inferring meaning, let's not be tempted to skip steps in the process. This is an example of how that can backfire. The word looks like the past participle of the verb *ganar*, but it is not. Like in several previous examples this word follows the conjunction "y" and thus relates to what comes before the conjunction, which in this case is the noun "personas." This tells us that "ganado" is a noun. Further investigation shows us that both "personas" and "ganado" are the direct objects of the verb "se alimentaba," which we now know means "ate." This tells us that the *cuélebre* ate both people and "ganado," and we can safely infer that "ganado" is a type of food. Thinking about it more, we easily reach the conclusion that "ganado" is likely some sort of animal rather than a plant, for if the *cuélebre* eats people, then it is likely not a vegetarian. In fact, "ganado" means *livestock*.

se deslizó (8)   We identify that this is a verb in the preterit tense, and the subject is *cuélebre*. Further context shows us that the *cuélebre* did this action "por los árboles" and that it then "llegó a la orilla de un lago" (to the shore of a lake). Therefore, the verb "se deslizó" is likely a verb of movement, bringing the *cuélebre* from where it woke up to the lake. This is sufficient to understand the text, but if we were to take it a step further, when we remember that the *cuélebre* has the body of a snake and therefore no legs or feet, then we see that "se deslizó" probably means *to slither* or *slide*.

ovejita (10)   We quickly identify that this word is a noun, and that it is also the direct object of the verb "vio" (*saw*). Another important clue is the preposition "a," which is often used before a direct object that denotes a human being or an animal, so we know that the noun probably is one of those two things. Further investigation shows us that the "ovejita" is eating "hierba" on the other side of the lake. The word "hierba" looks and sounds like *herbs*, so we assume that it probably is an animal and that it is grazing. We don't have enough information to say exactly what type of animal it is, but that is not vital to understand enough to comprehend the story. In case you are curious, "ovejita" means *small sheep* or *lamb*.

se acercó (10)   This word is a verb in the preterit tense and the subject of this verb is *cuélebre*. There is no direct object, but there is the preposition "hasta" (*until*) that precedes another verb "alcanzar" and the direct object "la ovejita." So you know that the *cuélebre* did something until it did something else to the "ovejita" . . . but what? As we look further, we see in the next clause that the *cuélebre* "abrió su boca" (*opened its mouth*). This gives us enough information to know what "se acercó" probably means. Working backwards from "abrió su boca," we deduce that the *cuélebre* opened its mouth to eat the "ovejita," but before being able to do so, the *cuélebre* must have caught or reached the "ovejita," and this is probably what "alcanzar" means. But since we know from the previous sentence that the sheep was on the other side of the lake, the *cuélebre* had to move towards it first. Therefore, "se acercó" means *approached*. Another way to confirm this is to change the verb to the infinitive form, which is *acercarse*. In this word, we see the preposition "cerca" (*near*), which gives us further evidence that our supposition is correct.

se la tragó (11)	We quickly identify that this word is a verb in the preterit tense, and again the subject is the *cuélebre*. Since this is the third verb in the preterit in this sentence, it is the third action in the sequence of events. We know that right before this verb, the *cuélebre* opened its mouth. This should be sufficient information to infer that "se la tragó" means *ate* or *swallowed*.
se asustó (14)	Again we start by identifying that this word is a verb in the preterit tense. This time, however, the subject is "un niño." It is also the second of three verbs in this sentence that are conjugated in the preterit tense, and all three have the same subject. The first and last actions in the sequence contain the basic verbs "vio" (*saw*) and "correr" (*ran*), so logically, the boy likely became scared after seeing the enormous *cuélebre* that was sleeping, and thus ran away, which is what "se asustó" means.
cazadores (15)	We identify that this word is a noun and is the direct object of the verb "llamó." An important clue again is that it follows the preposition "a," which means that this noun is either a human being or an animal. Since the subject of the verb "llamó" is the young boy, and he calls the "cazadores" after running away from the *cuélebre*, it makes sense that "cazadores" must be people, and people that can help him. This is sufficient information to establish understanding. In case you are still curious, "cazadores" are *hunters*.
arrastrarse (20)	This word is a verb, and it is in the infinitive form because it follows the conjugated verb "comenzó a." The subject is *cuélebre*. In this context, we know that the *cuélebre* woke up, felt sick, and "comenzó a arrastrarse" until it reached the sea. We have sufficient information to infer that this is a verb of motion, which is correct and sufficient for understanding the text. Thinking through it further, if we remember that the *cuélebre* felt sick because the sheep in its stomach was replaced with rocks, then we likely are visualizing movement to the sea that is labored and difficult. If this leads you to infer that this verb probably means *to drag*, you are correct.
se ahogó (21)	This words is also a conjugated verb and the subject is *cuélebre*. We know that this action occurred after the *cuélebre* reached the ocean and that, following this action, the beast rested for eternity at the bottom of the ocean. This information, paired with our prior knowledge that its stomach was filled with rocks, helps us infer that this verb means *drowned*.

As you practice inferring meaning of unfamiliar words using context clues, do not worry too much if you are not able to infer the *exact* meaning. Often, simply getting in the ballpark is good enough. The goal is to understand ideas, and if you are able to infer enough to understand correctly the overall idea being presented, you will perform well on most interpretive tasks.

CULTURE AND CONTENT ACROSS DISCIPLINES

Culture

When talking about culture, one has to consider the products, practices, and perspectives (for more detailed information, refer to the section on culture in Chapter 1). Sometimes the questions regarding culture will pertain to a certain attitude that is presented within the text, or it may ask you about a particular expression that is used and why.

PRÁCTICA

Read the passage and answer the questions that follow. As you read, try to identify some of the practices and perspectives that are demonstrated.

> A las cuatro merendamos juntos, pan y pasas, sentados en el sofá, y cuando nos levantamos, no sé por qué, mi padre no quiso que limpiara el espaldar que el albañilito había manchado de blanco con su chaqueta; me detuvo la mano y lo
>
> *Línea* limpió después sin que lo viéramos . . .
> *(5)* —¿Sabes, hijo mío, por qué no quise que limpiara el sofá? Porque limpiarle mientras tu compañero lo veía era casi hacerle una reconvención por haberlo ensuciado. Y esto no estaba bien: en primer lugar, porque no lo había hecho de intento, y en segundo lugar, porque le había manchado con ropa de su padre, que se la había enyesado trabajando; y lo que se mancha trabajando no ensucia;
> *(10)* es polvo, cal, barniz, todo lo que quieras, pero no suciedad. El trabajo no ensucia. No digas nunca de un obrero que sale de su trabajo: "Va sucio". Debes decir: "Tiene en su ropa las señales, las huellas del trabajo". Recuérdalo. Quiero mucho al albañilito: primero, porque es compañero tuyo, y además, porque es hijo de un obrero. —*Tu padre.*

1. ¿De qué se trata esta selección?
   (A) De la conducta apropiada de un anfitrión
   (B) De los modos de mantenerse limpio en casa
   (C) De la conducta apropiada de un huésped
   (D) De los modos de disciplinar a un hijo

2. ¿Por qué no quería el papá que su hijo limpiara el sofá de inmediato?
   (A) No quería que el albañilito viera a su hijo trabajando.
   (B) Quería que la madre lo hiciera.
   (C) Quería que el albañilito viera lo que había hecho.
   (D) No quería parecer descortés al invitado.

3. En las línea 9, ¿qué quiere decir ". . . lo que se mancha trabajando no ensucia"?
   (A) Indica que no puede ensuciarse trabajando.
   (B) Significa que el padre no vio que la chaqueta estaba sucia.
   (C) Significa que trabajar no es una desgracia.
   (D) Quiere decir que el padre se sentía superior a los obreros.

RESPUESTAS

Pregunta #1: A

The predominant cultural perspective that stands out is the importance of being a good host. The narrator is obviously young and still in the process of learning the importance of hospitality. This perspective is highlighted not only by what the father tells his son, but also by certain actions he takes, such as not cleaning the chalk stain left on the sofa.

Pregunta #2: D

As in the question prior, the action is not taken because the father does not want his guest to feel uncomfortable. This is indeed a cultural practice—not doing a particular action that may make someone feel uncomfortable.

Pregunta #3: C

This question asks you to reflect on the use of language in order to understand a particular cultural perspective. In this case, you must go beyond what the words are literally saying and focus on the general idea within the context. The father is teaching his son why it is important to respect those who work, regardless of the work they do. The saying also conveys a cultural perspective.

Content Across Disciplines

You can expect that the reading selections on the AP Spanish exam will deal with a number of topics pertaining to different disciplines. As you prepare for the exam, it is important to diversify your readings as much as possible in order to expose yourself to the vocabulary and ideas that pertain to different topics. Do not panic if you find yourself in front of a selection on a topic about which you know very little. Consider this as an opportunity to grow your knowledge of that particular subject.

PRÁCTICA

Read the passage and answer the questions that follow. As you read, try to identify (1) the subject matter to which the passage pertains, and (2) key vocabulary words that are common when talking about the subject.

En verano se ven menos horas de televisión, según los estudios de audiencia. Los días son más largos. Los espectadores encuentran elementos sustituidores de ocio fuera de su hogar habitual. La publicidad floja y disminuye la presión com-

Línea
(5) petitiva. Este año, sin embargo, y a excepción de Antena 3, que apenas modificará su programación, la lucha por ganar más cuota de pantalla no baja la guardia. La más agresiva es Telecinco, que prepara las maletas para situarse en las playas. En la de Marbella ya ha contratado a su alcalde para que haga de presentador.

Para los jóvenes, Telecinco ha preparado una versión reducida de *La quinta marcha,* que se emitirá al mediodía desde distintos emplazamientos turísticos y
(10) playeros. En esta misma línea de seguimiento a la audiencia consumidora de discos y refrescos, se mueve *Hablando se entiende la basca,* una versión del programa de Coll que se realizará en el mismo escenario de *Hablando se entiende la gente,* el teatro de la ONCE de Madrid. Chavales entre 10 y 17 años ofrecerán diariamente su espectáculo conducido por unos de los presentadores de *La quinta marcha.*

---

1. ¿Qué tendencias se han notado entre los televidentes españoles?
   (A) Durante el invierno miran menos porque están tan ocupados.
   (B) Durante el verano miran menos porque prefieren disfrutar del tiempo fuera de casa.
   (C) No hay diferencia entre el número de horas que miran en verano y en invierno.
   (D) Depende más de la edad del televidente cuánto miran en el verano.

2. ¿De dónde procede este trozo?
   (A) Es un folleto del Consejo de Turismo sobre la televisión.
   (B) Es un guión para los televidentes.
   (C) Es de una revista que investiga las novedades en la televisión.
   (D) Es de una obra literaria mostrando la vida moderna.

RESPUESTAS

Pregunta #1: B

The correct answer can be found in the first three sentences of the passage, where the main idea is basically restated verbatim.

Pregunta #2: C

The information presented in the passage is simply stating the facts as they appear. There is no reference to any other programming besides the three that are mentioned in the article (eliminating choice (B)), and it is too specific to be choice (A) or (D).

PRACTICE READING COMPREHENSION PASSAGES

In addition to reading comprehension, you should have identified that this article was about television and programming. There is a lot of vocabulary that can be extracted from this article that you can use when talking about television in general. These words include: *audiencia, espectadores, ocio, publicidad, programación, cuota de pantalla, presentador, emitir, programa, escenario, teatro,* and *espectáculo,* as well as the name of two television stations, Antena 3 and Telecinco. This information can be helpful to demonstrate your knowledge of Spanish culture. Looking at the questions, you could have also picked up on the word *televidente.* As you are making a list of vocabulary on any particular topic, remember to identify its function (verb, noun, adjective), and think about possible words in the same family (*espectáculo, espectacular, espectador; presentador, presentar, presentación,* and so on).

Finally, be sure to use the text to your advantage. Too often students make mistakes by not noticing the small details that can help them in their overall communication. For example, you should have noted that the word *programa* is masculine (line 11, ". . . versión del programa"), whereas the word *programación* is feminine. Although in this article there is no way to tell the gender of *programación,* later in the passage you will find the word "versión" preceded by *una,* which should be enough to tell you that *programación* is also a feminine noun, since both words end in *-ión.* Also, you should have identified that Antena 3 and Telecinco are television stations in Spain by the mention of two Spanish cities, Marbella (line 7) and Spain's capital, Madrid (line 13).

READING GRAPHS, TABLES, AND CHARTS

You can expect to have three graphs, tables, and/or charts as part of the exam. The first will be in Section I, Part A, the second in the Print and Audio Texts (combined) portion of Section I, Part B, and lastly as part of the Section II, Task 2 (Argumentative Essay). In each case these graphs, tables, or charts will relate thematically to the article that precedes it and/ or to the audio that follows. These require a slightly different approach than reading texts. In most cases, they make complex information easier to understand, but they can lead to confusion when they are misinterpreted. Below are some strategies you can use.

- Read the introduction and title of the graph, table, or chart.
- Read the labels on the graph, table, or chart, if applicable.
- Pay attention to any pattern printed on each section of a graph or pie chart, and use the key to understand what each pattern represents.
- Analyze the information gathered from the graph, table, or chart. Ask yourself what conclusions you can make from these and how they relate to the article seen beforehand and/or predict how they will relate to the audio that follows.

One of the more common mistakes students make when working with graphs, tables, or charts is to force a point of view that cannot be supported by the image. Often these graphics simply present information objectively and do not have a positive or negative point of view on the topic.

Bar graphs

Bar graphs show the relationship between groups or different categories. When reading a bar graph, make sure to:

- Read the introduction and title.
- Read the label on each axis.
- Determine the value that each bar represents.
- Analyze the relationship between each bar in the graph and how they compare or contrast with each other.

Práctica: El siguiente gráfico presenta la principal actividad que realizan los usuarios de internet en México. Se basa en datos compilados por INFOTEC en 2018.

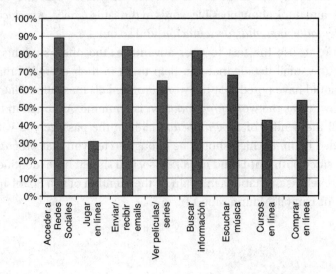

This graph presents data objectively, and there are several conclusions that can be made:

- Most people surveyed use internet to access social media.
- The top reasons to use internet is for communication and information rather than entertainment.
- It is apparent, since the combined percentages exceed 100%, that the people surveyed use internet for more than one purpose, such as chatting with friends, shopping, and accessing music and movies.
- Fewer than half the people surveyed use internet to play videogames or to take online courses.

Pie Charts

Pie charts show how different elements relate to a whole. Generally, the information presented in pie charts is measured with percentages, with the sum of the parts equal to 100 percent. A pie chart will be divided in sections with different colors and/or patterns with a key to indicate what each color and pattern means. When reading a pie chart, make sure to:

- Read the introduction and title.
- Read the label for each part of the pie.
- Understand what each part represents and how they relate to each other.
- Analyze each part in relation to the whole.

Práctica: El siguiente gráfico presenta el tipo de basura que se tira en la Patagonia, Argentina. Se basa en datos compilados por el gobierno de Argentina en 2018.

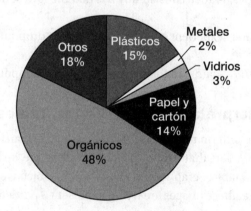

Like the previous bar graph, this pie chart presents information quite objectively. The main conclusion that can be drawn is that a higher percentage of trash thrown is organic, meaning that the original product came from a living being (plant, animal, and so on), while plastic trash is a distant third. It is unclear what "otros" may refer to, but we know what it is not (organic trash, plastic, paper, metal, or glass).

Tables

Unlike graphs and pie charts, tables list data about a specific subject. The data is lined up in columns and rows, with headings identifying each of the categories. When reading a table, you should:

- Read the introduction and title.
- Read the row and column headings.
- Determine the value of each of the numbers in the table (percentages, in tens, thousands, etc.).
- Read down from the left and then across to the right.

Práctica: La siguiente tabla presenta la tasa de abandono escolar prematuro de la población total de jóvenes entre 18 y 24 años. La información se basa en datos compilados por el Instituto Vasco de Estadística.

País	2013	2014	2015	2016	2017
Alemania	11,9	11,2	11,0	10,7	10,6
Francia	9,7	9,0	9,2	8,8	8,9
España	23,6	21,9	20,0	19,0	18,3
Italia	16,8	15,0	14,7	13,8	14,0
Reino Unido	12,4	11,8	10,8	11,2	10,6

As with the previous two graphs, this table presents data objectively. Several ideas that can be extracted from this table are the following:

- Of the five countries, France consistently has had the lowest dropout rates and Spain the highest.
- Both Italy and France experienced a slight increase in dropout rates between 2016 and 2017.
- Since 2013 and 2017, Spain had the biggest decrease in dropout rates.

Avoid Forcing Interpretation from Graphs, Tables, and Charts

As mentioned earlier, a common mistake is for students to force meaning or a point of view from the graph, table, or chart that cannot be supported by the image. Almost always, the information presented in tables, graphs, and charts will be objective and neutral. Avoid the temptation to suggest that these images are trying to present a particular point of view unless it is clear that this is what they are doing.

For example, the bar graph simply presents the types of activities that internet users do when using internet. It never suggests that people *prefer* to use internet to watch movies or listen to music, so making that claim would be incorrect.

Let's try another example with the pie chart. As mentioned earlier, the pie chart simply presents information about the type of trash that is thrown away. However, when we look at *vidrio*, glass, the percentage is quite low. Why is that? Do people in the region of Patagonia use less glass? Do they recycle glass more often than other products? We don't have enough information to answer these questions, so to make any of these claims would be an incorrect statement because it cannot be supported by the information in the chart.

Finally, the table presents dropout rates in several European countries between 2013 and 2017. One thing it does not show is *why* students dropped out, so one cannot make a statement as to why based solely on information from this table.

Section I, Part A

To briefly review the steps for reading:

When reading print texts

1. Read the introduction
2. Understand the format of the text
3. As you read
   a. underline key words that will remind you of the main ideas being presented
   b. identify people, places, and events
   c. use context clues to infer the meaning of unfamiliar words that you feel are important, and
   d. make note of any cultural elements (products, practices, or perspectives).

4. After you finish, evaluate the information to
   a. determine the tone and mood,
   b. determine the intended reader, and
   c. draw conclusions and make predictions based on the text.

When reading graphs, charts, or tables

1. Read the introduction
2. Read tables and graphs from the left column and move across
3. Remember that most graphics present information objectively, so don't try to force an interpretation that cannot be supported by the data

When answering questions

1. Carefully read the question and options
2. Select the option whose idea best reflects the information presented in the text

Finally, as mentioned in the introduction of this book, following some of the reading selections you will find some additional activities. These activities are not included in the AP exam. They are included here to give you additional practice in the skills that will help you further develop your interpretive and communicative proficiencies. After all reading activities, you will also find a "Cultural Awareness" section that will highlight the products, practices, and perspectives mentioned in the print texts. Use this as an opportunity to reflect on these aspects of culture and how they are similar or different than your own community in preparation for Task 4 (Cultural Comparison).

ANSWER SHEET
Reading Comprehension

Selección #1

1. Ⓐ Ⓑ Ⓒ Ⓓ
2. Ⓐ Ⓑ Ⓒ Ⓓ
3. Ⓐ Ⓑ Ⓒ Ⓓ
4. Ⓐ Ⓑ Ⓒ Ⓓ
5. Ⓐ Ⓑ Ⓒ Ⓓ
6. Ⓐ Ⓑ Ⓒ Ⓓ
7. Ⓐ Ⓑ Ⓒ Ⓓ

Selección #2

1. Ⓐ Ⓑ Ⓒ Ⓓ
2. Ⓐ Ⓑ Ⓒ Ⓓ
3. Ⓐ Ⓑ Ⓒ Ⓓ
4. Ⓐ Ⓑ Ⓒ Ⓓ
5. Ⓐ Ⓑ Ⓒ Ⓓ
6. Ⓐ Ⓑ Ⓒ Ⓓ
7. Ⓐ Ⓑ Ⓒ Ⓓ
8. Ⓐ Ⓑ Ⓒ Ⓓ
9. Ⓐ Ⓑ Ⓒ Ⓓ
10. Ⓐ Ⓑ Ⓒ Ⓓ
11. Ⓐ Ⓑ Ⓒ Ⓓ

Selección #3

1. Ⓐ Ⓑ Ⓒ Ⓓ
2. Ⓐ Ⓑ Ⓒ Ⓓ
3. Ⓐ Ⓑ Ⓒ Ⓓ
4. Ⓐ Ⓑ Ⓒ Ⓓ
5. Ⓐ Ⓑ Ⓒ Ⓓ

Selección #4

1. Ⓐ Ⓑ Ⓒ Ⓓ
2. Ⓐ Ⓑ Ⓒ Ⓓ
3. Ⓐ Ⓑ Ⓒ Ⓓ
4. Ⓐ Ⓑ Ⓒ Ⓓ
5. Ⓐ Ⓑ Ⓒ Ⓓ
6. Ⓐ Ⓑ Ⓒ Ⓓ
7. Ⓐ Ⓑ Ⓒ Ⓓ

Selección #5

1. Ⓐ Ⓑ Ⓒ Ⓓ
2. Ⓐ Ⓑ Ⓒ Ⓓ
3. Ⓐ Ⓑ Ⓒ Ⓓ
4. Ⓐ Ⓑ Ⓒ Ⓓ
5. Ⓐ Ⓑ Ⓒ Ⓓ
6. Ⓐ Ⓑ Ⓒ Ⓓ
7. Ⓐ Ⓑ Ⓒ Ⓓ

Selección #6

1. Ⓐ Ⓑ Ⓒ Ⓓ
2. Ⓐ Ⓑ Ⓒ Ⓓ
3. Ⓐ Ⓑ Ⓒ Ⓓ
4. Ⓐ Ⓑ Ⓒ Ⓓ
5. Ⓐ Ⓑ Ⓒ Ⓓ
6. Ⓐ Ⓑ Ⓒ Ⓓ
7. Ⓐ Ⓑ Ⓒ Ⓓ

Selección #7

1. Ⓐ Ⓑ Ⓒ Ⓓ
2. Ⓐ Ⓑ Ⓒ Ⓓ
3. Ⓐ Ⓑ Ⓒ Ⓓ
4. Ⓐ Ⓑ Ⓒ Ⓓ
5. Ⓐ Ⓑ Ⓒ Ⓓ
6. Ⓐ Ⓑ Ⓒ Ⓓ
7. Ⓐ Ⓑ Ⓒ Ⓓ
8. Ⓐ Ⓑ Ⓒ Ⓓ
9. Ⓐ Ⓑ Ⓒ Ⓓ
10. Ⓐ Ⓑ Ⓒ Ⓓ
11. Ⓐ Ⓑ Ⓒ Ⓓ

Selección #8

1. Ⓐ Ⓑ Ⓒ Ⓓ
2. Ⓐ Ⓑ Ⓒ Ⓓ
3. Ⓐ Ⓑ Ⓒ Ⓓ
4. Ⓐ Ⓑ Ⓒ Ⓓ
5. Ⓐ Ⓑ Ⓒ Ⓓ
6. Ⓐ Ⓑ Ⓒ Ⓓ
7. Ⓐ Ⓑ Ⓒ Ⓓ

Selección #9

1. Ⓐ Ⓑ Ⓒ Ⓓ
2. Ⓐ Ⓑ Ⓒ Ⓓ
3. Ⓐ Ⓑ Ⓒ Ⓓ
4. Ⓐ Ⓑ Ⓒ Ⓓ
5. Ⓐ Ⓑ Ⓒ Ⓓ
6. Ⓐ Ⓑ Ⓒ Ⓓ
7. Ⓐ Ⓑ Ⓒ Ⓓ

Selección #10

1. Ⓐ Ⓑ Ⓒ Ⓓ
2. Ⓐ Ⓑ Ⓒ Ⓓ
3. Ⓐ Ⓑ Ⓒ Ⓓ
4. Ⓐ Ⓑ Ⓒ Ⓓ
5. Ⓐ Ⓑ Ⓒ Ⓓ

Selección #11

1. Ⓐ Ⓑ Ⓒ Ⓓ
2. Ⓐ Ⓑ Ⓒ Ⓓ
3. Ⓐ Ⓑ Ⓒ Ⓓ
4. Ⓐ Ⓑ Ⓒ Ⓓ
5. Ⓐ Ⓑ Ⓒ Ⓓ

Selección #12

1. Ⓐ Ⓑ Ⓒ Ⓓ
2. Ⓐ Ⓑ Ⓒ Ⓓ
3. Ⓐ Ⓑ Ⓒ Ⓓ
4. Ⓐ Ⓑ Ⓒ Ⓓ
5. Ⓐ Ⓑ Ⓒ Ⓓ
6. Ⓐ Ⓑ Ⓒ Ⓓ
7. Ⓐ Ⓑ Ⓒ Ⓓ

Selección #13

1. Ⓐ Ⓑ Ⓒ Ⓓ
2. Ⓐ Ⓑ Ⓒ Ⓓ
3. Ⓐ Ⓑ Ⓒ Ⓓ
4. Ⓐ Ⓑ Ⓒ Ⓓ
5. Ⓐ Ⓑ Ⓒ Ⓓ

Selección #14

1. Ⓐ Ⓑ Ⓒ Ⓓ
2. Ⓐ Ⓑ Ⓒ Ⓓ
3. Ⓐ Ⓑ Ⓒ Ⓓ
4. Ⓐ Ⓑ Ⓒ Ⓓ
5. Ⓐ Ⓑ Ⓒ Ⓓ
6. Ⓐ Ⓑ Ⓒ Ⓓ
7. Ⓐ Ⓑ Ⓒ Ⓓ

Selección #15

1. Ⓐ Ⓑ Ⓒ Ⓓ
2. Ⓐ Ⓑ Ⓒ Ⓓ
3. Ⓐ Ⓑ Ⓒ Ⓓ
4. Ⓐ Ⓑ Ⓒ Ⓓ
5. Ⓐ Ⓑ Ⓒ Ⓓ
6. Ⓐ Ⓑ Ⓒ Ⓓ
7. Ⓐ Ⓑ Ⓒ Ⓓ

Selección #16

1. Ⓐ Ⓑ Ⓒ Ⓓ
2. Ⓐ Ⓑ Ⓒ Ⓓ
3. Ⓐ Ⓑ Ⓒ Ⓓ
4. Ⓐ Ⓑ Ⓒ Ⓓ
5. Ⓐ Ⓑ Ⓒ Ⓓ
6. Ⓐ Ⓑ Ⓒ Ⓓ
7. Ⓐ Ⓑ Ⓒ Ⓓ
8. Ⓐ Ⓑ Ⓒ Ⓓ
9. Ⓐ Ⓑ Ⓒ Ⓓ
10. Ⓐ Ⓑ Ⓒ Ⓓ
11. Ⓐ Ⓑ Ⓒ Ⓓ

Selección #17

1. Ⓐ Ⓑ Ⓒ Ⓓ
2. Ⓐ Ⓑ Ⓒ Ⓓ
3. Ⓐ Ⓑ Ⓒ Ⓓ
4. Ⓐ Ⓑ Ⓒ Ⓓ
5. Ⓐ Ⓑ Ⓒ Ⓓ
6. Ⓐ Ⓑ Ⓒ Ⓓ
7. Ⓐ Ⓑ Ⓒ Ⓓ

Selección #18

1. Ⓐ Ⓑ Ⓒ Ⓓ
2. Ⓐ Ⓑ Ⓒ Ⓓ
3. Ⓐ Ⓑ Ⓒ Ⓓ
4. Ⓐ Ⓑ Ⓒ Ⓓ
5. Ⓐ Ⓑ Ⓒ Ⓓ

Selección #19

1. Ⓐ Ⓑ Ⓒ Ⓓ
2. Ⓐ Ⓑ Ⓒ Ⓓ
3. Ⓐ Ⓑ Ⓒ Ⓓ
4. Ⓐ Ⓑ Ⓒ Ⓓ
5. Ⓐ Ⓑ Ⓒ Ⓓ
6. Ⓐ Ⓑ Ⓒ Ⓓ
7. Ⓐ Ⓑ Ⓒ Ⓓ

Selección #20

1. Ⓐ Ⓑ Ⓒ Ⓓ
2. Ⓐ Ⓑ Ⓒ Ⓓ
3. Ⓐ Ⓑ Ⓒ Ⓓ
4. Ⓐ Ⓑ Ⓒ Ⓓ
5. Ⓐ Ⓑ Ⓒ Ⓓ
6. Ⓐ Ⓑ Ⓒ Ⓓ
7. Ⓐ Ⓑ Ⓒ Ⓓ

Selección #21

1. Ⓐ Ⓑ Ⓒ Ⓓ
2. Ⓐ Ⓑ Ⓒ Ⓓ
3. Ⓐ Ⓑ Ⓒ Ⓓ
4. Ⓐ Ⓑ Ⓒ Ⓓ
5. Ⓐ Ⓑ Ⓒ Ⓓ
6. Ⓐ Ⓑ Ⓒ Ⓓ
7. Ⓐ Ⓑ Ⓒ Ⓓ
8. Ⓐ Ⓑ Ⓒ Ⓓ
9. Ⓐ Ⓑ Ⓒ Ⓓ
10. Ⓐ Ⓑ Ⓒ Ⓓ
11. Ⓐ Ⓑ Ⓒ Ⓓ

Selección #22

1. Ⓐ Ⓑ Ⓒ Ⓓ
2. Ⓐ Ⓑ Ⓒ Ⓓ
3. Ⓐ Ⓑ Ⓒ Ⓓ
4. Ⓐ Ⓑ Ⓒ Ⓓ
5. Ⓐ Ⓑ Ⓒ Ⓓ
6. Ⓐ Ⓑ Ⓒ Ⓓ
7. Ⓐ Ⓑ Ⓒ Ⓓ

Selección #23

1. Ⓐ Ⓑ Ⓒ Ⓓ
2. Ⓐ Ⓑ Ⓒ Ⓓ
3. Ⓐ Ⓑ Ⓒ Ⓓ
4. Ⓐ Ⓑ Ⓒ Ⓓ
5. Ⓐ Ⓑ Ⓒ Ⓓ
6. Ⓐ Ⓑ Ⓒ Ⓓ
7. Ⓐ Ⓑ Ⓒ Ⓓ
8. Ⓐ Ⓑ Ⓒ Ⓓ

Selección #24

1. Ⓐ Ⓑ Ⓒ Ⓓ
2. Ⓐ Ⓑ Ⓒ Ⓓ
3. Ⓐ Ⓑ Ⓒ Ⓓ
4. Ⓐ Ⓑ Ⓒ Ⓓ
5. Ⓐ Ⓑ Ⓒ Ⓓ
6. Ⓐ Ⓑ Ⓒ Ⓓ
7. Ⓐ Ⓑ Ⓒ Ⓓ

SELECCIÓN #1

Tema curricular: Los desafíos mundiales

La siguiente redacción presenta la opinión de un español ante la situación actual en su país. Fue publicado en la página web *LaRazon.es* en 2012.

OPINIÓN: Pagar en «B»
Por Idoia Arbillaga

En cierta ocasión, mientras comía en un exquisito restaurante con un bullicioso grupo de amigos, yo escuchaba—como solemos hacer los escritores aun sin darnos cuenta—las conversaciones de los comensales de otras mesas. Entre varios

Línea
(5) noruegos, un español, al parecer casado con una señora también noruega, afirmaba que lo que más le había sorprendido de su vida en el país del norte es que, siendo él asesor, nadie le admitía que regateara al Estado en el pago de impuestos ni en ninguna declaración. «No, no; debo pagar lo que me toca». Ese civismo responsable no existe en España, aquí reina el trapicheo, la falta de responsabilidad económica y social, aquí prevalece el «mientras yo me ahorre un euro . . .».

(10) Y el Estado somos todos, vieja frase, pero parece ser que nunca llegó a calar en nuestra conciencia como ciudadanos. Vas al taller mecánico y cuando sacas la tarjeta, te dicen, «¡Ah, ¿vas a querer factura? Es que entonces debo cobrarte más!». El viejo truco. Hasta para pagar 100 euros de un lavado de tapicerías de coche, en un centro comercial, me dijeron: «No, no, en metálico». ¿Tenemos todos la obliga-

(15) ción de llevar siempre 100 euros encima? El propio tejido económico que hemos construido se sustenta en el dinero negro, en el pago en B, en el fraude. Esta es la economía española, y esto es ajeno al sistema político de turno, aquí maquillaros contabilidades todos, trapicheamos todos y le escamoteamos al Estado todo lo que podemos. Así no, así España no alcanzará ninguna clase de prosperidad

(20) nunca, ninguna equidad económica ni legal con el resto de Europa. El saneo de la economía es trabajo arduo, de lustros, de concienciación social; los países nórdicos quedan muy lejos, geográfica . . . y moralmente.

www.larazon.es/detalle_hemeroteca/noticias/LA_RAZON_447644/
2166-opinion-pagar-en-b

---

1. ¿Qué evento le impulsó al autor escribir este comentario?
   - (A) Una conversación que tuvo con unos amigos
   - (B) Una discusión que oyó entre varios desconocidos
   - (C) El estado actual de la economía de España
   - (D) La prosperidad de los países nórdicos

2. ¿Qué le sorprendió al marido español de su estancia en Noruega?
   - (A) Que nadie pagara sus impuestos
   - (B) Que nadie fuera honesto
   - (C) Que todos engañaran el Estado
   - (D) Que todos pagaran lo que debían

3. ¿Qué diferencia señala el autor entre los noruegos y los españoles?
   (A) Los españoles suelen elaborar los estados financieros.
   (B) A los españoles no les gusta pagar impuestos.
   (C) Los noruegos suelen tener que pagar más impuestos.
   (D) Los noruegos tienen una menor conciencia social.

4. Según lo que se puede inferir del texto, ¿por qué prefieren los comerciantes españoles efectuar pagos con efectivo en vez de tarjeta de crédito?
   (A) Porque habrá un recibo del pago.
   (B) Porque no tienen que pagarle un porcentaje a una institución bancaria.
   (C) Porque es más fácil ocultar la venta y evitar pagar menos impuestos luego.
   (D) Porque no todos tienen la capacidad de aceptar tarjetas de crédito.

5. ¿Cuál de las siguientes frases comunica la misma idea que la frase "mientras yo me ahorre un euro . . ." (línea 9)?
   (A) Siempre y cuando me favorezca.
   (B) Tan pronto como gane más dinero.
   (C) En tanto que haya economizado suficientemente.
   (D) Hasta que me paguen.

6. ¿A qué se refiere el autor cuando pregunta, "¿Tenemos todos la obligación de llevar siempre 100 euros encima?" (líneas 14–15)?
   (A) A que muchos no tienen suficiente dinero para hacer las compras.
   (B) A lo ridículo de llevar tanto efectivo para que otros eviten los impuestos.
   (C) A que muchas tiendas no tienen la capacidad de aceptar tarjetas de crédito.
   (D) A que los dueños de las tiendas no aceptan billetes menos de 100 euros.

7. ¿Cuál de los siguientes adjetivos mejor describe el tono del autor?
   (A) Desilusionado
   (B) Fascinado
   (C) Engañado
   (D) Deseoso

Selección #1—Más práctica

Vocabulario en contexto—Use the context of the text to figure out the most probable meaning of the following words. Write a synonym or explain the word in Spanish in the blanks that follow. The numbers in parentheses indicate the line where the word is found.

Definición / Sinónimo

1. bullicioso (1)   _____

2. comensales (3)   _____

3. trapicheo (8)   _____

4. escamoteamos (18)   _____

Ampliando tu vocabulario—Usa el vocabulario y frases del texto para llenar las columnas según el tema. ¿Puedes pensar en un tema adicional?

Palabras / frases relacionadas con . . .

. . . el fraude	. . . la economía	. . . el civismo	_____
maquillaros contabilidades	*asesor impuestos*	*responsabilidad social*	

Cultural Awareness

Cultural practice: The article presents a common practice in Spain: paying under the table in cash for a number of products and services and thus avoid paying taxes on the product or service.

Cultural perspective: This article is also an opinion piece, and the author clearly feels that this continued practice will hinder Spaniards from reaching global economic prosperity.

Are the practice and/or perspective mentioned in this article similar to or different from what you have observed in your own community?

SELECCIÓN #2

Tema curricular: Los desafíos mundiales

Fuente #1: El siguiente artículo presenta información de cómo mantener una dieta con una mayor conciencia ecológica. El artículo fue publicado en *Eroski Consumer* en 2010.

Cómo seguir una dieta baja en carbono
Por Alex Fernández Muerza

Los alimentos son responsables de al menos el 20% de los gases de efecto invernadero (GEI) producidos en EE.UU., uno de los principales países causantes de este tipo de contaminación. El porcentaje podría ser incluso mayor si se tuvie-
Línea ron en cuenta las fuentes de emisión indirectas, según diversos estudios.

(5) Ahora bien, los alimentos individuales varían en sus huellas de carbono, y por ello, las decisiones de los consumidores y del sistema alimentario pueden contri- buir en gran medida a reducir los GEI. Es la reflexión de Thomas Tomich, director del Instituto de Agricultura Sostenible de la Universidad de California, en EE.UU. Su equipo trabaja en el proyecto "Dieta baja en carbono", que mide las emisiones
(10) de GEI en el ciclo de vida de los alimentos, desde que se elaboran, se transportan, hasta que llegan a la mesa.

El equipo de los investigadores californianos se suma a un movimiento cre- ciente que propugna un tipo de alimentación que tiene en cuenta su impacto en el calentamiento global. Los defensores de la dieta baja en carbono valoran
(15) la cantidad de GEI emitidos durante la producción, embalaje, procesamiento, transporte, preparación y transformación en residuo de los alimentos.

Según este criterio, los ciudadanos que quieran reducir su impacto en el cam- bio climático deberían aumentar el consumo de productos locales. Este tipo de alimentos, como defienden los localtarianos, evitan el transporte desde puntos
(20) lejanos, el uso de energía y la liberación de gases contaminantes.

Nathan Pelletier, investigador de la Escuela Universitaria Dalhousie para Estudios Medioambientales, en Halifax (Canadá), asegura que para seguir este tipo de dieta no sólo hay que fijarse en dónde se han producido los alimentos, sino también cómo. Pelletier señala que la principal contribución de la produc-
(25) ción alimentaria al cambio climático proviene de la ganadería. El 60% de los GEI asociados con carne de vacuno se relacionan con la emisión de metano o de nitrógeno procedentes del tratamiento del estiércol. Según un estudio de dicho investigador, para que un pez aumente de peso un kilo se necesita de uno a dos kilos de alimento; en el caso de una vaca la cantidad oscila entre 10 y 30 kilos.

(30) Los defensores de esta dieta recomiendan también reducir en lo posible el consumo de productos agropecuarios procedentes de explotaciones industriales. En estas instalaciones, la producción de verduras, frutas, lácteos, carne, etc., se lleva a cabo un uso intensivo de la energía y los recursos naturales, y se emplean productos químicos que contribuyen al calentamiento global. Como alternativa
(35) recomiendan el consumo de alimentos ecológicos, e incluso se alienta al auto consumo de alimentos procedentes de pequeños huertos urbanos.

Los productos frescos, de temporada, no envasados ni procesados, son otro de los alimentos estrella de una dieta baja en carbono. El empaquetado de productos requiere el uso de plástico y energía; de forma similar, la transformación (40) o congelación de un alimento para conservarlo y transportarlo conlleva el uso de energía y diversos procesos industriales que lanzan a la atmósfera diversos GEI. El agua mineral embotellada es una de las peores compras por la gran cantidad de recursos utilizados.

www.consumer.es/web/es/medio_ambiente/urbano/2010/04/05/192126.php

Fuente #2: El siguiente gráfico presenta la huella de carbono que se asocia con diferentes alimentos.

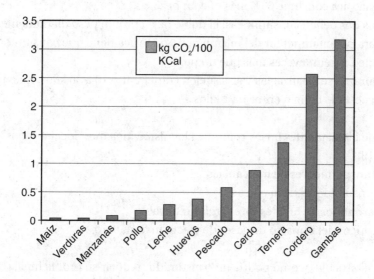

1. Según el artículo, ¿dónde queda Estados Unidos en la lista de países que producen gases invernaderos?
   (A) Es uno de los líderes en emisiones de gases invernaderos.
   (B) Es responsable por un quinto de las emisiones globales.
   (C) Es uno de los países con menor emisión global.
   (D) El artículo no presenta ninguna información acerca de este tema.

2. ¿Cómo se mide la huella de carbono de diversos alimentos?
   (A) Se basa en la energía usada para la crianza de ganado o el cultivo de plantas.
   (B) Se calcula la cantidad de residuos producidos por cada alimento.
   (C) Es basada en la preparación de los alimentos para ser consumidos.
   (D) Se incluyen todas fases de producción, desde el campo a la mesa.

3. ¿Qué debe considerar una persona que quiere seguir una dieta bajo en carbono?
   (A) La calidad de los alimentos y su frescura
   (B) La procedencia de los alimentos y su elaboración
   (C) El tipo de alimento y la cantidad que se debería consumir
   (D) El empaquetado y su valor nutritivo

4. ¿Por qué suele la ganadería tener una huella de carbono más alto que otros alimentos?
   (A) Porque hay más fincas de ganado que de cultivo de otros alimentos.
   (B) Porque hay más consumidores de ganado que de verduras.
   (C) Porque es más difícil transportarlos que otros alimentos.
   (D) Porque se requiere más energía para criar el ganado y hay más residuos.

5. ¿Qué dice el artículo en cuanto a la huella de carbono de un pez y una vaca?
   (A) Una vaca consume 60% más que un pez.
   (B) Los dos deben consumir casi el doble de su propio peso diariamente.
   (C) Para poder aumentar del mismo peso, una vaca tiene que consumir entre cinco a treinta veces más que un pez.
   (D) Durante su crianza, las vacas suelen comer entre 10 a 30 kilos, mientras los peces sólo comen entre 1 a 2 kilos.

6. ¿Cuál de las siguientes frases comunica la misma idea que "localtarianos" (línea 19)?
   (A) Transportadores de mercancías
   (B) Consumidores de lo cercano
   (C) Partidarios de fuentes de energías renovables
   (D) Críticos del impacto de gases de efecto invernadero

7. Según el artículo, ¿cómo podría un consumidor reducir su propia huella de carbono?
   (A) Evitar el consumo de productos de grandes granjas locales
   (B) Basar su dieta en los productos regionales y de temporada
   (C) Consumir más productos de lugares exóticos
   (D) Reducir la cantidad de consumo en general

8. ¿Qué tipo de información presenta el gráfico?
   (A) Las razones por las cuales hay que consumir un tipo de alimento en vez de otro.
   (B) La cantidad de dióxido de carbono que se asocia con diferentes alimentos.
   (C) Los alimentos que son más saludables a los consumidores.
   (D) La cantidad de calorías que cada alimento contiene.

9. Según el gráfico, ¿cuál de las siguientes afirmaciones es correcta?
   (A) La ganadería tiene un impacto ambiental más alto que el cultivo de frutas y verduras.
   (B) La producción de carne de ave perjudica más al ambiente que la de otras carnes.
   (C) El cultivo de manzanas impacta el ambiente tanto como el de verduras y maíz.
   (D) El maíz impacta menos al ambiente porque se ha reducido el consumo.

10. Basándote en la información de las dos fuentes, ¿cuál de las siguientes ideas sería una explicación por la cual gambas tienen la huella de carbono más alta en el gráfico?
    (A) Las gambas requieren mucha comida para que aumenten de peso.
    (B) Las gambas suelen ser congeladas para conservarlas y transportarlas.
    (C) La gente prefiere comer gambas a otros mariscos.
    (D) Hay que consumir una gran cantidad de gambas para satisfacer el hambre.

11. Si quisieras empezar un proyecto para promover una dieta baja en carbono en tu comunidad, ¿cuál de las siguientes publicaciones sería más apropiado para ayudarte?
    (A) *El granjero urbano: cómo crear tu propia huerta en tu ciudad*
    (B) *El impacto ambiental de la importación de alimentos*
    (C) *Ser vegetariano en 5 pasos*
    (D) *GEI y su impacto a nuestro planeta*

Selección #2—Más práctica

Ampliando tu vocabulario—Usa el vocabulario y frases del texto para llenar las columnas según el tema. ¿Puedes pensar en un tema adicional?

Palabras / frases relacionadas con . . .

. . . el daño al medio ambiente	. . . la elaboración de comida	. . . la conciencia ecológica	_____
gases de efecto invernadero (GEI) emisión	embalaje procesamiento	huellas de carbono reducir los GEI	

Cultural Awareness

Cultural practice: The article presents the importance of following a diet that has a small carbon footprint. Although the article uses data from several countries, the piece was published in a Spanish publication for a Spanish-speaking audience, and therefore reflects a perspective of this community.

How is the perspective mentioned in this article similar to or different from what you have observed in your own community?

SELECCIÓN #3

Tema curricular: La belleza y la estética

Introducción: El siguiente anuncio es para un evento de baile en Lima, Perú. Fue publicado en la página web del Ministerio de Cultura de Perú.

MUNICIPALIDAD DE LIMA TE INVITA AL XIII CONCURSO NACIONAL DE MARINERA LIMEÑA 2018

Con el propósito de preservar y revalorar las expresiones culturales de nuestra ciudad, la Gerencia de Cultura de la Municipalidad de Lima, organiza el XIII Concurso Nacional de Marinera Limeña 2018, el domingo 22 de julio en el Anfiteatro Nicomedes Santa Cruz del Parque de la Exposición.

Línea

(5) Este evento reunirá a más de 100 parejas de bailarines, de reconocidas escuelas de bailes de nuestro país, en seis distintas categorías: INFANTIL (8 a 11 años), PREJUVENILES (12 a 17 años), JUVENILES (18 a 21 años), ADULTOS (22 a 34 años), PREMAYORES (35 a 49 años) y MAYORES (50 años a más), quienes se disputarán premios que van desde los S/ 500 hasta S/ 5,000 soles, además de escapu-

(10) lario, bandas, trofeo y diplomas de honor.

Asimismo, se presentará la competencia de la categoría Campeón de Campeones, en la que participarán todos los campeones de los concursos de Marinera Limeña realizados por la Municipalidad de Lima, excepto los ganadores de los dos últimos años de la categoría Campeón de Campeones.

(15) Esta actividad se realiza con el fin de motivar a la población y que se encuentre con sus raíces y manifestaciones populares como lo son los bailes costumbristas y típicos del Perú, los mismos que constituyen el patrimonio inmaterial de la Humanidad, fortaleciendo y hacia la identidad nacional.

Lugar: Anfiteatro Nicomedes Santa Cruz, Parque de la Exposición

(20) **Dirección:** Av. 28 de Julio, Cercado de Lima

Fecha: 22 de julio

Hora: 9:00 am

Ingreso libre

1. ¿A quiénes se dirige principalmente este anuncio?

   (A) A estudiantes de baile
   (B) A bailarines profesionales
   (C) Al público limeño
   (D) A ganadores de concursos anteriores

2. ¿Cuál es una meta principal de este evento?

   (A) Seleccionar a los mejores bailarines del país
   (B) Conservar y apreciar un aspecto importante de la cultura peruana
   (C) Motivar a los espectadores a participar en el baile
   (D) Crear una identidad nacional

3. ¿Qué pueden ganar los concursantes?

   (A) Un premio monetario
   (B) Un trofeo o diploma
   (C) La oportunidad de competir en la categoría Campeón de Campeones en el futuro
   (D) La oportunidad de ganar cualquiera de las opciones mencionadas en opciones A, B, y C

4. ¿Quiénes pueden competir en la categoría Campeón de Campeones?

   (A) Los campeones de cualquier concurso de baile anterior que nunca han ganado esta categoría
   (B) Los que han ganado su categoría y que también han participado en esta categoría en años recientes
   (C) Los que han ganado un concurso del mismo patrocinador y que no han ganado esta categoría recientemente
   (D) Únicamente los campeones de categoría de este concurso que aún no han ganado esta categoría

5. Si quisieras más información de este evento, ¿cuál de las siguientes preguntas sería más apropiada para formular?

   (A) No veo la hora de este evento. ¿Cuál es la parada de autobús más cercana?
   (B) Me gustaría llevar a mi familia. ¿Cuánto nos costaría asistir?
   (C) Mi hija es bailarina y vivimos justo al lado del teatro. ¿Puede ella participar también?
   (D) Quiero inscribirme en un curso de baile para mantenerme en forma. ¿Qué tipo de baile me convendría más?

Cultural Awareness

Cultural product: This advertisement promotes an event in Lima, Perú, whose purpose is to celebrate a typical Peruvian dance, the *baile marinera*.

Cultural perspective: This advertisement also highlights the importance of preserving and appreciating traditional dances in Perú.

Does your community sponsor events similar to the one mentioned in this advertisement?

SELECCIÓN #4

Tema curricular: Las familias y las comunidades

En la siguiente carta, Pablo le escribe a su amigo de una fiesta que experimentó cuando estuvo en México.

Querido Javier,

Espero que todo te vaya bien. Acabo de pasar unas semanas en México para celebrar el día de los Reyes Magos con mis tíos y quería contarte de cómo me fue.

Línea

(5) Me divertí un montón, especialmente disfrutando de la rosca de Reyes. No sé si la has probado, pero es absolutamente deliciosa.

La rosca de Reyes es un bizcocho fino que contiene en promedio tres figuras de plástico en forma de niño y que simbolizan al hijo de Dios. Según me contó mi tía, es una tradición que vino de España en los primeros años del Virreinato y formó parte de las festividades de año nuevo para recordar la llegada a Jerusalén

(10) de los Reyes Magos. Desde entonces la rosca de Reyes es el centro de atención de la fiesta de cada seis de enero por ser una de las tradiciones más antiguas de la iglesia católica que recuerda este evento. Esto es muy distinto de lo que hacemos en Estados Unidos, donde la celebración es típicamente el veinticinco de diciembre.

(15) Según la religión católica, quién encuentre la figura deberá vestir y presentar al niño Dios en la iglesia durante la fiesta del Día de la Candelaria el 2 de febrero para celebrar los 40 días de su nacimiento. Mi hermano la encontró, pero se la dio a nuestro primo para que él lo entregara, dado que ya habríamos vuelto a casa. Mi tío nos dijo que desde la Edad Media las familias españolas acostumbra-

(20) ban a servir una merienda en la cual se partía la rosca de Reyes y que unos historiadores aseguran de que se trata de una costumbre romana que tomó la iglesia católica y la unió a la Navidad.

Los comerciantes aprovechan esta ocasión para incrementar sus ganancias mediante la venta de roscas de todos tamaños, pero mi tía nos la preparó y te

(25) aseguro que la de mi tía es la mejor rosca que hayas comido jamás. Ella la elaboró cuidadosamente con harina, azúcar, mantequilla y huevos hasta tener una pasta fina y después la puso en un molde y la adornó con trozos de fruta seca. Te aseguro que no has comido mejor bizcocho en tu vida.

Aunque tuvimos que volver a casa, la festividad continúa hasta el Día de la

(30) Candelaria, cuando las familias se reúnen nuevamente para celebrar la presentación del niño Dios en la iglesia. En ese momento se preparan y se comen tamales verdes, rojos y de dulce acompañado con atole de maíz. ¡Cuánto me encantaría estar de nuevo allí para gozar de ellos! Pero mi tía me dijo que esta tradición ha perdurado generaciones y que seguramente podré disfrutar de ella en el futuro.

(35) Bueno, me despido de ti. Lo he pasado súper bien con mis tíos, y espero que un día tengas también la oportunidad de experimentar esta fiesta tan bonita. Cuídate y nos veremos en la escuela.

Un abrazo,
Pablo

1. ¿Qué es una rosca de Reyes?
   (A) Es una figura pequeña que se presenta a la iglesia el 6 de enero.
   (B) Es un tipo de postre con pequeñas figuras escondidas adentro.
   (C) Es un tipo de regalo traído por los Reyes Magos.
   (D) Es una fiesta que tiene la familia durante el mes de enero.

2. ¿Cuándo se celebra esta tradición?
   (A) El veinticinco de diciembre
   (B) El seis de enero
   (C) El dos de febrero
   (D) Cuarenta días después del dos de febrero

3. ¿En qué consiste la costumbre?
   (A) Los miembros de la familia se visten en trajes romanos para ir a la iglesia.
   (B) Todos compran regalos para presentar al niño Jesús el Día de la Candelaria.
   (C) Todos compran o preparan una rosca para la fiesta en casa.
   (D) Se celebra el Día de los Reyes Magos visitando la iglesia con comida especial.

4. ¿Qué tiene que hacer el que encuentra la figura del niño?
   (A) Tiene que vestirse en traje romano para ir a la iglesia.
   (B) Tiene que preparar la fiesta para el Día de la Candelaria.
   (C) Tiene que llevarla a Belén.
   (D) Tiene que presentarse a la iglesia con la figura.

5. ¿De dónde procede la tradición de la rosca?
   (A) Tiene raíces durante la época colonial de México.
   (B) Empezó con el Nacimiento.
   (C) Tiene raíces en las costumbres de la iglesia católica medieval.
   (D) Los romanos empezaron la costumbre con una fiesta pagana.

6. ¿Qué permite esta costumbre?
   (A) Que toda la familia se reúna para ayudar a los comerciantes.
   (B) Que los comerciantes disfruten de un descanso de su negocio.
   (C) Que la iglesia estreche las relaciones con la comunidad comercial.
   (D) Que los niños se sientan parte de la comunidad religiosa.

7. ¿Por qué se molesta Pablo al fin de la carta?
   (A) Quiere poder entregar el niño en la iglesia.
   (B) No quiere perderse otra cena maravillosa.
   (C) No se va a repetir esta celebración por unos años.
   (D) No quiere volver a las clases.

Comparación cultural

SELECCIÓN #5

Tema curricular: La vida contemporánea

El siguiente fragmento del libro *Corazón: Diario de un niño*, de Edmundo de Amacis, relata un evento que experimentó el narrador con un joven obrero.

	A las cuatro merendamos juntos, pan y pasas, sentados en el sofá, y cuando nos levantamos, no sé por qué, mi padre no quiso que limpiara el espaldar que el albañilito había manchado de blanco con su chaqueta; me detuvo la mano y
Línea	lo limpió después sin que lo viéramos. Jugando, al albañilito se le cayó un botón
(5)	de la cazadora, y mi madre se le cosió; él se puso encarnado, y la veía coser; muy admirado y confuso, no atreviéndose ni a respirar. Después le enseñé el álbum de caricaturas, y él, sin darse cuenta, imitaba los gestos de aquellas caras, tan bien, que hasta mi padre se reía. Estaba tan contento cuando se fue, que se olvidó de ponerse al andrajoso sombrero, y al llegar a la puerta de la escalera, para manifes-
(10)	starme su gratitud, me hacía otra vez la gracia de poner el *hocico de liebre*.
	—¿Sabes, hijo mío, por qué no quise que limpiara el sofá? Porque limpiarle mientras tu compañero lo veía era casi hacerle una reconvención por haberlo ensuciado. Y esto no estaba bien: en primer lugar, porque no lo había hecho de intento, y en segundo lugar, porque le había manchado con ropa de su padre,
(15)	que se la había enyesado trabajando; y lo que se mancha trabajando no ensucia; es polvo, cal, barniz, todo lo que quieras, pero no suciedad. El trabajo no ensu- cia. No digas nunca de un obrero que sale de su trabajo: "Va sucio". Debes decir: "Tiene en su ropa las señales, las huellas del trabajo". Recuérdalo. Quiero mucho al albañilito: primero, porque es compañero tuyo, y además, porque es hijo de un
(20)	obrero. —*Tu padre.*

1. ¿De qué trata esta selección?
   (A) De la conducta apropiada de un anfitrión
   (B) De los modos de mantenerse limpio en casa
   (C) De la conducta apropiada de un huésped
   (D) De los modos de disciplinar a un hijo

2. Al levantarse del sofá, ¿qué le molestaba al hijo?
   (A) Que la ropa del visitante estaba sucia
   (B) Que se vieron algunas huellas del trabajo en el sofá
   (C) Que en la chaqueta del albañilito faltaba un botón
   (D) Que la chaqueta mostraba señales del trabajo

3. ¿Cómo se sentía el albañilito cuando observó a la mamá reparando la ropa?
   (A) Estaba muy triste.
   (B) Se avergonzó.
   (C) Se enojó.
   (D) Se arrepintió.

4. En la línea 15, ¿qué quiere decir "... lo que se mancha trabajando no ensucia"?
   (A) Indica que no puede ensuciarse trabajando.
   (B) Significa que el padre no vio que la chaqueta estaba sucia.
   (C) Significa que trabajar no es una desgracia.
   (D) Quiere decir que el padre se sentía superior a los obreros.

5. ¿Por qué no quería el papá que su hijo limpiara el sofá de inmediato?
   (A) No quería que el albañilito viera a su hijo trabajando.
   (B) Quería que la madre lo hiciera.
   (C) Quería que el albañilito viera lo que había hecho.
   (D) No quería parecer descortés al invitado.

6. ¿Qué determina la diferencia entre el hijo y el albañilito?
   (A) Los aspectos socio-económicos de los dos
   (B) El nivel de formación educativa de los dos
   (C) Las características personales de los dos
   (D) La edad de los dos

7. ¿Cómo es la relación entre el papá y el hijo?
   (A) Parece que el padre es muy exigente.
   (B) Parece que los dos gozan de relaciones muy estrechas.
   (C) Parece que el chico no le hace mucho caso al padre.
   (D) El chico parece ser muy mimado por su padre.

Cultural Awareness

Cultural perspective: In this fragment, the mother and father demonstrate the right conduct of being a good host, and the father takes the time to explain this importance to his son.

How is the perspective presented in this text similar to or different from your own community?

SELECCIÓN #6

Tema curricular: Los desafíos mundiales

En la siguiente carta, Susana, una joven española, le cuenta a su amiga una preocupación que ella tiene.

Querida Susana,

Ya se están aproximando las vacaciones de verano, y no puedo decirte cuánto me alegra poder descansar un poco. Las clases han ido bien, pero todavía tengo

Línea los exámenes del fin de curso . . . ¡qué rollo!

(5) Gracias por tu última carta en que me informaste de que habías adoptado un cachorro. ¿Por fin le has dado un nombre? Supongo que requiere mucha responsabilidad pero igual te llena de alegría. Me gustaría también tener un perrito, pero mi padre dice que tengo que enfocarme en los estudios y que volveremos a discutirlo en el otoño.

(10) Hablando de mascotas, es el tema de mi proyecto de investigación para la clase de ciencias sociales. Me entristeció enterarme de que este país encabeza la lista en abandono de mascotas, con más de cien mil perros abandonados anualmente. Para mí, no hay ningún motivo válido que justifique el abandono de estos pequeños seres de cuatro patas.

(15) Muchos creen que es durante el período estival cuando se da el mayor número de abandonos, pero hay que desmentir esta creencia (aunque sí, es cierta para los gatos). Hoy en día se mantiene estable a lo largo del año, siendo factores económicos el principal motivo seguido por camadas no deseadas. Si no quisieron una camada, ¿por qué no esterilizar a los perros para evitar que se abandonen

(20) a sus crías? ¡Y casi el diez por ciento de los casos de abandono es por la pérdida de interés! ¿Puedes creerlo?

¿Cómo crees que podemos reducir este problema? Seguro que hay que afrontarlo desde varios frentes, como mejorar la legislación. Pensando en este asunto, creo también que hay que poner en marcha más campañas, como unas de este-

(25) rilización para evitar camadas no deseadas y que fomenten la adopción de animales. ¿Qué opinas?

¿Y tú? ¿Qué vas a hacer con tu cachorro cuando vayas de vacaciones? ¿Lo vas a llevar contigo o tienes a alguien que lo va a cuidar? Desde hace varios años ha habido portales en que amantes de animales anuncian su disponibilidad de aco-

(30) ger a una mascota durante los días de vacaciones. Pero, ¿sabes qué?, también hay hoteles que han tomado la iniciativa de permitir la entrada de animales domésticos por un pequeño suplemento. Seguramente ya lo tienes todo pensado y planeado . . . simplemente quería pasarte unas ideas en caso de que las necesitaras.

Bueno, eso es todo que te voy a contar por ahora porque tengo que irme. Lo

(35) siento por haberme ido por las ramas con este asunto. Como puedes ver, me ha tocado bastante. Te prometo que en la próxima carta volveré al tema de la pregunta que me hiciste. Mientras tanto, espero que el fin del año escolar te vaya bien y aprovecho esta oportunidad para despedirme con un gran abrazo y beso.

Saludos a tu familia,

(40) Alicia

1. ¿Con qué propósito le escribe Alicia a Susana?

   (A) Para informarla de su proyecto
   (B) Para continuar a corresponder con ella
   (C) Para cambiar el tema de una conversación previa
   (D) Para despedirse de ella

2. Según Alicia, ¿cuál es la principal razón por el abandono de los perros?

   (A) Las familias van de vacaciones y no pueden cuidarlos.
   (B) No tienen suficiente dinero para mantenerlos.
   (C) Se deteriora la afección que tienen por ellos.
   (D) Los perros tienen muchas crías.

3. Según la carta, ¿cómo se compara la situación del abandono de mascotas en España con la de otros países europeos?

   (A) Es menor que de otros países.
   (B) Es igual que de otros países.
   (C) Es mayor que de otros países.
   (D) No tiene los datos para hacer una comparación.

4. ¿De dónde parece provenir la información que Alicia le presenta a su amiga?

   (A) Es resultado de su investigación.
   (B) Es su propia opinión del tema.
   (C) Es sentido común.
   (D) Es resultado de entrevistas.

5. ¿Cuál de las siguientes declaraciones mejor describe la solución al problema?

   (A) Hay que castigar a los que abandonan las mascotas.
   (B) Hay que concienciar más a la gente del problema.
   (C) Hay que hacerle frente desde múltiples ángulos.
   (D) Hay que crear más plataformas para el cuidado responsable de mascotas.

6. ¿Qué novedad menciona Alicia puede ayudar a reducir la tasa de abandono durante el período estival?

   (A) Una nueva campaña que promueve la esterilización de las mascotas
   (B) Una plataforma en que personas indican su capacidad de cuidar a las mascotas cuando el dueño está de vacaciones
   (C) Establecimientos de alojamiento que permiten la entrada de animales
   (D) Un movimiento que promueve la adaptación durante el período de vacaciones

7. ¿Qué comunica Alicia en el cierre de su carta cuando dice que se había ido «... por las ramas» (línea 30)?

   (A) Que se había desviado del tema de discusión anterior
   (B) Que este asunto no tiene una solución fácil
   (C) Que este es un tema que le importa mucho
   (D) Que es una persona bastante sensible

Identifica las siguientes partes de la correspondencia:

- El saludo
- La apertura
- El cuerpo
- El cierre
- La despedida

¿Qué tono usa la escritora? ¿Por qué?

Cultural Awareness

Cultural practice: This correspondence presents an unfortunate practice in Spain: how many pets are abandoned and the reasons for this abandonment. Unlike most cultural practices, this one is accidental, meaning that it is a result of circumstances rather than desire. There are other practices mentioned in this text, including the emergence of pet sitting opportunities and hotels that now have designated rooms for pets.

Cultural perspective: This correspondence also presents the view shared by many in Spain regarding the abandonment of pets, and how it is frowned upon and considered cruel.

How do the practices and perspectives presented in this text compare to those in your own community?

SELECCIÓN #7

Tema curricular: La ciencia y la tecnología

Introducción:

Fuente #1: El siguiente artículo se trata del uso de las diferentes redes sociales en España. Fue publicado en 2018 por DigitalNewsReport.es.

Facebook y WhatsApp siguen liderando en redes pero YouTube, Twitter e Instagram crecen entre los jóvenes

Casi la mitad de la población conectada en España continúa empleando Facebook (48%) para seguir, comentar o compartir noticias, al menos semanalmente. La popular red social, objeto de polémicas en el último año por la fil-
Línea
(5) tración de datos personales de usuarios a terceros, mantiene su liderazgo en uso informativo en todas las franjas de edad, seguido por el servicio hermano WhatsApp, que usa en relación con la actualidad informativa al menos uno de cada tres internautas de cualquier edad, y que continúa siendo el sitio o la aplicación más popular en uso general.

Los mayores crecimientos en uso de redes sociales y las mayores diferencias
(10) por edad están en YouTube (pasa de 67% a 74%), Twitter (sube del 33% al 39%) e Instagram (del 29%, llega al 36%). Las tres suben, en uso general, entre seis y siete puntos porcentuales en un año; esto sitúa a YouTube a la par de Facebook en uso general.

La encuesta del Digital News Report ha encontrado similitudes y diferencias
(15) en el uso que se hace de dos servicios de la misma empresa, Facebook y Whats-App, en relación con las noticias, tomando como base los internautas que han respondido que empleaban cada plataforma con finalidad informativa o de debate y opinión en torno a las noticias. No existe una distinción radical entre Facebook y WhatsApp, pero sí se observa cómo el consumo más pasivo de noticias (ver
(20) titulares y vídeos y hacer clic en enlaces), así como las interacciones más sencillas, como los 'me gusta' o compartir directamente una publicación, tienden a producirse con más frecuencia en Facebook, mientras que WhatsApp concentra la participación proactiva, dentro de grupos creados al efecto y debates privados.

La fuente de la noticia es el principal criterio que emplean los usuarios para
(25) decidir si leen o ven una información que encuentran en redes sociales. Sendas mayorías del 57% también consideran importantes aspectos tan distintos como, por una parte, el titular y la imagen con los que se presenta cada información, y por otra parte, la persona que comparte la noticia. Por último, las opiniones están divididas en cuanto a la relevancia del número de interacciones ('me gusta',
(30) comentarios o veces que se ha compartido) a la hora de determinar el interés de una información: casi una tercera parte lo considera importante, y son algunos más quienes no lo tienen en cuenta.

Fuente #2: La siguiente tabla presenta el porcentaje de usuarios de internet en España por tipo de actividad realizada en 2018. Los datos provienen del Instituto Nacional de Estadística.

Hombres y mujeres en España de 16 a 74 años		
Actividad realizada	**Mujeres**	**Hombres**
Recibir o enviar correos electrónicos	81,1	79,3
Telefonear o videollamadas a través de internet	37,3	39,0
Participar en redes sociales	64,4	70,5
Jugar o descargar juegos	36,0	31,1
Ver contenidos de video de sitios para compartir (p. ej. YouTube)	76,8	74,9
Vender bienes o servicios	14,8	11,4

1. ¿Cuál es el propósito del artículo?

    (A) Informar de los hábitos de uso de las redes sociales en España

    (B) Explicar las razones por las cuales los usuarios usan las redes sociales

    (C) Analizar cuáles son las redes sociales qué más se usan para encontrar y compartir noticias

    (D) Informar de los resultados de una encuesta sobre los efectos del uso de las redes sociales

2. ¿Qué información presenta el artículo sobre Facebook?

    (A) Su uso se ha bajado

    (B) Su uso ha generado controversia

    (C) Es el sitio predilecto para encontrar noticias

    (D) Es mayormente usado por los adultos

3. Según el artículo, ¿qué red social es la más usada por los jóvenes para dar y recibir noticias?

    (A) Facebook

    (B) YouTube

    (C) Twitter

    (D) Instagram

4. Según la información presentada en el artículo, ¿cuál es la red social más usada en uso general?

    (A) Facebook

    (B) WhatsApp

    (C) YouTube

    (D) Twitter

5. ¿Cómo se destacan YouTube, Twitter e Instagram en cuanto a su uso general?

    (A) Todas tienen el mismo nivel de importancia.

    (B) Han experimentado un crecimiento continuo.

    (C) Son tan populares como Facebook.

    (D) Su uso se ha incrementado entre los jóvenes.

6. Según el artículo, ¿cómo se diferencian Facebook y WhatsApp en como fuente de noticias?

   (A) No hay ninguna diferencia.
   (B) Los usuarios de WhatsApp tienden a interactuar más con otros usuarios.
   (C) Los usuarios de Facebook divulgan más noticias.
   (D) Las noticias se encuentran más fácilmente por WhatsApp.

7. ¿A qué se refiere el artículo cuando dice «La fuente de la noticia . . .» (línea 21)?

   (A) A la procedencia de la noticia
   (B) Al tipo de noticia
   (C) A la fiabilidad de la noticia
   (D) Al contenido de la noticia

8. Según el artículo, ¿qué impacto tienen los comentarios de otros en determinar el interés de una noticia?

   (A) Tienen un impacto enorme.
   (B) Tienen un impacto mínimo.
   (C) No tienen ningún impacto.
   (D) Para algunos son importantes y para otros no tanto.

9. ¿Qué información presenta la tabla?

   (A) Las acciones que realizan los usuarios de redes sociales en línea
   (B) El número de personas que realizan diferentes actividades por internet
   (C) Las actividades típicas que ambos sexos efectúan por internet
   (D) Las acciones preferidas por hombres y mujeres en internet

10. Según la información en la tabla, ¿cuál de las siguientes opciones mejor describe la actividad realizada más frecuentemente en línea?

    (A) Efectuar operaciones económicas
    (B) Comunicarse con otros
    (C) Entretenerse
    (D) Compartir fotos y videos

11. Si fueras a investigar el tema presentado en el artículo y en la tabla, ¿cuál de las siguientes publicaciones tendría la información que buscas?

    (A) *La conquista global de Facebook*
    (B) *La evolución de las comunidades virtuales en la península Ibérica*
    (C) *Redes sociales e internet: cómo usarlos para impulsar tu negocio*
    (D) *Siete motivos para usar internet y redes sociales en tu vida*

Cultural Awareness

Cultural practice: The article presents current habits in Spain regarding use of social media to access news, while the table presents current habits regarding use of the internet in general.

How do these compare to the use of social media and the internet in your community?

SELECCIÓN #8

Tema curricular: Las identidades personales

El siguiente fragmento, del libro *Tiempo Mexicano* por Carlos Fuentes publicado en 1973, relata el cambio social que ocurrió en México en el siglo XX.

	Entre los jóvenes de clase media, y a veces de clase obrera que con grandes sacrificios llegan a los estudios superiores, tiene lugar, por otra parte, la transformación cultural más interesante de la década. Quizás la historia cultural del
Línea	México independiente pueda dividirse en tres etapas. La primera, hasta finales
(5)	de la dictadura de Díaz, muestra una marcada tendencia—que las grandes excepciones, de Fernández de Lizardi a Posadas, no alcanzan a suprimir—a los que Antonio Caso llamó "la imitación extralógica": una cultura importada, como las mansardas que en las casas de la Colonia Juárez esperaban inútilmente la ventisca invernal. Pero a fines del Porfiriato, las novelas de Rabasa y Frías, la poesía
(10)	de Othón, los grabados de Posada anunciaban un descubrimiento: el de México por sí mismo. La Revolución, en esencia un paso del no ser, o del ser enajenado, al ser para sí, fue el acto mismo de ese descubrimiento—los actos coinciden con las palabras y la apariencia con el rostro: la máscara cae y todos los colores, voces y cuerpos de México brillan con su existencia real. Un país dividido en compar-
(15)	timientos estancos entra en contacto con sí mismo. Las formidables cabalgatas de la División del Norte y del Cuerpo del Noroeste por todo el territorio de la república son un abrazo y un reconocimiento: los mexicanos saben por primera vez cómo hablan, cómo cantan, cómo ríen, cómo aman, cómo beben, cómo comen, cómo injurian y cómo mueren los mexicanos.
(20)	Del choque revolucionario surgió una doble tendencia cultural, positivo en cuanto permitió a los mexicanos descubrirse a sí mismos, y negativa en cuanto llegó a un extremo chauvinista, tipificado popularmente en la frase "Como México no hay dos" que sólo acentúa nuestra forzosa relación bilateral con los Estados Unidos. Curiosa y suicida coincidencia de cierta izquierda y de la derecha cierta: la
(25)	xenofobia, la afirmación de la singularidad mexicana, la invención estimágtica de "ideas exóticas" para denigrar, sencillamente, las ideas que no se comprenden o se juzgan peligrosas para la ortodoxia de los unos o las ganancias de los otros.

1. ¿Cómo se diferencian los jóvenes modernos de los de la época del Porfiriato?
   - (A) Creen que saben más.
   - (B) No tienen identidad auténtica.
   - (C) Son más artísticos.
   - (D) Disfrutan de más oportunidades.

2. ¿Qué pasó en la primera etapa de la gran transformación mexicana?
   - (A) Estalló la rebelión contra la dictadura de Porfirio Díaz.
   - (B) Los mexicanos imitaron a las modas ajenas.
   - (C) El pueblo se escondió tras máscaras regionales.
   - (D) El país se dividió en varios departamentos.

3. ¿Cómo empezaron algunos a mostrar su independencia?
    (A) Unos artistas iniciaron unas nuevas tendencias artísticas.
    (B) La División del Norte se encontró con el Cuerpo del Noroeste.
    (C) Mexicanos de todas partes se juntaron en contra de Porfirio Díaz.
    (D) Unos mexicanos empezaron a pensar de una manera no muy lógica.

4. ¿Qué es lo que se veía al caer la máscara?
    (A) Se veía muchos colores brillantes.
    (B) Descubrieron que eran xenofóbicos.
    (C) Reconocieron sus diferencias regionales.
    (D) Se enteraron de cómo eran sus compatriotas.

5. ¿Qué aspecto positivo tiene la doble tendencia cultural mexicana?
    (A) Los mexicanos reconocieron sus semejanzas.
    (B) Supieron que tenían que juntarse para luchar contra los Estados Unidos.
    (C) Descubrieron el valor de la cultura autóctona.
    (D) Descubrieron que a todos les gustaron los colores vivos.

6. En las líneas 22–23, ¿qué quiere decir la frase *Como México no hay dos*?
    (A) Hay sólo una raza mexicana.
    (B) No se puede permitir influencias extranjeras en México.
    (C) No hay diferencias políticas entre los mexicanos.
    (D) Todas las regiones de México gozan de oportunidades iguales.

7. Últimamente ¿en qué consiste la transformación discutida en esta selección?
    (A) El fomento de revolución artística
    (B) La creación de regiones únicas
    (C) Un proceso de autoidentificación mexicana
    (D) El reconocimiento de la superioridad cultural mexicana

---

Cultural Awareness

Cultural perspective: In this fragment, the Mexican author Carlos Fuentes connects several key episodes in Mexican history to the formation of the culture and identity of its people.

Can you think of an event in recent history that had an effect on the identity and culture in your own community? How is the perspective of history impacting culture and identity similar to or different from that in your own community?

SELECCIÓN #9

Tema curricular: La ciencia y la tecnología

El siguiente artículo se trata de cómo internet afecta la reputación de individuos. El artículo fue publicado en *http://LaNacion.com* en 2010.

El desafío de mantener una reputación en internet

El prestigio siempre ha sido algo de lo que preocuparse. Construir una identidad era tarea de una vida, incluso de varias. En tiempos medievales bastaba echar una ojeada al escudo de armas, que garantizaba el buen nombre del portador.

Línea

(5) Yelmos y flores de lis fueron sustituidos por los contactos, gente importante que respaldaba la propia fama.

Hoy, internet se ha apropiado de las herramientas para labrarse una buena reputación. Ni cartas de recomendación ni blasones familiares. El linaje ha sido sustituido por el historial de Google.

La notoriedad nunca fue tan democrática como ahora. Cualquiera puede

(10) acceder a la red y defenderse en ella sin dinero ni intermediarios. Sólo méritos y un público casi ilimitado. Pero al igual que en la Edad Media, bullen los rumores que se extienden como la pólvora y que, también de manera democrática, salpican las reputaciones.

"Antes, si crecías en un pueblo, sabías quién era hijo de quién y, si te metías

(15) en líos, todos se enteraban. Ahora, ese pueblo es Facebook o Twitter. Si cometes un error, todos lo saben". Andy Beal es uno de los mayores expertos mundiales en reputación online y ha asesorado, entre otros, a Microsoft y Motorola. Asegura que los jefes consultan Google y Facebook para saber más sobre sus empleados: "Al menos una vez al año, supervisarán tu actividad online para encontrar algo

(20) que pueda hacerte prescindible. Muchos gerentes se hacen amigos tuyos en las redes sociales para vigilarte".

Medir la reputación y mejorarla es tarea de profesionales. En España, despuntan las primeras consultoras especializadas. Estudian la presencia en internet de la empresa, institución o particular que les contrata y generan contenido positivo

(25) sobre ellas (texto, fotos y vídeos sobre lo que hacen y dicen, cuanto más, mejor). Si el daño ya está hecho, solicitan a blogs, foros y webs que retiren los comentarios injuriosos sobre sus clientes.

La mayoría de los expertos minimizan los riesgos y se sienten molestos por la distorsión mediática: "El miedo vende", dice Neus Arqués, de la consultora Man-

(30) fatta. "Antes, para llegar a grandes audiencias, hacía falta dinero para pagar a un responsable de comunicación. Ahora, cualquiera, incluso un autónomo, puede llegar más allá de su barrio".

No todos los rumores son infundados. "Hay gente que merece su mala fama", afirma Victor Puig, de Overalia. Pero incluso estos, señala Oriol Gifra, de Cus-

(35) tomer Hunt, tienen derecho a limpiar su reputación: "Esto es como si van a un abogado: yo les defenderé, sean inocentes o no".

¿Cómo hacer para no perder el buen nombre en el lodazal de insultos anónimos que puede ser la red? Jeremiah Owyang se presenta como «estratega web» y es columnista de *Forbes:* «Debes apropiarte de tu nombre en internet

(40) antes de que otro lo haga». Blindarse ante posibles ataques, tal y como hace la Casa del Rey, que ha ido comprando y cerrando los dominios web con el nombre de los hijos del Príncipe y las Infantas a medida que estos nacían.

En el medievo, bastaba una mala salida al campo de batalla para perder la vida. Si el caballero no había dejado descendencia, desaparecía su nombre. Hoy,

(45) quien deja huella en internet lo hace para siempre. Borrarse de las redes sociales no garantiza nada, la información sigue ahí.

1. Según el artículo, ¿cómo se podía distinguir la reputación de alguien en la época medieval?
   (A) La gente importante solía llevar flores.
   (B) Se llevaban insignias para confirmar su prestigio.
   (C) Los de buena reputación portaban armas.
   (D) Había cartas que comprobaban la reputación de una persona.

2. ¿A qué se refiere el artículo cuando dice que para realizar una identidad en la antigüedad ". . . era tarea de una vida, incluso de varias" (línea 2)?
   (A) A que muchos participaban en la creación de una identidad
   (B) A que para tener una buena reputación se debía quitarles la vida a otros
   (C) A que la notoriedad era algo que sólo se podía alcanzar después de la muerte
   (D) A que alcanzar notoriedad tardaba mucho, incluso varias generaciones

3. ¿Qué dificultad se encuentra al mantener una buena reputación tanto con el uso actual de internet como en la antigüedad?
   (A) Alcanzar fama todavía requiere que el individuo tenga un linaje particular.
   (B) La reputación de un individuo puede ser dañada por el chisme.
   (C) Encontrar suficiente público para poder respaldar los méritos de alguien.
   (D) Se carece de unas herramientas vitales para crear una buena reputación.

4. De acuerdo al artículo, ¿por qué acuden unos directivos a redes sociales?
   (A) Para evaluar conducta de sus empleados afuera del ámbito laboral
   (B) Para poder estar al tanto de las comunidades virtuales
   (C) Para hacerse amigos de los trabajadores
   (D) Para encontrar a más aspirantes para un puesto particular

5. ¿Qué puede hacer una empresa para poder mejorar su reputación?
   (A) Contratar a un abogado que la defienda aunque merezca su mala reputación
   (B) Participar más en foros y blogs y escribir comentarios positivos de sus clientes
   (C) Pedir ayuda a compañías concentradas en la formación y restauración de reputaciones en la red
   (D) Apoderarse de todo contenido en internet que tenga que ver con la empresa

6. ¿Qué comunica el artículo en el último párrafo (líneas 43–46)?
   (A) Que en la actualidad es más fácil recibir una buena o mala reputación
   (B) Que en la antigüedad era más fácil recibir o perder una buena reputación
   (C) Que en la antigüedad la muerte del cabeza de familia significaba la desaparición de la identidad y reputación familiar
   (D) Que en la actualidad la identidad y reputación de alguien perdura mucho más que antes

7. Imagina que quieres informarte más en cómo crear y mantener una buena reputación en internet. ¿Cuál de los siguientes artículos te serviría más?
   (A) *Reputación online: prevenir es mejor que curar*
   (B) *La privacidad personal en la era de internet*
   (C) *Diez recomendaciones para la gestión de redes sociales*
   (D) *Guía para identificar a los trolls en tu blog*

Selección #9—Más Práctica

Vocabulario en contexto—Use the context of the text to figure out the most probable meaning of the following words. Write a synonym or explain the word in Spanish in the blanks that follow. The numbers in parentheses indicate the line where the word is found.

Definición / Sinónimo

1. echar una ojeada (2–3) _____

2. labrarse (6) _____

3. metías en líos (14–15) _____

4. blindarse (40) _____

Cultural Awareness

Cultural perspective: This article presents the challenges of keeping a good profile on the internet.

How is the perspective presented on this topic in this article similar to or different from the one in your own community?

SELECCIÓN #10

Tema curricular: La belleza y la estética

Este anuncio es para un concurso patrocinado por un instituto de educación secundaria en España.

Concurso de Tarjetas de Navidad

Navidad 2011

Bases y entrega de trabajos

Premios

Primer Premio

30 €

Segundo Premio

20 €

1° Podrán participar todos los alumnos matriculados durante el presente curso en la ESO.

2° El tamaño de las tarjetas será A5 (la mitad de un A4 210x297 mm) para darles el tradicional formato de tarjeta.

3° El nombre, apellidos y curso deberá figurar en el reverso de la tarjeta.

4° El tema de las tarjetas será cualquier imagen o composición que sugiera, evoque o suscite el concepto de la Navidad en España.

5° Los trabajos no podrán ser copia íntegra ni parcial de otras tarjetas.

6° El plazo de entrega será hasta el 28 de noviembre de 2011.

7° La entrega se hará en la Jefatura de Estudios del centro.

Tarjeta ganadora el curso 2010-2011

Fallo del Jurado

1° El Jurado estará compuesto por tres profesores del centro, un administrativo y un representante del Equipo Directivo.

2° Cualquier trabajo podrá ser impreso para tarjeta de felicitación institucional del centro.

3° La presentación a concursado implica la concesión del permiso para ser impreso.

4° Una selección de las obras podrá ser expuesta en el instituto.

5° El fallo del jurado y el lugar y fecha de la entrega de premios se harán públicos el la página Web del centro el día 15 de diciembre.

6° La presentación a concurso implica la aceptación de estas bases.

1. ¿Qué promociona este anuncio?
   (A) Los trabajos de unos estudiantes
   (B) Una competición escolar
   (C) Una representación de una fiesta de Navidad
   (D) Una muestra de arte estudiantil

2. ¿Quiénes calificarán los trabajos?
   (A) Maestros y representantes del cuerpo estudiantil
   (B) Unos profesores y el director de la escuela
   (C) Personal docente y administrativo
   (D) Varios miembros de la junta directiva y unos profesores

3. ¿Cuál de las siguientes es una norma que se acepta al entregar las tarjetas?
   (A) Que pueden ser publicadas y mandadas a la comunidad escolar
   (B) Que cualquier trabajo podrá ser expuesto en la página web de la escuela
   (C) Que las tarjetas serán exhibidas en una zona pública de la escuela
   (D) Que se otorgarán los premios el 15 de diciembre

4. ¿Qué otra información incluye el folleto?
   (A) Un ejemplar de una tarjeta típica
   (B) La fecha de comienzo del evento
   (C) El lugar de la entrega de premios
   (D) La tarjeta vencedora del año anterior

5. Si fueras un estudiante en esta escuela y quisieras participar en este evento según las normas establecidas, ¿cuál de los siguientes temas escogerías?
   (A) Belén, cuna de Jesús
   (B) Nochebuena madrileña
   (C) Crisol de celebraciones navideñas del mundo
   (D) Recorrido histórico de los tres Reyes Magos de Oriente

---

Cultural Awareness

Cultural practice: This article presents a competition in which students create Christmas cards celebrating the Christmas season in Spain.

How is this practice similar to or different from those in your own community?

Tema curricular: Las familias y las comunidades

Este anuncio promueve una tradición típica de Venezuela. Fue publicado en
http://Venezuelatuya.com.

La hallaca

Uno de los platos más reconocidos y elaborados que se presenta en la gastronomía venezolana es sin lugar a dudas la hallaca. Esta obra maestra de nuestra culinaria es el más tradicional de los platos que engalanan las festividades navideñas en nuestra Venezuela.

Línea

(5)   La hallaca es el resultado del proceso histórico que ha vivido nuestra sociedad.

Desde su cubierta de hojas de plátano hasta los detalles que adornan y componen su guiso, pasando por su ingrediente primordial, la masa de maíz coloreada con onoto, la hallaca es la expresión más visible del mestizaje del venezolano. Cada ingrediente tiene sus raíces: la hoja de plátano, usada tanto por el negro

(10) africano como por el indio americano, es el maravilloso envoltorio que la cobija; al descubrirla, traemos al presente nuestro pasado indígena, pues la masa de maíz coloreada con onoto es la que nos recibe con su esplendoroso color amarillo; luego, en su interior se deja apreciar la llegada de los españoles a estas tierras, carnes de gallina, cerdo y res, aceitunas, alcaparras, pasas . . . todo picado fina-

(15) mente, guisados y maravillosamente distribuidos se hacen parte de un manjar exquisito. Sus ingredientes, todos partes de diferentes raíces se complementan armoniosamente en la hallaca, expresión del mestizaje y colorido del que es parte nuestro pueblo.

La palabra "Hallaca" proviene del guaraní y deriva de la palabra "ayúa" ó

(20) "ayuar" que significa mezclar o revolver, de estas palabras se presume que "ayuaca" sea una cosa mezclada, que por deformación lingüística paso a llamarse "ayaca". Otra versión presume que la palabra procede de alguna lengua aborigen del occidente del país, cuyo significado es "envoltorio" o "bojote".

Sea cual sea el origen de esta palabra, sabemos que "la hallaca" es comple-

(25) tamente venezolana, tanto por su nombre como por su confección y es orgullo de nuestra cocina, pues ella sin distinciones sociales se presenta espléndida en la mesa navideña de todos los venezolanos, aportando un toque de maravilloso gusto y sabor a nuestra navidad.

En el mes de diciembre cuando las fiestas navideñas desbordan la alegría del

(30) venezolano, la hallaca es parte importante de la celebración, se intercambian, se regalan, se venden . . . en fin, en las fiestas de navidad para el venezolano no puede faltar la tan reconocida hallaca.

Para su preparación existen diversas recetas, pues en cada región del país hay recetas tradicionales, además como en la mayoría de los platos venezolanos cada

(35) familia le aporta su sazón y varía su confección.

1. ¿Qué simboliza la *hallaca*?
   (A) La integración intercultural del país
   (B) La cultura de los indígenas en Venezuela
   (C) La llegada de los españoles a tierra venezolana
   (D) La variedad de ingredientes autóctonos del país

2. Según el artículo, ¿cuál es el ingrediente principal de la *hallaca*?
   (A) Las hojas de plátano
   (B) La masa de maíz
   (C) La carne
   (D) El guisado

3. ¿A qué se refiere el autor cuando escribe ". . . se deja apreciar la llegada de los españoles" (línea 13)?
   (A) A que los españoles tuvieron el mayor impacto en la creación de la *hallaca*
   (B) A que los españoles trajeron nuevas técnicas culinarias
   (C) A que los españoles contribuyeron ingredientes no endémicos
   (D) A que los españoles disfrutaron de las tierras venezolanas

4. ¿Cuántas culturas son representadas en la preparación de la *hallaca*?
   (A) Dos
   (B) Tres
   (C) Cuatro
   (D) Más de cuatro

5. ¿Qué significa la frase "ella sin distinciones sociales se presenta espléndida en la mesa" (líneas 26–27)?
   (A) Que las cocina venezolana es magnífica pero modesta
   (B) Que las cenas navideñas suelen ser muy ricas
   (C) Que toda clase de gente goza de este plato
   (D) Que la *hallaca* es la más bella de todas las comidas venezolanas

---

Cultural Awareness

Cultural product: This reading presents a typical dish served during Christmas time in Venezuela and its origins.

How is product presented in this article similar to or different from one in your own community?

SELECCIÓN #12

Tema curricular: Las identidades personales y públicas

Este fragmento de la novela *Rosaura a las diez*, del escritor argentino Marcos Denevi, relata las primeras impresiones que tienen unas chicas al conocer a otra persona por primera vez.

	Entonces comenzaron entre ellas una de esas conversaciones en que a mí, aunque esté presente, no me dan intervención, porque van a decir cosas que saben que yo no he de admitirles, y hablando entre ellas y diciéndolo todo ellas
Línea	ligerito, quieren convencerme antes de que yo les ataje la palabra en la boca.
(5)	—Y no parece que tenga veintiséis años.
	—No ha hablado en ningún momento.
	—¡Nos miraba, y en qué forma!
	—Parecía asustada.
	—No, asustada no. Sorprendida, maravillada, estupefacta.
(10)	—Y mucha desenvoltura no aparenta tener.
	—Les digo que es una santita que nunca salió de su casa. Por eso ahora anda así.
	—Y se vino vestida bien modestamente.
	—Tenía una media corrida.
(15)	—Y los zapatos llenos de polvo.
	—El collar es una fantasía de dos por cinco.
	—Oigan, ¿no será sorda? ¿No será que no oye lo que se le dice y por eso nos miraba así?
	—Pero no, si cuando yo le pregunté . . .
(20)	—Pues algo raro hay en ella. Todavía no sé lo que es, pero ya lo sabré. Déjenme estudiarla.
	Y yo me acordé de aquellas manchas rojas en el antebrazo de Rosaura, ¡y sentí una indignación!
	—¡Vean qué tres serpientes he traído yo al mundo!—exclamé, mirándolas
(25)	con furia—. La señorita Eufrasia, al lado de ustedes, es Santa Eufrasia. No quería decirles nada, pero veo que es necesario. La pelea de Rosaura con el padre fue como para llamar a la policía. Tiene los brazos llenos de cardenales.
	Me miraron, horrorizadas.

1. ¿Quién narra lo que pasa en este trozo?
   (A) La señorita Eufrasia
   (B) Una de las chicas
   (C) La mamá de las chicas
   (D) Una chica huérfana

2. ¿De qué hablan?
   (A) De una joven que está visitando a la familia.
   (B) De una chica que es compañera de clase en la escuela.
   (C) De una santa que visitaba la casa.
   (D) De una joven pobre que visitaron en su casa.

3. ¿Con qué intenciones hablan las tres chicas?
   (A) Para conocer mejor a la chica
   (B) Para adivinar la identidad de la chica
   (C) Están chismeando
   (D) Les interesa ayudarle

4. En la línea 25, ¿qué quiere decir la frase "La señorita Eufrasia, al lado de ustedes, es Santa Eufrasia"?
   (A) Que las chicas son tan buenas como si fueran santas.
   (B) Que a la narradora le parece que las tres chicas son muy crueles.
   (C) Que la narradora cree que una persona cualquiera puede ser santa.
   (D) Que la narradora no cree que la señorita Eufrasia sea santa.

5. ¿Qué quiere la narradora que hagan las tres chicas?
   (A) Que ellas se callen.
   (B) Que ellas sean más piadosas.
   (C) Que las chicas la conozcan mejor.
   (D) Que las tres le muestren más respeto.

6. ¿Por qué se quedan horrorizadas las tres chicas?
   (A) No pueden creer que les hable la narradora con tanta franqueza.
   (B) Les ofende que haya intervenido la narradora en sus conversaciones.
   (C) Dudan que la narradora les haya dicho la verdad.
   (D) Les escandalizan los hechos del caso que acaba de decirles la narradora.

7. ¿Qué puede ser el pensamiento central de este trozo?
   (A) A las mujeres les gusta chismear todo el tiempo.
   (B) Los pobres no tienen ningunos derechos.
   (C) No se debe juzgar sin saber todos los datos del caso.
   (D) La intolerancia tiene raíces en la falta de comunicación.

Cultural Awareness

Cultural perspective: This fragment presents a classic situation in which people from different backgrounds meet each other for the first time. The young girls' comments about Rosaura's appearance anger their mother, who reprimands them for their insolence. The perspective presented here is to not pass judgment of others without knowing who they are.

How is the perspective presented in this fragment similar to or different from one in your own community?

SELECCIÓN #13

Tema curricular: La vida contemporánea

Este trozo proviene de la compañía *LACSA* y detalla una de sus políticas.

Emitido por: AERONAVES NACIONALES:

Boleto de pasaje y del talón de equipaje
Aviso sobre limitaciones de responsabilidades sobre equipajes:

Línea

(5)

Las limitaciones de responsabilidad del transportista sobre el equipaje facturado, serán de aproximadamente (U.S.) $9.07 por libra y sobre el equipaje no facturado serán de (U.S.) $400.00 por pasajero.

Noticia importante
BIENVENIDOS A BORDO

Estimado Pasajero:

(10)

Para mayor comodidad y seguridad, si Ud. interrumpe su viaje por más de 48 horas le solicitamos que reconfirme su intención de usar la continuidad o el retorno de su viaje. Para tal efecto le rogamos que informe a nuestras oficinas en el lugar donde Ud. intenta reanudar su viaje con 48 horas de anticipación a la hora de salida de su vuelo. La no reconfirmación de su salida podría traer como consecuencia la cancelación de su reserva. Esperamos su colaboración para

(15)

seguir brindándole nuestro tradicional servicio.

CUPÓN DE REEMBOLSO

El reembolso solo se hará al pasajero, a menos que se indique otra persona en la parte inferior de esta casilla, caso en el cual, solo podrá hacerse a la persona designada y no al pasajero, siempre y cuando entregue este cupón, los cupones

(20)

que no hayan sido usados y el talón de exceso de equipaje. El presente reembolso está sujeto a las tarifas, normas y regulaciones del transportador, así como a las leyes y demás disposiciones gubernamentales.

1. Este trozo parece ser
   (A) de un folleto de una línea aérea.
   (B) de un contrato entre un pasajero y una línea aérea.
   (C) el documento de embarque que se le entrega para poder embarcar.
   (D) de un anuncio para Aeronaves Nacionales.

2. Si Ud. tiene reservas para un vuelo de vuelta el doce de diciembre, a las catorce horas
   ¿para cuándo tendrá Ud. que reconfirmar su vuelo?
   (A) El 9 de diciembre, a las siete de la mañana
   (B) El 10 de diciembre, a las dos de la tarde
   (C) El 11 de diciembre, a las cuatro de la tarde
   (D) El 12 de diciembre, a la una de la tarde

3. Se necesita un *talón de equipaje* para
   (A) probar responsibilidad financiera de la línea aérea.
   (B) poder llevar el equipaje de mano en la cabina.
   (C) declarar el valor y peso del equipaje.
   (D) reclamar el equipaje al aduanero.

4. ¿Qué propósito tiene el cupón de reembolso?
   (A) Para que otra persona pueda usar el boleto que no se ha usado
   (B) Para que la línea aérea pague al pasajero por usar los servicios de ésta
   (C) Para que el gobierno le pague la parte que no se ha usado
   (D) Para que la línea aérea pague la parte que no se ha usado

5. Las palabras *nuestro tradicional servicio* indica
   (A) que la línea esta muy orgullosa de su servicio.
   (B) que es una vieja línea tradicional.
   (C) que es una línea establecida y reconocida.
   (D) que su servicio es igual al de cualquier otra línea.

Cultural Awareness

Cultural practice: This fragment presents several policies from a Costa Rican airline.

How are the policies in this document similar to or different from those of airlines in your own community?

SELECCIÓN #14

Tema curricular: La belleza y la estética

En esta carta, Javier le escribe a su amigo sobre una experiencia que tuvo la noche anterior.

Querido Pablo,

¿Cómo estás? Te quería escribirte anoche, pero estaba demasiado metido en mis propios pensamientos. Fui al cine con Sebastián y unos amigos suyos de la
Línea secundaria. Ya sabes cuánto me gusta ver películas, pero la verdad es que esta vez
(5) no disfruté la experiencia. Para empezar, nosotros llegamos tarde y las butacas estaban casi llenas. Afortunadamente pudimos encontrar suficiente asientos, pero tuvimos que separarnos y me quedé con dos jóvenes muy parlanchines: no dejaron de platicar durante toda la película . . . ¡qué horror! Además, la película fue una tontería: demasiado énfasis en la acción y efectos especiales y ninguna
(10) consideración en desarrollar la trama. Y para colmo, al juntarse de nuevo el grupo, todos la alababan como si fuera la mejor del año. Yo me quedé quieto durante el camino a casa porque no quería ser aguafiestas.

Al llegar a casa empecé a pensar en cómo los gustos de cada uno son tan distintos. Para mí, ir al cine es una experiencia íntima que empieza el momento
(15) en que entro la sala. No entiendo cómo a alguien no le molestaría llegar tarde y perderse los tráilers. Además, no soporto cuando la gente habla durante la película. Me encanta poder discutir las películas, pero se debería hacer después de que haya terminado. Esta reflexión me hizo pensar en qué opinan otros de su experiencia en el cine. Pensé en que seguramente para los dos jóvenes a mi lado,
(20) el compañerismo era una parte de su diversión, y que ver una película en el cine es un evento que compartes con los que te rodean. Por eso no se molestaron por el hecho de que la película ya había empezado y disfrutaron de ella, aunque me pareció pésima.

A causa de esta reflexión, me di cuenta de que posiblemente mi experiencia
(25) podría haber sido diferente si hubiera cambiado mi actitud. Al contemplar la película de nuevo, pude ver elementos graciosos en ella, y me pregunté si no disfruté de la película por ser mala, o simplemente porque estaba tan frustrado de antemano que no iba a gozarla de todas formas. Creo que lo que he aprendido es que la diversión es distinta para cada persona, y cuando un grupo decide hacer
(30) algo juntos es imposible complacer a todos, y el fraternizar es una parte intrínseca de la experiencia así que hay que abandonar las expectativas personales y no frustrarse tanto si algo sale diferente de lo que uno quiere. ¿Qué piensas tú? Lo siento por escribirte una carta tan filosófica, pero me ayuda poder vocalizar mis pensamientos y compartirlos.
(35) Bueno, me despido de ti y espero tu respuesta. Salúdale a toda tu familia y espero que nos veamos pronto.

¡Un abrazo!
Javier

1. Según la carta, ¿qué se puede afirmar sobre la relación entre Javier y las personas con quienes fue al cine?
   (A) El vínculo de amistad es bastante fuerte.
   (B) Son todos amigos de la escuela.
   (C) Los demás no se llevan bien con Javier.
   (D) Javier se siente un poco apartado del grupo.

2. ¿Qué hicieron los dos jóvenes durante la película?
   (A) Conversaron.
   (B) Lucharon.
   (C) Se durmieron.
   (D) Se enfermaron.

3. ¿Por qué no participó Javier en la discusión después de la película?
   (A) Porque estaba demasiado enojado.
   (B) Porque no quería ser pesimista.
   (C) Porque estaba cansado.
   (D) Porque no le caía bien el grupo.

4. Según la reflexión personal de Javier, ¿cuál de las siguientes afirmaciones mejor refleja su opinión de la experiencia de ir al cine?
   (A) Es más divertido ir con un grupo.
   (B) Es algo profundo y personal.
   (C) Es una experiencia que hay que hacer con otras personas.
   (D) Es un evento que se disfruta más solo.

5. ¿Por qué cree Javier que los otros gozaron más la experiencia que él?
   (A) Porque les gustan las películas de acción
   (B) Porque la película tuvo buenos efectos especiales
   (C) Porque la compartieron con sus amigos
   (D) Porque son más optimistas que él

6. En la carta, ¿cuál es el significado de la frase "todos la alababan" (línea 11)?
   (A) Todos debatían la película.
   (B) Todos celebraban la película.
   (C) Todos criticaban la película.
   (D) Todos maldecían la película.

7. A base de su reflexión, ¿qué cambio se nota en Javier?
   (A) Llega a ser más comprensivo.
   (B) Aumenta su frustración.
   (C) Se deprime un poco.
   (D) Siente vergüenza por su actitud.

Cultural Awareness

Cultural perspective: This fragment presents a perspective of a young man in regards to the movies and to certain behaviors exhibited by his friends.

How are the perspectives presented in this correspondence similar to or different from those in your own community?

SELECCIÓN #15

Tema curricular: Las identidades personales y públicas

En el siguiente fragmento, el narrador habla de su experiencia en Guatemala.

Patrocinado por el Instituto de Cultura e invitado por el Instituto

Guatemalteco, vengo a pasar un mes en Guatemala. A mi regreso, todos, amigos, parientes, colegas y hasta simples conocidos, me han asediado con su curiosidad por este país, del que por desgracia tan poco se conoce en Europa. Un

Línea
(5)

mes, por modo cierto, es muy poco tiempo para llegar al conocimiento de cualquier cosa importante y desde luego mucho menos para captar las esencias tan complejas y los matices tan variopintos de un país como Guatemala.

En todos los medios sociales en los que me he desenvuelto, la cortesía natural y algo más importante y sincero, como es la cordialidad, son la regla. En cada momento de mi vida allí, he tenido la sensación entrañable de encontrarme en

(10)

mi propio país y también de que "el solo hecho de ser español" ya era algo importante en Guatemala. Esto no implica, ni mucho menos, en el nativo o residente, servilismo ni ausencia de un lógico y acertado orgullo nacional, sino que si los "peninsulares" nos colocamos en la natural posición de hermanos, ellos como hermanos nos acogen.

(15)

Lo que no aceptan, y hacen muy bien, es la actitud más o menos veladamente "paternalista" y protectora, que el desconocimiento de la realidad hace adoptar a muchos de los que intentan "españolear" en América. Creo sinceramente que la única razón de los alientos que los guatemaltecos han prodigado a mis modestas actuaciones públicas se ha debido a mi sentir, sinceramente expresado, de que

(20)

tanto más tenía yo que aprender de ellos, como ellos de mí.

El intelectual guatemalteco es curioso de todos los saberes, hábil conversador, que sabe escuchar y decir—cada cosa a su tiempo—y de una cultura extensa e intensa, sin el mal de la pedantería. Como uno de los más gratos recuerdos de esta mi entrañable Guatemala, tengo el del "redescubrimiento" del apacible colo-

(25)

quio—hoy casi olvidado entre nosotros—con el designio más de aprender que de enseñar, el sentido de la mutua comprensión y la tolerancia liberal que preside toda mente selecta.

1. ¿Quién es el autor de este trozo?
   (A) Es guatemalteco que actualmente vive en España.
   (B) Es turista casual en Guatemala.
   (C) Es embajador cultural español en Guatemala.
   (D) Es un peninsular invitado por una organización guatemalteca.

2. ¿Qué actitud mostraba este autor?
   (A) Se sentía muy superior por ser español entre guatemaltecos.
   (B) Se sentía bien acogido.
   (C) Se sentía muy humillado porque los guatemaltecos eran tan inteligentes.
   (D) Se sentía muy dispuesto a regresar a su país cuanto antes.

3. ¿Qué característica de los guatemaltecos le impresionó más?
   (A) La envidia que le tenían porque era europeo.
   (B) Lo pedante que eran los guatemaltecos intelectuales.
   (C) Su gran curiosidad intelectual en cuanto a todo el mundo.
   (D) Su soberbia que no les permitió admitir la superioridad española.

4. ¿Qué crítica implícita hay en lo que dice este autor?
   (A) Critica a sus propios compatriotas.
   (B) Critica a los europeos con negocios en Guatemala.
   (C) Critica a los guatemaltecos por ser tan serviles.
   (D) Critica la pereza guatemalteca.

5. ¿Qué revela la actitud de los guatemaltecos en cuanto a las relaciones con los españoles?
   (A) Los guatemaltecos siempre han entendido mejor a los españoles que al revés.
   (B) Los guatemaltecos siempre han entendido peor a los españoles que al revés.
   (C) Las dos nacionalidades siempre se han tratado como iguales.
   (D) Nunca se han entendido bien.

6. ¿Qué sugiere que se aprenda de los guatemaltecos?
   (A) Sugiere que se aprenda a apreciar el arte de no hacer nada.
   (B) Sugiere que todo el mundo imite la sinceridad de los guatemaltecos.
   (C) Sugiere que todos viajen a Guatemala para experimentar esta cultura.
   (D) Sugiere que todos los intelectuales sean más pedantes, tal como los guatemaltecos.

7. ¿Cómo sería posible caracterizar a este escritor?
   (A) Muy sincero pero ingenuo.
   (B) Muy pensador.
   (C) Intenso.
   (D) Es un mentiroso.

SELECCIÓN #16

Tema curricular: Las familias y las comunidades

Fuente #1: El siguiente texto trata del papel que deben jugar los padres en la educación de sus hijos. Fue publicado en 2011 en la página web *www.planetamama.com.ar*.

La importancia de los padres en la educación

La importancia de las funciones paternales, reside en que no se trata sólo de nutrir y cuidar a los hijos, sino también de brindarles la protección y la educación necesaria para que se desarrollen como personas sanas, buenas y solidarias. Pero,

Línea una pregunta que se hacen últimamente los investigadores es: ¿acaso, tener un
(5) hijo convierte automáticamente a una persona en padre o madre? Para la ley, ser padre o madre es una condición que se asigna por el derecho que da la consanguinidad o la adopción; la misma supone el cuidado responsable y la satisfacción de las necesidades de los hijos; sin embargo, no todos los niño/as reciben de sus padres este tipo de atención en cantidad y calidad suficientes.

(10) El buen trato implica también, que los padres faciliten al niño el desarrollo de sus capacidades de aprendizaje y obtención de conocimientos mediante estimulación adecuada, experimentación y refuerzos positivos. También es indispensable que el niño pueda experimentar y descubrir bajo control el mundo que lo rodea, para aprender a relacionarse con su medio, adquirir libertad y seguridad.

(15) Los niños se animan a explorar su entorno y a tener nuevas experiencias a partir de la seguridad que les brinda la presencia de sus padres u otros adultos significativos que lo protegen.

Los niños necesitan aprender a modular sus emociones, deseos, pulsiones y comportamientos y a manejar sus frustraciones, así como también, a cumplir con
(20) deberes y obligaciones para consigo mismos y para con los demás.

Las normas y reglas de conducta son bien tratables cuando se basan en el derecho a la vida y a la integridad, en la igualdad de derechos para todos y en la aceptación de las diferencias, fomentan el desarrollo de la autonomía, la responsabilidad y el buen desempeño. Pero, para que los niños las puedan respetar
(25) e incorporar, los padres deben facilitar a sus hijos las conversaciones que les adjudiquen sentido.

Finalmente, los niños/as necesitan aceptar las normas que son legitimadas por los valores de su cultura. Interiorizar normas y reglas mediante los valores positivos de buen trato, como la justicia, la tolerancia, la solidaridad, la ayuda
(30) mutua, etc., a fin de permitir que se sientan dignos, seguros y confiados en su comunidad.

Dice Jorge Bradury: "Tratar bien a un niño es también darle los utensilios para que desarrolle su capacidad de amar, de hacer el bien y de apreciar lo que es bueno y placentero. Para ello debemos ofrecerles la posibilidad de vivir en con-
(35) textos no violentos, donde los buenos tratos, la verdad y la coherencia sean los pilares de la educación".

Fuente #2: El siguiente gráfico representa el porcentaje de adolescentes que opinan quiénes o qué les transmiten valores.

Valores	Padres	Profesores	Otros medios
Respeto a los mayores	78,1	42,1	7,3
Solidaridad	77,2	40,3	10,9
Esfuerzo	75	46,8	9,7
Paciencia	72,8	35,7	4,8
Fuerza ante dificultades	72,1	36,5	9,3
Lealtad	69,3	39,2	11,3
Sinceridad	65,8	41	11,6

1. ¿Cuál es el propósito del artículo?
   (A) Examinar distintos problemas relacionados con la crianza de niños
   (B) Exponer las causas de las dificultades que enfrenta la gente joven
   (C) Describir el valor de la enseñaza paternal y todo que esto conlleva
   (D) Criticar la falta de atención que reciben algunos niños

2. ¿Qué técnica usa el autor para comunicar sus ideas?
   (A) Defiende su argumento central con datos específicos.
   (B) Incorpora las opiniones de una variedad de expertos.
   (C) Presenta sucesos de su propia experiencia.
   (D) Explica las destrezas necesarias y los beneficios de ellas.

3. Según el artículo, ¿cuáles son los deberes de los padres a sus hijos?
   (A) Educar a los niños de la importancia de la buena conducta.
   (B) Proveerles protección y oportunidades educativas.
   (C) Alimentarles y asegurar que estén bien cuidados.
   (D) Crear un ambiente de solidaridad y de respeto.

4. ¿Qué les proveen los padres a sus hijos cuando les dan nuevas experiencias?
   (A) Un sentimiento de seguridad
   (B) Un aumento en el deseo de aprender
   (C) Desarrollo de su capacidad cognitiva
   (D) Más autoestima cuando crecen

5. Según el artículo, ¿cuál es un factor que ayuda a animar a los niños que exploren más el ambiente que los rodea?
   (A) Su propia búsqueda de estimulación cognitiva
   (B) El deseo de ser independiente
   (C) La protección que proveen los padres
   (D) El nivel de estímulo que hay en el entorno

6. ¿Cómo pueden los niños mejor entender las normas y concepto de buena conducta?
   (A) Tras el diálogo con los padres
   (B) A través de las experiencias en la vida
   (C) Al ser más autónomos
   (D) Cuando son más maduros

7. ¿Qué aspecto de la formación del niño *no* es incluido en este artículo?
   (A) La buena conducta
   (B) El respeto hacia los demás
   (C) El éxito escolar
   (D) El estímulo cognitivo

8. Según el artículo, ¿cuál de las siguientes frases sería el mejor ejemplo de "buen trato" (línea 29)?
   (A) Crear un ambiente libre de violencia y maltrato.
   (B) Proveer seguridad y estimulación cognitiva.
   (C) Demostrar un profundo sentimiento de respeto y valoración hacía la dignidad y necesidad de otros.
   (D) Saber manejar sus propias emociones e impulsos.

9. ¿Qué tipo de información presenta la tabla?
   (A) Los valores de más prestigio según la sociedad
   (B) La fuente de aprendizaje de los valores de los jóvenes
   (C) La responsabilidad que tienen distintos grupos en la educación de los jóvenes
   (D) El promedio de la importancia que se asocia a cada valor

10. Según la tabla, ¿dónde tienen los profesores más impacto?
    (A) En instalar la importancia de trabajo duro
    (B) En su capacidad de crear compañerismo
    (C) En su habilidad de comunicar la importancia de honestidad
    (D) En mantener la calma en situaciones frustrantes

11. ¿Cuál de las siguientes afirmaciones se comprueba a base del artículo y la tabla?
    (A) Ha habido un decremento en el papel de los padres a la transmisión de valores a sus hijos.
    (B) Los profesores y otros medios son más eficaces a transmitir ciertos valores.
    (C) Los padres son los más importantes para transmitir los valores a los jóvenes.
    (D) Ciertos valores son mejor transmitidos por unos medios que por otros.

Cultural Awareness

Cultural perspective: The article and accompanying table present opinions regarding the impact that parents do have and should have in their child's education.

How are the perspectives presented in these documents similar to or different from those in your own community?

SELECCIÓN #17

Tema curricular: La vida contemporánea

En el siguiente fragmento, del libro *Y van dos . . .* de Marcelo Menasche, el narrador narra las experiencias que tuvo después de tomar una decisión importante.

Cuando vi a Dora por tercera vez en brazos de un amigo diferente no esperé más. Y tomé una decisión: no la volvería a ver en mi vida.

Dicen que el mejor remedio para estas cosas es viajar; hasta tal punto debe ser
Línea cierto que tuve una vez una novia que, después de haberme hecho sufrir como
(5) inocente en el infierno me recomendó ella misma el cambio de lugar. Cosa que me inspiró el doble temor de que esa mujer me estaba tomando por imbécil y tenía comisión por envío de clientes a un balneario.

Como estábamos en pleno febrero bien podía elegir Mar del Plata, "la aristocrática playa". La vida agitada y tonta del balneario me haría olvidar.

(10) Reuní unos pesos, unas camisas y saqué un boleto "fin de semana". Subí al vagón, no sin pensar un poco, involuntariamente, en la posible aventura de viaje.

Es realmente asombroso, pero es el caso que los "magazines" ilustrados y las escritoras americanas tienen una pasión morbosa por ese tema: Irremediablemente, sube al tren "momentos antes de la salida" (¡qué gracia! bueno fuera
(15) "momentos después de la salida"), el joven escritor, elegante, atlético y famoso. La casualidad quiere que la bella y misteriosa viajera lea en ese mismo instante su última novela. (Un detalle siempre es "su última novela"; podría suceder, tratándose de un escritor prolífico y famoso, que la hermosa joven leyese la penúltima o la antepenúltima. Pero según parece hay un consorcio de escritores
(20) de esta categoría y nadie puede introducir innovaciones al estilo de la sociedad que es intangible). Una conversación se entabla pronto, sobre todo cuando los dos interlocutores son jóvenes.

1. ¿Por qué decidió visitar Mar del Plata?
   (A) Porque todos los aristócratas iban allí en el invierno.
   (B) Porque habría mucha actividad para pasar el tiempo.
   (C) Porque todos los escritores estarían allí.
   (D) Porque podría leer muchos libros.

2. ¿Qué desea olvidar este narrador?
   (A) Una novela que leyó
   (B) Un negocio fracasado
   (C) Una relación amorosa
   (D) Una joven que leyó su novela

3. ¿En qué tema tienen las escritoras americanas *una pasión morbosa*?
   (A) Los amores fracasados
   (B) La posibilidad de aventuras inesperadas
   (C) Conversaciones casuales en trenes
   (D) Viajes ferrocarrileros con autores famosos

4. ¿Qué hizo al subir al vagón?
   (A) Entabló una conversación con un escritor.
   (B) Observó el encuentro de dos otros pasajeros.
   (C) Empezó a leer una novela a una joven.
   (D) Imaginó una aventura entre dos personas.

5. ¿Qué parece opinar el narrador del joven escritor?
   (A) Admira su atleticismo.
   (B) Envidia su popularidad.
   (C) Se enoja que tenga tanto éxito.
   (D) Lo odia porque es famoso.

6. En las líneas 18–19, ¿cuál es el tono de las palabras *que la hermosa joven leyese la penúltima o la antepenúltima*?
   (A) Sarcástico
   (B) Irónico
   (C) Trágico
   (D) Chismoso

7. ¿Cuál es la actitud del narrador en este trozo?
   (A) Está deprimido.
   (B) Parece muy desilusionado.
   (C) Está muy enamorado.
   (D) Tiene buen sentido de humor.

Cultural Awareness

Cultural perspective: This fragment presents a perspective of an Argentine male narrator following a lost love affair. During part of his narration, he ridicules the idyllic world that he feels American magazines present.

How are the perspectives presented in this fragment similar to or different from those in your own community?

SELECCIÓN #18

Tema curricular: Las familias y las comunidades

El siguiente texto se trata de un evento académico promovido por las instituciones educativas de la Asociación para la Enseñanza en Cali, Colombia, en 2010.

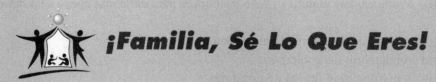

¡Familia, Sé Lo Que Eres!

JUSTIFICACIÓN:

Línea
(5)

La familia, cómo dudarlo, ocupa un merecido y privilegiado lugar en la historia de los hombres y, en nuestra época, no podría ser de otra manera. Los más pequeños llegan a ella como una tela en blanco, tal y como llegaban y sequirán haciendo su arribo a la existencia los niños de ayer, los de hoy y los de mañana. Y depende de unas condiciones óptimas-desarrolladas al interior de hogares sanos con relaciones funcionales estables, enmarcadas en principios y valores que, claramente sabemos no pueden ser negociables ni convertirse en relativos ni ponerse de moda o ser desechables o subjectivos- que los retoños se asomen a la sociedad para cumplir con el fin grandioso de ser, cada uno, persona humana.

(10)

OBJETIVOS GENERALES:

1. Reflexionar alrededor de las funciones indelegables e intransferibles de la familia en el proceso formativo de la persona humana.
2. Analizar a profundidad el significado de ser y hacer familia en una sociedad, para generar acciones en pro de su promoción, defensa y educación.

(15)

3. Promover una nueva cultura empresarial de atención y relación complementaria entre la vida familiar y la vida laboral de las personas.

TEMÁTICAS:

Claves para fundar, cuidar y desarrollar una familia sólida.

"Todos queremos ser amados y amar sólidamente y no líquida o frágilmente".

(20)

▪ Criterios y orientaciones fundamentales para fundar, cuidar y desarrollar una familia sustent able en el tiempo con unidad y armonía.
▪ Reflexiones acerca del gran desafío de cuidar el vínculo con la persona que hemos elegido para compartir la vida.

PERMANENCIA Y CAMBIO EN LA FAMILIA DEL SIGLO XXI.

(25)

▪ La familia es una entidad, viva y dinámica que no responde a necesidades fisiológicas de protección o reproducción, visión simplista de la sociología biologista, ni es un mero constructor teológico implementado para subyugar ideológicamente la libertad como lo pretende el relativismo liberal. Por lo tanto, la familia es una nueva realidad que trasciende la realidad de los contrayentes, hombre y mujer quienes desde su diversidad permiten crear ese

(30)

mundo tan rico del amor familiar.

NUEVA CULTURA EMPRESARIAL: LA INTEGRACIÓN FAMILIA—TRABAJO.

▪ Las políticas familiares en general y las polítcas empresariales como medios de integración familia-trabajo para la salud personal, familiar y social.

1. ¿Cuál es el propósito de este evento?
    (A) Explorar la función de los padres en el ámbito familiar y exponer cómo hay que criar a los hijos
    (B) Definir y promover los valores inherentes de la familia, su impacto en el ser humano, y su importancia social
    (C) Justificar las razones por las cuales hay que explorar la vida familiar más a fondo
    (D) Promocionar cambios sociales y laborales para darle más apoyo a las familias

2. ¿A quiénes parece ser dirigido este folleto?
    (A) A miembros del gobierno
    (B) A matrimonios, novios y educadores
    (C) A empleados y jefes de compañías locales
    (D) A funcionarios de la iglesia

3. ¿A qué se refiere la frase "como una tela en blanco" (líneas 3–4)?
    (A) A la inocencia de los niños
    (B) Al color de la tez de los niños
    (C) A cómo deben vestirse los pequeños
    (D) Al tamaño de los bebés cuando nacen

4. ¿Cómo define el folleto a una familia?
    (A) Es algo que va más allá del pensamiento preestablecido.
    (B) Es una unión necesaria biológica.
    (C) Es vital para balancear la vida con el mundo laboral.
    (D) Es un pilar importante de los mandatos religiosos.

5. Imagina que necesitas más información del seminario y que le mandas un mensaje por correo electrónico a la Asociación para la Enseñanza. ¿Cuál de las siguientes preguntas sería más apropiada?
    (A) Buenos días, ¿me podría quitar de la lista de correos electrónicos para estos tipos de eventos?
    (B) ¿Me podría decir cuáles van a ser los temas en que se va a enfocar este seminario?
    (C) ¿Qué hay? Mi esposa y yo estaremos allí. Nos vemos entonces.
    (D) A mi novia y a mí nos gustaría asistir. ¿Acaso hay un costo?

Cultural Awareness

Cultural perspective: This text presents the perspective of the importance of family.

Cultural product: This text presents an event that took place in Colombia in which participants are taught to reflect on the importance of family.

How are the products and perspectives presented in this text similar to or different from those in your own community?

SELECCIÓN #19

Tema curricular: Los desafíos mundiales

La siguiente carta es de una estudiante a su profesor en que habla de un artículo que leyó que le llamó la atención.

Profesor Sánchez,

Ante todo quiero agradecerle por ser un profesor tan inspirador. Verdaderamente disfruté mucho su clase y estoy interesado más que nunca en el servicio
Línea social y buscar oportunidades en que yo pueda ayudar a los menos afortunados.
(5) Por eso quisiera comentarle de un proyecto que descubrí que me ha dejado muy entusiasmada y me gustaría poder compartirlo con usted.

El otro día estaba leyendo el periódico y leí un artículo de una organización que se llama "Payasos sin Fronteras". ¿Los conoces? Estuve muy conmovida por los logros de este grupo y el impacto que ha tenido durante los últimos veinte años. El
(10) grupo toma la iniciativa de darles apoyo emocional a las poblaciones refugiadas de todo el mundo mediante la risa. Hasta ahora ha hecho más de diez mil actuaciones en casi cien países, haciéndoles reír a más de tres millones de niños y niñas.

Después de leer el artículo, decidí investigarlos más. Descubrí que empezaron en 1993, cuando un grupo de estudiantes de una escuela en Barcelona le invitaron
(15) a un payaso que les acompañara a un campo de refugiados en Croacia, durante la guerra de los Balcanes. Desde aquel día, este grupo ha crecido hasta contar con secciones en varios países europeos, Estados Unidos, Canadá y Sudáfrica. Los miembros son típicamente artistas profesionales que han llevado un largo recorrido en los circos, teatros, u otras disciplinas y que trabajan como voluntarios en
(20) los proyectos internacionales y aunque la organización les paga todos los gastos para llevar a cabo la labor, no reciben ninguna compensación ni salario.

El artículo me dejó muy emocionada, y me pregunté si se pudiera llevar a cabo un proyecto parecido o formar una sección en nuestra comunidad. Sé que muchos están sufriendo ahora por la crisis económica, y un proyecto como éste
(25) podría por lo menos brindarles a los niños más impactados unos momentos de alivio. ¿Conoce usted a alguien que pueda ayudarme con esta iniciativa? ¿Tiene unos consejos para ayudarme? También, sería un gran honor si usted pudiera participar de alguna forma, aunque sea de forma mínima. Su curso y su pasión por los desafortunados me han dado la motivación de buscar estas oportunida-
(30) des, y nada me haría más feliz que poder trabajar a su lado.

Le agradezco por todo lo que ha hecho por mí y espero que considere mi invitación y que me pueda ayudar de cualquier forma posible.

Atentamente,
Luisa Ramírez

1. ¿Con qué propósito le escribe Luisa a su profesor?
   (A) Para agradecerle su ayuda
   (B) Para informarle de algo que descubrió
   (C) Para pedirle ayuda
   (D) Para informarle de algo y pedirle ayuda

2. ¿Cuál es la función primaria Payasos sin Fronteras?
   (A) Llamar la atención a los problemas mundiales
   (B) Recaudar fondos para ayudar a los refugiados
   (C) Hacerles reír a todos los niños del mundo
   (D) Traer humor y felicidad a los que están sufriendo

3. ¿Qué les provee la organización a los payasos que deciden participar?
   (A) Reembolso de los gastos personales y de viaje
   (B) Pagamento de producción y de transporte
   (C) Apoyo emocional y moral
   (D) Entrenamiento profesional

4. ¿Quiénes suelen ser los voluntarios de esta organización?
   (A) Artistas de todos tipos de disciplinas
   (B) Gente experimentada en diferentes espectáculos para niños
   (C) Estudiantes universitarios con ganas de viajar
   (D) Personas interesadas en desarrollar proyectos internacionales

5. ¿Cómo se puede describir la relación entre Luisa y el profesor?
   (A) Es una relación bastante fría.
   (B) Se conocen personalmente.
   (C) Son amigos.
   (D) Ella ha sido estudiante de él.

6. Si Luisa quisiera investigar más los impactos de esta organización que menciona en su carta, ¿cuál de las siguientes publicaciones le ayudaría más?
   (A) *La solidaridad caminando de la mano de la risa*
   (B) *Desplazamiento y conflictos globales*
   (C) *El que ríe vive mejor*
   (D) *Los retos de ser payaso*

7. Según la carta, ¿cuál de los siguientes adjetivos mejor describe el estado emocional de Luisa?
   (A) Inspirada
   (B) Desilusionada
   (C) Preocupada
   (D) Frustrada

Cultural Awareness

Cultural product: This correspondence presents a group from Spain whose mission is to help bring emotional support to people who have been displaced.

How are this group and its mission similar to or different from non-profit groups in your own community?

SELECCIÓN #20

Tema curricular: La belleza y la estética

El siguiente artículo trata de un baile tradicional. Fue publicado en la página web de la Alcaldía de Ibagué en Colombia.

El Sanjuanero

El Sanjuanero tolimense, más que una danza es un lenguaje representativo de la idiosincrasia del departamento. Su nombre original es el *Contrabandista*,
Línea melodía oficializada en 1988 como la danza insignia del departamento. Fue com-
(5) puesto por el maestro *Cantalicio Rojas*.

La coreografía del *Sanjuanero Tolimense* es el resultado de la investigación de Inés Rojas Luna (QEPD), quien recogió diferentes representaciones folclóri-cas de todo el Tolima. Rojas Luna logró mezclar los rajaleñas que se bailan en el sur del departamento con los bambucos característicos del norte, en munici-
(10) pios como Líbano, Fresno y Villahermosa. Esta danza representa las estrategias de conquista y el idilio que vivían los campesinos tolimenses en las épocas de antaño.

Empieza con el coqueteo, pasa por el enamoramiento y termina con el sím-bolo del matrimonio. Es una coreografía mestiza, en la que se combinan pasos
(15) indígenas (movimientos suaves sobre la tierra) con la influencia española (pasos fuertes, donde se levantan los cuerpos).

En otros tiempos, los hombres utilizaban este baile para estar cerca de la mujer a la que amaban y para formalizar el noviazgo en medio de la fiesta.

Historia

(20) Nadie sabe con exactitud dónde, cuándo, ni cómo se inició la antiquísima celebración sanjuanera que nos llama a los tolimenses en el mes de junio. Todos conocemos la historia moderna de la festividad a partir de 1959 cuando el patriarca conservador Adriano Tribín Piedrahita, decidió crear el Festival Folclórico, casi como una extensión de la Alianza por la Paz, iniciativa que pro-
(25) puso como elemento catalizador para alcanzar la convivencia y reconciliación de las convulsionadas regiones del país.

Pero para llegar a ese punto de la historia moderna del *San Juan* muchos acontecimientos históricos, económicos, políticos y sociales debieron sucederse; no exactamente en Ibagué, sino en el llano tolimense, en las encomiendas,
(30) haciendas y caseríos tornados en poblaciones, localizadas estas a orillas del río Grande de la Magdalena. Lo cierto es que el *San Juan* como celebración llega a estas tierras con el influjo español, se entremezcla con las tradiciones aborígenes, amalgamado por la evangelización de las misiones católicas, con el propósito de convertir a los pueblos nativos considerados paganos. La relación estrecha
(35) surgida entre conquistadores y conquistados, luego entre encomenderos y enco-mendados, y posteriormente entre señores y jornaleros, hizo que el *San Juan* iniciara su camino hacia la modernidad y la festividad que hoy observamos.

1. Según el artículo, ¿qué representa el *Sanjuanero Tolimense*?
   (A) Las diversas lenguas que se hablan en esta región
   (B) Las investigaciones hechas por una antropóloga famosa
   (C) Los rasgos y el carácter de la provincia
   (D) La historia de la conquista de esta parte del país

2. ¿Qué escenifica el baile?
   (A) Las tradiciones de la gente indígena y los españoles
   (B) Un cortejo típico del pasado
   (C) Unos cuentos folklóricos
   (D) Los bailes característicos del norte y del sur de Colombia

3. ¿Qué es "bambuco" (línea 8)?
   (A) Es un tipo de música.
   (B) Es un departamento del país.
   (C) Es una representación teatral.
   (D) Es un conjunto de pueblos.

4. Según el artículo, ¿cuál fue el propósito original del Festival Folclórico?
   (A) Servir de evento unificador para diversas facciones en conflicto
   (B) Darle homenaje a la cultura del departamento
   (C) Llamar la atención a diversos asuntos políticos y económicos
   (D) Representar la llegada de los españoles en el siglo XVII

5. ¿A qué se refiere la palabra "tornados" (línea 29) en el texto?
   (A) A los tumultos que existían en aquel entonces
   (B) A la ubicación de diversos pueblos
   (C) A la peculiaridad de la tierra colombiana
   (D) Al crecimiento de habitantes en una parte de la provincia

6. ¿Qué adjetivo mejor describe la fiesta de *San Juan*?
   (A) Religiosa
   (B) Moderna
   (C) Heterogénea
   (D) Pagana

7. Al escribir un ensayo sobre el tema del artículo, quisieras buscar más información.
   ¿Cuál de las siguientes publicaciones te serviría más?
   (A) *Ferias y fiestas del Tolima*
   (B) *Bailes folclóricos españoles*
   (C) *Una historia concisa de América Latina*
   (D) *Guía práctico del altiplano colombiano*

Cultural Awareness

Cultural product: This text presents a type of dance in Colombia.

How is this dance similar to or different from those in your own community?

SELECCIÓN #21

Tema curricular: La vida contemporánea

Fuente #1: El siguiente artículo trata del tema de ser vegetariano. Fue publicado en *www.laopinion.com.*

Hasta qué punto conviene ser vegetariano. La Opinión Digital
(*www.laopinion.com/salud/salud_nutrition.html*)

Realmente, la carne, como cualquier otro alimento excepto la leche materna para su descendiente en el primer período de la vida de los mamíferos, no es indispensable para la nutrición del hombre, pero es un valioso componente de

Línea gran riqueza nutritiva en las dietas de muchas personas que gozan de buena salud

(5) y no ejerce en los sujetos normales los efectos nocivos que el vegetarianismo le atribuye. Existe la creencia popular de que la alimentación vegetariana es más saludable que una que incluya carne u otros productos derivados de animales.

Lo cierto es que todo tipo de alimentación cuenta con beneficios nutritivos y puede también presentar aspectos problemáticos.

(10) La selección de alimentos que escoge la persona es el factor que determina si una alimentación es saludable o no. Si se elige una alimentación vegetariana, es importante asegurarse de ingerir cantidades suficientes de vitamina B_{12} y calcio, especialmente durante la adolescencia.

Una alimentación vegetariana bien planeada tiende a incluir niveles menores

(15) de grasa saturada y colesterol, así como niveles más altos de fibra y elementos nutrientes derivados de las plantas que una alimentación no vegetariana.

Especialistas en nutrición del programa de Extensión Cooperativa de la Universidad de California citan diversas investigaciones que indican que una alimentación con tales características puede reducir el riesgo de desarrollar diabetes,

(20) presión arterial alta, problemas del corazón y obesidad.

Sin embargo, los beneficios mencionados pueden obtenerse también con una alimentación que incluya productos animales. Con una planificación cuidadosa y el consumo de carnes magras y productos animales con poca grasa, así como frutas y verduras, se puede llevar una alimentación con poca grasa saturada y

(25) colesterol y rica en fibra y nutrientes derivados de plantas.

Además, el consumo de productos animales facilita obtener las cantidades recomendables de calcio, zinc, hierro y vitamina B_{12}.

Fuente #2: La siguiente tabla presenta una guía para una dieta vegetariana. Fue publicado en la página web *www.macroestetica.com* en 2009.

Grupo de alimentos	Raciones diarias sugeridas	Tamaños de la ración
Panes, cereales, arroz y pasta	6 o más	1 rebanada de pan, ½ bollo, ½ taza de cereal cocido, arroz o pasta, 30g de cereal seco
Vegetales	4 o más	½ taza cocidos o 1 taza crudos, ½ taza jugo de verduras
Frutas	3 o más	1 pieza de fruta, ½ taza de jugo de fruta, ½ taza de fruta enlatada o cocida
Leguminosas y otros sustitutos de carne	2 a 3	½ de leguminosas cocidas, 120g de tofú, 240 ml de leche de soja, 45g de queso de soja, 2 cucharadas de crema de cacahuate, 90g de hamburguesa de tofú
Productos lácteos (opcional)	No más de 3	1 taza de leche o yogur, 45g de queso natural, 60 g de queso procesado
Huevos (opcional)	3 a 4 a la semana	1 huevo o 2 claras, ½ taza de sustituto de huevo
Grasas, dulces y alcohol	Pocas cantidades	Aceite, margarina y mayonesa, aderezos para ensalada, gaseosas, dulces, cerveza, vino y bebidas destiladas

1. ¿Cuál es el propósito del artículo?
   - (A) Persuadir a que los lectores sigan una dieta vegetariana
   - (B) Analizar cómo una dieta vegetariana puede reducir el riesgo de contraer unas enfermedades
   - (C) Criticar la creencia de que seguir una dieta vegetariana es más saludable que otras dietas
   - (D) Presentar información de lo que uno debe tener en cuenta al pensar en ser vegetariano

2. ¿Qué técnica usa el autor del artículo para apoyar una de sus ideas?
   - (A) Cita varias anécdotas de su propia experiencia.
   - (B) Incluye resultados de unos estudios.
   - (C) Hace referencia a unas estadísticas.
   - (D) Incorpora varios dichos y proverbios.

3. ¿Cuál de las siguientes afirmaciones mejor resume la opinión presentada en el artículo en cuanto al consumo de carne?
   - (A) Perjudica tanto como acusa el pensamiento vegetariano.
   - (B) Es esencial para obtener ciertas vitaminas y minerales.
   - (C) Aunque provee algún beneficio, causa muchos más problemas a la salud.
   - (D) Forma parte de una dieta saludable, siempre que sea baja en grasa.

4. Según el artículo, ¿qué alimento es absolutamente necesario para el ser humano?
   (A) Comidas ricas en fibra durante la edad adulta
   (B) Alimentos que contienen mucho calcio durante la juventud
   (C) La leche materna durante la primera parte de la vida
   (D) Frutas y verduras en la vejez

5. ¿A qué se refiere "la selección de alimentos" (línea 10) en cuanto a su impacto a llevar una dieta saludable?
   (A) A elegir una determinada cantidad de comida
   (B) A seleccionar solo comidas de alta calidad
   (C) A escoger diversas comidas con una variedad de valores nutritivos
   (D) A evitar las comidas con grasa

6. Según el artículo, ¿qué beneficio aporta el consumo de carne?
   (A) Provee la grasa necesaria en una dieta.
   (B) Aprovisiona ciertas vitaminas y minerales.
   (C) Reduce el riesgo de algunas enfermedades.
   (D) Suministra fibra y otros nutrientes que se encuentran también en plantas.

7. ¿Qué información presenta la tabla?
   (A) Un menú diario típico de una persona vegetariana
   (B) Los tipos y cantidades de comidas que forman una saludable dieta vegetariana
   (C) El valor nutritivo de ciertos alimentos en relación a otros
   (D) Los alimentos más saludables para llevar una dieta balanceada

8. Si fueras de seguir la tabla al pie de la letra, ¿cuál es la cantidad mínima de pan, cereales, pasta y arroz que deberías consumir en un día?
   (A) Dos bollos y una taza de pasta
   (B) Una rebanada de pan, un bollo y una taza de cereal cocido
   (C) Dos rebanadas de pan y una taza de arroz
   (D) Dos tazas de arroz y una rebanada de pan

9. Según la tabla, ¿cuál de los siguientes alimentos no se debería consumir diariamente?
   (A) Una naranja
   (B) Huevo duro
   (C) Queso fresco
   (D) Un sándwich de crema de cacahuete

10. ¿Cuál de las siguientes afirmaciones del artículo se puede verificar en la tabla?
    (A) El consumo de carne en poca cantidades es beneficioso para la salud.
    (B) No es indispensable el consumo de carne para la nutrición.
    (C) Hay que consumir una variedad de alimentos vegetarianos.
    (D) La alimentación vegetariana es más saludable que una que incluye carne.

11. Al preparar una presentación para tu clase sobre el mismo tema del artículo y la tabla, quisieras buscar más información. ¿Cuál de las siguientes publicaciones te ayudaría más en tu preparación?

(A) *Los beneficios ecológicos de ser vegetariano*

(B) *10 efectos nocivos del consumo de carne y otros productos animales*

(C) *La ética de matar por comida*

(D) *La dieta vegetariana: una opción posible, sana y científica*

Selección #21—Más Práctica

Ampliando tu vocabulario—Usa el vocabulario y frases del texto para llenar las columnas según el tema. ¿Puedes pensar en un tema adicional?

Palabras / frases relacionadas con . . .

. . . la buena salud	. . . la mala salud	_____
nutrición	efectos nocivos	
gozan de buena salud	aspectos problemáticos	

Cultural Awareness

Cultural perspective: The article presents an opinion on certain considerations one should make when considering becoming a vegetarian, while the table presents suggested daily intake of a vegetarian diet.

How are the perspectives presented in these texts similar to or different from those in your own community?

SELECCIÓN #22

Tema curricular: La ciencia y la tecnología

En la siguiente carta, un estudiante le escribe a su profesor acerca de un artículo que leyó.

Estimado Profesor Morales,

Le escribo para agradecerle por haberme recibido ayer en su oficina y comentarle que disfruté mucho la charla que tuvimos sobre la ética de modificar células.
Línea
(5) Al volver a casa investigué más el asunto y encontré un artículo que me hizo pensar más en el tema y quería compartir mis pensamientos con usted.

El autor relata la historia de una niña de cuatro años que padece leucemia y sus padres decidieron traer al mundo otra hija para ser la donante de células madre provenientes de su cordón umbilical. La pregunta esencial es que si se pudiera salvar a un hijo al manipular células, ¿lo haría?

(10) Entiendo que modificar células presenta muchos problemas. Por un lado, la Iglesia Católica está completamente en contra de la idea porque cada persona es un don de Dios, y al modificar las células una persona pierde su dignidad inherente. Por otro lado, esta modificación le puede salvarle la vida a la niña, y podría curar otras enfermedades.

(25) Otra idea que surgió es el hecho de cómo se sentiría la otra niña, la que nació para salvarle a su hermana. ¿Cómo le van a justificar los padres la razón por la cual vino al mundo? ¿Fue porque querían otra hija o porque fue por el ansia del bienestar de la otra?

Temo que no haya una respuesta correcta o fácil a este asunto. Algunos cientí-
(20) ficos ven una distinción entre una persona y un conjunto de células. Argumentan que aunque el embrión tiene la potencialidad de transformarse en persona, no lo es, y esto es diferente de cuando es feto que sí ya tiene vida. Creo que todos compartimos la misma opinión de que crear un feto para hacer uso de sus órganos y después descartar el individuo es una idea espantosa. La cuestión es que si hay
(25) que poner un conjunto de células en la misma categoría.

Personalmente tengo más preguntas que respuestas. Por un lado entiendo el argumento de los científicos y la razón de los padres, pero también comprendo el peligro y el dilema ético que el desarrollo de estas prácticas puede llevar. ¿Dónde ponemos el límite? ¿Tenemos el derecho de usar la ciencia para cambiar nuestro
(30) destino? ¿Quién decide si es permisible o no?

Este tema es algo que seguramente me va a seguir rondando en la cabeza y no veo la hora de poder discutirlo más a fondo con usted. Otra vez, agradezco el tiempo que tuvo para mí.

Atentamente,
(35) Julio Benavides

1. ¿Por qué le escribe el estudiante al profesor?
   (A) Para informarle de un acontecimiento en el mundo de la medicina
   (B) Para presentarle los resultados de una investigación
   (C) Para continuar una conversación que tuvieron
   (D) Para debatir un asunto que le causó molestia

2. ¿Qué historia le relata el estudiante al profesor?
   (A) De los avances científicos en la modificación de células
   (B) De la decisión que tomó una familia
   (C) De la polémica que existe entorno a la modificación de células
   (D) De las complicaciones médicas que tuvo una pequeña niña

3. ¿A qué se refiere el autor de la carta cuando dice que para la Iglesia Católica cada persona es un "don de Dios" (línea 12)?
   (A) A que cada persona es tal y como debería ser.
   (B) A que las personas son muy religiosas.
   (C) A que los científicos deben tener más fe.
   (D) A que también las personas enfermas son gente digna.

4. ¿Qué dilema presenta el autor de la carta que posiblemente van a enfrentar los padres mencionados?
   (A) Decidir si quieren tomar medidas para salvarle la vida a su hija
   (B) Proveer para dos hijas, una de la cual es enferma
   (C) Explicarle a una hija el motivo de traerla al mundo
   (D) Determinar si la modificación de células es una práctica ética

5. ¿Qué debate presenta el autor de la carta en cuanto al uso de células?
   (A) Si las células que se usan efectivamente ya tienen vida.
   (B) Si el embrión se puede convertir en persona.
   (C) Si hay que crear un feto para usar los órganos.
   (D) Si las personas son formadas de un grupo de células.

6. ¿Qué quiere comunicar el autor de la carta cuando dice que el tema le "va a seguir rondando" (línea 31)?
   (A) Que este tema le está causando dolor de cabeza.
   (B) Que no puede dejar de pensar en él.
   (C) Que no tiene la capacidad de pensar más.
   (D) Que el tema es demasiado complejo para él.

7. ¿Cuál de las siguientes afirmaciones describe mejor al autor de la carta?
   (A) A pesar de que acaba de enterarse de este tema, tiene las ideas bien claras.
   (B) Es un experto del tema, aunque no tiene opiniones muy fuertes.
   (C) Le fascina el asunto y quiere aclarar sus propias ideas.
   (D) Le interesa el tema, pero necesita ayuda para poder explicarse mejor.

Cultural Awareness

Cultural perspective: This text presents the perspective of a student in regards to the ethics of stem cell research and cloning cells in general.

How is the perspective presented in this text similar to or different from those in your own community?

SELECCIÓN #23

Tema curricular: La ciencia y la tecnología

El siguiente artículo trata sobre los acuarios. El artículo original fue publicado en *Eroski Consumer* en 2010.

Línea

Los acuarios proliferaron en plena fiebre científica de comienzos del siglo veinte en las ciudades costeras. Cien años más tarde se llaman oceanarios y su misión de acercar el mundo marino, exhibiendo una recreación natural de su fauna y su flora, se ha afianzado. Cumplen además la triple function de conservar,
(5) investigar y concienciar de la necesidad de proteger el planeta. Con el convencimiento de que se salvaguarda mejor lo que se conoce, el espectador de estos escaparates acuáticos contempla el resultado de un trabajo preciso de biólogos y profesionales que velan por el funcionamiento perfecto unas instalaciones complejas y una organización eficaz. Todo para lograr acercar la biodiversidad de
(10) los mares y mostrar el ecosistema, el patrimonio universal que se esconde debajo del agua.

A primera hora de la mañana comienza la actividad en el complejo laberinto de zonas privadas y espacio público. La parte franca, la que disfrutan los visitantes, la conforman salas de cristal recorridas por pasillos. Antes de que estos accedan,
(15) se inspeccionan los acrílicos y el metacrilato, se observa el agua y se comprueba que reine la armonía dentro de ella. En el otro lado del cristal la actividad se multiplica. Se toman pruebas de agua, se controlan los filtros, los sensores, los vasos, las tuberías y los comprensores, las tomas de mar y las bombas que permiten el intercambio del agua. Pese a que todo el sistema está informatizado, la inspec-
(20) ción visual es constante.

Los miles de animales y plantas que pueblan las aguas llegan del mar o son criados en cautividad, pero sea cual sea su procedencia, antes de pasar a convivir en la reproducción oceánica del oceanario salvan una cuarentena. A pesar de que la imitación es perfecta y flora y fauna viven en un habitat idéntico, las
(25) nuevas incorporaciones pueden suponer un peligro de alteración de los ácidos y microorganismos. Para evitarlo, todas las especies, grandes o pequeñas, viven sus primeros días en el acuario en pequeños tanques esperando el momento de pasar a las aguas definitivas. La cuarentena es un proceso complicado pero de vital importancia porque es donde se consigue que los peces se aclimaten, se
(30) acostumbren al alimento que recibirán, y también donde se les desparasita y se les cura las heridas. Cuando el pez está en óptimas condiciones puede pasar a la exposición.

En el acuario no hay corrientes que limpien las aguas, ni los animals pueden huir de un foco intoxicado. La limpieza es clave. Todos los días se sifona la su-
(35) ciedad del fondo, ya sean excrementos, algas o restos de comida. Se realiza de manera mecánica con herramientas específicas para cada espacio, pero cuando el tamaño del vaso impide la manipulación de mangueras son los buzos quienes se encargan de mantener la higiene de paredes, suelo y decorados.

Visitar un acuario es tener la oportunidad de imaginar un viaje en el subma-
(40)   rino del capitán Nemo, el protagonista de 20.000 leguas de viaje submarino. Tras
los cristales reina la vida inalcanzable del fondo de los océanos. Pero un acuario
no es solo la suma de recipientes con millones de metros cúbicos de agua en
los que se expone el ciclo de animales y plantas, en los que se pueden ver peces
tropicales, corales, atunes, medusas, tortugas. También son centros científicos
(45)   que realizan labores de investigación y conservación de la fauna y la flora marina.
Se desarrollan proyectos medioambientales ahora más necesarios que nunca,
porque vivimos un tiempo en que la salud de algunos mares, deteriorada por la
actividad humana, pone en riesgo la salud de todo el planeta.

(revista.consumer.es/web/es/20100501/actualidad/informe1/75560.php)

1. ¿Cuál será el propósito de un acuario?
    (A) Crear la ilusión de la vida submarina en la superficie del mar
    (B) Rescatar a animales marítimos heridos por pescadores deportivos
    (C) Enseñar al público de su responsabilidad para cuidar del ecosistema oceánico
    (D) Atraer al público para enriquecer la ciudad donde está el patrimonio universal

2. ¿Qué es la cuarentena (líneas 23 y 28)?
    (A) Un tipo de vaso en el que se guardan animales para observarlos.
    (B) Un tipo de tratamiento que recibe un animal enfermo para curarlo.
    (C) El tiempo necesario para preparar el acuario para recibir el animal.
    (D) Un modo mediante el cual se acierta que se adapte el animal al medio
         ambiente nuevo.

3. ¿Cómo se limpia el vaso grande del acuario?
    (A) Hay peces que comen materias dañosas en el acuario.
    (B) Hay buceadores encargados de mantener la limpieza.
    (C) Hay herramientas mecánicas que se utilizan para limpiarlo.
    (D) Hacen correr chorros de agua para intercambiar las aguas.

4. ¿Cómo se mantiene todo un sistema tan complejo en el acuario?
    (A) Con mucha tubería
    (B) Por inspección visual
    (C) Por ciencia de ordenador
    (D) Con bombas y mangueras

5. ¿Por qué le gusta tanto al público visitar el acuario?
    (A) Lo inaccesible y secreto siempre le fascinan al público.
    (B) Le gusta visitar al Capitán Nemo cuando visitan el acuario.
    (C) Al público le encanta la idea de ser animal acuático.
    (D) Le atrae la oportunidad de aprender del alimento procedente del mar.

6. ¿Qué importancia tiene el acuario?
   (A) Es la única manera de salvar las especies en peligro de desaparecer.
   (B) No hay otro lugar donde se puede observar la vida inútil del mar.
   (C) Las indagaciones científicas logradas allí son imprescindibles.
   (D) Al visitar el acuario los niños se entusiasman por hacerse científicos.

7. Según el artículo, ¿a qué se atribuye el deterioro del mar?
   (A) Al descuido del ser humano
   (B) Al calentamiento global de las aguas
   (C) Al maltrato del océano por los marineros
   (D) A la sobreproducción de la industria pescadera

8. ¿Cuál de las siguientes frases sería el mejor título para este artículo?
   (A) *Guía básica para montar un acuario*
   (B) *Cómo cuidar a tus peces*
   (C) *El mar entre cuatro paredes*
   (D) *Ventajas y desventajas de un acuario*

Cultural Awareness

Cultural product: This text presents information about aquariums and how they function.

How are the aquariums presented in this text similar to or different from those in your own community?

SELECCIÓN #24

Tema curricular: Las familias y las comunidades
Introducción: La siguiente selección trata de un festival en Valencia, España.

El origen de la fiesta de las Fallas se sitúa en los últimos años del siglo XV, cuando los carpinteros de la ciudad, en vísperas de la fiesta de su patrón San José, quemaban frente a sus talleres, en las calles y plazas públicas, los trastos inser-

Línea
(5)

vibles junto con los artilugios de madera que empleaban para elevar los candiles que les iluminaban mientras trabajaban en los meses de invierno.

En la actualidad, son más de 350 las fallas que se queman en la ciudad de Valencia la noche del 19 de marzo, durante la tradicional cremà. Estos impresionantes monumentos de cartón piedra que invaden las calles tras la plantà, el 15 de marzo, compiten en ingenio y belleza, desde unas estructuras piramidales

(10)

que garantizan una perfecta caída y posterior conversion en cenizas, satirizando sobre los últimos acontecimientos de la vida política, social y cultural.

Las fallas van tomando poco a poco la ciudad transformándola en un auténtico espectáculo que cobra más fuerza a medida que se acerca su fin. Quien visite Valencia durante los días previos a la llamarada final se verá irremediablemente

(15)

envuelto por la fiesta. Tendrá ocasión de pasearse entre las fallas que se instalan en cada esquina mientras escucha la música de las bandas o come chocolate con buñuelos; sentir que los cimientos retumban todos los días a las 14,00 horas, con la mascletà que se dispara desde la plaza del Ayuntamiento; ver una corrida de toros; asistir a la ofrenda a la Virgende los Desamparados, el 17 y el 18 de marzo,

(20)

que convierte la fachada de la Basílica en un auténtico tapiz de flores y la plaza de la Virgen en un jardín; o disfrutar de la magia de los castillos de fuegos artificiales que llegan a su punto culminante la noche del 18 de marzo, nit del foc.

(www.pueblos-espana.org/comunidad+valenciana/valencia/valencia/)

---

1. ¿A quién(es) es dirigido este informe?
   (A) A gente que busca participar en un festival tranquilo.
   (B) A los que sufren de piromanía.
   (C) A turistas que quieren experimentar un evento local.
   (D) A jóvenes aficionados de los fantoches.

2. ¿Cuál fue el origen de las Fallas?
   (A) La gente quería honrar al alcalde de la ciudad de Valencia.
   (B) Tuvo origen en la dedicación de candiles en la Basílica durante la cremà.
   (C) Unos carpinteros quemaron sus desperdicios y otros objetos en público.
   (D) Alguna gente hizo fuegos en las calles para iluminar la ciudad de noche.

3. Actualmente, ¿cómo se hacen las fallas?
   (A) Los artesanos las hacen de cartón.
   (B) Los carpinteros las hacen de madera.
   (C) Los valencianos las producen con piedras.
   (D) La gente las construyen de artilugios.

4. ¿Dónde se sitúan las fallas?
   (A) En la plaza del Ayuntamiento
   (B) En los jardines
   (C) En la Basílica
   (D) En las esquinas

5. ¿Con qué motivo se construyen las fallas?
   (A) Para mostrar la dedicación religiosa
   (B) Para conmemorar figuras sacadas de la historia
   (C) Para burlarse cómicamente de personas actuales
   (D) Para satírizar las grandes figuras religiosas de hoy y del pasado

6. ¿Qué es la mascletà (línea 18)?
   (A) Fuegos artificiales diurnos
   (B) Una corrida de toros
   (C) Fuegos artificiales nocturnos
   (D) Un desfile de carrozas

7. ¿Qué pasa durante la última noche?
   (A) Toda la gente se reúne en la plaza de la Basílica y del Ayuntamiento.
   (B) Hay un espectáculo tremendo de fuegos artificiales.
   (C) La Virgen aparece vestida de flores delante de la Basílica.
   (D) Hay obras de magia en los castillos de fuegos artificiales.

Cultural Awareness

Cultural practice: This text presents a festival that happens in Valencia, Spain, in March.

Cultural product: In addition to the festival, the text mentions the creation of structures that are a key part of the festival.

How are the practices and products presented in this text similar to or different from those in your own community?

ANSWER KEY

Reading Comprehension

Selección #1
1. **B**	3. **B**	5. **A**	7. **A**
2. **D**	4. **C**	6. **B**	

Selección #2
1. **A**	4. **D**	7. **B**	10. **B**
2. **D**	5. **C**	8. **B**	11. **A**
3. **B**	6. **B**	9. **A**	

Selección #3
1. **C**	3. **D**	5. **A**
2. **B**	4. **C**	

Selección #4
1. **B**	3. **D**	5. **C**	7. **B**
2. **B**	4. **D**	6. **D**	

Selección #5
1. **A**	3. **B**	5. **D**	7. **B**
2. **B**	4. **C**	6. **A**	

Selección #6
1. **B**	3. **C**	5. **C**	7. **A**
2. **B**	4. **A**	6. **C**	

Selección #7
1. **C**	4. **B**	7. **A**	10. **B**
2. **C**	5. **D**	8. **D**	11. **B**
3. **A**	6. **B**	9. **C**	

Selección #8
1. **D**	3. **A**	5. **C**	7. **C**
2. **A**	4. **D**	6. **B**	

Selección #9
1. **B**	3. **B**	5. **C**	7. **A**
2. **D**	4. **A**	6. **D**	

Selección #10
1. **B**	3. **A**	5. **B**
2. **C**	4. **D**	

Selección #11
1. **A**	3. **C**	5. **C**
2. **B**	4. **B**	

Selección #12
1. **C**	3. **C**	5. **B**	7. **C**
2. **A**	4. **B**	6. **D**	

Selección #13

1. **B**
2. **B**
3. **A**
4. **D**
5. **A**

Selección #14

1. **D**
2. **A**
3. **B**
4. **B**
5. **C**
6. **B**
7. **A**

Selección #15

1. **D**
2. **B**
3. **C**
4. **A**
5. **A**
6. **B**
7. **B**

Selección #16

1. **C**
2. **D**
3. **B**
4. **B**
5. **C**
6. **A**
7. **C**
8. **C**
9. **B**
10. **A**
11. **C**

Selección #17

1. **B**
2. **C**
3. **B**
4. **D**
5. **B**
6. **A**
7. **B**

Selección #18

1. **B**
2. **B**
3. **A**
4. **A**
5. **D**

Selección #19

1. **D**
2. **D**
3. **B**
4. **B**
5. **D**
6. **A**
7. **A**

Selección #20

1. **C**
2. **B**
3. **A**
4. **A**
5. **D**
6. **C**
7. **A**

Selección #21

1. **D**
2. **B**
3. **D**
4. **C**
5. **C**
6. **B**
7. **B**
8. **A**
9. **B**
10. **B**
11. **D**

Selección #22

1. **C**
2. **B**
3. **A**
4. **C**
5. **A**
6. **B**
7. **C**

Selección #23

1. **C**
2. **D**
3. **B**
4. **B**
5. **A**
6. **C**
7. **A**
8. **C**

Selección #24

1. **C**
2. **C**
3. **A**
4. **D**
5. **C**
6. **A**
7. **B**

ANSWERS EXPLAINED

SELECCIÓN #1

1. **(B)** In lines 2–3, the narrator states that he was listening to diners next to him while in a restaurant ("unos comensales de otras mesas"). Be careful not to be tempted to select option (C), for although the entire tone of the article relates to the economic situation in Spain, it is the overheard discussion that sparked this reflection and written commentary.

2. **(D)** The text states that a Spaniard was surprised that while in Norway, nobody cheated the state while paying taxes or on their tax returns ("nadie le admitía que regateara al Estado en el pago de impuestos ni en ninguna declaración"). The one word that may cause difficulty when answering this question is the verb *regatear*, which literally means to haggle or to bargain, but in this case, it also means to cheat. If you were not sure, one thing to do is look at the following sentence, where the narrator says, "Ese civismo responsable no existe en España . . . ," and you could infer that the idea communicated before must inherently be a form of civility. Another strategy is to look at all the other answers. Options (A), (B), and (C) are all negative, while (D) stands out as the only positive answer.

3. **(B)** The answer to this question is found specifically in lines 8–9, where the author, when speaking about Spain, writes, ". . . la falta de responsabilidad económica y social . . . ." Since paying taxes is a social and economic responsibility, this is the best answer.

4. **(C)** Following along the train of thought that the main criticism here is how Spaniards like to cheat the state, option (C) is the only option that explains how the practice cheats the state. In line 12, the worker at a mechanic shop reacts to the narrator pulling out his credit card by saying that he will charge more money if the narrator wants a receipt. One can infer that paying by credit card will leave evidence of the sale, and therefore lead to having to pay taxes on that money earned. Forcing the customer to only pay cash ("metálico") can help hide the true amount earned for services, and therefore reduce the amount of taxes owed at the end of the fiscal year.

5. **(A)** The word *ahorrar* means to save, as in to save money (*salvar* is to save lives), and *euro* is the currency used in most Western European countries. The expression, whether in English or in Spanish, is meant to indicate that one person is willing to do the action as long as it benefits himself or herself, and, in this case, it is by cheating the state. Options (B) and (D) are incorrect because they refer to being paid and receiving money from elsewhere, not cheating someone money that is due to them. Option (C) is incorrect because it refers to economizing, or spending money carefully.

6. **(B)** This is a rhetorical statement that criticizes how one has to carry loads of cash so that others can avoid their civic and economic duties. A careful reading of each of the other options will clearly indicate that there is no evidence in the text to support it, but that it also does not follow the theme of the entire article.

7. **(A)** The adjective *desilusionado* means discouraged or disappointed. This is not to be confused with the adjective disillusioned in English, which means to be free from false belief, although *desilusionado* can also have this meaning. However, in this case, this is the best adjective because the overall tone of the piece is one of being disappointed with the way Spanish society is as it relates to the economy. Options (B) and (D) are clearly incorrect because they express a more positive attitude, and option (C) is incorrect

because, although the author criticizes people for being disingenuous, the author herself is not cheated or fooled.

Vocabulario en contexto: The following are possible answers. Remember, if you do not know a synonym, use circumlocution (explain the meaning with different words).

1. ruidoso, con mucha gente

2. personas que comparten una mesa, clientes en un restaurante

3. engaño, eludir una responsabilidad

4. robar, evitar, engañar

Ampliando tu vocabulario

. . . el fraude	. . . la economía	. . . el civismo	. . . la desilusión
maquillar contabilidades	*asesor*	*responsabilidad social*	*sorprendido*
dinero negro	*impuestos*	*civismo*	*no admitir*
fraude	*económico*	*moralmente*	*no alcanzar ninguna prosperidad*
falta de responsabilidad	*pago*	*pagar lo que me toca*	
escamotear al Estado	*prosperidad*	*la obligación*	
el trapicheo	*equidad económica*	*saneo*	
no legal	*ahorre*	*concienciación social*	
	regatear		
	cobrar(le)		

SELECCIÓN #2

1. **(A)** Pay close attention to the question, and you will see that it is asking where the USA ranks globally in greenhouse gas emissions. You can easily find the answer to this question in lines 2 and 3, where it states, ". . . uno de los principales países causantes de este tipo de contaminación." Don't be confused by option (B), because the 20% in line 1 refers to the percentage of greenhouse gases produced in the USA that are derived from food.

2. **(D)** The answer to this question is found in lines 10–11, where it talks about how the carbon footprint (*huella de carbono*) is measured (". . . en el ciclo de vida de los alimentos, desde que se elaboran, se transportan, hasta que llegan a la mesa."). In other words, consider all phases of production.

3. **(B)** The answer to this question requires a full reading of several paragraphs. The first half of the answer is found in the fourth paragraph (". . . consumo de productos locales."). While the second half is found in the last paragraph ("no envasados ni procesados"). Often a student may be tempted to choose option (A) because of the word "frescos," which is mentioned in line 37, but there is nothing in the text to support the first part of this answer ("la calidad"). Foods of high quality may not have a low carbon footprint, because they could include meats from foreign countries, which have high transportation costs.

Remember that when selecting an answer, you have to make the *best* choice, and given the context, option (B) is the only one fully supported by the text.

4. **(D)** This answer is supported by evidence in lines 25–29, where it talks about how emissions of nitrogen and methane caused by manure and the amount of food that a cow needs to eat to gain a certain amount of weight.

5. **(C)** If you got this answer correct, then you did a great job avoiding some obvious traps. Options (A) and (D) both include percentages and numbers from the text, but they are incorrect in their interpretation of these numbers. The number 60% refers to the percentage of greenhouse gasses emitted from raising cattle that comes from their manure, not the amount of food that they eat. The numbers 10 and 30 refer to the amount, in kilograms, of food that cows need to eat to gain one kilogram of weight. Fish only need to eat between 1 and 2 kilos to gain the same weight. It does not say that as they are raised, they *only* eat 10–30 kg or 1–2 kg of food respectively, which is what option (D) is suggesting. Option (C) says that to gain the same amount of weight (1 kg), a cow has to eat between five and thirty times what a fish needs to eat, which is the correct way to interpret these numbers.

6. **(B)** This should have been a pretty easy question, given that the word "local" is in "localtariano," and the word "cercano" means near. The word *localtarian* is also more and more being used in English and has the same meaning.

7. **(B)** If you have understood the entire article, this question should be pretty easy to answer. In order to reduce one's carbon footprint when it comes to food, one has to eat fresh foods that are in season (therefore avoiding refrigeration and the use of preservatives) and are local (to avoid transportation costs). Some may argue that option (A) is a possibility, but the article explicitly states to avoid consuming products from large farming industries ("productos agropecuarios procedentes de explotaciones industriales") and instead opt to purchase foods from small urban gardens ("pequeños huertos urbanos").

8. **(B)** When answering questions that deal with overall meaning of a passage, graph, or table, it is always wise to read the introduction first. By doing so, you will clearly see that this graph simply presents the carbon footprint associated with different foods, therefore making option (B) the obvious choice.

9. **(A)** This question can be a little tricky to answer, but you have to go with the option that you are best able to defend. Since there are no numbers on the actual bars on the graph, one has to estimate their total $kgCO_2/100kCal$ impact. Implementing a process of elimination may be helpful to identify the correct answer. Option (B) is clearly incorrect because "carne de ave" includes "pollo," which clearly contributes less than other meats, such as "cerdo," "ternera," and "cordero." Option (D) is the next choice to be eliminated because, although "maíz" is the lowest on this list, there is nothing in the graph that explains why it is the lowest, and therefore we have to discount it as a possible correct answer. Option (C) is tough to defend because, although on the graph it is evident that "manzanas" is more than "maíz" and "verduras," do we really know if it is just as bad as both "maíz" and "verduras" combined? Option (A), on the other hand, is clearly obvious because "ganadería" includes all livestock that feed on grass, therefore including "ternera" (veal) and "cordero" (lamb). If there is one obvious answer and one that is not so clear, always opt for the obvious one rather than trying to force another option.

10. **(B)** To get this answer correct, you have to refer back to the information you learned in the article. Remember that some reasons for a high carbon footprint associated with food are transportation and preservation costs. *Gambas* (shrimp) have to be kept frozen and often are shipped large distances, especially to those communities living inland. Option (A) is incorrect because there is no data indicating how much shrimp need to eat to gain weight (and one can assume that it is probably not more than what fish need, which is far less than cows need). Options (C) and (D) refer to personal preferences and eating habits, which is not supported anywhere in the texts.

11. **(A)** Remember to read the question carefully. The project is to promote a low carbon-footprint diet in your community. Option (A) is the best answer because it completes the same goals as mentioned in question 7: eat local foods that are in season. Options (B) and (D) are incorrect because, although they will provide more information on how importing foods affects the environment and the negative effects of greenhouse gasses, it may not necessarily give solutions to help you with this particular project. Option (C) is not the best answer because there is nothing in the article that says being a vegetarian will minimize your carbon footprint. If you are a vegetarian with a passion for imported fruits and vegetables, it will completely negate the goals of this project.

Ampliando tu vocabulario—Usa el vocabulario y frases del texto para llenar las columnas según el tema. ¿Puedes pensar en un tema adicional?

Palabras / frases relacionadas con . . .

. . . el daño al medio ambiente	. . . la elaboración de comida	. . . la conciencia ecológica	_____
gases de efecto invernadero (GEI)	embalaje	huella de carbono	
	procesamiento	reducir los GEI	
emisión	envasado	dieta baja en carbono	
calentamiento global	procesado	recursos naturales	
	plástico		
residuos	congelación	alimentos ecológicos	
gases contaminantes	conservar		
	agua embotellada		
productos químicos			

SELECCIÓN #3

1. **(C)** The advertisement is for the general public since the dancers have already been selected. The adjective *limeño* refers to a resident of Lima, Perú.

2. **(B)** The answer to this question is clearly found in lines 1 and 2, and then restated in lines 20–23. Some might be tempted to select answer A, for in this competition there will be winners. However, the stated goal of the advertisement is not to pick the best dancers in the nation, but rather to preserve a cultural practice.

3. **(D)** There are a number of prizes that are mentioned in lines 13 through 15. These include monetary prizes as well as diplomas and trophies. In addition, lines 16–17 present the *Campeón de Campeones* category, which is where the winners of past competitions compete. Although the text never says what each category winner receives, one can safely assume that the winner will win one of the prizes mentioned in lines 13–15 and qualify to compete in an upcoming *Campeón de Campeones* event.

4. **(C)** The answer is found in lines 16–19, where it states that any champion of a contest sponsored by the *Municipalidad de Lima* can compete except for those who have won this category sometime in the past two years.

5. **(A)** When answering questions that force you to think beyond the text, a good idea is to think of the most logical option. In this case, option A is logical because the text does give information about the location of the event, but nothing about how to get there. Option B is not logical because the text says that the cost is free (line 28). Option C is incorrect because this text is inviting the general public, not looking for dancers. Option D is also not a good option because the author of this text would not necessarily know how to answer this, nor does it have anything to do with the event that the author is promoting.

SELECCIÓN #4

1. **(B)** The answer to this question is found in lines 6–7, where it states that the *rosca* is ". . . un bizcocho fino . . . que contiene en promedio tres figures de plástico . . . ." The adjective "delicioso" in line 5 proves that the "bizcocho" is a type of food, therefore making option (B) the correct answer because it is the only option that mentions a type of food ("postre").

2. **(B)** This information is found in lines 10–11, which says that the *rosca* is ". . . el centro de atención de la fiesta de cada seis de enero . . . ." The other dates make reference to different activities, but not the eating of this food.

3. **(D)** Pay close attention to this question, for unlike questions 1 and 2, it refers now to the event, not the food. Although there are two events mentioned in this text (*el Día de los Reyes Magos* and *el Día de la Candelaria*), the main event is *el Día de los Reyes Magos* because the author of this letter was not able to stay long enough to experience the second celebration. *El Día de los Reyes Magos*, or Epiphany as it is known in English, is an event that celebrates the arrival of the three kings (also known as wise men) to Bethlehem to visit the infant Jesus. Although the text itself does not explicitly say what actions are taken besides eating the *rosca de Reyes*, you can infer that the family goes to church because in lines 30–31, when talking about the actions surrounding *el Día de la Candelaria*, it says

that families ". . . se reúnen nuevamente para celebar la presentación del niño Dios en la iglesia." The key word is "nuevamente" (once again), meaning that they had met earlier to do a similar celebration, which is celebrating with food and going to church. Option (A) is incorrect because the only reference to Romans is in line 21, where it states that some historians believe that this tradition has Roman origins. Option (B) is incorrect because in lines 15–16 it says that only the person who finds the plastic figure in the *rosca de Reyes* has to dress up and present gifts, not everyone. Option (C) is incorrect because not everyone prepares or purchases a *rosca*, only one is made per family.

4. **(D)** This information is found in lines 15–16, where it says, ". . . quién encuentre la figura deberá vestir y presantar al niño Dios en la iglesia . . . ."

5. **(C)** You can find the answer in lines 19–20, where it speaks to how long this current tradition has been in place. Some might be tempted to select option (D), and although some historians believe that it has Roman origins, it is not clear if the current Catholic religious celebration began in Roman times since Romans were pagans, thus making option (D) an answer difficult to prove.

6. **(D)** This is another question in which process of elimination can help you clearly identify the correct answer. There is nothing explicitly stated in the text that will help you answer this question. Rather you have to consider the message as a whole. Does this tradition make it so that families come together to help merchants? Not really, so option (A) can be eliminated. Does this celebration allow merchants to take a break? No, because they actually take advantage of this time to expand their earnings (lines 23–24), thus option (B) can be eliminated. Does this celebration tighten relations between the church and merchants? No. Merchants take advantage of this celebration to gain more money, but the church almost definitely is not using this as a financial gain, but rather to celebrate an important part of its history (eliminate option (C)). Does this celebration allow children to feel a part of the religious community? Well, yes. They get to remember an important religious event, eat delicious food and, if they find the plastic figure, they will have to present it at church. By the process of elimination, option (D) is the clear answer.

7. **(B)** The penultimate paragraph contains this information. Pablo mentions all the foods that will be prepared for the *Día de la Candelaria*, and is upset that he will not be there to partake. Option (A) is incorrect because Pablo did not find the plastic figure, his brother did, and therefore Pablo could not present it even if he wanted to. Option (C) is incorrect because this celebration is a yearly event. Option (D) is incorrect because he never mentions not wanting to return to school. In fact, he simply states that he will see his friend in school, and one could infer that he could be looking forward to it.

Selección #4—Más Práctica

When answering these questions, consider how you and your family celebrate a religious holiday during the months of December and January. Consider the products used (food, gifts, etc.), the practices (do you go to a religious establishment, home of a family member, etc.), and perspectives (why do you and your family do these activities?). If you don't know about the King Cake in New Orleans, you may want to do some research on it and compare/contrast it to the *rosca de Reyes* mentioned in the text. This will give you an example of how communities in the United States and in Spanish-speaking countries celebrate important events.

SELECCIÓN #5

1. **(A)** To answer this question, you have to read the entirety of the passage. The passage talks about the visit of a construction worker or bricklayer (*albañil*) to the house of the narrator. The family treats this guest with the utmost respect, and the father stops his son from cleaning the back of the sofa where the worker was sitting and accidentally stained in white (probably due to having dust on his clothes from being at work earlier that day). The father keeps the son from cleaning the back of the couch because he does not want his guest to feel bad for having stained it. Therefore, option (A) is the best answer because it refers to the proper conduct of a host (*anfitrión*) when he has a guest.

2. **(B)** The answer is found in lines 2–3 where the narrator says, "... no quiso que limpiara el espaldar que el albañilito había manchado de blanco ..." (I did not want me to clean the back of the couch that the guest had stained in white). The word "huellas" means footprints or remnants, and, in this case, refers to the white dust that came off the jacket of the guest as he was sitting at the couch.

3. **(B)** This may be a difficult question to answer if you don't know the vocabulary in the options. However, these are words that you should know and learn if you don't. *Avergonzarse* means to be embarrassed, *enojarse* means to be upset/angry, and *arrepentirse* means to be regretful or sorry. In line 5 of the text, the *albañilito* becomes "encarnado," or red faced, meaning he is embarrassed. The word *encarnar* comes from the prefix *en* and the noun *carne* (meat). In other words, *encarnar* means to turn the color of meat, or flesh colored (red).

4. **(C)** This is a quote that you cannot take literally and have to understand it in context to find out its true meaning. The father is trying to communicate to his son why he did not want him to clean up the stain left by the guest. He says that any dirt or dust on the worker is a result of hard work, and therefore should not be considered a disgrace or embarrassment, but rather a source of pride because that person has put in a tough day.

5. **(D)** This answer follows the same train of thought throughout the story. The hosts do not want to embarrass the guest, for that would be rude ("descortés").

6. **(A)** Throughout the text you can tell there is a definite socioeconomic class difference between the two characters. The *albañilito* is dusty, dirty, has buttons falling off his clothes, and has a raggedy hat ("ajandroso sombrero"). The family, on the other hand, cares for their belongings, such as the immediate impulse to want to clean the couch once it was stained and sewing the button back on the jacket. There is nothing in the text that can be used to evaluate the level of education between the son and the worker because they could be both of school age and attending the same school, making options (B) and (D) not the best choices. Option (C) is not the best answer because it is inferred that the boy and the worker are friends, and therefore there are no major personality differences.

7. **(B)** The fact that the father takes the time at the end of the passage to explain to his son why he did not want him to clean the couch shows a true devotion from the father to his son. The fact that his son writes about this memory of his father shows that the son really respects his father, therefore making option (B) the best answer. Option (A) is incorrect because the father is not demanding, he just wants to teach his son the right etiquette in a non-confrontational way. Options (C) and (D) are incorrect because the son does learn from his father, and there is nothing in the text to suggest that he is spoiled by his father.

SELECCIÓN #6

1. **(B)** The answer is clearly found in line 5, where Alicia informs the reader that this is in response to a letter that Susana previously wrote. Option A and C are not correct, for even though she does change the topic of discussion and does inform Susana of her project, this is not the reason for this exchange.

2. **(B)** The answer can be found in line 15, where Alicia says that *factores económicos* are the main reason. Therefore, one can safely assume that the family does not have enough money to care for the animals.

3. **(C)** Line 10 says that her country *encabeza la lista*. If we look carefully at the verb, we see that it includes the noun *cabeza*, which means head. Therefore, this verb means *at the top of* or *leads* the list.

4. **(A)** Although Alicia never mentions explicitly where she got her information, she delves into this topic because she is working on a research project for one of her classes. All the facts that she provides about animal abandonment are quite specific, and therefore we can safely assume that she knows this as a result of her investigation.

5. **(C)** Lines 19–22 show the reader that there is not one solution to this problem, making option C the best answer.

6. **(C)** The key word here is "novedad", which means that it is something new, and the only novelty that Alicia mentions is that certain hotels are now offering rooms in which pets are allowed, making option C the best answer. Don't be tempted to select option B, for Alicia says that this platform has been around for several years, and therefore is not a novelty.

7. **(A)** The expression *irse por las ramas* means *to go off on a tangent*. We can clearly see this is what Alicia does in this letter, especially because she apologizes for having dedicated the majority of this correspondence on animal abandonment and for not addressing the question Susana asked in her previous letter (line 31).

Selección #6—Más Práctica

It is always a good idea to note how interpersonal writings are structured and the tone that is used throughout. This is an informal correspondence, so both the greeting ("Querida") and goodbye ("Saludos a tu familia") are appropriate for this context as well as the use of "tú" throughout. Also note the division. First the opening, where Alicia talks briefly about her school and asks a question about Susana's puppy. Next comes the body, which fills lines 9 through 28. Finally comes the closing, in lines 29–33. Not only is this correspondence organized by being divided into paragraphs, there is also organization of thought throughout. One idea leads to another, which helps the reader follow the train of thought. It is a good idea to notice the structural and organizational elements of correspondences, as they will help you become a better writer in the Free Response Task 1: Email Reply portion of the exam.

SELECCIÓN #7

1. **(C)** In line 2 the article clearly presents that the angle it is investigating is which social media sites are used in regards the news and all activities that surround it (sharing, commenting, and so on).

2. **(C)** Lines 3–4 show that Facebook still leads in terms of its *uso informativo* (to become informed). The article also mentions that Facebook has encountered some controversy, but that is a side bar and not the main data presented in the text.

3. **(A)** Be careful not to jump to premature conclusions, for although the title of the article says that the use of YouTube, Twitter, and Instagram is growing among younger people, the article also states in line 4 that the use of Facebook for informative purposes leads all age ranges (*todas las franjas de edad*), which is what the question is asking.

4. **(B)** The answer is found in line 6–7, where it says that WhatsApp continues to be the most popular in terms of general use.

5. **(D)** The answer to this question is clearly seen in the title, where it states that the use of these sites is increasing in young people. Option A is not correct, for all three sites have different percentages of usage. Option B is also incorrect, for we are only presented with the data for this past year, and there is no way of knowing if this growth is similar or different than in previous years. Option C is also incorrect because, although the text does say that YouTube is as popular as Facebook when it comes to general use, the text does not say the same about the other two social media platforms.

6. **(B)** The answer to this question can be found in lines 16–20, where the text states that interactions in Facebook tend to be more passive, while in WhatsApp the participants tend to engage each other in debates, and so on.

7. **(A)** The word *fuente* refers to the source, which is where the news comes from.

8. **(D)** The answer can be found in lines 25–27, where the author says that opinions are divided in terms of whether the number of likes or interactions a news story gets has a direct effect on user interest in the story. For some people it does, while for many more it does not.

9. **(C)** Careful with this question, for although the article talks about social media platforms, the introduction to this table clearly states that it is presenting what types of activities internet users do on internet. This rules out option A because it refers exclusively to social media platforms, and not internet in general. Option B is incorrect because the table gives percentages, not number of people. Option D is incorrect because the table simply presents what internet users do and does not present whether they enjoy doing these activities or not.

10. **(B)** The activity that has the highest percentage is sending and receiving emails, which is a type of communication. Some may argue that if we were to combine some of these categories, other options could also be correct. However, be careful when doing so, for one of the pitfalls some students fall into is when they try to force an interpretation that cannot be backed up by the evidence given. For example, some students may argue that Option C (*entretenerse*) could be correct if we were to combine playing videogames, participating in social media sites, and watching videos like on YouTube. However, the

graph never says that the use of social media and watching videos is for entertainment purposes. It could be that people watch videos as part of a homework assignment or for research. It could be that people use social media for business purposes or to maintain contact with family. They may not necessarily *enjoy* it, but do it because it is a necessity. Therefore, unless a graph or table explicitly tells you *why* people do the actions they are doing, we cannot force our own interpretation and have to simply accept the data as presented to us.

11. **(B)** Both sources specify use of internet and social media in Spain, making option B the best answer. Option A is all about Facebook, which the table does not mention. Option C refers to using these tools for business purposes, which is never mentioned in the article. Option D is incorrect because both the article and table present objective data and are not trying to persuade a habit.

SELECCIÓN #8

1. **(D)** The passage talks about the social evolution of Mexico during part of the 20th century, and how a compartmentalized society now has become more integrated. The first few lines speak to the changes that have happened, one of which is that both middle-class and working-class youth can go on to study in the university ("estudios superiores"). This, along with the information in lines 14–15, where the text mentions "Un país dividido en compartimientos . . . entra en contacto con sí mismo," implying that the unification and discovery of their own country gives the Mexican people more opportunities to learn about themselves.

2. **(A)** The Mexican revolution is the event that began the great transformation, for it broke with the cultural history that existed up to that point. Option (B) refers to part of the culture before the transformation began, and since it is not part of the transformation itself, it is an incorrect option. The revolution was an act of self-discovery, and therefore the masks of isolation that existed beforehand fell (lines 13–14), thus making option (C) incorrect. Option (D) is incorrect because there is nothing in the text to support the division of Mexico into states during this period.

3. **(A)** The theme throughout this passage is the self-discovery of Mexico as a nation comprised of many colors, cultures, and people. The passage says that the beginning of this self-identity came through art (lines 9–11), in which authors and artists started seeing Mexico for what it really was.

4. **(D)** Don't be limited to the information in lines 13 and 14, which mention the mask falling ("la máscara cae"). The "colores, voces y cuerpos de México" refer to the recognition of who the Mexican people really are, as described later in lines 17–19.

5. **(C)** This answer may be difficult if you don't know the meaning of the word "autóctona" (autochthonous, or native to a land or area), and if this is the case, then it is a good word to learn. However, you can use the process of elimination to find the right answer. The "doble tendencia" referenced in the question is found in line 20, where the author says that a positive aspect was that the Mexicans were able to discover themselves ("descubrirse a sí mismos"). You can eliminate option (A) because the discovery implies learning something new, not recognizing similarities. Option (B) can be eliminated because there is nothing in the text to suggest an impending battle with the United States, and the only

time the United States is mentioned is in the negative aspect of the "doble tendencia," not the positive aspect that this question asks. Finally, option (D) can be eliminated because there is nothing to suggest that they liked the same colors, and the "colores" mentioned refer to the diversity of the people.

6. **(B)** The idea behind the saying is that there is no equal to Mexico, there is only one. The author introduces the saying by stating that it typifies a chauvinist extreme that came as a result of the great transformation. The use of the word "chauvinista" implies that one feels superior to another, and in this case, the "other" are those outside of Mexico, or foreign influences ("influencias extranjeras"), thus making option (B) the best answer. Some may be tempted to select option (A), but it is not correct because Mexican is not a race, but rather a community formed of many different races.

7. **(C)** By this point, this answer should be pretty clear. The transformation is the discovery of Mexico as a country comprised of many different people and accepting this as the new reality. Yes, art did play a part in this self-discovery, but it is not the focus of the transformation that this passage discusses, therefore making option (A) incorrect. Option (D) is incorrect because although there is a sense of superiority as a result of this self-discovery, the passage is focused on the process of self-discovery, not the consequences afterward. There is nothing in the text to support option (B) as a viable answer.

SELECCIÓN #9

1. **(B)** The answer is clearly found in lines 2–3, where the text says, ". . . bastaba echar una ojeada al escudo de armas, que garantizaba el buen nombre del portador." The word *escudo de armas* means coat of arms, and is the insignia of a family.

2. **(D)** When you look at the phrase referenced, it suggests that identity was a work of a lifetime and, in some cases, many lives. Option (D) communicates this same message.

3. **(B)** The information needed to answer this question can be found in lines 11–13, where it states that "los rumores . . . se extienden como la pólvora y que . . . salpican las reputaciones." The words *rumores* and *chismes* are synonyms and refer to one way that reputations could be damaged both in the past and present.

4. **(A)** Lines 17–21 mention the bosses who use search engines and social media sites to find out more about their employees and of "gerentes [que] se hacen amigos tuyos en las redes sociales para vigilarte." Don't be tempted to select option (C) simply because it mentions becoming friends with coworkers online. The article mentions that bosses do so in order to watch (*vigilar*) their employees rather than for social and friendship reasons.

5. **(C)** In lines 22–23, the text mentions "consultoras" whose job is to "medir la reputación y mejorarla" (evaluate and improve or recover online reputations). Don't be tempted to select option (B) because the company does not participate in these forums, but rather the contracted consultants do.

6. **(D)** The paragraph mentions that in medieval times, when a knight without descendents died on the field then "desaparecía su nombre," while in modern times the information is still there, thus lasting a whole lot longer ("la información sigue ahí").

7. **(A)** With these types of questions that put you in a hypothetical situation, it is very important to understand the scenario in which you are placed. Here you want to find

out more about how to create and keep a good reputation; therefore, the best option is to learn how to take steps to prevent a bad reputation in the first place, making option (A) the best answer.

Selección #9—Más Práctica

1. echar una ojeada (2–3)   *mirar*

2. labrarse (6)   *crearse, formarse, cultivarse*

3. meterse en líos (14–15)   *meterse en problemas, dificultarse*

4. blindarse (40)   *protegerse, defenderse*

SELECCIÓN #10

1. **(B)** This should be a simple question to answer, simply because both the introduction and the title mention "concurso," which is a competition.

2. **(C)** The word "docente" means teacher or members of the education community. In the section titled *Fallo del Jurado*, it mentions "tres profesores . . . un administrativo y un representante del Equipo Directivo." Option (C) is the only answer that most broadly covers the bases, for it says both teachers and administrators. Options (A) and (B) are incorrect because students don't participate in the judging, and neither does the school director. Option (D) is incorrect because it says that various members of the board of directors will participate, and the text says that only one will be involved (the other non-teacher is an administrator).

3. **(A)** The information needed to answer this question is under number 2 of the "Fallo del Jurado," where it states that any work can be printed and used as a season's greetings card from the school. One can safely assume that these cards will be sent to members of the school community.

4. **(D)** The image at the bottom right of the advertisement has a picture of last year's winning drawing, as indicated by the caption below it. The word "ganadora" is the adjective of the verb *ganar*, which means to win.

5. **(B)** Number 4 in the section titled *Bases y entrega de trabajos* says that the theme needs to be about Christmas in Spain. The only option that indicates that a part of Spain will be represented is option (B). Remember that the word *madrileño* is an adjective to describe someone or something from Madrid. Also, *Nochebuena* is the night before Christmas. Don't be tempted to select option (D) simply because Spain does celebrate the *Reyes Magos*. The "recorrido" or route the three kings took was in the Middle East, not in Spain.

SELECCIÓN #11

1. **(A)** The *hallaca* symbolizes the "mestizaje del venezolano," which is comprised of "el negro africano," "el indio americano," and "la llegada de los españoles." Remember that the word *mestizo* means of mixed race.

2. **(B)** The three main ingredients are the banana leaf, the *masa de maíz* (corn dough), and the *guiso* (stew), which is a combination of meats, olives, capers, and raisins. However, a careful reading will show that the banana leaf is only used as a wrapper ("envoltorio");

therefore, it cannot be the main ingredient. The meat and *guiso* are one and the same, because the meat is part of the *guiso*, which also includes other ingredients. Therefore, the only lone ingredient that stands out is *masa de maíz*.

3. **(C)** The context in which this line is used talks about the contributions each community made to the creation of this dish. The arrival of the Spaniards contributed capers, raisins, and olives. One can safely assume that these ingredients were not found in Venezuela before the arrival of the Spaniards, making option (C) the best answer.

4. **(B)** This question elaborates on the information you should have already learned in order to answer question 1. The three cultures are African, European, and indigenous.

5. **(C)** "... sin distinciones sociales ..." means without social distinctions. Therefore, people from all social classes and races can enjoy this meal.

Selección #11—Más Práctica

You may want to think about dishes that you and your family eat during holidays or celebrations and what cultures influenced the creation of these dishes. For instance, most people will eat turkey during Thanksgiving, and you may want to research why turkey and not another animal is eaten. Also, the side dishes may differ somewhat in different parts of the country. Why? You already have information regarding a dish served in Venezuela and its influences, now you simply need to dig a little deeper into dishes that you and your community enjoy during celebrations, and you will have two great examples to use on any oral presentation pertaining to cultural significance of food and/or how people celebrate different types of celebrations.

SELECCIÓN #12

1. **(C)** Passages that tend to come from works of literature can always be tricky, so it is best to read the entire passage first before answering the questions. The answer to this question can be found in line 24, when the narrator exclaims "¡Vean qué tres serpientes he traído yo al mundo!" The expression *traer al mundo* means to give birth, so that means that the narrator is the mother of the three girls who are gossiping.

2. **(A)** The verb "hablaban" in the question refers to what the girls were talking about earlier in the passage. A careful reading will show at the end that this person is Rosaura, and she had a physical altercation with her father that has left her with bruises on her arms ("brazos llenos de cardenales"). You can then assume that Rosaura must have come to the narrator's home, who is now taking care of her, and her three daughters are talking about their first impressions of Rosaura.

3. **(C)** By reading the dialogue, you can tell that the girls are gossiping about Rosaura. They talk about her clothes, how she looked scared, and one of the girls at the end of the dialogue wants to "estudiarla" (study her more) because there is something strange about Rosaura ("algo raro hay en ella").

4. **(B)** Although we don't know who Eufrasia is based solely on this fragment, when the mother says that compared to how her daughters are acting now (which is not very nice) Eufrasia could be a saint, we can infer that Eufrasia probably is not a very nice person. Therefore, the intent of this declaration is to emphasize how cruel the girls are being at this moment.

5. **(B)** The adjective *piadoso* means pious or compassionate. You can infer based on the mother's reaction that she is not appreciative of the way her daughters are talking about Rosaura, and when she mentions the bruises on her arm, she wants the girls to understand that this is a person who has suffered and therefore needs some compassion. Some would argue that option (D) is also a possibility, but it is not the best answer because the mother does not necessarily want the daughters to respect Rosaura. She simply does not want them to criticize her without knowing all the hardship that she has suffered.

6. **(D)** The girls are "horrorizadas" immediately following the revelation that Rosaura has bruises all over her arms from the horrible fight with her father. One might argue that option (A) is a possibility, but the girls would have to be pretty spoiled to react that way, and we don't have enough background knowledge in this fragment alone to say whether this is the case. Also, the fact that the mother reprimanded them suggests that she is not afraid to draw the line when it comes to unacceptable behavior, and therefore it is quite probable that the girls have been scolded before.

7. **(C)** Based on the fragment and all the explanations for the previous answers, this should be pretty clear. The girls in this fragment are making fun of someone's appearance and peculiarities without knowing all the facts.

SELECCIÓN #13

1. **(B)** Be careful when answering this question, because all of the options indicate that this has something to do with an airline. The title of the document says that this is a notice of conditions and responsibilities about luggage (". . . limitaciones de responsabilidades sobre equipajes"), therefore making this more of an informative legal document. You can eliminate option (A) because the word *folleto* means brochure, and it is unlikely that this type of information would be included in a promotional document. The same goes for option (D) since this is not an advertisement, and option (C) can be excluded because it is not a boarding pass.

2. **(B)** Line 12 says that the passenger should contact the airlines 48 hours before the departure time before resuming an interrupted flight. Remember that in many Spanish-speaking countries they use military time, so 14:00 hours is 2:00 P.M.

3. **(A)** The *talón de equipaje* is a baggage check, and in this document it provides the reimbursement policy of the airline in case the luggage is lost. This is part of the "limitaciones de responsabilidad del transportista," the airline.

4. **(D)** The word *reembolso* means reimbursement, and the reimbursement coupon would be logically paid by the airline company for services not rendered.

5. **(A)** Be careful with the word "tradicional" in this statement because it can lead one to think that it means traditional or old. However, in context with the words "seguir brindándoles" (to keep serving), it shows that the company is looking forward to offering its typical services, of which it is proud. Options (B) and (C) suggest that the airline is old and well established, information that cannot be determined from the text. One cannot confirm the veracity of option (D) either because there is no other airline mentioned in the text.

SELECCIÓN #14

1. **(D)** In the first paragraph of the correspondence, Javier talks about being separated from Sebastián and some of his friends, and that he did not enjoy the film as much as the rest of the group, so he could not partake in the conversation that followed. All this confirms that Javier felt a little excluded from the rest of the group during this outing.

2. **(A)** The verb *platicar* in line 8 is a synonym of *hablar* or *charlar*. The adjective *parlanchín* used in line 7 is similar to the English noun parlance, meaning the way or manner in which one speaks. If you could not figure out what this verb means in context, you probably could easily eliminate options (C) (they fell asleep) and (D) (they became ill) because they probably would not have been something they would have done repeatedly throughout the entire movie. If you are able to eliminate two options, you have raised your chances of being correct if you need to guess.

3. **(B)** In lines 8–9 Javier describes the movie as being a "tontería," yet the rest of the group he is with acted as if it were "la major del año." Therefore, he did not speak because he did not want to be a spoilsport ("aguafiestas"). The word *aguafiestas* literally means water on a party, like raining on a party, and means that something ruins a fun event.

4. **(B)** The answer to this question is found in the first half of the second paragraph, where Javier talks about his personal reflection on the event once he arrived home. He says, "ir al cine es una experiencia íntima," meaning that, for him, it is a very personal and meaningful experience. His frustration with the other moviegoers is enough information to easily eliminate options (A) and (C) from the list. However, he never states that he prefers to go alone, and in fact he says that he really enjoys talking about the movie after it has ended, so one can safely assume that he enjoys going with other people, as long as they like to arrive on time and don't talk during the movie. Based on this information, you can comfortably eliminate option (D).

5. **(C)** Although Javier has a very particular idea of what the movie-going experience should be like, the reader can see that as he is writing, he is coming to the realization that not everyone is made the same, and maybe he should have had a different reaction to the events that transpired. Line 20 shows his realization that maybe the others had more fun simply because they were enjoying the experience of being together.

6. **(B)** In order to answer this question correctly, you will need to use context clues to figure out the meaning of this verb. In the previous sentence, you can see that the narrator disliked the film by calling it "una tontería." However, the rest of the group "la alababan" as if it were the best movie of the year. Therefore, you can safely assume that the verb *alabar* means something positive, so you can eliminate options (C) and (D) for being negative. You could also eliminate option (A) because if they were debating about the film, Javier probably would have engaged in this debate. In case you have not already figured it out, the verb *alabar* means to praise.

7. **(A)** You can tell in the final paragraph that Javier's tone changes as he becomes more understanding of the experience he had. You can see this change when he uses words like *aprender* (line 28) and "abandoner las expectativas personales y no frustrarse tanto" (lines 31–32). One may be tempted to choose option (D), but the tone that comes across is not necessarily one of embarrassment, but rather of understanding, therefore making option (A) the best answer.

SELECCIÓN #15

1. **(D)** The introduction to this text clearly states that this person is not from Guatemala; therefore, you could eliminate option (A) without even having read a single word of the text itself. We don't know much about the narrator except that, based on the title, he was invited to spend a month in Guatemala. Therefore option (B) is not correct because he is visiting the country on a more official capacity than simply being a tourist. This leaves options (C) and (D), and the only thing to suggest the profession of the narrator is in line 18–19 where he refers to his own "modestas actuaciones públicas," which could suggest that he is a performer of some sort. However, we don't have enough information to say that he is a cultural ambassador, but we do know that he was invited by the Instituto de Cultura, a Guatemalan organization, so we have enough evidence to comfortably select option (D).

2. **(B)** The adjective *acogido* means accepted or embraced, and this is clearly seen when he talks about the "cortesía natural" and "cordialidad" he experienced, and how the Guatemalans "nos acogen" (line 14). One may be tempted to select option (C), but although he may have felt a little humbled, it is not because the Guatemalans were so much smarter than him.

3. **(C)** This is another example where the process of elimination can help tremendously. The narrator is highly impressed with the Guatemalan people, and therefore options (A) and (D) can quickly be dismissed because they both refer to negative attributes (envy and arrogance). Even if you do not know what *soberbia* means, the rest of the sentence in option (D) that says "no les permitió admitir la superioridad española" should be enough to convey a negative attribute. Option (B) can be quite complicated, especially if you don't know what the word *pedante* means. However, if you look at line 23 in the text, the narrator says "sin el mal de la pedantería," and therefore you could infer that *pedantería* is a negative noun. *Pedante* means pretentious, and the adjective pedant also exists in English.

4. **(A)** The narrator praises the Guatemalan people and on several occasions makes indirect criticisms about his own country. This is seen in statements such as how little Guatemala is known in Europe and how he rediscovered the art of conversing, which, says the narrator, is almost forgotten in his country. You could easily eliminate options (C) and (D) since they criticize Guatemala, and there is no mention of economics, so you can safely eliminate option (B).

5. **(A)** The narrator speaks of the *peninsulares* and Guatemalans as *hermanos*, so they clearly have a bond. However, one can clearly infer that Guatemalans have a much better understanding of the world outside of them than the outside world has of them. This can be seen in the statements "por desgracia tan poco se conoce en Europa" (line 3) and "no aceptan . . . la actitud . . . protectora, que el desconocimiento de la realidad hace adoptar a muchos de los que intentan 'españolear' en América" (lines 15–17). Based on the latter statement alone, you can easily eliminate option (C), and because they do have a bond, you can eliminate option (D).

6. **(B)** Here is another example where the process of elimination can be helpful. The word *pedante* makes another appearance here, and if you learned anything from question 3, then you can safely eliminate option (D) from contention. You can also eliminate option (A) because it really has nothing to do with the overall message of the text. Option (C)

could be a possibility, but it really does not answer the question. The question asks what does the narrator suggest we learn, and the answer is not that one learns to travel to Guatemala, but rather how to apply some of the positive qualities in their own life.

7. **(B)** You probably easily eliminated options (C) and (D) because the narrator is clearly not intense nor does he appear to be a liar. A careful reading of option (A) indicates why it too should be eliminated. The narrator may be sincere, but he is not naïve. Option (B) is clearly the best choice, for he is reflecting on his experience and writing quite eloquently.

SELECCIÓN #16

1. **(C)** The introduction and title of the text clearly indicate the purpose of this reading. As with most objective texts, its purpose is to inform, not persuade, so you can easily eliminate options (A) and (D). Option (B) is incorrect because the text focuses on the parents, not young people.

2. **(D)** This is an example where the process of elimination can be quite helpful. There are no specific examples or case studies (eliminate option (A)), the author does not introduce his/her own voice in this article (eliminate option (B)), and although there is a quote from one expert, it is only a singular expert, and not plural (which eliminates option (C)). The author simply presents the skills needed and how they are beneficial to their children, making option (D) the best answer.

3. **(B)** The answer to this is found in the first two sentences, which state that the role of parents is to nurture, raise, protect, and educate their children. You can safely eliminate options (A) and (D) because they each only provide one responsibility, and the question is looking for multiple *deberes*. Option (C) has two, but they are to feed and ensure that they are well cared for, which is not the best answer because feeding is not mentioned in this text, probably because it is considered common sense. Option (B) is the best answer because it restates two of the obligations stated explicitly in the text.

4. **(B)** The information can be found in lines 15–17. Option (A) is incorrect because although children do feel secure when having experiences under the protection of their parents, that is not the benefit that the child experiences. One could argue that having new experiences has both cognitive and self-esteem benefits, but the text does not say so, and therefore it would be quite a stretch to prove these as correct answers, so options (C) and (D) are not the best choices. The text does say that children "se animan a explorer su entorno y a tener nuevas experiencias," meaning that they start to take the initiative to learn and make discoveries on their own.

5. **(C)** As stated in the previous question, the way children become more comfortable exploring their surroundings is from the feeling of being protected by their parents.

6. **(A)** The answer is found in the line that states: ". . . para que los niños puedan respetar e incorporar, los padres deben facilitar a sus hijos las conversaciones que les adjudiquen sentido." Therefore, the article suggests that parents should speak with their children in order to better internalize proper social conduct.

7. **(C)** This should be clearly obvious, since there is no reference to schooling. Remember that in Spanish the word *educación* can also mean social and life lessons, not simply academic knowledge.

8. **(C)** Following the expression *buen trato* are several examples, such as justice, tolerance, solidarity, etc. These are all qualities that are expressed in option (C). Don't be tempted by the word *trato* to think that it means treatment because it does not. Many non-native Spanish students make this mistake, and that can cause one to pick option (A) instead. When in doubt, look at other words surrounding the word(s) in question. Using context clues will often help you identify the true meaning of a word.

9. **(B)** When presented with a general question, such as the purpose or reason for a text, always look at the introduction and title. By reading the introduction, you can see that this table presents from whom or where they learn certain values. This makes option (B) the obvious choice.

10. **(A)** To answer this question, you have to find the highest percentage under the heading *Profesores*. Here you can see that the value that adolescents most attribute to learning from professors is *esfuerzo*, or hard work, making option (A) the clear answer.

11. **(C)** This should be an easy question to answer, for the article solely discusses the importance of parents in instilling values in children, and the table confirms this. There is no evidence to suggest that there is a decrease in parents properly raising their children, making option (A) incorrect, and options (B) and (D) are clearly incorrect because the evidence in the table alone contradicts these statements.

SELECCIÓN #17

1. **(B)** The narrator wants to go on a trip because he wants to forget his girlfriend. In lines 8–9, he says that he chooses *Mar del Plata* because the "vida agitada" will help him forget. One can assume that the agitated life he is referring to means a lot of frivolous activities. Don't be tempted to pick option (A) simply because of the word "aristócratas." *Mar del Plata* is known as "la playa aristócrata," but it does not mean that many aristocrats will be there, nor is that the reason the narrator is going.

2. **(C)** As in the previous explanation, the narrator wants to go to forget about his ex-girlfriend, whom he saw in the arms of a "friend" too many times.

3. **(B)** The narrator boards a train to his destination and immediately starts imagining a possible encounter between a young writer and a young lady. In line 11, the narrator states, "no sin pensar un poco" (not without thinking a little) in a possible adventure. The imagined story is of a writer who boards the train at the last minute, and as he enters the coach, he sees a young lady reading his last novel. The "pasión morbosa" refers to the type of story, which is a chance encounter on a train that may lead to an amorous relationship, which is often written about but hardly ever happens in real life.

4. **(D)** As in the previous explanation, all the events from the end of line 13 on are part of the imagination of the narrator.

5. **(B)** As the narrator imagines this chance encounter, he goes off on a tangent about how these types of stories always have the young lady reading the last novel, and therefore the young author obviously has to be a famous prolific writer. One can note that there is a condescending tone, which is likely due to a sense of envy. To say the narrator hates or is angry at the character he has created is probably too harsh. Remember that the narrator is imagining this story, and he is probably projecting the type of fame he wishes he could have.

6. **(A)** As with the previous example, the narrator questions why in these types of stories the young lady is always reading the latest novel. If the author was so famous and prolific, why could it never be the second-to-last or third-to-last novel. Obviously the narrator is not searching for an answer; he is simply poking fun at the convenience of it all.

7. **(B)** When considering the passage as a whole, option (B) becomes the obvious choice. The narrator has his heart broken, wants to leave to forget, boards a train, and imagines a chance encounter between two young individuals. One gets the sense that the narrator is ridiculing the story he is imagining, and therefore the prevailing mood is that this probably won't happen (although the narrator probably secretly wishes that it would happen to him). This makes *desilusionado* the best option because there is a sense of loss of hope for the author. To say that he is depressed (option (A)) is a little too severe an emotion for this story, and there is nothing to suggest that he is still in love or that he has a good sense of humor about losing his girlfriend, therefore eliminating options (C) and (D).

SELECCIÓN #18

1. **(B)** The answer to this is found in the section titled *Objetivos generales*, where each of the bullet points states the objectives of this publication. The text simply is trying to define the importance of family values and how they benefit individual humans and society as a whole.

2. **(B)** This is another question where the process of elimination is key. The text obviously is directed at families, as per its title. Therefore, you can safely eliminate options (A), (C), and (D).

3. **(A)** ". . . como una tela en blanco . . ." literally means a white canvas. This refers to the innocence of children, since the proverbial canvas will be painted by the experiences they have as they grow.

4. **(A)** The text is trying to promote a deeper understanding of what it means to have a family and its role in both the individual and society. Lines 25–30 speak to its importance and how it goes beyond the simple unification of bride and groom, therefore having a deeper meaning and importance than simply a union.

5. **(D)** With these types of questions, you have to identify what is *not* in the text. In the introduction to the text, it states that this is promoting an event, and therefore if you were interested in attending this seminar, you might want to know if there is a fee, making option (D) the best answer.

SELECCIÓN #19

1. **(D)** Make sure that you read all options before making your selection. Some individuals may stop at (B) without realizing that option (C) is also correct. Option (D) is correct because it has both answers. Luisa writes to inform her professor about a program that she has discovered, and she asks him if he would be interested in helping her.

2. **(D)** This is the best answer because it addresses the scope of *Payasos sin fronteras*, which is to give emotional support to refugee populations around the world. Options (A) and (C) are incorrect because they cover too wide a scope, and option (B) is incorrect because

the text never mentions raising money as a primary goal, although it certainly could help their cause.

3. **(B)** This information can be found in lines 20–21, where the text says that the organization pays all expenses to cover the production. This would include transportation and production costs, but not personal expenses.

4. **(B)** In lines 17 through 19, the text shows that the volunteers are professional artists who have worked in circuses, theater, and other performance disciplines. Of the options, option (B) is the best because it speaks of shows and performances. Be careful if considering option (A) because "todos tipos de artistas" also could include painters, sculptors, musicians, etc., and this group is almost solely performance artists.

5. **(D)** This is clearly seen in the opening of the correspondence, where Luisa remembers how inspiring her teacher was to her. They probably don't know each other on a friendly basis because she still refers to him as *Profesor*, which implies a more formal relationship, therefore eliminating options (B) and (C).

6. **(A)** The goal of this organization is to provide emotional support and solidarity to refugees through laughter, making option (A) the clear answer. Option (B) could deal with causes for refugees, but it does not achieve the goal of the investigation, which is to learn more about the organization *Payasos sin fronteras*. Options (C) and (D) are too generic and have nothing to do with the goal of this organization.

7. **(A)** Reading the entire card, it is clear that Luisa is inspired, for she wants to create her own project to help the youth in her community.

Selección #19—Más Práctica

To answer these questions, think about service and volunteer programs in your community. Some ideas can include soup kitchens, English as a second language classes that are given to immigrants, etc. If you don't know of any programs, you can reasearch some online.

SELECCIÓN #20

1. **(C)** The first sentence of the text speaks to how the dance is "representativo de la idiosincrasia del departamento." The word *idiosincrasia* means trait. Don't be confused by the word *lengua*, for it is still a dance, but one that "communicates" the qualities and peculiarities of this part of Colombia.

2. **(B)** Lines 12–13 explain what the dance dramatizes. It includes all parts of an amorous union, from flirting to the wedding.

3. **(A)** This is a tricky answer to figure out, but it can be done! A dance typically includes two aspects: movement and music. The choreography of the dance as created by mixing the dance, or movement, from a type of dance in the south of the state, with the *bambuco*, from the north. In this context, the options could be dance, music, or both. When you look at the options, it is evident that options (B) and (D) can be eliminated, and since the *bambuco* refers to a part of how the choreography was created, it probably is not a theatrical representation, therefore eliminating option (C).

4. **(A)** This information is found in lines 23–25, where it says that the creation of the festival was to achieve coexistence and reconciliation between the regions of the country that were in turmoil.

5. **(D)** Don't be influenced by the English word *tornado*. Use the context to figure out the meaning of this word. In line 29, the text mentions the *haciendas* (ranch) and *caseríos* (village) that turned into *poblaciones* (large settlements), in other words, became larger.

6. **(C)** Lines 30–36 describe how the celebration began from Spanish influence, but then it combined with local traditions and, throughout the generations, kept evolving as a mixture of elements from populations from different extremes (conquerors and those conquered, aristocrats and day workers). Therefore, the best description of the *San Juan* celebration is that it is a combination of a variety of influences, making it heterogeneous, or varied and mixed.

7. **(A)** The *Sanjaunero* is unique to the state of Tolima, as stated in the first two paragraphs. Therefore, to find out more information about celebrations in this area, it only makes sense to find a publication based on this region.

SELECCIÓN #21

1. **(D)** This passage presents the pros of having a vegetarian diet, but it also argues that eating meat in moderation has its merits. The author is not necessarily trying to convince the reader of one diet over another, but says that if the reader chooses to follow a vegetarian diet, he/she should also supplement with vitamins and minerals (lines 11–12).

2. **(B)** Lines 17–20 are where the author introduces the results of several investigations on the benefits of having a specific type of diet. The author summarizes the results, and because he/she does not present any actual data from the investigation, option (C) cannot be a possibility.

3. **(D)** Although the article states that by eating animal products ". . . facilita obtener las cantidades recomendables de calcio, zinc, hierro y vitamina B12," the author never mentions that this is the only place one can get these vitamins and minerals, only that consuming meat is a good source of these. Therefore, option (B) is not the best answer. The author does say that eating lean meats along with fruits and vegetables is a healthy diet.

4. **(C)** The information needed for this answer is in lines 1–3. Be careful when reading because the author says that meats and other foods *with exception of mother's milk* is not essential for human nutrition. Options (A), (B), and (D) are all true for a generally healthy diet, but they are not absolutely essential, which is what the question is asking.

5. **(C)** This fragment follows the sentence in lines 8–9 where the author says that all foods have benefits but could also have problematic areas. Therefore, *selección de alimentos* refers to the types of foods that are being selected, and one should consider supplementing the food with something else in case the food does not contain the vitamins and minerals that one should have (an idea presented in lines 11–13).

6. **(B)** As with the explanation for question 3 in this section, in lines 26–27 the author says that eating animal products is a good source of minerals and vitamins. One can misread the information contained in lines 23–25 and think that fiber is derived from meat, and thus be tempted to select option (D), but the article here (and in lines 15–16) says that the fiber necessary is derived from fruits and vegetables, not meats.

7. **(B)** Again, with questions of purpose, one has to always read the introduction first. The introduction says that this is a guide (*guía*), and the first two columns give general examples and guidelines. This is definitely not a menu, nor does it provide the nutrient content of the foods listed; therefore, you can easily eliminate options (A) and (C). Because the table gives general examples of foods in each category, and foods that absolutely have to be consumed, option (D) can also be eliminated.

8. **(A)** The table says that for breads and cereals, one should consume 6 or more portions. The third column provides an example of what a portion should be. Option (A) is the only choice that provides 6 or more portions. Let's do the math: $2 \times bollos$ = 4 portions (½ *bollo* is one portion) + 1 × *taza de pasta* = 2 portions (½ *taza de pasta* is one portion) = 6 portions. Following this example, you will see that all other options fall short of the 6 recommended portions per day.

9. **(B)** This should be a pretty simple question to answer, for not only are *huevos* optional, but the guide also suggests that they only be consumed 3 or 4 times a week. Although milk products are also optional, they can be consumed daily, just no more than 3 servings per day. If you don't know what *cacahuete* is, it means peanut, and *crema de cacahuete* is peanut butter and is located in the *Leguminosas y otros sustitutos de carne* category.

10. **(B)** The table never mentions meat, and eggs are not considered meat. Therefore, you can easily eliminate options (A) and (D), because there would have to be information in the table to suggest that meat is either beneficial or not for one of these options to be true. Option (C) is not the best answer. The table does give a list of various vegetarian products, but remember that the question asks what statement made in the article can be supported by the table. Since the article never mentions that one has to consume a variety of vegetarian products, option (C) is not correct. The article does explicitly state that consumption of meat is not essential for human nutrition, and the table does provide a list of non-meat foods that one can consume to hit all the nutritional needs. You can therefore use the information in the table to validate the statement in the article, and this is why option (B) is the best answer.

11. **(D)** This should have been pretty straightforward. Options (A) and (C) are obviously out of place for neither the article nor the table talk about environmental benefits or ethical reasons for being a vegetarian. The article does mention briefly that consumption of meats high in fat content can be bad for your health, but it is by no means the overall message of the text. In addition, this cannot be verified by any information in the table, so option (B) can be safely eliminated. Both the article and the table provide information on guidelines that one should follow if he or she is considering becoming vegetarian, making option (D) the correct answer.

Selección #21—Más Práctica

> **Ampliando tu vocabulario**—Usa el vocabulario y frases del texto para llenar las columnas según el tema. ¿Puedes pensar en un tema adicional?
>
> ### Palabras / frases relacionadas con . . .
>
> | . . . la buena salud | . . . la mala salud | _____ |
> |---|---|---|
> | nutrición | efectos nocivos | |
> | gozar de buena salud | aspectos problemáticos | |
> | saludable | grasa saturada | |
> | beneficios nutritivos | colesterol | |
> | vitamina | riesgo | |
> | fibra | diabetes | |
> | nutrientes | presión arterial alta | |
> | | obesidad | |

SELECCIÓN #22

1. **(C)** In the opening of the letter, Julio refers to a conversation that he had with the professor, and that led to his research sometime thereafter. Since he is continuing to talk about the same topic of the original discussion, this is a continuation, and therefore option (C) is the best answer.

2. **(B)** The *historia* that the question references refers to that of the family who made a certain decision in order to try and save their daughter's life. The daughter indeed has medical issues, but her issues are not the story, but rather the actions that the family took to address these issues. Therefore, option (D) is not an option. Although the author also mentions the controversy (*polémica*), he does not summarize the story of this controversy, so option (C) cannot be considered an option.

3. **(A)** You probably could figure out that the word *don* is part of the verb *donar* (to gift) and adjective *donación* (a gift). Therefore, the expression means that everyone is a gift from God, and therefore should accept himself or herself as he or she is.

4. **(C)** The information needed to answer this question can be found in lines 15–19. This is where the author continues his thoughts on the moral dilemma that the family in question will probably face. The family has already made the decision they did, so options (A) and (D) can be eliminated because they speak of actions that have already happened as if they hadn't yet. Option (B) is incorrect because there is nothing in the text to suggest that the family will feel burdened from having to raise two young girls.

5. **(A)** The answer to this question can be found in the fifth paragraph, where the author is debating whether cells do have life and should be considered human. Option (B) is incorrect because the author states that scientists believe this to be true already, and he later rejects the statement that option (C) makes. Option (D) is irrelevant because the author never brings up this question.

6. **(B)** The word *rondar* means to wander or to haunt. By using context clues, you could figure this out on your own. In the previous paragraph, he mentions that he has ". . . más preguntas que respuestas . . . ," and he closes his letter by saying, ". . . no veo la hora de poder discutirlo más a fondo . . . ," therefore implying that he has not achieved closure on this issue. Therefore, you could infer that *rondar* means something that has not gone away, which is close enough to deduce that (B) is the best answer.

7. **(C)** By now you should comfortably be able to eliminate options (A) and (B) from this list. He is obviously no expert on the subject and still has questions about it. Option (D) is not the best answer because of the statement ". . . necesita ayuda para explicarse mejor." His issue is not that he can't explain himself, it is that he still does not know what side of the argument he is willing to support.

SELECCIÓN #23

1. **(C)** Be careful with this question, for it is not asking what the purpose of the article is, but rather what the purpose of an *acuario* is. Although options (A) and (B) are certainly true of aquariums, they are not the purpose mentioned in the text. Aquariums are spaces intended to ". . . conserver, investigar y concienciar de la necesidad de proteger el planeta," therefore making option (C) the best answer.

2. **(D)** You may have guessed from context that *cuarentena* is Spanish for quarantine. As stated in lines 28–30, *la cuarentena* is a process, so option (A) can be excluded since that refers to an object. Option (B) is partially correct because it is part of the process, but option (D) is the best answer because it inherently comprises two elements of the process (adapting to the new environment and to the new food). Option (C) is incorrect because the period is solely to treat the animal, not the space that the animal will occupy.

3. **(B)** The word *buzo* is a scuba diver, and they are the ones responsible for cleaning the larger tanks (lines 37–38). The word *buceador* is a synonym, and the verb is *bucear*. It is a good word to add to your vocabulary in case you did not already know it. If you did not know it, then you still could have figured out the correct answer by the process of elimination, and by seeing the similarities between the two words *buzo* and *buceador*. Remember that the letter "c" when next to the letters "e" or "i" has a soft sound, like the letter "s." When next to the vowels "a," "o," or "u," it has a sound like the letter "k." In the case of the word *buzo*, the letter "c" changes to "z" in order to keep the soft sound.

4. **(B)** Lines 15–20 contain all the information you need to answer this question. Although there are mechanized systems in place, visual inspection is key to ensuring that all aspects of the operation are functioning well. Options (A), (C), and (D) all include parts of the operation, but option (B) is the one that oversees all those parts.

5. **(A)** The information needed to answer this question is in lines 39–41. They speak about the opportunity to visit the depths of the ocean, like Captain Nemo. Don't be tempted to select option (B) simply because it references the captain, he is not at the aquarium. Options (C) and (D) may be individual preferences, but they are not mentioned in the text.

6. **(C)** The word *imprescindible* means essential and communicates the same idea presented in line 46 that scientific projects done at aquariums are "más necesarios que nunca." Don't be tempted to select option (B), for the adjective *inútil* makes this completely false.

7. **(A)** This answer is almost taken verbatim from lines 47–48. Options (C) and (D), although possibly true, are too specific, and the article does not go into specifics.

8. **(C)** Although nowadays there are aquariums of all shapes and sizes, your basic aquarium will probably be square shaped. Therefore, the four *paredes* refer to the see-through walls of the aquarium, making this the best answer. Options (A) and (B) are not appropriate because they are geared to setting up an aquarium at home, and this article does not deal with this topic. Option (D) is not correct because the article does not give any information on this topic.

SELECCIÓN #24

1. **(C)** The text is about *las Fallas*, a celebration in Valencia, Spain. Since the reading gives a brief history and overview of the festivities, it is most likely aimed to attract tourists to the area. By no means is it a tranquil celebration, so you can easily eliminate option (A), and if you suffer from pyromania and you know it, you probably don't want to go to this celebration and be surrounded by flames, thus eliminating option (B). Option (D) is incorrect because the *fantoches*, or puppets, are burned at the end.

2. **(C)** Lines 2–4 give the history of the *fallas*. The carpenters would burn scraps of wood and leftover contraptions on the eve of the celebration of *San José*.

3. **(A)** Line 8 says that the constructions are made out of "cartón piedra," or paper mache (plasterboard). Note that the word *piedra* modifies the word *cartón*, so it is not the main material used, thus eliminating option (C).

4. **(D)** You can find the answer in lines 15–16, where it says that these structures ". . . se instalan en cada esquina. . . ."

5. **(C)** This might be a little difficult to understand if you don't pay attention to punctuation. The answer you seek begins in line 9 and continues in lines 10–11. In line 9, it says that the structures compete with each other in ingenuity and beauty while satirizing the latest political, social, and cultural events. The information in between describes how the structures are shaped, thus ensuring a smooth fall and burning. Pay attention to the use of punctuation so that you can keep track of the ideas being communicated.

6. **(A)** In the text, the *mascletà* is the object of the passive voice form of the verb *disparar* (shoot). Therefore, the *mascletà* is something that is shot every day at 2:00 P.M., which is what option (A) communicates. The word *diurno* means during the daytime.

7. **(B)** The "castillos de fuegos artificiales" that the text mentions at the end refers to the size of the fireworks, not that they are in castles. This is why option (D) is incorrect. If you identified that it was some sort of spectacle with fireworks, you could then easily have eliminated options (A) and (C).

PART THREE
Listening Comprehension

General Considerations

3

The listening comprehension part of the exam consists of two parts: Print and Audio Texts (combined) and Audio Texts. The questions and multiple-choice answers for all questions in this section will be printed in your test booklet. Before each audio selection is played, you will be given time to read the introduction and preview the questions and multiple choice options. The audios all come from authentic sources, and can include interviews, presentations, advertisements, and so on. Each audio will be played twice.

FORMAT OF THE EXAM

The listening comprehension part of the exam is divided into the following parts:

Print and Audio Texts (combined)—This portion includes two reading and listening activities and a total of 17 questions. The first activity will pair an article with a listening source, the second will be a graph, table, or chart paired with a listening source.

- **Article and audio** (10 questions) For this first activity you will have 4 minutes to read the article and then two additional minutes to read the introduction to the audio source and preview the questions. After the audio plays once, you will then have one minute in which you start answering the questions before the audio is played again. Following the second playing of the audio, you will have 15 seconds per question to finish answering the questions. You can expect to have 10 questions on this section, 4 questions about information in the article, 4 about information in the audio, and 2 relating to both sources. This means that you will have a total of 2 minutes 30 seconds after the second listening of the audio to finish answering the questions.

- **Graph, table, chart and audio** (7 questions) For this activity you will have one minute to read the graph, table, or chart, and then have one additional minute to read the introduction to the audio source and preview the questions. After the audio plays once, you will have one minute in which you start answering the questions before the audio is played again. Following the second playing of the audio, you will have 15 seconds per question to finish answering the questions. You can expect to have 7 questions in this section, 3 about information in the graph, table, or chart, 3 about information in the audio, and 1 relating to both sources. This means that you will have a total of 1 minute 45 seconds after the second listening to finish answering the questions.

Audio Texts—This portion includes three listening activities and a total of 18 questions. Before each activity, you will be given one minute to read the introduction and to preview the questions and multiple choice answers. Following the first listening of the audio, you will have one minute to start answering the questions. Following the second listening of the audio, you will have 15 seconds per question to finish answering the questions. You can expect the following types of audio files: interview (5 questions), instructions (5 questions), and a presentation (8 questions).

TYPES OF QUESTIONS

The types of questions in this section are very similar to those in Part A, Reading Comprehension. You can expect the following types of questions in the listening section.

- **UNDERSTAND CONTENT.** Identify the main idea and details.
- **THINK CRITICALLY.** Identify the purpose of the text, the target audience, point of view of its author, the tone or attitude, and how the author communicates his/her ideas; be able to separate fact from opinion and make predictions based on information presented in the text.
- **UNDERSTAND MEANING.** Infer the meaning of unfamiliar words and expressions using context clues; comprehend a wide variety of vocabulary, idioms, and cultural expressions.
- **UNDERSTAND CULTURE AND CONTENT ACROSS DISCIPLINES.** Identify practices, products, and perspectives of Hispanic cultures as well as information pertaining to other disciplines, such as science, geography, history, art, and so on.

STRATEGIES FOR LISTENING COMPREHENSION
Before You Listen

- **READ THE INTRODUCTION AND TITLE.** All listening selections will have a brief introduction about the text and its source. This information is helpful to get you thinking about what information will be presented, as well as the possible point of view of the author and intended audience.
- **READ THE QUESTIONS AND MULTIPLE-CHOICE ANSWERS.** You will have plenty of time to read the questions and preview the answers. Use this time to gather as much information about the selection as possible.

During the First Listening

- **IDENTIFY THE MAIN IDEA.** Listen for repetition of words or phrases and for words that are topically related.
- **VISUALIZE WHAT YOU HEAR.** Imagine in your mind's eye what is being said. This will help you understand the overall ideas
- **IMAGINE.** If the topic deals with an unfamiliar subject matter, try to imagine what it would be like to be in that situation or to experience the setting or event that is discussed.
- **FOCUS ON WHAT YOU DO KNOW AND NOT ON WHAT YOU DON'T KNOW.** Don't get hung up on single words you don't understand. Focus on what you do understand and use contextual clues to help you figure out the gist of ideas that may not be entirely clear.
- **EVALUATE THE INFORMATION BEING PRESENTED.** Is the speaker trying to persuade the listener? Is the speaker stating facts or opinions? What evidence, if any, does the speaker present?

- **FOCUS ON THE MESSAGE, NOT THE DISTRACTIONS.** Often there will be background noise as you listen or in the audio itself. These noises can include traffic sounds or music. Don't let the background noises distract you from focusing on the message that is being delivered.

During the Second Listening

- **TAKE NOTES OF KEY WORDS.** You will have space in your exam book to take notes. However, limit these notes to individual words and not phrases. Make sure that the words you do write down will help you remember the main ideas of the listening passage.
- **CONFIRM AND CLARIFY.** You should already have understood the main idea of the listening passage, so during the second listening you want to focus on identifying a few details that support the main idea. You can also use this time to confirm the information you understood the first time and to help clarify any doubts that you may have had.

STRATEGIES FOR IMPROVING LISTENING COMPREHENSION

Like reading, the best way to become a better listener is to practice regularly. Here are a couple of suggestions that will make you a better listener.

- **LISTEN TO A LOT OF AUTHENTIC SPANISH.** Nothing improves listening comprehension than a lot of practice, so listen to as much Spanish as you can. Make sure that you listen to authentic audio sources that were produced for a Spanish-speaking audience. Do not shy away from audios that include a lot of visual and/or audio distractions, such as background noises and music. The more you become accustomed to listening to Spanish with distractions in the background, the better prepared you will be for this exam.
- **VISUALIZE AS YOU LISTEN.** If you can picture what the words say, you are more likely to remember them. If you practice with a video source, try listening to the video first with your eyes closed and see if you visualized correctly what you heard.
- **TAKE NOTES OF KEY WORDS.** Practice taking notes of key words that will help you remember the main ideas of the listening passage. Avoid writing down whole sentences or phrases, because this will take a lot of time and it may cause you to not hear part of the audio.

Section I, Part B—Listening Comprehension: Print and Audio Texts (Combined)

4

The first section of the test includes both print and audio texts. You will be given the theme of the activity and a brief introduction to each source. The print source will be either an article or some sort of image, table, or graph to study before listening to the audio source. You will be given four minutes to read the article or one minute to look over any graphs or tables before the audio begins. While reading, you should implement all of the reading strategies that are highlighted in the Reading Comprehension portion of this book. The audio source will either be a dialogue, narrative, or some other type of speech sample. Before listening to the audio file the first time, you will have an additional minute to read a preview of the selection and look over the questions that you will be asked. After listening to the audio selection, you will have an additional minute to begin answering the questions. After the selection has played the second time, you will have 15 seconds per question to finish answering them. You may take notes during the audio section, but they will not be scored.

STRATEGIES FOR READING

- Understand the format of the print text.
- Read the introduction and scan the passage to get the general idea. Predict what the selection may be about.
- Reread more carefully to
  - identify key vocabulary words (underline them),
  - identify characters,
  - identify the setting, and
  - understand what is happening.
- Use background knowledge.
- Evaluate the information you have gleaned from the piece to
  - determine the tone and mood of the piece,
  - determine the intended reader, and
  - draw conclusions about the piece.
- Read the chart from the left column and then across.

STRATEGIES FOR LISTENING

- Read the introduction and questions to each sample.
- Concentrate while you listen.
- Evaluate the information being presented.
- Follow the thread of the conversation.
- Visualize, if you can.
- Take note of key words that lead to ideas.
- Focus on what you understand and don't get hung up on what you don't understand. Use contextual clues to help you understand unfamiliar words or phrases.
- Remember that you will hear the audio twice. Listen the first time for overall theme and general ideas, and use the second listening to take notes on specific details.

ANSWER SHEET
Print and Audio Texts

Selección #1

1. Ⓐ Ⓑ Ⓒ Ⓓ
2. Ⓐ Ⓑ Ⓒ Ⓓ
3. Ⓐ Ⓑ Ⓒ Ⓓ
4. Ⓐ Ⓑ Ⓒ Ⓓ
5. Ⓐ Ⓑ Ⓒ Ⓓ
6. Ⓐ Ⓑ Ⓒ Ⓓ
7. Ⓐ Ⓑ Ⓒ Ⓓ
8. Ⓐ Ⓑ Ⓒ Ⓓ
9. Ⓐ Ⓑ Ⓒ Ⓓ
10. Ⓐ Ⓑ Ⓒ Ⓓ

Selección #2

1. Ⓐ Ⓑ Ⓒ Ⓓ
2. Ⓐ Ⓑ Ⓒ Ⓓ
3. Ⓐ Ⓑ Ⓒ Ⓓ
4. Ⓐ Ⓑ Ⓒ Ⓓ
5. Ⓐ Ⓑ Ⓒ Ⓓ
6. Ⓐ Ⓑ Ⓒ Ⓓ
7. Ⓐ Ⓑ Ⓒ Ⓓ
8. Ⓐ Ⓑ Ⓒ Ⓓ
9. Ⓐ Ⓑ Ⓒ Ⓓ
10. Ⓐ Ⓑ Ⓒ Ⓓ

Selección #3

1. Ⓐ Ⓑ Ⓒ Ⓓ
2. Ⓐ Ⓑ Ⓒ Ⓓ
3. Ⓐ Ⓑ Ⓒ Ⓓ
4. Ⓐ Ⓑ Ⓒ Ⓓ
5. Ⓐ Ⓑ Ⓒ Ⓓ
6. Ⓐ Ⓑ Ⓒ Ⓓ
7. Ⓐ Ⓑ Ⓒ Ⓓ

Selección #4

1. Ⓐ Ⓑ Ⓒ Ⓓ
2. Ⓐ Ⓑ Ⓒ Ⓓ
3. Ⓐ Ⓑ Ⓒ Ⓓ
4. Ⓐ Ⓑ Ⓒ Ⓓ
5. Ⓐ Ⓑ Ⓒ Ⓓ
6. Ⓐ Ⓑ Ⓒ Ⓓ
7. Ⓐ Ⓑ Ⓒ Ⓓ
8. Ⓐ Ⓑ Ⓒ Ⓓ
9. Ⓐ Ⓑ Ⓒ Ⓓ
10. Ⓐ Ⓑ Ⓒ Ⓓ

Selección #5

1. Ⓐ Ⓑ Ⓒ Ⓓ
2. Ⓐ Ⓑ Ⓒ Ⓓ
3. Ⓐ Ⓑ Ⓒ Ⓓ
4. Ⓐ Ⓑ Ⓒ Ⓓ
5. Ⓐ Ⓑ Ⓒ Ⓓ
6. Ⓐ Ⓑ Ⓒ Ⓓ
7. Ⓐ Ⓑ Ⓒ Ⓓ

Selección #6

1. Ⓐ Ⓑ Ⓒ Ⓓ
2. Ⓐ Ⓑ Ⓒ Ⓓ
3. Ⓐ Ⓑ Ⓒ Ⓓ
4. Ⓐ Ⓑ Ⓒ Ⓓ
5. Ⓐ Ⓑ Ⓒ Ⓓ
6. Ⓐ Ⓑ Ⓒ Ⓓ
7. Ⓐ Ⓑ Ⓒ Ⓓ

Selección #7

1. Ⓐ Ⓑ Ⓒ Ⓓ
2. Ⓐ Ⓑ Ⓒ Ⓓ
3. Ⓐ Ⓑ Ⓒ Ⓓ
4. Ⓐ Ⓑ Ⓒ Ⓓ
5. Ⓐ Ⓑ Ⓒ Ⓓ
6. Ⓐ Ⓑ Ⓒ Ⓓ
7. Ⓐ Ⓑ Ⓒ Ⓓ

Selección #8

1. Ⓐ Ⓑ Ⓒ Ⓓ
2. Ⓐ Ⓑ Ⓒ Ⓓ
3. Ⓐ Ⓑ Ⓒ Ⓓ
4. Ⓐ Ⓑ Ⓒ Ⓓ
5. Ⓐ Ⓑ Ⓒ Ⓓ
6. Ⓐ Ⓑ Ⓒ Ⓓ
7. Ⓐ Ⓑ Ⓒ Ⓓ
8. Ⓐ Ⓑ Ⓒ Ⓓ
9. Ⓐ Ⓑ Ⓒ Ⓓ
10. Ⓐ Ⓑ Ⓒ Ⓓ

Selección #9

1. Ⓐ Ⓑ Ⓒ Ⓓ
2. Ⓐ Ⓑ Ⓒ Ⓓ
3. Ⓐ Ⓑ Ⓒ Ⓓ
4. Ⓐ Ⓑ Ⓒ Ⓓ
5. Ⓐ Ⓑ Ⓒ Ⓓ
6. Ⓐ Ⓑ Ⓒ Ⓓ
7. Ⓐ Ⓑ Ⓒ Ⓓ

Selección #10

1. Ⓐ Ⓑ Ⓒ Ⓓ
2. Ⓐ Ⓑ Ⓒ Ⓓ
3. Ⓐ Ⓑ Ⓒ Ⓓ
4. Ⓐ Ⓑ Ⓒ Ⓓ
5. Ⓐ Ⓑ Ⓒ Ⓓ
6. Ⓐ Ⓑ Ⓒ Ⓓ
7. Ⓐ Ⓑ Ⓒ Ⓓ
8. Ⓐ Ⓑ Ⓒ Ⓓ
9. Ⓐ Ⓑ Ⓒ Ⓓ
10. Ⓐ Ⓑ Ⓒ Ⓓ

SELECCIÓN #1

Tema curricular: Las identidades personales

Primero tienes cuatro minutos para leer la fuente número 1

Fuente #1: El siguiente artículo trata de la poeta Sor Juana Inés de la Cruz.

Sor Juana Inés de la Cruz. Mujer moderna en el siglo XVIII

De niña gozó de todo un mundo de letras, debido a su estancia con su abuelo materno, quien le abrió las puertas de la literatura. A la edad de nueve años, la joven Juana de Asbaje y Ramírez de Santillana, su nombre completo, ya había aprendido el latín, a causa de toda la literatura a su alcance. Su nombre recorrió *Línea* todo la región, hasta llegar a oídos del Virrey de Nueva España. La invitó a la corte, (5) y allí permaneció como dama de honor para la Virreina la Marquesa. Parece que pasó varios años disfrutando de una vida que correspondía al nivel social al que se había levantado. Pero por ser hija natural, la oportunidad de casarse le resultó remota.

(10) Después de dos años, la joven tan encantadora y lista renunció los placeres de la corte y se dedicó a la iglesia, entrando en el convento de San Jerónimo donde cumplió el término de sus años en este mundo. Una vez internada en el convento, se dedicó a las letras, amontonando una impresionante biblioteca de unos 4.000 libros, una cantidad asombrosa en aquel entonces. Floreció intelectualmente y (15) concentró los esfuerzos en estudiar todo un rango de asuntos, de la teología, la pintura, la ciencia, y, sobre todo, las letras. A medida que pasaban los años, su renombre aumentaba a la vez, hasta que se dio con un padre celoso de su potencia e influencia. La buena monja se empeñaba en reclamar su fidelidad a la voluntad de Dios en cuánto investigaba. Sus razonamientos no persuadieron a los (20) obstinados clérigos. Resignada, Sor Juana no quiso continuar su carrera literaria. Se sometió, rindiendo sus pertenencias a los pobres. Murió poco después, una de las estrellas de la literatura colonial de México, sin que lo quisieran sus detractores. Unas de sus palabras más famosas se encuentran en los famosos versos de una redondilla.

(25)
Hombres necios que acusáis
a la mujer sin razón,
sin ver que sois la ocasión
de lo mismo que culpáis;
. . .

(30)
Bien con muchas armas fundo
que lidia vuestra arrogancia,
pues en promesa e instancia
juntáis diablo, carne y mundo.

Tienes dos minutos para leer la introducción y prever las preguntas.

> **Fuente #2:** Esta grabación trata de Michelle Bachelet, quien fue elegida la primera presidenta de Chile. El reportaje fue presentado en el programa *Nuestra América* el 16 de enero de 2006.

Track 1

1. ¿Cuál es el propósito del artículo?
   (A) Exponer una biografía breve de una literata
   (B) Presentar los desafíos de ser mujer en el siglo XVIII
   (C) Mostrar los pasos necesarios para hacerse poeta
   (D) Hacer una reseña sobre los beneficios de seguir una vida religiosa

2. Según el artículo, ¿por qué nunca podía Juana contraer matrimonio?
   (A) Porque había decidido ser monja.
   (B) Porque no había pretendientes en la corte.
   (C) Porque era demasiado enfocada en los estudios.
   (D) Porque llevaba una deshonra.

3. En el artículo, ¿cuál es el mejor significado de la frase "se empeñaba . . . investigaba" (líneas 18–19)?
   (A) Que Sor Juana se dio cuenta que poco a poco estaba perdiendo su fe.
   (B) Que ella tuvo que afirmar que no había renunciado su convicción religiosa.
   (C) Que su lealtad a la vida religiosa era más fuerte que nunca.
   (D) Que sus investigaciones le habían aclarado los mandamientos de Dios.

4. ¿Por qué decidió abandonar la literatura?
   (A) Fue una causa de polémica en su convento.
   (B) Decidió dedicarse a ayudar a los pobres.
   (C) Se interesó en otras materias académicas.
   (D) Careció de inspiración para componer más obras literarias.

5. Según la fuente auditiva, ¿cuál fue el margen de victoria de la presidenta?
   (A) De casi 100 puntos
   (B) De un poco más de 50 puntos
   (C) De un poco menos de 50 puntos
   (D) De menos de 10 puntos

6. ¿Cuál fue la reacción de la población chilena ante su victoria?
   (A) La mayoría protestó en las calles.
   (B) Muchos se exiliaron.
   (C) La gente festejó su elección.
   (D) Miembros del ejército participaron en actos de violencia.

7. ¿Qué prometió hacer la nueva presidente?
   (A) Representar a los que la apoyaron
   (B) Crear más trabajo para todos
   (C) Dirigir el país para el bienestar de todos
   (D) Reducir el número de analfabetos en su país

8. ¿Cuál era el mayor problema que se encontraba en Chile en aquel entonces?
   (A) Miles seguían apoyando una dictadura militar.
   (B) Había una gran disparidad entre las clases sociales.
   (C) La población indígena carecía de educación.
   (D) Había más mujeres que hombres en busca de empleo.

9. ¿Qué tienen en común las dos fuentes?
   (A) Muestran lo difícil que es ser mujer en el mundo latino.
   (B) Presentan a mujeres que se destacaron en su propio país.
   (C) Resaltan lo importante de nunca abandonar los sueños.
   (D) Llaman la atención a la desigualdad social por razón de género.

10. ¿Cuál de las siguientes afirmaciones de América Latina, tanto en el presente como en el pasado, se puede apoyar usando información presentada en ambas fuentes como evidencia?
   (A) Sigue habiendo un gran número de gente en paro.
   (B) Las mujeres suelen enfrentar más retos que los hombres en todos aspectos de la vida.
   (C) Las clases y estigmas sociales tienen un impacto en el bienestar de una persona.
   (D) Todavía persiste una desigualdad en el acceso a educación.

Selección #1—Más Práctica

Análisis literario: ¿Qué figura retórica usa Sor Juana de la Cruz en la primera estrofa de su redondilla?
   (A) Metáfora
   (B) Hipérbole
   (C) Apóstrofe
   (D) Personificación

Cultural Awareness

Cultural perspective: Both these texts present the role of women in the Spanish-speaking world.

How are the perspectives presented in these texts similar to or different from what you have observed in your own community?

Tema curricular: La belleza y la estética

Primero tienes cuatro minutos para leer la fuente número 1.

Fuente #1: El siguiente artículo trata de un barrio en Buenos Aires, Argentina. Fue publicado en la página web *http://Alojargentina.com*.

La Boca
(*http://Alojargentina.com*)

En un barrio típico de inmigrantes de los más distintos orígenes, entre los que se destacan griegos, yugoslavos, turcos e italianos, sobre todo genoveses. La calle Caminito, de apenas 100 metros de longitud, es peatonal. Es una calle *Línea* tan pequeña como particular. En ella no hay puertas. Algunas ventanas, algún (5) balcón lleno de plantas y de ropas colgadas a secar. Sus paredes pintadas de diferentes colores recuerdan a Venecia. En ellas hay todo tipo de murales, cerámicas y distintos adornos. Al principio era simplemente un ramal del ferrocarril, lleno de tierra, yuyales y piedras. Al lugar se lo llamaba "la curva", la que luego se convirtió en "un caminito" que acortaba distancias. Ese fue el famoso "caminito" (10) por el que transitaba a diario Juan de Dios Filiberto, quien luego escribió el tango que lleva su nombre. La iniciativa de ponerle ese nombre a la calle surgió nada menos que de su amigo Benito Quinquela Martín. Hoy es una calle turística, no sólo visitada por los extranjeros, sino por argentinos de todo el país, orgullosos de ese lugar tan pintoresco. El Club Atlético Boca Juniors, ubicado en Brandsen (15) 805, es uno de los clubes de fútbol más importantes del país y fue fundado por cinco jóvenes habitantes del barrio de la Boca en 1905. El nombre de la institución fue tomado directamente del barrio, pero se le agregó la palabra "Juniors" que le daba a la denominación algo más de prestigio, contrastando con la fama de "barrio difícil" que se había ganado la Boca por aquel entonces. Su estadio de (20) fútbol tiene capacidad para 50.000 espectadores y en su barrio social y deportivo se practican otras disciplinas deportivas.

Tienes dos minutos para leer la introducción y prever las preguntas.

Fuente #2: Esta grabación trata de un pueblo en México. Fue publicado en la página web *www.mexicodesconocido.com.mx*.

Track 2

1. ¿Cuál es el propósito del artículo?
   (A) Contar la historia de un equipo de fútbol profesional
   (B) Comentar sobre el desarrollo de una calle de Buenos Aires
   (C) Describir cómo se ha evolucionado un barrio porteño
   (D) Relatar la influencia de los inmigrantes en la capital argentina

2. ¿Cómo se podría describir la calle Caminito?
   (A) Peculiar
   (B) Común
   (C) Simple
   (D) Rústico

3. ¿Cómo recibió la calle el nombre "caminito"?
   (A) Por su forma de línea recta
   (B) Por ser una calle que abreviaba la ruta de muchos
   (C) Por ser un destino turístico
   (D) Por su apariencia pintoresca

4. A base de toda la información presentada en el artículo, ¿cómo se podría describir la gente que vive en este barrio?
   (A) Muchos se sentirán molestos por la cantidad de turistas.
   (B) Será gente diversa pero orgullosa de su barrio.
   (C) Los residentes serán grandes aficionados del fútbol.
   (D) Los habitantes serán expertos en bailar el tango.

5. ¿Cuál es el propósito de la fuente auditiva?
   (A) Narrar la historia de Santa Clara del Cobre
   (B) Explicar las razones por la cual fue nombrada Pueblo Mágico
   (C) Describir el pueblo como destino turístico
   (D) Detallar el proceso de producción de artesanía

6. Según la fuente auditiva, ¿cómo se distingue esta comunidad?
   (A) Por sus viviendas y plazas
   (B) Por tener una influyente comunidad indígena
   (C) Por su producción de objetos hechos de cobre
   (D) Por haber inventado una nueva técnica de elaborar el metal

7. ¿A qué se refiere la fuente auditiva cuando afirma que un techo "se ilumina con los rayos del sol"?
   (A) A que hay una representación del sol encima.
   (B) A que el techo brilla como el sol.
   (C) A que refleja la luz del sol.
   (D) A que ilumina como si fuera de día.

8. ¿A quiénes les interesaría más visitar este pueblo?
   (A) A empresarios y fabricantes
   (B) A artistas y excursionistas
   (C) A indígenas y extranjeros
   (D) A funcionarios y empresas inmobiliarias

9. ¿Qué tienen en común las dos fuentes?
   (A) Las dos resaltan las características del lugar.
   (B) Las dos destacan los productos de cada comunidad.
   (C) Tanto el audio como el artículo muestran los cambios que han ocurrido a través de los años.
   (D) Las dos fuentes señalan la influencia de varias culturas en el desarrollo de la comunidad.

10. Si fueras a escribir sobre la información de las dos fuentes, ¿cuál sería el mejor título para tu ensayo?
    (A) La magia del color local
    (B) Características de un pueblo latinoamericano
    (C) Ventajas de vivir en una comunidad autóctona
    (D) El crisol cultural argentino

Cultural Awareness

Cultural product: Both these texts present peculiar places in Argentina and Mexico and how they reflects the character of the people who live there.

How are these places similar to or different from those in your own community?

SELECCIÓN #3

Tema curricular: La vida contemporánea

Tienes un minuto para leer la fuente número 1.

Fuente #1: Esta tabla presenta algunas ventajas e inconvenientes de asistir a una universidad grande.

¿Por qué elegir una universidad grande?	
Ventajas	**Inconvenientes**
• Conocer y convivir con todo tipo de gente y gente de distintas carreras • Variedad de instalaciones de acuerdo a las necesidades de cada carrera • Buen ambiente debido a la variedad de estudiantes • El prestigio, tratándose de una universidad que abarca mucho puede ser muy fuerte, y por ende un arma importante al egresar • Gran variedad de oportunidades sociales y de trabajo • Mucha gente conocerá la universidad, y por ende es una carta de presentación reconocida por todos • Los profesores suelen ser de alta calidad	• Las clases son muy grandes • Muchos profesores se interesan más por sus propias investigaciones que en enseñar las clases • Muchos cursos, especialmente los preliminares, suelen ser enseñados por asistentes de profesores • Posibilidad de no destacarse por la gran cantidad de estudiantes • Más burocrático que personal • Más competición para las becas

Tienes dos minutos para leer la introducción y prever las preguntas.

Fuente #2: La siguiente grabación trata de unos beneficios de asistir a una universidad pequeña. Es basada en información publicada en la página web *www.collegeboard.com*.

Track 3

1. Según la información proveída en la tabla, ¿cuál es un beneficio de asistir una universidad grande?
    (A) No hay que preocuparse por perderse en la muchedumbre.
    (B) Los cursos básicos suelen ser más fáciles porque los catedráticos no los suelen enseñar.
    (C) Hay más ocasiones de participar en ferias y seminarios.
    (D) Todo está más al alcance del estudiante.

2. Basándote en la información de la tabla, ¿cuál sería un reto de asistir a una universidad grande?
    (A) La variedad de eventos sociales pueden afectar negativamente los estudios.
    (B) Sería más difícil desarrollar amistades verdaderas por la gran cantidad de estudiantes.
    (C) Los asistentes de profesores no son capacitados para controlar sus clases.
    (D) Hay más barreras y limitaciones relacionados con el inscribirse y diseño de los estudios.

3. ¿Para qué tipo de persona sería apropiado asistir a una universidad grande?
    (A) Una persona autónoma que, aunque le gusta socializar, prefiere ser más incógnita que el ombligo del mundo.
    (B) Una persona introvertida que frecuentemente necesita ayuda de consejeros y profesores por una variedad de asuntos.
    (C) Una persona a quien le encanta entablar debates con su profesor y otros estudiantes durante las clases.
    (D) Una persona que quiere que su universidad tenga un fuerte sentido de comunidad y ambiente unido.

4. Según la fuente auditiva, ¿cuál es un beneficio de asistir a una universidad pequeña?
    (A) Hay amplias oportunidades de formar partes de diferentes grupos sociales.
    (B) Existe una relación más personal entre los docentes y los estudiantes.
    (C) Las carreras son menos competitivas que en las grandes universidades.
    (D) Los profesores suelen enseñar sus clases mejor que los en las grandes universidades.

5. ¿Cómo se distinguen las universidades pequeñas en cuanto a las carreras que ofrecen?
    (A) Hay tantas carreras como ofrecen las universidades grandes.
    (B) Los estudiantes tienden a seguir varias carreras de estudio.
    (C) Se animan a los estudiantes a que personalicen sus investigaciones.
    (D) Los profesores y estudiantes trabajan juntos para crear las distintas carreras que se ofrecen cada año.

6. ¿Qué recomendación ofrece la grabación para una persona que esté preocupada en un aspecto de asistir a una universidad pequeña?
   (A) Conversar con estudiantes actuales para informarse de las oportunidades de ocio
   (B) Conocer bien a los profesores y asesores para enterarse del apoyo que la universidad ofrece
   (C) Buscar en el catálogo de cursos unas carreras de estudio que le interesa
   (D) Investigar si las universidades efectivamente son capaces de cumplir con los intereses de los estudiantes

7. Según la tabla y la fuente auditiva, ¿cuál de las siguientes afirmaciones es correcta?
   (A) Las universidades grandes suelen ser de renombre, mientras las más pequeñas son de menos prestigio.
   (B) Hay tantas oportunidades de formar parte de un grupo social en las universidades pequeñas como en las grandes.
   (C) En las universidades grandes, los profesores son más experimentados que los en las universidades pequeñas.
   (D) El entorno en los dos tipos de universidades es igualmente agradable, según la personalidad del estudiante.

Cultural Awareness

Cultural perspective: The print and audio texts present certain perspectives on making a decision on what type of college or university to attend.

How are the perspectives presented in these texts similar to or different from what you have observed in your own community?

SELECCIÓN #4

Tema curricular: La belleza y la estética

Tienes cuatro minutos para leer la fuente número 1.

Fuente #1: El siguiente artículo trata de un tipo de música popular en México. Fue publicado en la página web *http://InfoMorelos.com*.

El corrido
(http://InfoMorelos.com)

El corrido es una parte central de la música popular mexicana. Se ha convertido en una de las fuentes más eficientes para la difusión de las historias heroicas o románticas. Estas historias, frecuentemente se ubican en el ambiente de
Línea la revolución de 1910; sin embargo, ahora también se abarcan temas como el
(5) narcotráfico y la política contemporánea. Los temas más populares y difundidos son el amor engañado, la queja del débil frente al poderoso, el énfasis en actos guerreros, la habilidad especial en el manejo de las armas y el desafío después de haber sufrido alguna injusticia.

En los tiempos de la revolución, los cantantes viajeros recitaban los corridos
(10) en las calles o las plazas públicas, para comunicar novedades acerca de los acontecimientos importantes, así como lo habían hecho los trovadores de la Edad Media. La fuerte difusión de los corridos también tiene que ver con la venta de los textos impresos en papel de colores en las ferias y fiestas populares. Estas impresiones frecuentemente estaban ilustradas por el entonces totalmente descono-
(15) cido artista José Guadalupe Posada. Estas hojas servían frecuentemente para la difusión de ideas revolucionarias. Eran algo así como celdas de lo subversivo que, normalmente, fueron ignoradas por parte de la censura, ya que estas hojas se consideraban como "asuntos del populacho" sin importancia.

El musicólogo Vicente T. Mendoza opina que el primer corrido fue "Macario
(20) Romero," que data del año 1898 y surgió en el estado de Durango. El texto relata un acontecimiento del año 1810.

El corrido es recitado o cantado y tiene parte de sus raíces en la música popular española. La voz principal a veces es apoyada por un refrán cantado por un coro. El acompañamiento consiste principalmente en instrumentos de cuerda, tales
(25) como la guitarra, el violín y el guitarrón. A veces también tocan instrumentos de viento, sobre todo trompeta.

Sin embargo, frecuentemente una guitarra basta para cantar los corridos, presentando historias de infidelidad, borracheras, tragedias familiares, atrevidas aventuras y amores a un público que escucha sorprendido, admirado o indignado.
(30) Además existen diferentes concursos para la composición y representación de corridos. Hoy en día, Chabela Vargas, Amparo Ochoa, Cuco Sánchez, Vicente Fernández y otros son los intérpretes más destacados de los corridos tradicionales, mientras que los Tigres del Norte son el representante más conocido del corrido contemporáneo.

Tienes dos minutos para leer la introducción y prever las preguntas.

Fuente #2: La siguiente grabación trata de la música clásica. Se basa en un artículo publicado en la página web *www.buscarinformación.com*.

Track 4

1. Durante la revolución, ¿cuál era la función primaria de los corridos?
   (A) Entretener a la gente
   (B) Investigar la historia de México
   (C) Proveer noticias de diferentes sucesos
   (D) Criticar varios aspectos de la sociedad mexicana

2. ¿Cuál es uno de los temas de los corridos?
   (A) El comercio de libros y textos
   (B) Las injusticias cometidas durante la revolución
   (C) La vida y las obras de diferentes héroes
   (D) Las fiestas y ferias populares de México

3. ¿Qué otro impacto tuvieron los corridos?
   (A) Causaron una polémica que llevó a la censura de algunos corridos.
   (B) Inspiraron una representación gráfica de las letras de algunas canciones.
   (C) Cambiaron los gustos y filosofía de la sociedad.
   (D) Hicieron que la gente aprendiera más de la música española.

4. ¿Cuál es una característica del corrido?
   (A) Es una mezcla de varios estilos musicales de América Latina.
   (B) Sólo hay una persona que canta.
   (C) Se usan instrumentos acústicos y eléctricos.
   (D) Es cantada por un conjunto cuyos miembros tocan y cantan.

5. Según la grabación, ¿qué tipo de música se puede denominar "música clásica"?
   (A) Música que une varios instrumentos en una orquesta
   (B) La música compuesta entre la edad media y el barroco
   (C) Sólo la música compuesta por Bach y Beethoven
   (D) La música que incorpora los estilos de diferentes épocas

6. ¿Cómo se caracteriza la música clásica?
   (A) Es compleja y resulta difícil de entender.
   (B) Es melancólica por tratar de temas serios.
   (C) Es elegante y asequible, pero merece profunda atención.
   (D) Es principalmente para los adinerados.

7. Según la fuente auditiva, ¿quiénes gozan de la música clásica?

    (A) Los aficionados de la época medieval

    (B) Mayormente la gente mayor

    (C) Tanto los mayores como los jóvenes

    (D) Principalmente la juventud

8. ¿Cómo se destacó la música clásica?

    (A) Por lograr unir varios instrumentos distintos para una representación

    (B) Por ser la primera en perfeccionar la unión entre el canto e instrumentos

    (C) Por ser la primera rama musical que creyó obras dramáticas

    (D) Por su capacidad de ser relevante en diferente épocas

9. ¿Qué tienen en común la música clásica y los corridos?

    (A) Los dos tienen sus orígenes antes del siglo XIX.

    (B) Los dos incorporan una gran variedad de instrumentos de todos tipos.

    (C) Los dos presentan historias de la antigüedad.

    (D) Los dos gozan de bastante popularidad en el presente.

10. ¿Por quiénes parecen ser adaptados los dos estilos musicales?

    (A) Los corridos son para la clase obrera, y la música clásica es para los más educados.

    (B) La música clásica es para los catedráticos, y los corridos son para los guerreros.

    (C) Los corridos son para los a quienes les gusta festejar, y la música clásica es para los que favorecen lo dramático.

    (D) La música clásica es para los que tienen gustos más refinados, y los corridos son para la gente que busca romance.

Cultural Awareness

Cultural product: The print text presents a type of music that is famous in Mexico.

How is this particular music similar to or different from what you have observed in your own community?

SELECCIÓN #5

Tema curricular: Los desafíos sociales

Tienes un minuto para leer la fuente número 1.

Fuente #1: El siguiente anuncio trata de unas razones por participar en una manifestación. Se basa en un anuncio publicado por la UGT, una organización sindical obrera en España.

Razones para participar este sábado ¡Juntos podemos hacer una diferencia!	
Las reformas laborales del gobierno hacen el despido más fácil, más rápido y más barato.	Impulsa la privatización de los servicios públicos, como el transporte, educación y sanidad.
El empresario tiene todo el poder, la flexibilidad interna facilita la movilidad, la modificación de jornada, horario y modificación de salarios.	Perjudican el empleo público, incrementan la jornada, reducen días libres, nos quitan la paga de navidad . . .
Fomenta la inestabilidad de los jóvenes, que los condena al subempleo y al desempleo.	Reduce las prestaciones por desempleo, elimina subsidio y reduce la prestación desde el 6° mes.
Seguro que tienes más razones . . . ¡ponlas aquí!	

Tienes dos minutos para leer la introducción y prever las preguntas.

Fuente #2: En la siguiente conversación, dos amigos hablan de un evento que quieren preparar.

Track 5

1. ¿Cuál es el propósito principal de esta manifestación?
   (A) Proponer cambios a los beneficios que ofrecen las empresas
   (B) Criticar las injusticias en el mundo del trabajo
   (C) Pedir aumentos de sueldo y cantidad de tiempo libre
   (D) Impulsar reformas de la gestión pública

2. ¿Cuál parece ser la queja global de los manifestantes?
   (A) Los jóvenes no tienen tantas oportunidades como los demás.
   (B) El gobierno no le está prestando atención a los deseos del público.
   (C) Las compañías privadas tienen demasiado dominio.
   (D) La legislación laboral es anticuada.

3. ¿Qué quieren los organizadores de esta manifestación?
   (A) Quieren que los participantes dejen sus trabajos.
   (B) Invitan a que la gente añada sus propias molestias.
   (C) Mandan que los empresarios no despidan a tanta gente.
   (D) Proponen que se dé un sobresueldo durante los días festivos.

4. En la conversación, ¿qué están planeando estos hombres?
   (A) Una huelga
   (B) Un carnaval
   (C) Una lucha
   (D) Una feria

5. ¿Por qué están insatisfechos los dos?
   (A) Los dos hombres piensan que no pueden mejorar su situación.
   (B) Ellos opinan que merecen más pago.
   (C) La empresa está por quebrar y no puede pagarles.
   (D) Los otros empleados no desean cooperar con su plan.

6. ¿Qué resolución proponen los dos?
   (A) Proponen que la compañía les permita trabajar la semana que viene.
   (B) Proponen que la compañía les reembolse por el tiempo perdido del trabajo.
   (C) Recomiendan que la compañía acepte el ascenso de cincuenta dólares.
   (D) Sugieren que el árbitro les permita regresar al empleo sin contrato para que puedan mantener la producción.

7. ¿Qué tienen en común la fuente escrita y la auditiva?
   (A) Los dos buscan aumento de sueldo.
   (B) Los dos buscan una solución lo más antes posible.
   (C) Los dos se quejan de la falta de contratos.
   (D) Los dos buscan armar un grupo para luchar contra las injusticias.

Cultural Awareness

Cultural practice: The print and audio texts present a common practice in many Spanish-speaking countries: going on strike or holding a social protest.

How is the practice presented in these texts similar to or different from what you have observed in your own community?

SELECCIÓN #6

Tema curricular: La ciencia y la tecnología

Tienes cuatro minutos para leer fuente número 1.

Fuente #1: La siguiente tabla presenta medidas de prevención ante un terremoto.

Consejos y medidas de prevención ante un sismo		
Antes	**Durante**	**Después**
• Identifique y marque las zonas más seguras en casas, escuelas, oficinas, edificios y calles para ubicarse en ellas. • Aléjese de ventanales y cables de alta tensión. • Identifique lugares seguros cercanos para la concentración de personas, como parques o casas de familiares. Póngase de acuerdo con los familiar para ubicarse en ellos. • Identifique las rutas de evacuación y realice simulacros preventivos de comportamiento. • Coloque los muebles de manera que los pasillos queden despejados. • Tenga un botiquín, botellas de agua, lámparas y pilas y un radio, siempre a la mano.	• Mantenga la calma y ayude a que otros hagan lo mismo. • No corra, no grite y no empuje a nadie, muchas veces hay más accidentes durante la evacuación, que por efectos del sismo. • Colóquese bajo los escritorios, mesas fuertes o en los sitios marcados como seguros como son los marcos de puertas y junto a pilares de contención de edificios. • Aléjese de ventanas que puedan romperse con el movimiento. • Si es posible salir a la calle, colóquese en lugares alejados de cables de alta tensión.	• Salga de los edificios y casas y permanezca un buen rato fuera de ellos. • Revise los daños externos antes de entrar nuevamente y los internos antes de que su familia entre. • No utilice gas, aparatos eléctricos ni encienda cerillos. • Encienda un radio de pilas, para mantenerse informado. Atienda las indicaciones del personal de protección civil siempre. • Esté preparado para las réplicas, a veces estas son menores y frecuentemente con mayores consecuencias. • Evite saturar las líneas telefónicas, para que los servicios de emergencia puedan atender las llamadas de urgencia.

Tienes dos minutos para leer la introducción y prever las preguntas.

Fuente #2: En la siguiente conversación, dos mujeres hablan de un evento que ocurrió la noche anterior.

Track 6

1. Según la información en la tabla, ¿qué preparativos puedes hacer en la casa?
    (A) Determinar la mejor forma de salir de la casa en caso de un sismo
    (B) Comprar reservas de comestibles en caso de que estés atrapado
    (C) Identificar los edificios públicos en su barrio para poder refugiarse en ellos
    (D) Situar los muebles para que no obstruyan el paso de salida

2. ¿Por qué hay que mantener la calma durante un sismo?
    (A) Porque el desorden puede aumentar el número de heridos.
    (B) Porque el nerviosismo puede causarles mucha tensión a los demás.
    (C) Porque la tranquilidad ayuda a que se encuentren lugares de refugio.
    (D) Porque la calma ayuda a que otros se tranquilicen.

3. ¿Por qué hay que quedarse afuera de los edificios después de un sismo?
    (A) Porque es más fácil que los socorristas te encuentren.
    (B) Porque es posible que el personal de protección necesite tu ayuda.
    (C) Porque es probable que la estructura haya sido dañada.
    (D) Porque es más fácil revisar los daños desde el exterior.

4. Según la conversación ¿qué acontecimiento comentan estas mujeres?
    (A) La noche anterior lanzaron muchos cohetes.
    (B) La noche anterior sufrieron un bombardeo.
    (C) La noche anterior hubo una plaga de insectos.
    (D) La noche anterior hizo muy mal tiempo.

5. ¿Qué molestia adicional ha sufrido la segunda narradora?
    (A) No tiene electricidad en la casa.
    (B) No tiene agua corriente en la casa.
    (C) No tiene plantas en el huerto.
    (D) No tiene ningunas gotas.

6. ¿Qué remedio hay para el problema de la segunda narradora?
    (A) Todo estará arreglado pronto, ese mismo día.
    (B) El ayuntamiento le ha prometido hacer reparaciones mañana.
    (C) Ella esperará hasta que brille el sol para colgar la ropa al aire.
    (D) No hay remedio, tendrá que esperar mucho tiempo.

7. Según la conversación y la información de la tabla, ¿qué preparativos deberían haber tomado las dos mujeres que les habría ayudado durante este evento?

(A) Localizar el lugar más seguro de refugio en su casa

(B) Tener guardado una linterna, botellas de agua y radio

(C) Colocar los muebles de manera que queden despejados los pasillos

(D) Identificar las rutas de evacuación y realizar simulacros preventivos

---

Cultural Awareness

Cultural perspectives: The print and audio texts present how different communities prepare for and react to environmental challenges, such as earthquakes or a bad storm.

How are the perspectives presented in these texts similar to or different from what you have observed in your own community?

SELECCIÓN #7

Tema curricular: Las familias y las comunidades

Tienes un minuto para leer fuente número 1.

Fuente #1: El siguiente gráfico indica lo que suelen publicar los adolescentes en redes sociales en 2005 y 2011.

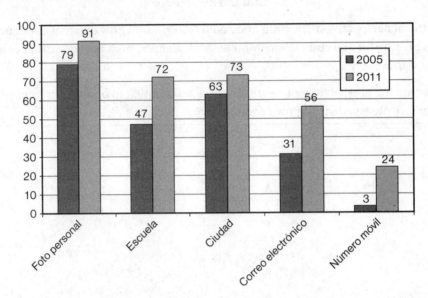

Tienes dos minutos para leer la introducción y prever las preguntas.

Fuente #2: En la siguiente entrevista, Gemma Martínez, investigadora de la Universidad del País Vasco, habla sobre la próxima generación de usuarios de ordenadores. La entrevista original fue publicada en la página *www.consumer.es* en 2010.

Track 7

1. Según el gráfico, ¿qué tipo de información ha tenido el mayor cambio porcentual?
   - (A) La foto de la persona
   - (B) Información de la escuela
   - (C) La dirección de su casa
   - (D) El número de su celular

2. ¿Qué tipo de información ha tenido menor incremento porcentual?
   - (A) La resistencia a proveer información de contacto
   - (B) Proporcionar un elemento visual del usuario
   - (C) Ofrecer información acerca del lugar de formación académica
   - (D) Información de la vivienda del usuario

3. Según el gráfico, ¿qué se podría decir ha sido el mayor cambio?
   (A) Ha aumentado el uso de correo electrónico entre los adolescentes.
   (B) Los adolescentes tienen más orgullo de su escuela y ciudad.
   (C) Los jóvenes son más inclinados para proveer información personal.
   (D) Los jóvenes tienden a acudir más a redes sociales para encontrar amigos.

4. Según la entrevista, ¿cuál es un problema que puede encontrar un menor al navegar por la red?
   (A) No tiene la capacidad de distinguir las páginas adecuadas para su edad.
   (B) No sabrá qué hacer si abre páginas con contenido inadecuado.
   (C) Los padres no siempre están presentes para poder darle ayuda.
   (D) Puede causarle molestia buscar las páginas a que quiere acceder.

5. Según Gemma Martínez, ¿cómo pueden los padres mejor ayudar a sus hijos en cuanto a navegar por la Red?
   (A) Discutir con sus hijos los riesgos asociados con ciertas páginas y conducta
   (B) Bloquear los sitios que contienen contenido que no es apropiado
   (C) Vigilar a sus hijos cada vez que usen el internet
   (D) Instalar filtros para monitorear la acción de sus hijos cuando navegan

6. ¿Cuál de las siguientes preguntas sería más apropiada para que Gemma Martínez continuara la entrevista?
   (A) ¿A qué edad es permisible que un niño tenga perfil en Facebook?
   (B) ¿Hay ejemplos en que la Red puede fomentar valores y el aprendizaje?
   (C) ¿Cómo pueden los padres mejor saber lo que es y no es apropiado?
   (D) ¿Cómo se diferencian los padres y los hijos en cuanto a su capacidad de manejar el internet?

7. Según el gráfico y la fuente auditiva, ¿qué se puede deducir de impacto del internet en la sociedad?
   (A) Los jóvenes son menos cautelosos con la información que publican y no siempre son conscientes de lo que puede ocasionar un uso no responsable.
   (B) Los adolescentes son más expertos con la tecnología y los padres son incapaces de impedirles que actúen de cierta forma.
   (C) El internet ha reemplazado la vida real, y tanto los jóvenes como los padres lo usan más como una herramienta para socializar y comunicarse.
   (D) Los adolescentes guardan su información personal en internet para que sea más asequible para los demás.

Cultural Awareness

Cultural practice: The print text presents the habits of adolescents on social media.

Cultural perspective: The audio passage presents the perspectives of an expert on the use of technology.

How are the practices and perspectives presented in these texts similar to or different from what you have observed in your own community?

SELECCIÓN #8

Tema curricular: La ciencia y la tecnología

Tienes cuatro minutos para leer fuente número 1.

Fuente #1: El siguiente artículo trata de la energía eólica. Fue publicada en la página web *www.enbuenasmanos.com*.

¿Qué es la energía eólica?

La energía eólica es la energía producida por el viento. La utilización de este tipo de energía por el hombre no es nada nuevo pues se viene haciendo desde tiempos remotos.

Línea
(5) Las ventajas de la energía eólica ya eran aprovechadas por los babilonios y los chinos hace más de 4.000 años para bombear agua para regar los cultivos y en la Edad Media era el viento el encargado de mover los molinos para moler el grano y, por supuesto, era la energía utilizada por los barcos.

Hoy día se aprovecha esta energía para, mediante un generador, transformarla en electricidad.

(10) Son muchas las ventajas de la energía eólica, estas son algunas de ellas:

- Los costes de producción de este tipo de energía son relativamente bajos, pueden competir en rentabilidad con otras fuentes de producción de energía: centrales térmicas de carbón, centrales de combustible, etc.

- Otra de las ventajas de la energía eólica es que es una energía limpia, para su
(15) producción no es necesario un proceso de combustión. Es un proceso limpio que no perjudica a la atmósfera, la fauna, la vegetación y no contamina el suelo ni las aguas.

- Los modernos molinos de viento pueden ser instalados en zonas remotas, no conectadas a la red eléctrica, para conseguir su propio suministro.

(20) - Una de las mayores ventajas de la energía eólica es que es inagotable, sostenible y no contaminante.

- La utilización de la energía eólica para la generación de electricidad no incide sobre las características fisicoquímicas del suelo, ya que no se produce ningún contaminante que le perjudique, ni tampoco vertidos o grandes movimientos
(25) de tierras.

- La energía eólica no altera los acuíferos y la producción de electricidad a partir de esta energía no contribuye al efecto invernadero, no destruye la capa de ozono ni genera residuos contaminantes.

A pesar de todas las ventajas de la energía eólica esta también tiene algunas des-
(30) ventajas:

- La fuerza del viento es muy variable, por lo que la producción de energía no es constante.

- Los modernos molinos de viento son estructuras grandes y todavía bastantes caras.

(35) • Hay quien está en contra de los aerogeneradores porque producen una alteración sobre el paisaje.
 • Las turbinas son ruidosas.
 • Los parques eólicos son un peligro para las aves, las palas de los molinos han matado a muchas de ellas.
(40) • Hoy por hoy las empresas de energía eólica dependen de subsidios de los gobiernos pues todavía no son competitivas.

Tienes dos minutos para leer la introducción y prever las preguntas.

Fuente #2: La siguiente fuente auditiva trata de los beneficios de la energía solar. Se basa en un artículo de David Dickson, director de SciDiv.net.

Track 8

1. ¿Cuál es el propósito del artículo?
   (A) Contar la historia del uso de energía eólica
   (B) Mostrar los efectos positivos y problemas del viento
   (C) Presentar los pros y contras del uso de energía producida por el viento
   (D) Convencer a que se hagan cambios en nuestras fuentes de energía

2. ¿Cómo se usaba el viento en la antigüedad?
   (A) Para poder sacar agua potable de la tierra.
   (B) Ayudaba con la agricultura.
   (C) Se usaba para cosechar los granos.
   (D) Se usaba en la fabricación de naves y barcos.

3. ¿Cuáles son unos beneficios de la energía eólica?
   (A) Es barato producir e instalar los molinos.
   (B) La energía producida es constante y abundante.
   (C) No produce ningún contaminante y no contribuye a la huella de carbono.
   (D) No afecta negativamente ni a la fauna ni al medioambiente.

4. Según la información proveída en el artículo, ¿quién estaría más dispuesto a usar energía eólica?
   (A) Un jubilado que acaba de comprarse una cabaña en las montañas para poder disfrutar de la vista y la tranquilidad.
   (B) Una pareja que quiere mudarse al campo y piensa construirse una casa autosuficiente, apartada de la red eléctrica.
   (C) Una persona que piensa trasladar su empresa a una zona remota y necesita una fuente fiable de energía.
   (D) Un grupo de ornitólogos que necesita energía para su nueva instalación de observatorios, los cuales se encuentran en la ruta de aves migratorias.

5. Según la fuente auditiva, ¿qué quiere comunicar el locutor acerca de la energía solar cuando dice que es "el último recurso de energía renovable"?

(A) Que se debe usar después de agotar todos otros recursos.

(B) Que dura más tiempo que otras energías.

(C) Que es la más reciente de las energías renovables.

(D) Que es la energía renovable con más uso variado.

6. ¿Qué papel desempeña Fondo Clima Verde?

(A) Suministra apoyo financiero para extender el uso de energías renovables en países en vía de desarrollo.

(B) Provee dinero para combatir el calentamiento global y la pobreza.

(C) Participa en conferencias para alcanzar mayor conciencia del medio ambiente y energías renovables.

(D) Presiona las compañías de energía y el gobierno a que integren planes de energía renovable en el desarrollo del país.

7. ¿Qué problema todavía existe con la energía solar?

(A) La tecnología todavía está en su infancia.

(B) El proceso de convertir la luz del sol en energía no es muy rápido.

(C) Los paneles solares son poco eficientes.

(D) El precio de los dispositivos sigue siendo demasiado alto.

8. ¿Qué obstáculo se encuentra en cuanto a la difusión de la energía solar globalmente?

(A) Grupos de presión y ayuda gubernamental todavía favorecen el uso de energía de recursos tradicionales.

(B) No hay suficiente evidencia de que puede ser una forma alternativa viable.

(C) Esta energía beneficia mayormente a los países que se encuentran en la línea ecuatorial.

(D) Todavía no resulta claro qué beneficios medioambientales ofrece esta alternativa.

9. ¿Qué tienen en común las dos fuentes?

(A) Hacen referencia a las ventajas y desventajas de usar estos tipos de energía renovable.

(B) Presentan los beneficios que estas energías aportan a la flora y fauna.

(C) Muestran algunos de los desafíos que todavía enfrentan estas energías alternativas.

(D) Resaltan la creciente popularidad de tratar de incorporar estas energías.

10. ¿Qué tienen en común las dos formas de energía alternativa?
    (A) Ofrecen un bajo coste de producción.
    (B) No proveen energía constante.
    (C) Necesitan una forma de batería para almacenar la energía que producen.
    (D) Benefician de abundantes fuentes de energía.

Cultural Awareness

Cultural perspective: The print and audio texts present certain perspectives on alternative energy.

How are the perspectives presented in these texts similar to or different from what you have observed in your own community?

SELECCIÓN #9

Tema curricular: Los desafíos mundiales

Tienes un minuto para leer la fuente número 1.

Fuente #1: El siguiente gráfico representa las razones por las cuales jóvenes entre 10 y 17 años abandonan los estudios escolares en seis países de América Latina. Se basa en datos de SITEAL publicados en 2010.

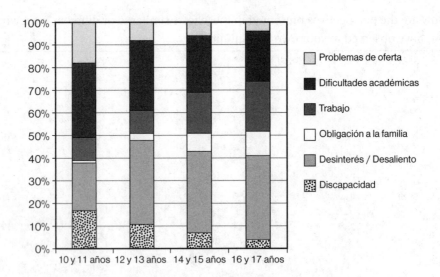

Tienes dos minutos para leer la introducción y prever las preguntas.

Fuente #2: El siguiente reportaje trata del asunto de la preparación de jóvenes latino-americanos al entrar en el mundo laboral. El reportaje fue publicado en Radio Naciones Unidas en 2012. La grabación dura aproximadamente cuatro minutos.

Track 9

1. Entre los estudiantes de 12 y 13 años, ¿cuál es la razón principal por abandonar los estudios?
   (A) No entienden las materias académicas.
   (B) Necesitan apoyar a la familia económicamente.
   (C) Prefieren perseguir otras actividades que el estudio.
   (D) Les resulta difícil llegar a las escuelas.

2. ¿Qué factor ha incrementado más durante los años?
   (A) Los jóvenes tienen que asumir roles típicamente reservados para los padres.
   (B) Los estudios tienden a ser más difíciles.
   (C) Los estudiantes tienen menos tiempo para dedicarse a los estudios.
   (D) Les falta interés a las familias que sus hijos continúen con los estudios.

3. Según el gráfico, ¿qué les ayudaría más a los estudiantes entre 10 y 11 años continuar con los estudios académicos?
   (A) Introducción de programas de becas y subsidios
   (B) Programas de apoyo y fortalecimiento académico
   (C) Mayor involucramiento de los padres
   (D) Mejoramiento de la disponibilidad de escuelas en zonas rurales

4. Según la fuente auditiva, ¿cuántos en América Latina carecen de las destrezas básicas para cumplir el trabajo?
   (A) El 25% de la población latinoamericana
   (B) El 50% de la población latinoamericana
   (C) 200 millones de jóvenes
   (D) Un cuarto de la población joven

5. Según Marisol Sanjinés, ¿qué hay que hacer para mejorar el problema?
   (A) Mandar que todos los jóvenes se queden en las escuelas hasta cumplir la secundaria
   (B) Aumentar la inversión de 1 dólar por persona a 10 a 15 dólares por persona
   (C) Proveer oportunidades a los que abandonaron los estudios en que pueden conseguir ciertas habilidades
   (D) Proporcionar equipo a los agricultores para facilitarles el trabajo en el campo

6. Al fin de la entrevistas, ¿qué comunica la cita de la joven en cuanto la situación en que se encuentran muchos jóvenes?
   (A) Que los jóvenes son incapaces de controlar sus propios destinos
   (B) Que están a la merced de las acciones o inactividad de la generación actual
   (C) Que están sufriendo y los mayores hacen muy poco para ayudarlos
   (D) Que son mayormente ignorados por la generación anterior

7. ¿Qué se puede afirmar sobre el gráfico y la fuente auditiva?
   (A) Los dos presentan unas causas por el abandono escolar en América Latina.
   (B) Los dos exponen unas consecuencias de abandonar los estudios.
   (C) La fuente auditiva presenta unas soluciones para reducir las causas que presenta el gráfico.
   (D) El gráfico presenta las razones que llevan a la situación que la fuente auditiva trata de solucionar.

Cultural Awareness

Cultural practice: The print texts presents the reasons students in several Latin American countries drop out of school, while the audio presents the preparedness of young Latin Americans entering the workforce.

How are the practices presented in these texts similar to or different from what you have observed in your own community?

Tema curricular: La vida contemporánea

Tienes cuatro minutos para leer la fuente número 1.

Fuente #1: El artículo trata de unas razones por las cuales una persona no recibe un contrato después de tener una entrevista. Se basa en un artículo publicado en la página web *www.pymex.pe.*

---

10 razones por las que no es contratado después de una entrevista laboral

Si está desempleado o ya tiene un empleo pero decide cambiarlo, sea cual sea su opción, la búsqueda y selección de personal son su asunto principal ahora. Muchas veces luego de una entrevista (en la que todo parecía andar bien)
Línea el resultado no es el esperado y pues no lo llaman. Debe continuar buscando
(5) hasta que logre el puesto de trabajo deseado.

Los paradigmas de selección para los encargados de recursos humanos no son los mismos, pero si coinciden en muchos aspectos. Veamos algunas razones por las cuales no fue seleccionado, luego de ello podrá reflexionar y tendrá más claro cuales son sus áreas a mejorar:

(10) **1. Llegó tarde**—La puntualidad es una de las cualidades que todo empleador busca en sus candidatos.

2. Su CV no está bien redactado—Las faltas de ortografía y mala redacción juegan un punto en contra y lo toman como falta de profesionalismo.

3. La información consignada no es verdadera—Las personas encargadas de
(15) recursos humanos muchas veces contrastan la información o solicitan referencias. El día que encuentren algo que no coinciden no se detendrán a preguntarle por qué mintió, simplemente no lo llamarán.

4. No sabe nada de la empresa—Es conveniente antes de asistir a una entrevista de trabajo conocer al menos la información básica de la empresa: rubro,
(20) años en el mercado, premios, etc.

5. Mala reputación online—Puede que esté a punto de obtener el trabajo tan esperado, pero a la persona encargada de selección se le ocurrió buscar su nombre en Google. Depende de Ud. que los resultados de la búsqueda no lo perjudiquen.

(25) **6. Dio comentarios negativos de sus anteriores trabajos**—No hay nada de malo decir los motivos de salida de otros centros laborales, lo malo es extenderse demasiado y hacer de esta respuesta una forma de desprestigio total a la institución que alguna vez le dio trabajo.

7. Mostrar excesivo interés por el sueldo—Es necesario saber cuanto será
(30) el monto del salario entre otras condiciones, pero si muestra solo interés en el dinero su entrevistador puede tomarlo como la única motivación por la cual Ud. accedió a una entrevista.

8. No tiene experiencia—Si aun no tiene una experiencia relevante pues manténgase activo y trate de involucrarse en proyectos de corto plazo al *(35)* menos. Más de uno o dos meses sin trabajar deja una impresión negativa en los encargados de selección de personal.

9. Se mostró desinteresado—No muestre desesperación, pero demostrar un poco de interés en la oferta no le cae mal a nadie. Trate de ser cordial y respetuoso.

(40) **10. Su presentación personal no estuvo acorde a la entrevista**—La primera impresión sí cuenta en estas ocasiones, busque una vestimenta y accesorios sobrios.

Tienes dos minutos para leer la introducción y prever las preguntas.

Fuente #2: En la siguiente fuente auditiva, el psicólogo Dr. Esteban Prado ofrece unos consejos para una entrevista de trabajo. La grabación fue publicada por el periódico El Comercio y dura aproximadamente 3 minutos y 10 segundos.

Track 10

1. ¿Para quién es dirigido este informe?
   (A) A los jefes de grandes empresas que buscan ampliar su personal
   (B) A empleados que están pensando en dejar su trabajo
   (C) A estudiantes que van a graduarse de la universidad
   (D) A solicitantes que activamente están buscando trabajo

2. ¿Qué no se debería divulgar durante una entrevista?
   (A) La información que sabe de la empresa
   (B) La antipatía que tiene para el empleo previo
   (C) La razón por la cual quiere la entrevista
   (D) Su interés acerca de cualquier oferta que reciba

3. Según la información presentada en el informe, ¿cómo puede el entrevistado mejor prepararse de antemano?
   (A) Saber cuánto paga el puesto para no hacer esa pregunta durante la entrevista
   (B) Revisar el currículum para averiguar que esté bien escrito y que los datos sean verídicos
   (C) Pasar unos meses únicamente buscando el puesto perfecto
   (D) Publicar en redes sociales la mala experiencia que tuvo en su trabajo previo

4. ¿Qué comunica el autor de la ropa que se debe llevar a una entrevista?
   (A) Que debe llamar la atención
   (B) Que debe mostrar su personalidad
   (C) Que debe ser de última moda
   (D) Que debe ser moderada

5. Según la fuente auditiva, ¿a qué se refiere la "película" que menciona Dr. Prado?
   - (A) A cómo el candidato quiere ser recordado después de la entrevista
   - (B) A la representación visual de las calificaciones del candidato
   - (C) Al hecho de que las entrevistas suelen ser filmadas
   - (D) A que muchos entrevistadores son gente famosa

6. Según Dr. Prado, ¿en qué aspecto es mejor equivocarse en una entrevista?
   - (A) En la forma en que se presenta al entrevistador
   - (B) En el tono que usa para referirse al entrevistador
   - (C) En las preguntas que se hacen al entrevistador
   - (D) En el volumen con que se habla al entrevistador

7. Según Dr. Prado, ¿qué habilidad tienen muchos entrevistadores?
   - (A) Son capaces de saber si alguien está contando falsedades.
   - (B) Casi nunca se equivocan en el uso de *tú* y de *usted*.
   - (C) Tienen la capacidad de crear un ambiente relajante.
   - (D) Saben hacer las preguntas adecuadas en cada situación.

8. Según la fuente auditiva, ¿qué debe hacer el entrevistado durante la entrevista?
   - (A) Cerrar la entrevista debidamente
   - (B) Engrandecer las experiencias que tuvo en los trabajos previos
   - (C) Participar activamente, tanto en hacer como contestar preguntas
   - (D) Ocultar los miedos y bajo autoestima que tiene

9. ¿Qué información tienen en común las dos fuentes?
   - (A) La importancia de mostrar interés por el puesto y la compañía
   - (B) La importancia de vestirse bien para la entrevista
   - (C) El beneficio de tener experiencia
   - (D) La forma en qué uno debe actuar durante la entrevista

10. A base de la información del informe y de la fuente auditiva, ¿qué pregunta sería más apropiada para terminar una entrevista?
    - (A) ¿Cuáles son los desafíos que enfrenta la organización en este momento?
    - (B) ¿Cuánto paga el puesto y puedo trabajar desde mi casa?
    - (C) ¿En cuánto tiempo puedo recibir un ascenso?
    - (D) ¿A qué se dedica exactamente esta empresa?

Cultural Awareness

Cultural perspective: The print and audio texts present certain perspectives on how to best be prepared to get a job.

How are the perspectives presented in these texts similar to or different from what you have observed in your own community?

ANSWER KEY

Print and Audio Texts (Combined)

Selección #1
1. **A**
2. **D**
3. **B**
4. **A**
5. **D**
6. **C**
7. **C**
8. **B**
9. **B**
10. **C**

Selección #2
1. **C**
2. **A**
3. **B**
4. **B**
5. **B**
6. **C**
7. **C**
8. **B**
9. **A**
10. **A**

Selección #3
1. **C**
2. **D**
3. **A**
4. **B**
5. **C**
6. **A**
7. **D**

Selección #4
1. **C**
2. **C**
3. **B**
4. **D**
5. **A**
6. **C**
7. **C**
8. **B**
9. **D**
10. **A**

Selección #5
1. **B**
2. **C**
3. **B**
4. **A**
5. **B**
6. **C**
7. **D**

Selección #6
1. **D**
2. **A**
3. **C**
4. **D**
5. **B**
6. **A**
7. **B**

Selección #7
1. **D**
2. **B**
3. **C**
4. **B**
5. **A**
6. **B**
7. **A**

Selección #8
1. **C**
2. **B**
3. **C**
4. **B**
5. **C**
6. **A**
7. **D**
8. **A**
9. **C**
10. **D**

Selección #9
1. **C**
2. **A**
3. **B**
4. **D**
5. **C**
6. **B**
7. **D**

Selección #10
1. **D**
2. **B**
3. **B**
4. **D**
5. **A**
6. **B**
7. **A**
8. **C**
9. **A**
10. **A**

ANSWERS EXPLAINED

SELECCIÓN #1

1. **(A)** From the beginning of the text, which talks about her childhood, to the very end, with her death, it is clear that this is a mini-biography of Sor Juana Inéz de la Cruz.

2. **(D)** The key to answering this question is in line 8, where it says that she was a "hija natural." This means a child born out of wedlock, which during those times was considered a high dishonor.

3. **(B)** In lines 18–20, we see how, due to the actions of a jealous priest, she had to work to defend her faithfulness in God. The words "fidelidad" and "voluntad" should be good hints to select this option as the best answer.

4. **(A)** You can identify this answer in line 20, where it states that Sor Juana resigned herself to abandoning her literary career. She did so because she was unable to convince the clergymen that her study and works of literature did not interfere with her faith.

5. **(D)** The audio states that Bachelet earned just over 53% of the votes, and that Pinera earned 46%. Therefore, she won this election by less than 10 percentage points.

6. **(C)** Following Bachelet's victory, the audio says that there was ". . . una explosión de alegría en su coalición . . . ," meaning that people celebrated her victory. Don't focus too much on the word *explosión* and think of it as an act of violence. Also, although the audio says that hundreds of thousands of people flooded the streets, it was to *vitorear*, or cheer, not protest.

7. **(C)** As a part of her victory speech, Bachelet said that she would govern for all Chileans, including ". . . los que votaron por ella y los que no lo hicieron."

8. **(B)** The second part of the audio presents the problem at the time that Bachelet was elected. The speaker repeats the word *desigualdad* several times, as in "desigualdad social" and "desigualdad de ingresos." Therefore, this inequality between social classes is the main issue at hand.

9. **(B)** Remember that the verb *destacar* means to stand out. Both Bachelet and Sor Juana stood out among their contemporaries at the time. Option (A) is incorrect because, although Sor Juana encountered difficulties in her time, the audio never mentions Bachelet having similar issues. Option (C) is also incorrect because Sor Juana had to abandon her study of literature, which she loved. Option (D) is incorrect because if there was gender inequality, then Bachelet would not have been voted president.

10. **(C)** When answering this question, remember that the answer has to be validated by both sources. The best answer is option (C) because Sor Juana suffered from her dishonor of being born out of wedlock (not her fault), and the audio talks about the social inequality that exists in Chile. Therefore, both sources provide information showing that social class differences and marks of shame do affect the well-being of people.

SELECCIÓN #1—MÁS PRÁCTICA

Análisis literario: (C) apóstrofe. In this literary device, the speaker (*voz poética*) addresses all men. This direct reference to men in general, and not to one specific person, makes it an example of apostrophe. You have probably learned several literary devices from your English class, and they are helpful to know, especially if you want to take AP Spanish Literature and Culture down the road.

SELECCIÓN #2

1. **(C)** The text deals with the neighborhood known as *La Boca* in Buenos Aires. The majority of the text describes the peculiarities and characteristics of this area. Don't be tempted to select option (D) simply because of the word *inmigrantes*, as this answer refers to their influence in all of Buenos Aires, whereas the text only deals with a particular neighborhood in Buenos Aires.

2. **(A)** The text describes this street as having multicolored buildings but without any doors. This would make it quite odd or unique, thus making option (A) the correct answer.

3. **(B)** In line 9, the text says that the street was named as such because ". . . acortaba distancias." The verb *acortar* means to make shorter, a synonym of the verb *abreviar*.

4. **(B)** Because this neighborhood is so peculiar and unique, one must infer that the people who live there are too, or would have to be. In addition, they probably feel a sense of pride for their neighborhood, therefore making option (B) the best answer.

5. **(B)** At the very beginning of the audio, the speaker says that the town was recently named *pueblo mágico*. Therefore, the purpose of this audio is to explain why it received this honor.

6. **(C)** The word *cobre* appears several times in the audio. It means copper, and it has been used in this area for many generations. The copper is found in artisanal works and living structures, and there is also a museum dedicated to this metal.

7. **(C)** Read the answers carefully to distinguish the difference in meaning from one to the other. The roofs illuminate because they reflect light, making option (C) the best answer. All the other options suggest that there is something embedded in the roof itself that gives it light or an image. In other words, the light is produced from the roof, and not by reflecting light.

8. **(B)** One gets the impression from this audio that this is a small town that is very close knit and proud of their history and artisanal culture. Therefore, it is unlikely that businessmen and large corporations would be attracted, making options (A) and (D) incorrect. Option (C) could be a possibility, but it is quite exclusive, meaning that it does not include people who are not either indigenous or foreigners. Option (B) is the best choice because it refers to travelers and artists, and that comprises the majority of people (both local and foreign) who would be interested.

9. **(A)** Both the audio and the text describe the peculiarities of a small town and neighborhood. Although there is mention of the products from Santa Clara del Cobre, there is no mention of original products from La Boca, making option (B) incorrect. Furthermore, option (D) is incorrect because the audio does not talk about the influences from different cultures.

10. **(A)** The text and audio use the word *color* in their presentations, and the word *color* can also refer to sights, sounds, and people from the area. Option (B) is incorrect because La Boca is not a town. Option (C) is incorrect because neither the text nor the audio want to persuade the audience to move to these areas by citing their benefits, and option (D) is incorrect because Santa Clara del Cobre is not in Argentina.

SELECCIÓN #3

1. **(C)** This is a question where the process of elimination can help. Options (A) and (B) can be eliminated because they are in the *Inconvenientes* section of the text. Option (D) is not the best answer because it says that everything is within reach, and one can assume that in a big university, this probably isn't the case. Option (C) is the best answer because the text says that there are a variety of opportunities in bigger universities, and that can include the events mentioned in option (C).

2. **(D)** This answer suggests that classes cannot be personalized based on the need of the student, which is true and falls under the category of bureaucracy. All the other options, although possible, are on an individual level, not across the board, whereas option (D) is probably true for all students.

3. **(A)** This question requires you to consider all of the qualities of the personalities presented. A benefit mentioned in the text of a large university is the social opportunities, and a negative is the possibility of not standing out as a person. The student described in option (A) is someone who likes to socialize, but not stand out, thus making this the best answer. All other profiles include a trait that would make this person encounter some difficulty based on the information presented in the text.

4. **(B)** The audio says that a benefit of small universities includes ". . . los asesores conocen muy bien a los estudiantes . . . ." Remember that the word *docente* means teacher. All other options are negated in the audio.

5. **(C)** Toward the end of the audio, the speaker says that small schools offer the opportunity for students to ". . . desarrollar especialidades creativas, individuales enfocadas en áreas de interés específicas," which is the same idea communicated in option (C).

6. **(A)** Midway through the audio, the speaker says that students should speak with other students in order to learn more about social life and what non-academic activities are available (". . . hablen con estudiantes para entender cómo es la vida social y qué tipo de actividades no académicas existen.").

7. **(D)** Remember that to answer these questions, you have to have proof from both sources. There is nothing to suggest that smaller schools are not prestigious. The text says that larger schools tend to be more prestigious, but option (A) is incorrect because it says that they are all prestigious. This absolute declaration makes it incorrect. Option (B) is incorrect because the audio explicitly refutes this idea. Option (C) is incorrect because there is nothing in the audio or text that references the experience of the teachers. Option (D) is correct. Both the audio and text present pros to large and small schools, so it is ultimately up to the student to decide what is best according to his or her personality.

SELECCIÓN #4

1. **(C)** Lines 9–12 have all this information. In line 10, it says "comunicar novedades" (to communicate news), which is a synonym of the word *suceso* in the answer.

2. **(C)** You can find this information at the beginning of the first paragraph, where it says that the *corrido* has become one of the most efficient ways to spread heroic and romantic stories. Be careful with option (B), for it is not correct because of the word *injusticia*. There is nothing in the text to suggest that the *corridos* criticized the revolution, but rather simply communicated events.

3. **(B)** In lines 12–15, you can read about how the *corridos* were associated with the sale of "textos impresos . . . ilustradas por . . . José Guadalupe Posada." Option (A) is incorrect because in lines 16–18 we see that these texts were ignored by the censors due to the subtlety in the way that they conveyed pro-revolution messages.

4. **(D)** The key information is found in paragraph 4, where it mentions how there is a main voice accompanied by a chorus, and that there are several instruments used. Although in the following paragraph the text says that often a *corrido* only needs a singer with a guitar, there is nothing to suggest that this is the norm.

5. **(A)** Be careful when answering this question, for you may be tempted to select options (B) or (C). Option (B) is incorrect because the audio states at the beginning that classical music is often referred to as music that was composed from medieval to contemporary times, and option (B) limits itself to only two time periods within this range. Option (C) is incorrect because the audio presents this as the idea of some purists, but does not argue this as being the case. The audio does define classical music as ". . . la unión de varios instrumentos para dar paso al desempeño de una orquesta . . . ," thus making option (A) the best answer.

6. **(C)** About halfway through the audio, the speaker says that classical music is ". . . seria, para un oido especial o más refinado . . . ," and continues with ". . . no en el sentido de ser grave e inaccesible." One can then understand that the audio argues that classical music is refined and elegant, but accessible to all listeners. Option (A) is wrong because it communicates the opposite idea of the audio text. Option (B) is incorrect because it uses the word *serio* out of context and, therefore, communicates a different idea than what the audio text means to communicate. At the end of the audio, the speaker mentions ". . . las personas más cultas . . ." and ". . . la élite . . . ," but if you listen carefully, you will hear that the speakers says the music was arranged by them ". . . adaptada por las personas más cultas . . . ," not *for* them (*para* ellos). The difference between the preposition *por* and *para* in this case is what makes option (D) incorrect.

7. **(C)** Be careful with this question, for although it comes later in the list, the information needed to answer it is in the beginning of the audio. The audio text says that classical music ". . . siempre ha contado con un gran número de seguidores y entusiastas de todas las edades," meaning young and old alike. Don't assume that all questions will always follow in the order of the audio or print text. The comprehension portion of the exam will test how well you have understood the entirety of the passage.

8. **(B)** At the beginning of the second half of the audio, the speaker describes classical music as being ". . . la primera rama musical que unió perfectamente el despempeño

de los instrumentos con las voces de personas," thus making option (B) the only correct answer.

9. **(D)** Both the print and audio texts mention that this music is still prevalent in today's society. Option (A) is incorrect because classical music has much older origins. Option (B) is incorrect because the *corrido* includes only a few different instruments, while classical music has a bunch. Finally, option (C) is incorrect because classical music does not necessarily tell stories from antiquity.

10. **(A)** As with the explanation for question 6 in this section, the key word is the preposition *por.* Classical music was arranged by the upper class, while you can tell that the origins of the *corridos* were from members of the working class. All other options, although maybe true for individual tastes, do not satisfy the overarching ideas that both the print and audio texts present.

Selección #4—Más Práctica

If you are having trouble thinking of a style of music in your own community, consider hip-hop, rap, country, and metal music. Although most of these styles, except country music, are quite different, you may be surprised to learn how their origins are not far removed from those of the *corrido*.

SELECCIÓN #5

1. **(B)** By reading this advertisement, you will quickly see that all statements are negative toward labor reforms. Therefore, the purpose of this document is to criticize as a way to promote change.

2. **(C)** Read carefully in order to select the best answer. Options (B) and (D) are incorrect because in the former it is not known whether the government is paying attention to the group's desires, and there is nothing to confirm that the current legislation is antiquated. Option (A) is tricky because the text says that ". . . fomenta la inestabilidad . . ." (encourages instability), but it is not clear whether or not this instability is a reality at the time of publication of this document. What is clear is that this group believes that the business owner has all the power, and that can lead to a number of other issues.

3. **(B)** At the very bottom of the advertisement, the group invites the reader to add additional reasons to participate in this protest. Some may opt for option (C), but note that, although this may be an inherent desire, what the group is trying to achieve with this protest is labor reforms.

4. **(A)** The word *huelga* is a strike, which is when people stop working to protest conditions and to try to achieve their demands.

5. **(B)** Toward the end of the dialogue, one of the speakers mentions "Pidamos un ascenso de cincuenta dólares al mes como mínimo . . . ," which proves that they are not happy with the money they are being paid. There is nothing in the audio to suggest that the company is going belly up, so option (C) is not a correct choice.

6. **(C)** As in the explanation for question 5, the two speakers want a raise, and if they get it, they both agree to ". . . empezar de nuevo el martes por la mañana."

7. **(D)** Option (A) is incorrect because the ad never mentions wanting an increase in salary. Option (B) is incorrect because there is no time frame in the ad indicating when they want this to be accomplished, and option (C) is incorrect because, once again, the ad does not mention contracts.

SELECCIÓN #6

1. **(D)** The key word in the question is *preparativos*, meaning that you can find this information in the first column of the table. The fifth bullet has all the information you need to answer this question. If you carefully read all the other options, you will see that there is nothing in this column to support their claims.

2. **(A)** Again, the key word is *durante*, so this means you have to look at the second column. The second bullet says to remain calm because disorder is the leading cause of accidents during an earthquake.

3. **(C)** The third column does not give this information explicitly, but one can easily infer from the second bullet that the reason to leave the building is because it may be damaged. The second bullet says that one needs to check the building for damage, which implies that it may have become structurally unsound. Option (A) could easily be removed, for there is nothing in the text to support it, and option (B) is incorrect because, although the text does say to help others, this is not the main reason for leaving a building. Option (D) is incorrect because, although it is probably true that one can better observe any structural damage from outside, the main reason to leave the building is to avoid the chance that it may fall on you. Once outside, then you can start looking at it more carefully to see if it is safe to re-enter.

4. **(D)** This should be pretty straightforward, for the two speakers mention the *tormenta* right from the beginning. The "espectáculo pirotécnico" one of the speakers refers to is used to describe the lightning during the storm.

5. **(B)** Toward the very end of the dialogue, one speaker asks the other if water has been restored. The other responds negatively, but says that she hopes it will soon because she has a lot of laundry to do.

6. **(A)** The last person to speak says that she called the municipality and they would take care of it "… esa misma mañana." Therefore, the solution will be taken care of that same day.

7. **(B)** Since the event that took place in the audio is not an earthquake, you must consider which of the preparations in the table would be most logical for a family before a thunderstorm. The best choice is option (B), for a storm could cut electricity, and the family would need a radio to be able to hear any important news announcements.

SELECCIÓN #7

1. **(D)** This question in essence is a math problem. For *Número móvil*, the increase is 700%. There is no other category that even breaks 100% increase.

2. **(B)** A quick look at the graph shows that the two categories with the least change are *foto personal* and *ciudad*, respectively. Therefore, you should easily be able to eliminate

options (A) and (C) from contention. A careful reading of option (D) will show you that the answer includes *vivienda*, which is another word for one's house. Because the category *ciudad* suggests that it comprises more of simply the house in which the user lives, this, too, is not the best option.

3. **(C)** Although there has been an increase in all categories, the biggest increases occur with providing email address and phone numbers, both of which are personal contact information.

4. **(B)** The speaker, Gemma Martínez, twice mentions that a minor can get into problems if that minor does not understand the privacy policies of the site he/she is entering or if the content is inappropriate. In either case, the child won't know what to do, and that is why parents need to be vigilant.

5. **(A)** This information comes at the very end of the audio text, where the speaker says that parents and children need to speak about which sites are being visited most often, and what dangers are associated with them.

6. **(B)** Option (A) is irrelevant to this discussion since the speaker never mentions social media or Facebook. Options (C) and (D) have already been addressed in the audio. The speaker exclusively speaks of the dangers, and not of the benefits, of using the internet. Therefore, it is quite appropriate to ask her what benefits are available.

7. **(A)** Because both the graph and the audio show that young people are more prone to publicizing personal information and don't really understand the risks associated with this, option (A) is the clear correct answer.

SELECCIÓN #8

1. **(C)** This should be pretty clear-cut because the article is largely divided into two sections: *ventajas* and *desventajas* (pros and cons).

2. **(B)** This information can be found in lines 4 and 5, where the text speaks about how the ancient Chinese and Babylonians used wind to help pump (*bombear*) water for their crops.

3. **(C)** Be careful when making this selection. Although the text says that the cost is relatively low, it continues by saying that it is on par with coal-fired power stations, which is not cheap for the common user, therefore making option (A) incorrect. Options (B) and (D) are in the *desventajas* section, so they too should be eliminated.

4. **(B)** This is the best option because it includes benefits mentioned in the text. Read carefully through the other options, and you will clearly see that they include at least one element from the *desventajas* section of the text.

5. **(C)** The word *último* means latest, as in the most recent. Do not be tricked by the false cognate *ultimate* into translating this word as meaning *the best*. If you think about it, solar energy technology has not been around that long in relation to wind and water energy.

6. **(A)** In the first third of the audio text, the speaker mentions *Fondo Clima Verde* and says, ". . . busca recaudar y distribuir alrededor de US$30 mil millones . . . para ayudar a los países en desarrollo."

7. **(D)** The speaker mentions two issues with solar technology: poor efficiency and high costs. However, the speaker continues by saying that technology has debilitated the technology barrier, whereas at the end of the audio the speaker says, ". . . los costos de capital de los dispositivos solares siguen siendo considerables . . . ," meaning that their cost is still a problem.

8. **(A)** The information needed to answer this question comes at the very end of the audio, where the speaker says that government subsidies frequently still follow the interests of traditional energy companies (such as coal and oil).

9. **(C)** Remember that the correct answer has to include information from both sources. The audio source does not present the pitfalls of using solar energy (except for price, which is only one, not multiple), thus eliminating option (A). The audio does not mention the direct benefits to animals, so option (B) can safely be eliminated as well. Option (D) is also incorrect because there is no reference in either text as to the popularity increase.

10. **(D)** Both the text and audio speak to the abundance of energy that can be harnessed using these technologies. Neither one is cheap (eliminate option (A)), and although wind energy may be inconsistent, it is unclear whether or not the same is true for solar (eliminate option (B)). Finally, there is no mention in the text that wind energy has some sort of battery.

SELECCIÓN #9

1. **(C)** The graph shows that the leading cause for abandoning school in this age group is because of disinterest. Therefore, it can safely be assumed that these students are interested in pursuing other activities (whether legal or illicit).

2. **(A)** If you look at all the categories, only one has increased significantly, and that is the white part of the column, or *Obligación a la familia*. One can safely assume that this obligation is some sort of help to the family, a role and responsibility that is traditionally that of the parents.

3. **(B)** The biggest area of concern for this age group is that they are struggling with their studies. Therefore, the biggest help would be tutoring and programs to help the students overcome these difficulties.

4. **(D)** Careful when answering this question. The audio says ". . . 25% de esos jóvenes están trabajando en situaciones donde se les paga muy poco . . . nos muestra que los jóvenes salen al mercado del trabajo sin las destrezas necesarias. . . ." 25% of youth is one fourth of the youth population, therefore making option (D) the only correct answer.

5. **(C)** About halfway through the audio, Marisol Sanjinés mentions that young people ". . . necesitan una segunda oportunidad u otras vías para ir adquiriendo estas competencias o destrezas necesarias para poder tener un empleo . . . ." Don't be tempted to select option (B) simply because the same numbers are mentioned. The audio text says that every dollar invested in education gives a return of $10–$15 over the productive lifetime of that person. It does not say that they need to raise the investment from $1 to $10 or $15.

6. **(B)** The young person at the end of the audio says that they can either be victims of the failure of the generation that preceded them, or they can be protagonists of their own destiny. In other words, she is asking for help and says that the previous generation is the one that needs to take action by providing the means for young people to succeed academically and in life.

7. **(D)** The sole function of the graph is to present the reasons for abandoning studies, and the audio presents what needs to be done to rectify the issue, making option (D) the best answer. Options (A) and (B) are incorrect because, in the first case, the audio does not say why young people abandon their studies, and, in the second case, the graph does not show the consequences that this abandonment has. Option (C) is incorrect because it is the opposite of what the graph and audio present.

SELECCIÓN #10

1. **(D)** The title gives all the information you need. The target audience is someone who has just had an interview but has not been hired. Remember that the word *solicitante* means applicant or candidate.

2. **(B)** Line 25 explicitly says that making negative comments about previous work experience is a reason that one was not hired. The word *antipatía* means dislike and is the opposite of *simpatía*.

3. **(B)** The second item in the list makes reference to the writing of the résumé. Poor spelling and editing shows lack of professionalism by the candidate.

4. **(D)** The last item on the list refers to the dress that a candidate has to consider wearing. The word *sobrio* may be a little problematic, but you can overcome this obstacle with a little ingenuity. There is not a whole lot of context to help you with meaning, so the best strategy is the process of elimination. The first option says clothing that draws attention. A candidate probably does not want his clothing to garner more attention than his or her credentials, and also clothing that draws attention may be positive or negative. Option (B) is probably not a good choice because, depending on one's personality, there could be many types of dress, and this could cause issues in an interview. Option (C) says that it has to be of the latest style and trend. Well, this may be true for certain types of jobs, like in the fashion industry, but is probably not true for most job interviews. In addition, option (C) is too similar to option (A), for they both will draw attention. The last option has the adjective *moderada*, which you probably already inferred to mean moderate. This means that it is neither flashy nor underdressed, which is a safe bet for any type of interview.

5. **(A)** Although *película* does mean movie, in this context it refers to the image or memory that the interviewer has of the candidate following the interview.

6. **(B)** In the first third of the audio, the speaker says that it is better ". . . equivocarse usando el usted que el tú . . . ." As you probably already know, it is better to be overly polite at the beginning than to come across as rude.

7. **(A)** Toward the end of the audio, the speaker mentions that many interviewers are trained to study body behavior and can tell if someone is "fingiendo," or pretending. Therefore, it is always best to tell the truth.

8. **(C)** Halfway through the audio, the speaker says that it is best that the interviewee ask questions that are appropriate within the context. Remember that these comprehension questions will not necessarily always go in order, so make sure that you listen to the entirety of the passage before beginning to answer.

9. **(A)** Both the audio and the text make reference to showing interest in the position, albeit in different ways. The text shows that being disinterested (number 9 in the list) could be a reason that one was not hired, and therefore one should show interest. The audio says that it is important that the candidate ask appropriate questions, and inherently this will demonstrate that the candidate is interested in the work and in learning more about what the job entails.

10. **(A)** When considering these options, ask yourself what would be the most appropriate question to ask in this situation. A good question is presented in option (A), for the candidate may be interested in some of the challenges that the company faces as a way to determine whether or not he or she can help overcome these challenges. Options (B) and (C) are not good choices because they show too much interest in compensation and advancement, and that is something the text explicitly says is a negative. Option (D) is also not a good option because it shows that the candidate has no background knowledge on the company, and hence probably would not be hired.

Section I, Part B— Listening Comprehension

5

Section I, Part B of the test consists of up to three selections that will be a combination of long narratives, interviews, short lectures, instructions, or some other type of speech sample. These selections will be between two and five minutes in length. You may take notes on this section, but they will not be scored.

You should practice before taking the exam to see if you do better taking notes, or if you do better simply trying to recall information from memory. The advantage of notes is that you have a cue to jog your memory about the content of the speech sample. However, you should avoid writing whole sentences. Instead, practice identifying and writing down key words that will help you recall the ideas presented in the sample.

Some of the following selections are longer than those you will see on the AP exam, but they will allow you to practice your ability to listen for main ideas and details.

STRATEGIES FOR LISTENING

- Read the introduction and questions to each sample.
- Concentrate while you listen.
- Evaluate the information being presented.
- Follow the thread of the conversation.
- Visualize, if you can.
- Take notes of key words that lead to ideas.
- Focus on what you understand and don't get hung up on what you don't understand. Use contextual clues to help you understand unfamiliar words or phrases.
- Remember that you will hear the audio twice. Listen the first time for overall theme and general ideas, and use the second listening to take notes on specific details.

ANSWER SHEET
Audio Texts

Selección #1

1. (A) (B) (C) (D)
2. (A) (B) (C) (D)
3. (A) (B) (C) (D)
4. (A) (B) (C) (D)
5. (A) (B) (C) (D)
6. (A) (B) (C) (D)
7. (A) (B) (C) (D)

Selección #2

1. (A) (B) (C) (D)
2. (A) (B) (C) (D)
3. (A) (B) (C) (D)
4. (A) (B) (C) (D)
5. (A) (B) (C) (D)
6. (A) (B) (C) (D)
7. (A) (B) (C) (D)
8. (A) (B) (C) (D)

Selección #3

1. (A) (B) (C) (D)
2. (A) (B) (C) (D)
3. (A) (B) (C) (D)
4. (A) (B) (C) (D)
5. (A) (B) (C) (D)

Selección #4

1. (A) (B) (C) (D)
2. (A) (B) (C) (D)
3. (A) (B) (C) (D)
4. (A) (B) (C) (D)
5. (A) (B) (C) (D)

Selección #5

1. (A) (B) (C) (D)
2. (A) (B) (C) (D)
3. (A) (B) (C) (D)
4. (A) (B) (C) (D)
5. (A) (B) (C) (D)
6. (A) (B) (C) (D)
7. (A) (B) (C) (D)
8. (A) (B) (C) (D)

Selección #6

1. (A) (B) (C) (D)
2. (A) (B) (C) (D)
3. (A) (B) (C) (D)
4. (A) (B) (C) (D)
5. (A) (B) (C) (D)
6. (A) (B) (C) (D)
7. (A) (B) (C) (D)

Selección #7

1. (A) (B) (C) (D)
2. (A) (B) (C) (D)
3. (A) (B) (C) (D)
4. (A) (B) (C) (D)
5. (A) (B) (C) (D)
6. (A) (B) (C) (D)
7. (A) (B) (C) (D)
8. (A) (B) (C) (D)

Selección #8

1. (A) (B) (C) (D)
2. (A) (B) (C) (D)
3. (A) (B) (C) (D)
4. (A) (B) (C) (D)
5. (A) (B) (C) (D)
6. (A) (B) (C) (D)
7. (A) (B) (C) (D)

Selección #9

1. (A) (B) (C) (D)
2. (A) (B) (C) (D)
3. (A) (B) (C) (D)
4. (A) (B) (C) (D)
5. (A) (B) (C) (D)
6. (A) (B) (C) (D)

Selección #10

1. (A) (B) (C) (D)
2. (A) (B) (C) (D)
3. (A) (B) (C) (D)
4. (A) (B) (C) (D)
5. (A) (B) (C) (D)

Selección #11

1. (A) (B) (C) (D)
2. (A) (B) (C) (D)
3. (A) (B) (C) (D)
4. (A) (B) (C) (D)
5. (A) (B) (C) (D)
6. (A) (B) (C) (D)
7. (A) (B) (C) (D)

Selección #12

1. (A) (B) (C) (D)
2. (A) (B) (C) (D)
3. (A) (B) (C) (D)
4. (A) (B) (C) (D)
5. (A) (B) (C) (D)

SELECCIÓN #1

Tema curricular: La vida contemporánea

Primero tienes un minuto para leer la introducción y prever las preguntas.

> **Introducción:** El siguiente audio es una entrevista con Ana Nemesio, surfista que cuenta de su taller de yoga y cómo se aplica al surf. La entrevista fue publicada en RTVE en junio de 2015. La grabación dura dos minutos treinta segundos.

Track 11

1. ¿Cuál es el propósito de la entrevista?
   (A) Revelar lo difícil que es hacer el surf y el yoga
   (B) Exponer la cantidad de lesiones que el surf y la yoga pueden provocar
   (C) Informar sobre la utilidad del yoga al surf
   (D) Proponer que los surfistas hagan yoga para mejorarse en las competiciones de surf

2. Según Ana Nemesio, ¿qué aporta el surf?
   (A) Experiencias maravillosas pero con dolor corporal
   (B) Sensaciones de fatiga y cansancio
   (C) Emociones de alegría y de entusiasmo
   (D) Efectos poco placenteros pero con beneficios físicos

3. ¿Qué afirma Ana Nemesio en cuanto a las lesiones que experimentan los que hacen el surf?
   (A) Los hombres mayormente son los que encuentran lesiones haciendo el surf.
   (B) La mayoría de las lesiones se encuentran en la parte superior del cuerpo.
   (C) Muchas lesiones se producen en la parte inferior del cuerpo.
   (D) Las lesiones suelen ser más duras que las que se experimentan en otros deportes.

4. ¿A qué se reviere Ana Nemesio cuando dice que la práctica del yoga es "una cuestión de inversión del futuro"?
   (A) Al número de surfistas que van a dedicarse al yoga
   (B) Al incremento de la calidad del surf y de perduración de poder practicar el deporte
   (C) Al hecho que el yoga puede prolongar las lesiones causadas por el surf
   (D) A que el yoga es un deporte menos costoso que el surf

5. Según la entrevista, ¿cuál de las siguientes opciones no es un beneficio mencionado que aporta el yoga al surf?
   (A) Hace que a uno le guste más el surf
   (B) Mejora la postura del surfista
   (C) Aumenta la fuerza física y flexibilidad
   (D) Incrementa el equilibrio y elasticidad

6. ¿Cuál de las siguientes afirmaciones mejor refleja el éxito del taller de yoga?
   (A) A los adultos les gusta, pero a los niños no tanto.
   (B) A los niños les gusta, pero a los adultos no.
   (C) A ambos adultos y niños les gusta, y los dos grupos participan activamente y con vigor.
   (D) A ambos adultos y niños les gusta, pero los adultos son un poco más perezosos que los niños.

7. Si quisieras investigar el tema un poco más a fondo, ¿cuál de las siguientes publicaciones sería más útil?
   (A) *Los mejores destinos del mundo para surfear*
   (B) *La importancia de practicar el yoga desde niños*
   (C) *Deportes en sintonía: cómo mejorar tu entrenamiento de surf*
   (D) *Los beneficios de ser surfista*

Cultural Awareness

Cultural perspective: The audio presents the usefulness of yoga and how it can help one become a better surfer.

How are the perspectives presented in this audio similar to or different from what you have observed in your own community?

SELECCIÓN #2

Tema curricular: Los desafíos mundiales

Primero tienes un minuto para leer la introducción y prever las preguntas.

> **Introducción:** El siguiente audio, titulado *Efectos de la soledad*, trata de la soledad en la tercera edad. Es una producción del programa *Cuaderno mayor* y fue emitido por Radio 5 en junio de 2015. La grabación dura aproximadamente tres minutos.

Track 12

1. ¿Cuál es el propósito del audio?
   (A) Exponer unas causas y los efectos de la vida solitaria
   (B) Llamar la atención a un problema anteriormente desconocido
   (C) Destacar las consecuencias de los que eligen vivir en soledad
   (D) Motivar a que el público tome medidas para afrontar problemas relacionados con la soledad

2. ¿Qué usa la locutora para poder apoyar su presentación?
   (A) Citas de personas que han sido afectadas por la soledad
   (B) Datos procedentes de varias investigaciones y citas proporcionadas por expertos
   (C) Sus propias opiniones del tema
   (D) Interpretaciones de comentarios hechos por unos expertos

3. Según la grabación, ¿cuál de las siguientes opciones no es un factor que provoca el asilamiento?
   (A) Problemas financieros
   (B) El no compartir la vivienda con otros
   (C) Problemas asociados con la salud
   (D) Conflictos entre miembros familiares

4. ¿Qué información provee la grabación en cuanto al número de mayores que viven en soledad?
   (A) Menos hombres mayores viven en soledad que mujeres mayores.
   (B) La minoría de los mayores vive en soledad.
   (C) La mayoría de la población mayor vive en soledad.
   (D) La mayoría de los mayores que viven en soledad tiene más de 85 años.

5. ¿Qué se sabe de la situación en cuanto al número de personas que vive en soledad?
   (A) La mayoría de ellas son de tercera edad.
   (B) Ha incrementado en años recientes.
   (C) Ha provocado más problemas de salud.
   (D) Muchas de ellas no tienen familiares.

6. Según la grabación, ¿con qué frecuencia recibe una visita una persona que vive en soledad?

    (A) Una vez o menos cada siete días

    (B) Típicamente más de una vez cada siete días

    (C) Una vez o menos cada treinta días

    (D) La mayoría no recibe visitas

7. ¿Por qué dice la grabación que hay que afrontar la soledad como un "problema social"?

    (A) Porque se prevé que la población mayor va a aumentar, y por consiguiente los problemas asociados con la soledad.

    (B) Porque los que viven en soledad experimentan varios problemas con la salud, tanto físicos como sicológicos.

    (C) Porque todavía no se han encontrado soluciones para combatir los efectos que produce la vida solitaria.

    (D) Porque el público en general no sabe de las causas y efectos de la vida solitaria.

8. Si quisieras formar parte de un programa cuya meta es de solucionar el problema mencionado en la grabación, ¿cuál de las siguientes sería la mejor?

    (A) *Adopta un anciano*

    (B) *Ahorro para la jubilación*

    (C) *Jóvenes contra la injusticia social*

    (D) *Fundación del corazón: deporte y ejercicio para mayores*

Cultural Awareness

Cultural practice: The audio presents a practice that affects the elderly in Spain.

Cultural perspective: The audio also presents a perspective relating to the effects that loneliness has on the elderly.

How are the practices and perspectives presented in this audio similar to or different from what you have observed in your own community?

SELECCIÓN #3

Tema curricular: Las familias y las comunidades

La siguiente grabación trata del sistema de votación en Chile. Fue publicado el 12 de julio de 2017 en la página web de la Biblioteca del Congreso Nacional de Chile / BCN. La grabación dura aproximadamente dos minutos, cuarenta y dos segundos.

Track 13

1. ¿Cuál es el propósito de esta grabación?

   (A) Animar a la gente a que vote
   (B) Describir algunos derechos que tienen los votantes
   (C) Informar sobre cambios en el sistema de votación
   (D) Promover cambios en el sistema de votación

2. Según la grabación, ¿quiénes pueden votar?

   (A) Los que tienen más de 18 años el día de la votación
   (B) Sólo los que cumplen 18 años el día de la votación
   (C) Los que tienen 18 años o más del día de la votación
   (D) Todos los que cumplen años el día de la votación

3. ¿A qué se refiere la grabación cuando dice que el documento de identidad o pasaporte tiene que estar "vigente"?

   (A) A que los documentos tienen que ser actuales
   (B) A que los documentos tienen que ser verdaderos
   (C) A que los documentos no pueden ser de otro país
   (D) A que los documentos deben pertenecer a la persona que los presenta

4. ¿Cuántas horas típicamente están abiertas las mesas para votar?

   (A) 18 horas
   (B) 2 horas
   (C) 4 horas
   (D) 12 horas

5. Si quisieras más información sobre el tema presentado en la grabación, ¿cuál sería la pregunta más apropiada para formular?

(A) Mi abuelo quiere votar pero está en una silla de ruedas. ¿Hay un centro específico donde tiene que votar?

(B) ¿Soy inmigrante a Chile? ¿También puedo votar?

(C) ¿Hay un local específico en que me corresponde votar o puedo ir a cualquier local?

(D) Tengo que trabajar en Alemania durante seis meses. ¿Todavía puedo votar en las elecciones presidenciales de Chile?

Cultural Awareness

Cultural practice: The audio presents the practice of voting in Chile.

How is this practice similar to or different from what you have observed in your own community?

SELECCIÓN #4

Tema curricular: La belleza y la estética

Primero tienes un minuto para leer la introducción y prever las preguntas

> **Introducción:** El siguiente audio trata del Día Internacional de la Juventud. La grabación fue publicada en agosto de 2014 en la página ecuatoriana Radialistas Apasionadas y Apasionados (*www.radioalistas.net*). La grabación dura un minuto veintisiete segundos.

Track 14

1. ¿Qué tipo de grabación es esta?
   (A) Una canción al estilo hip hop
   (B) Un reportaje de la música rap
   (C) Un anuncio para un evento venidero
   (D) Un fragmento de una obra teatral

2. ¿Cómo se describiría la actitud de la mujer y del hombre al comienzo de la grabación?
   (A) De condena
   (B) De asombro
   (C) De apoyo
   (D) De apatía

3. ¿Qué aspecto del joven se critica?
   (A) Su afición por la patineta
   (B) Su forma de moda
   (C) La forma en que habla
   (D) Su gusto musical

4. ¿Qué quiere el joven que los demás hagan?
   (A) Que respeten sus decisiones de ocio
   (B) Que no rechacen los gustos de los demás
   (C) Que participen también en un deporte
   (D) Que actúen de la misma manera que él

5. ¿Con cuál de los siguientes refranes estaría más de acuerdo el rapero de la grabación?

    (A) Dime con quién andas y te diré quién eres.

    (B) La ociosidad es madre de todos los vicios.

    (C) Por la facha y el traje, se conoce al personaje.

    (D) No juzgues un libro por su portada.

Cultural Awareness

Cultural product: The audio presents an advertisement for an upcoming event that celebrates the youth.

Cultural perspective: The audio also inherently presents a perspective about how young people are seen and how they should be seen.

How are the products and perspectives presented in this audio similar to or different from what you have observed in your own community?

SELECCIÓN #5

Tema curricular: Los desafíos mundiales

Primero tienes un minuto para leer la introducción y prever las preguntas.

Introducción: El siguiente audio es un fragmento de una entrevista sobre emisoras de radio que sirven zonas rurales de América Latina. La grabación fue publicada en febrero de 2016 por Radio Naciones Unidas, Nueva York, y dura cuatro minutos quince segundos.

Track 15

1. ¿Cuál es el propósito de esta entrevista?
   (A) Promocionar las emisoras de radio que sirven las poblaciones rurales
   (B) Exponer el papel que tienen unas emisoras de radio en diferentes zonas rurales
   (C) Proponer que las emisoras más potentes transmitan en zonas rurales
   (D) Informar sobre la comercialización de radios locales

2. ¿Qué se sabe de la población a quien se dirigen las radios campesinas?
   (A) La mayoría son oyentes de las radios campesinas.
   (B) Es gente que vive en un territorio bastante extenso y diverso.
   (C) Es mayormente muy pobre.
   (D) Se preocupa mayormente por asuntos económicos.

3. ¿Cuáles de las siguientes no es un papel de las radios campesinas?
   (A) Informar a la gente de asuntos locales y globales
   (B) Promover y reforzar las identidades de la gente de la zona
   (C) Servir como una fuente de aprendizaje
   (D) Estimular el comercio de bienes en diferentes mercados

4. ¿Qué quiere comunicar el Profesor Rivadeneyra cuando dice que las comunidades rurales "tienen en la radio un aliado"?
   (A) Que la radio no los hace sentir tan aislados
   (B) Que mucha gente en estas comunidades escucha la radio para entretenerse
   (C) Que la radio les ofrece conocimiento para poder mejorarse
   (D) Que la radio les brinda oportunidades económicas a los oyentes

5. Según la entrevista, ¿qué comunidades son las mencionadas que benefician de un sistema de alerta temprana?
   (A) Las comunidades cercanas al mar
   (B) Las poblaciones que se encuentran al pie de los Andes
   (C) Las comunidades andinas que viven en alturas superiores a unos 3.000 m s. n. m.
   (D) Todas comunidades rurales, no importa su ubicación

6. En cuanto a temas económicos, ¿qué información proveen las radios campesinas a sus oyentes?
   (A) Consejos de cómo adaptarse ante un clima cambiante
   (B) Pronósticos de las tendencias económicas
   (C) Información sobre la el cambio climático y su impacto global
   (D) Recomendaciones para el mejor tipo de animal que criar en estas zonas

7. ¿Cuál de las siguientes ideas destaca el Profesor Rivadeneyra en cuanto a la nutrición?
   (A) Una madre expectante bien nutrida favorece un buen parto y crianza.
   (B) Las madres y niños en zonas rurales tradicionalmente no se nutren bien.
   (C) Las madres deben nutrirse bien durante los primeros tres años de su vida.
   (D) Los niños y las madres carecen de oportunidades de nutrirse bien.

8. ¿Qué pregunta sería más apropiada hacerle al Profesor Rivadeneyra al fin de su entrevista?
   (A) ¿Conoce usted el nombre de un programa específico de las radios campesinas que haya tenido un impacto positivo en un asunto que ha mencionado?
   (B) ¿Sabe usted cómo reciben fondos estas emisoras?
   (C) ¿Nos podría informar de unos tipos de desastres climáticos que impulsarían el uso del sistema de alerta temprana?
   (D) ¿En qué países de América Latina se encuentran emisoras de este tipo?

Cultural Awareness

Cultural product: The audio presents the creation of radio stations specifically designed for farmers.

How is the product presented in this audio similar to or different from what you have observed in your own community?

SELECCIÓN #6

Tema curricular: La vida contemporánea

Primero tienes un minuto para leer la introducción y prever las preguntas.

Introducción: La siguiente grabación pertenece a una serie titulada *Pueblos con encanto*, que trata de varias localidades de La Rioja, una comunidad autónoma en el noreste de España. Esta grabación fue producida por Producciones Laboreo (España) en marzo de 2014 y dura aproximadamente dos minutos y medio.

Track 16

1. ¿Cuál es el propósito de esta grabación?
   (A) Animarle al oyente de tomarse unas vacaciones
   (B) Destacar las características más llamativas de unos pueblos riojanos
   (C) Hacer un viaje virtual de una localidad
   (D) Estimular el interés de visitar La Rioja

2. Según la grabación, ¿cuál de las siguientes opciones mejor describe Arnedo en la actualidad?
   (A) Ha logrado balancear el desarrollo con la preservación de su pasado histórico.
   (B) Su población es formada por un crisol de diversas razas.
   (C) Mantiene viva varias costumbres culturales de su historia medieval.
   (D) Es un centro industrial y de fuerte carácter artístico.

3. ¿Cuál de las siguientes opciones tuvo el impacto más grande en el desarrollo de Arnedo?
   (A) La conversión de palacios en museos
   (B) La fabricación del calzado
   (C) El descubrimiento de minerales preciosos y fósiles en la zona
   (D) La llegada de importantes figuras religiosas

4. ¿Qué aspecto de la iglesia de Santo Tomás llama más la atención?
   (A) Su tamaño
   (B) Su arquitectura
   (C) Su localidad
   (D) Sus parroquianos

5. Basándose en la información provista en la grabación, ¿por qué son importantes las cuevas de los Cien Pilares?
   (A) Son usadas para ceremonias religiosas.
   (B) Todavía hay gente que vive en ellas.
   (C) Son valiosas para el estudio de poblaciones antiguas.
   (D) Es la atracción turística más popular de la zona.

6. Al fin de la grabación, el locutor menciona los *fardelejos*. ¿Qué es un *fardelejo*?
   (A) Un tipo de comida
   (B) Una persona típica de la zona
   (C) Un tipo de calzado
   (D) El nombre que se les da a los visitantes

7. Si quisieras saber más información del tema presentado, ¿cuál de las siguientes sería la pregunta más apropiada hacerle al locutor de esta grabación?
   (A) ¿Hace cuánto tiempo que la industria del calzado ha existido en Arnedo?
   (B) ¿Me podría dar un ejemplo de algo que recuerde el pasado musulmán de Arnedo?
   (C) ¿Cuán lejos de Logroño, la capital de La Rioja, queda Arnedo?
   (D) ¿Ofrece Arnedo actividades de ocio en la naturaleza?

Cultural Awareness

Cultural product: The audio presents a town in the northern part of Spain.

Cultural perspective: The audio also explains why this area is special and worth visiting.

How does this town compare to those in your own community?

SELECCIÓN #7

Tema curricular: Las identidades personales y públicas

Primero tienes un minuto para leer la introducción y prever las preguntas.

> **Introducción:** En el siguiente audio, Fidel Revilla Castro, santero cubano, explica aspectos de la santería a los presentadores del programa de radio español *El canto del grillo*. La grabación fue publicada por RTVE en febrero de 2016 y dura cuatro minutos cuatro segundos.

Track 17

1. ¿Cuál es el propósito de esta presentación?
   (A) Presentar la historia de una religión española
   (B) Informar sobre el origen y unas características de una religión de las Américas
   (C) Presentar las particularidades de una religión africana
   (D) Dar una crítica de las influencias ajenas en la religión

2. ¿Cómo se puede mejor definir la *santería*?
   (A) Es el resultado de una mezcla de dos culturas.
   (B) Fue creado por los africanos que vinieron a trabajar en Cuba.
   (C) Es una religión con varios aspectos problemáticos.
   (D) Es una creación de los que colonizaron las Américas.

3. ¿Cómo define Fidel Revilla Castro las religiones africanas y la católica?
   (A) Los africanos eran idólatras, mientras los católicos veneraban las representaciones de figuras religiosas.
   (B) Los africanos veneraban las representaciones de figuras religiosas, mientras los católicos eran idólatras.
   (C) Las dos veneraban las representaciones religiosas.
   (D) Las dos eran idólatras.

4. ¿Qué aspecto de la *santería* se considera algo problemático?
   (A) El deseo de salvar a las personas
   (B) Unos de los métodos que se practican
   (C) Que no se pueden resolver todos los problemas
   (D) Su aplicación de la fe en sus tratamientos

5. ¿Qué ejemplo usa Fidel Revilla Castro para clarificar la idea de "la alquimia"?
   (A) Presenta varios trabajos que los santeros cumplen en sus procedimientos.
   (B) Explica la forma en que los santeros se limpian.
   (C) Explica el uso de plantas como parte de un tratamiento.
   (D) Presenta unas influencias negativas que pueden afectarle a alguien.

6. ¿Cómo se podría mejor definir el "baño de florecimiento" a alguien que no haya escuchado esta grabación?

    (A) Es un tipo de rito religioso.

    (B) Es como un tratamiento homeopático.

    (C) Es una pócima o bebida medicinal.

    (D) Es una influencia negativa.

7. Basándose en esta presentación, ¿con cuál de las siguientes declaraciones estaría de acuerdo Fidel Revilla Castro?

    (A) La santería es una religión pagana.

    (B) En la santería la fe lleva un papel poco importante.

    (C) Para entender la santería, se necesita conocimiento de los astros.

    (D) La mayoría de la gente cubana practica la santería.

8. ¿Cuál de las siguientes técnicas usa Fidel Revilla Castro para comunicar su mensaje?

    (A) Incorpora citas de distintos santeros.

    (B) Desarrolla sus ideas usando ejemplos.

    (C) Presenta las ideas más importantes en forma de lista.

    (D) Relata acontecimientos históricos y su influencia actual.

Cultural Awareness

Cultural product: The audio presents a religion that was created in Cuba.

Cultural perspective: The audio also presents certain rituals that are a part of this religion.

How does this religion and its practices compare with or differ from what you have observed in your own community?

SELECCIÓN #8

Tema curricular: Las identidades personales y públicas

Primero tienes un minuto para leer la introducción y prever las preguntas.

> **Introducción:** El siguiente audio, titulado Tecún Umán, trata de un capitán indígena k'iche', héroe nacional de Guatemala por su lucha contra los españoles. La grabación fue emitida por el grupo ArmadilloSound (Guatemala) en junio de 2015. La grabación dura aproximadamente dos minutos y medio.

Track 18

1. ¿Cuál de las siguiente opciones mejor describe el tipo de relato presentado en el audio?
   (A) Es una biografía.
   (B) Es un relato histórico.
   (C) Es un cuento de ficción.
   (D) Es una leyenda.

2. ¿En qué siglo se supone probablemente ocurrieron los evento narrados en esta historia?
   (A) Durante el siglo XV
   (B) Durante la colonización de las Américas
   (C) Durante la independencia de Guatemala
   (D) Es imposible predecir a base del audio

3. ¿Qué le causó miedo a Tecún Umán?
   (A) La posibilidad de enfrentar al enemigo solo
   (B) El tamaño del ejército español
   (C) La alucinante figura que avanzaba hacia él
   (D) El poder mítico que tenía don Pedro

4. ¿Cuál es el "destino" al que don Pedro se refiere cuando le habla a Tecún Umán?
   (A) La victoria a manos de los invasores
   (B) La muerte de muchos indígenas en la batalla
   (C) La inevitable derrota de los españoles
   (D) La batalla que iba a ocurrir

5. ¿Qué le sorprendió a Tecún Umán durante la batalla?
   (A) Que hubiera subestimado la fuerza del caballo
   (B) Que los caballos no contuvieran el espíritu del jinete
   (C) Que hubiera matado al caballo
   (D) Que los españoles no tuvieran un dios

6. ¿Qué consecuencia tuvo el error cometido por Tecún Umán?
   (A) Supo cómo matarle a don Pedro
   (B) Perdió su única lanza
   (C) Don Pedro lo mató
   (D) Perdió su espíritu guardián

7. ¿Qué recuerda la historia de Tecún Umán hoy en día?
   (A) Cada lucha que enfrenta el pueblo indígena
   (B) El plumaje de un ave endémico de la zona
   (C) El color rojo que se le pone en el pecho de un recién nacido
   (D) Los homenajes que se hacen a los dioses

Cultural Awareness

Cultural product: The audio presents a legend from Guatemala about an indigenous leader.

How is this legend similar to or different from what you have observed in your own community?

SELECCIÓN #9

Tema curricular: La ciencia y la tecnología

Primero tienes un minuto para leer la introducción y prever las preguntas

Introducción: En la siguiente entrevista, la subdirectora ejecutiva de la Agencia de Gestión de Emergencia de Desastres del Caribe habla de la experiencia del Caribe en el manejo de los desastres naturales. La entrevista fue transmitida el 23 de mayo de 2013 por Radio Naciones Unidas. La grabación dura aproximadamente tres minutos y treinta segundos.

Track 19

1. ¿Cuál es el propósito de la entrevista?
   (A) Revelar los desafíos que se encuentran en el Caribe para afrontar los desastres naturales
   (B) Exponer la cantidad e impacto de desastres naturales en la región
   (C) Informar sobre el sistema que existe en el Caribe para hacer frente a los desastres naturales
   (D) Proponer unos cambios al manejo de ayuda que existe actualmente

2. Según la entrevista, ¿cómo ha cambiado la región del Caribe en los últimos 30 a 50 años?
   (A) Ha habido un incremento en el número de desastres naturales.
   (B) Los países se han modernizado para minimizar el número de víctimas.
   (C) Los desastres naturales han sido más devastadores que nunca.
   (D) En Haití se ha visto una disminución en la pérdida de vida.

3. ¿Cómo se destaca el modelo caribeño?
   (A) Ha tenido una gran cantidad de inversión de varias fuentes.
   (B) Cuenta con la colaboración de muchos de los países de la región.
   (C) Ha prevenido la muerte de millones de sus ciudadanos.
   (D) Ha minimizado los efectos de los desastres naturales a la infraestructura.

4. ¿Qué quiere comunicar la subdirectora ejecutiva cuando dice "El terremoto puso sobre el tapete la vulnerabilidad de ciudades caribeñas"?
   (A) Que el evento hizo descubrir un punto débil en el sistema
   (B) Que el sismo causó mucho daño a las zonas urbanas
   (C) Que no se revelaron de inmediato los efectos del terremoto
   (D) Que el terremoto hizo la localidad más vulnerable a otros desastres

5. Según la entrevista, ¿qué elemento es esencial para la gestión de emergencia?
   (A) Tener líderes capaces de afrontar diferentes situaciones
   (B) La coordinación entre diferentes entidades de ayuda y rescate
   (C) Restaurar los servicios de comunicación lo más antes posible
   (D) Prestar atención inicialmente a las áreas que sufrieron más daño

6. Si quisieras investigar el tema un poco más a fondo, ¿cuál de las siguientes publicaciones sería más útil?
   (A) *Prepárate: 5 pasos preparatorios para sobrevivir cualquier desastre natural*
   (B) *Los desastres naturales más catastróficos del siglo XIX*
   (C) *Prevenir los riesgos y mitigar las consecuencias de desastres naturales*
   (D) *Enciclopedia de los riesgos naturales del Caribe*

Cultural Awareness

Cultural practice: The audio presents certain actions that are taking place in the Caribbean to become better prepared for natural disasters.

How are the practices mentioned in this audio similar to or different from what you have observed in your own community?

SELECCIÓN #10

Tema curricular: La ciencia y tecnología

Primero tienes un minuto para leer la introducción y prever las preguntas.

Introducción: El siguiente podcast trata de unas consideraciones que hay que hacer cuando se piensa viajar a un país exótico. El podcast original fue publicado por Radio 5 en 2011.

Track 20

1. ¿Cuál es el propósito del mensaje?
   (A) Informar sobre las enfermedades que se puede contagiar en lugares exóticos
   (B) Promover unos medicamentos que ayudan a los viajeros no enfermarse
   (C) Recomendar unos pasos para evitar enfermedades cuando se viaja
   (D) Dar un panorama de los diferentes medicamentos para varias enfermedades

2. Según la grabación, ¿qué es importante hacer cuando uno decide vacunarse?
   (A) Escoger una vacuna que sea efectivo contra los riesgos en la zona que desea visitar
   (B) Recordar que las vacunas son más eficaces durante el verano
   (C) Buscar un centro de vacunación que ofrece el servicio deseado
   (D) Pedir una vacuna unas semanas antes del viaje

3. Según la grabación, ¿cuándo hay que pedir consulta al médico?
   (A) Cuando sabes que has contagiado una enfermedad durante tu viaje
   (B) Antes de viajar a un lugar exótico
   (C) Antes como medida de precaución y cuando experimentas síntomas durante el viaje
   (D) Cuando no experimentas un viaje placentero

4. A base de la entrevista, ¿cuál de las siguientes afirmaciones es correcta?
   (A) Con un poco de cautela, se puede mitigar la posibilidad de enfermarse al viajar a un lugar exótico.
   (B) Las enfermedades que se pueden contagiar en lugares exóticos pueden ser muy dañinas si no se tratan a tiempo.
   (C) Hay que investigar bien las vacunas de antemano para saber cuáles serán más efectivas contra las enfermedades de un lugar particular.
   (D) Las enfermedades en lugares exóticos son peligrosos porque son más intensos durante el verano cuando a los españoles les gusta viajar.

5. ¿Qué pregunta sería más apropiada para el Doctor Agustín Benito al final de su presentación?
   (A) ¿Hay otras cosas que uno puede hacer para no exponerse a posibles enfermedades aparte de vacunas y medicamentos?
   (B) ¿Puede darnos un ejemplo de cómo uno puede contagiarse?
   (C) ¿Hay una vacuna que nos pueda proteger de todas las enfermedades o tenemos que buscar vacunas particulares?
   (D) Si me enfermo, ¿dónde puedo conseguir información de los centros médicos en el área?

Cultural Awareness

Cultural perspective: The audio presents ideas about how best to prepare before visiting an exotic location.

How does the perspective presented in this audio compare with or differ from what you have observed in your own community?

SELECCIÓN #11

Tema curricular: Las familias y las comunidades

Primero tienes un minuto para leer la introducción y prever las preguntas.

> **Introducción:** La siguiente grabación trata de la Tomatina, una fiesta en Buñol, España. La grabación dura aproximadamente tres minutos.

Track 21

1. ¿A qué público se dirigiría esta grabación?
   (A) A estudiantes de español
   (B) A empresarios de una compañía turística
   (C) A visitantes al municipio
   (D) A aficionados de los deportes extremos

2. Según la grabación, ¿cuál de las siguientes afirmaciones mejor describe la fiesta?
   (A) Es relativamente nueva.
   (B) Es difícil de entender.
   (C) Incluye una mezcla de varias culturas.
   (D) Es bastante violenta.

3. ¿Por qué se celebra la Tomatina?
   (A) Para vender muchos tomates
   (B) Para protestar contra el gobierno
   (C) Para entretener a la población valenciana
   (D) Para honrar la tradición de su historia

4. ¿Cómo se originó la celebración?
   (A) Un joven se enfadó con un vendedor de tomates.
   (B) Un gigante de un desfile atacó a un espectador.
   (C) Algunas personas se vieron envueltas en un disturbio.
   (D) Una persona le quitó el disfraz a otra en una pelea.

5. ¿Qué reacción provocó el acontecimiento original?
   (A) El Ayuntamiento no quiso permitir una repetición.
   (B) El gobierno distribuyó tomates para mejorar la fiesta.
   (C) Los vendedores trajeron más y más tomates para dárselos al público.
   (D) El público observó la prohibición del Ayuntamiento contra la fiesta.

6. Hoy en día, ¿cómo se ha mejorado la fiesta?

   (A) Sólo se permiten tomates.

   (B) Se organizaron más juegos.

   (C) La gente lleva palos para defenderse.

   (D) Se usa jabón para limpiar los palos con jamón.

7. Imagina que tienes que dar una presentación oral a tu clase sobre el tema de la grabación y necesitas información adicional para ampliar tu presentación. ¿Cuál de las siguientes publicaciones te sería más útil?

   (A) *Cuando el tomate es un arma de destrucción masiva*

   (B) *Gastronomía y cultura en España - historia del tomate*

   (C) *Juegos tradicionales de la comunidad valenciana*

   (D) *Conozca todo sobre el tomate*

Cultural Awareness

Cultural product: The audio presents an annual festival in Spain.

Cultural practice: The audio also presents certain practices that are a part of this festival.

How does this festival and its practices compare with or differ from what you have observed in your own community?

SELECCIÓN #12

Tema curricular: La belleza y la estética

Primero tienes un minuto para leer la introducción y prever las preguntas.

> **Introducción:** El siguiente podcast trata sobre cómo convertirse en mejor escritor. El podcast original fue publicado por podcast Aprendiendo a escribir en 2011. La grabación dura aproximadamente tres minutos, cuarenta segundos.

Track 22

1. ¿Cuál es el propósito del informe?
   (A) Dar consejos para hacerse escritor profesional
   (B) Presentar información útil para escribir mejor
   (C) Informar sobre los retos de convertirse en escritor
   (D) Presentar maneras en que unos escritores tuvieron éxito

2. Según el presentador, ¿por qué no les gustan a unas personas sus sugerencias?
   (A) Porque son unos pasos complicados.
   (B) Porque se tarda mucho tiempo perfeccionarlas.
   (C) Porque no contienen la magia que ofrecen otras sugerencias.
   (D) Porque ya son escritores exitosos.

3. ¿Qué dice el presentador acerca de los escritores profesionales?
   (A) Que se tranquilizan en cuanto hayan alcanzado su objetivo.
   (B) Que les resulta más fácil ser publicados.
   (C) Que siguen desarrollando su capacidad.
   (D) Que les suele tomar una vida entera cumplir su meta.

4. ¿Con cuál de las siguientes afirmaciones estaría de acuerdo el presentador?
   (A) La culminación de cada escritor es de ser publicado.
   (B) Cuanto más escribes, más oportunidades tendrás para que el público conozca tu obra.
   (C) Hay que encontrar un tema que les agrade al público para que tu obra sea publicada.
   (D) Los mejores escritores son los que imitan las técnicas de los grandes escritores.

5. ¿Cuál de las siguientes técnicas utiliza el presentador para comunicar su mensaje?

    (A) Incluye citas de editores profesionales.

    (B) Utiliza varias anécdotas de escritores famosos.

    (C) Da ejemplos concretos de métodos que utilizan los grandes escritores.

    (D) Presenta su propia experiencia y opiniones.

Cultural Awareness

Cultural perspective: The audio presents the opinion of one man on what one must do in order to become a better writer.

How does perspective compare with or differ from what you have observed in your own community?

ANSWER KEY

LISTENING COMPREHENSION

Selección #1

1. **C**	3. **B**	5. **A**	7. **C**
2. **A**	4. **B**	6. **D**	

Selección #2

1. **A**	3. **D**	5. **B**	7. **A**
2. **B**	4. **A**	6. **C**	8. **A**

Selección #3

1. **B**	3. **A**	5. **C**
2. **C**	4. **D**	

Selección #4

1. **C**	3. **B**	5. **D**
2. **A**	4. **B**	

Selección #5

1. **B**	3. **D**	5. **C**	7. **A**
2. **B**	4. **C**	6. **A**	8. **B**

Selección #6

1. **C**	3. **B**	5. **C**	7. **D**
2. **A**	4. **B**	6. **A**	

Selección #7

1. **B**	3. **A**	5. **C**	7. **A**
2. **A**	4. **B**	6. **B**	8. **B**

Selección #8

1. **D**	3. **C**	5. **B**	7. **B**
2. **B**	4. **A**	6. **C**	

Selección #9

1. **C**	3. **B**	5. **B**
2. **B**	4. **A**	6. **C**

Selección #10

1. **C**	3. **C**	5. **C**
2. **D**	4. **A**	

Selección #11

1. **C**	3. **C**	5. **A**	7. **C**
2. **A**	4. **C**	6. **B**	

Selección #12

1. **B**	3. **C**	5. **D**
2. **B**	4. **B**	

ANSWERS EXPLAINED

SELECCIÓN #1

1. **(C)** The interview is based entirely around the benefits of yoga for surfing, making this the clear choice. Option (A) is incorrect because there is no reference to the difficulty of yoga or surfing. Option (B) is incorrect because, although the interview does mention the number of injuries that surfing can cause, it never states that yoga also causes injuries. Option (D) is incorrect because, although one can deduce that because yoga can make one a better surfer, that this can translate into better performances in surfing competitions, this is never explicitly stated nor is it the reason for this interview.

2. **(A)** Ana Nemesio states that surfing is a sport that combines the good ("sensaciones estupendas") with the bad ("lesiones"), making option (A) the only logical answer. Options (B) and (C) are incorrect because they focus solely on the negatives (option (B)) or only on the positive (option (C)). Option (D) is incorrect because it is the opposite of option (A).

3. **(B)** During the interview, the only two body parts mentioned are "hombros" (shoulders) and "lumbares" (lower back), both of which are in the upper part of the body. Be careful with option (A) because you don't want to confuse *hombros* with *hombres*. Option (C) is clearly incorrect because it refers to the wrong part of the body, and option (D) is incorrect because there is never any mention as to how the injuries experienced in surfing compare to those in other sports.

4. **(B)** Ana Nemesio states that in order to surf well and for a long time, one must take good care of his or her body. We therefore can infer that yoga can accomplish this goal, making option (B) the best answer. Option (A) is incorrect because there is no reference, direct or indirect, to the number of surfers who are going to take on yoga. Option (C) is incorrect because yoga does not prolong injuries, but rather helps prevent them, and option (D) is incorrect because there is never any reference to the cost of yoga *vs.* surfing.

5. **(A)** Be careful with this question, for it is asking which of the options is *not* mentioned. Options (B), (C), and (D) are all clearly stated in the audio, whereas option (A) is not.

6. **(D)** By listening to the entirety of Ana Nemesio's response to the success of the yoga workshop, the adverb most often repeated is "*bien*," making options (A) and (B) incorrect because they assume that one group did not enjoy it. Ana Nemesio does say that the adults were more "vago" (lazy), making option (C) incorrect. Although the adults were not as energetic as the younger kids, this does not mean that they disliked the program (at least, not from Ana's point of view).

7. **(C)** This was a tough question, and it requires one to make some inferences in order to find the correct answer. Remember to focus first on what the question is asking. The theme of the interview is the benefits of yoga for surfing, two different sports in which the practice of one is advantageous for practicing the other. This makes option (C) the best answer because it refers to at least two sports by using the plural form of *deportes*, and refers to how the harmony (*sintonía*) between these sports can improve surf training. Options (A), (C), and (D) all ignore the relationship between surfing and another sport, making them incorrect answers.

SELECCIÓN #2

1. **(A)** The audio provides an objective overview of loneliness, making option (A) the best answer. There is nothing in the audio to suggest that this issue was unknown beforehand, therefore option (B) is incorrect. Option (C) is incorrect because it refers solely to those who choose to live a solitary life, whereas the audio speaks to all the elderly who live a solitary life, whether by choice or not. Option (D) is incorrect because, although a listener may feel inclined to help solve this issue, this is not the main purpose of the audio.

2. **(B)** The audio mentions "estudios," "encuestas," and "expertos," therefore indicating that the information provided is based on facts and expert opinion. This makes option (B) the best answer. The speaker does not directly quote people who live alone, making (A) incorrect, nor does she inject her own opinion or interpret those of others, thus making options (C) and (D) also incorrect.

3. **(D)** Be careful when reading this question because it is asking which of the following does _not_ lead to loneliness and isolation. Options (A), (B), and (C) are all stated in the audio ("vivir solo," "no dotar de buena salud," and "insolvencia económica"). There is nothing that mentions family strife or conflict that leads to this isolation. Note, the audio mentions "situaciones de duelo," which is a good idiomatic expression to know. It means *grief*, as in the emotion that one feels following the death of a loved one.

4. **(A)** This answer is an example of testing to see if the listener is focusing on the idea being communicated over the words being used. The audio states that of all the elderly who live alone, "la mayoría son mujeres", which means that the minority are men. Read carefully what each answer is saying because options (B) and (C) cannot be substantiated by the audio text, and option (D) is clearly incorrect, as the audio states that 42% of the elderly who live alone are older than 85.

5. **(B)** The audio states the following: ". . . se ha producido un aumento en el número de hogares unipersonales . . . ," which is the same idea that option (B) communicates using different words. Although some or all the information presented in options (A), (C), and (D) could be true, there is nothing in the audio to substantiate these claims, therefore making them incorrect choices.

6. **(C)** The answer to this question largely rests on whether or not you understood the word "mensual," meaning *month*, which would automatically eliminate options (A) and (B) from contention. The audio continues to say, "una visita . . . y en algunos casos, estas visitas no existen," making option (D) incorrect because most get visitors, albeit infrequently.

7. **(A)** Toward the end of the recording, the speaker mentions that ". . . esta situación se puede incrementar a tenor [*in relation*] de las expectativas demográficas . . . ," which implies that in the future, social demographics will be comprised of more elderly people. There is nothing in the audio to substantiate options (C) and (D), and, although the statement made in option (B) is partially correct, there is nothing in the audio to say that all of those who live alone suffer from these problems, nor is it clear how this is a social problem.

8. **(A)** Option (A) is the clear answer to this question because it is the one that most directly addresses the issue that the audio presents. If one were to "adopt" an elderly person, that means that they would be establishing a relationship with that person, thus alleviating his/her feeling of loneliness. Option (B) is self-serving, for it will help someone who is not yet retired save money, but it does not address those who are currently in need. Option (C) is too general in nature because "injusticia social" can cover multiple areas, including political issues, problems with education, economic issues, etc. Option (D) is also incorrect because, although it promotes exercise and health benefits, it is unclear whether there is a social aspect of this program, for many exercises can be done alone at home.

SELECCIÓN #3

1. **(B)** The audio throughout details who can vote, what identification is needed, and some information regarding access to voting. All these are best categorized as some of the citizen's rights to vote. There is nothing in the audio text to suggest that what is described is somehow different than in the past, making option (C) incorrect, and there is also nothing indicating that the audio is trying to persuade its audience, thus making options (A) and (D) incorrect.

2. **(C)** Most of the answer options for this question look similar, but they communicate different ideas. The audio clearly states that voters must have had their 18th birthday by the time they vote, making option (C) the correct choice. Options (A) and (D) are saying that only those who have birthdays on the day of voting can vote, while option (B) is saying that one has to be older than 18 in order to vote.

3. **(A)** Remember that the adjective *actual* is a false cognate, and means *current* or *up to date*, which is what *vigente* also means. Even if you forgot this, option (A) is still the best option because the other ones don't make common sense. One would expect any document to be real and not fake, making option (B) incorrect, and common sense also says that, in order to vote, a person would need a valid identification document issued by the country in which he is voting and that the document pertains to that person and not to someone else, thus making options (C) and (D) also incorrect.

4. **(D)** The audio states that the voting tables must begin operating at 8:00am and close at 18:00 hours, which is 6:00pm. The audio also states that, as an exception, tables can open at 9:00am or 10:00am, but those are outlier cases and not the norm.

5. **(C)** When answering these types of questions, remember to select the option that is both logical within the context and whose answer was not already given in the text. In this case, the audio already addresses how immigrants and expatriates can vote, as well as access to voting for those with disabilities, thus making options (A), (B), and (D) incorrect. The audio does not mention whether or not there is a designated voting location for voters, making option (C) a logical choice.

SELECCIÓN #4

1. **(C)** You can tell at the very end of the recording that this is advertising the *Día internacional de la juventud*, which makes option (C) the best answer. Although there is some rapping in the recording, this is not a song, therefore eliminating option (A), and this is definitely not a news report, making option (B) also incorrect. Option (D) is incorrect because, although parts of this recording are like a play, it is not a theater production.

2. **(A)** Both the lady and the man at the beginning of the recording are quite critical of the clothing, piercings, and tattoos of the young man they are looking at. Options (B) and (C) are incorrect because they both refer to positive emotions (*asombro* means surprise or admiration, *apoyo* means support), and they are definitely not apathetic, making option (D) also incorrect.

3. **(B)** The recurring critique from the man and the woman at the beginning and the defense from the rappers all relate to his clothing and style. The young man being critiqued is indeed a skater, but skating itself is never being targeted, therefore making option (A) incorrect. There is nothing in the audio to suggest that his way of speaking is being criticized, thus eliminating option (C), and, although you, the listener, may not like his rapping, there is nothing in the audio that suggests that his musical taste is being criticized, which takes option (D) off the table.

4. **(B)** Around the one minute mark, the youth says that others should *ser más abiertos, tratar de comprender mejor*, in other words, not reject what others enjoy to do or their style. Option (A) is incorrect because the critique is never about his choice of sport, and he mentions his sport as an example of something that he enjoys, but not that it is something that needs to be respected. Options (C) and (D) are incorrect because there is nothing in the audio to support them.

5. **(D)** This is a tough question if you have trouble understanding sayings or proverbs. However, you should be able to identify the meaning of option (D) because its literal translation is *Don't judge a book by its cover*. This saying communicates the same message of the recording because it asks others to not critique the youth simply because they have a different style, and it is what's inside that counts. If you are unfamiliar with the other sayings in the list, they mean *Show me who your friends are, and I'll tell you who you are* (option (A)), *Idleness is the mother of all vices* (option (B)), and *Clothes make the man* (option (C)). It is a good idea to learn a few proverbs and sayings in Spanish, because using them appropriately in your communicative tasks as part of your topic development can really help elevate your overall performance.

SELECCIÓN #5

1. **(B)** The purpose of this interview is to show how *radios campesinas* (rural radio stations) are benefitting the audience they serve. Option (A) is incorrect because the interview is not trying to promote or advertise (*promocionar*), but is to rather inform about these radio stations. Option (C) is also incorrect because the word "proponer" implies that the interview has another agenda beyond informing, and (D) is incorrect because there is nothing in the audio to suggest that rural radio stations are becoming more commercial.

2. **(B)** Professor Rivadeneyra states that these stations serve a vast territory, and he also mentions that some of these communities live in the Andes mountains, therefore making (B) the best answer. Options (A), (C), and (D) are incorrect because there is never any reference to how many people in these communities listen to the radio nor of their social status or of their interests.

3. **(D)** Be careful when reading this question because there are three correct answers, and you are asked to identify the one that is *not* correct. The audio mentions the first three options as being roles that community radios play, but never mentions option (D).

4. **(C)** In this question, you have to use context to figure out the best meaning of the word *aliado* (ally). Option (C) is the best answer because, just like the question beforehand, community radio provides information and knowledge that can help these communities better manage their conditions and environments. Option (A) is not correct because there is no reference to whether or not listeners feel less isolated by listening to the radio, or whether they listen to it for entertainment purposes, making option (B) also incorrect. Option (D) is incorrect because there is never any mention that these radio stations don't provide economic opportunities to their listeners.

5. **(C)** The audio states that the communities that are most affected are those 3,500 meters above sea level (*m. s. n. m.* means *metros sobre nivel del mar*). Don't be distracted by words such as *mar*, which may lead you to select incorrect option (A).

6. **(A)** The speaker mentions this information at least twice in the audio, and the idea is that the radio programs help teach communities how to learn how to adapt (*adaptarse*) to a changing climate (*clima cambiante*). Note how the form of words is different in the answer than was used in the audio. This is done to see if you are listening for specific words or listening to the whole idea. If you were only listening for specific words, you may have selected one of the other options, which contain specific words from the audio (*económico, cambio climático*) but do not communicate ideas that are stated in the audio text.

7. **(A)** The speaker highlights the importance of nutrition for expectant mothers and how this will have a positive impact on the gestation, birth, and childrearing during the first few months. Options (B) and (D) are incorrect because, although the temptation exists to deduce that people who live in rural areas may likely have less access to medical care and/or resources, and this could result in poor nutrition, there is nothing in the audio that explicitly states this to be true. Remember that the argument could also be made that because they live in rural areas, their nutrition is actually healthier because they eat a lot of vegetables, grains, fruits, etc. Always validate your answers with the text. Finally, option (C) is a little tricky. It is incorrect because the printed answer says that the mother has to nourish herself during her first three years of life, but the audio says that the mother has to nourish herself during the first three years of her *baby's* life.

8. **(B)** When you see questions like these, you have to pick the response whose answer was not already given in the audio or print text. There is never any mention as to how these community radio stations are funded. Are they government funded? Do volunteers run these radio stations? Do they rely on revenue from advertising like the big stations? All other questions have already been answered in the audio text. Option (A) was answered at the end (*La radio saludable*), option (C) was answered when talking about

the *sistema de alerta temprana* and several weather conditions were mentioned, and option (D) was answered throughout the interview where several countries, including Bolivia, Perú, and Colombia, were mentioned.

SELECCIÓN #6

1. **(C)** The purpose of this audio is to give a quick overview of Arnedo, a city in La Rioja. Since this overview is done via audio, it can also be considered a virtual tour. Some may be enticed to select option (B) because the introduction states that the series is dedicated to several towns in La Rioja. But note that the question asks about this particular audio, not the series, therefore making option (B) incorrect. Options (A) and (D) are very similar, and, although one who listens to this audio may want to take a vacation and possibly take it to La Rioja, that is a secondary benefit of the audio, and not its primary purpose.

2. **(A)** The audio mentions the "simbiosis perfecta entre modernidad y tradición" (fusion of modernity and tradition), making option (A) a clear choice. Option (B) is incorrect because, although different civilizations occupied the area at one time, there is nothing in the audio to suggest that the town's population today is comprised of many different races. There is nothing in the audio that refers to cultural customs, and, although it mentions the shoe industry (*industria de calzado*) several times, the shoe industry is not a custom, therefore making option (C) incorrect. Option (D) is incorrect because, although Arnedo has a strong shoe industry, there is no mention of its arts scene. Most museums mentioned showcase items extracted from the local mines (*fósiles y minerales*) and archeological sites, as well as the evolution of the shoe industry.

3. **(B)** This is the clear option not only because the audio directly states it (*una ciudad cuyo crecimiento ha ido paralelo al desarrollo de una notable industria del calzado*), but also because there are museums dedicated to this craft, and it is an important part of the industry today.

4. **(B)** The audio states that the church is admired for its beauty and structural originality ("belleza y originalidad constructiva"), thus making option (B) the clear choice. Don't forget that the word "tamaño" means *size* and "parroquiano" means *patron* or *parishioner*, as in a member of a local church.

5. **(C)** When talking about the caves, the audio gives three bits of information: (1) their location (in the mountain behind the church), (2) their use today (as *bodegas*, or wine cellars), and (3) their archaeological importance (because people used to live in them). Based on the last bit of information, one can infer that those people were from ancient civilizations, therefore making option (C) the best answer.

6. **(A)** There are two important clues in the audio that this is the correct answer. They are "postre" (dessert) and "¡Buen provecho!" (enjoy your meal!). Don't be distracted by the word "típico" in both the recording and in option (B). Just because the same word is used, it does not mean that it is the correct answer.

7. **(D)** When answering hypothetical questions such as these, remember to select the most logical and appropriate response. The audio highlights some of the cultural, historical, and food attractions of this area, and, although options (A), (B), and (C) may seem like appropriate questions, they have already been answered in the audio (the audio states

that the shoe industry has been around since the 11th century, the *fardelejo* is from Arab origin, and at the beginning of the audio it states that Arnedo is located 48 km from the capital of La Rioja). Option (D) is a logical question because a visitor to the town may also want to know if there are any outdoor activities that can be enjoyed.

SELECCIÓN #7

1. **(B)** This is the best answer because it includes all aspects of the presentation. Although the speaker uses *santería* in Cuba as an example, this religion is also practiced in other areas of Central and South America, particularly in areas that border the Caribbean. Options (A) and (C) are incorrect because they ignore the combination of cultures that helped form *santería*. Option (D) is incorrect because the speaker never criticizes the religion, but rather gives an honest (and personal) description of it.

2. **(A)** *Santería* is a result of syncretism between African religions and Catholic beliefs when slaves from Africa were brought to the island of Cuba to work in the sugarcane fields. Option (B) is incorrect because it suggests that African slaves created this religion upon arriving in the new world, which is not entirely correct since the current religion is partially based on ideas and practices that originated in Africa. This is the same reason option (D) is incorrect. It ignores the African influence found in the religion. Finally, option (C) is incorrect because the idea that *santería* is problematic is a matter of opinion, not fact. The speaker only gives one example that is considered problematic, but then goes on to discount this notion.

3. **(A)** This answer may have been more difficult if you did not know the meaning of the word *idólatra* (idolatry, or the worshiping of idols). The speaker in the audio makes reference to how the religions from Africa worship rocks (*piedras*), tools (*herramientas*), and sea shells (*caracol)*, which are types of idols. The Catholics, on the other hand, revere God through images, not the images themselves.

4. **(B)** The speaker makes direct reference to how the *santeros* resolve issues through faith and alchemy, which is his way of referring to specific procedures and actions that the *santeros* use. Options (A), (C), and (D) are incorrect because it is not the *santeros'* desire to heal or whether or not they can solve all problems or that they have faith that is problematic to others, but rather their actual actions.

5. **(C)** The speaker gives only one example of the use of "alchemy" in *santería*, and that is the *baño de florecimiento*, which we learn is a bath with many herbs, such as *salvia* (sage), *menta* (mint), and *lavanda* (lavender). Option (A) is incorrect because the speaker never mentions multiple jobs, but only gives one example, and it is not of a job, but of an actual treatment. Option (B) is not correct because the audio never makes reference to how the *santeros* cleanse themselves. You may have chosen this answer by focusing on *lavarse*, but remember that this is a reflexive verb and, therefore, refers back to the subject. The example given in the audio is how *santeros* help others. Finally, option (D) is incorrect because, although the speaker does mention negative influences, they are an example of the symptom that the alchemy seeks to cure, not a definition of the alchemy itself.

6. **(B)** Remember that *baño* means bath and, as explained in the previous answer, a *baño de florecimiento* is a bath with many herbs, which is most like a homeopathic procedure as the speaker himself states (*"situaciones de homeopatía"*). Option (A) is incorrect

because it is not a religious rite or ceremony, but rather a treatment (*tratamiento*). Option (C) is incorrect because it is not a drink, but rather a bath, and option (D) is incorrect because the bath itself is not a negative influence, but rather serves to rid one of negative influences.

7. **(A)** A pagan religion is a non-monotheistic religion, meaning that it involves belief in more than one deity. Since *santería* includes the devotion to idols, this makes option (A) the best answer. Option (B) is incorrect because faith is indeed important in *santería*. There is nothing in the audio to support option (C), and the word *astro* is only mentioned once at the end in another context. There is never any mention in the audio as to how many people in Cuba practice *santería*, therefore making option (D) incorrect.

8. **(B)** This question asks you to look at *how* the speaker delivers his message. He does give a brief explanation as to the origins of *santería*, but then gives specific examples of a practice that is done in *santería*. The speaker never quotes another *santero*, thus making option (A) incorrect, and he does not present the information in a list form, making option (C) also incorrect. Be careful with option (D), for, although the speaker does give some historical background as to the origins of *santería*, he never mentions any specific historical event (*acontecimiento*) nor how it continues to influence *santería* today.

SELECCIÓN #8

1. **(D)** The story, although based in fact, is a legend because it (1) includes supernatural elements, such as an "espíritu guardián" that comes to speak to Tecún Umán and (2) at the end uses the story to teach a lesson, which is why the Quetzal bird has a red chest. One might argue that option (C) is also a possibility, but the reason it is not the *best* answer is that "cuentos" tend to be a lot longer and don't have the purpose of teaching a lesson or explaining a natural phenomenon.

2. **(B)** It is clear from the words such as "conquistador" and "conquista" that this story takes place during the colonization of the Americas, therefore making option (B) the correct answer. Option (A) is incorrect because the 15th century comprises the years 1400–1499, and since the Americas were discovered in October of 1492, it is highly unlikely that a full-scale colonization effort was organized in less than seven years.

3. **(C)** The first part of the audio speaks to the imposing figure of don Pedro riding his horse. Since horses were foreign animals to this land, the sight of don Pedro approaching was what would have caused Tecún Umán to feel some fear, therefore making option (C) the best answer. One could argue that option (B) could also be a possibility, but the size of the Spanish army is not mentioned until quite a bit later in the audio, so it is not the best answer.

4. **(A)** Don Pedro asks Tecún Umán to surrender (*rendirse*) several times and asks him to accept his destiny. One can infer that this destiny is the inevitable victory that the Spanish army would have, therefore making option (A) the best answer. Option (B) is incorrect because the audio never mentions how many natives die in battle, and option (C) is incorrect because the Spanish eventually win, not lose. Option (D) is incorrect because don Pedro wants Tecún Umán to surrender, not engage in battle.

5. **(B)** Just as Tecún Umán had a guardian spirit in the form of the Quetzal bird that lands on his shoulder, he felt that the horse contained the spirit of its rider, or *jinete*. When Tecún Umán kills don Pedro's horse but don Pedro does not die, Tecún Umán is

surprised to realize that the horse is simply an animal, not the guardian spirit, therefore making option (B) the correct answer. If you did not know what the word *jinete* meant, you may have had some difficulty with this question. A good strategy when you find yourself in this situation is to eliminate the other options one by one. Option (A) is incorrect because it implies that the horse was stronger than it really was. Tecún Umán kills the horse pretty quickly, so this statement is untrue. Option (C) is incorrect because it would not surprise Tecún Umán that he killed the horse since it was the horse he was aiming for all along. Finally, Option (D) is incorrect because there is really nothing in the audio to substantiate it. The Spaniards clearly state that God is on their side, so Tecún Umán clearly knew that they believed in at least a god.

6. **(C)** The mistake of Tecún Umán thinking that the horse and rider were spiritually connected cost him his life. It was at the moment of realization when ". . . la lanza de don Pedro le atravesó directamente en su corazón . . ." (don Pedro's spear went straight through Tecún Umán's heart).

7. **(B)** The phenomenon this legend teaches is why a certain bird, the Quetzal, has a red chest. Earlier in the audio you meet the Quetzal, for it is the ". . . espíritu guardián con la forma del ave de Quetzal . . . ," so when they mention the Quetzal at the end, you should already know that it is a bird (*ave*). Don't be scared of the word "endémico." It means *endemic* or *local to particular region*. Even if you do not know what "endemic" means, you still have enough information to select it as the correct choice. Don't be tempted to choose answers simply because they contain many words that are mentioned in the audio text, as is the case with Option (C). Focus on whether or not the idea being communicated is correct.

Expansión

Now that you have learned about a legendary hero from Guatemala, can you think of a legendary hero from your own community? You may also want to consider more fictional figures, such as Paul Bunyan, if you are a United States resident. Do you know of landmarks in the United States that were "built" by Paul Bunyan? If you don't, you may want to research this and other legends and internalize key words so that you can tell these stories in Spanish. This is the type of practice that will pay huge dividends on the oral presentation portion of the exam.

SELECCIÓN #9

1. **(C)** The purpose of this audio is to inform, not persuade, so you can easily eliminate option (D) from contention. The only question is whether it is presenting problems or showing what the area is doing to combat these problems. Since the speakers talk about the development of infrastructure over the past fifty years and, although they certainly could use more, it is enough to prove that this audio is showing the system in place and how it works. Option (A) is not the best answer, for it suggests that there are only challenges, and the audio clearly provides examples of systems in place that, although not perfect, do address many of the challenges.

2. **(B)** Liz Riley says that there has been ". . . inversión significativa en infraestructura nueva . . ." and that the damages caused by natural phenomena have impacted ". . . la infraestructura, no tanto a la pérdida de vidas . . ." (with exception of Haiti).

3. **(B)** The speaker says that the Caribbean is one of the best-prepared regions because of their ". . . mecanismo intergubernamental de coordinación de respuesta . . ." where all countries that participate can take advantage of the resources of each country. This means that several countries work well with each other to minimize the effects that natural disasters can have.

4. **(A)** The speaker uses the earthquake in Haiti to point out the vulnerabilities in some cities in the region, where she says that many of the basic services are located. If a natural disaster takes out a city, then the services also will be destroyed, so they have to come up with plans to minimize this impact.

5. **(B)** Liz Riley provides this information at the very end of the interview, when she says, "En momentos de crisis el liderazgo y la cohesión de los dirigentes en un frente unido para dirigir al pueblo es fundamental." The word *gestionar* in the question means to manage, and one can see that the speaker believes that there has to be a coordinated effort between multiple entities to help in a time of crisis.

6. **(C)** Since the audio deals with how to minimize the effects of loss of life during a natural disaster, option (C) is the only publication that suggests it is on the same topic. A good word to learn is *mitigar*, which means to minimize.

SELECCIÓN #10

1. **(C)** The majority of the audio is spent giving recommendations about what travelers need to do in order to ensure that they stay healthy. Although a list of diseases and illnesses are mentioned at the beginning, the bulk of the audio is spent on how to avoid these.

2. **(D)** The word *vacuna* means vaccine, and the doctor says that the vaccine needs to be administered ". . . con suficiente antelación . . . entre uno o dos meses antes del viaje. . . ."

3. **(C)** In the second half of the audio, the doctor says that one needs to go to the doctor "previamente al viaje" and ". . . al mínimo momento en que puedas tener algún tipo de simtomatología . . . ," in other words, the moment one has any symptom.

4. **(A)** The purpose of the audio is not to scare the listener, but rather to give some tips that can be used to minimize one becoming sick while visiting an exotic location. Options (B) and (D) focus more on the illnesses, and not preventative measures, so they are not the best options. Option (C) is not the best choice either because the audio gives advice on how to avoid all illnesses in general, not specific ones.

5. **(C)** When answering these types of questions, always consider what is most appropriate. Options (A), (B), and (D) are incorrect because the doctor has already answered them.

SELECCIÓN #11

1. **(C)** As you can tell from the audio, this event is not aimed at any particular age group or demographic. Even though young people will probably be more attracted to it, the purpose of the audio is to talk about the *Tomatina* and its history. Therefore, it is most likely directed to anyone interested in visiting this part of Spain.

2. **(A)** The celebration as it is known today began in 1945, which is relatively recent considering Spain as a country that has been around for over 500 years (since its unification, of course).

3. **(C)** Although the celebration started as a protest, it is now a fun event, with no additional intent other than to provide entertainment for locals and tourists alike.

4. **(C)** In the middle of the audio, the speaker mentions how a fight broke out because a young man wanted to be a part of a parade, and he hit some of the people in the parade. This led to a bigger fight, and someone decided to use vegetables as ammunition, and the rest is history.

5. **(A)** The audio continues by saying how a group of people congregated the next year at the same spot with "cajones de tomates," but that the government did not approve and, year after year, "prohibía la batalla vegetal."

6. **(B)** Toward the end of the audio, the speaker mentions a number of additional activities that take place in today's festival. These include "carreras de sacos" (sack races) and "cucañas" (having to climb to the top of a greasy pole).

7. **(C)** When selecting a publication on the festival, try to find one that deals with the spirit of the festivity today. The third publication is on traditional games in the Valencia community, where the *Tomatina* takes place. This is the best option because it clearly deals with the topic. Don't be tempted to pick option (A), because although tomatoes are used, they certainly should not be considered weapons of mass destruction. Options (B) and (D) seem to deal with tomatoes as a food item, not as part of a celebration.

SELECCIÓN #12

1. **(B)** Both the introduction to the audio and the majority of the audio itself indicate that this piece is about becoming a better writer. The speaker in the audio does mention several times that one can become a professional, but also explicitly states that becoming a professional writer "... no debería ser su meta" (should not be your goal).

2. **(B)** At the beginning of the audio, the speaker says that many don't like his answers because they either look for "... una solución rápida ..." or "... una fórmula mágica ...." Therefore, you can safely assume that the speaker believes that becoming a better writer is a long process.

3. **(C)** The speaker urges one to keep reading and writing, and at one point says that he has never met a professional writer who said that he or she has learned enough and could not get better ("... aprendí suficiente. Más no puedo mejorar.").

4. **(B)** At the end of the audio, the speakers says, "... cuanto más fortalezca su escritura, más fácil será alcanzar la segunda meta ...," and *la segunda meta* is to find your market or readership. Although the speaker does mention that writers may not get published because of the theme they chose to write about, he does not suggest that writers adapt their themes to their public, but rather continue to try and find their own voice, and the readers will come.

5. **(D)** This presentation is solely based on the speaker's own experiences. The only time he gives some sort of quote ("... aprendí suficiente. Más no puedo mejorar.") is one he invents because he said that he never heard anyone say that to him.

PART FOUR
Writing Skills

General Considerations

6

DESCRIPTIONS OF THE WRITING TASKS OF THE EXAM

The writing portion of the exam is divided into two tasks: Task 1: Email Reply and Task 2: Argumentative Essay. Both types of responses require that you showcase your ability to communicate effectively in Spanish on the assigned task. In Task 1: Email Reply, your main objective is to maintain a formal exchange. For Task 2: Argumentative Essay you will have to clearly present and defend your point of view about a question printed in your test book.

SCORING THE WRITING TASKS

The grading of the writing samples is holistic, meaning that they are analyzed as a whole. No specific item or aspect of language has any point value. Rankings proceed along a continuum from strong, good, fair, weak, and poor. The difference between each level largely hinges on your treatment of the topic within the context of the task and on language use. A common misconception is that if you can write well in Spanish, you will score well on this portion of the exam. However, that is only true if what you write is relevant within the context of the task. Therefore, before putting pen to paper, you need to clearly understand the task. Here are some strategies when approaching the writing portions of the exam:

- Read the introduction and understand the instructions.
- Address the task assigned as fully as you can.
- Use a formal tone throughout. This not only includes the choice of register, but also choice of ideas. *What* you say is as important as *how* you say it.
- Time yourself as you write. Your goal for Task 1: Email Reply is to write for 10 minutes. Your goal for Task 2: Argumentative Essay is to write for 35 minutes. This will give you enough time to proofread what you write.
- Always proofread your writings. Look for mistakes with language use but more importantly ensure that your ideas are clearly understood by an unsympathetic reader.

Section II, Part A—Task 1: Email Reply

7

The first part of Section II is the Interpersonal Writing task. For this task you are to write a formal response to an email. In your test book, you will be given an email and a brief description of the reason you received this email. You then have 15 minutes to read the email and respond. In your response, you have to do the following:

- Write a response that clearly maintains the exchange
- Use a formal tone throughout
- Answer all questions asked in the original email
- Ask more information about something mentioned in the original message or is relevant to the topic of the message.

SCORING YOUR EMAIL

Your score will be based on how well you are able to accomplish this task and can roughly be broken into the following categories:

1. **What you were able to do.**

   - Did you maintain the exchange?
   - Did you answer all questions and elaborate on your answers?
   - Did you ask a question relating to the topic?
   - Did you use a formal tone throughout?

2. **How you were able to do it.**

   - Is your response fully comprehensible?
   - Did your use of language show some sophistication?
   - Is your response well organized?

If you answered yes to all the above questions, your performance on this section likely will score in the high range. There are some criteria that are more important than others. For example, a response that includes sophisticated language but fails to maintain the exchange will earn a low score. This usually happens when the student misunderstands something in the original message, and this causes a response that is not entirely on task. Likewise a response in which the student attempts to maintain the exchange but whose language ability makes the reply mostly incomprehensible will also earn a low score.

A great way to understand how you will be evaluated is to put yourself in the shoes of the recipient. Imagine that you are the person who sent the original printed in the test and you receive the response. Does it address all your questions and concerns? Is the tone appropriate? Did the student put heart and soul into the response? If the email does all this, then you are on the path to scoring a "5".

STRATEGIES FOR TASK 1: EMAIL REPLY

The following is a guideline about how you should budget your time.

Read the introduction and the mail (2 to 3 minutes).

- Identify who sent this email and why.
- Identify the questions you need to answer. Underline them so that you can refer back to them quickly.
- Make note of any information that is mentioned that you could ask for more details about.
- Make note of any cultural references in the original message (origin of the author, and so on).

Writing your reply (8 to 10 minutes).

- Use the formal register throughout your response.
- Structure your response correctly (greeting, opening, body, closing, goodbye).
- Respond to all the questions being asked and elaborate briefly on your responses.
- Request more information about something that was mentioned or about something related to the theme.
- Vary your vocabulary.
- Keep your ideas simple and clear.
- Include a variety of tenses and/or moods, if appropriate. Do not try to force the use of different tenses or moods, as this will count against you if it makes your response confusing.
- If you make a mistake, draw a line through it and keep writing.

After you finish writing (2 to 5 minutes)

- Proofread your reply to make sure that . . .

  - . . . you have addressed all the elements in the email, including asking for more details;
  - . . . you have used a variety of vocabulary;
  - . . . your ideas are clear and concise; and
  - . . . you used correct orthography, punctuation, and paragraphing.

WRITING YOUR EMAIL

As you prepare to write your email, you need to consider how the message should be structured. A good email should be divided into the following 5 sections:

1. **GREETING.** Should be appropriate for a formal correspondence.
2. **OPENING.** These are one or two sentences in which you acknowledge receipt of the message and convey any feelings and emotions from having read this message and/or in which you make a general comment related to the topic.

3. **BODY.** This is the bulk of your response. Answer the questions asked in the original email and elaborate briefly on each answer. Be creative with your elaboration but make sure that the ideas you write are appropriate for a formal situation. Include a question that is relevant and appropriate within the context.
4. **CLOSING.** This is one or two sentences in which you again express your gratitude to the recipient of the email, reiterate some of the information mentioned in the body, and/or express that you look forward to hearing back from this person soon.
5. **GOODBYE.** Should be appropriate for a formal correspondence.

Here are a few examples of simple greetings, openings closings, and goodbyes appropriate for a formal situation.

Formal greetings	Opening comments
■ Estimado(a) Señor(a) ■ Buenos días, Señor(a)	■ Le agradezco mucho por su mensaje. ■ Espero que todo esté bien con usted.

Closing comments	Formal goodbyes
■ Muchas gracias por su amable atención. ■ Quedo a la espera de su respuesta. ■ Quedo a su disposición para facilitarle cualquier otra información.	■ Le saluda cordialmente ■ Atentamente ■ Respetuosamente

In addition to ensuring that your language use is appropriate for a formal correspondence, you also need to pay attention to organization of thought. This is where transitions can be useful and they should be incorporated in your response. Here are some useful transitions that you can use often in your email replies:

Uses of transitions	Examples	
To introduce an idea	*Para empezar . . .*	*En primer lugar . . .*
To add to ideas	*Además . . .*	*También . . .*
To contrast ideas	*En cambio . . .* *No obstante . . .*	*Por otro lado . . .* *Sin embargo . . .*
To change topic	*Con respecto a . . .*	*En cuanto a . . .*
To show effect	*Como resultado . . .* *Debido a lo anterior . . .* *Entonces . . .*	*Por consiguiente . . .* *Por eso . . .* *Por esa razón . . .*
To give examples	*Por ejemplo . . .*	*En particular . . .*
To finalize	*Finalmente*	*Para concluir*

You should practice incorporating transitions in all your speaking and writing activities. Often you will find that you can easily use 4–5 in a simple email response. They will help you organize your thoughts and make your response sound more sophisticated.

SAMPLE EMAIL REPLY

DIRECTIONS: You will write a reply to an email that you received. You have 15 minutes to read the message and write your reply.

Your reply should include an appropriate greeting and closing and should answer all the questions and requests in the original message. In addition, your reply should ask for more details about something that was mentioned in the message. You should use a formal tone in your response.

Vas a escribir una respuesta a un mensaje de correo electrónico. Tienes 15 minutos para leer el mensaje y escribir tu respuesta.

Tu respuesta debe incluir un saludo y despedida apropiada y contestar a todas las preguntas y peticiones del mensaje original. También tu respuesta debe pedir más información de algo mencionado en el mensaje original. Debes usar el tono formal en tu respuesta.

Tema curricular: Las identidades personales y públicas

Este mensaje electrónico es de María José Martínez Vargas, directora de un programa a que has solicitado. Te escribe para informarte que has sido seleccionado finalista.

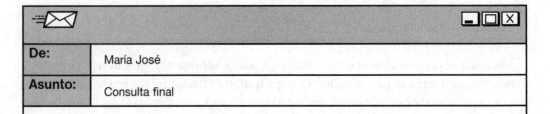

De:	María José
Asunto:	Consulta final

Apreciado/a candidato/a,

Me complace mucho comunicarle que ha pasado a la última fase de nuestro proceso de selección. Hemos recibido solicitudes de muchos candidatos, y es un gran honor simplemente poder llegar hasta este punto. Como ya sabrá, nuestro proyecto este verano tiene la meta de armar una exposición de los grandes héroes y su influencia la cultura e identidad de un país que será expuesta en el museo municipal. Es un proyecto ambicioso, por eso necesitamos un equipo dedicado y motivado.

Para poder ayudarnos con la finalización de la selección de candidatos, favor de contestar las siguientes preguntas:

1. ¿Quién es su héroe o heroína nacional favorito/a y por qué le gusta tanto?

2. Si fuera seleccionado/a, ¿cómo piensa usted incluir a esta persona en nuestra exposición?

Agradezco de antemano su amable atención a esta petición.

Respetuosamente,

María José Martínez Vargas

Directora

Response

By now you should know well the directions of this task, which are the following:

1. Reply to the email
2. Answer all questions asked
3. Ask an appropriate question related to the topic
4. Use a formal tone

The first step in your response is to read the introduction. This is a crucial step because it gives you the context of the correspondence. For this email, we learn the following important information:

1. You have applied for this position (so it is something of obvious interest to you).
2. You have _not_ received the position but are a finalist for it.
3. The person who is writing to you is the director of the program, and she is female.

You need to be aware of all this information because it will help you craft your response. Remember, you don't want to give the impression that you have already won the job, for this won't be maintaining the exchange. You also need to imagine that you _really_ want the job, so your response needs to show that you are a motivated candidate who wants this position.

As you begin to put pen to paper, you need to think quickly about how you will answer the questions she has asked. In her email, María José wants to know the following:

1. Who is your favorite national hero and why?
2. How do you plan on showcasing this person at the exposition?

Since the term "hero" can be vague, you have the freedom to pick anyone. It can be a sports hero, a historical figure, and so on. It really does not matter whether the person you select is indeed your favorite hero in real life; the most important part is that you convey that this person is your favorite hero in your response.

The next part is to figure out how you would include this figure in the exposition. You will have to be creative here, but anything that would be appropriate in a museum setting could work.

The last part is to identify something that you may need to know more about. In this email, there are several questions that you could ask. Here are a few:

1. How many candidates are finalists?
2. When will the exposition take place?
3. How long will the exposition last?
4. How many people will form the team?
5. What types of resources will be available to assemble the exposition?
6. Is this a paid position?
7. When will the selected candidates be announced?
8. When in the summer is the exposition?

Once you have identified the questions you need to answer and thought of a question that you could ask, it is time to write your response. The first step is to address the recipient appropriately, which can be tricky sometimes because, as in this case, the person to whom you are writing has four names. In Spanish cultures, people generally have two last names: the first is the paternal last name and the second is the mother's maiden name. It is customary to only use the paternal last name, which in this case would be Martínez. However, if you are unsure, you could simply write her whole name out or simply refer to her as _directora_, which is the title she uses at the end of her email.

Sample Response

Here is what a sample response could look like:

Estimada Directora,

En primer lugar quisiera agradecerle por haberme seleccionado como finalista. Estoy muy emocionado saber que tengo la oportunidad de participar en esta fantástica exposición.

Para contestar a sus preguntas, de niño, siempre me han fascinado los grandes héroes nacionales, pero si fuera de solamente escoger uno, sería José Martí. Me fascina tanto porque a través de su literatura ayudó a crear una identidad cubana, que sirvió de fuerza unificadora para la gente de la isla. También, murió en batalla tratando de liberar su país de los españoles.

En la exposición, me gustaría incorporar ejemplos de su literatura para mostrar cómo sirvió para crear esta identidad nacional. Sería interesante incorporar partes de sus Versos Sencillos, y crear talleres donde los visitantes pueden mejor comprender su obra y formar versos originales que definan su propia identidad cultural.

Me emociona muchísimo saber que soy finalista. ¿Sabe usted cuándo van a seleccionar al solicitante ganador?

Muchísimas gracias otra vez por correspondencia, y quedo a su disposición para facilitarle cualquier otra información.

Atentamente,

Javier Benavidez

As you look over this response, make note of the following:

1. The organization of the response into the five distinct portions (greeting, opening, body, closing, goodbye)
2. Use of transitions (*En primer lugar . . .*, *Para contestar a sus preguntas . . .*, *También . . .*)
3. Elaboration following the answer of each question
4. Use of formal tone throughout
5. Use of a variety of verb moods and tenses (present, preterit, conditional, imperfect subjunctive)

Also note what is *not* in the response, such as your email address or the date. These elements are not required for this task and are simply a waste of time.

EMAIL REPLY #1

Tema curricular: Los desafíos mundiales

Este mensaje electrónico es del señor Javier Gaitán, el presidente del Club Planeta Verde. Él está planeando publicar un informe sobre la situación del medio ambiente. Has recibido este mensaje porque vives en la comunidad en que se ubica este club.

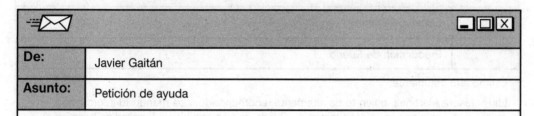

De:	Javier Gaitán
Asunto:	Petición de ayuda

Apreciado/a participante,

Nuestro club está preparando un informe especial sobre la situación del medio ambiente en nuestra comunidad. El tema será una investigación sobre la consciencia general en cuanto a temas relacionados con el medio ambiente. Esperamos poder publicar nuestro informe para el mes que viene.

El informe incluirá información obtenida de una variedad de fuentes, y consiguiente les estamos escribiendo a todos los miembros de nuestra comunidad para pedirles que nos ayuden con este proyecto. ¿Le gustaría ayudarnos? Si desea participar, por favor conteste las siguientes preguntas:

☼ ¿Está preocupado por la conservación del medio ambiente? ¿Por qué?

☼ ¿Está usted dispuesto/a a modificar su forma de vida y su bienestar para conservar el planeta? ¿Por qué?

Le rogamos que conteste estas preguntas a la mayor brevedad posible, y le damos las gracias de antemano por su ayuda.

Atentamente,

Javier Gaitán

Presidente
Club Planeta Verde

EMAIL REPLY #2

Tema curricular: La belleza y la estética

Este mensaje te lo envió el Profesor Gutiérrez, profesor de teatro de tu escuela. Te escribe porque quiere hacerte encargo del decorado para la obra de teatro *Sueño*, que va a estrenar el próximo mes.

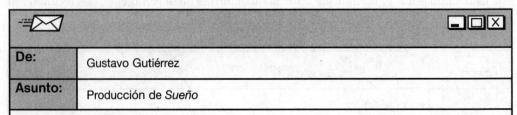

De:	Gustavo Gutiérrez
Asunto:	Producción de *Sueño*

Estimado/a estudiante,

La Profesora Martínez, quien te ha altamente recomendado, nos mandó tu información, y quiero que participes en la producción de *Sueño* el mes que viene. La obra se basa en el drama del siglo XVII *La vida es sueño* de Calderón de la Barca. Estamos muy emocionados por esta producción, y pensamos que va a ser un exitazo.

Como sabes, crear el decorado es una de las tareas más complicadas de cualquier producción, y por eso necesitamos un experto como tú. La Profesora Martínez me aseguró que no hay nadie mejor que tú y que tienes el tiempo para ayudarnos. Estamos contando con tu experiencia.

Dado que queremos estrenar la obra en treinta días, tenemos que empezar de inmediato. Necesito saber qué materiales piensas que vas a necesitar y el cálculo anticipado de gastos. Tienes el taller de la escuela a tu disposición, pero te pido que me informes si haya alguna herramienta especial que necesites para completar el trabajo. Finalmente, te pido que me des el número de personal que piensas vas a necesitar para ayudarte cumplir este trabajo.

Quedo atento para tu pronta respuesta, para así terminar el proceso de planificación y empezar la producción.

Un saludo cordial,

Dr. Gustavo Gutiérrez

Profesor de Teatro

EMAIL REPLY #3

Tema curricular: La vida contemporánea

Este mensaje electrónico es de la señora Carmen Cienfuegos, la directora de *Voluntariado Universal.* Has recibido este mensaje porque has aceptado participar en uno de sus programas en Argentina.

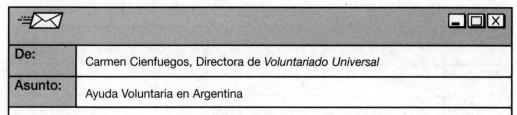

De:	Carmen Cienfuegos, Directora de *Voluntariado Universal*
Asunto:	Ayuda Voluntaria en Argentina

Estimado voluntario/a,

Muchas gracias por su respuesta y por haber aceptado participar en nuestro programa. Aunque somos una compañía bastante joven, debido al la generosidad de nuestros voluntarios hemos podido crecer rápidamente y aumentar nuestros programas. Trabajamos con niños y jóvenes socialmente marginados que viven bajo la línea de la pobreza, y creamos actividades con el fin de mejorar las condiciones de su vida. Como voluntario, su trabajo será de trabajar estrechamente con los chicos y ayudar a crear un ambiente saludable y feliz, compartiendo afecto y risas.

Tenemos dos programas distintos, uno en el suburbio de Buenos Aires, y el otro trabajando con la comunidad indígena en la jungla de Misiones. Las dos localidades presentan retos distintos, ya que en Misiones se presentan problemas con el alcance de elementos básicos, como agua potable y atención sanitaria, y en Buenos Aires hay todos los problemas y peligros típicos de un barrio pobre de una metrópolis. Ofrecemos programas de dos a cuatro semanas, y para poder finalizar nuestra lista, quisiera que nos proveyera la siguiente información:

- Primero, queremos aprovechar de los talentos e intereses de los voluntarios. Por lo tanto, ¿nos podría precisar en qué programa quiere participar y por qué?
- Segundo, para poder tener los mejores equipos, buscamos formar los grupos con voluntarios que tengan distintos talentos. ¿Nos podría proveer información de cualquier talento y/o habilidad que tenga y cómo esto puede beneficiar al grupo?

Le rogamos que nos provea esta información en cuanto pueda. Quedo atenta a su pronta respuesta y estoy pendiente para cualquier consulta que necesite.

Le saluda cordialmente,

Carmen Cienfuegos
Directora
Voluntariado Universal

EMAIL REPLY #4

Tema curricular: Las identidades personales y públicas

Eres estudiante en el colegio y tu escuela va a patrocinar una mesa redonda sobre la religión. Una profesora tuya, quien va a ser uno de los panelistas, quiere incorporar las ideas de varios estudiantes. Te manda un mensaje electrónico pidiendo que la ayudes en prepararse para la discusión.

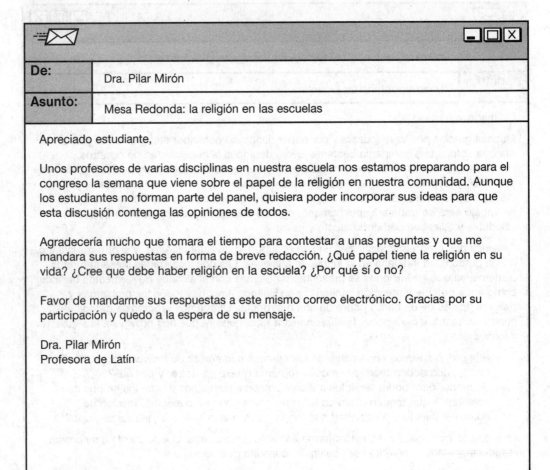

De:	Dra. Pilar Mirón
Asunto:	Mesa Redonda: la religión en las escuelas

Apreciado estudiante,

Unos profesores de varias disciplinas en nuestra escuela nos estamos preparando para el congreso la semana que viene sobre el papel de la religión en nuestra comunidad. Aunque los estudiantes no forman parte del panel, quisiera poder incorporar sus ideas para que esta discusión contenga las opiniones de todos.

Agradecería mucho que tomara el tiempo para contestar a unas preguntas y que me mandara sus respuestas en forma de breve redacción. ¿Qué papel tiene la religión en su vida? ¿Cree que debe haber religión en la escuela? ¿Por qué sí o no?

Favor de mandarme sus respuestas a este mismo correo electrónico. Gracias por su participación y quedo a la espera de su mensaje.

Dra. Pilar Mirón
Profesora de Latín

EMAIL REPLY #5

Tema curricular: Las familias y las comunidades

Un periodista de una revista popular está preparando un artículo sobre las diferentes tradiciones que se celebran en distintas comunidades. Te manda un mensaje electrónico pidiendo que respondas a unas preguntas para ayudarlo en terminar su trabajo.

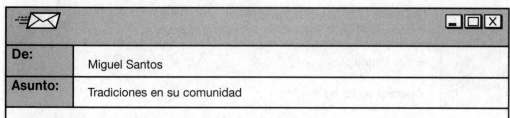

De:	Miguel Santos
Asunto:	Tradiciones en su comunidad

Querido lector,

Como parte de nuestra iniciativa de reseñar la diversidad en nuestro magnífico país, nuestra revista ha lanzado una nueva serie de artículos sobre las diversas costumbres y tradiciones que se celebran en distintas comunidades. El objetivo de este proyecto es de resaltar y celebrar el crisol de culturas que nos rodea. Hemos recibido mucha información de la Navidad y el Día de Independencia, y queremos expandir esta serie a incluir celebraciones que sean menos conocidas o particular de una región.

Por esta razón, le invitamos a responder a las siguientes preguntas, y esperamos que nos pueda contestar de manera más completa posible.

- ¿Hay una tradición particular que se celebra en su región? ¿Cuál es? ¿Por qué se celebra? ¿Cuándo se celebra?
- ¿Cómo se celebra esta tradición? ¿Hay una comida particular que se come o una vestimenta típica?

Sus respuestas son muy importantes para nosotros. Muchas gracias por su participación y ayuda en este proyecto.

Atentamente,

Miguel Santos
Periodista

Tema curricular: La ciencia y la tecnología

Eres estudiante a punto de empezar tu primer semestre en la universidad y un decano te escribe un mensaje electrónico. Quiere saber tus opiniones sobre si se debería permitir el uso de teléfonos celulares en las aulas.

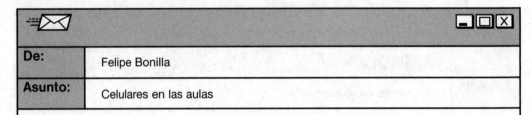

De:	Felipe Bonilla
Asunto:	Celulares en las aulas

Estimado/a estudiante,

La Universidad Nacional de Sucre está actualmente realizando una investigación sobre los beneficios y riesgos de permitir el uso de teléfonos celulares en las aulas durante las clases. Para poder tener una comprensión completa de los positivos y negativos, estamos poniéndonos en contacto con todos los docentes y estudiantes y pidiéndoles que participen en una encuesta. Los resultados se publicarán en un informe que se presentará en un congreso el otoño que viene.

¿Se anima a participar en esta encuesta? Esperamos que sí, y le invito a que conteste las siguientes preguntas:

- ¿Cree que el uso del celular afecta el rendimiento académico de los estudiantes? ¿Cómo?
- ¿En qué situaciones cree que es permisible el uso del celular en la sala de clase?

Agradezco de antemano la pronta atención que pueda prestar a contestar estas preguntas y quedo a su disposición para cualquier consulta.

Cordialmente,

Felipe Bonilla
Decano
Facultad de Filología
Universidad Nacional de Sucre

EMAIL REPLY #7

Tema curricular: Los desafíos mundiales

Recibes un mensaje electrónico de Annet Romero, asistente ejecutiva del alcalde en tu ciudad. Están pensando en implementar unas reformas a unos programas sociales y quiere saber tu opinión sobre el asunto.

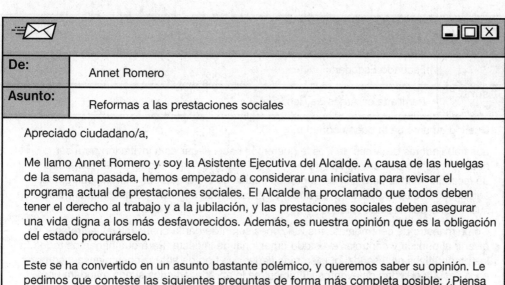

De: Annet Romero

Asunto: Reformas a las prestaciones sociales

Apreciado ciudadano/a,

Me llamo Annet Romero y soy la Asistente Ejecutiva del Alcalde. A causa de las huelgas de la semana pasada, hemos empezado a considerar una iniciativa para revisar el programa actual de prestaciones sociales. El Alcalde ha proclamado que todos deben tener el derecho al trabajo y a la jubilación, y las prestaciones sociales deben asegurar una vida digna a los más desfavorecidos. Además, es nuestra opinión que es la obligación del estado procurárselo.

Este se ha convertido en un asunto bastante polémico, y queremos saber su opinión. Le pedimos que conteste las siguientes preguntas de forma más completa posible: ¿Piensa usted que proveer prestaciones a los desempleados les ayuda o los perjudica? ¿Quién debería ser principalmente responsable para asegurar que los en paro o los de bajos ingresos tengan un adecuado estándar de vida?

Como siempre, un placer disfrutar del punto de vista de nuestros queridos ciudadanos, aunque no coincida con el nuestro. Me despido cordialmente esperando su contestación.

Un cordial saludo,

Annet Romero
Asistente Ejecutiva del Alcalde

EMAIL REPLY #8

Tema curricular: La vida contemporánea

Acabas de recibir un mensaje electrónico del gerente de tu restaurante favorito. Te escribe porque quiere que participes en un evento para recaudar fondos para un nuevo parque infantil.

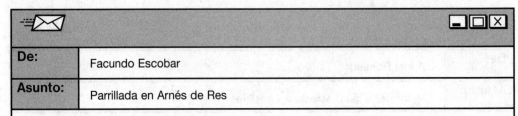

De:	Facundo Escobar
Asunto:	Parrillada en Arnés de Res

Querido amante de la buena comida,

Los trabajadores de Arnés de Res le queremos hacer llegar esta invitación para ser nuestro maestro de ceremonias de nuestra parrillada la semana que viene, con el fin de recaudar fondos para un nuevo parque infantil en el Parque San Martín. Queremos agradecerle su apoyo durante los años, y con su ayuda el nuevo parque infantil no será un sueño, sino por fin una realidad.

Como maestro de ceremonias, sus funciones serán de dar la charla inicial, entretener y divertir al público y controlar el estado emocional de la fiesta. Para que hagamos todos los preparativos necesarios, quisiéramos saber qué tipo de actuaciones piensa incorporar en la fiesta y el orden de eventos. También, se lo agradeceríamos si nos mandara una sinopsis de su charla.

Finalmente, como usted es uno de nuestros mejores clientes, le mandaremos una libreta de cupones para que pueda disfrutar de descuentos especiales en nuestro restaurante.

Quedamos a su disposición para facilitarle otra información.

Reciba un cordial saludo,

Facundo Escobar
Gerente
Arnés de Res

EMAIL REPLY #9

Tema curricular: Las familias y las comunidades

Eres estudiante y recibes un mensaje electrónico de tu profesor pidiendo información de tu proyecto final del curso.

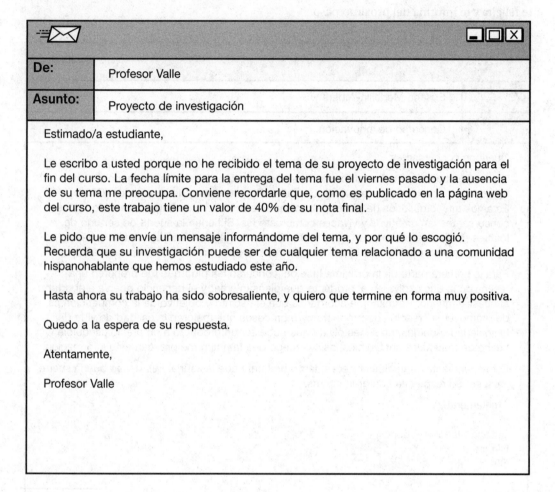

De: Profesor Valle

Asunto: Proyecto de investigación

Estimado/a estudiante,

Le escribo a usted porque no he recibido el tema de su proyecto de investigación para el fin del curso. La fecha límite para la entrega del tema fue el viernes pasado y la ausencia de su tema me preocupa. Conviene recordarle que, como es publicado en la página web del curso, este trabajo tiene un valor de 40% de su nota final.

Le pido que me envíe un mensaje informándome del tema, y por qué lo escogió. Recuerda que su investigación puede ser de cualquier tema relacionado a una comunidad hispanohablante que hemos estudiado este año.

Hasta ahora su trabajo ha sido sobresaliente, y quiero que termine en forma muy positiva.

Quedo a la espera de su respuesta.

Atentamente,

Profesor Valle

EMAIL REPLY #10

Tema curricular: La belleza y la estética

Eres un estudiante de diseño que acaba de calificarse a la siguiente ronda de un concurso de productos innovadores. Recibes un mensaje electrónico de la directora del concurso en que te felicita y te informa del próximo paso.

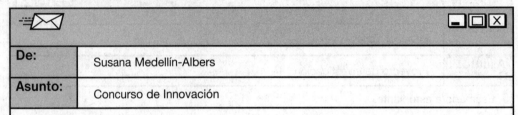

De:	Susana Medellín-Albers
Asunto:	Concurso de Innovación

Queridos concursantes,

Quiero felicitarles por haber sido seleccionados semifinalistas en la categoría de "Producto Innovador" para el primer Concurso Panamericano de Innovación (CPI). Estamos muy orgullosos de poder patrocinar este evento y que hayamos tenido tantos concursantes tan creativos y vivaces como ustedes. Si tienen la suerte de ser uno de los tres finalistas, estarán a un paso más cercano de ganarse uno de los tres premios monetarios y un contrato de trabajo con la célebre compañía INFOTEK por un año.

Para la primera parte de la próxima fase del concurso les pido que me preparen una reseña en la que expliquen el producto que piensan crear y el beneficio que va a aportar al nuestro mundo. Permítanme acordarles que el espíritu y objetivo de la competición es de promover la creación de productos y/o procesos que mejoran la calidad de vida de la sociedad. Además, no se les olvide que debe ser un producto a un precio asequible y hecho de materiales sostenibles, así les ruego que también me provean esta información.

Estoy pendiente de cualquier necesidad o pregunta que les surja. Les deseo buena suerte y espero su respuesta con gran interés.

Atentamente,

Susana Medellín-Albers
Directora
CPI

Section II, Part A–Task 2: Argumentative Essay

8

Task 2: An Argumentative Essay showcases your ability to argue your point of view on a particular topic. You will be given a question to answer three sources that present different points of view on the topic. Your task is to interpret the information presented on the topic in the sources, and then use it to support your argument. The first source is an article, the second is a chart, graph, or table, and the third is a listening source. You will be given 6 minutes to read the question and sources 1 and 2. You then will hear the audio played twice, with a 2 to 3 second pause in between. You then have 40 minutes to write your essay. Your Argumentative Essay must include the following:

- A clear answer to the question presented for this task
- Integration of all three sources in support of the overall argument
- Organization of thought
- Appropriate language for a presentational essay

SCORING YOUR ARGUMENTATIVE ESSAY

Your score will be based on how well you are able to accomplish this task and can roughly be broken into the following categories:

1. **What you were able to do.**

   - Did you answer the question with a clear thesis?
   - Did you incorporate information from all three sources in support of your argument?
   - Does your argument drive the essay and is there frequent elaboration?

2. **How you were able to do it.**

   - Is your response fully comprehensible?
   - Did your use of language show some sophistication?
   - Is your response well organized?

   As with Task 1: Email Reply, it is important to remember that these two categories work together. If you answered yes to all the above questions, your essay will likely score in the high range. There are some criteria that are more important than others. For example, a response that does not clearly answer the question or in which the student starts the essay by defending one viewpoint but ends up defending another will not score well. Likewise a response in which the student clearly tries to answer the question but whose language ability makes the reply mostly incomprehensible will also earn a low score.

   Another key element is to understand that your argument has to be the driving force of the essay, not the information in the sources. The information from the sources should serve as support for your ideas, not the other way around. Student essays whose argument relies heavily on summarizing information from the sources generally score in the 3 range. Also, you need to include at least one piece of information from each source. Failing to include information from one source in support of the essay will jeopardize your ability to earn a "5", even if all other parts of your response merit a score of a "5"

STRATEGIES FOR TASK 2: ARGUMENTATIVE ESSAY

The following is a guideline about how you should budget your time.

Read the question of the essay (30 seconds).

- Underline key words of the question so that it is absolutely clear what you need to answer.

Read source 1 (4 minutes).

- Read the introduction to the article.
- Read the title of the article.
- As you read, underline key words and phrases that will help you remember key ideas about the text.
- Focus on what it is you do know. Use context clues to infer the meaning of unfamiliar words, but do not spend too much time trying to decipher complicated information.
- When you finish reading, write down a few key words from the text that best summarize the point of view of the article.

Read source 2 (2 minutes).

- Read the introduction to the graph, chart, or table.
- Read the title of the graph, chart, or table.
- Analyze the information and come up with one or two ideas that clearly can be defended by the information in the graph, chart, or table. Remember that almost always this information presents objective data, and does not have a particular point of view. Don't force a point of view unless it is clearly presented in the graphic.

Listen to source 3 (5-7 minutes)

- Read the introduction to source 3 when directed to do so. Make a prediction of the point of view that this audio might take. Generally speaking, the audio will contain information that presents a different point of view than the article.
- Listen to the audio the first time to get a general idea of the overall argument. Visualize as you listen.
- When you listen the second time, take notes of key words that will help you remember one or two ideas from the audio source relating to the topic.
- Focus on what it is you understand and don't get hung up on what you don't understand. Use contextual clues to help you understand unfamiliar words or phrases.

Writing your essay (35 minutes)

- Begin by rereading the question you have to answer.
- Make a decision as to your answer to the question.
- Structure your essay correctly (introduction, body, and conclusion).
- Present your argument and use information from the sources to support your argument. Cite the sources as you use them.

- Vary your vocabulary. Make sure that you also use vocabulary from the sources correctly.
- Make sure that your ideas are clear and succinct.
- Include a variety of tenses and/or moods, if appropriate. Do not try to force the use of different tenses or moods, as this will count against you if it makes your response confusing.
- If you make a mistake, draw a line through it and keep writing.

After your finish writing (5 minutes)

- Proofread your essay and ensure that . . .

  - . . . you clearly answered the question;
  - . . . your overall argument is clear and supported by information from the sources;
  - . . . your ideas are clear to an unsympathetic reader; and
  - . . . you used correct orthography, punctuation, and paragraphing.

WRITING YOUR ARGUMENTATIVE ESSAY

When writing your essay, you should imagine that you are writing to someone who probably is not familiar with the topic. Therefore, your essay should be organized in such a way that you help guide the reader through your train of thought. Here is a general outline of how your essay should be organized:

- Introduction (1 paragraph).

  - Present the topic of the essay,
  - Present the two points of view on the essay, and
  - Clearly state your thesis.

- Body (2 paragraphs).

  - Paragraph #1

    o Begin by introducing your first idea that defends your thesis.
    o Use evidence from one or two of the sources to support your idea. Cite the sources as you use them.
    o Finish by elaborating why your idea is valid.

  - Paragraph #2

    o Begin by presenting the opposite point of view.
    o Use evidence from one of the sources as evidence to support this opposite point of view. Cite the source as you use it.
    o Reject this point of view and reaffirm your own point of view. Use information from the sources to support this rejection and reaffirmation. Cite the sources as you use them.

  - Conclusion (1 paragraph).

    o Restate your thesis.
    o Summarize the evidence that you used to prove your thesis.
    o Make a final remark or call to action that gives your essay a sense of closure and ending.

Citing Sources

When you cite sources, be as brief as possible. You can write something as simple as "Según fuente # . . ." or write "F#" in parenthesis after you present the idea from the source.

USEFUL VOCABULARY

One way to ensure that your essay flows well is to use transitional phrases. Here is a list that you can use. Practice using them regularly so that you will remember them easily on the exam.

To introduce an idea	*Como punto de partida . . .* *Para empezar . . .*
To add to an idea	*Además . . .* *En segundo lugar . . .*
To explain an idea	*Por ejemplo . . .* *Para ilustrar . . .*
To contrast	*Por otro lado . . .* *Sin embargo . . .* *No obstante . . .*
To compare	*De la misma manera . . .*
To show a result	*Por consiguiente . . .* *Como resultado . . .* *Debido a lo anterior . . .*
To conclude or summarize	*Por fin . . .* *En suma . . .* *Para concluir . . .*

SAMPLE ARGUMENTATIVE ESSAY

Tema curricular: La ciencia y la tecnología

Primero tienes seis minutos para leer el tema del ensayo, la fuente número 1 y la fuente número 2.

Tema del ensayo: ¿Es verdaderamente necesario dormir ocho horas para tener una vida saludable?

Fuente #1

Introducción: El siguiente artículo, escrito por Pablo Bejerano, cuestiona la verdad si dormir ocho horas es necesario. El artículo fue publicado en la página web *http://Blogthinkbig.com.*

El tiempo ideal de sueño varía de una persona a otra, pero las investigaciones demuestran que las ocho horas diarias no son necesarias.

Dormir es una de las partes más importantes de nuestro día a día. No en vano lo más probable es que sea la actividad en la que empleemos más tiempo a lo largo de nuestra vida. Por supuesto, el resto de tareas diarias se ven condicionadas

Línea
(5)
por las necesidades de reposo que requiere el organismo. Pero, ¿cuántas horas necesitamos dormir realmente? No son ocho, como dicta la creencia popular, y no necesariamente resulta beneficioso alargar el tiempo de sueño.

Hoy en día, cuando los niveles de productividad se estudian al detalle y se trata de optimizar al máximo el rendimiento en el trabajo, cobra cada vez más importancia el descanso. Ya hace tiempo que se desmontó el mito de las

(10)
ocho horas diarias de sueño y, aunque no hay una sola idea concluyente de cuántas horas necesitamos dormir, se puede tomar como referencia lo que han descubierto algunos investigadores.

Uno de los especialistas en sueño más prestigiosos, Daniel Kriple, ha constatado en su último estudio que la gente que duerme entre 6,5 horas y 7,5 horas, además

(15)
de vivir más tiempo, es más feliz y más productiva. Otra de las claves que apunta tiene que ver con dormir más de las ocho horas tradicionales. Según sus conclusiones, dormir 8,5 horas podría ser peor que dormir 5 horas.

Estas cifras pueden variar ligeramente de unas personas a otras, pues no todo el mundo tiene las mismas necesidades debido a su genética, complexión e incluso

(20)
a su actividad diaria. ¿Pero qué ocurre si dormimos menos de lo necesario? Una de las creencias extendidas es que perdemos capacidad para enfrentarnos a nuestras tareas. No es del todo cierto. Una persona falta de sueño puede llevar a cabo las mismas funciones que otra que sí haya descansado bien.

La diferencia—nada desdeñable—está en que la persona que ha dormido

(25)
poco tiene más dificultad para recuperar la concentración. Y es que todos nos distraemos constantemente, pero cuando el cerebro se encuentra en buenas condiciones tiene más facilidad para volver a centrarse, algo mucho más costoso cuando hay falta de sueño. Además, alguien con este impedimento para concentrarse no repara en su déficit, algo que contribuye a la infravaloración del

(30)
sueño.

La siesta puede convertirse en otra de las claves para mejorar la calidad del sueño. De hecho, algunos historiadores han señalado que hasta hace pocos siglos era habitual la práctica de segmentar el sueño en dos etapas. El escritor Michael S. Hyatt afirma que diariamente duerme la siesta alrededor de las tres de la tarde,

(35)
cuando nota que su productividad cae en picado. Tras el reposo cuenta con otra hora y media de alto rendimiento.

Eso sí, las recomendaciones siempre hablan de no excederse en el tiempo de siesta, que no supere los 25 minutos o media hora. Este hábito lógicamente lleva a estar menos cansado, de lo que se deriva que se tenga mejor ánimo, algo que

(40)
constituye una base sólida para estar más contento.

Fuente #2
Introducción: La siguiente tabla presenta las horas recomendadas de sueño según la National Sleep Foundation.

Edad	Horas recomendadas
Recién nacidos	14–17
Bebés	12–15
Niños y preescolares	10–14
Escolares y adolescentes	8–11
Adultos jóvenes y adultos	7–9
Adultos mayores	7–8

Fuente #3
Introducción: El siguiente audio trata del tema de si se debe dormir ocho horas o no. Es un fragmento de la grabación titulada "Dormir o no dormir", y fue emitida por Radio Ciudad del Mar (Cuba) en octubre de 2012. La grabación dura aproximadamente tres minutos y medio.

Track 23

Response

By now you should know well the directions of this task, which are the following:

- You are to write an argumentative essay in which you answer the question with your own viewpoint.
- You must use information from all three sources in support of your argument.
- When you use information from the sources, cite them appropriately.
- Organize your essay.

The first step is to read the question and underline key words. In this case, the key words are "necesario dormir ocho horas" and "vida saludable." One could argue that there are three possible responses to this question.

1. Yes, it is important to sleep 8 hours as part of a healthy lifestyle.
2. No, it is not important to sleep 8 hours to maintain a healthy lifestyle.
3. Maybe . . . for some it is important while for others it is not important.

It is easiest to take a definitive position, such as defending one of the first two options. You only have 40 minutes to write, so you want to defend the idea that is easiest for you to defend. It does not matter whether or not you personally believe the idea that you defend, the strength of your argument in the essay is what will be evaluated.

The next step is to read the sources. Make sure that you do the following:

- Read the introduction and title.
- As you read, underline key words that will help you remember important ideas from the source.
- Try to find at least one good idea from each source.

Here are some ideas that you can extract from the sources in this example.

- Fuente #1—Sleeping 8 hours isn't necessary, and some studies show that sleeping more than 8 hours can have worse effects than sleeping less than 5 hours and that those who sleep 6.5 to 7.5 hours are more productive and happier.
- Fuente #2—The National Sleep Foundation recommends that young children sleep much more than 8 hours, while adults can sleep 7–8 hours.
- Fuente #3—The interviewees feel that sleeping 8 hours is vital to keep healthy and to perform adequately.

Now that you have an idea from each source, go back and re-read the question. Once you have done so, choose what side of the argument you plan to defend and begin writing your essay. Here is a sample essay:

Sample Essay

El sueño es una parte fundamental de nuestra salud y bienestar. Aunque todos concuerdan que es vital que la gente tenga la oportunidad de recuperarse de los esfuerzos físicos y mentales que nos enfrentan diariamente, no hay consenso del número de horas que hay que dormir. Unos dicen que hay que dormir un mínimo de ocho horas diariamente, mientras otros dicen que no son necesarios. Para mí, creo que es imprescindible que la gente duerma ocho horas como mínimo porque beneficia la calidad de nuestra productividad y ayuda a mantener una vida sana.

Como punto de partida, dormir ocho horas es beneficioso para la salud mental y física. Nosotros nos encontramos en un mundo lleno de estímulos, y muchas veces es difícil manejar todas las expectativas que nos rodean. Estudiantes, por ejemplo, tienen un sinfín de obligaciones académicas, y es común que ellos trasnochen completando un proyecto o estudiando para un examen. Pero no dormir lo suficiente puede causar peor rendimiento (fuente #3). Además, puede llevar a problemas físicos. Según la fuente #3, no dormir lo suficiente aumenta el riesgo de contraer enfermedades, tal como la obesidad y cáncer. Los expertos concuerdan, y el prestigioso National Sleep Foundation recomienda un mínimo de 8 horas para todas las edades, y cuanto menos años uno tiene, más tiene que dormir. Por consiguiente, es lógico que la gente duerma ocho horas cada día.

Por otro lado, hay unos que argumentan que dormir ocho horas no es necesario. Ellos argumentan que alguien que duerme menos de ocho hora puede llevar a cabo las mismas funciones que alguien que haya dormido ocho horas, y hacen referencias a estudios que muestran que dormir más de ocho horas es peor que dormir menos de cinco horas (fuente #1). Sin embargo, también admiten que dormir menos de ocho horas afecta la capacidad de poder concentrarse (fuente #1), una consecuencia bastante grave particularmente si es un estudiante tomando un examen u operador de equipo pesado donde la falta de concentración puede causarle fracasar un examen o matar a alguien. Por lo tanto, no parece que valga la pena poner a sí mismo o a otros a riesgo por la falta de sueño.

Para concluir, a mi parecer es imprescindible que durmamos lo suficiente cada noche, y tanto los expertos como la muchedumbre están de acuerdo que lo suficiente equivale a ocho horas diarias (fuentes #2 y #3). Dormir ocho horas no sólo permite que uno pueda llevar a cabo bien sus responsabilidades, sino también ayuda a prevenir trastornos físicos. Con todos los beneficios que aporta, ¿quién no dormiría ocho horas?

As you look over this response, make note of the following:

1. The organization of the response into the three distinct portions (introduction, body, conclusion)
2. The organization of each of the portions:
   a. Introduction—Introduces the topic, presents the contrasting points of view, and then clearly presents a thesis.
   b. Body #1—Introduces an idea in support of the thesis, Uses evidence from sources 3 and 2 in support of the idea.
   c. Body #2—Presents the other point of view. Uses evidence from source 1 to support this point of view. Rejects the point of view, and goes back to defending original thesis.
   d. Conclusion—Reaffirms thesis, summarizes evidence to support thesis, and closes the essay with a final comment.
3. The information from the sources serves to support the argument
4. Use of transitional phrases (*Como punto de partida . . . , por ejemplo . . . , Además . . . , Por consiguiente . . . , Por otro lado . . . , Por lo tanto . . . , Para concluir . . .*)
5. Elaboration throughout
6. Use of a variety of verb moods and tenses (present, present subjunctive) and a wide range of vocabulary

ENSAYO #1

Tema curricular: La vida contemporánea

Primero tienes seis minutos para leer el tema del ensayo, la fuente número 1 y la fuente número 2.

Tema del ensayo: ¿Se debería eliminar los deberes de las escuelas?

Fuente #1: El siguiente artículo trata de los deberes escolares. Fue publicado en la página web Global Voices en Español (*es.globalvoices.org*) en 2016.

¿Para qué sirven los deberes escolares? Un debate en España

¿Tiene sentido que una niña o una niño tengan que permanecer largas horas después de clase haciendo deberes? ¿Tiene sentido que padres e hijos acaben peleando porque hacer los deberes significa decir "no" a jugar, ir al parque, ver la

Línea televisión o simplemente tumbarse a la bartola?

(5) España es uno de los países donde más deberes se mandan: 6,5 horas de media a la semana frente a las 4,9 de media en los 34 países miembros de la Organización para la Cooperación y el Desarrollo Económicos (OCDE). En Colombia los estudiantes dedican el mismo número de horas a la semana a hacer deberes en casa que los españoles; en Argentina y Chile sólo cuatro. Una encuesta

(10) de la Organización Mundial de la Salud publicada en marzo pasado, muestra a España como uno de los países con un mayor porcentaje de niños y niñas que se sienten "presionados" por las tareas para casa, una presión que aumenta a medida que los niños crecen.

Y no es que España como país sea precisamente "el primero de la clase".

(15) El sobre-esfuerzo no se traduce en un mejor rendimiento escolar. Así lo pone de manifiesto el informe del Programa para la Evaluación Internacional de Alumnos (PISA, por sus siglas en inglés). El rendimiento educativo de España en matemáticas, lectura y ciencias permanece por debajo de la media de los países de la OCDE. Además, la equidad en los resultados educativos ha empeorado.

(20) Los alumnos con un nivel socio-económico favorecido superan a los alumnos menos favorecidos en 34 puntos en matemáticas en 2012, una diferencia 6 puntos superior a la observada en 2003.

¿Sirven los deberes?

El debate no es reciente. Para unos, los deberes son una medida educativa

(25) necesaria, que hace que los escolares se esfuercen y les ayuda a asentar el conocimiento. Para otros son un abuso, producto de la falta de planificación, que acrecienta las desigualdades entre los escolares. La OCDE advierte que los deberes son una carga para los alumnos con desventajas socioeconómicas, algo

(30) que también señala un informe de la Fundación BBVA y el Instituto Valenciano de Investigaciones Económicas.

El informe PISA reconoce que los deberes sí pueden servir para mejorar los resultados, pero la tendencia actual es reducir su cantidad. En 2003 la media era de 5,9 horas a la semana, una hora más que en 2012. Países cuyos sistemas educativos destacan como los primeros del mundo, presentan una carga mucho *(35)* menor: 2,8 horas a la semana en Finlandia o 2,9 en Corea del Sur. Numerosos expertos en educación coinciden en la necesidad de reducir las tareas escolares que realizan los niños españoles.

Los deberes a examen en España

Eva Bailén es madre de tres hijos, y su propia experiencia familiar con los *(40)* deberes la llevó a iniciar una petición en change.org por la racionalización de los deberes en el sistema educativo español, una petición que se ha convertido ya en todo un movimiento. Eva lanzó su petición hace poco más de un año, en marzo de 2015, y obtuvo un respaldo inmediato. En un mes consiguió 100.000 firmas, y hoy ya supera las 205.000.

Fuente #2: El siguiente gráfico presenta el tiempo medio (en minutos) por semana que dedican los estudiantes a la instrucción y tareas escolares. Se basa en datos publicados por la OCDE (Organización para la Cooperación y Desarrollo Económicos) en 2012.

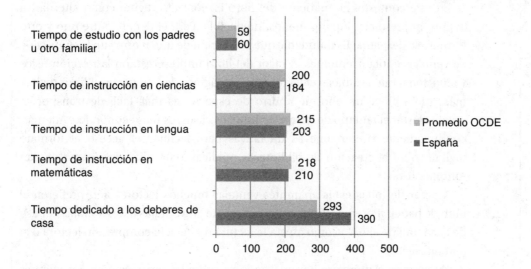

Fuente #3: El siguiente audio trata un debate sobre los deberes escolares. El audio forma parte de la serie titulada *Por la educación* en RTVE. Fue emitido en octubre de 2015 y dura aproximadamente tres minutos.

Track 24

Apuntes:

ENSAYO #2

Tema curricular: La belleza y la estética

Primero tienes seis minutos para leer el tema del ensayo, la fuente número 1 y la fuente número 2.

Tema del ensayo: En la era digital y con todo el acceso a tabletas y otros medios de comunicación, ¿vale la pena seguir imprimiendo libros?

> **Fuente #1:** El siguiente artículo trata de los beneficios que todavía aporta el libro impreso. Fue publicado por el Centro Nacional de Innovación e Investigación Educativa (España) en 2015.

El libro impreso frente al libro digital: hacia una convivencia pacífica

Los nuevos avances tecnológicos y la influencia que estos ejercen en la conducta de la sociedad han producido, como en tantos otros aspectos de nuestra vida, un cambio en los hábitos lectores y en las formas de aprendizaje.

Línea
(5) Nos encontramos rodeados de ordenadores, tabletas, móviles, televisiones, vídeos, videojuegos y herramientas afines como internet y las redes sociales que favorecen el acceso continuo a la información. El aprendizaje puede surgir en cualquier momento y en cualquier lugar, solo es necesario alguien con ganas de aprender y acceso tecnológico a la información que necesita.

En este contexto, la aparición del libro en formato digital como alternativa
(10) al libro impreso era, cuanto menos, predecible. Pero el debate entre uno y otro formato se perpetúa. Es indudable que la elección de uno u otro supone una serie de ventajas e inconvenientes. A favor del libro impreso estaría la relación física y emocional que establece el lector con las páginas. Por su parte, el libro digital, más "frío", ofrece un enorme ahorro de espacio, es más fácil de transportar,
(15) puede ajustar el tamaño de letra y, en muchos casos, es más económico. Además, continuamente surgen nuevas iniciativas para facilitar el acceso al formato digital, como la creación de bibliotecas públicas 100% digitales (como en San Antonio, Texas).

A pesar de todas estas aparentes ventajas muchos lectores aún prefieren el
(20) libro de papel. ¿Por qué? ¿Cuáles son realmente las ventajas o desventajas del uso de cada uno de ellos? ¿Cómo afecta la lectura digital a la compresión lectora o al aprendizaje?

Numerosos estudios se han realizado ya sobre las virtudes e inconvenientes de la utilización de libros digitales frente a los libros impresos, pero los datos
(25) obtenidos, lejos de ser concluyentes, son contradictorios en muchos aspectos. Por ejemplo, los estudios realizados por Anne Mangen en el Reading Centre of the University of Stavanger o los llevados a cabo por Jean-Luc Velay de la Universidad de Aix-Marseille, indican que leer libros impresos favorece la comprensión lectora; por otro lado, un reciente estudio llevado a cabo por Jim Johnson de la
(30) Universidad Estatal de Indiana o el realizado por la psicóloga Sara Margolin de la Universidad Brockport, señalan justamente lo contrario, que el soporte no afecta a la comprensión lectora.

Otros estudios, como el llevado a cabo por Anne Campbell de la Open University of Scotland, concluyen que los dispositivos móviles promueven

(35) una lectura más profunda pero un menor aprendizaje activo. En España también se han desarrollado estudios sobre lectura digital. Entre ellos destaca el proyecto Territorio Ebook de la Fundación Germán Sánchez Ruipérez que recoge algunos indicios sobre los cambios que el soporte digital puede provocar en las generaciones futuras.

Fuente #2: El primer gráfico presenta el precio medio del libro en papel vs. digital entre 2011–2014. Fue publicado por el Observatorio de la Lectura y el Libro, un organismo perteneciente al Ministerio de Educación, Cultura y Deporte de España. El segundo gráfico presenta los resultados de una encuesta hecho por un estudio titulado *Estudio sobre el uso de los libros electrónicos en las bibliotecas universitarias de Castilla y León,* publicado en la página web de la Universitat de Barcelona en 2013.

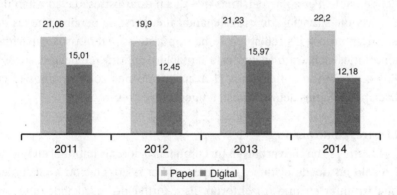

Uso de la versión electrónica frente a la impresa

Fuente #3: El siguiente audio titulado *Un libro digital puede ser cientos de veces más barato que uno impreso* trata de los beneficios económicos y sociales de libros digitales. Fue emitido por Radio Naciones Unidas en abril de 2014 y dura aproximadamente tres minutos y medio.

Track 25

Apuntes:

ENSAYO #3

Tema curricular: La ciencia y la tecnología

Primero tienes seis minutos para leer el tema del ensayo, la fuente número 1 y la fuente número 2.

Tema del ensayo: ¿Es beneficioso o perjudicial experimentar estrés en la vida?

Fuente #1: El siguiente artículo, titulado "El estrés nuestro de cada día", trata del impacto del estrés en la vida cuotidiana. El artículo original fue publicado en 2008 en la página web *www.consumer.es.*

Línea

(5)

(10)

Raro es el día en que la palabra estrés no forme parte de nuestro vocabulario habitual. Algunos expresan así sus penas laborales, otros lo hacen para pedir ayuda y muchos más de los que pensamos recurren a este vocablo para despertar admiración: "qué persona más exitosa y ocupada", es su frase. En lo que casi todos coinciden, sin embargo, es en que el nivel de estrés actual está por encima del deseable. Pero, ¿las personas que dicen estar estresadas lo están de verdad? Se vive una situación de estrés cuando una persona percibe que las demandas de su entorno y los retos que se ha impuesto superarán sus capacidades para afrontarlos con éxito y que esta situación pondrá en peligro su estabilidad. Es decir, cuando anticipamos el fracaso y no nos conformamos (y cuando lo hacemos solemos deprimirnos), tendemos a estresarnos.

El estrés como aliado

(15)

(20)

(25)

El estrés se ha convertido en un compañero de viaje habitual en nuestras vidas. No sólo no puede evitarse, sino que facilita la adaptación a cualquier cambio que irrumpa en nuestro entorno. Esta forma de reaccionar ante problemas, demandas y peligros, viene predeterminada por una actitud innata de lucha/huida heredada de nuestros antepasados: sobrevivieron aquellos que, ante situaciones amenazantes para su integridad física (ver un enemigo) o que informaban de la posibilidad de obtener un beneficio (cobrar una presa), mejor activaban su organismo. Dilatación de pupilas para aumentar la visión periférica y permitir una mayor entrada de luz en la oscuridad, músculos tensados para reaccionar con más velocidad y fuerza, aumento de la frecuencia respiratoria y cardiaca para mejorar la oxigenación y aportar mayor flujo de sangre al cerebro y al resto de órganos vitales, son algunos de los cambios que les proporcionaba una clara ventaja sobre sus enemigos y sus presas.

Pero el inconveniente de este fabuloso mecanismo de adaptación es que genera un importante desgaste del organismo y un alto consumo de energía, por lo que es necesario desarrollar unos cuidados y un periodo de recuperación del que no siempre somos conscientes.

Fuente #2: El siguiente gráfico presenta los síntomas asociados con el estrés. Fue publicado originalmente en el blog *La Coctelera* en 2008.

Síntomas frecuentes

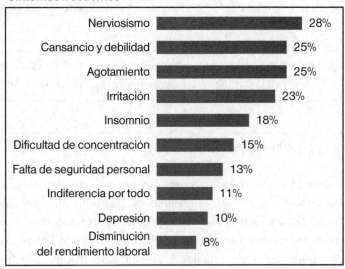

Fuente #3: La siguiente entrevista es con José Buendía, profesor de psicopatología de la Universidad de Murcia. La grabación dura aproximadamente 2 minutos y 30 segundos.

Track 26

Apuntes:

ENSAYO #4

Tema curricular: Las familias y las comunidades

Primero tienes seis minutos para leer el tema del ensayo, la fuente número 1 y la fuente número 2.

Tema del ensayo: ¿Es la responsabilidad de los padres o de los docentes educar a los niños y jóvenes?

Fuente #1: El siguiente artículo provee unos consejos a los padres de cómo educar valores a sus hijos. Fue publicado en la página web *http://enfermedadesytratamientos.com* en 2013.

Consejos para educar a tu hijo en la responsabilidad y la disciplina

La sociedad actual está en continuo proceso de transformación, y estos cambios, también se dan en la enseñanza. Hasta los años sesenta no existían escuelas mixtas, los alumnos/as se dirigían a sus profesores/as de usted.

Línea

(5) Actualmente hay muchos aspectos diferentes en lo que a materia de enseñanza se refiere y podíamos llegar a hablar de un alumnado distinto. Muchos niños/as no tienen un ejemplo de modelo adulto en sus casas y, por ende, tampoco lo ven en los maestros. En muchas ocasiones los niños/as ven a sus profesores como colegas, ya que sus padres también lo son para ellos. Y lo que ocurre es que muchos padres y madres no quieren estropear los momentos que pasan con sus hijos/as con una

(10) serie de negativas, exigiéndoles responsabilidades . . . No quieren llevar a cabo la educación de antaño y dan paso a una educación permisiva.

Ciertamente hay ventajas en la educación actual:

—Se tiene más en cuenta al niño/a, llegando a conocer mejor sus etapas y necesidades.

(15) —Se le explican las cosas, se le escucha y todo este conjunto de cambios hace que los niños/as de hoy en día sean mucho más asertivos, aunque corremos el riesgo de no exigir el esfuerzo suficiente, limitando las responsabilidades y llegando a un consentimiento excesivo.

Para no caer en esta trampa podemos seguir los siguientes consejos:

(20) —Tenemos que ser estrictos con nuestros hijos/as. Cuando decimos que "no", tenemos que llevar ese "no" hasta el final, sin importarnos la insistencia que lleven a cabo.

En relación con esto mismo, es muy importante que tanto el padre como la madre estén dentro de la misma línea educativa y, entre otras cosas, esto implica

(25) no ceder cuando el otro progenitor exige . . .

—Hay que exigir responsabilidades de acuerdo a la edad del niño/a.

—Controlar el tiempo que pasa viendo la tele o jugando a videojuegos. A medida que aumenta la edad, podemos ir aumentando el tiempo que pasa delante de la consola . . .

(30)　　No podemos permitir que nuestros hijos sólo busquen la estimulación visual por medio de una pantalla, que no sean capaces de crearla en su mente. Vamos a facilitar que puedan emocionarse con el simple hecho de contarles una historia, un cuento . . .

　　　　—En relación con lo anterior, es muy importante que dediquemos un tiempo,
(35)　todos los días para hablar y jugar con nuestros hijos/as . . .

　　　　—Debemos intentar comer en familia, al menos una vez al día, sin la tele encendida, fomentando el dialogo, los buenos hábitos y modales.

　　　　—Es conveniente realizar actividades con nuestros hijos, por ejemplo, los fines de semana. Vamos a intentar que con alguna de estas actividades que hacemos
(40)　juntos, en familia, se estimulen aspectos como la creatividad, el deporte, el respeto al medio ambiente, a los demás, el trabajo en equipo, . . .

Fuente #2: El siguiente gráfico muestra los resultados de un estudio patrocinado por la Fundación Hogar del Empleado (FUHEM) y publicado en noviembre de 2007.

Porcentaje de profesores, familias y alumnos que considera que los siguientes factores tienen bastante o mucha influencia en la educación.

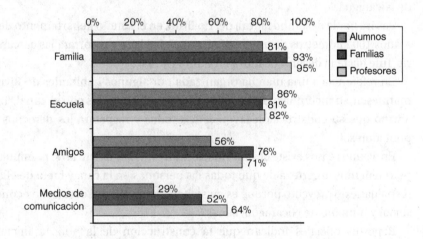

Fuente #3: El siguiente audio es un fragmento de un documental titulado *Redes—La revolución educativa*. En el fragmento, el psicólogo Robert Roesner ayuda a redefinir el papel de profesores y maestros en la educación de los jóvenes. Fue emitido por RTVE en 2010, y dura aproximadamente cuatro minutos.

Track 27

Apuntes:

ENSAYO #5

Tema curricular: Los desafíos mundiales

Primero tienes seis minutos para leer el tema del ensayo, la fuente número 1 y la fuente número 2.

Tema del ensayo: ¿Se debería permitir que se construya el canal de Nicaragua?

Fuente #1: El siguiente texto trata de la construcción del Canal de Nicaragua. Fue publicado en la página web *Nuestromar.org* en 2013.

Continúan preparativos para emprender el Canal de Nicaragua

La clasificación de tierras y bienes accesorios avanza con rigor en la ruta donde se construirá la vía interoceánica en Nicaragua, aseguró el miembro de la Comisión del Gran Canal, Telémaco Talavera, en recientes declaraciones.

Línea

(5)   Según Talavera, se prevé que el estudio, realizado por expertos nicaragüenses y extranjeros, esté listo el próximo 15 de octubre y una vez culminado la empresa china HKND, concesionaria del proyecto, iniciará negociaciones para el pago de indemnizaciones a los dueños de territorios afectados.

La longitud del canal, cuya ruta fue anunciada en julio último, será de aproximadamente 278 kilómetros, de los cuales un tramo de 105 estará en el lago

(10)   de Nicaragua.

Pasará por la desembocadura del río Brito, en el sureño departamento de Rivas, a unos 100 kilómetros de esta capital, cruzará el lago y recorrerá las cercanías del río Tule hasta la desembocadura en Punta Gorda.

En referencia a una marcha organizada por algunos habitantes de Rivas para

(15)   manifestar su inconformidad con las labores relacionadas con el canal, Talavera afirmó que su construcción favorecerá a todos y respetará los derechos de los pobladores.

En algunos casos existe desinformación, en otros la influencia de manipuladores, pero tenemos la certeza de que todas las personas en la ruta y fuera de ella van a

(20)   respaldar este proyecto porque es en su beneficio y para el desarrollo económico, social y humano de Nicaragua, señaló.

Reportes oficiales indican que la construcción de la obra, a iniciarse en diciembre próximo y cuya duración se estima en cinco años, generará alrededor de 50 000 empleos y otros 200 000 en una etapa posterior.

(25)   Además del canal, se trabajará en subproyectos como un aeropuerto, varias carreteras, una zona de libre comercio, complejos turísticos y dos puertos, uno del lado del océano Pacífico y otro en el Atlántico.

Fuente #2: La siguiente tabla presenta la comparación entre el Canal de Nicaragua y el Canal de Panamá. Se basa en datos recopilados por el Gobierno de Nicaragua.

Detalles del proyecto		
	Canal de Nicaragua	Canal de Panamá
Profundidad	22 m	13,8 m
Longitud	286 km	80 km

El canal de Nicaragua tendrá la capacidad de recibir barcos de hasta 250.000 toneladas métricas, y hasta 285 m de largo.

Fuente #3: En el siguiente audio, la abogada ambientalista nicaragüense Mónica López Baldotano, presenta las razones para las que quiere detener la construcción del Canal Interoceánico de Nicaragua. La grabación fue publicada en noviembre de 2015 por RTVE y dura aproximadamente cuatro minutos.

Track 28

Apuntes:

ENSAYO #6

Tema curricular: La ciencia y la tecnología

Primero tienes seis minutos para leer el tema del ensayo, la fuente número 1 y la fuente número 2.

Tema del ensayo: Descargas ilegales: ¿afectan o no afectan negativamente a las industrias de entretenimiento?

> **Fuente #1:** El siguiente texto presenta un argumento que las descargas ilegales de música no afectan negativamente a esta industria. Fue publicado en la página web Asociación de Internautas (*www.internautas.org*) el 20 de marzo de 2013.

La UE es clara: la "piratería" de música no perjudica a los propietarios de los derechos de autor

Un estudio publicado esta misma mañana por el *Joint Research Centre* de la Unión Europea afirma algo que ya ha sido comentado en otras ocasiones: que la piratería de música en internet no afecta negativamente a las ventas en los canales de pago o legales.

El estudio de la Unión Europea llega a estas conclusiones después de analizar el comportamiento de 16 mil internautas de UK, Francia, Alemania, Italia y España. Este análisis se concentra en conocer los hábitos de los europeos, midiendo la
Línea relación entre las visitas a páginas web de descarga de música frente a opciones
(5) legales y de pago o streaming.

Además de destacar el hecho de que un alto número de visitas a páginas de descargas se corresponden con un número también elevado de visitas a canales legales, el estudio que fue realizado con la ayuda de Nielsen destaca también las siguientes conclusiones:

(10) ▪ Parece que la mayoría de la música que es consumida ilegalmente por los individuos de nuestra muestra no habría sido comprada si las páginas de descargas ilegales no estuviesen disponibles
▪ Los servicios de streaming de música tienen un efecto todavía mayor, al creerse que tienen un efecto de estímulo hacia el pago de contenidos
(15) ▪ Nuestras conclusiones sugieren que la piratería de música digital no debería ser vista como una preocupación para los propietarios de los derechos de autor. Además, nuestros resultados indican que nuevos métodos de consumo como el *streaming* de música afectan positivamente a los propietarios de dichos derechos

(20) Aunque el estudio fue realizado analizando Internautas de los cinco países mencionados anteriormente, es importante destacar que existen diferencias significativas entre los países. En España e Italia, por ejemplo, el número de clicks en páginas de descarga gratuita de música fueron mucho mayores que en el resto de países. Y en clicks a páginas legales de contenidos, España fue segunda por la
(25) cola, sólo superada por Italia.

Con este informe se vuelve a destacar que no existe una relación tan estrecha entre piratería y pérdida de ventas, y que la primera no tiene un efecto significativo y negativo sobre la segunda. Eso sí, el informe vuelve a poner de relieve otro detalle que se ha apuntado en previas ocasiones, y es que en la Europa (30) del sur (principalmente España e Italia), una mayor proporción de usuarios se decantan por la descarga gratuita de música, en vez de optar por los canales de pago y *legales*.

Fuente #2: El primer gráfico muestra los tipos de multimedia obtenida por los encuestados que hicieron descargas ilegales durante los últimos 12 meses. El segundo muestra cuánto pagarían los encuestados por descargarla legalmente.

Tipos de descargas ilegales

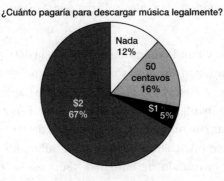

¿Cuánto pagaría para descargar música legalmente?

Fuente #3: El siguiente audio presenta los resultados de la lucha contra descargas ilegales. Fue publicado por el programa *Entre paréntesis* en Radio 5 (España) en marzo de 2015. La grabación dura aproximadamente tres minutos cuarenta y cinco segundos.

Track 29

Apuntes:

ENSAYO #7

Tema curricular: Las familias y las comunidades

Primero tienes seis minutos para leer el tema del ensayo, la fuente número 1 y la fuente número 2.

Tema del ensayo: ¿Es una buena idea tener servicio militar obligatorio para los jóvenes?

Fuente #1: El siguiente texto critica el servicio militar obligatorio. Fue publicado en la página web *http://suramericapress.com* en octubre de 2011.

¿El Servicio Militar Obligatorio instruye a los jóvenes?

Pese a que algunos sectores conservadores e individualidades califican a los objetores de: "antipatriotas, desviados sociales, cobardes" y muchos otros adjetivos que no vale repetir en este artículo, lo cierto es que los/as jóvenes que impulsan esta campaña están proponiendo algo nuevo para la sociedad, tienen el valor y el coraje de pensar y proponer una sociedad más pluralista, con mayores libertades y elevar la responsabilidad y autonomía juvenil en la construcción de una patria para todos y todas, llena de colores de esperanza y vida.

Los que defienden la idea de que el Servicio Militar Obligatorio es una escuela de aprendizaje para los jóvenes, donde se enseñan valores patrióticos, que ayuda a disminuir la delincuencia juvenil, deberían tener muy en cuenta los siguientes datos, que dicen totalmente lo contrario y muestran a varios militares en situación de prepotencia, alcoholismo y violencia, lejos de ser un "ejemplo" para la sociedad:

- El sub oficial Víctor Ramón Guerrero Brizuela del Comando de Ingeniería en estado de ebriedad atropella y mata a un motociclista, el hecho ocurrió sobre la ruta I, km 21 Posta Ybycuá, de la ciudad de Capiatá. (fecha: 21-03-2010)
- El Sargento ayudante de la Fuerza Militar Fernando Carracela Cristaldo disparó contra un motociclista en la ciudad de Asunción, 2 impactos de balas dieron en la moticicleta de la víctima, el militar fue detenido y se comprobó que estaba en estado de ebriedad, tenía en su poder una pistola 9mm, escopeta calibre 12 y arma blanca. (fecha: 27-09-2010)
- El Teniente de Infantería Rubén Gustavo Pratt Moreira, fue denunciado por los vecinos de Luque por escuchar música a todo volumen, en estado de ebriedad, haciendo alarde de su arma 9mm en la cintura, al llegar la policía, el militar reaccionó prepotentemente y no quiso someterse a la prueba de alcotest. (fecha: 30-10-2010).
- Sub oficial Teniente de infantería, Joel Alejandro Velázquez Meza, a bordo de su motocicleta realizaba disparos en la vía pública en estado de ebriedad en la ciudad de Fernando de la Mora, uno de los periódicos nacionales titulaba el hecho: "Motocicleta, alcohol y arma de fuego derivan en detención de Militar". (fecha: 30-07-2011)

Línea (5) ... (10) ... (15) ... (20) ... (25) ... (30)

A estos hechos de particular irresponsabilidad, de homicidios incluso, protagonizados por militares le podríamos agregar muchos otros casos similares, *(35)* además de mencionar los últimos casos de tortura ocurridos recientemente en la Academia Militar (Academil), varias irregularidades y violaciones de derechos humanos de los cuarteles donde según algunos "se hace patria".

Fuente #2: La siguiente tabla presenta la política de alistamiento en diferentes países del mundo. Se basa en datos recopilados por el autor.

País	Política de alistamiento
Bolivia	Obligatorio
Chile	Obligatorio
Costa Rica	No hay fuerzas armadas
España	No obligatorio
Paraguay	Obligatorio

Fuente #3: El siguiente audio, titulado *Ley fácil—Servicio militar,* es una dramatización creada por la Biblioteca del Congreso Nacional de Chile (BCN). Trata de las responsabilidades de los ciudadanos chilenos en cuanto al servicio militar. La grabación dura aproximadamente dos minutos y medio.

Track 30

Apuntes:

ENSAYO #8

Tema curricular: Los desafíos mundiales

Primero tienes seis minutos para leer el tema del ensayo y las fuentes número 1 y 2.

Tema del ensayo: ¿Ayuda o perjudica el ecoturismo a una comunidad?

Fuente #1: El siguiente artículo trata de las ventajas del ecoturismo. El artículo original fue publicado en la página web *Ciberamerica.org*.

Principios, ventajas y potencialidades del ecoturismo
(*www.ciberamerica.org/Ciberamerica/Castellano/Areas/turismo/ecoturismo*)

En este momento la aportación económica del ecoturismo es de suma importancia, sobre todo por parte de las autoridades, y en algunos países ya es parte de un turismo que ha llegado a ser el principal proveedor de divisas *Línea* derivadas del uso de la tierra. Dos ejemplos de buenas prácticas a la hora de
(5) distribuir los ingresos de esta actividad son los de Costa Rica y Belice, lo que indujo a numerosos gobiernos o entidades privadas a enviar misiones a estos países, con el propósito de aprovechar la experiencia acumulada.

En este sentido, lo más apropiado es un turismo cuidadosamente regulado, practicado por personas genuinamente interesadas en la naturaleza, dispuestas
(10) a causar el menor disturbio posible y respetuosas de las costumbres locales. Una técnica para reducir tal impacto es la "zonificación" de áreas protegidas, delimitando las áreas más frágiles con acceso restringido mientras que en otras áreas se permita sólo la visita manteniéndose en el sendero todo el tiempo.

Las áreas protegidas tienen una importante función. En efecto, el uso por
(15) parte de ecoturistas supone la generación de beneficios, tanto tangibles (empleos locales, por ejemplo) como otros (biodiversidad, protección de aguas y suelos). El ecoturismo en muchas instancias ha favorecido la conservación de la naturaleza. Tales argumentos se aplican también a la conservación de los parques marinos y su influencia beneficiosa sobre la productividad para la pesca en áreas cercanas
(20) o a veces situadas a considerable distancia. Hay que evitar que ambos sectores, la pesca y la llegada de ecoturistas compitan. Las zonas protegidas de arrecifes de coral han evitado su possible destrucción y permitido la recuperación de la pesca, especialmente de alevines en estas áreas, además de proveer nuevos empleos. Un proceso similar se ha llevado acabo en humedales y otros entornos.
(25) Por otro lado, el fomento del ecoturismo favorece la conservación de la biodiversidad.

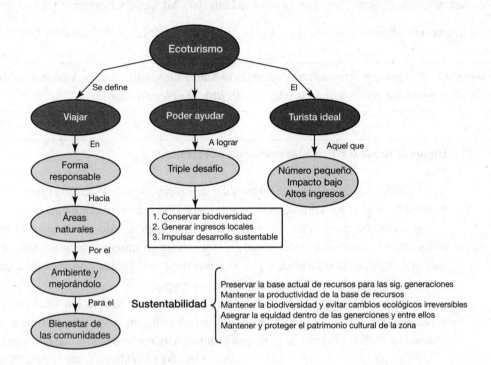

Track 31

Apuntes:

ENSAYO #9

Tema curricular: La vida contemporánea

Primero tienes seis minutos para leer el tema del ensayo y las fuentes número 1 y 2.

Tema del ensayo: ¿Existe de veras una perfecta dieta para llevar una vida saludable?

Fuente #1: El siguiente artículo trata de los problemas de seguir una dieta de moda. El artículo original fue publicado en la página web *http://Enplenitud.com.*

Dietas de moda. Crítica a las promesas milagrosas

La estética ha dejado de ser monopolio de las mujeres. Los hombres también quieren lucir bien y no dudan en consultar para obtener un mejor estado físico.

Las dietas de moda circulan con soluciones mágicas que dicen resolver el problema a la brevedad, descuidando el hecho que en muchos casos se trata de una enfermedad, la obesidad, y por lo tanto debe ser tratada con seriedad. La salud no tiene precio y tampoco es un acto de magia.

A lo largo del tiempo, los modelos van cambiando y, lo que era ideal en el Renacimiento, está lejos de ser aceptado socialmente en este siglo. Hombres y mujeres no dudan a la hora de optar por productos light y largas horas de gimnasio.

Una amplia información es la que circula sobre cómo liberarse de la pesadilla de la gordura. En general, son recetas mágicas que prometen resultados increíbles en muy corto tiempo; pero luego de varios intentos y sin conseguir el tan ansiado logro, los "dietantes" pierden las esperanzas, hasta que aparece una nueva alternativa milagrosa.

El charlatanerismo prolifera cada vez más, basándose en dietas absurdas y promesas de curación definitiva.

Es un negocio, y se basa en la falta de lectura crítica y en la credulidad popular, pero lo que ofrece es tentador y ¿quién no intentó alguna vez las famosas dietas de la Luna, la Sopa, la Fuerza Aérea, la Disociada, etcétera?

El remedio es sencillo: intentar comer de forma más ordenada, tratando de evitar aquellos alimentos de alto valor calórico, pero sin sufrir grandes privaciones.

Realizar actividad física y si es posible consultar a un nutricionista con el fin de obtener la información adecuada para lograr una alimentación balanceada.

El objetivo: sentirse bien, y alcanzar el peso ideal, que no es aquel que marcan las tablas o las fórmulas, sino el que nos permitirá llegar a una mayor longevidad con una mejor calidad de vida.

Mucho es lo que se podría hablar de este tema pero, resumiendo: una dieta prefabricada, general y adaptable a cualquier persona no es más que un producto para vender. Está en cada uno analizar la situación para evitar frustraciones futuras.

No debemos olvidar que se trata de la salud y así como no se busca en revistas el remedio para la presión, tampoco debería hacerse en este caso.

Línea

(5)

(10)

(15)

(20)

(25)

(30)

Fuente #2: El siguiente gráfico presenta el consumo ideal de la dieta mediterránea. El gráfico original fue publicado en la página web *www.enterbio.es* el tres de marzo de 2013.

Fuente #3: La siguiente grabación, titulada "El vegetarianismo y la dieta vegetariana", trata de las recomendaciones de los teóricos de seguir una dieta vegetariana. Se basa en un artículo publicado en *http://Terra.com*.

Track 32

Apuntes:

ENSAYO #10

Tema curricular: La belleza y la estética

Primero tienes seis minutos para leer el tema del ensayo y las fuentes número 1 y 2.

Tema del ensayo: En un mundo globalizado en que muchas comunidades se están mezclando, ¿todavía se puede decir que la gastronomía refleja la cultura de un país?

Fuente #1: El siguiente texto trata de un nuevo restaurante en Venezuela. El artículo original fue publicado por *http://nebraskamagazine.blogspot.com* en enero 2016.

"Cow", restaurante y carnicería gourmet, llega a Maracaibo con un concepto único

Con una concepción completamente diferente, en donde se mezcla un restaurante de carnes y hamburguesas al estilo americano y una carnicería con los cortes más finos del mercado, Cow abre sus puertas en Maracaibo para ofrecer calidad, buen servicio y un excelente concepto gastronómico.

Línea

(5)

"Uno de nuestros claros objetivos es brindar una buena atención y destacar como innovadores. Me di la tarea de recorrer las carnicerías más prestigiosas de Venezuela y ninguna es tan completa como Cow, porque aquí podrás almorzar, desayunar, cenar, tomar un café, un jugo o simplemente hacer compras de carnes, pan o embutidos", destacó Gamaliel López, creador del concepto.

(10)

Asimismo, explicó que el slogan "simple, caliente y sabroso" fue pensado porque en el área del restaurante no sólo probarán la mejor comida, sino que además siempre estará recién hecha y a la temperatura ideal para degustarla.

En el área de carnicería, Cow ofrece cortes Premium, piezas completas y asesoría personalizada; es decir, un chef siempre estará recomendándole cortes,

(15)

recetas y estilos de preparación, con el propósito de ofrecer una atención VIP y única en Maracaibo. Pero si de desayunos se trata, Cow tienta a sus clientes a hacerlo como todo un rey, con desayunos cinco estrellas.

"Quisimos hacer un sitio gourmet muy completo. Desayunos al estilo hotel, hamburguesas americanas, estación de cafés hechos por expertos, set de jugos y

(20)

frutas, además de la carnicería", resaltó López.

Hamburguesas de otro mundo

Para quien ande en busca de la auténtica hamburguesa americana, Cow es el lugar indicado. "En esta onda de hamburguesas gourmet, hacía falta una que representara el verdadero sabor de la hamburguesa. Por eso, en nosotros

(25)

decidimos hacer las mejores", dijo Gamaliel López, gerente general del lugar.

Absolutamente todos los ingredientes son hechos por el restaurante, en donde además podrán comprar su combo "crudo" para preparar dichas hamburguesas en su propia casa. El pan, otra de las grandes sensaciones de Cow, siempre está fresco y los expertos ya los pronostican como el mejor de la ciudad; pero bastará

(30)

con visiten el lugar para que se den cuenta de todo por ustedes mismos.

Fuente #2: El siguiente gráfico presenta los resultados de una encuesta por la Universidad San Ignacio de Loyola en Perú. Los encuestados eran entre diferentes edades y todos respondieron a la pregunta "¿A qué se debe la diversidad de nuestros platos?"

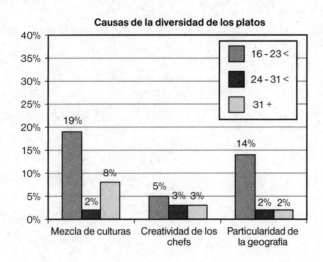

Causas de la diversidad de los platos

Fuente #3: La siguiente grabación es una entrevista entre un turista de la ruta gastronómica española y Ramón Inique, natural de Barcelona. La grabación dura aproximadamente dos minutos, quince segundos.

Track 33

Apuntes:

PART FIVE
Speaking Skills

General Considerations 9

DESCRIPTIONS OF THE SPEAKING TASKS OF THE EXAM

The speaking portion of the exam is divided into two tasks: Task 3: Conversation and Task 4: Cultural Comparison. Both tasks require that you showcase your ability to communicate effectively in Spanish in formal and informal situations. In Task 3: Conversation, you will engage in a simulated conversation. The context of this conversation could be formal or informal, and in your test book you will be given an outline indicating the flow of the conversation. For Task 4: Cultural Comparison, your task is to give a formal oral presentation on a specific topic. In your presentation, you need to compare a community from the Spanish-speaking world with your own community. The question you need to answer will be printed in your test book.

SCORING THE SPEAKING TASKS

The grading of the speaking samples is holistic, meaning that they are analyzed as a whole. No specific item or aspect of language has any point value. Rankings proceed along a continuum from strong, good, fair, weak, and poor. The difference between each level largely hinges on your how well you complete the task. Here are some strategies when approaching the speaking portions of the exam:

- Read the introduction and understand the task you have been assigned to complete.
- For Task 3: Conversation, identify if the context is formal or informal. For Task 4: Cultural Comparison, remember to use a formal tone throughout.
- Address the task as fully as you can and make sure *what* you say is appropriate within the context of the task.
- Speak for the entire allotted time.
- Do not use English unless there is absolutely no Spanish equivalent.

Section II, Part B— Task 3: Conversation

10

The third task of Section II is the Conversation. For this task you are to participate in a simulated conversation. As you begin this task, you will be given a set of directions, an introduction to the conversation, and an outline showing you the flow of the conversation. You will have one minute to read the directions and one additional minute to read the introduction and outline of the conversation. In the outline, the shaded parts indicate the part of the conversation that has already been recorded, and your part is the unshaded part. Following the two minutes, the conversation will begin. Each speaking prompt will be given only once. After each time the other person speaks, you will have 20 seconds to record your response. You can expect to have to respond a total of 5 different times throughout the entire conversation. Typically you won't be expected to initiate the conversation.

SCORING YOUR CONVERSATION

Your score will be based on how well you are able to accomplish this task and can roughly be broken into the following categories:

1. **What you were able to do.**

   - Did you maintain the exchange?
   - Was it clearly appropriate within the context of the task?
   - Did you provide all information with frequent elaboration?
   - Did you use an appropriate tone throughout?

2. **How you were able to do it.**

   - Were your responses fully comprehensible?
   - Did your use of language show some sophistication?

Remember that these two categories work together, and if you answered yes to all the above questions, your reply will score in the high range. One way to know if you are on the path to success is to put yourself in the shoes of the other person in this conversation. Was this a successful conversation? Did you receive all the information you needed? Was it fully comprehensible? If you answered yes to all of these questions, then you are on your way to earning a "5" on this task.

STRATEGIES FOR TASK 3: CONVERSATION

Because of its design, this task is inherently the most artificial of the communicative tasks. It requires you to be able to think on your feet and be able to improvise quickly. One great way to prepare for this is to really immerse yourself in the role you have been asked to play. This will help you be more engaged in this conversation and could lead to a better score.

The following is a guideline about how you should budget your time.

Read the introduction and flow of the conversation (2 minutes).

- Identify with whom you will be conversing and any information about this person.
- Identify immediately the tone that you should use (formal or informal).
- Identify the context of this conversation and where it is taking place (home, school, a sporting event, and so on).
- Make note of any specific type of reactions you are expected to make. Jot down key words that may help you with this reaction. For example, if you are asked to respond negatively, you could jot down *No creo que* (then use the subjunctive). If you are asked to thank someone you could jot down *muchas gracias por* (then use the infinitive form of a verb).

As you speak (20 seconds per response).

- Follow the printed outline. Make a check mark after each prompt so you don't lose your place as you are speaking.
- Try to visualize the person with whom you are speaking. Speak with energy and emotion. If this person is supposed to be your friend, act like he or she is your friend. If this person is a teacher, act more formally and with more respect.
- Answer any questions directly. Do not repeat the question before you answer it.
- Speak for the entire 20 seconds. Do not leave long pauses.
- Speak calmly. Do not try to rush the information. If you sound nervous, the conversation will feel awkward.
- Elaborate often. Be creative with your responses and give lots of information.
- Correct yourself if you make a mistake.

What happens if during the conversation you fail to understand a question?

Because the speaking prompts are only spoken once, at times students may have difficulty understanding a question that was asked. If this happens, the best thing to do is to respond by telling the person that you did not understand the question and then use the rest of the response time to elaborate on something mentioned earlier. The worst thing you can do if you don't understand a question is to say "uhhh" or "ummm" or not say anything at all. This task is evaluating your speaking ability, and therefore you need to provide something that can be evaluated.

USEFUL VOCABULARY

Here is a list of useful phrases and vocabulary that may come in handy during Task 3: Conversation.

To greet someone	*Buenos días* (formal) *Hola, ¿qué tal?* (informal)
To show positive emotion	*¡Qué bien!* *¡Cuánto me alegra!*
To suggest an idea	*Yo recomiendo que . . .* (+ present subjunctive) *Sería mejor que . . .* (+ imperfect subjunctive)
To respond negatively	*No creo que . . .* (+ present subjunctive) *Desafortunadamente no . . .* (+ present indicative)
To thank someone	*Muchas gracias por . . .* (+ infinitive verb) *Agradezco su (tu) . . .* (+ noun)
To end a conversation	*Tengo que irme. Nos vemos.* (Informal) *Adiós.* (Formal and informal) *Hasta luego.* (Formal and informal)

SAMPLE CONVERSATION

Below is a sample of a script similar to the sort you will see on the informal speaking part. Following the script are the steps you will follow to fulfill this part of the exam.

DIRECTIONS: You will now take part in a simulated conversation. First, you will have 1 minute to read a preview of the conversation, including the script for both parts. Then, the conversation will begin and follow the script. Each time it is your turn to speak, you will have 20 seconds to respond.	Ahora vas a participar en una conversación simulada. Primero, tendrás un minuto para leer la introducción y el esquema de la conversación. Después, empezará la conversación, siguiendo el esquema. Cada vez que te toque hablar, tendrás 20 segundos para responder.
You should engage in the conversation as much and as appropriately as possible.	Debes participar en la conversación de la forma más completa y apropiada posible.

1. **Tema curricular:** *La belleza y la estética*

   Tienes un minuto para leer la introducción y el esquema de la conversación.

   > **Introducción:** Esta es una conversación con Paco, un amigo tuyo que te ha llamado pidiendo que lo llamaras. Quiere invitarte a un evento en tu escuela.

Track 34

Paco:	Contesta el teléfono.
Tú:	Salúdalo y explica la razón por tu llamada.
Paco:	Continúa la conversación.
Tú:	Reacciona apropiadamente.
Paco:	Continúa la conversación.
Tú:	Reacciona apropiadamente dando detalles.
Paco:	Continúa la conversación.
Tú:	Responde afirmativamente con detalles.
Paco:	Continúa la conversación.
Tú:	Finaliza los planes. Despídete.
Paco:	Concluye la conversación.

2. Note that in the exam, every time it is your turn to speak, you will have 20 seconds to do so. When the speaker finishes, you will hear a tone and then have 20 seconds to respond. The tone will sound at the end of 20 seconds indicating that you should stop speaking and listen to the next part. You should engage in the conversation as much as possible.

NOTE

For the purpose of this sample only, we are providing the following dialogue script with a sample conversation for your reference. You can practice speaking the sample responses, so that you can become more comfortable with the flow and pace of the conversation.

Paco:	Hola
Tú:	Hola Paco, ¿cómo estás? Hace much tiempo que no hablamos. ¿Cómo van las cosas? Acabo de salir de mi clase de ciencias. ¡Qué aburrido! El profesor no dejó de hablar y no contestó ninguna pregunta. Pero, no quiero molestarte con estas cosas. Te llamo porque recibí tu mensaje. Cuéntame, ¿qué novedad tienes?
Paco:	Ah, sí, gracias por llamarme. Querría invitarte a acompañarme a la escuela este fin de semana. Hay un drama buenísimo que se da, se llama *Sueño*.
Tú:	¿De veras? ¡Qué divertido! Ya sabes cuánto me fascinan las obras de teatro. No recuerdo la última vez que fui a una obra. He oído muy buenas cosas de esta obra, y no veo la hora de poder acompañarte. Muchas gracias por pensar en mí.
Paco:	Me dijeron que nuestro compañero de clase es fantástico en el drama. Interpreta el papel del rey. Como recuerdas, leímos una parte de este drama en la obra *La vida es sueño* en la clase de español hace un mes. Me gustaron esos versos de "¿Qué es la vida? Una ilusión,". . . etcétera.
Tú:	Miguel es un actor muy talentoso, y seguro que un día ganará el premio Oscar por una actuación suya. La verdad es que aunque recuerdo haber leído este drama, no puedo recordar muy bien la trama. Desafortunadamente no tengo tan buena memoria como tú.
Paco:	Sí, los otros de la clase ya han ido y dicen que les gustó. ¿Te gustaría ir conmigo? Te invito.
Tú:	Obviamente que me gustaría ir. Tengo unas tareas que completar antes pero seguro que voy a poder asistir contigo. Si la obra es tan buena como dicen los demás, va a ser una noche para no olvidar.
Paco:	¡Estupendo! Te encontraré enfrente del teatro a las siete.
Tú:	Perfecto. Entonces, por qué no planeamos tomar algo después. Ya sabes que no me gusta comer tan pronto, y creo que tendremos suficiente tiempo para tomarnos un cafecito. Mira, tengo que irme porque tengo un montón de tarea. Pero muchas gracias otra vez. Te veré el sábado.
Paco:	De acuerdo amigo. Nos vemos.

3. The recording is finished. You will check to see that your voice was recorded.

Now study the model above and complete the practice exercises that follow. This will give you enough practice, so that when you get to the exam, the task will be familiar to you. You can easily imagine your own sample conversations with a little practice. The more you practice, the more comfortable and relaxed you will be and the better your speech sample will be.

DIRECTIONS: You will now take part in a simulated conversation. First, you will have 1 minute to read a preview of the conversation, including the script for both parts. Then, the conversation will begin and follow the script. Each time it is your turn to speak, you will have 20 seconds to respond.

You should engage in the conversation as much and as appropriately as possible.

Ahora vas a participar en una conversación simulada. Primero, tendrás un minuto para leer la introducción y el esquema de la conversación. Después, empezará la conversación, siguiendo el esquema. Cada vez que te toque hablar, tendrás 20 segundos para responder.

Debes participar en la conversación de la forma más completa y apropiada posible.

CONVERSACIÓN #1

Tema curricular: *La vida contemporánea*

Tienes un minuto para leer la introducción y el esquema de la conversación.

Introducción: Tú estás de viaje. Te encuentras en una ciudad desconocida y te has perdido en el centro, no muy lejos del hotel. Tienes que preguntar a alguien cómo se llega al hotel. Entras en una tienda para preguntar a un dependiente cómo llegar allá.

Track 35

Dependiente:	Te salúda.
Tú:	Responde apropiadamente. Hazle una pregunta.
Dependiente:	Contesta a la pregunta. Te hace una pregunta.
Tú:	Responde que no tienes la dirección.
Dependiente:	Te pide otros nombres.
Tú:	Nombrale otro lugar.
Dependiente:	Responde con otra pregunta.
Tú:	Dale otro descriptivo. Pídele la dirección.
Dependiente:	Te dice que la reconoce. Te instruye cómo llegar.
Tú:	Reaccióna. Despídete del dependiente.

CONVERSACIÓN #2

Tema curricular: *Los desafíos mundiales*

Tienes un minuto para leer la introducción y el esquema de la conversación

> **Introducción:** Imagina que estás en una entrevista con un profesor tuyo para recibir una beca este verano para estudiar más a fondo un asunto relacionado con el medio ambiente.

Track 36

Profesor Sánchez:	Te saluda y empieza la conversación.
Tú:	Saluda y responde apropiadamente.
Profesor Sánchez:	Continúa la conversación y te hace otra pregunta.
Tú:	Contesta la pregunta ofreciendo detalles.
Profesor Sánchez:	Continúa la conversación y te hace otra pregunta.
Tú:	Contesta la pregunta con detalles.
Profesor Sánchez:	Continúa la conversación.
Tú:	Contesta negativamente, y ofrece una alternativa.
Profesor Sánchez:	Termina la conversación y se despide.
Tú:	Termina la conversación y despídete.

CONVERSACIÓN #3

Tema curricular: *Las identidades personales y públicas*

Tienes un minuto para leer la introducción y el esquema de la conversación.

Introducción: Tú eres un estudiante nuevo en una escuela. Tu familia acaba de mudarse a esta nueva ciudad y tú tienes que cultivar un nuevo grupo de amigos en la escuela.

Track 37

Cristina:	Saluda y te hace una pregunta.
Tú:	Saluda y responde apropiadamente.
Cristina:	Continúa la conversación y te hace otra pregunta.
Tú:	Reacciona apropiadamente con detalles.
Cristina:	Continúa la conversación y te hace otra pregunta.
Tú:	Contesta la pregunta con detalles.
Cristina:	Continúa la conversación y te invita a un evento.
Tú:	Contesta negativamente, y ofrece una alternativa.
Cristina:	Termina la conversación y se despide.
Tú:	Termina la conversación y despídete.

CONVERSACIÓN #4

Tema curricular: *La vida contemporánea*

Tienes un minuto para leer la introducción y el esquema de la conversación.

> **Introducción:** Este verano necesitas encontrar empleo para ahorrar dinero para la universidad. Tienes una entrevista con la gerenta de una compañía donde quieres obtener empleo. Imagina la conversación entre tú y la gerenta.

Track 38

Gerenta:	Te saluda.
Tú:	Responde apropiadamente.
Gerenta:	Te hace una pregunta.
Tú:	Explícale tus razones.
Gerenta:	Reacciona de buena manera. Te hace otra pregunta.
Tú:	Responde. Cuéntale algo que has hecho. Expresa tus esperanzas. Pregúntale cuánta experiencia hace falta para el trabajo.
Gerenta:	Te contesta. Te ofrece un puesto.
Tú:	Reacciona favorablemente. Acepta.
Gerenta:	Te responde
Tú:	Dale las gracias. Despídete te de ella.

CONVERSACIÓN #5

Tema curricular: *La ciencia y la tecnología*

Tienes un minuto para leer la introducción y el esquema de la conversación.

> **Introducción:** Para la próxima edición del periódico de tu revista estudiantil necesitas entrevistar al director de la cafetería de su escuela porque los alumnos acaban de hacer una encuesta sobre la comida en la cafetería y la falta de comida nutritiva en el menú.

Track 39

Director:	Te saluda.
Tú:	Respóndele apropiadamente.
Director:	Comentario sobre sus relaciones con los estudiantes. Te hace una pregunta.
Tú:	Explícale el propósito de la visita. Hazle una pregunta.
Director:	Contesta a la pregunta.
Tú:	Cuéntale los resultados de la encuesta. Hazle otra pregunta.
Director:	Te hace una pregunta de respuesta.
Tú:	Comunica los deseos de los estudiantes.
Director:	Propone una idea.
Tú:	Reacciona favorablemente.
Director:	Responde con sus deseos.
Tú:	Despídete de él.

CONVERSACIÓN #6

Tema curricular: *Las familias y las comunidades*

Tienes un minuto para leer la introducción y el esquema de la conversación.

> **Introducción:** Imagina que ves a Luis durante el almuerzo un día. Está un poco molesto y tú quieres saber por qué.

Track 40

Tú:	Salúdale y pregunta por su estado de ánimo.
Luis:	Te informa de lo que lo está molestando.
Tú:	Reacciona y trata de consolarlo.
Luis:	Continúa la conversación y te hace otra pregunta.
Tú:	Contesta la pregunta con detalles.
Luis:	Continúa la conversación y te invita a un evento.
Tú:	Contesta la pregunta con detalles.
Luis:	Continúa la conversación y te invita a un evento.
Tú:	Contesta negativamente y ofrece una alternativa. Despídete.
Luis:	Saluda y te hace una pregunta.

CONVERSACIÓN #7

Tema curricular: *La belleza y la estética*

Tienes un minuto para leer la introducción y el esquema de la conversación.

> **Introducción:** Imagina que eres una estudiante y que estás en el norte, en febrero, y necesitas una blusa de cierto estilo para un papel en un drama en la escuela. Vas a comprarla. Entras en una tienda y hablas con una dependienta sobre lo que necesitas.

Track 41

Dependienta:	Se dirige a ti.
Tú:	Responde apropiadamente. Explícale lo que necesitas.
Dependienta:	Comenta sobre tu pedido. Comenta sobre la mercancía. Ofrece mostrártela.
Tú:	Agradécele. Dile lo que buscas en particular.
Dependienta:	Te sugiere algo. Te hace una pregunta.
Tú:	Contesta la pregunta. Expresa una preferencia. Hazle otra pregunta.
Dependienta:	Contesta. Expresa una opinión.
Tú:	Responde.
Dependienta:	Concluye el trato.
Tú:	Expresa gratitud.
Dependienta:	Te responde. Te invita a volver.

CONVERSACIÓN #8

Tema curricular: *La vida contemporánea*

Tienes un minuto para leer la introducción y el esquema de la conversación.

Introducción: Imagina que trabajas en un restaurante. Un día un cliente entra para almorzar. Parece que es la primera vez que esta persona ha venido al restaurante.

Track 42

Tú:	Dirígete apropiadamente al cliente. Hazle una pregunta.
Cliente:	Responde. Pide más información.
Tú:	Responde. Hazle otra pregunta.
Cliente:	Te pide información.
Tú:	Nombra unos platos.
Cliente:	Te pide una sugerencia.
Tú:	Sugiere uno de los platos que acabas de nombrar. Descríbelo con más detalle.
Cliente:	Acepta tu sugerencia. Te hace una pregunta.
Tú:	Nombra la selección.
Cliente:	Completa su selección.
Tú:	Termina la conversación.

CONVERSACIÓN #9

Tema curricular: *La ciencia y la tecnología*

Tienes un minuto para leer la introducción y el esquema de la conversación.

> **Introducción:** Un día te despiertas con síntomas tan malos que no puedes asistir a tus clases. Tienes que llamar a la enfermera de la oficina médica de tu doctor para pedir una cita.

Track 43

	Suena el teléfono.
Enfermera:	Saluda.
Tú:	Responde apropiadamente. Explica el motivo de tu llamada.
Enfermera:	Te hace una pregunta.
Tú:	Explica tus síntomas.
Enfermera:	Te hace otras preguntas.
Tú:	Contesta. Haz una pregunta.
Enfermera:	Comenta sobre tu estado. Hace una pregunta.
Tú:	Explica que sí, pero con una condición.
Enfermera:	Responde.
Tú:	Responde apropiadamente. Despídete.
Enfermera:	Se despide.

CONVERSACIÓN #10

Tema curricular: *Las identidades personales y públicas*

Tienes un minuto para leer la introducción y el esquema de la conversación.

> **Introducción:** Imagina que estás en un café con tu amiga Carlota. Ella te pidió que la encontraras porque quiere hablarte de un problema que tiene.

Track 44

Tú:	Saluda y empieza la conversación.
Carlota:	Te explica su dilema.
Tú:	Reacciona y pídele más información.
Carlota:	Continúa la conversación y te hace una pregunta.
Tú:	Contesta la pregunta con detalles.
Carlota:	Continúa la conversación y te hace otra pregunta.
Tú:	Contesta la pregunta con detalles.
Carlota:	Continúa la conversación y te hace otra pregunta.
Tú:	Contesta negativamente explicando por qué. Termina la conversación y despídete.
Carlota:	Termina la conversación y se despide.

Section II, Part B—Task 4: Cultural Comparison

11

The final task of Section II is the Cultural Comparison. For this task you are to answer a question printed in your test book. In your response, you need to use an example from a community in the Spanish-speaking world and one from your own community as evidence to support your answer. You will have one minute to read the directions and four minutes to read the question and prepare your presentation. You then will have two minutes to present.

SCORING YOUR CULTURAL COMPARISON PRESENTATION

Your score will be based on how well you answer the question and your knowledge of the target cultures. Your overall grade can be broken into the following categories:

1. **What you were able to do.**

   - Is your treatment of the topic clearly effective?
   - Do you clearly compare your own community with the target culture?
   - Do you demonstrate good understanding of the target culture?

2. **How you were able to do it.**

   - Was your response fully comprehensible?
   - Was your response well organized and cohesive?
   - Did your use of language show some sophistication?

As with all other tasks in Section II, these two categories work together. If you answered yes to all the above questions, your reply will score in the high range.

STRATEGIES FOR TASK 4: CULTURAL COMPARISON

Cultural knowledge is vital in your ability to answer this question. You can use information that you have learned from any source, including materials that you may have read; conversations with native speakers; programs on television, radio, and the internet; and any experiences that you may have had first-hand. The best way to be prepared to talk about the possible topics is by familiarizing yourself with as much culture from the Spanish-speaking world as possible.

The following is a guideline about how you should budget your time.

Read the introduction question (4 minutes).

- Underline key words from the question.
- Identify a key example from <u>one</u> Spanish-speaking community and one from your own community.
- Create a flow chart like the following to help organize your ideas.

Palabras clave de la pregunta			
Evidencia			
	¿Dónde?	**Descripción del ejemplo**	**¿Cómo responde a la pregunta?**
Comunidad hispanohablante			
Mi comunidad			

As you speak (2 minutes).

- Relax! Your presentation does not have to be exhaustive. It simply is a sample that demonstrates that you have good knowledge of Spanish-speaking communities and your own community, and that you can present your ideas clearly and concisely.
- Organize your presentation with a brief introduction (10 seconds max.) in which you inform your audience of your topic.
- Begin your body with an example from the Spanish-speaking world. Use the flow chart as you present your ideas.
- Present your second example from your own community. Explain how it is similar or different than the one used for the Spanish-speaking community.
- If you have time, give a conclusion. However, a conclusion is not necessary.
- Speak for the entire 2 minutes. Do not end too early and make sure you get in both examples before the 2 minutes expire.
- Correct yourself if you make a mistake.

It is quite difficult to give a detailed oral presentation in two minutes, and most students will not be able to finish within the allotted time. This does not mean, however, that your goal should be not to finish, but rather it should be to give the strongest presentation you can, regardless of whether or not you finish it in two minutes.

USEFUL VOCABULARY

Just like with Task 2: Argumentative Essay, any formal presentation is enhanced by the use of transitional phrases. Here are some that will be helpful.

To introduce an idea	*Como punto de partida . . .* *Para empezar . . .*
To add to an idea	*Además . . .* *En segundo lugar . . .*
To explain an idea	*Por ejemplo . . .* *Para ilustrar . . .*
To contrast	*Por otro lado . . .* *Sin embargo . . .* *No obstante . . .*
To compare	*De la misma manera . . .*

To show a result	Por consiguiente . . . Como resultado . . . Debido a lo anterior . . .
To conclude or summarize	Por fin . . . En suma . . . Para concluir . . .

SAMPLE CULTURAL COMPARISON PRESENTATION

DIRECTIONS: You will now prepare an oral presentation for your class on a specific topic. You will have 4 minutes to read the topic and prepare your presentation. Then, you will have 2 minutes to record your presentation.

In your presentation, compare your own community to one of the Spanish-speaking world with which you are familiar. You should demonstrate your understanding of cultural features of the Spanish-speaking world. Your presentation should also be well organized.

Ahora vas a preparar una presentación oral para tu clase de español sobre un tema cultural. Primero, tendrás 4 minutos para leer el tema y preparar tu presentación. Después, tendrás 2 minutos para grabarla.

En tu presentación, compara tu comunidad con una del mundo hispanohablante con el que estés familiarizado. Debes demostrar tu comprensión de los aspectos culturales en el mundo hispanohablante. También, tu presentación debe ser bien organizada.

Tema curricular: Las familias y las comunidades

Tema de la presentación: ¿Qué papel tienen las compañías e instituciones privadas para mejorar el bienestar de una comunidad?

Compara tus observaciones de las comunidades en que has vivido con tus observaciones del una región del mundo hispanohablante que te sea familiar. Puedes referirte a lo que has estudiado, vivido, observado, etc.

Response

The first step is to read the directions to the task and the question. It is a good idea to underline key words so that you know exactly what you need to talk about. The questions will be very general by design, and therefore there are many ways to answer them. Your job is to come up with one good example from your own community and one from a Spanish-speaking country that answers the question. You need to move quickly and jot down a quick outline or flow chart. Here is an example of one way to answer the question above.

Palabras clave de la pregunta	Compañías e instituciones privadas; mejorar el bienestar; comunidad		
Evidencia			
	¿Dónde?	**Descripción del ejemplo**	**¿Cómo responde a la pregunta?**
Comunidad hispanohablante	*Colombia*	*Crépes y Waffles—restaurante que contrata a mujeres cabeza de familia*	*Beneficios: vivienda, seguro médico* *Oportunidad a las mujeres de superarse* *Confianza, mejora autoestima*
Mi comunidad	*Estados Unidos*	*Tom's Shoes—Compañía de ropa* *Donación: sistema de agua sana; fundaciones ayudan a los sin hogar*	*Ayuda a los clientes sentir que están contribuyendo a mejorar la comunidad*

Sample Speaking Response

The following is an example of an oral presentation. Note how it follows the flow chart above.

Buenos días. Estoy aquí para presentarles cómo las compañías e instituciones privadas mejoran el bienestar de una comunidad.

Como punto de partida, en Colombia hay una compañía que se llama Crépes y Waffles. Es una cadena de restaurants cuyos empleados son mayormente mujeres cabeza de familia. Esta compañía no solo les ofrece a las mujeres una forma de mantener a su familia, sino también les ofrece muchos beneficios como el seguro médico y ayuda financiera adicional para poder comprarse una vivienda. Por consiguiente, estas mujeres tienen la oportunidad de superarse y esto ayuda a mejorar su confianza y autoestima. De la misma manera, en los Estados Unidos hay una compañía que se llama Tom's Shoes. Es una compañía que produce ropa pero que también hace una donación por cada producto que alguien compra. Estas donaciones han ayudado a varias comunidades. Por ejemplo Tom's Shoes ha donado dinero para financiar un sistema de agua sana en barrios pobres y ha donado dinero a fundaciones que ayudan a los sin hogar. Además de ayudar a las comunidades que reciben las donaciones, también ayuda a los clientes sentir que están contribuyendo a mejorar la comunidad mundial.

Para concluir, Tom's Shoes y Crépes y Waffles son ejemplos de compañías que actualmente tienen un impacto positivo en mejorar el bienestar de sus comunidades. Si más compañías tuvieran la misma consciencia social, el mundo sería un mejor lugar para todos. Muchas gracias por su amable atención.

NÚMERO 1

Tema curricular: Los desafíos mundiales

Tema de la presentación: ¿Qué impacto tienen los inmigrantes en la economía de un país?

Compara tus observaciones acerca de las comunidades en las que has vivido con tus observaciones de una región del mundo hispanohablante que te sea familiar. En tu presentación, puedes referirte a lo que has estudiado, vivido, observado, etc.

NÚMERO 2

Tema curricular: Los desafíos mundiales

Tema de la presentación: ¿Cuál es la importancia de crear espacios naturales protegidos?

Compara tus observaciones acerca de las comunidades en las que has vivido con tus observaciones de una región del mundo hispanohablante que te sea familiar. En tu presentación, puedes referirte a lo que has estudiado, vivido, observado, etc.

NÚMERO 3

Tema curricular: Los desafíos mundiales

Tema de la presentación: ¿Qué desafíos tienen que enfrentar las comunidades con respecto al tráfico?

Compara tus observaciones acerca de las comunidades en las que has vivido con tus observaciones de una región del mundo hispanohablante que te sea familiar. En tu presentación, puedes referirte a lo que has estudiado, vivido, observado, etc.

NÚMERO 4

Tema curricular: Los desafíos mundiales

Tema de la presentación: ¿Quién es responsable por el bienestar social de una sociedad?

Compara tus observaciones acerca de las comunidades en las que has vivido con tus observaciones de una región del mundo hispanohablante que te sea familiar. En tu presentación, puedes referirte a lo que has estudiado, vivido, observado, etc.

NÚMERO 5

Tema curricular: La ciencia y la tecnología

Tema de la presentación: ¿Cuál es el impacto del uso de teléfonos inteligentes en una comunidad?

Compara tus observaciones acerca de las comunidades en las que has vivido con tus observaciones de una región del mundo hispanohablante que te sea familiar. En tu presentación, puedes referirte a lo que has estudiado, vivido, observado, etc.

NÚMERO 6

Tema curricular: La ciencia y la tecnología

Tema de la presentación: ¿Cuál es la actitud de la gente con respecto a mantener un equilibrio entre el avance y el bienestar de nuestro planeta?

Compara tus observaciones acerca de las comunidades en las que has vivido con tus observaciones de una región del mundo hispanohablante que te sea familiar. En tu presentación, puedes referirte a lo que has estudiado, vivido, observado, etc.

NÚMERO 7

Tema curricular: La ciencia y la tecnología

Tema de la presentación: ¿Cuál es la actitud de la gente con respecto al impacto del ser humano en los fenómenos naturales?

Compara tus observaciones acerca de las comunidades en las que has vivido con tus observaciones de una región del mundo hispanohablante que te sea familiar. En tu presentación, puedes referirte a lo que has estudiado, vivido, observado, etc.

NÚMERO 8

Tema curricular: La ciencia y la tecnología

Tema de la presentación: ¿Cuál es la actitud de la gente con respecto a los avances en la ciencia y la tecnología?

Compara tus observaciones acerca de las comunidades en las que has vivido con tus observaciones de una región del mundo hispanohablante que te sea familiar. En tu presentación, puedes referirte a lo que has estudiado, vivido, observado, etc.

NÚMERO 9

Tema curricular: La vida contemporánea

Tema de la presentación: ¿Cuál es la actitud de la gente con respecto a tener un título universitario?

> Compara tus observaciones acerca de las comunidades en las que has vivido con tus observaciones de una región del mundo hispanohablante que te sea familiar. En tu presentación, puedes referirte a lo que has estudiado, vivido, observado, etc.

NÚMERO 10

Tema curricular: La vida contemporánea

Tema de la presentación: ¿Qué aspectos del tiempo libre y el ocio valoran más los jóvenes?

> Compara tus observaciones acerca de las comunidades en las que has vivido con tus observaciones de una región del mundo hispanohablante que te sea familiar. En tu presentación, puedes referirte a lo que has estudiado, vivido, observado, etc.

NÚMERO 11

Tema curricular: La vida contemporánea

Tema de la presentación: Al viajar a otro país para conocer mejor su cultura, ¿qué consideraciones son importantes tener en cuenta?

> Compara tus observaciones acerca de las comunidades en las que has vivido con tus observaciones de una región del mundo hispanohablante que te sea familiar. En tu presentación, puedes referirte a lo que has estudiado, vivido, observado, etc.

NÚMERO 12

Tema curricular: La vida contemporánea

Tema de la presentación: ¿Qué importancia tienen las tradiciones en una comunidad?

> Compara tus observaciones acerca de las comunidades en las que has vivido con tus observaciones de una región del mundo hispanohablante que te sea familiar. En tu presentación, puedes referirte a lo que has estudiado, vivido, observado, etc.

NÚMERO 13

Tema curricular: Las identidades personales y públicas

Tema de la presentación: ¿Qué importancia tienen las figuras históricas en el orgullo nacional de un país?

> Compara tus observaciones acerca de las comunidades en las que has vivido con tus observaciones de una región del mundo hispanohablante que te sea familiar. En tu presentación, puedes referirte a lo que has estudiado, vivido, observado, etc.

NÚMERO 14

Tema curricular: Las identidades personales y públicas

Tema de la presentación: ¿Qué elementos de una cultura mejor definen su identidad?

> Compara tus observaciones acerca de las comunidades en las que has vivido con tus observaciones de una región del mundo hispanohablante que te sea familiar. En tu presentación, puedes referirte a lo que has estudiado, vivido, observado, etc.

NÚMERO 15

Tema curricular: Las identidades personales y públicas

Tema de la presentación: ¿Qué aspectos de la vida cotidiana influencian la autoestima de una persona?

> Compara tus observaciones acerca de las comunidades en las que has vivido con tus observaciones de una región del mundo hispanohablante que te sea familiar. En tu presentación, puedes referirte a lo que has estudiado, vivido, observado, etc.

NÚMERO 16

Tema curricular: Las identidades personales y públicas

Tema de la presentación: ¿Cuál es la actitud de la gente con respecto a aprender una lengua extranjera?

> Compara tus observaciones acerca de las comunidades en las que has vivido con tus observaciones de una región del mundo hispanohablante que te sea familiar. En tu presentación, puedes referirte a lo que has estudiado, vivido, observado, etc.

NÚMERO 17

Tema curricular: Las familias y las comunidades

Tema de la presentación: ¿De qué forma han cambiado las estructuras de la familia?

> Compara tus observaciones acerca de las comunidades en las que has vivido con tus observaciones de una región del mundo hispanohablante que te sea familiar. En tu presentación, puedes referirte a lo que has estudiado, vivido, observado, etc.

NÚMERO 18

Tema curricular: Las familias y las comunidades

Tema de la presentación: ¿Cuál ha sido la influencia de redes sociales en las relaciones interpersonales?

> Compara tus observaciones acerca de las comunidades en las que has vivido con tus observaciones de una región del mundo hispanohablante que te sea familiar. En tu presentación, puedes referirte a lo que has estudiado, vivido, observado, etc.

NÚMERO 19

Tema curricular: Las familias y las comunidades

Tema de la presentación: ¿Qué beneficios aportan la vida urbana y la campestre?

> Compara tus observaciones acerca de las comunidades en las que has vivido con tus observaciones de una región del mundo hispanohablante que te sea familiar. En tu presentación, puedes referirte a lo que has estudiado, vivido, observado, etc.

NÚMERO 20

Tema curricular: Las familias y las comunidades

Tema de la presentación: ¿Cuál es la actitud de la gente con respecto a comer juntos?

> Compara tus observaciones acerca de las comunidades en las que has vivido con tus observaciones de una región del mundo hispanohablante que te sea familiar. En tu presentación, puedes referirte a lo que has estudiado, vivido, observado, etc.

NÚMERO 21

Tema curricular: La belleza y la estética

Tema de la presentación: ¿Qué influencia tienen las películas y programas de televisión a la cultura de la gente?

Compara tus observaciones acerca de las comunidades en las que has vivido con tus observaciones de una región del mundo hispanohablante que te sea familiar. En tu presentación, puedes referirte a lo que has estudiado, vivido, observado, etc.

NÚMERO 22

Tema curricular: La belleza y la estética

Tema de la presentación: ¿Quién importancia tiene la música en la vida de los jóvenes?

Compara tus observaciones acerca de las comunidades en las que has vivido con tus observaciones de una región del mundo hispanohablante que te sea familiar. En tu presentación, puedes referirte a lo que has estudiado, vivido, observado, etc.

NÚMERO 23

Tema curricular: La belleza y la estética

Tema de la presentación: ¿De dónde viene la inspiración para la creación artística?

Compara tus observaciones acerca de las comunidades en las que has vivido con tus observaciones de una región del mundo hispanohablante que te sea familiar. En tu presentación, puedes referirte a lo que has estudiado, vivido, observado, etc.

NÚMERO 24

Tema curricular: La belleza y la estética

Tema de la presentación: ¿Qué función tiene el arte en reflejar la vida y los valores de una sociedad?

Compara tus observaciones acerca de las comunidades en las que has vivido con tus observaciones de una región del mundo hispanohablante que te sea familiar. En tu presentación, puedes referirte a lo que has estudiado, vivido, observado, etc.

PART SIX
Practice Tests

PART SIX
Practice Tests

ANSWER SHEET
Practice Test 1

SECTION I

PART A

1. Ⓐ Ⓑ Ⓒ Ⓓ
2. Ⓐ Ⓑ Ⓒ Ⓓ
3. Ⓐ Ⓑ Ⓒ Ⓓ
4. Ⓐ Ⓑ Ⓒ Ⓓ
5. Ⓐ Ⓑ Ⓒ Ⓓ
6. Ⓐ Ⓑ Ⓒ Ⓓ
7. Ⓐ Ⓑ Ⓒ Ⓓ
8. Ⓐ Ⓑ Ⓒ Ⓓ
9. Ⓐ Ⓑ Ⓒ Ⓓ
10. Ⓐ Ⓑ Ⓒ Ⓓ

11. Ⓐ Ⓑ Ⓒ Ⓓ
12. Ⓐ Ⓑ Ⓒ Ⓓ
13. Ⓐ Ⓑ Ⓒ Ⓓ
14. Ⓐ Ⓑ Ⓒ Ⓓ
15. Ⓐ Ⓑ Ⓒ Ⓓ
16. Ⓐ Ⓑ Ⓒ Ⓓ
17. Ⓐ Ⓑ Ⓒ Ⓓ
18. Ⓐ Ⓑ Ⓒ Ⓓ
19. Ⓐ Ⓑ Ⓒ Ⓓ
20. Ⓐ Ⓑ Ⓒ Ⓓ

21. Ⓐ Ⓑ Ⓒ Ⓓ
22. Ⓐ Ⓑ Ⓒ Ⓓ
23. Ⓐ Ⓑ Ⓒ Ⓓ
24. Ⓐ Ⓑ Ⓒ Ⓓ
25. Ⓐ Ⓑ Ⓒ Ⓓ
26. Ⓐ Ⓑ Ⓒ Ⓓ
27. Ⓐ Ⓑ Ⓒ Ⓓ
28. Ⓐ Ⓑ Ⓒ Ⓓ
29. Ⓐ Ⓑ Ⓒ Ⓓ
30. Ⓐ Ⓑ Ⓒ Ⓓ

PART B

31. Ⓐ Ⓑ Ⓒ Ⓓ
32. Ⓐ Ⓑ Ⓒ Ⓓ
33. Ⓐ Ⓑ Ⓒ Ⓓ
34. Ⓐ Ⓑ Ⓒ Ⓓ
35. Ⓐ Ⓑ Ⓒ Ⓓ
36. Ⓐ Ⓑ Ⓒ Ⓓ
37. Ⓐ Ⓑ Ⓒ Ⓓ
38. Ⓐ Ⓑ Ⓒ Ⓓ
39. Ⓐ Ⓑ Ⓒ Ⓓ
40. Ⓐ Ⓑ Ⓒ Ⓓ
41. Ⓐ Ⓑ Ⓒ Ⓓ
42. Ⓐ Ⓑ Ⓒ Ⓓ

43. Ⓐ Ⓑ Ⓒ Ⓓ
44. Ⓐ Ⓑ Ⓒ Ⓓ
45. Ⓐ Ⓑ Ⓒ Ⓓ
46. Ⓐ Ⓑ Ⓒ Ⓓ
47. Ⓐ Ⓑ Ⓒ Ⓓ
48. Ⓐ Ⓑ Ⓒ Ⓓ
49. Ⓐ Ⓑ Ⓒ Ⓓ
50. Ⓐ Ⓑ Ⓒ Ⓓ
51. Ⓐ Ⓑ Ⓒ Ⓓ
52. Ⓐ Ⓑ Ⓒ Ⓓ
53. Ⓐ Ⓑ Ⓒ Ⓓ
54. Ⓐ Ⓑ Ⓒ Ⓓ

55. Ⓐ Ⓑ Ⓒ Ⓓ
56. Ⓐ Ⓑ Ⓒ Ⓓ
57. Ⓐ Ⓑ Ⓒ Ⓓ
58. Ⓐ Ⓑ Ⓒ Ⓓ
59. Ⓐ Ⓑ Ⓒ Ⓓ
60. Ⓐ Ⓑ Ⓒ Ⓓ
61. Ⓐ Ⓑ Ⓒ Ⓓ
62. Ⓐ Ⓑ Ⓒ Ⓓ
63. Ⓐ Ⓑ Ⓒ Ⓓ
64. Ⓐ Ⓑ Ⓒ Ⓓ
65. Ⓐ Ⓑ Ⓒ Ⓓ

Practice Test 1

SECTION I, PART A

Interpretive Communication: Print Texts

Time: Approximately 40 minutes

> **DIRECTIONS:** Read the following passages. After each passage there are a number of questions for you to answer, based on the information provided in the reading selection. For each question, choose the response that is best according to the selection and mark your answer on the answer sheet.
>
> Lee los siguientes textos. Cada texto va acompañado de varias preguntas que debes contestar, según la información en el texto. Para cada pregunta, elige la mejor respuesta según el contexto y escríbela en la hoja de respuestas.

Tema curricular: Las familias y las comunidades

Introducción: El siguiente fragmento, que trata de un rito de pasaje, proviene del cuento *Pequeñeces* por P. Luis Coloma.

La orquesta dio principio al acto, tocando magistralmente la obertura de *Semíramis*. El rector, anciano religioso, honra y gloria de la Orden a que pertenecía, pronunció después un breve discurso, que no pudo terminar. Al fijarse sus
Línea apagados ojos en aquel montón de cabecitas rubias y negras, que atentamente
(5) le miraban, apiñadas y expresivas como los angelitos de una gloria de Murillo, comenzó a balbucear, y las lágrimas le cortaron la palabra.

—¡No lloro porque os vais!—pudo decir, al cabo—. ¡Lloro porque muchos no volverán nunca! . . .

La nube de cabecitas comenzó a agitarse negativamente y un aplauso espon-
(10) táneo y bullicioso brotó de aquellas doscientas manitas, como una protesta cariñosa que hizo sonreír al anciano en medio de sus lágrimas.

El secretario del colegio comenzó a leer entonces los nombres de los alumnos premiados: levantábanse estos ruborosos y aturdidos por el miedo a la exhibición y la embriaguez del triunfo; iban a recibir la medalla y el diploma de manos del
(15) arzobispo, entre los aplausos de los compañeros, los sones de la música y los bravos del público, y volvían presurosos a sus sitios, buscando con la vista en los ojos de sus padres y de sus madres la mirada de inmenso cariño y orgullo legítimo, que era para ellos complemento del triunfo.

1. ¿Qué evento narra este fragmento?
   (A) Una fiesta religiosa
   (B) Un concierto de música clásica
   (C) La otorgación de premios después de un concurso
   (D) Una celebración escolar

2. ¿Por qué no pudo terminar el rector su discurso?
   (A) Se conmovió.
   (B) Vio una aparición.
   (C) Alguien lo interrumpió.
   (D) Se le olvidó lo que iba a decir.

3. ¿A qué se refieren las "cabecitas" (líneas 4 y 9)?
   (A) A unos ángeles
   (B) A una obra de arte
   (C) A los jóvenes
   (D) A los padres

4. ¿Qué adjetivo mejor describir la relación entre el rector y el público a que habla?
   (A) Odiosa
   (B) Indiferente
   (C) Hostil
   (D) Afectuosa

5. ¿Quiénes son los "premiados" (línea 13)?
   (A) Jóvenes universitarios
   (B) Niños pequeños
   (C) Miembros de la iglesia
   (D) Ex miembros de una escuela

6. ¿Qué emoción predomina en este fragmento?
   (A) Tristeza
   (B) Alegría
   (C) Nostalgia
   (D) Molestia

7. ¿Cuál de lo siguiente sería el más probable de ocurrir inmediatamente después de esta escena?
   (A) El comienzo de las clases
   (B) Un sermón de regaño
   (C) Un festejo entre familiares
   (D) Un recorrido musical por diferentes estilos

Tema curricular: La vida contemporánea

Introducción: La siguiente fuente es un anuncio de una compañía en el sector de viajes que les pueda interesar a sus clientes.

Línea

(5)

(10)

Ahora, visitar a familiares y amigos le cuesta hasta un 35 por ciento menos de nuestras tarifas ya rebajadas. Aeronaves quiere celebrar con usted su nuevo y cómodo servicio a Mérida, México, y a Tegucigalpa, Honduras, vía Houston, ¡con tarifas superespeciales! Y para celebrar en grande, se han rebajado las tarifas a todas las ciudades que sirve en Latinoamérica. Pero apúrese, porque debe comprar sus boletos de ida y vuelta, mínimo 7 días antes de viajar, y sólo tiene hasta el 8 de febrero para comprarlos. La nueva y comodísima terminal internacional de Aeronaves en el aeropuerto hace más fácil que nunca viajar a Latinoamérica, incluyendo los trámites de aduana e inmigración. Además, cada vez que viaja con Aeronaves, gana millaje con nuestro programa Número Uno, una de las maneras más rápidas de ganar viajes gratis. ¡Inscríbase y comience a ganar!

(15)

(20)

Estas tarifas están basadas en la compra de boletos de ida y vuelta, los que deben adquirirse no más tarde del 8 de febrero, o sea una semana en adelante. Los boletos deben comprarse un mínimo de 7 días antes de viajar. La máxima estadía es de 60 días y todos los viajes deben terminar el 23 de marzo del año actual, o antes. El importe de los boletos no es reembolsable. Hay un cargo de US$75 si se hacen determinados cambios en las reservaciones. Solicite los detalles. Estas tarifas son para viajes que se originan en Tejas. El servicio a Guayaquil comenzará el 6 de febrero. Estas tarifas están sujetas a la aprobación del gobierno y pueden cambiar sin previo aviso.

8. ¿Qué anuncia en esta selección?
   (A) Maneras de conseguir viajes gratuitos con el programa Número Uno
   (B) Una nueva manera de facilitar los trámites de aduana e inmigración
   (C) Consejos para saber cuándo es mejor comprar boletos aéreos
   (D) Una venta de vuelos con destino a unos países al sur de EE.UU.

9. ¿Con qué motivo se promueve esta oferta?
   (A) Se celebran el Año de la Familia.
   (B) Se celebran el establecimiento del programa Número Uno.
   (C) Se celebra su nuevo servicio del nuevo aeropuerto.
   (D) Se celebra iniciar vuelos con destinos distintos para la línea.

10. Una persona puede aprovechar esta oferta con tal de que . . .
    (A) compre el boleto sin hacer ningunos cambios en el itinerario.
    (B) se salga rumbo al sur de Tejas en el viaje.
    (C) se inscriba en el programa Número Uno.
    (D) permanezca más de dos meses en su destino.

11. Si por alguna razón una persona no puede usar el boleto, ¿qué recurso tiene?
    (A) Se puede recibir un reembolso por el precio del boleto.
    (B) Se puede cambiarlo con un pago adicional.
    (C) Se puede usarlo para recibir un descuento en otro boleto.
    (D) No se ofrecen reembolsos ni modificaciones.

12. ¿En qué mes habría aparecido este texto?
    (A) En el mes de enero
    (B) En el mes de febrero
    (C) En el mes de marzo
    (D) En el mes de abril

SELECCIÓN #3

Tema curricular: Los desafíos mundiales

Fuente #1

Introducción: El siguiente artículo trata del envejecimiento de la población en España. El artículo original fue publicado en *Eroski Consumer* en 2005.

Abuelos en adopción

El envejecimiento de España se ha convertido en una realidad creciente. La población mayor de 65 años en nuestro país es siete veces mayor que la registrada a comienzos del siglo XX. En concreto, más de siete millones de españoles
Línea se hallan dentro de la denominada tercera edad y más de un millón, el 20%, vive
(5) solo todo el año, una cifra que se multiplica durante los meses de verano. Para ellos, la soledad se ha convertido en uno de los problemas más graves al que se enfrentan, tanto es así que según las estadísticas les preocupa más que otras cuestiones como la salud y las pensiones tan ajustadas que reciben muchos de ellos.

El papel que en la actualidad ocupan nuestros mayores poco tiene que ver con
(10) el de generaciones anteriores. Diluido el concepto de 'barrio', sobre todo en las grandes ciudades, donde incluso se les trataba de 'Don', las relaciones humanas en los núcleos urbanos se han modificado y ha dejado de ser habitual que, por ejemplo, los vecinos se dirijan a ellos para preguntarles si necesitan algo.

La ONG Solidarios, consciente de esta necesidad de compañía tan demandada
(15) por los mayores, trabaja desde el año 1995 con más de 600 voluntarios en el programa 'Acompañamiento de ancianos', del que se benefician cerca de 1.000 ancianos en todo el país. Su iniciativa consiste en poner en contacto a la persona que ofrece la compañía y al anciano que demanda un acompañante.

A esta preparación se suman los 'cursos de cuidados', centrados en las tareas
(20) prácticas que deben llevar a cabo en su compañía; cómo promover actividades de ocio, conocimientos básicos para los más enfermos, minusválidos o personas con discapacidad física y mental.

Una vez seleccionada la pareja, el programa fija en dos horas el tiempo que deben pasar juntos. En ese tiempo el voluntario se adapta a los deseos o necesidades de
(25) la persona mayor: puede acompañarle al médico, realizar trámites administrativos, llevarle a una cafetería con sus amigos o quedarse en casa charlando con él. La ONG advierte de que no se puede superar este tiempo de compañía. No obstante, el voluntario suele hacer un seguimiento de su pareja por teléfono, le pregunta sobre su salud, si ha tomado la medicación, etc.

(30) Respecto a la financiación del proyecto, éste cuenta con la colaboración de Iberdrola para promocionar la campaña de ayuda a los mayores 2005 y cubrir los gastos mínimos de transporte de los voluntarios y las necesidades más urgentes de los ancianos: taxis adaptados, sus traslados en metros y autobuses, etc.

Fuente #2

Introducción: La siguiente tabla presenta la tasa de dependencia en España en 2012 y la predicción para el año 2052. Se basa en datos del Instituto Nacional de Estadísticas en 2012.

Años	Mayores de 64 años	Menores de 16 años	Total (mayores de 16 y menores de 64 años)
2012	26,14	24,25	50,39
2022	33,30	24,81	58,11
2032	45,24	22,49	67,73
2042	62,23	24,27	88,50
2052	73,09	26,41	99,50

La tasa de dependencia se expresa en porcentaje. Las cifras representan la relación entre la población de menores de 16 años y mayores de 64 años por cada 100 miembros de la población entre 16 años y 64 años.

13. ¿Cuál es el propósito del artículo impreso?
    (A) Presentar la situación demográfica en España en este momento
    (B) Analizar cómo se puede afrontar el envejecimiento en España
    (C) Informar sobre una iniciativa para ayudar a los de tercera edad
    (D) Resumir las causas y efectos del envejecimiento en general

14. ¿Qué usa el autor para apoyar sus afirmaciones iniciales?
    (A) Datos específicos
    (B) Testimonios de los de tercera edad
    (C) Opiniones de varios expertos
    (D) Sólo usa su propia convicción

15. ¿A qué se refiere el número 20% (línea 4)?
    (A) Al porcentaje de población mayor en relación a la población española
    (B) Al incremento de la población de tercera edad desde el siglo XX
    (C) Al porcentaje de la población mayor de 65 años que vive sola durante el verano
    (D) Al porcentaje de gente de tercera edad que tiene que cuidarse sola

16. Según el artículo, ¿qué cambios se ha notado en la sociedad en general?
    (A) Los de tercera edad tienden a ser más independientes.
    (B) El vínculo entre los residentes de una comunidad no es tan estrecha como antes.
    (C) Hay menos recursos para la gente mayor de 65 años.
    (D) La población mayor de 65 años se enferma más que anteriormente.

17. ¿Qué ofrece la ONG Solidarios a los de tercera edad?
    (A) Apoyo emocional y financiero
    (B) Cursos de capacidades básicas
    (C) Compañerismo afectuoso
    (D) Oportunidades de servir de voluntarios en la comunidad

18. ¿Qué se puede deducir es la función primaria de los acompañantes?
    (A) Desarrollar una relación personal
    (B) Proveer ayuda médica
    (C) Comunicarse con su pareja diariamente
    (D) Darles apoyo emocional

19. ¿Cómo financia la ONG Solidarios los gastos de su programa?
    (A) Recibe dinero de los mayores.
    (B) Recauda fondos con la ayuda de otra compañía.
    (C) Los voluntarios pagan sus propios gastos.
    (D) Depende de la caridad de otras organizaciones.

20. ¿Cuál de las siguientes afirmaciones mejor resume el artículo?
    (A) Hay un crecimiento de programas en España para darles apoyo a los que más lo necesitan.
    (B) Se necesitarán más jóvenes voluntarios en los próximos años para ayudar con los problemas sociales.
    (C) Hay que entrenar bien a los voluntarios para que cumplan debidamente con las tareas asignadas.
    (D) Continuará habiendo un aumento en el número de gente de tercera edad que necesitará ayuda personal.

21. ¿Qué información presenta la tabla?
    (A) Los aumentos constantes en tasa de dependencia de cada población estudiada
    (B) El incremento de porcentaje de población total española que dependerá de los demás
    (C) El crecimiento de la población total en España
    (D) El aumento de los sectores demográficos de España en relación a la Unión Europea

22. Según la tabla, ¿qué pasará en 2022?
    (A) 33,30% de la población será mayor de 64 años.
    (B) 58,11% de la población total será inactiva.
    (C) Por cada 10 personas en edad de trabajar, habrá casi 6 que no estaría en edad
        de hacerlo.
    (D) Casi un cuarto de la población no tendrá suficientes años para trabajar.

23. ¿Cuál de las siguientes afirmaciones es correcta a base del artículo y la tabla?
    (A) Se necesitará ampliar programas de cuidado para los mayores de 64 años durante
        las próximas décadas.
    (B) Con el aumento de la población joven, habrá más voluntarios para cuidar a los
        de tercera edad.
    (C) El incremento de jubilados significa que habrá más trabajo para ellos en edad
        de hacerlo.
    (D) Los menores de 16 años formarán parte del grupo de voluntarios para cuidar
        a los de la tercera edad.

SELECCIÓN #4

Tema curricular: Las familias y las comunidades

> **Introducción:** Este texto es una carta de Julio a sus padres.

Queridos y amados padres:

Estoy en la azotea de mi casa y contemplo un hermoso atardecer de noviembre, los campos ya se están secando y el color dorado aparece por doquier, los recuerdos se agolpan en mi mente, ahora que soy joven, voy madurando poco

Línea a poco como esos campos que ahora contemplo, que con tanto ahínco cuida

(5) el labrador; así pienso en ustedes amados padres, cuanto amor, cuanto cariño, cuanto esmero han puesto en mí para ser el joven que soy ahora con una vida por delante, con un campo lleno de ilusiones.

A papá por enseñarme a amar a mi prójimo, gracias por enseñarme a ser fuerte y no doblegarme ante una derrota, gracias también por hacer de mi un hombre

(10) que desea triunfar y forjar la templanza en todo mi ser.

A ti mamá, por inculcarme la ternura, el amor y el deseo inmenso de verme un triunfador que sepa dar afecto, amor, regalar caricias, abrazos, y sobre todo saber apreciar las cosas que nos da la vida.

Quiero que sepan que los amo, los aprecio, los adoro y este amor que les tengo,

(15) no se podría pagar ni con todo el oro del mundo, por que es amor único.

Termino estas líneas viendo el horizonte y hermoso atardecer, donde muere el día y empieza la oscura noche, solo que en mi vida nace la esperanza y el deseo inmenso de vivir para agradecer a Dios el tenerlos y disfrutar de su presencia.

Padre, madre, benditos sean ahora y siempre.

(20) Con cariño su hijo:

Julio

24. ¿Por qué les escribe esta carta el autor a sus padres?
    (A) Para informarles de unos planes que tiene previsto
    (B) Para gratificarles por todo lo que le han hecho
    (C) Para despedirse de ellos antes de irse
    (D) Para compartir su creencia y fe

25. ¿Con qué relaciona el cuidado que sus padres le dieron?
    (A) Con la casa en que vive actualmente
    (B) Con la fe que tiene
    (C) Con la persistencia de los campesinos
    (D) Con los triunfos que experimentó en la vida

26. ¿A qué se refiere el autor de la carta cuando escribe ". . . un campo lleno de ilusiones" (línea 8)?
    (A) Al entusiasmo que tiene por la vida delante
    (B) A la vista casi irreal de su casa
    (C) Al tamaño del campo que tiene delante
    (D) A la cantidad de trabajo que tiene que hacer

27. ¿Qué características suyas les atribuye a sus padres?
    (A) A su padre, el cariño; a su madre, el amor
    (B) A su padre, la fortaleza; a su madre, su compasión
    (C) A su padre, el respeto por los héroes; a su madre, el deseo de triunfar
    (D) A su padre, la prudencia; a su madre, la tenacidad

28. ¿Qué perspectiva cultural predomina en la carta?
    (A) La creencia religiosa
    (B) El amor a los demás
    (C) El valor del trabajo duro
    (D) La solidaridad en la familia

29. ¿Qué figura retórica incluye el autor en su carta para comunicar sus ideas?
    (A) Metáfora
    (B) Símil
    (C) Cacofonía
    (D) Repetición

30. Según la carta, ¿cuál de las siguientes afirmaciones describe mejor la personalidad del autor?
    (A) Es solitario.
    (B) Es cauteloso.
    (C) Es optimista.
    (D) Es valiente.

SECTION I, PART B

Interpretive Communication: Print and Audio Texts (Combined)

Time: Approximately 55 minutes

DIRECTIONS: You will listen to several audio selections. The first two also include print texts. When there is a print text, you will have an additional amount of time to read it.

For each audio selection, you will have a designated amount of time to read the introduction of the selection and to preview the questions and answers that follow. Each audio selection will be played twice.

Following the first listening, you will have one minute to begin answering the questions. After the second listening, you will be given 15 seconds per question to finish answering. For each question, select the best answer according to the selection and mark your answer on your answer sheet.

Vas a escuchar a varias grabaciones. Las primeras dos van acompañadas de textos escritos. Cuando hay un texto escrito, tendrás tiempo adicional para leerlo.

Para cada selección auditiva, vas a tener un tiempo determinado para leer la introducción de la selección y prever las preguntas que siguen. Vas a escuchar cada fuente auditiva dos veces.

Después de escuchar cada selección la primera vez, vas a tener un minuto para empezar a contestar las preguntas. Después de escucharla la segunda vez, vas a tener 15 segundos por pregunta para terminarlas. Para cada pregunta, elige la mejor respuesta según el contexto y escríbela en la hoja de respuestas.

SELECCIÓN #1

Tema curricular: La familia y las comunidades

Fuente #1: Primero tienes un minuto para leer fuente número 1.

Introducción: El siguiente gráfico presenta los pasos recomendados para poder elegir una universidad. Se basa en información publicada en *Guiat.net*

Track 45

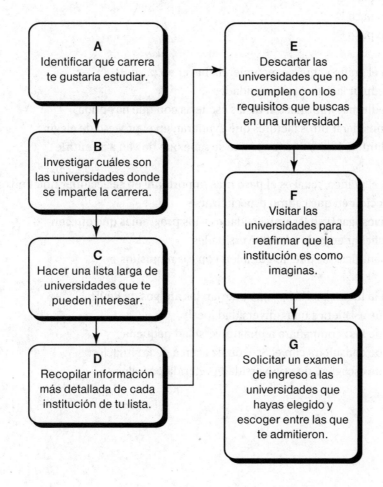

Fuente #2: Ahora tienes un minuto para leer la introducción y prever las preguntas.

Introducción: La siguiente fuente auditiva trata de una conversación entre Raúl, un estudiante, y Sr. Gómez, su consejero. Hablan del futuro estudiantil de Raúl. La grabación dura aproximadamente tres minutos.

31. Según el gráfico, ¿cuándo se debe profundizar la investigación de la universidad a que uno piensa asistir?
    (A) En paso B
    (B) En paso C
    (C) En paso D
    (D) En paso F

32. Según el gráfico, ¿qué se recomienda hacer en paso E?
    (A) Reducir la lista de universidades
    (B) Pedir más información de las escuelas con que hay duda
    (C) Considerar otros factores que ayudarán en el proceso de elegir
    (D) Eliminar las instituciones que se sabe que no van a admitirle

33. Según el gráfico, ¿cuál es el paso más importante en seleccionar una universidad?
    (A) Decidir en qué campo especializarse
    (B) Investigar bien las universidades y los programas que ofrecen
    (C) Solicitar entrada a las universidades
    (D) Identificar las que no cumplen con tus requisitos

34. Según la fuente auditiva, ¿qué querían los amigos de Raúl?
    (A) Que asistiera a una universidad local
    (B) Que los acompañara a una universidad pequeña
    (C) Que consultara con el Sr. Gómez acerca de la situación
    (D) Que escogiera una universidad preferida por ellos

35. Según la conversación, ¿qué problemas sufrió Raúl este año?
    (A) No tuvo éxito en la clase de ciencias.
    (B) A ninguno de sus profesores le gustaba.
    (C) No estudiaba idiomas por falta de interés.
    (D) No pidió ayuda cuando le faltaba comprensión.

36. Basándote en la conversación, ¿qué tipo de universidad seleccionará Raúl?
    (A) Una universidad pequeña en una ciudad grande
    (B) Una universidad grande en una ciudad cercana
    (C) Una universidad pequeña en una ciudad lejana
    (D) Una universidad grande en una ciudad lejana

37. A fin de cuentas, ¿qué tipo de alumno es Raúl?
    (A) Mezquino
    (B) Considerado
    (C) Consciente
    (D) Astuto

38. Según la conversación y el gráfico, ¿en qué paso se encuentra Raúl?
    (A) En el paso A
    (B) En el paso B
    (C) En el paso C
    (D) En el paso D

SELECCIÓN #2

Tema curricular: Los desafíos mundiales

Fuente #1: Primero tienes cuatro minutos para leer fuente número 1.

Introducción: El siguiente fragmento trata de la agricultura de la civilización incaica. Fue publicada en la página web *www.holistica2000.com.*

Track 46

La destrucción de la agricultura incaica—Fragmento.

Por Antonio Elio Brailovsky y Dina Foguelman
(*www.holistica2000.com.ar/ecocolumna226.htm*)

      El imperio incaico fue un espectacular ejemplo de eficiencia en el manejo de la tierra y en el respeto al equilibrio ecológico de la región. Ningún sistema posterior consiguió alimentar a tanta población sin degradar los recursos naturales. Los

Línea incas basaron su civilización en una relación armónica con su ambiente natural,

(5) integrado por los frágiles ecosistemas andinos, y desarrollaron complejos y delicados mecanismos tecnológicos y sociales que les permitieron lograr una sólida base económica sin deterioros ecológicos.

      Se pueden ver aún las terrazas de cultivo, construidas como largos y angostos peldaños en los faldeos de las montañas, sostenidos por piedras que retenían la

(10) tierra fértil. Las terrazas cumplían la función de distribuir regularmente la humedad. Allí el agua de lluvia iba filtrándose lentamente desde los niveles superiores a los inferiores, utilizándose plenamente la escasa cantidad de líquido disponible. En las áreas más lluviosas y en las de mayor pendiente, las terrazas permitían evitar la erosión, al impedir que el escurrimiento superficial del agua de lluvia

(15) arrastrara las partículas del suelo. También facilitaron el aprovechamiento de los diversos pisos ecológicos.

      El suelo de las terrazas se mezclaba con guano, el excremento de aves marinas acumulado en las islas y costas. Este recurso era cuidadosamente administrado, porque de él dependía en buena medida la alimentación de la población: para

(20) extraerlo, cada aldea tenía asignada una parte de isla o costa, marcada con mojones de piedra que no era permitido alterar.

      Había muy poco suelo que fuera naturalmente apto para el cultivo y había que construirlo metro a metro. Había que ir a buscar el agua a las nacientes de los arroyos y encauzarla mediante una red de canales. A veces, al cruzar un valle, era

(25) necesario sostener el canal sobre columnas para que el nivel del agua no perdiese altura, construyéndose acueductos similares a los romanos.

Fuente #2: Tienes dos minutos para leer la introducción y prever las preguntas.

Introducción: Esta grabación titulada *El uso del suelo en América Latina* trata de las tendencias en la agricultura latinoamericana. Se basa en un artículo publicado en la página web *www.eurosur.org*. La grabación dura aproximadamente tres minutos, veinte segundos.

39. ¿Cuál es el propósito del artículo impreso?
    (A) Narrar la ruina de un antiguo sistema de agricultura
    (B) Presentar las características del cultivo de la tierra de los incas
    (C) Elogiar las innovaciones de la civilización incaica
    (D) Promover el uso sostenible de tierras como hicieron nuestros antepasados

40. ¿Qué impacto tuvo la agricultura de los incas a su alrededor?
    (A) Cambió la frecuencia de lluvias en distintas zonas.
    (B) Disminuyó los recursos naturales del área.
    (C) Perjudicó al medioambiente.
    (D) Se mantuvo en equilibrio con el entorno.

41. Según el artículo, ¿cuál era un beneficio del uso de las terrazas?
    (A) Suministraban el flujo de agua.
    (B) Aseguraban que el guano se escurriera.
    (C) Facilitaban el acceso a la cosecha.
    (D) Fortalecían las laderas de las montañas.

42. En el artículo, ¿a qué se refiere la frase "de él dependía en buena medida la alimentación de la población" (línea 19)?
    (A) Al guano, que servía de alimento para la gente incaica.
    (B) Al ambiente en que vivían las aves, que les proveía comida a las aldeas.
    (C) Al administro del excremento, para asegurar que hubiera suficiente para el cultivo.
    (D) Al suelo que se mezclaba con guano, que solo no era suficientemente fértil.

43. ¿Cuál de los siguientes adjetivos mejor describiría a los Incas en cuanto a su agricultura?
    (A) Innovadores
    (B) Trabajadores
    (C) Inconscientes
    (D) Explotadores

44. Según la fuente auditiva, ¿qué cambio se ha notado en la agricultura de América Latina?
    (A) Se han encontrado más áreas de cultivo.
    (B) Particularmente en Brasil y en México, se ha reducido la cantidad de tierra cultivable.
    (C) Se cultivan diferentes plantas ahora que anteriormente.
    (D) Más tierras están siendo designadas para la agricultura.

45. Según la fuente auditiva ¿qué impacto tiene la ganadería?
    (A) Ha impulsado la creación de ranchos.
    (B) Es en parte responsable por la reducción de los bosques.
    (C) Ha aumentado las tierras destinadas al cultivo.
    (D) Ha llegado a ocupar más de 50% de las tierras de cultivo de América Latina.

46. ¿A qué se refiere la fuente auditiva cuando dice que las actividades agropecuarias ". . . tienen mayor incidencia sobre el medio ambiente . . ."?
    (A) A que las actividades que ocurren en zonas no urbanas son más dañinas
    (B) A que muchas actividades en este sector se encuentran en zonas peligrosas
    (C) A que las actividades en este sector mayormente tienen lugar encima de la tierra
    (D) A que son las que más impactan el entorno

47. ¿Qué predicción hace la fuente auditiva en cuanto al futuro de la agricultura?
    (A) Que no habrá suficiente tierra cultivable para sostener el cultivo
    (B) Que habrá modificaciones del suelo por el uso de químicos
    (C) Que será cada vez más caro poder expandir las tierras cultivables
    (D) Que el uso de la genética mejorará el rendimiento de producción agrícola

48. Imagina que quieres escribir un informe que contiene las ideas presentadas en las dos fuentes, ¿cuál de las siguientes publicaciones sería más apropiado?
    (A) *El impacto del cultivo de frijoles y maíz en América Latina*
    (B) *Implementando prácticas agrarias del pasado para superar retos del presente*
    (C) *Teorías sobre la destrucción de nuestras tierras cultivables*
    (D) *El cultivo de la soja y la ganadería: el futuro de comestibles para una población creciente*

SELECCIÓN #3

Tema curricular: La belleza y la estética

Primero tienes un minuto para leer la introducción y prever las preguntas.

Introducción: La siguiente entrevista, titulada *Concurso de hip hop en Colombia,* trata de un evento de música en Colombia. La entrevista original fue publicada por Radio Naciones Unidas el 31 de mayo de 2012 en Estados Unidos. La grabación dura aproximadamente tres minutos.

Track 47

49. ¿Cuál es el propósito del concurso?
   (A) Mostrar como el hip hop le ha cambiado la vida a unos jóvenes colombianos
   (B) Destacar el papel del hip hop en la comunidad
   (C) Servir como un ámbito para promover la seguridad y convivencia ciudadanas
   (D) Presentar los diversos estilos musicales de varias regiones de Colombia

50. ¿Quiénes pueden participar en este evento?
   (A) Artistas musicales y visuales de varias ciudades
   (B) Músicos hip hop de distintos países
   (C) Jóvenes a quienes les gusta la música hip hop
   (D) Todos los interesados en el género del hip hop

51. ¿En qué se va a enfocar el festival?
   (A) En exponer los diferentes temas asignados
   (B) En presentar a los ganadores del concurso
   (C) En grabar la música de los artistas
   (D) En convertirse en un nuevo evento nacional

52. Según la entrevistada, ¿qué representa el hip hop para los jóvenes?
   (A) Es una forma en que pueden expresarse.
   (B) Es una manera en que aprenden de temas que no conocen.
   (C) Es una oportunidad para sobresalir en la sociedad.
   (D) Es una herramienta que les trae mucha belleza en su vida.

53. ¿Qué más se espera de este evento?
   (A) Que se reduzca el consumo de drogas durante el concurso
   (B) Que la gente cambie su opinión de los jóvenes
   (C) Que los jóvenes entiendan que el hip hop trae beneficios
   (D) Que se repita este evento en años sucesivos

SELECCIÓN #4

Tema curricular: Las identidades personales y públicas

Primero tienes un minuto para leer la introducción y prever las preguntas.

> **Introducción:** Esta grabación titulada El *Popol Vuh*. La grabación dura aproximadamente tres minutos.

Track 48

54. ¿Qué narraba el *Popol Vuh*?
    (A) La historia de una tribu mexicana
    (B) La procedencia de los maya quiché
    (C) La conversión de los indígenas al cristianismo
    (D) La conquista de los indígenas por los españoles

55. ¿De qué materia se crearon los hombres?
    (A) De materia vegetal
    (B) De la tierra del altiplano
    (C) De los dioses gemelos de la muerte
    (D) Del aliento de Hunahpú y Xbalanqué

56. ¿Cómo era el primer texto impreso después de la conquista española?
    (A) Apareció en lengua quiché.
    (B) Fue una traducción al español.
    (C) Tomó la antigua forma pictórica.
    (D) Combinó ambas lenguas a la vez.

57. ¿Dónde se conserva una copia del primer libro impreso en español y quiché?
    (A) En la universidad de Guatemala
    (B) En una universidad estadounidense
    (C) En Francia, donde un abad francés lo dejó
    (D) En España, donde un padre dominicano lo depositó

58. ¿Qué significa que el *Popol Vuh* sea el "Libro del Consejo"?
    (A) Significa el petate sobre el cual se sentaban los reyes indígenas.
    (B) Significa los orígenes de los linajes indígenas.
    (C) Significa la autoridad de los gobernantes de las tribus.
    (D) Significa la narrativa de la creación del mundo.

SELECCIÓN #5

Tema Curricular: La vida contemporánea

Primero tienes un minuto para leer la introducción y prever las preguntas.

> **Introducción:** La siguiente grabación es una entrevista con José Antonio de Urbina, diplomático y autor del libro *El arte de invitar*. La grabación dura aproximadamente 3 minutos 40 segundos.

Track 49

59. ¿A quién se dirige este experto del protocolo internacional?
    (A) A los presidentes de naciones
    (B) A cualquiera deseosa de asegurar que los huéspedes se sientan en casa
    (C) A los directores de protocolo contratados para arreglar cenas
    (D) A los anfitriones de huéspedes ilustres en funciones formales

60. ¿Cuál es el propósito de tener un protocolo?
    (A) Para que el hombre sea tratado como si fuera rey en su casa
    (B) Para que todos los invitados al Palacio Real se comporten cortésmente
    (C) Para facilitar la comunicación y respetar la dignidad de cada persona
    (D) Para que una persona se sienta confiada al aceptar una invitación

61. ¿Dónde debe sentarse a una pareja o un matrimonio?
    (A) Siempre se coloca al hombre cerca de una señora o señorita guapa.
    (B) Hay que colocar a la señora al lado de otra para que puedan conversar.
    (C) Hay que alternar los géneros para promocionar conversación.
    (D) Es buena idea separarlos para evitar disputas durante la cena.

62. ¿Por qué no se sientan las mujeres en las puntas de la mesa?
    (A) Es más difícil emparejar este sitio, y por eso no se pone a una señora allí.
    (B) Es un sitio peligroso y para evitar que alguien le roce, no se la pone allí.
    (C) Es más fácil entablar conversación con otra persona que esté al lado.
    (D) Es mala suerte colocarlas en ese sitio, por eso no se lo hace.

63. ¿Qué remedio hay cuando un invitado no puede venir, dejándolo con doce?
    (A) Se puede matar a uno de los invitados.
    (B) Siempre se puede invitar a una persona más y contar con la ausencia de una.
    (C) Se puede invitar a otro amigo íntimo al último momento.
    (D) Se puede llamar a un invitado y cancelar la invitación.

64. ¿Con qué autoridad habla esa persona en la narrativa?
    (A) Es director de protocolo del Palacio Real Española.
    (B) Es director de una escuela para los embajadores españoles.
    (C) Es director de mayordomos del Palacio Real Española.
    (D) Es director de información para invitados al Palacio Real Española.

65. Imagina que tienes que dar una presentación oral sobre el mismo tema y quieres investigarlo más. ¿Cuál de los siguientes libros sería más apropiado citar?
    (A) *Organización de reuniones y eventos*
    (B) *El manual de las buenas maneras*
    (C) *Como evitar incomodidades en una amistad*
    (D) *Pasos para elevar la autoestima de los demás*

SECTION II

Interpersonal Writing: Email Reply

Time: 15 minutes

> **DIRECTIONS:** You will write a reply to an email that you received. You have 15 minutes to read the message and write your reply.
>
> Your reply should include an appropriate greeting and closing and should answer all the questions and requests in the original message. In addition, your reply should ask for more details about something that was mentioned in the message. You should use a formal tone in your response.

> Vas a escribir una respuesta a un mensaje de correo electrónico. Tienes 15 minutos para leer el mensaje y escribir tu respuesta.
>
> Tu respuesta debe incluir un saludo y despedida apropiada y contestar a todas las preguntas y peticiones del mensaje original. También tu respuesta debe pedir más información de algo mencionado en el mensaje original. Debes usar el tono formal en tu respuesta.

Tema curricular: Las identidades personales y públicas

> **Introducción:** El siguiente mensaje electrónico es de tu profesor a quien le has pedido que le escribieras una carta de recomendación para enviarla con tu solicitud de ingreso a una universidad.

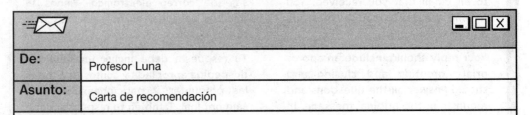

Apreciados estudiantes,

Primero quiero tomar la oportunidad de agradecerles por haberme pedido que les escriba su carta de recomendación para la universidad. Es una parte integral de su solicitud a la universidad y entre todos los profesores que podían haber escogido, me siento muy orgulloso de que me hayan seleccionado a mí. Es un trabajo en que pongo mucho esfuerzo y ánimo y dedico a cada carta la atención que merece.

Como parte de este proceso, siempre me gusta conocer un poco mejor a mis estudiantes. Tengo bien claro lo que pueden hacer académicamente, pero no tanto el aspecto personal, por ejemplo sus creencias e intereses. Por eso me gustaría que tomaran el tiempo para considerar las siguientes preguntas y que me contesten individualmente con sus respuestas con ejemplos si pueden:

- ¿A qué tipo de persona admiran ustedes? ¿Qué cualidades creen son importantes en una persona? ¿Por qué?

- ¿Creen que ustedes encarnen estas mismas cualidades? ¿Por qué sí o no?

Debo salir para una conferencia en dos días así que me harían un gran favor si me pudieran mandar sus respuestas lo más antes posible para que tenga la oportunidad de contemplarlas durante mi viaje.

Saludos cordiales,

Profesor Eduardo Luna

Presentational Writing: Argumentative Essay

Time: Approximately 55 minutes

Track 50

DIRECTIONS: You will now write a persuasive essay. The essay topic is based on the following three print and audio sources. First, you will have 6 minutes to read the essay topic and the printed sources. Next, you will hear the audio material twice. Then, you will have 40 minutes to plan and write your essay.

In your essay you should make reference to specific information from the three source materials. Do not simply summarize what is contained in the sources. Incorporate them into your essay and cite them in the proper manner. In addition, you should also clearly present your own viewpoints on the topic and defend them thoroughly. Your essay should be organized into clear paragraphs and you should use appropriate vocabulary and grammar.

Ahora vas a escribir un ensayo persuasivo. El tema del ensayo se basa en las siguientes fuentes escritas y auditivas. Primero, tendrás 6 minutos para leer las fuentes impresas. Después, vas a escuchar la fuente auditiva dos veces. Finalmente, tendrás 40 minutos para planear y escribir tu ensayo.

En tu ensayo, debes hacer referencia a información específica de las tres fuentes. Debes evitar simplemente resumir la información de las fuentes. Incorpórala en tu ensayo e identifícalas apropiadamente. Además, debes presentar claramente tus propios puntos de vista y defenderlos bien. Tu ensayo debe ser organizado en distintos párrafos bien desarrollados y debes usar vocabulario y gramática apropiada.

Tema curricular: Los desafíos mundiales

Primero tienes seis minutos para leer el tema del ensayo, la fuente número 1 y la fuente número 2.

Tema del ensayo: ¿Beneficia o perjudica la inmigración a un país?

Fuente #1

Introducción: El siguiente texto trata del impacto que han tenido los inmigrantes haitianos a la República Dominicana. El artículo fue publicado en la página web Global Voices (*es.globalvoices.org*) en julio de 2009.

República Dominicana: El costo financiero de los inmigrantes haitianos indocumentados

Los países de República Dominicana y Haití comparten la misma isla, llamada comúnmente La Española desde que fuera descubierta en 1492 por Cristóbal Colón. La República Dominicana y Haití son dos naciones independientes, con cultura, creencias y sistemas totalmente diferentes. A pesar de la cercanía, la evolución también ha sido diferente en términos de economía y desarrollo. Mientras la República Dominicana ha venido fortaleciendo su democracia desde 1966, Haití ha estado sumido en el caos político desde la caída de Papa Doc Duvalier, y de nada ha valido la intervención internacional: hoy Haití es el país más pobre de toda América y la República Dominicana disfruta de una de las economías más grandes en el Caribe y Centro América.

A pesar de estos obvios contrastes, es la proximidad de estos dos países lo que ha entrelazado sus destinos. Son muchos los haitianos que cada día se pasan ilegalmente al otro lado de la isla, donde a menudo consiguen trabajo como obreros de la construcción o se dedican a la venta ambulante de frutas, dulces y artículos de poca monta. Otros llegan contratados con permisos especiales para trabajar en plantaciones de caña de azúcar.

Una buena parte de los haitianos que llegan ilegalmente a la República Dominicana se dedica a pedir limosna en las calles y, luego de establecerse en un lugar fijo, a la tumba y quema de árboles, una práctica que ha dejado a Haití deforestado en más de un 90%. Estos ejemplos visibles a menudo dejan en los dominicanos una estereotipada visión negativa de los haitianos. Sin embargo una minoría llega legalmente con la intención de estudiar, muchas veces con becas, y suele constituir un ejemplo positivo.

A pesar de estos ejemplos positivos de haitianos, muchos dominicanos piensan que la inmigración haitiana en República Dominicana está fuera de control. Hombres, mujeres y niños llegan a diario a territorio dominicano, la mayoría de su cuenta, otros forman parte de redes que se dedican a abusar de la dignidad humana, pues los colocan en puntos estratégicos de las ciudades a pedir, todo bajo la mirada indiferente de agentes de tránsito que prefieren ignorar el panorama. Se estima que hay cerca de un millón de haitianos indocumentados en la

Línea
(5)

(10)

(15)

(20)

(25)

(30)

RD, y la situación ha llegado tan lejos que hasta hay niños haitianos en funciones de limpiavidrios y limpiabotas. Manuel Vólquez, de Diario Digital Dominicano, lo resume así:

(35)   «Los haitianos se desplazan por el país como hormigas y han desplazado a nuestros obreros en sectores importantes de la economía como son la construcción y los negocios informales. Han llegado tan lejos que hasta usan niños en las avenidas para mendigar, han asimilado nuestra cultura y nuestras costumbres. ¿Cosas de la transculturización y la globalización?»

(40)   Esto tiene su impacto sobre el estado dominicano, que destina una parte importante de sus recursos en dar atenciones médicas gratuitas a estos inmigrantes, muchas veces en detrimento de los propios dominicanos. En diciembre del año pasado, el director de Salud de la regional Sur, doctor Bolívar Matos, informó que los procedimientos médicos para los inmigrantes haitianos que ingresan ilegalmente a las provincias de San Juan y Elías Piña conllevan un gasto anual de

(45)   55 millones de pesos.

Fuente #2

Introducción: La siguiente tabla muestra el crecimiento del producto interno bruto (PIB) de diferentes países europeos entre 1995 y 2005. Se basa en datos publicados en *www.cataluñacaixa.com*.

Crecimiento medio anual del PIB real		
Impacto de la inmigración sobre el aumento del PIB per cápita., 1995–2005		
	PIB real per cápita	PIB per cápita sin inmigrantes
Irlanda	5,87	1,07
Grecia	3,42	–0,62
Suecia	2,51	–0,77
España	2,60	–0,64
Finlandia	3,18	0,16
Alemania	1,28	–1,52
Reino Unido	2,39	–0,15
Portugal	1,80	–0,63
Italia	1,01	–1,17

Fuente #3

Introducción: La siguiente grabación, titulada *El Museo del Barrio celebra 30 años de excelencia promoviendo el arte latino en los Estados Unidos*—trata del impacto de la comunidad latina en Estados Unidos. El artículo original fue publicado en 2006 por *http://elmuseo.org*. La grabación dura aproximadamente dos minutos treinta segundos.

SECTION II

Interpersonal Speaking: Conversation

Time: Approximately 10 minutes

Track 51

<table>
<tr>
<td>

DIRECTIONS: You will now take part in a simulated conversation. First, you will have 1 minute to read a preview of the conversation, including the script for both parts. Then, the conversation will begin and follow the script. Each time it is your turn to speak, you will have 20 seconds to respond.

You should engage in the conversation as much and as appropriately as possible.

</td>
<td>

Ahora vas a participar en una conversación simulada. Primero, tendrás un minuto para leer la introducción y el esquema de la conversación. Después, empezará la conversación, siguiendo el esquema. Cada vez que te toque hablar, tendrás 20 segundos para responder.

Debes participar en la conversación de la forma más completa y apropiada posible.

</td>
</tr>
</table>

Tema curricular: La vida contemporánea

Tienes un minuto para leer la introducción y el esquema de la conversación.

> **Introducción:** Esta es una conversación con Eva, una amiga tuya que te llama y te dice que sus padres acaban de darle permiso para invitarte a Florida durante las vacaciones escolares de primavera.

Eva:	Te saluda y te da las noticias.
Tú:	Salúdala y reacciona a sus noticias. Pide detalles.
Eva:	Continúa la conversación.
Tú:	Reacciona apropiadamente. Hazle una pregunta.
Eva:	Continúa la conversación.
Tú:	Ponte de acuerda con ella. Agrega un deseo propio.
Eva:	Continúa la conversación.
Tú:	Reacciona apropiadamente.
Eva:	Continúa la conversación y te ofrece una alternativa.
Tú:	Acepta apropiadamente. Despídete.
Eva:	Concluye la conversación.

SECTION II

Presentational Speaking: Cultural Comparison

Time: Approximately 6 minutes

> **DIRECTIONS:** You will now prepare an oral presentation for your class on a specific topic. You will have 4 minutes to read the topic and prepare your presentation. Then, you will have 2 minutes to record your presentation.
>
> In your presentation, compare your own community to one of the Spanish-speaking world with which you are familiar. You should demonstrate your understanding of cultural features of the Spanish-speaking world. Your presentation should also be well organized.

> Ahora vas a preparar una presentación oral para tu clase de español sobre un tema cultural. Primero, tendrás 4 minutos para leer el tema y preparar tu presentación. Después, tendrás 2 minutos para grabarla.
>
> En tu presentación, compara tu comunidad con una del mundo hispanohablante con el que estés familiarizado. Debes demostrar tu comprensión de los aspectos culturales en el mundo hispanohablante. También, tu presentación debe ser bien organizada.

Tema curricular: Las identidades personales y públicas

Tema de la presentación: ¿Qué importancia tienen los deportes en una comunidad?

> Compara tus observaciones de las comunidades en que has vivido con tus observaciones de una región del mundo hispanohablante que te sea familiar. Puedes referirte a lo que has estudiado, vivido, observado, etc.

ANSWER KEY
Practice Test 1

SECTION I

PART A

1. D	11. B	21. B
2. A	12. A	22. C
3. C	13. C	23. A
4. D	14. A	24. B
5. B	15. D	25. C
6. B	16. B	26. A
7. C	17. C	27. B
8. A	18. A	28. D
9. D	19. B	29. A
10. B	20. D	30. C

PART B

31. C	43. A	55. A
32. A	44. C	56. D
33. A	45. B	57. B
34. D	46. D	58. C
35. D	47. B	59. B
36. A	48. B	60. C
37. C	49. C	61. C
38. A	50. A	62. A
39. B	51. D	63. C
40. D	52. A	64. A
41. A	53. B	65. B
42. C	54. B	

ANSWER SHEET
Practice Test 2

PART A

1. Ⓐ Ⓑ Ⓒ Ⓓ
2. Ⓐ Ⓑ Ⓒ Ⓓ
3. Ⓐ Ⓑ Ⓒ Ⓓ
4. Ⓐ Ⓑ Ⓒ Ⓓ
5. Ⓐ Ⓑ Ⓒ Ⓓ
6. Ⓐ Ⓑ Ⓒ Ⓓ
7. Ⓐ Ⓑ Ⓒ Ⓓ
8. Ⓐ Ⓑ Ⓒ Ⓓ
9. Ⓐ Ⓑ Ⓒ Ⓓ
10. Ⓐ Ⓑ Ⓒ Ⓓ
11. Ⓐ Ⓑ Ⓒ Ⓓ
12. Ⓐ Ⓑ Ⓒ Ⓓ
13. Ⓐ Ⓑ Ⓒ Ⓓ
14. Ⓐ Ⓑ Ⓒ Ⓓ
15. Ⓐ Ⓑ Ⓒ Ⓓ
16. Ⓐ Ⓑ Ⓒ Ⓓ
17. Ⓐ Ⓑ Ⓒ Ⓓ
18. Ⓐ Ⓑ Ⓒ Ⓓ
19. Ⓐ Ⓑ Ⓒ Ⓓ
20. Ⓐ Ⓑ Ⓒ Ⓓ
21. Ⓐ Ⓑ Ⓒ Ⓓ
22. Ⓐ Ⓑ Ⓒ Ⓓ
23. Ⓐ Ⓑ Ⓒ Ⓓ
24. Ⓐ Ⓑ Ⓒ Ⓓ
25. Ⓐ Ⓑ Ⓒ Ⓓ
26. Ⓐ Ⓑ Ⓒ Ⓓ
27. Ⓐ Ⓑ Ⓒ Ⓓ
28. Ⓐ Ⓑ Ⓒ Ⓓ
29. Ⓐ Ⓑ Ⓒ Ⓓ
30. Ⓐ Ⓑ Ⓒ Ⓓ

PART B

31. Ⓐ Ⓑ Ⓒ Ⓓ
32. Ⓐ Ⓑ Ⓒ Ⓓ
33. Ⓐ Ⓑ Ⓒ Ⓓ
34. Ⓐ Ⓑ Ⓒ Ⓓ
35. Ⓐ Ⓑ Ⓒ Ⓓ
36. Ⓐ Ⓑ Ⓒ Ⓓ
37. Ⓐ Ⓑ Ⓒ Ⓓ
38. Ⓐ Ⓑ Ⓒ Ⓓ
39. Ⓐ Ⓑ Ⓒ Ⓓ
40. Ⓐ Ⓑ Ⓒ Ⓓ
41. Ⓐ Ⓑ Ⓒ Ⓓ
42. Ⓐ Ⓑ Ⓒ Ⓓ
43. Ⓐ Ⓑ Ⓒ Ⓓ
44. Ⓐ Ⓑ Ⓒ Ⓓ
45. Ⓐ Ⓑ Ⓒ Ⓓ
46. Ⓐ Ⓑ Ⓒ Ⓓ
47. Ⓐ Ⓑ Ⓒ Ⓓ
48. Ⓐ Ⓑ Ⓒ Ⓓ
49. Ⓐ Ⓑ Ⓒ Ⓓ
50. Ⓐ Ⓑ Ⓒ Ⓓ
51. Ⓐ Ⓑ Ⓒ Ⓓ
52. Ⓐ Ⓑ Ⓒ Ⓓ
53. Ⓐ Ⓑ Ⓒ Ⓓ
54. Ⓐ Ⓑ Ⓒ Ⓓ
55. Ⓐ Ⓑ Ⓒ Ⓓ
56. Ⓐ Ⓑ Ⓒ Ⓓ
57. Ⓐ Ⓑ Ⓒ Ⓓ
58. Ⓐ Ⓑ Ⓒ Ⓓ
59. Ⓐ Ⓑ Ⓒ Ⓓ
60. Ⓐ Ⓑ Ⓒ Ⓓ
61. Ⓐ Ⓑ Ⓒ Ⓓ
62. Ⓐ Ⓑ Ⓒ Ⓓ
63. Ⓐ Ⓑ Ⓒ Ⓓ
64. Ⓐ Ⓑ Ⓒ Ⓓ
65. Ⓐ Ⓑ Ⓒ Ⓓ

Practice Test 2

![decorative striped bar]

SECTION I, PART A

Interpretive Communication: Print Texts

Time: Approximately 40 minutes

> **DIRECTIONS:** Read the following passages. After each passage there are a number of questions for you to answer, based on the information provided in the reading selection. For each question, choose the response that is best according to the selection and mark your answer on the answer sheet.
>
> Lee los siguientes textos. Cada texto va acompañado de varias preguntas que debes contestar, según la información en el texto. Para cada pregunta, elige la mejor respuesta según el contexto y escríbela en la hoja de respuestas.

Tema curricular: La vida contemporánea

> **Introducción:** El siguiente fragmento se trata de cuando dos amigos encuentran la muerte de un conocido. Proviene del cuento "El tesoro misterioso" de Guillermo Le Queux, publicado en 1909.

—¡Muerto! ¡Y se ha llevado su secreto a la tumba!

—¡Jamás!

—Pero se lo ha llevado. ¡Mira! Tiene la quijada caída. ¡No ves el cambio, hombre!

Línea —¡Entonces, ha cumplido su amenaza, después de todo!

(5) —¡La ha cumplido! Hemos sido unos tontos, Reginaldo . . . ¡verdaderamente tontos!—murmuré.

—Así parece. Confieso que yo esperaba confiadamente que nos diría la verdad cuando comprendiese que le había llegado el fin.

—¡Ah! tú no lo conocías como yo—observé con amargura.—Tenía una voluntad

(10) de hierro y un nervio de acero.

—Combinados con una constitución de caballo, porque, si no, haría mucho tiempo que se hubiera muerto. Pero hemos sido engañados . . . completamente engañados por un moribundo. Nos ha desafiado, y hasta el último momento se ha burlado de nosotros.

(15) —Blair no era un tonto. Sabía lo que el conocimiento de esa verdad significaba para nosotros: una enorme fortuna. Lo que ha hecho, sencillamente, es guardar su secreto.

—Y dejarnos sin un centavo. Aunque hemos perdido miles, Gilberto, no puedo menos de admirar su tenaz determinación. Recuerdo que ha tenido que atravesar

(20) por momentos aciagos, y ha sido un buen amigo, pero muy bueno, con nosotros; por lo tanto, creo que no debemos abusar de él, aun cuando nos cause mucho sentimiento el hecho de que no nos haya dejado su secreto.

—¡Ah, si esos labios blancos pudiesen hablar! Una sola palabra, y los dos seríamos hombres ricos—exclamé con pena, contemplando la cara pálida del muerto, con

(25) sus ojos cerrados y su barba afeitada, que yacía sobre la almohada.

1. ¿Qué efecto produce el hecho que el autor comienza la narración *in medias res* (en medio de la acción)?
   (A) Ayuda a proveer detalles significativos a la trama.
   (B) Facilita que el lector conozca mejor a los personajes principales.
   (C) Ayuda a presentar diferentes puntos de vista acerca del evento.
   (D) Produce un aire dramático y entusiasma al lector que siga leyendo.

2. ¿Quién ha muerto?
   (A) Reginaldo
   (B) Gilberto
   (C) Blair
   (D) No es posible saber por este fragmento

3. ¿Qué se puede inferir de la muerte del hombre?
   (A) Murió de repente.
   (B) Fue asesinado.
   (C) Se sabía que iba a morir.
   (D) Murió al aire libre.

4. ¿Qué se sabe del fallecido?
   (A) Era de carácter tierno.
   (B) Confiaba con los demás.
   (C) Compartía información íntima.
   (D) Era una persona adinerada.

5. ¿Qué quiere comunicar uno de los protagonistas cuando dice que el muerto "ha tenido que atravesar por momentos aciagos" (líneas 19–20)?
   (A) Ha experimentado mucho éxito.
   (B) Mantuvo buenas relaciones con todos.
   (C) Tuvo unas situaciones de mala suerte.
   (D) Supo manejar bien todos tipos de negocios.

6. ¿Por qué quieren los protagonistas saber el secreto del fallecido?
   (A) Porque conocían bien al hombre muerto
   (B) Porque no quieren que el hombre siga burlándose de ellos
   (C) Porque les traería mucha riqueza
   (D) Porque eran muy buenos amigos de él

7. ¿Qué actitud en este fragmento?
   (A) Tristeza
   (B) Asombro
   (C) Frustración
   (D) Alivio

SELECCIÓN #2

Tema curricular: La vida contemporánea

> **Fuente #1**
>
> **Introducción:** El siguiente artículo trata de un equipo de fútbol en Colombia. Fue publicado en la revista *Semana* en 2006.

Era la 'cenicienta' del torneo colombiano, eterno colero; los rivales lo miraban con desdén; del General Santander, su estadio, decían que era el más grande del mundo porque nunca se llenaba y si sólo dos veces bajó a segunda división es porque apenas a partir de 1992 se implantó el descenso en el país.

Línea

(5)   Hoy el Cúcuta Deportivo es el campeón defensor del fútbol colombiano, está entre los mejores ocho clubes del continente después de golear al Toluca y fue el primero de los 16 equipos de la Copa Mustang en conseguir su clasificación a los cuadrangulares semifinales.

Pero tras ocho años en la B, serios problemas económicos y con el estadio

(10)   incompleto y destartalado, apareció en el panorama Ramiro Suárez Corzo. Una de las banderas de su campaña a la Alcaldía de Cúcuta fue salvar al club y lo primero que hizo cuando asumió en 2004 fue liderar la compra del equipo pese al deseo de Pachón por mantenerlo. Al final el negocio se hizo por 1.200 millones de pesos.

La inyección de capital no se hizo esperar y sólo un año después se logró el

(15)   ascenso. Pero las aspiraciones iban más allá de cambiar los viajes en bus de la B por el de aviones en la A, y para reaparecer en primera se buscó a Jorge Luis Pinto como entrenador. Una reunión de tres minutos fue suficiente para llegar a un acuerdo y Pinto, apenado, le dijo a Suárez que alargaran la reunión para que no pensaran que no era seria.

(20)   La gestión del hoy seleccionador nacional tuvo éxito inmediato. En el primer semestre de 2006 clasificó a los cuadrangulares semifinales y solo tres puntos separaron al equipo de disputar la final. En el segundo intent se logró el campeonato, que significó el fruto recogido tras tanto sufrimiento. La transformación de la institución incluía también un nuevo escudo que al comienzo fue resistido.

(25)   Hasta el obispo de la ciudad afirmó que en su diseño se veían cachos y garras como de demonio.

La clave del Cúcuta no es un secreto. El club tiene el apoyo de todos, desde el Alcalde hasta el último habitante del departamento, lo que ha permitido que su patrimonio haya ascendido a 4.000 millones. Con una nómina de jugadores desahuciados

(30)   por otros equipos, el plantel sabe que más que nombres, tiene hombres.

(www.semana.com/wf_InfoArticulo)

Fuente #2

Introducción: La siguiente tabla presenta las estadísticas del Cúcuta Deportivo en 2012.

Cúcuta Deportivo	
Liga	Primera – Liga Postobón
Posición	18 / 18
Ganados	3 (16,67%)
Empate	2 (11,11%)
Perdidos	13 (72,22%)
Puntos (por partido)	11 (0,61)
Goles a favor (por partido)	12 (0,67)
Goles en contra (por partido)	35 (1,94)
Más de 2.5 goles	9 (50%)
Menos de 2.5 goles	9 (50%)
Sin goles en contra	2 (11,11%)
Sin goles	10 (55,56%)

8. ¿Cuál es el propósito del artículo?
   (A) Detallar las claves para el éxito en los deportes
   (B) Informar sobre los sucesos de un club deportivo
   (C) Resumir la última temporada de un deporte
   (D) Resaltar la importancia de apoyo local para los deportes

9. ¿Qué tipo de deporte se jugaba en el General Santander?
   (A) Tenis
   (B) Fútbol
   (C) Fútbol americano
   (D) Juegos olímpicos

10. ¿Por qué se llamaba al club la 'cenicienta' del continente?
   (A) Porque jugaba en un estadio arruinado
   (B) Porque perdía continuamente y casi nunca podía progresar
   (C) Porque había muchos aficionados que los apoyaban
   (D) Porque tras unos cambios estratégicos, el club empezó a tener suerte

11. Entre 1992 y 2004, ¿qué sucedió para el club?
   (A) El estadio se derrumbó.
   (B) Se adoptó una bandera nueva.
   (C) Hubo un nuevo liderazgo.
   (D) Se cambiaron los buses por aviones.

12. ¿Qué se puede inferir fue la causa por la que la entrevista con Pinto duró poco tiempo?
    (A) Era una conversación poco seria.
    (B) El entrenador ya había sido contratado.
    (C) Pinto sentía vergüenza y no quería prolongar el proceso.
    (D) El club le coincidió un contrato muy favorable.

13. ¿Qué pasó con el club en 2006?
    (A) Gozó de más éxito.
    (B) Perdió su nuevo escudo.
    (C) Recibió la bendición del obispo.
    (D) Sufrió una pérdida en el campeonato.

14. ¿Cuál sería la clave del triunfo?
    (A) Hay un nuevo patrimonio.
    (B) Ahora se obtiene más plata.
    (C) Hay respaldo de la municipalidad y del pueblo.
    (D) Hay mayor confianza gracias al nuevo estadio.

15. Según la tabla, ¿en qué posición terminó el Cúcuta Deportivo en 2012?
    (A) Primera
    (B) Tercera
    (C) Última
    (D) No se puede contestar a base de la tabla.

16. ¿Cuál fue la diferencia en el total de goles durante la temporada?
    (A) Marcaron más goles que sufrieron.
    (B) Sufrieron más goles que marcaron.
    (C) Sufrieron tantos goles como marcaron.
    (D) No marcaron goles esta temporada.

17. Basándote en la información de las dos fuentes, ¿qué cambio se ha notado entre 2006 y 2012?
    (A) El Cúcuta ha tenido más éxito que nunca.
    (B) El equipo ha marcado menos goles.
    (C) Ha habido un nuevo patrocinador de la liga.
    (D) Otros equipos se han enterado del secreto del Cúcuta.

18. Según la información en el artículo y las estadísticas en la tabla, ¿cuál de las siguientes situaciones es más probable?
    (A) Si tiene otra temporada como ésta, va a ganar el campeonato.
    (B) Si tiene otra temporada como ésta, va a bajar a la segunda división.
    (C) Si tiene otra temporada como ésta, puede calificarse para las semifinales.
    (D) Esta temporada es parecida a la de que gozó en 2006.

SELECCIÓN #3

Tema curricular: La belleza y la estética

> **Introducción:** El siguiente anuncio trata de un anuncio para un evento de literatura. Fue publicada en la página web *www.escritores.org* en 2013.

PREMIO NACIONAL DE LITERATURA JUVENIL

El Ministerio de Culturas y Turismo, Entel y Santillana convocan a la primera versión del Premio Nacional de Literatura Juvenil, de acuerdo con las siguientes bases:

Línea
(5)
Participantes: Podrán optar al Premio todas las personas mayores de edad de nacionalidad boliviana que residan en Bolivia.

Presentación de la obra: El concursante deberá enviar en un sobre cerrado bajo el rótulo 1er. Premio Nacional de Literatura Juvenil una obra literaria para lectores juveniles de entre 13 y 18 años, escrita en lengua castellana, que sea original, rigurosamente inédita y que no haya sido premiada anteriormente en ningún otro
(10) concurso, ni corresponda a autores fallecidos con anterioridad al anuncio de esta convocatoria. La obra juvenil tendrá una extensión mínima de 60 páginas y un máximo de 80 páginas tamaño carta, numeradas, mecanografiadas a doble espacio por una sola cara, con letra de 12 puntos. Deberán enviarse dos ejemplares impresos, anillados, encuadernados o cosidos, y un CD con el texto completo en
(15) formato Word. Es obligatorio adjuntar un sobre cerrado con el título de la obra y el pseudónimo del autor que contendrá: Una hoja con los datos del autor —nombre y apellidos, dirección, correo electrónico y teléfono(s) de contacto—; una declaración firmada aceptando expresamente las bases y condiciones de este Premio, garantizando que la obra no se halla pendiente del fallo en ningún otro concurso
(20) y que el autor tiene la libre disposición de todos los derechos sobre la obra; y una fotocopia de la cédula de identidad. De faltar algunos de estos requisitos, la novela juvenil no será considerada en el concurso.

Recepción de obras: El plazo de admisión de los originales vence el día viernes 12 de julio de 2013. En caso de envíos por correo, se aceptará la fecha de recepción
(25) con el sello de origen.

Premio: El premio para el ganador será de Bs. 15.000 (quince mil bolivianos), de los que se detraerán los impuestos que fueran aplicables según la legislación boliviana. El monto es único e indivisible y cubre los derechos de autor de la primera edición de mil ejemplares.

(30) **Otras consideraciones**: La editorial Santillana se reserva el derecho de opción preferente para la publicación de cualquier otra narración juvenil presentada al Premio que, no habiendo alcanzado el galardón, sea considerada de su interés.

19. ¿Cuál es el propósito del anuncio?

    (A) Promover el conocimiento de la literatura entre los jóvenes

    (B) Reclutar a jóvenes a que entreguen su obra favorita

    (C) Promocionar un evento para la creación literaria original

    (D) Proporcionar información sobre las diferentes formas de crear una obra

20. ¿A quién se dirige el anuncio?

    (A) A todos los amantes de la literatura

    (B) A los jóvenes bolivianos

    (C) A los residentes de Bolivia que sean mayores de cierta edad

    (D) A los bolivianos de tercera edad

21. ¿Qué se puede inferir de las obras literarias mencionadas en este anuncio?

    (A) Son de la literatura boliviana.

    (B) Son cuentos típicos de la literatura latinoamericana.

    (C) Son novelas bastante cortas.

    (D) Son ejemplares de literatura popular.

22. ¿Qué recibe el autor de la novela ganadora?

    (A) Un premio monetario equivalente a quince mil bolivianos

    (B) Un poco menos de Bs. 15.000 y la publicación de su obra

    (C) 15.000 bolivianos y un contrato con una empresa editorial

    (D) Un premio monetario, publicación de su obra, y ser exceptuado de pagar impuestos

23. ¿Qué ocurre a las obras que no ganaron el premio?

    (A) No reciben un premio pero todavía pueden ser publicadas.

    (B) Son publicadas para que todos las disfruten.

    (C) Son regaladas a la editorial para ser publicadas en el futuro.

    (D) El anuncio no menciona esta información.

24. Necesitas más información que no está publicada en el anuncio y le llamas al organizador para clarificar tus dudas. ¿Cuál de las siguientes preguntas sería más apropiada?

    (A) "Perdona, ¿qué ocurre si mi entrega no contiene toda la información pedida?"

    (B) "Vivo lejos de la sede y tengo que enviar mi entrega. Aunque sé que la puedo mandar a tiempo, ¿qué pasa si llega después de la fecha límite publicada?"

    (C) "Si mi entrega no gana, ¿qué proceso hay para pedir que la consideren otra vez?"

    (D) "Si mi entrega gana, ¿cuánto suele ser quitado por los impuestos?"

SELECCIÓN #4

Tema curricular: Los desafíos mundiales

> **Introducción:** Lo siguiente es una carta abierta al Presidente de la República de Uruguay sobre un asunto del medio ambiente. La carta original fue publicada en *El Observador* en 2010.

Sr. Presidente,

Me dirijo a Usted por este medio para conocer su opinión, sus respuestas a la infinidad de interrogantes que hoy nos formulamos los productores rurales de cuatro
Línea departamentos ante la presencia de la Minera Aratirí que avanza en sus trabajos de
(5) prospección y exploración en la búsqueda de hierro en una zona ganadera, donde los directamente afectados, los superficiarios, no hemos tenido una sola respuesta oficial al respecto, aún habiéndola solicitado en más de una oportunidad.

La Minera cavaría inmensos huecos en el corazón del país ocasionando una alteración permanente y definitiva del paisaje, de la red de drenaje, dada la
(10) imposibilidad de devolver a la zona su estructuración inicial. Esta alteración trae consecuencias ecológicas, sociales, económicas dramáticas ya que rompe una cadena productiva que será imposible reconstruir.

Sabemos que "las aguas ácidas representan un grave riesgo ambiental ya que alteran las características químicas de las aguas receptoras contaminándolas y
(15) causando impactos en los ecosistemas", así lo dicen informes técnicos de profesionales expertos en la materia. Sabemos que con la crisis mundial de alimentos se vienen tiempos de valorización de los productos agrícolas (materias primas agropecuarias). Sabemos de la necesidad de control de sectores estratégicos como el rural y el agro negocio. Sabemos que un país como Brasil está legislando
(20) para impedir la extranjerización de la tierra previendo la crisis de alimentos y la escasez del agua.

Y si sabemos todo esto . . .

¿Es posible que estemos hipotecando nuestras fértiles praderas naturales en proyectos mineros que producen alteraciones irreversibles en ecosistemas
(25) naturales y que estemos hipotecando la salud y el futuro de nuestro país, el de nuestros hijos y nietos y que además no estemos informados?

No Señor Presidente, no es posible.

Por lo tanto queremos conocer su opinión y queremos ejercer nuestros derechos como ciudadanos, queremos ser escuchados, que nuestra opinión sea también
(30) válida, queremos ser atendidos porque todos ansiamos lo mejor para el País Natural que codician los extranjeros.

Atentamente,

Rosina Mascheroni

18 de diciembre de 2010

25. ¿Cuál es el propósito de esta carta?

(A) Que el presidente se entere de unos problemas medioambientales

(B) Solicitar trabajo en una compañía minera que se ubica en su zona

(C) Que el gobierno preste atención a las preocupaciones de unos ciudadanos

(D) Saber exactamente qué planes tiene el gobierno para el futuro del país

26. ¿A qué se refiere la autora cuando dice ". . . la infinidad de interrogantes . . ." (líneas 2–3)?

(A) A las inquietudes del pueblo

(B) A las demandas del gobierno

(C) A las preguntas de la compañía minera

(D) A la alta demanda de minerales de su zona

27. ¿Cuál es la preocupación más grande con Minería Aratirí?

(A) Que no permite que los locales puedan solicitar trabajo

(B) Que les quitará todo el hierro de su zona

(C) Que hará un daño permanente a la tierra

(D) Que no les permite seguir trabajando con la ganadería

28. ¿Qué se puede inferir acerca de la compañía minera?

(A) Es una filial de una compañía extranjera.

(B) Ha tenido éxito previo en Brasil.

(C) Es una de las compañías más prósperas de Uruguay.

(D) Ha tomado medidas para el sostenimiento ecológico.

29. ¿De qué manera comunica la carta su mensaje sobre el impacto de la compañía minera?

(A) Cuenta una historia previa de la compañía.

(B) Incluye opiniones de la población afectada.

(C) Relata unas experiencias de su propia situación.

(D) Se refiere a datos y hechos específicos.

30. ¿Qué perspectiva cultural representa la carta?

(A) Devoción a la tradición ganadera y de agricultura

(B) Cautela ante el progreso

(C) Valor de la democracia

(D) Importancia del respaldo gubernamental

SECTION I, PART B

Interpretive Communication: Print and Audio Texts (Combined)

Time: Approximately 55 minutes

DIRECTIONS: You will listen to several audio selections. The first two also include print texts. When there is a print text, you will have an additional amount of time to read it.

For each audio selection, you will have a designated amount of time to read the introduction of the selection and to preview the questions and answers that follow. Each audio selection will be played twice.

Following the first listening, you will have one minute to begin answering the questions. After the second listening, you will be given 15 seconds per question to finish answering. For each question, select the best answer according to the selection and mark your answer on your answer sheet.

Vas a escuchar a varias grabaciones. Las primeras dos van acompañadas de textos escritos. Cuando hay un texto escrito, tendrás tiempo adicional para leerlo.

Para cada selección auditiva, vas a tener un tiempo determinado para leer la introducción de la selección y prever las preguntas que siguen. Vas a escuchar cada fuente auditiva dos veces.

Después de escuchar cada selección la primera vez, vas a tener un minuto para empezar a contestar las preguntas. Después de escucharla la segunda vez, vas a tener 15 segundos por pregunta para terminarlas. Para cada pregunta, elige la mejor respuesta según el contexto y escríbela en la hoja de respuestas.

SELECCIÓN #1

Tema curricular: Los desafíos mundiales

Fuente #1: Primero tienes un minuto para leer fuente número 1.

Introducción: El siguiente gráfico presenta la cantidad de remesas, en millones de dólares, que se ha mandado a El Salvador. Se basa en información publicada del Banco Nacional de Reserva de El Salvador.

Track 52

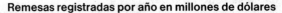
Remesas registradas por año en millones de dólares

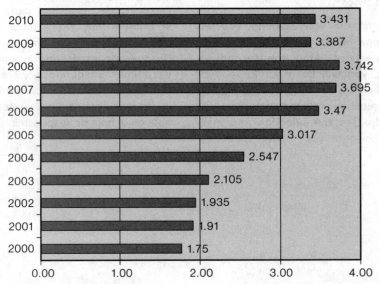

Año	Millones de dólares
2010	3.431
2009	3.387
2008	3.742
2007	3.695
2006	3.47
2005	3.017
2004	2.547
2003	2.105
2002	1.935
2001	1.91
2000	1.75

Fuente #2: Ahora tienes un minuto para leer la introducción y prever las preguntas.

Introducción: La siguiente fuente auditiva es una entrevista con el embajador de El Salvador en Radio Naciones Unidas. El tema es la migración y desarrollo en El Salvador. La entrevista original fue publicada en Nueva York por Radio Naciones Unidas el 23 de octubre de 2012. La grabación dura aproximadamente tres minutos, treinta segundos.

31. Según la tabla, ¿cuánto dinero fue enviado a El Salvador en 2003?
    (A) Dos mil ciento cinco dólares
    (B) Dos dólares, ciento cinco centavos
    (C) Dos millones, ciento cinco dólares
    (D) Dos mil millones, ciento cinco mil dólares

32. Según la tabla, ¿qué se puede afirmar de las remesas a El Salvador?
    (A) Ha habido un incremento constante.
    (B) Ha empezado a disminuir cada año.
    (C) Recientemente hubo un descenso en relación a años anteriores.
    (D) Recientemente hubo un ascenso en relación a años anteriores.

33. ¿Qué se puede deducir de la tabla que ocurrió entre el año 2000 y 2006?
    (A) Casi se duplicó la cantidad de dinero enviado a El Salvador.
    (B) Más salvadoreños emigraron a países con economías más prósperas.
    (C) Los emigrantes ganaron más dinero durante esta época.
    (D) La economía salvadoreña experimentó una crisis económica.

34. Según la entrevista, ¿cuál es la preocupación fundamental del gobierno salvadoreño?
    (A) Preservar la historia de su país
    (B) Crear condiciones para favorecer la permanencia en El Salvador
    (C) Facilitar el proceso de emigración a otros países
    (D) Subministrar documentación a la población inmigrante de su país

35. ¿Qué iniciativa está tratando de emplear el gobierno salvadoreño?
    (A) Documentar a sus connacionales
    (B) Abrir vías de migración a Canadá, España y Australia
    (C) Asegurar que las remesas sigan una parte integral de su economía
    (D) Obligar a los indocumentados que regresen a su país

36. En la entrevista, ¿a qué se refiere el embajador cuando dice que "el inmigrante se vaya olvidando de su terruño"?
    (A) A una razón por la cual no van a volver a El Salvador
    (B) A una posible causa de la reducción de la remesas
    (C) Al deseo de los inmigrantes de invertir en su país sede
    (D) A que los inmigrantes van a perder las tierras de su familia

37. ¿Qué opina el embajador en cuanto a las remesas?
    (A) Aportan muchos beneficios a la economía salvadoreña.
    (B) Hay que encaminarlas en inversiones para mejorar el país.
    (C) No son tan productivas como eran anteriormente.
    (D) Muchas familias no saben qué hacer con ellas.

38. De acuerdo al gráfico y la fuente auditiva, ¿qué se puede deducir de la situación en El Salvador?
    (A) Carecen de las oportunidades económicas para sostener a una familia.
    (B) A los salvadoreños les gusta compartir sus riquezas.
    (C) Los salvadoreños en el extranjero han ganado más durante los años.
    (D) Las familias en El Salvador tienen una mejor vida por la migración a otros países.

SELECCIÓN #2

Tema curricular: La ciencia y la tecnología

Fuente #1: Primero tienes cuatro minutos para leer fuente número 1.

Introducción: El siguiente artículo trata de la importancia de dormir bien. Fue publicado en la página web *www.consumer.es* el 22 de octubre de 2012.

Track 53

Para estudiar más no es beneficioso sacrificar el descanso nocturno y, menos, hacerlo antes de un examen. Al contrario, suele ser contraproducente, ya que el rendimiento óptimo se logra cuando hay un equilibrio entre las horas dedicadas
Línea al estudio y al dormir, según los resultados de un trabajo reciente llevado a cabo
(5) en la Universidad de California en Los Ángeles (EE.UU.). Aunque no significa que no haya que estudiar, sino que hay que tener en cuenta que las horas de sueño pueden ser determinantes para el éxito académico.

Dormir para retener lo aprendido

Investigaciones anteriores ya habían constatado que lo aprendido se retiene
(10) mejor si se duerme justo después de hacerlo. Un trabajo de la Universidad estadounidense de Notre Dame señalaba que la memoria de lo aprendido era superior en los que habían dormido justo después de estudiar, respecto de los que habían dormido tras un día de vigilia.

Otro estudio presentado durante la reunión anual de la Asociación Americana
(15) para el Avance de la Ciencia, en 2010, llevado a cabo por investigadores de la Universidad de California en Berkeley, confirma que una de las principales funciones del sueño es la de "limpiar" la memoria a corto plazo para dejar sitio libre para más información. Los autores concluían que una noche sin dormir puede reducir la capacidad de asimilar conocimientos en casi un 40%, ya que las
(20) regiones cerebrales implicadas en el almacenaje no funcionan de forma correcta durante la falta de sueño.

Las mejores horas para estudiar y dormir

Muchas de las personas que estudian por la noche dicen hacerlo porque se concentran mejor, rinden más y tienen menos interrupciones y distracciones. Un tra-
(25) bajo de 2008 del Hospital Quirón de Valencia desbancó esta arraigada costumbre en muchos alumnos. Muchos especialistas aseguran que el periodo de máximo aprovechamiento coincide con la mañana, decrece a lo largo de la tarde y, sobre todo, de la noche, por lo que conviene trabajar la mayor parte de la materia al comienzo del día y dejar el repaso o la tarea más fácil para la última hora de la
(30) jornada.

39. ¿Qué técnica usa el autor en los primeros párrafos del artículo para comunicar su idea?
    - (A) Presenta su opinión con ejemplos cotidianos.
    - (B) Incluye anécdotas de diferentes expertos.
    - (C) Provee ideas contrarias de varios grupos.
    - (D) Incluye datos para apoyar el tema.

40. En el artículo, ¿qué comprobaron los investigadores en cuanto al retener la información estudiada?
    - (A) Que se retiene más fácilmente si se duerme lo suficiente
    - (B) Que se retiene mejor si se trasnocha estudiando
    - (C) Que se retiene mejor si se duerme inmediatamente después
    - (D) Que se retiene mejor el día después de estudiar

41. Según el artículo, ¿a qué se refiere el autor cuando dice "las regiones cerebrales implicadas en el almacenaje no funcionan" (líneas 19–20)?
    - (A) A que el cerebro pierde la capacidad de memorizar
    - (B) A la reducción de la capacidad de guardar información
    - (C) A la incapacidad de entender información nueva
    - (D) A la falta de capacidad de distinguir una cosa de otra

42. Según el artículo, ¿cuándo es el mejor tiempo para estudiar?
    - (A) Durante la noche cuando hay menos distracciones
    - (B) Por la tarde, después del almuerzo
    - (C) Después del desayuno y antes del mediodía
    - (D) Cuando quiera uno, siempre que tome un estimulante

43. Según el Podcast, ¿qué se menciona que es un valor en la sociedad?
    - (A) El equilibrio de trabajo y descanso
    - (B) La capacidad de saber cuándo ser productivo
    - (C) El alto rendimiento en el ámbito laboral
    - (D) Descansar lo suficiente para poder ser más productivo

44. ¿Con qué propósito incluye la fuente auditiva una cita de Sócrates?
    (A) Para presentar que el valor del descanso no es novedoso
    (B) Para subrayar la importancia de la productividad
    (C) Para añadir más ejemplos a los beneficios del descanso
    (D) Para exponer otra hipótesis del valor del ocio

45. Según la psicóloga de la fuente auditiva, ¿cuándo hay que aprovecharse del descanso?
    (A) En el ámbito laboral
    (B) Fuera del trabajo y de los deberes domésticos
    (C) Tanto en el trabajo como fuera
    (D) En las actividades de ocio y de tiempo libre

46. ¿Cómo diferencia la psicóloga del Podcast el tiempo libre del ocio?
    (A) El tiempo libre es el tiempo que uno tiene para divertirse.
    (B) El ocio es el tiempo que se pasa con la familia.
    (C) El ocio es el tiempo para realizar actividades domésticas.
    (D) El tiempo libre es el tiempo para alimentarse y echarse una siesta.

47. ¿En qué coinciden la fuente escrita y la auditiva?
    (A) Presentan la importancia del descanso en la productividad.
    (B) Citan personajes históricos para apoyar sus ideas.
    (C) Mencionan los beneficios de tomar tiempo libre.
    (D) Critican el énfasis de la sociedad en ser productivos.

SELECCIÓN #3

Tema curricular: Las identidades personales y públicas

Primero tienes un minuto para leer la introducción y prever las preguntas.

Introducción: La siguiente grabación, titulada "¿Dónde está la felicidad?", se trata sobre el tema de la felicidad de los hombres. Fue publicada en *http://mariacristinasalas.blogspot.com* en 2011. La grabación dura aproximadamente tres minutos cuarenta segundos.

Track 54

48. ¿Cuál de los siguientes mejor resume la búsqueda del hombre como se menciona en la fuente auditiva?
   (A) Encontró lo que buscaba al encontrarse con un sabio.
   (B) Al desenvolver el paquete, descubrió la respuesta a su pregunta.
   (C) Todavía se quedó perplejo de lo que había encontrado.
   (D) Al verse en el espejo, encontró lo que buscaba.

49. ¿A qué se refiere la frase "se postró ante él y habló entre sollozos"?
   (A) A la humildad con que el hombre se presentó ante el sabio
   (B) Al apuro que tenía el hombre para encontrar la respuesta a su pregunta
   (C) A la compasión que tuvo el sabio para el hombre
   (D) A la confusión que tenía el hombre al ver al sabio

50. ¿Cuál de las siguientes frases mejor describe al sabio?
   (A) Es un hombre insensato.
   (B) Es un hombre mayor.
   (C) Es un hombre inquieto.
   (D) Es un hombre ocupado.

51. ¿Cómo es la actitud del hombre hacia el paquete regalado?
   (A) Confuso
   (B) Ansioso
   (C) Resignado
   (D) Tímido

52. Según el cuento, ¿cómo se describe el templo?
    (A) Lujoso
    (B) Descuidado
    (C) Arreglado
    (D) Protegido

53. ¿Qué ocurrió cuando el hombre colocó el pedazo que tenía en el espejo?
    (A) Se vio a si mismo por primera vez.
    (B) Se dio cuenta que estaba en el lugar incorrecto.
    (C) Pudo comprender la función de la palabra inscrita.
    (D) Sintió más delirio y confusión.

54. ¿Cuál es la moraleja del cuento?
    (A) Hay que meditar para encontrar la felicidad.
    (B) La felicidad se obtiene al viajar.
    (C) La verdadera felicidad se encuentra en un pedazo, que al colocarlo bien, hace uno lleno.
    (D) Sólo nosotros podemos darnos la felicidad.

SELECCIÓN #4

Tema curricular: La belleza y la estética

Primero tienes un minuto para leer la introducción y prever las preguntas.

> **Introducción:** La siguiente grabación, titulada Día Internacional del Libro y del Derecho de Autor, fue publicada en Radio Naciones Unidas en 2012. La grabación dura aproximadamente tres minutos, cuarenta segundos.

Track 55

55. ¿Cuál es el propósito de esta selección?
    (A) Mostrar el impacto que ha tenido el festival a unos autores
    (B) Revelar lo que les inspiró a unos autores a la lectura
    (C) Resaltar la importancia de empezar a leer cunado eres joven
    (D) Informar sobre unos autores y sus recuerdos infantiles

56. ¿Qué tipo de cuentos se le leían a Carmen Boullosa?
    (A) Cuentos para jóvenes
    (B) Trozos de cuentos para niños
    (C) Partes de novelas famosas
    (D) Cuentos cómicos de diversos géneros

57. Según Carmen Boullosa, ¿qué le fascinaba de los libros para niños aparte del cuento?
    (A) Que eran cuentos marginalizados
    (B) Que había una gran variedad
    (C) Que eran historias de grandes autores
    (D) Que eran agradables a la vista

58. ¿Por qué empezó Sergio Ramírez a escribir cuentos?
    (A) Para que el género que tanto le gustaba no desapareciera
    (B) Para continuar a revivir las historias de su niñez
    (C) Para poder exponer los misterios que le fascinaban tanto
    (D) Para explorar más el universo y mundos extraños

59. ¿Por qué escogió Santiago Roncagliolo su primera novela?
    (A) Porque su padre se lo había recomendado
    (B) Porque le fascinaba el tema
    (C) Porque le interesaba la portada
    (D) Porque no podía escoger cómics

60. ¿Qué se puede deducir de los tres autores?
    (A) Son todos aficionados de la gran literatura
    (B) Su amor por la literatura se fomentó a través de diversas experiencias
    (C) Llegaron a ser autores por la influencia de sus padres
    (D) Sienten mucho orgullo de formar parte del Día Internacional del Libro

SELECCIÓN #5

Tema curricular: La ciencia y la tecnología

Primero tienes un minuto para leer la introducción y prever las preguntas.

> **Introducción:** La siguiente grabación trata de la dieta mediterránea. La grabación proviene del programa titulado Alimento y Salud emitido por Radio 5 en España. Fue publicada en abril de 2013 y dura aproximadamente dos minutos, treinta segundos.

Track 56

61. ¿Cuál es el propósito de la grabación?
   (A) Informar sobre un estudio hecho de la dieta mediterránea
   (B) Presentar las características de la dieta mediterránea
   (C) Dar consejos a base de estudios para cómo mantener una dieta saludable
   (D) Contar por qué la dieta mediterránea es mejor que otras dietas

62. ¿Qué sugiere el presentador acerca de la dieta mediterránea?
   (A) Que todavía hacen falta más pruebas para averiguar sus beneficios
   (B) Que se ha sabido por mucho tiempo que es la dieta más saludable
   (C) Que hay diversos motivos por la cual la dieta es tan saludable
   (D) Que las investigaciones comprobaron un conocimiento previo

63. ¿Qué se puede inferir del estudio hecho?
   (A) Que fue completada en Estados Unidos
   (B) Que varios países participaron en él
   (C) Que los participantes eran todos españoles
   (D) Que los participantes padecían de mala salud

64. ¿Por qué se paró la investigación prematuramente?
   (A) Para ofrecerle a un grupo los beneficios que experimentaban los demás
   (B) Porque a los investigadores se les acabaron las finanzas para continuar el estudio
   (C) Porque unos participantes sufrieron unos problemas médicos
   (D) Para poder analizar los resultados de su investigación

65. ¿Con cuál de las siguientes afirmaciones estaría más de acuerdo Dr. Ramón Estuch, el coordinador del estudio?
   (A) La dieta mediterránea es más saludable por ser baja en grasa.
   (B) Otros países deberían considerar emular la dieta mediterránea.
   (C) Los con sobrepeso deben limitar el consumo de grasas vegetales.
   (D) Es una obligación de los políticos cambiar los hábitos de consumo de la gente.

SECTION II

Interpersonal Writing: Email Reply

Time: 15 minutes

DIRECTIONS: You will write a reply to an email that you received. You have 15 minutes to read the message and write your reply.

Your reply should include an appropriate greeting and closing and should answer all the questions and requests in the original message. In addition, your reply should ask for more details about something that was mentioned in the message. You should use a formal tone in your response.

Vas a escribir una respuesta a un mensaje de correo electrónico. Tienes 15 minutos para leer el mensaje y escribir tu respuesta.

Tu respuesta debe incluir un saludo y despedida apropiada y contestar a todas las preguntas y peticiones del mensaje original. También tu respuesta debe pedir más información de algo mencionado en el mensaje original. Debes usar el tono formal en tu respuesta.

Tema curricular: Las identidades personales y públicas

Introducción: El siguiente mensaje electrónico es de la editora de *Apreciarte* una revista dedicada al mundo artístico. La revista esta lanzando un nuevo blog relacionado al arte, y quiere que sus suscritores contribuyan sus ideas.

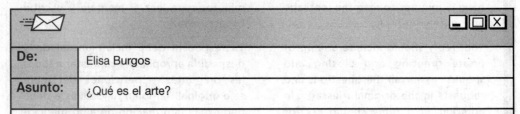

De:	Elisa Burgos
Asunto:	¿Qué es el arte?

Querido suscritor,

Es mi placer informarle que la revista *Apreciarte* está a punto de lanzar un nuevo blog completamente dedicado al arte. Estamos muy orgullosos de este nuevo proyecto para que nuestros estimados y muy valorados lectores contribuyan y compartan sus ideas de la belleza del arte. La idea es de proponer un tema diferente cada mes y dejar que la gente lo discuta y que presente su opinión.

Antes del lanzamiento del blog, quisiéramos darles el honor a nuestros queridos suscritores a que ellos sean los primeros contribuyentes. Por esa razón, queremos invitarle a usted a que responda a las siguientes preguntas:

– ¿Cómo define usted el arte?

– Para usted, ¿qué hace que una obra de arte sea superior a otra?

No ponemos límite a su respuesta, así tome la oportunidad de expresarse tanto como quiera. Cuanto más pueda contribuir, mejor para el blog.

Le agradezco de antemano por su valioso tiempo y por considerar su participación en este proyecto tan emocionante.

Atentamente,

Elisa Burgos
Editora General *Apreciarte*

SECTION II

Presentational Writing: Argumentative Essay

Time: Approximately 55 minutes

Track 57

Tema curricular: La vida contemporánea

Primero tienes seis minutos para leer el tema del ensayo, la fuente número 1 y la fuente número 2.

Tema del ensayo: ¿Es importante seguir los estudios después de la escuela secundaria?

Fuente #1

Introducción: El siguiente texto trata de la formación universitaria y su relevancia en el mercado laboral. El artículo fue publicado por *Eroski Consumer* en agosto de 2013.

¿Estudiar en la universidad me garantiza un empleo?

La formación universitaria está muy valorada en el mercado laboral, pero desde 2005, la tasa de paro ha aumentado un 7,4% entre universitarios y un 1,2% entre doctorados

Por Azucena García

No es un secreto. La tasa de paro ha aumentado desde 2007, ¿pero cómo ha afectado a los estudiantes que cada año salen de la universidad con un título bajo el brazo? El anuario "Datos y cifras del sistema universitario español", relativo al curso 2012–2013, del Ministerio de Educación, revela que la tasa de desempleo se ha incrementado entre ellos, aunque en menor medida que entre la población total. Mientras la tasa general pasó del 8,3% en 2007 al 21,6% en 2011, entre la población con educación superior no doctor ascendió del 5,4% al 12,8% y entre los doctorados, del 2,7% al 3,9%. "Estos datos ponen de manifiesto que la educación universitaria disminuye el riesgo de paro", asegura el informe.

La conclusión es halagüeña, pero conviene profundizar. Estar empleado no siempre implica desempeñar la tarea para la que se ha recibido formación. "Muchos trabajadores solamente consiguen empleos inferiores a la cualificación que poseen (subocupación)", detalla el informe "Panorama de la educación. Indicadores de la OCDE 2013". ¿Cuántos son muchos? "Un 36% de los titulados universitarios", de acuerdo a otro informe de la Fundación Conocimiento y Desarrollo (Fundación CYD).

La tasa de ocupación entre los graduados superiores ha descendido desde 2007 en nuestro país, pero también la media de la UE-27 ha registrado una caída. En concreto, en 2012, el informe de la Fundación CYD revela una tasa de ocupación española siete puntos inferior a la media europea. Por franja de edad, la mayor tasa de ocupación fue para los graduados superiores de 45 a 49 años (82,5%), mientras que la más baja—aparte de los mayores de 60 años (49,4%)—fue para el grupo de 25 a 29 años (66,6%) y de 30 a 34 años (77,2%).

El estudio de la OCDE concluye que "existe un posible exceso de oferta de titulados universitarios". Si bien reconoce que un mayor nivel de estudios aumenta las posibilidades de contratación, de tener un empleo estable y de adquirir mayores salarios, revela que no garantiza el futuro en el terreno laboral.

Línea

(5)

(10)

(15)

(20)

(25)

Fuente #2

Introducción: El gráfico muestra las tasas de paro por nivel de formación para la población de 20–24 años y de 30–44 años en el periodo 2006–2010 en España. Se basa en estadísticas de la INE en 2010.

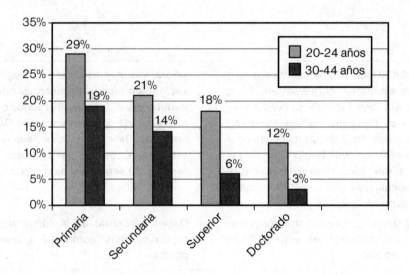

Fuente #3

Introducción: El siguiente reportaje trata de la vida moderna en Hispanoamérica. La conversación dura aproximadamente dos minutos.

SECTION II

Interpersonal Speaking: Conversation

Time: Approximately 10 minutes

Track 58

<table>
<tr><td>

DIRECTIONS: You will now take part in a simulated conversation. First, you will have 1 minute to read a preview of the conversation, including the script for both parts. Then, the conversation will begin and follow the script. Each time it is your turn to speak, you will have 20 seconds to respond.

You should engage in the conversation as much and as appropriately as possible.

</td><td>

Ahora vas a participar en una conversación simulada. Primero, tendrás un minuto para leer la introducción y el esquema de la conversación. Después, empezará la conversación, siguiendo el esquema. Cada vez que te toque hablar, tendrás 20 segundos para responder.

Debes participar en la conversación de la forma más completa y apropiada posible.

</td></tr>
</table>

Tema curricular: La vida contemporánea

Tienes un minuto para leer la introducción y el esquema de la conversación.

> **Introducción:** Imagina que has oído un anuncio clasificado de un puesto vacante este verano para un salvavidas en la piscina municipal. El ayuntamiento prefiere contratar a una persona que sea responsable y que tenga prueba de habilidad para el trabajo.

Empleada:	Te saluda y te da las noticias.
Tú:	Salúdala y explícale la razón por qué llamas.
Empleada:	Continúa la conversación. Te hace una pregunta.
Tú:	Contesta la pregunta con detalles.
Empleada:	Continúa la conversación. Te hace otra pregunta.
Tú:	Responde con detalles.
Empleada:	Continúa la conversación.
Tú:	Reacciona positivamente. Explícale una condición.
Empleada:	Continúa la conversación. Te hace otra pregunta.
Tú:	Responde apropiadamente. Despídete.
Empleada:	Concluye la conversación.

SECTION II

Presentational Speaking: Cultural Comparison

Time: Approximately 6 minutes

DIRECTIONS: You will now prepare an oral presentation for your class on a specific topic. You will have 4 minutes to read the topic and prepare your presentation. Then, you will have 2 minutes to record your presentation.

In your presentation, compare your own community to one of the Spanish-speaking world with which you are familiar. You should demonstrate your understanding of cultural features of the Spanish-speaking world. Your presentation should also be well organized.

Ahora vas a preparar una presentación oral para tu clase de español sobre un tema cultural. Primero, tendrás 4 minutos para leer el tema y preparar tu presentación. Después, tendrás 2 minutos para grabarla.

En tu presentación, compara tu comunidad con una del mundo hispanohablante con el que estés familiarizado. Debes demostrar tu comprensión de los aspectos culturales en el mundo hispanohablante. También, tu presentación debe ser bien organizada.

Tema curricular: La ciencia y la tecnología

Tema de la presentación: ¿Cómo ha cambiado la tecnología en cuanto a la manera en que uno se relaciona con los demás hoy en día?

Compara tus observaciones de las comunidades en que has vivido con tus observaciones del una región del mundo hispanohablante que te sea familiar. Puedes referirte a lo que has estudiado, vivido, observado, etc.

ANSWER KEY
Practice Test 2

SECTION I

PART A

1. D	11. C	21. C
2. C	12. D	22. B
3. C	13. A	23. A
4. D	14. C	24. D
5. C	15. C	25. C
6. C	16. B	26. A
7. C	17. C	27. C
8. B	18. B	28. A
9. B	19. C	29. D
10. B	20. C	30. A

PART B

31. C	43. C	55. B
32. A	44. A	56. C
33. B	45. C	57. D
34. A	46. D	58. A
35. A	47. A	59. C
36. B	48. D	60. B
37. B	49. A	61. A
38. A	50. B	62. D
39. D	51. B	63. C
40. A	52. B	64. A
41. B	53. C	65. B
42. C	54. D	

PART SEVEN

Appendices

Audioscripts

PART B, SECTION I

Listening Comprehension: Audio and Print Texts (Combined)

Selección número 1, Fuente número 2

Programa *Nuestra América,*
La Habana, 16 de enero 2006
Michelle Bachelet, nueva presidenta de Chile
Santiago de Chile, 15 de enero. Michelle Bachelet ganó hoy las elecciones chilenas tras derrotar al derechista Sebastián Piñera, lo que la convertirá en la primera presidenta de Chile, reportó EFE.

El Ministerio del Interior chileno informó hoy de que, con el 97,71% de los votos escrutados, Bachelet obtuvo el 53,49% frente al 46,50% de Piñera.

El derrotado candidato de la derecha, Sebastián Piñera, reconoció su derrota y felicitó a su rival, a quien deseó "el mayor de los éxitos".

La victoria de Bachelet causó una explosión de alegría en su coalición, en donde el senador democratacristiano Andrés Zaldívar afirmó que la electa presidenta gobernará para todos los chilenos, "los que votaron por ella y los que no lo hicieron".

Diversas agencias de prensa se referían en la noche de ayer a que casi medio millón de chilenos se lanzaron a las calles para vitorear a Michelle Bachelet, agitando banderas y cantando *Vuelvo*, la canción mítica del grupo local Illapu, que narra la emoción de miles de exiliados durante la dictadura militar, entre ellos la presidenta electa.

El gobierno de Bachelet, que tomará posesión de su cargo el 11 de marzo, será el cuarto de la coalición de centroizquierda Concertación por la Democracia desde 1990, destacó EFE.

Desigualdad: Reto para Próximo Presidente
Santiago de Chile, 15 de enero.
—El próximo presidente enfrentará el desafío de altos niveles de desigualdad social y desempleo. Organismos oficiales confirman que el 20% más acaudalado de los chilenos percibe 15 veces más que el 20 más pobre, y de esa cifra de poderosos, el 1% resulta particularmente concentrador de riquezas.

Chile está ubicado entre los 15 primeros países (de 130) con peor desigualdad de ingresos a nivel mundial y según el Instituto Nacional de Estadísticas, aún 532.607 personas se mantienen analfabetas: 258.262 hombres y 274.345 mujeres. De acuerdo con el último censo, existe un 4,7% de indigentes, es decir 728.063 personas, mientras un 14,08% enfrenta el desamparo no indigente (2.179.653).

Selección número 2, Fuente número 2

Track 2

Santa Clara del Cobre es nombrada nuevo "Pueblo Mágico"

Por Elizabeth Cruz

Nombrado recientemente como Pueblo Mágico, el pueblo colonial de Santa Clara del Cobre, Michoacán, se caracteriza por haber conservado a través de generaciones la tradición artesanal del metal que le da nombre, ya que cada pieza es el resultado de calor, martillazos y la vasta imaginación de cada uno de los hombres que han hecho de estos artículos su forma de vida.

Santa Clara es una pequeña localidad que ofrece a sus visitantes no sólo el encanto de sus artesanías, sino la belleza de sus casas blancas con techos de teja roja, de entre las que destaca un kiosko con techo de cobre que se ilumina con los rayos del sol en medio de la plaza principal.

Aunque se tiene conocimiento que los antiguos indígenas de la región ya utilizaban el metal para la creación de diversos artículos como hachas, aretes y otros objetos ornamentales, fue hasta la llegada del obispo Vasco de Quiroga cuando se perfeccionaron las técnicas artesanales existentes, pues fue él quien introdujo el proceso de fundición y martillado que persiste hasta nuestros días.

En Santa Clara también es posible visitar el Museo del Cobre, donde se exponent antiguos objetos encontrados en el lugar, fabricados por los tarascos, así como piezas artísticas ganadoras de concursos nacionales e internacionales. Asimismo, existe una escuela-taller y una cooperativa que lleva el nombre de Vasco de Quiroga, además de la Casa del Artesano, lugares donde se imparte capacitación y preparación para los nuevos artistas.

Para una mejor experiencia de viaje, te recomendamos visitar este nuevo "Pueblo Mágico". *(www.mexicodesconocido.com.mx/notas/91469-Santa-Clara-del-Cobre-es-nombradanuevo-%E2%80%9CPueblo-M%C3%A1gico%E2%80%9D)*

Selección número 3, Fuente número 2

Track 3

Las ventajas de las universidades pequeñas

¿A su hija o hijo le encantan las clases de pequeños grupos con discusiones en las que tiene prioridad la participación activa y el conocimiento directo? En ese caso, su hijo o hija debería plantearse ir a una universidad pequeña. Algunas posibles ventajas asociadas con las universidades de menor tamaño son clases de tamaño pequeño, oportunidades directas de conocimiento, especialidades diseñadas de forma individual, fuerte sistema de asesoría, y los asesores conocen muy bien a los estudiantes, gran sentido de comunidad, los catedráticos, no asistentes, enseñan la mayoría de las clases, y oportunidad de conocer bien a los profesores.

Si bien las universidades pequeñas suelen ofrecer un fuerte sentido de comunidad, el entorno también dificulta a los estudiantes salirse o entrar en grupos sociales con la misma facilidad que permite una universidad con miles de alumnos. Cuando usted y su hija o hijo visiten una pequeña universidad, hablen con estudiantes para entender cómo es la vida social y qué tipo de actividades no académicas existen.

Las pequeñas universidades son perfectas para aquellos estudiantes que se sienten bien en entornos de pequeños grupos, se sienten estimulados por altos niveles de interactuación entre profesores y alumnos, y que están interesados en desarrollar especialidades creativas, individuales enfocadas en áreas de interés específicas.

Generalmente las universidades pequeñas son capaces de cumplir con los intereses únicos de su hijo o hija y sus necesidades. Al contrario de los establecimientos más grandes, las universidades de menor tamaño alientan a los estudiantes a explorar áreas distintas a su campo de estudios.

(www.collegeboard.com/padres/buscar/explorar)

Selección número 4, Fuente número 2

Música Clásica

Por lo general, "música clásica" es un término que se usa para referirse a la música culta o académica compuesta en el medioevo, renacimiento y barroco hasta el período contemporáneo; los más puristas consideran a la música clásica sólo como la compuesta en el período clásico, que se extiende entre los tiempos finales de J. S. Bach y el fin de la vida de Beethoven. El interés por la música clásica podría parecer algo anacrónico, pero la verdad es que hoy goza de gran popularidad, tal vez no como las corrientes populares por razones obvias, pero siempre ha contado con un gran número de seguidores y entusiastas de todas las edades. Música tan antigua como la del medioevo y el renacimiento cobran fuerza e interés entre la juventud, reviviendo instrumentos hermosos e impresionantes como, por ejemplo, la viola de gamba, instrumento popular entre los nobles de los siglos XV y XVII.

Para referirnos a la música clásica, uno debe hacer una gran distinción entre ésta y las otras ramas de la música. Ésta es claramente más seria, para un oído especial o más refinado; en todo caso nos referimos por "seria" al hecho de ser característicamente profunda y estudiada, y no en el sentido de ser grave e inaccesible.

La música clásica se caracteriza por ser la primera rama musical que unió perfectamente el desempeño de los instrumentos con las voces de personas. Al mismo tiempo se debe mencionar que la música clásica logra la unión de varios instrumentos para dar paso al desempeño de una orquesta como tal. Con ello se logra una potente dramatización a través de la música en sí. Entre los instrumentos de música clásica más conocidos están el violín, el piano de cola, el violonchelo, el contrabajo, el arpa, la trompeta, el trombón, la flauta, el clarinete y los instrumentos de percusión.

Desde sus inicios la música clásica fue adaptada por las personas más cultas de cada sociedad. Aquellas que tenían el acceso a manuscritos y por supuesto, eran parte integral de alguno de los distintos estamentos que conformaban la elite en sus respectivas épocas.

(www.buscarinformacion.com/musica/musica_clasica.html)

Selección número 5, Fuente número 2

(Sound of a crowd of people talking)

NAR 1: Compadre. Escúcheme. Tenemos que organizar este grupo para ponernos en manifiesto contra esta administración.

NAR 2: Estoy de acuerdo. Hace seis meses que trabajamos sin contrato y no van a concedernos ningunos ascensos si no hacemos algo.

NAR 1: ¡Qué va! Siempre nos han tratado como si fuéramos esclavos. Mañana podremos mostrarles nuestra fuerza en un desfile por las calles del centro.

NAR 2: Pues, llamaré a todos los líderes del turno de la noche con quienes trabajo.

NAR 1: Y yo llamaré a los otros de mi turno. Podremos alcanzar cien hombres para una manifestación si llamamos a todos los que están con nosotros.

NAR 2: Con un poco de suerte podríamos negociar un contrato nuevo para el lunes si el árbitro tratara con nosotros de la manera que queremos. Pidamos un ascenso de cincuenta dólares al mes como mínimo, lo cual no es tanto como merecemos y veremos qué dicen.

NAR 1: Si nos lo otorgara, podríamos empezar de nuevo el martes por la mañana. Y de esta manera la empresa tendría la producción que desea sin perder mucho tiempo.

NAR 2: De acuerdo. Todo esto debería mostrarles que queremos que nos tomen en serio.

Track 6

Selección número 6, Fuente número 2

NAR 1: Esa tormenta que pasó por aquí anoche fue la más espantosa que jamás he visto en la vida. Perdimos toda la electricidad y llovió a cántaros con un rato de granizos que destruyeron todo, todo lo que tuvimos en el huerto. ¿Sufrieron ustedes mucho daño?

NAR 2: Era igual con nosotros. Y lo peor sucedió cuando tratamos de abrir los grifos en la cocina y no salió nada, ni una gota de agua. Pasamos una noche muy mala.

NAR 1: ¡Ya lo creo! Y con todo el tronar y relampaguear los pobres niñitos se agarraron de mi esposo y de mí toda la noche por el susto que tuvieron.

NAR 2: Gracias a Dios los míos tienen bastante edad para no temer tanto el ruido. De veras fue el mayor espectáculo pirotécnico que jamás hayamos visto. Y esta mañana ¡fíjate cuánto brilla el sol, como si no hubiera pasado ni una nube por el cielo!

NAR 1: Sí, se siente la limpieza del aire esta mañana. ¿Y ahora? ¿Les han restablecido el agua?

NAR 2: Llamamos al ayuntamiento para decirles de nuestro problema y nos prometieron volver a ponérnosla esta misma mañana. Sería en buena hora porque hoy tengo que lavar mucha ropa sucia.

Track 7

Selección número 7, Fuente número 2

¿Es recomendable que los padres de un menor se creen un perfil en la red social de su hijo para aconsejarle?

Por Jordi Sabate Martí

Introducción del interlocutor y Gemma Martínez, investigadora de la Universidad del País Vasco:

A diferencia de sus progenitores, las próximas generaciones de jóvenes serán nativos digitales. Crecerán vinculados de una manera íntima al ordenador y a una cultura digital que a sus padres se les antojará casi marciana. Por ello, númerosos expertos en educación y sociología alertan de que deben acompañarles durante sus primeros años de navegación por internet, así como asesorarles en el mundo de las redes sociales.

Interlocutor: ¿Es malo que el menor utilice las redes sociales?

Gemma Martínez: La respuesta adecuada sería: depende. Si un menor entra en una red social sin tener nociones básicas sobre las normas de privacidad que ha de seguir en este entorno (contactos que debe y no debe aceptar, publicación de información personal o fotos, accesibilidad a su perfil, etc.), puede ser perjudicial. En cambio, si el menor utiliza bien esta herramienta, el uso de redes sociales y otras soluciones de comunicación servirá para reforzar los lazos de amistad con sus amigos. Los padres no pueden olvidar, en el caso concreto de las redes sociales, que los menores de catorce años no pueden acceder.

Interlocutor:	¿Es perjudicial que los menores accedan a contenidos sexuales o violentos online?
Gemma Martínez:	Si un menor de nueve años accede de forma accidental a contenidos sexuales o violentos, puede suponer para él una situación de incomodidad y malestar porque carece de la capacidad para analizar de forma crítica esos contenidos. Ahí es donde la figura de los padres cobra un papel imprescindible. Para un adolescente, el hecho de encontrarse con contenidos sexuales o violentos no es tan grave, ya que se le presupone una capacidad crítica para evitarlos.
Interlocutor:	¿Cómo pueden los padres discernir entre lo bueno y lo malo de internet?
Gemma Martínez:	Los padres sólo pueden discernir qué es apropiado para sus hijos en internet si ellos usan también la red. Por fortuna, entre 2005 y 2006, el número de padres usuarios de internet con hijos que también navegan ha aumentado de modo considerable. Pero en el caso de España, un 15% de los padres cuyos hijos utilizan internet desconocen el medio.
Interlocutor:	Parece que los padres responsables deben hoy en día esforzarse más para educar a sus hijos porque han de asimilar conceptos nuevos. ¿Es así?
Gemma Martínez:	A los padres no se les exige más que antes, sino algo diferente. Los padres [dicen] que sus hijos saben más que ellos y eso no es del todo cierto.

Un niño puede manejar internet con más rapidez que sus padres porque desde edades muy tempranas se enfrenta al ordenador. En cambio, un adulto tiene capacidad crítica y una visión más objetiva de los contenidos beneficiosos o perjudiciales con los que su hijo se encuentra en internet. El comportamiento del menor en la red es similar al de la vida real, pero en este caso los padres no han de perder de vista que internet cuenta con las posibilidades de anonimato e inmediatez. |
Interlocutor:	¿Los padres irán siempre por detrás de sus hijos en el aprendizaje digital? ¿Sería buena idea dejarse guiar por ellos en este nuevo mundo?
Gemma Martínez:	No todos los padres van por detrás de sus hijos en el aprendizaje digital. Pero hay resultados recientes que demuestran que en Europa los padres aumentan su uso de internet.
Interlocutor:	¿Hay que vigilar todo lo que hace un hijo en internet?
Gemma Martínez:	Con los adolescentes, un padre no puede navegar con ellos porque ya han adquirido una cierta madurez personal y estar a su alrededor mientras utilizan internet puede suponer una intromisión en su intimidad. A estas edades, muchos menores también han desarrollado las habilidades suficientes como para desinstalar filtros del ordenador y borrar todo rastro de sus acciones en internet.

En cambio, si la comunicación entre padres e hijos acerca de lo que hacen en internet es de confianza, los padres tienen que saber cuáles son los sitios que más frecuenta y cuáles son los posibles peligros para él. |

Track 8

Selección número 8, Fuente número 2

¡Energía solar para la gente!

Por David Dickson, director, *SciDiv.net*

En principio, la energía solar es una solución casi perfecta para las necesidades energéticas de los países en desarrollo. Es universal y de acceso gratuito, particularmente cerca de la línea ecuatorial, donde se encuentran muchos de estos países.

La energía solar es el último recurso de energía renovable. Su uso no agota las reservas, ni emite mucho dióxido de carbono a la atmósfera, convirtiéndola en la respuesta ideal al desafío del cambio climático.

Uno de los logros de la última conferencia sobre el clima—que con frecuencia se pasa por alto—fue el acuerdo sobre el Fondo Clima Verde, que busca recaudar y distribuir alrededor de US$30 mil millones anuales en los próximos tres años para ayudar a los países en desarrollo a expandir el uso de sus tecnologías renovables e integrarlas en sus planes de desarrollo.

El Fondo refleja la aceptación creciente de que el desarrollo de las fuentes de energía renovables es crucial para sacar de la pobreza a los más pobres del mundo de un modo ambientalmente sostenible.

Pero el fracaso de los gobiernos para alcanzar un compromiso pone de relieve que la política energética ha sido y es altamente política. Poderosos intereses (que puede incluir los de los consumidores en el mundo desarrollado) a menudo tienen la misma influencia en la política que las oportunidades tecnológicas.

Si la energía solar contribuye efectivamente al desarrollo sostenible, debe ser una parte integral de las estrategias de innovación basadas en la comunidad.

Hasta hace poco, la barrera principal para la captación de la energía solar era la poca eficiencia—y el relativamente alto costo—de convertirla en una forma utilizable. Pero los avances científicos están debilitando rápidamente esta barrera. Las tecnologías fotovoltaicas, que usan reacciones químicas para convertir la luz del sol en electricidad avanzan rápidamente, al igual que las baterías usadas para almacenar electricidad hasta que se la necesite.

A medida que los costos de conversión y almacenamiento disminuyen, el potencial de la tecnología solar para ayudar a las comunidades pobres inevitablemente aumentará.

Si las ventajas del juego en el campo económico fueran prioritarias, la combinación de gran necesidad/gran demanda y la caída de costos sería suficiente para garantizar la rápida difusión de la energía solar a lo largo del mundo en desarrollo.

Desafortunadamente el campo de juego no está nivelado. Los costos de capital de los dispositivos solares siguen siendo considerables, especialmente para los pobres. Y los subsidios gubernamentales para la energía producida por las fuentes no renovables—destinadas ostensiblemente a mantener asequibles sus precios—con frecuencia han distorsionado el mercado siguiendo los intereses de los proveedores de energía convencional.

Track 9

Selección número 9, Fuente número 2

¿Están los jóvenes de América Latina preparados para enfrentarse al mundo laboral?

Más de ocho millones de jóvenes de entre 15 y 24 años de América Latina y el Caribe no han completado la escuela primaria y carecen de las habilidades más básicas para encontrar un trabajo decente.

Un informe de la UNESCO afirma que sin habilidades como la capacidad de entender un periódico o de hacer ejercicios matemáticos básicos, esos adolescentes están condenados a empleos precarios y mal pagados.

Prácticamente la mitad de la población de la región tiene menos de 25 años.

En una entrevista con Radio ONU, Marisol Sanjinés, una de las autoras del informe, explicó que los jóvenes salen de la escuela sin las habilidades y la formación que requieren las empresas que deberían contratarlos.

Los latinoamericanos son una población muy joven, si pensamos que el 50% de la población total de la región tiene menos de 25 años. El 25% de esos jóvenes están trabajando en situaciones donde se les paga muy poco, se les paga menos de $1,25 al día. Entonces nos muestra que los jóvenes salen al mercado del trabajo sin las destrezas necesarias para enfrentarlo, y entonces están teniendo que tomar trabajos los cuales les están pagando muy poco".

"Entonces cuéntame qué porcentaje de jóvenes carecen de las destrezas básicas de las que me hablaba que en principio deberían adquirirse durante la educación primaria".

"Bueno, en líneas generales, nosotros decimos que son en América Latina más de 8 millones de personas que están entre la edad de 15 y 24 años, es decir uno de cada doce latinoamericanos y caribeños no ha terminado los estudios primarios. Entonces necesitan una segunda oportunidad u otras vías para ir adquiriendo estas competencias o destrezas necesarias para poder tener un empleo y tener una vida digna y próspera, ¿no? Entonces es una cifra bastante elevada. Claro que si comparamos con otras regiones tal vez no, pero en América Latina esa es la situación".

"¿Qué está fallando y qué medidas pueden adoptar los gobiernos y las instituciones educativas para mejorar esta situación"?

"Bueno, fíjate que hay la calidad del aprendizaje. Nosotros tenemos como . . . como una de las . . . de las recomendaciones es que no solo se necesita poner a todos los niños en la escuela sino que también se tiene que mejorar la calidad de la enseñanza. Luego, también hay que buscar vías alternativas para esos 200 millones de jóvenes en el mundo entero que no tienen competencias, ¿no? Entonces de buscar, que sea el sector privado, los gobiernos, tiene que buscar unas vías alternativas donde los jóvenes puedan adquirir las competencias que los lleven al trabajo. Hablando con jóvenes indígenas, ellos nos decían que en el campo ellos tienen básicamente las destrezas que han venido recibiendo de una familia a otra, pero eso no es suficiente para enfrentar el mercado, ellos necesitan mejorar las destrezas en el campo con mejores sembreríos, de mejores semillas, mejores resultados para poder vivir del campo, ¿no? Una última . . . última idea que tenemos fuerte en el informe es el concepto de inversión. Nosotros pensamos y lo hemos medido en el informe que por cada . . . por cada dólar que se invierte en la educación de los jóvenes, esto representa 10 o 15 dólares a lo largo de la vida productiva de esa persona. Entonces cuando hablamos de qué es lo que se debe hacer, es una inversión . . . es una inversión en cada futuro. Decía una joven esta mañana al lanzamiento del informe "nosotros los jóvenes podemos ser víctimas del fracaso de la generación que nos antecede o nos pueden ayudar a ser protagonistas en nuestro propio destino". Esta es la disyuntiva que está abierta para los jóvenes y hay que escucharla".

Escuchamos a Marisol Sanjinés, una de las autoras del informe de la UNESCO sobre el nivel educativo y las habilidades de los jóvenes. Emma Reverter, Naciones Unidas, Nueva York.

Track 10

Selección número 10, Fuente número 2

Sugerencias para una entrevista de trabajo

EP: En una entrevista, lo ideal es que el empleado, el colaborador, pueda mostrar una imagen, una película con la que se va a quedar la persona que le está entrevistando en este momento. Los enemigos en este momento son . . . eh . . . los miedos, las inseguridades, la baja autoestima, el estrés, la tensión, todo eso que juega en contra del empleado en este momento. Entonces, si tenemos que dar sugerencias . . . eh . . . específicas . . . eh . . . podríamos decir que primero desde el saludo, el saludar . . . en nuestra cultura . . . eh . . . tenemos esta diferencia entre usar el tú y el usted. Es mejor equivocarse usando el usted que el tú . . . es un criterio clave. Otra es el estrechar la mano, el dar la mano es la forma en cómo se saluda en estos contextos. Eh . . . esperar a que le inviten a tomar asiento antes que uno mismo . . . eh . . . se siente. Esa persona tiene que ir a escuchar antes de hablar, porque eso va a favorecer la comunicación y que sea de una manera relajada, efectiva, y que la otra persona se de una buena . . . eh . . . imagen de este individuo que está siendo entrevistado. Em . . . es importante también . . . eh . . . es bien visto en las entrevistas de trabajo que esta persona haga preguntas. Normalmente creemos que el entrevistado va solo a responder, que las preguntas las debe dar la otra persona, pero es muy importante que se hagan preguntas, preguntas obviamente adaptadas al contexto. Es importante que haya un contacto visual, al hablar. Eh . . . es muy importante . . . eh . . . la posición corporal, se dice que si es que uno está sentado la posición ideal es llenando toda la superficie del asiento de esta persona. Es muy importante . . . eh . . . que el nivel de voz sea adecuado al nivel de voz de la persona que está realizando, dirigiendo la entrevista. Normalmente la gente por dar una buena imagen tiende a fingir, y el problema de fingir se traduce en lenguaje corporal, y por no decir la mayoría de las entrevistas ahora son técnicas, son gente que está entrenada en programación neurolingüística y puede detectar a través del lenguaje corporal si una persona está fingiendo o está contando. Entonces en este sentido es mejor . . . eh . . . contar algo, que a lo mejor no es tan maravilloso pero que es real, a contar algo muy maravilloso que no es real, porque eso le va a quitar oportunidades a la persona que está siendo entrevistad-a. Por eso es importante que antes de ir a una entrevista, uno la planifique: ¿cuáles van a ser las cosas que yo voy a decir? . . . eh . . . ¿cómo las voy a decir? Sobre todo, como les dije, ¿cuál va a ser mi forma de cerrar la entrevista? ¿Qué es lo que yo puedo decir de manera sintética, si es posible en una frase, que le va a dejar pensando al otro que yo soy la mejor opción?

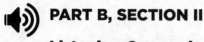

PART B, SECTION II

Track 11 **Listening Comprehension**

Selección número 1

Locutor: Estamos en Doniños en la final del campeonato de España del surf 2015. Entre las diferentes actividades que se han programado en la playa, se han realizado nuevos talleres de yoga aplicados al mundo de surf, y tenemos con nosotros, pues, a la persona encargada de repartir estos talleres Ana Nemesio

Ana: Hola, buenos días.

Locutor: Bueno, pues, la pregunta es clara. ¿Cuáles son los beneficios del surf . . . del yoga aplicado al mundo del surf?

Ana: Pues, a ver, la práctica del surf es muy dura, muy dura. Eh . . . nos aporta muchísimas sensaciones estupendas, pero es muy sacrificada a nivel físico. Entonces, con el yoga lo que conseguimos es intentar compensar las múltiples lesiones que el surfing nos puede provocar. Además es una cuestión de inversión de futuro. Si lo que más nos gusta es surfear y queremos hacerlo el mayor tiempo posible con la mejor calidad, tenemos que cuidar nuestro cuerpo porque va a ser nuestro instrumento encima de la tabla. El surfing genera muchas lesiones a nivel de hombros, eh . . . problemas en los lumbares, entonces con el yoga, pues, intentamos compensar. Es una práctica que nos ayuda a corregir estos defectos en las líneas y de postura y además aporta mucha flexibilidad, mucha flexibilidad y fuerza. Es una práctica, pues, eh . . . que ayuda a prevenir muchas lesiones. Entonces eh . . . se trabaja en equilibrio, se trabaja en la flexibilidad, se trabaja en coordinación, torsiones, eh . . . una serie de . . . de ventajas que nos van a ayudar a practicar mejor el surfing que es porque nos gusta.

Locutor: Y además de monitor eso tú practicas surfing habitualmente, ¿no?

Ana: Pues, sí. La verdad es que me gusta mucho y fue un poco lo que me llevó también a descubrir el yoga. No tengo el nivel para competir, pero en el agua me divierto que creo que es lo más importante.

Locutor: Y, ¿qué tal ha sido la respuesta de la gente aquí en Doniños? ¿Cómo ha sido la participación de los chicos y las chicas en tus talleres?

Ana: Pues tengo que decir que sobre todo los veo súper contentos. Las chicas y los chicos muy bien. Los adultos un poquito más vagos, pero bien, muy bien, una . . . un ambiente muy bueno de verdad. Muy a gusto.

Locutor: Pues Ana, encantado haberte tenido aquí con nosotros y suerte.

Ana: Muchas gracias.

Locutor: Esto ya es todo desde Doniños.

Track 12

Selección número 2

Locutor: Cuaderno mayor

Locutora: La soledad es un factor de riesgo para la depresión, el deterioro cognitivo, la morbilidad y la mortalidad entre las personas mayores. Así lo atestiguan diferentes estudios en los que se reconoce que algunos de los factores que provoca el aislamiento tienen que ver con vivir solo, no gozar de buena salud y de solvencia económica o las situaciones de duelo. En España se contabiliza un 1.853.700 personas mayores que viven en soledad, de las cuales la mayoría son mujeres. Concretamente, el 72,2%. Y de los mayores que viven solos, 368.400 tienen más de 85 años, es decir el 42% de ellos. Según la Encuesta Continua de Hogares de 2014 se ha producido un aumento en el número de hogares unipersonales, situación ante la cual alertan los expertos en geriatría y gerontología de a que consideran que puede provocar problemas en la salud de los *seniors*. Las encuestas también reflejan que estas personas apenas reciben una visita mensual de alguien conocido de su entorno social, y en algunos casos, estas visitas no existen. Se trata de personas que sufren problemas de salud asociados con la soledad. Además de la depresión, la soledad se relaciona con enfermedades cardiovasculares, hipertensión y demencia. Incluso existe un vínculo muy fuerte con la mortalidad temprana. Tienen problemas ligados a la movilidad y un mayor riesgo de caídas, lo que conlleva a un riesgo también mayor, de que se produzcan fracturas. Suelen tener más problemas económicos lo cual repercute en su alimentación y también en su higiene. Los expertos reconocen que esta situación se puede incrementar a tenor de las expectativas demográficas, por lo que es fundamental afrontarlo como un problema social que incide en la salud y la calidad de vida de las personas mayores. Además instan a buscar fórmulas para prevenir las consecuencias negativas de la sociedad que se impone como un modo de vida casi mayoritario en las sociedades modernas. Si necesita más información sobre este asunto, puede visitar la página *www.balancedeladependencia.com*. Juani Loro, Radio 5 Todo Noticias.

Track 13

Selección número 3

Cómo votar

Detalla instrucciones y datos útiles orientados al votante. 2017

¿Quiénes pueden votar?

Todos los chilenos y chilenas y extranjeros que tengan cumplidos 18 años de edad el día de la votación y que se encuentren inscritos en el padrón electoral. La inscripción es automática por lo que no se requiere que la persona concurra a la oficina del Servicio Electoral. En el caso de los extranjeros, deben llevar viviendo más de cinco años en el territorio nacional. También se incluyen en el padrón los nacionalizados por gracia y los hijos de chilenos que lleven un año viviendo en Chile.

¿Los chilenos que viven o están en el extranjero tienen derecho a voto?

Si, una reforma constitucional y una ley aprobadas por el Congreso Nacional establecieron que los ciudadanos chilenos con derecho a sufragio que se encuentren fuera de Chile pueden emitir su voto en las elecciones para presidente o presidenta de la República, en las primarias presidenciales que hagan los partidos o pactos electorales y en los plebiscitos nacionales.

No podrán emitir sufragio en las elecciones de senadores, diputados, alcaldes, concejales y consejeros regionales.

Para ello, deben inscribirse en los consulados de Chile en el exterior.

¿Qué documentos necesito para votar?

La cédula nacional de identidad o el pasaporte, en el caso de los chilenos. En el caso de los extranjeros, la cédula de identidad para extranjeros. Sea cual sea el documento de identidad que use, debe estar vigente.

¿Puedo votar si perdí mi cédula de identidad?

Si no tiene su cédula de identidad, puede usar su pasaporte, siempre que esté vigente. Tenga en cuenta que no sirve el comprobante de cédula de identidad en trámite que entrega el Registro Civil en caso de extravío.

¿Hasta qué hora puedo ir a votar?

Las mesas deben cerrar a las 18:00, siempre que no queden pendientes electores que deseen sufragar. Si se da este caso, se debe esperar a recibir estos votos antes de cerrar.

Las mesas deben iniciar su funcionamiento a las 8:00 A.M. Excepcionalmente pueden empezar a funcionar a las 9:00 o 10:00 A.M., según si la mesa pudo constituirse con todos sus vocales designados.

¿Puedo votar si soy no vidente?

Sí. Los no videntes cuentan con una plantilla especial que posee ranuras correspondientes a cada candidato. Estas plantillas estarán disponibles el día de la elección en la Oficina Electoral de cada recinto en que funcionen mesas receptoras.

¿A quién debo dirigirme si soy una persona con discapacidad y necesito ayuda para llegar a la mesa de votación?

A las personas en situación de discapacidad se les permite ir acompañados de un mayor de edad hasta la mesa de votación e ingresar con él a la cámara secreta. También pueden solicitar, mediante lengua de señas o por escrito al presidente de la mesa, ser asistido en el mismo acto de votar.

Track 14

Selección número 4

Mujer:	Esa juventud de ahora. ¡Mire nada más esa ropa!
Hombre:	¡Ayyyy, sí, ya no respetan a nadie!
Mujer:	¿Cómo les dejarán salir de su casa con esos tatuajes y ese montón de aretes? ¡Mire!
Control Rapeando:	Sí, claro, cresta, patineta, pantalón ancho. Ser diferente, consciente, cuerpo, alma, vida, mente. Así, con mis botas, gorra, capucha, faldas rotas, tatuado el corazón de cariño esperanza presente niño. No me juzgue, mi señora, por mi ropa, me mira hasta ahora. Adentro vale lo que sueño, lo que creo es en mi empeño. Llenas de valor y conciencia rebeldía tanta paciencia. Tu sonido diverso diversa entendámonos nuestra fuerza.

Joven:	Yo, como joven quiero divertirme con una patineta. A lo mejor el hijo de esta persona que no entiende si quiere divertir con un balón. O sea, simplemente ser más abiertos, tratar de comprender mejor. Y verle el lado positivo de las cosas que a fin de cuentas es un deporte, que haces es un hobby, es, no sé que, una distracción . . . .
Control Rapeando:	Todos y todas a cambiar el mundo sin importar lo que por fuera luzco.
Locutora:	12 de agosto Día Internacional de la Juventud

Selección número 5

Track 15

Locutora:	En América Latina, las radios locales tienen un rol informativo, cultural y formativo que ayuda a romper el aislamiento de ciertas áreas rurales. En los Andes de Perú y Bolivia, por ejemplo, un conjunto de emisoras han creado un sistema de información para enfrentar el cambio climático. Otro ejemplo es la llamada "radio saludable", en Perú, orientada a la formación sobre nutrición materno-infantil. Nos cuenta más detalles sobre el trabajo de las radios campesinas en América Latina Carlos Rivadeneyra, Profesor de la Universidad de Lima.
Carlos Rivadeneyra:	En América Latina la radio campesina y también llamada y conocida como las radios locales, son emisoras de radio que cubren zonas muy amplias que están poco atendidas por las emisoras más potentes y de carácter comercial que existen en las ciudades. La radio entonces campesina, rural y comunitaria, se convierte en una emisora no solamente para conocer lo que sucede en diferentes zonas de un territorio, de un país o de varios países, sino también para fomentar y fortalecer las identidades de los ciudadanos y las ciudadanas. En ese sentido el rol, por un lado, es cultural, el rol también es informativo, y el rol es formativo, porque la radio puede ser un eficiente medio para fortalecer la educación y las capacidades de los grupos sociales, básicamente rurales, que tienen que enfrentar a diferentes cambios, a diferentes retos, también de mercado, y que tienen en la radio un aliado para poder vincularse con otros espacios, conocer más experiencias y también dar a conocer las propias.
Locutora:	¿Podría usted profundizar algo más en este tema y darnos ejemplos de cómo la radio ha generado impactos positivos sobre la reducción de riesgo de desastres?
Carlos Rivadeneyra:	En los últimos años en los países andinos, Ecuador, Colombia, Perú y Bolivia, se ha venido debutando diferentes proyectos de asistencia inmediata ante las emergencias por la variabilidad climática. En los Andes de Perú y Bolivia se pudo establecer hace dos años un sistema de información para enfrentar el cambio climático que impacta sobre todo en los principales medios de vida y subsistencia de las comunidades rurales alto-andinas. Estamos hablando de comunidades que están encima de los 3.500 metros sobre el nivel del mar, y estas comunidades tienen que tener sistemas de información y alerta temprana ante eventos climáticos: llámese nevadas, heladas, friages, vientos muy fuertes, lluvias muy copiosas y extensas de territorios que afectan los pastos y sus crianzas. Y esto afecta de inmediato en la vida económica

y en la calidad de vida de las familias rurales. También la radio prepara la población para que sus crianzas, sus cultivos y estilo de vida vayan adaptándose a los problemas de los cambios del clima.

Locutora: ¿Cuál es el papel de la radio en la mejora de la seguridad alimentaria y la nutrición en las zonas afectadas por las catástrofes?

Carlos Rivadeneyra: Yo considero que hay por lo menos dos roles. El primero es adaptarse a los cambios del clima para tener medios de vida de subsistencia, tener pastos para las crianzas, los animales, tener cultivos que resisten los climas más inclementes y adversos, de tener labores culturales agronómicas para tener cultivos en determinadas zonas, en determinados lugares, para que estos sean menos afectados por los problemas del clima. Pero otro lado también está de educación y la orientación en nutrición materna infantil. No nos olvidemos que la nutrición de los seres humanos es fundamental en los primeros tres años de vida, pero incluso en el vientre materno, el feto que está por nacerse alimenta de la madre, y si la madre está bien nutrida, también podrá tener un buen parto y una buena crianza en los primeros meses de vida del bebé. En el Perú se hizo una experiencia interesante que se llama la Radio Saludable, que brinda orientación a las madres rurales con hijos pequeños o gestantes para que puedan estar preparadas de la mejor manera para tener y facilitar buena nutrición a sus pequeños hijos.

Selección número 6

Track 16

Pueblos con encanto. Un breve recorrido virtual por los pueblos riojanos.

Locutor: Pueblos con encanto, Arnedo. A orillas de las aguas del río Cidacos descansa la hermosa población de Arnedo, a apenas 48 kilómetros de la capital riojana. Simbiosis perfecta entre modernidad y tradición, Arnedo ha sabido adaptarse a los nuevos tiempos y convertirse en una próspera villa sin perder un ápice del encanto medieval que la caracterizó siglos atrás. Hablar de Arnedo es rememorar los orígenes romanos de la bella Arenetum, así llamada por ubicarse sobre una vasta plataforma de arena, es evocar su pasado musulmán, cuando fue bastión de la poderosa dinastía de los Banu Qasi, y es también admirar la vida comercial de una ciudad cuyo crecimiento ha ido paralelo al desarrollo de una notable industria del calzado, que comenzó a gestarse en la zona hacia el siglo XI.

Entre sus monumentos destaca la iglesia de Santo Tomás, fabuloso templo del siglo XVI, causante de admiración de propios y ajenos por su belleza y originalidad constructiva. A espaldas del templo se eleva el cerro de San Miguel, de gran valor antropológico, pues allí se hallan las cuevas de los Cien Pilares, habitadas por el hombre durante largos años y hoy utilizadas como bodegas.

Otra visita recomendada es la del palacio del Arzobispo Argáiz. Esta notable mansión renacentista del siglo XVII, antaño propiedad del Don José Argáiz, arzobispo de Granada, aloja hoy el Museo de Ciencias Naturales. Se trata de uno de los museos más visitados de la ciudad por la fascinante colección de minerales y fósiles que expone junto a una valiosa colección de objetos encontrados en los yacimientos de Atapuerca.

Museo destacado es el del calzado Callaghan. La evolución de la industria del calzado en Arnedo, desde sus inicios en el siglo XIX hasta la actualidad, queda reflejada en este interesante museo, promovido por Callaghan, una de las marcas principales del calzado local.

El museo, ubicado en un hermoso palacete, da a conocer los antiguos procesos productivos a pequeña escala, con las primeras alpargatas de yute, y ofrece una visión general de los cambios en la moda del calzado a lo largo de la historia.

Y terminamos esta visita virtual a Arnedo disfrutando de uno de sus más típicos postres, de origen árabe, los fardalejos. ¡Buen provecho!

Selección número 7

(Música)

Track 17

Fidel Revilla Castro: La misión y el propósito de este negocio, por así decirlo, es un poco fundar eh . . . y profundizar en las personas, de una forma u otra, eh . . . el sentido de lo que es la religión . . . africana, por así decirlo, o la santería, como popularmente se llama. El concepto de la santería aplicada en estos tiempos es la eh . . . la combinación de dos religiones o dos culturas: africanas y española. Nosotros, nuestros santos son tan católicos como cualquier santo español. Y, eh . . . ¿cómo se inició esta religión? Bueno, muy fácilmente se inicia, o se crea o nace, en el acontecimiento de la . . . de tiempos atrás donde los, los eh . . . españoles quisieron, o colonizaron las Américas, y cuando llevaron su cultura, también, también llevaron su religión. Al llevar la religión, pues entonces incluyeron también lo que es de . . . de África, estos negros africanos que vinieron a trabajar lo que es la . . . la caña de azúcar en Cuba, ¿no? Y ellos también llevaron su tradición y su religión. ¿Qué pasa con esto? En la religión católica, se venera la imagen, y en la religión africana, se venera lo que es la piedra, la rela . . . la herramienta, y el caracol. Son los tres requisitos elementales para eh . . . profesar o tener fe en alguna . . . en ese tipo de religión. Ahora, ¿cuál es el problema de la santería? ¿Cuál es lo que verdaderamente trifulca la santería y . . . y se crea una polémica con respecto a esto? El problema es que el procedimiento donde verdaderamente los santeros resolvemos nuestros problemas. Y es muy sencillo: nosotros aplicamos la fe, pero aplicamos la alquimia, que es cómo se hacen los trabajos, los diferentes trabajos tanto para salvar como para eh . . . hacer posible que se hagan ciertas determinadas cosas. Por ejemplo, el alquimia se utiliza cuando tú te vas a hacer un baño de florecimiento, ahora lo voy a explicar, como te vas a hacer un baño de florecimiento es un . . . es . . . se hace cuando una persona por ejemplo está . . . yo lo voy a explicar en el aspecto religioso: cuando una persona está saturada o está cargada, está bajo las influencias negativas, pues alguna vez nos creamos nosotros estas propias influencias negativas, pues entonces un bañito por ejemplo con salvia, un bañito por ejemplo con menta, un bañito por ejemplo con lavanda, ¿verdad? Eso relaja y refresca, ¡qué sí! Pues, mira, eso se está utilizando ahora como eh . . . situaciones de eh . . . homeopatía para liberar las historias del arma y del karma y todo igual. Bueno, esos son tradiciones que nosotros aplicamos y tenemos efectivamente que la hacemos para los diferentes tipos de rituales y cosas. Trabajamos siempre con la naturaleza, o sea cualquier cosa que nosotros hacemos trabajamos siempre con las hojas, con las plantas, con las hojuela, con cosas totalmente naturales de la tierra y que verdaderamente hacemos posible de que los acontecimientos astralmente ni se detengan, ni se corrompan. Simplemente que la persona desde su propio yo, desde su propio miedo, desde su propia duda, pues entonces sea capaz a resolver sus propias situaciones siempre cuando no . . . no pierda nunca eh . . . el aspecto en la fe.

Selección número 8

Track 18

El poderoso conquistador español, don Pedro de Alvarado, llegó cabalgando en su caballo. Era una figura majestuosa e intimidante, y su caballo, un animal extranjero en Guatemala, se veía exótico y magnífico. Frente al enemigo, Tecún Umán sintió un aleteo de miedo en lo íntimo de su corazón. En este momento, su *nahual*, un espíritu guardián con la forma del ave de quetzal, se posó en su hombro. El gorjeo melódico del quetzal le dio un poco de consuelo, como si le dijera: "No estás solo. Estaré contigo hasta el final".

—Ríndete, Tecún Umán—gritó don Pedro.—Tenemos armas mejores y un ejército más fuerte. Hasta el dios está en nuestro lado. ¡Ríndete al destino!

—No—respondió Tecún Umán con dignidad. No creo que los dioses hubieran querido que nos rindiéramos sin luchar.

Entonces empezó la batalla de la conquista. De repente, Tecún Umán tuvo un ramalazo de inspiración. Asumió que el caballo era el *nahual* de Don Pedro. Así que pensó que si mataba al caballo, a Don Pedro se le perdería su espíritu guardián y se moriría. El caballo estaba a su alcance. ¡Fue la perfecta oportunidad! Clavó su lanza en el cuerpo del caballo . . . .

El caballo relinchó de dolor y cayó, pero Don Pedro no se murió. En este momento Tecún Umán se dio cuenta de que había hecho un gran error. Los españoles no tenían *nahuales*: el caballo fue un animal y nada más. Al momento siguiente, la lanza de Don Pedro le atravesó, directamente en su corazón. Sintió un dolor agudo en el pecho, antes de que todo se desvaneciera en la oscuridad.

Se dice que hoy en día, los quetzales nacen con el pecho de rojo brillante, como recuerdo del héroe valiente que luchó contra viento y marea para preservar la dignidad de su gente.

Selección número 9

Track 19

Los países del Caribe son afectados por una amplia gama de desastres naturales como las tormentas tropicales, huracanes, sequías, actividades volcánicas, terremotos, inundaciones y deslizamientos de tierra.

La región también se encuentra expuesta a peligros tecnológicos y biológicos, por ser un importante punto de tránsito y trasbordo de cargamentos peligrosos.

Liz Riley es la subdirectora ejecutiva de la Agencia de Gestión de Emergencia de Desastres del Caribe. Ella participó en la Cuarta Reunión de la Plataforma Mundial para la Reducción de Riesgos de Desastres celebrada en Ginebra.

LR: Una de las cosas a la que tenemos que prestar más atención es a la exposición a esos fenómenos naturales, y esto tiene mucho que ver con el desarrollo. En los últimos 30 a 50 años en el Caribe, ha habido una inversión significativa en infraestructura nueva y los principales indicadores que tenemos sobre los peligros naturales ahora están relacionados a la pérdida y a daños a la infraestructura, no tanto a la pérdida de vidas, al menos que se mire específicamente a Haití.

Riley explicó que los estados del Caribe han desarrollado un abarcador enfoque global de la gestión de desastres.

LR: El Caribe es una de las regiones mejor preparadas en la respuesta a los desastres. Fuimos la primera en desarrollar un mecanismo intergubernamental de coordinación de respuesta, que permite a los estados aprovechar los recursos de cada uno de los países participantes en el apoyo de cualquier estado afectado, y esto fue durante un buen tiempo algo exclusivo del Caribe. De hecho el modelo caribeño se ha utilizado con frecuencia en la estructuración de arreglos similares en el resto del mundo.

El devastador terremoto de Haití ofreció importantes lecciones a los países de la región, apunta Riley.

LR: El terremoto puso sobre el tapete la vulnerabilidad de ciudades caribeñas porque vimos que en lo fundamental la capital haitiana, Puerto Príncipe, quedó destruida. En el Caribe mucha de la infraestructura fundamental, los servicios básicos, frecuentemente se concentran en las ciudades principales porque los países son muy pequeños, esto aumenta la vulnerabilidad. Cuando estas instalaciones y servicios no funcionan, esto tiene serias implicaciones en el apoyo que se puede dar al resto del país.

Otra experiencia aprendida fue la relacionada con la continuidad del gobierno en medio de un desastre natural de gran envergadura.

LR: Esto ha recibido mucha atención por los jefes de estado de CARICOM después que vimos interrupciones de las comunicaciones entre los mecanismos del gobierno en Haití. En momentos de crisis el liderazgo y la cohesión de los dirigentes en un frente unido para dirigir al pueblo es fundamental.

La subdirectora ejecutiva de la agencia de gestión de emergencia de desastres del Caribe también subrayó que la experiencia haitiana los ha hecho trabajar en el establecimiento de normas constructivas que garanticen la resistencia antisísmica de la infraestructura. Jorge Miyares, Naciones Unidas, Nueva York.

Track 20

Selección número 10

MM: La fiebre amarilla, la disentería, el cólera, algunos tipos de meningitis y hepatitis, el tétanos, la fiebre tifoidea, la rabia, son enfermedades que están muy controladas en el primer mundo pero tenemos encima las vacaciones y cada vez son más demandados los destinos exóticos, países donde estas patologías sí son por desgracia mucho más frecuentes. Si está planeando uno de esos viajes para este verano, sepa que entre las previsiones ha de estar su salud. El doctor Agustín Benito es director del Centro Nacional de Medicina Tropical del Instituto de Salud Carlos III.

AB: Muchas de estas enfermedades . . . eh . . . simplemente necesitan unas pautas en el país donde están ubicadas para poder . . . eh . . . eh . . . para no vivir con ellas. Muchas de ellas son transmitidas por vectores que son mosquitos o insectos, ¿no? Está claro que estos te tienen que picar porque son hematófagos, necesitan la sangre para desarrollarse . . . eh . . . sus ovariolas y poder tener su ciclo de vida. Entonces simplemente como medidas preventivas ya es un paso importante que es pues ponerte repelente para los insectos e ir con, con camisas cómodas de algodón, de manga larga, y protegerte los espacios donde te puedan picar, eso es por un lado. Y por otro lado pues la profilaxis y medicamentos . . . eh . . . que te van a recomendar y aparte mucha de ellas son vacunables, ¿no?

MM: La vacunación efectivamente es una ayuda muy importante en la prevención de las enfermedades infecciosas. Pero para que las vacunas o el tratamiento que se estime pertinente y efectivo tienen que ser dispensados con suficiente antelación. Entre uno y dos meses antes del viaje es un tiempo prudente para realizar los trámites en los más de sesenta centros de vacunación internacional de España que dependen del servicio de sanidad del exterior del Ministerio de Sanidad.

AB: Normalmente previamente al viaje lo ideal es hacer este tipo de consulta en primer lugar porque . . . porque . . . porque todo el mundo queremos viajar en los períodos estivales . . . en los períodos vacacionales. ¿Qué ocurre? Que al final hay una gran demanda de esos servicios . . . de . . . de . . . de las unidades y servicios de atención a viajeros o a profesionales que van a ir de viaje. Y estos centros de vacunación, entonces claro, requieren un tiempo mínimo que yo creo está bien, lo que tú has comentado, un par de meses antes ponerte en contacto para que te den cita porque previamente se tiene que vacunar obviamente un mínimo de quince días tiene que tener para que la vacuna te empiece a funcionar o hacer efecto, ¿no? Y luego por el tema de la profilaxis porque te van a recomendar medicación en función del riesgo que tienen algunas de las enfermedades al área donde vas a definir.

Y el último consejo es que en cuanto llegues a una zona donde sea un área afectada por cualquier tipo de patología tropical o . . . o . . . o olvidada al mínimo momento en que puedas tener . . . eh . . . algún tipo de sintomatología febril etcétera, etcétera, te encuentres mal, pues acudir a estos centros, a estas unidades de consejo a viajeros y medicina tropical que . . . eh . . . requieren y están a disposición de cualquier, de cualquier persona en cualquier . . . eh . . . centro que ya digo que están en todos los registrados del Ministerio de Sanidad.

MM: Los viajes a países exóticos pueden resultar de los más placenteros e interesantes pero también tienen sus riesgos, riesgos que convienen prevenir como nos ha contado el Doctor Agustín Benito, director del Centro Nacional de Medicina Tropical del Instituto de Salud Carlos III. Manuel Moraga para Radio 5 Toda Noticias.

Selección número 11

La Tomatina: fiesta del tomate en España

Track 21

El pueblo español de Buñol tiene una larga historia que se remonta a más de 50 mil años. Sin embargo, en la actualidad es conocido por una fiesta que se festeja desde hace sólo 60: la Tomatina. Es uno de los días más célebres del calendario valenciano, en el que se lleva a cabo la lucha vegetal más grande del mundo con 30 mil personas y 200 toneladas de tomate. Si pensabas que tal cosa era imposible, entérate en esta nota.

Buñol es una ciudad en el centro de Valencia y ha sido testigo fiel de la historia española. Ocupada por romanos, árabes, moros y franceses, las influencias extranjeras son apreciables en muchos de los edificios, pero también en pequeñas cosas de la vida diaria. Como toda fiesta de pueblo, cada habitante contará su propia versión de los hechos. Nosotros elegimos contarles una de las versiones de cómo empezó la Tomatina; la menos increíble, pero la que más se acerca a la verdad.

Corría el año 1945 y se estaba celebrando en el centro de la ciudad un desfile de "Gigantes y Cabezudos". Parece que en esa época todos se peleaban por participar y disfrazarse. Según cuentan, un joven que quería ser parte del desfile, golpeó a uno de los que estaban disfrazados, tirándolo al suelo. Este hombre, totalmente indignado, comenzó a golpear a todo el mundo, iniciando una verdadera batalla campal. De pronto, a alguien se le ocurrió utilizar las verduras de un puesto de hortalizas cercano como munición y todos lo imitaron, abriendo los cajones de tomate que estaban en exhibición.

Como siempre, el orden público se hizo presente y se multó a los revoltosos. Fue tan memorable el episodio que al año siguiente se congregaron en la plaza con una gran cantidad de cajones de tomates. Todo el pueblo participó de la ya conocida "Tomatina", a pesar de la desaprobación del gobierno que año tras año, prohibía la batalla vegetal.

Las actividades más comunes son, en primer lugar, las carreras de sacos, o carreras de embolsados. En ellas unas cuantas personas introducen la parte inferior de su cuerpo en sacos de tela e intentan llegar a la meta, saltando. Otro juego tradicional son las "cucañas", que se celebran en España en casi todas las fiestas populares. Para las cucañas es necesario el tronco de un árbol o un palo pulido. En la cima del palo se cuelga un trofeo, en este caso un jamón, y luego se enjabona toda la superficie de madera. El ganador es aquella persona que pueda subir el palo enjabonado y tomar el trofeo.

Track 22

Selección número 12

Yo estaba escribiendo profesionalmente por más de dos décadas y también he enseñado a hacerlo por casi el mismo período de tiempo. En cada conferencia, en cada encuentro, en cada clase, siempre alguien de la audiencia no deja de preguntar, ¿cómo puedo convertirme en un mejor escritor? En general, no suelen disfrutar de mi respuesta. Seguro, solo hay que practicar la propia escritura y leer para estudiar los métodos de los otros escritores, todos los días. No les suele gustar mi repuesta por una o dos razones. Algunas personas buscan una solución rápida, una fórmula mágica que los convierte en buenos escritores a partir de tres fáciles pasos. Aunque mi sugerencia consiste en solo dos pasos, es obvio que implica un proyecto a largo plazo. El resto de las personas harán una mueca de desprecio a los primeros porque se consideran verdaderos escritores, pero verdaderamente no les gusta mi respuesta más que a los demás. Creen simplemente que poseen un don que debe ser desencadenado por la misma magia que ha tocado a los escritores exitosos. La simple verdad es que no existe otra forma de mejorar su escritura que practicar continuamente. Escriba todos los días. Experimente. Planee, corrija y vuelva a corregir. Propóngase desafíos, fechas límites y competiciones. Empújese usted y su escritura lo recompensará . . . se lo prometo. Escriba algo inspirado en un escritor que admire y luego escriba algo completamente propio. Sin embargo, no es suficiente escribir sobre la nada o en una torre de marfil, también deberá leer la escritura de los otros. Lea todo lo que pueda, lea ficción, no ficción, poesía y letras de canciones. Lea sobre argumentación y persuasión. Lea textos informativos y biográficos. Lea sobre ciencias y sobre fantasía. Lea a escritores talentosos. Lea a aquellos que todavía están buscando su propio camino en la escritura. Usted estará leyendo para inspirarse y para adquirir confianza. Estará leyendo para enriquecer su vocabulario y su almacenamiento de procedimientos. Estará leyendo para aprender más acerca de ritmos y patrones de lenguaje. Estará leyendo para que a la hora de escribir, pueda desarrollar su propia y única voz. El proceso de aprendizaje para volverse un mejor escritor no es un trabajo de un fin de semana o incluso de un semestre. Aprender a ser un buen escritor es el trabajo de una vida entera. No conozco a un solo escritor profesional que se haya sentado y dicho: "Ya aprendí suficiente. Más no puedo mejorar". Sin duda, le tomará toda una vida alcanzar el estatus de profesional, pero esa no debería ser su meta. Si piensa en esos términos, estará reteniendo su potencial. Por ejemplo, quizás la razón por la que no aceptaron un proyecto suyo en particular no tuvo nada que ver con su forma de escribir, sino que se pudo haber debido al tema que trata, a las necesidades particulares del editor, o incluso al estado de ánimo de la persona que leyó el manuscrito. Lo cierto es que no podrá decidir cuándo se convertirá en un autor publicado, en un escritor profesional. Pero sí podrá controlar su técnica, podrá mejorar su escritura. Créame, cuanto más fortalezca su escritura, más fácil será alcanzar la segunda meta. Cuando llegue al punto de obtener escritura de calidad regularmente, encontrará su mercado. Si puede escribir, el resto vendrá solo.

SAMPLE PRESENTATIONAL WRITING

Locutor:	De mi pueblo. Dormir o no dormir, eso es el problema. Algunas personas alardean de dormir poco para aprovechar el tiempo al máximo, mientras otras se regodean en la complacencia de un colchón molido, como práctica habitual que colinda con la holgazanería. Los extremos son siempre malos, sentencia un psicólogo, dejando en suspenso el tema como si no quisiera tomar partido. Pero, ¿cuál es su punto de vista?
Hombre:	Bueno, mi punto de vista es que el cuerpo humano necesita descansar, descansar y dormir no menos de ocho horas. Eso es . . . ah no sé, cuando son niños que necesitan más tiempo de descanso o por el cuerpo . . . como mínimo ocho horas deben descansar.
Mujer:	No sé, pero se supone que al máximo . . . medio . . . ocho horas, porque si no . . . la actividad diaria se vuelve muy difícil. Ejemplo, trasnocharte una noche y dormiste dos horas, al levantarte a las siete de la mañana, la . . . eh . . . la actividad diaria no es igual . . . rindes menos. Se supone que debes dormir ocho horas.
Locutor:	Las sociedades modernas imponen un ritmo diario muy agitado que roba tiempo al sueño. Sus consecuencias ya aparecen en aumentos en el riesgo de contraer enfermedades, tales como cardiopatías, irregularidades hormonales, obesidad, diabetes y variadas formas de cáncer se asocian actualmente al insuficiente descanso del sistema nervioso. ¿Qué opinión le merece tal afirmación?
Mujer:	Se supone que es verdad. La vida diaria es muy agitada. Pero hay que buscar tiempo para que todas estas enfermedades no . . . no progresen. Eliminar la obesidad, eliminar la . . . tratar de no . . . buscar actividades que no llevan a la cardiopatía. Hacer mucho ejercicio físico para tener una buena salud.
Hombre:	Bueno, según los estudios que se han determinado, el estrés, el de no relajar el cuerpo, el sueño, y unas series de cosas más, es que provoca la cardiopatía, y son irregulares hormonales también. En ello, bueno, puede que sea la obesidad, pero . . . muy difícil. Sí, lo que sí se debe dormir, como mínimo, como mínimo, son ocho horas diarias. Ocho horas diarias, y . . . en caso de que sean . . . no sé de qué . . . guardia nocturna o . . . otro que tenga que cumplirlo como lo hace él, descanso, más o menos según cinco horas, cuatro horas, en todas esa . . . es . . . nada menos siento que en el . . . en la etapa que estamos viviendo . . . el estrés es lo imprescindible en estos tipos de enfermedades. El . . . no descans . . . el no descansar y el sueño que eso es lo más, lo más preciado, que para el cuerpo humano.

PRESENTATIONAL WRITING: ARGUMENTATIVE ESSAY

Ensayo número 1

Fuente número 3

El ministro de educación Iñigo Méndez de Vigo se ha comprometido a debatir con la comunidad educativa el traído y llevado asunto de los deberes escolares, el titular del departamento considera "interesante" la propuesta de la Confederación de Asociaciones de Padres de suprimir las tareas que los chavales llevan a casa. La CEAPA, confederación de padres mayoritaria en la escuela pública, ha defendido en un comunicado que desaparezcan los deberes escolares. Y no es un tema nuevo, desde hace años la comunidad educativa está dividida: deberes sí, deberes no. Pero, ¿cuáles son los argumentos? Los detractores de los deberes consideran que alargan en exceso la jornada de los niños, que sobrecargan su agenda, y que este tipo de tareas debieran de realizarse dentro del horario escolar. Entre quienes apuestan por los deberes está la Confederación Católica de Padres de Alumnos, la CONCAPA considera que ayudan a reforzar lo aprendido y que además permiten que se establezca una buena comunicación entre hijos y padres y con el entorno escolar que también es muy importante. Mientras tanto el ministro Méndez de Vigo ha reabierto el diálogo con la idea de encontrar puntos de encuentro, pero hay que saber que cada centro educativo tiene libertad para programar qué tipo de tareas extraescolares han de tener sus alumnos. La mayoría de los pedagogos establecen una serie de premisas a tener en cuenta en todo este asunto, y en eso casi todo el mundo está de acuerdo. Por ejemplo, los deberes deben de ser un complemento al aprendizaje y no una forma de cumplir con el programa de la asignatura cuando falta tiempo en clase. También deben aportar un enfoque que enriquezca al chaval, por ejemplo que sirvan para que experimente, para que busque en internet, consulte libros, explore. En otras palabras, disfrute del conocimiento por voluntad propia y con más libertad que la que se les ofrece en la enseñanza arreglada. Los expertos lo definen como desarrollo de las competencias. Y desde luego no han de suponer un conflicto para las familias. Muchos padres llegan cansados a casa y resulta difícil encontrar un espacio para hacer los deberes. Por cierto, los deberes son de los niños, no de los padres. Y eso significa que el papel del adulto es el de orientar. Quizás simplemente hay que estar allí, cercano y presente cuando hacen esas tareas. Los padres no pueden asumir el papel de docentes. Por cierto les ofrezco una curiosidad. Finlandia es un país referente en calidad educativa. Los informes de la OCD lo sitúan en los primeros puestos en resultados académicos y en otros muchos marcadores. Pues bien, allí sí existen los deberes, aunque quizás no responden al modelo español. Lo que sí existe en este país nórdico son bastantes medidas que permiten conciliar la vida laboral y familiar. Aurora Campuzano, Radio 5 Todo Noticias.

Ensayo número 2

Track 25 **Fuente número 3**

Jorge Miyares:

"La Lectura en la Era de los Móviles" es el título de un estudio publicado por la Organización de la ONU para la Educación, la Ciencia y la Cultura (UNESCO), con motivo del Día Mundial del Libro y del Derecho de Autor, que se celebra este 23 de abril. La pesquisa, la primera de su tipo sobre la lectura en dispositivos móviles en los países en desarrollo, afirma que en la actualidad cientos de miles de personas utilizan los teléfonos móviles en esos Estados para leer libros en su totalidad. La UNESCO asegura que un uso eficiente de esta tecnología puede ser de gran ayuda para eliminar el analfabetismo que aún padecen más de 770 millones de personas. Uno de los autores del informe, Mark West, ofreció declaraciones a los medios de prensa de la UNESCO y compartió los principales hallazgos del estudio.

Mark West (Traducido):

El estudio corrobora que la tecnología móvil es una forma viable y legítima para acceder a textos. Hay muchas personas que dudan de que con una pantalla tan pequeña en blanco y negro pueda servir para leer libros enteros. Pero hemos acumulado suficientes evidencias que demuestran que hay personas en el mundo en desarrollo que están haciéndolo. Y son con frecuencia personas que tienen acceso muy limitado a oportunidades educativas.

Jorge Miyares:	Las tecnologías móviles ofrecen ventajas muy particulares para acceder a textos en los países en desarrollo, explica West.
Mark West (Traducido):	No hay dudas de que es así. En términos de costo, el precio de un libro electrónico es de entre dos y tres centavos, si es libre de derechos de autor. En cambio, es el mismo libro, su versión impresa, puede costar unos diez dólares. Por lo que el libro electrónico es de 300 a 500 veces más barato que uno en soporte físico. También sabemos que los libros impresos son más difíciles de distribuir en áreas remotas donde los niveles de analfabetismo son altos, y donde los aparatos móviles ya han penetrado estas zonas. La ONU estima que seis mil millones de personas tienen acceso a dispositivos móviles que funcionan. Por lo que hoy la posibilidad de llegar a las personas no tiene precedentes.
Jorge Miyares:	Según la UNESCO el porciento de mujeres analfabetas es superior al de los hombres. Sin embargo el estudio afirma que las mujeres usan más esos dispositivos para leer que los hombres. ¿Pudiera utilizarse esta tecnología para promover la educación entre las mujeres? Mark West comenta.
Mark West (Traducido):	Definitivamente creemos que sí. Uno de los principales hallazgos del estudio es que las mujeres y las niñas tienden a leer mucho más en estos dispositivos que los hombres. Dicho esto, hay muchos más hombres que incursionan en este tipo de lectura, pero leen en menor cantidad. Sabemos que a nivel mundial hay más mujeres analfabetas que los hombres, dos de cada tres analfabetos son mujeres. Y también sabemos que ellas tienen menos posibilidades de ser dueña de uno de estos dispositivos móviles que los hombres. Y uno de los hallazgos del estudio es que si las mujeres tuvieran un mayor acceso a estos, sería una forma de combatir el analfabetismo entre ellas.

 Ensayo número 3

Track 26 **Fuente número 3**

Sra. Bassi:	Todos hablamos mucho del estrés, pero, ¿cómo se define?
Prof. Buendía:	Hay una gran confusión respecto al estrés. Nos encontramos conpersonas que se lo toman como una patología, pero no lo es. El estrés surge cuando un individuo no puede cambiar de forma adecuada toda la presión que está recibiendo. El trabajo, la familia y otros factores, si no se pueden controlar ni canalizar, o determinadas situaciones, si son duraderas y agudas, pueden dar lugar a ciertas enfermedades, pero el estrés en sí no es una patología, sino un factor desencadenante de trastornos.
Sra. Bassi:	¿Reúne un amplio abanico de síntomas?
Prof. Buendía:	Sí, una persona que es muy vulnerable a nivel intestinal sufrirá trastornos digestivos; otras, problemas dermatológicos o trastornos de ansiedad o depresión.
Sra. Bassi:	¿Puede precisar?

Prof. Buendía: Se aprecian dos grandes fuentes de estrés. Unas veces el problema está en la familia, donde se viven cambios y modificaciones en la estructura familiar. Cuando a alguien le falla la familia, se apoya sobre todo en el trabajo e, incluso, puede que aumente su ritmo laboral. Y cuando la dificultad está en el trabajo, "burnout", estrés o "mobbing", la persona afectada se refugia en la familia.

Sra. Bassi: ¿Qué le parece la idea de trabajar las 60 ó 65 horas que propone la Unión Europea?

Prof. Buendía: Me parece desproporcionado e innecesario en una sociedad como la nuestra, eso es propio de un entorno donde es necesario para subsistir físicamente. Las personas no viven para trabajar, trabajan para vivir. En una investigación internacional se preguntó por qué merecía la pena vivir, la pregunta clave que resuelve el estrés, y respondieron que "para amar, trabajar y disfrutar". Una persona que se centre en lograr esas metas en su vida tendrá menos riesgos de enfermar por estrés que una persona que lo ponga todo en poseer bienes, dominar y subyugar.

Ensayo número 4

Track 27

Fuente número 3

Locutora: "Las escuelas existen tanto para el desarrollo de los estudiantes como para el de sus familias y de los educadores".—Robert Roeser. ¿Es hoy más difícil la convivencia en las aulas? ¿Están bien preparados los maestros para acompañar al niño hasta su adolescencia con una educación que englobe emociones e inteligencia social? Las necesidades de un adulto para vivir en [una] sociedad no son las mismas que hace cincuenta años, ni los son tampoco las condiciones de vida de los adolescentes, ni las tecnologías que rodean a todos. Sin embargo, los programas educativos han cambiado muy poco en el último siglo. Hoy en Redes, el sicólogo Robert Roeser nos ayuda a redefinir el papel de profesores y maestros, y a buscar en la ciencia unas propuestas para mejorar la educación de futuros ciudadanos.

Locutor: Si hay algo de lo que estamos casi seguros hoy en día es que debemos, no tenemos más remedio que transformar la educación de nuestros maestros. Descartemos de momento las responsabilidades de la familia a la hora de incidir sobre los niños. Lo que sí sabemos es que no nos sirven maestros que sólo destilen contenidos académicos en las mentes de los treinta niños que forman su clase a veces gritando casi todo el rato. Hoy sabemos que es importantísimo el que estos maestros aprendan a gestionar las emociones básicas universales de sus alumnos.

Locutor: Lo que me parece más revelador de este congreso que estáis celebrando aquí, en Washington, entre educadores, científicos y personas del mundo de las prácticas contemplativas, es que la gente, creo, se acaba de dar cuenta de que la culpa no es de los estudiantes ni de los padres, ni siquiera del estado. Realmente

	lo que necesita un cambio radical es la formación de los profesores. Hay que replantear la profesión de docente. ¿Te parece demasiado radical . . . como postura?
Robert Roeser (traducido):	No creo que no es nada radical. Creo que va incluso más allá de lo que tú sugieres. Como el mundo ha cambiado tanto desde el punto de vista de su interconexión económica, cultural, con la inmigración, realmente . . . ehm . . . tenemos que pensar en la educación en ambos sentidos: para los estudiantes pero también para los profesores. Se trata de habilidades como la de regular nuestras emociones, la de ser competentes en la interacción con personas de distintas culturas, la de responsabilizarnos no solo de nuestras propias acciones sino del bienestar de los demás. Todas estas habilidades tal y como las vemos tendrían que formar parte de la educación del siglo XXI, y eso significa que queremos que sean parte de la formación de los profesores, pero también que se impartan en la enseñanza primaria, secundaria y, ¿por qué no?, también en la terciaria.
Maestra:	La verdad es que en estos cuatro, cinco últimos años, la realidad ha cambiado significativamente. Eh . . . los alumnos ya no más provienen de familias la mayoría . . . de niveles socioeconómicos y culturales muy bajos. Este año, por ejemplo, tenemos un 60% de los alumnos que provienen de . . . de países diferentes, sobre todo Bolivia, Ecuador, Marruecos. En general, bueno hay un nivel . . . bastante bajo . . . un nivel académico bajo. Tenemos problemas de ausentismo, y una desmotivación general en el alumnado aquí . . . .

Ensayo número 5

Track 28

Fuente número 3

Locutor:	El pasado seis de noviembre la Comisión del Gran Canal Interoceánico de Nicaragua ha dado luz verde a esta gigantesca obra que unirá el Océano Pacífico con el Mar Caribe, atravesando el Lago de Nicaragua, el mayor lago de agua dulce de América Central. Saludamos ya a Mónica López Valdotano, una abogada ambientalista nicaragüense que ha ido a Madrid para recabar ayuda internacional para detener la construcción de ese gran canal interoceánico. Mónica, muy buenas tardes.
Mónica:	Hola, muy buenas tardes. Muchas gracias por el espa[cio].
Locutor:	Háblenos de este Lago de Nicaragua. ¿El lago realmente está en peligro como nos asegura?
Mónica:	Sí, mira, para poder hacer el proyecto del canal ellos tienen que dragar dentro del lago . . . eh . . . una franja de más de 105 kilómetros. Es una cantidad de remoción de tierra, roca y sedimento . . . eh . . . digamos, para decírtelo en otras palabras, la mayor remoción de tierra en la historia de la humanidad que cualquier proyecto de infraestructura ha tenido que hacer. Ahora, eso significa . . . ehm . . . afectar el lago no solo por, por . . . por . . . por fenómeno . . . eh . . . lógico de contaminación que

generan los propios buques, de verdad, o lo que puede suceder en el escenario de un . . . de un derrame petrolero, sino el hecho de que no hay ninguna garantía de . . . de la integridad del lago en tanto no está claro cómo van a manejar la salinidad. Otra vez que esto va a conectar el Pacífico con el Atlántico y a diferencia de . . . de . . . del caso de Panamá, realmente estamos hablando, en el caso nicaragüense, de un lago de más de 8.000 kilómetros cuadrados que realmente es una fuente estratégica de recursos. Por eso nosotros hemos insistido que es inaceptable que el gobierno haya emitido el permiso ambiental para el proyecto cuando el mismo estudio ambiental dice claramente que no hay suficiente estudio hecho sobre el gran Lago Cocibolca para poder realmente preparar un plan que impida que estos daños ocurran.

Locutor: Existiendo un Canal de Panamá ya de más ampliado, ¿este proyecto además es necesario?

Mónica: Es una excelente pregunta porque nosotros también hemos denunciado que ni la empresa HKND Group ni el gobierno han publicado lo que . . . lo primero que deberían de haber de publicado, que son los estudios de factibilidad comerciales. Es decir, ¿realmente el comercio marítimo mundial necesita un nuevo canal en una zona donde hay ya un canal de Panamá ampliado? Esa discusión, según expertos que hemos consultado entre puertos marítimos mundial han dicho sinceramente no le ven la necesidad de eso gran mega . . . megabuques que . . . que teóricamente pasarían por Nicaragua. Lo cual significa que se está empeñando al país en función de . . . de un negocio transnacional sobre el cual ni siquiera hay certidumbre de su necesidad.

Habláis de impacto ambiental, también hay impacto lo has citado en la comunidades que viven en las zonas de las obras. Concretamente, ¿a qué comunidades va a afectar este proyecto?

Bueno, mira, son tres departamentos del país. En esos territorios . . . eh . . . habitan mayormente población campesina rural, es decir gente que produce los alimentos que consumimos en Nicaragua. Este . . . arroz, frijoles, yuca, quequisque, ganado, leche, ehm . . . son . . . son zonas altamente productivas del país y también eh . . . territorios de pueblos indígenas que están reconocidos en la legislación nicaragüense protegido por las convenciones internacionales. O sea, prácticamente la afectación es . . . es directamente sectores populares productores de alimento y población . . . eh . . . indígena, lo cual obviamente agrava todavía más la situación en el sentido de que estamos hablando de un desplazamiento forzoso de más de 119.000 personas que . . . que además nos preocupa el hecho de que las van a forzar a establecerse en los pocos . . . las pocas áreas protegidas que nos quedan entre ellos reserva Indio Maíz y reserva Bosawas, ambas reconocidas internacionalmente por su importancia biológica.

Ensayo número 6

Fuente número 3

Track 29

Locutora:	La lucha contra las descargas ilegales en internet no parece estar dando los resultados esperados, a tenor de lo que dice un estudio que ha realizado el Observatorio de Piratería y de Hábitos de Consumo de Contenidos Digitales. Ese informe dice que el año pasado el acceso ilegal a contenidos en internet subió siete puntos a respeto a 2013, del 51% al 58%. Uno de cada dos usuarios que accede ilegalmente a esos contenidos, lo justifica con el argumento de que ya paga la conexión a internet. Antonio Guisasola, presidente de la Coalición de Creadores e Industrias de Contenidos y presidente de Promusicae, buenas tardes.
Antonio:	Hola buenas tardes.
Locutora:	El dato es demoledor: seis de cada diez descargas digitales son ilegales. Parece mentira a estas alturas.
Sr. Guisasola:	Bueno primeramente que sigamos en estas cifras, ¿no?, dado que llevamos bastantes años invocando el problema y pidiendo apoyo y hasta ahora no se ha encontrado una solución, no hay solución efectiva.
Locutora:	El informe ofrece una visión más completa que otros anteriores sobre . . . sobre este problema, el de la piratería digital, porque incluye por primera vez datos referidos a series de televisión, que cada vez tienen más seguidores, y a partidos de fútbol. O sea, estamos ante el dibujo más completo hasta ahora, ¿no?, de esta realidad.
Sr. Guisasola:	Sí, efectivamente pensamos también en los contenidos contribuyendo muchísimo peso, como son las, las series de televisión. Cada más . . . que es la problemática de que cuando alguien se engancha en una serie de alguna manera se baja temporadas enteras lo cual tiene una repercusión muy importante, y por supuesto el . . . el fútbol de pago que también en diferentes sectores en el que la piratería tiene mucha importancia. Y allí tiene la problemática un poco difícil porque lo que se consume realmente allí son . . . son directo realmente, no son emisiones de partidos en directo, no catálogos, pero prueba que . . . que es algo muy importante, creíamos que el observatorio sería más completo si estos contenidos estuvieran también reflejados allí.
Locutora:	Y lo de la música es . . . espectacular, ¿no? ¿Qué porcentaje tiene el mercado pirata respeto al mercado legal en internet?
Sr. Guisasola:	Bueno, pues, el mercado pirata en valor multiplica pues prácticamente por cincuenta lo que es el valor del mercado legal, ¿no?, es . . . estamos hablando de un mercado entorno a 170 millones mientras que el mercado pirata en . . . en valor está cerca de los 7 mil [millones], o sea, que es . . . que es una cifra totalmente disparatada. Es verdad que no todo eso se convierte . . . se podría convertir en . . . en mercado legal, pero lo que quedamo . . . lo que sí es refleja es que más del 90% de lo que se consuma es, de una forma, paralela al mercado legal.
Locutora:	Llaman muchísimo a la atención los argumentos de quienes piratean estos contenidos. Decía yo que la mitad argumentan que ya pagan la conexión a internet. Pero es que dos de cada diez creen que no están haciendo daño a nadie. Antonio Guisasola, ¿qué les contestamos desde aquí?

Sr. Guisasola:	Bueno, yo creo que es un . . . es una visión que . . . que en el fondo puede ser . . . parecer verdad, ¿no? Cuando . . . cuando alguien se encuentra todos los días con que si busca música en un buscador cualquiera, el primer resultado que son parte de páginas generales, uno accede a ellas sin ningún problema, se baja contenido que quiera, y esas páginas se ven allí durante meses. Se publicitan empresas, pues, más o menos serias, y además, pues, dan una apariencia de una legalidad que . . . que al final la gente . . . pues según uno de los sitios es una actividad muy legal pero desde luego, si fuera tan claramente ilegal no estaría allí, ¿no? Y desde luego es lo que vimos que efectivamente que . . . que estas páginas son limpias, de que son de la web, y desde luego el primer resultado cuando uno busca Alejandro Sanz o Larrio, no se ve una página pirata que no . . . es una página legal donde uno puede acceder a su música o desde luego sus películas o sus libros, ¿no? Es lo que vimos . . . es que evidentemente la gente . . . yo no creo tampoco que se llame engaño que saben que todo cuando gratis es dudoso que sea legal, pero en cualquier caso lo que hay que hacer es evitar esa posibilidad de . . . de acceder a ellos en ningún problema, y a como resultado . . . prioritario, . . . cómo hacen . . . cómo hacen una búsqueda.
Locutora:	Claro, parece demasiado fácil.

Ensayo número 7

Fuente número 3

Track 30

El programa Ley fácil de la Biblioteca del Congreso Nacional presenta: Servicio militar.

Pablo:	Hola Claudio.
Claudio:	Hola Pablo, ¿qué tal? ¿Qué andas?
Pablo:	Aquí mirando algún regalo para mi hijo que cumple años la próxima semana.
Claudio:	Y, ¿cuánto cumple Tomás?
Pablo:	Diecisiete
Claudio:	Diecisiete ya. ¡Cómo pasa el tiempo!
Pablo:	Sí diecisiete años. Ya le falta un año para salir del colegio, para votar . . .
Claudio:	Pero ya va a inscribirse en el servicio militar.
Pablo:	Oye, calma. ¿No hay que hacer eso el próximo año cuando cumple dieciocho?
Claudio:	No, Pablito. Eso es la cosa. Cuando Tomás cumpla los diecisiete, tiene que ir al Registro Civil a actualizar domicilio o residencia. Y va a pasar de inmediato a formar parte del registro militar. Es una especie de inscripción automática.
Pablo:	No me digas.
Claudio:	Así es. Porque después el Registro Civil envía a la Dirección General de Movilización Nacional los datos de quienes cumplan dieciocho. Para que así, cada año en el mes de abril se publique en la base de conscripción. En el fondo es una lista de quiénes podrían hacer el servicio.
Pablo:	Pero, ¿eso significa que lo van a llamar sin derecho al pataleo?
Claudio:	No necesariamente. A los dieciocho ya se puede ir a un cantón de reclutamiento a incluirse si alguien quiere hacerlo de forma voluntaria. Y después, los llamados se hacen por sorteo para completar las vacantes que no se llenaron con voluntarios.

Pablo:	Ya. Veo que cambió sistema de inscripción. Pero, ¿supongo que todavía corren las excepciones?
Claudio:	Sí, todavía se puede postergar si Tomás está estudiando, haciendo su práctica, o cursando cuarto medio. Y obvio, que han incluido los que tienen incapacidades físicas o psíquicas, los condenados a pena aflictiva y los que tienen inhabilidades morales calificadas.
Pablo:	De todas formas, no creo que Tomás lo haga aunque fuera voluntario. A él nunca le interesó el ejército. Le gustan los aviones.
Claudio:	Ah . . . pero el servicio militar también se puede hacer en la fuerza aérea, defensa civil y la armada. Es posible que Tomás haga durante su cuarto medio un curso especial de instrucción, que equivale haber hecho el servicio.
Pablo:	Ah . . . como para salir del paso del tiro y no preocuparse después.
Claudio:	Así que convérsalo con Tomás. No le gustarán los uniformes, pero que sepa que la cosa ya no es como antes.
Pablo:	Esto fue una producción de la Biblioteca del Congreso Nacional y la Radio de la Cámara de Diputados de Chile.

Ensayo número 8

Fuente número 3

Track 31

Narrador:	Hoy tenemos el placer de acoger al señor Benavides y al señor Domínguez. El señor Domínguez es presidente de Los Pescadores Artesanales de Puerto Aurora. El señor Benavides es director de la Fundación de Conservación de las Islas Galápagos en Ecuador. Bienvenidos, señores. Estamos para hablar unos momentos de los efectos de la Ley de Régimen Especial para la Conservación y Desarrollo Sustentable de la Provincia de Galápagos, ambos para el Parque y para el pueblo que vive cerca de él.
Sr. Benavides:	Le agradezco mucho la oportunidad de hablar un poco de la actualidad del Parque Galápagos porque hoy como antes, se ve amenazado por actividades humanas en varios sectores. Como se sabe, la Ley Especial de Galápagos que el Congreso Nacional promulgó en 1999 tenía por objetivo garantizar la conservación del ecosistema. Hasta el año 1971 no se veían fauna ni flora exóticas allí, ni había tanta presura de la actividad humana en el campo y los pueblos.
Sr. Domínguez:	También para nosotros no encontramos ningunos problemas. Pudimos mantener a nuestras familias con la pesca, pero actualmente es bien difícil.
Narrador:	¿A qué se atribuye la dificultad, Sr. Domínguez?
Sr. Domínguez:	Parece que hoy, con la escasez de pez, casi no se puede mantener a la familia. Nosotros también nos encontramos en conflicto con pescaderos industriales y los pescadores atraídos para la pesca deportiva. También parece que las aguas están llenas de barcos privados de turistas. Esto no cuenta los barcos grandes con ejércitos de turistas que vienen para pasar el día.
Sr. Benavides:	Para nosotros dentro del Parque, se ven los efectos que han causado esas invasiones, ambas de pescadores y turistas. Los pescadores reclaman sus

antiguos derechos, pero el hecho es que hay más demanda que surtido. Nosotros propusimos cuotas en las toneladas de peces de varias especies para aliviar la situación, pero. . . .

Sr. Domínguez: El hecho es que nosotros los pescadores artesanales tenemos el derecho de pescar en estas aguas porque llevamos siglos de hacerlo. Los otros no deben tener los mismos derechos.

Sr. Benavides: No sólo es cuestión de derechos. El problema es que actualmente los pueblos cerca del Parque introducen flora y fauna y microorganismos al Parque que antes no se veían. Pero allí están. La ley nos obliga proteger el Parque como patrimonio de la nación. También vemos el deterioro del campo a causa de la agricultura y todo el desarrollo para el ecoturismo.

Narrador: Los turistas sí llevan desarrollo económico, pero nos queda ver si ese desarrollo puede reemplazar los antiguos modos de sostenerse. Actualmente hay una gran cantidad de yates pequeños, barcos de carga, y cruceros internacionales que navegan por las islas, dejando residuos a menudo.

Sr. Domínguez: Los recursos están allí. Para los turistas, la naturaleza, para los pueblos en las islas, las huertas, para nosotros, los peces, de todo tipo, tiburón, calamar, pulpo, pepino de mar, atún, canchalagua, de todo. Las actividades pesqueras en la provincia marina son nuestro patrimonio.

Sr. Benavides: De acuerdo, pero al agotar los recursos, no tendremos nada. No hay alternativa más que el desarrollo sustentable.

Narrador: Entonces todavía le queda al gobierno regular los permisos de pesca artesanal, así como los del turismo y la actividad agrícola.

Ensayo número 9

Fuente número 3

Track 32

El vegetarianismo y la dieta vegitariana.

Recomendaciones de los teóricos del vegetarianismo

- Consumir pan integral o arroz moreno en lugar de pan blanco y arroz refinado.
- Dar una gran importancia a los frutos secos como fuente de proteína dentro de una comida.
- Favorecer el consumo de legumbres y pastas elaboradas con harina integral.
- Dentro de los productos lácteos consumir yogurt natural descremado.
- En la dieta vegetariana estricta se incluye la leche de soja en polvo.
- La única comida en la que debe aparecer regularmente una pequeña cantidad de azúcar o miel es el desayuno, ya que el organismo no puede digerirlo a otra hora.

Razones para excluir la carne

Algunas de las razones que aducen los vegetarianos para excluir la carne como producto destinado a la nutrición del ser humano son las siguientes:

- Ni la contextura física ni la dentadura del hombre corresponde a la de un animal carnívoro.
- Nuestros jugos digestivos carecen de la acidez necesaria para digerir la carne y es sólo por el hábito que el estómago se adapta a esa función. Incluso aseguran que un

hombre que no haya ingerido nunca carne al hacerlo por primera vez, experimenta una especie de intoxicación semejante a la alcohólica.

- La descomposición de toda sustancia animal produce toxinas mucho más peligrosas que las procedentes de la descomposición vegetal.

Ensayo número 10

Fuente número 3

Track 33

Turista:	Ya están cambiando las costumbres en cuanto a la comida, ¿verdad?
Ramón:	Sin duda. La facilidad de conseguir comestibles de todas partes del mundo remite a la integración de sabores desconocidos anteriormente en la gastronomía nacional.
Turista:	¿Pero no es que le faltaban a los cocineros productos locales y especialidades de renombre?
Ramón:	Claro que no. ¿Quién no ha oído de las famosas tapas de Barcelona? Hoy se encuentran en plenitud de libros de recetas. Hasta en Nueva York es de moda ir de tapas y probarse lo mejor del orgullo de la cocina española. Pero también se puede encontrarlas en Londres, en París, en Tokio, pues . . . por todo el mundo.
Turista:	Sí, los he visto en las librerías. Pero de las que me he probado, no tienen el mismo sabor que una tapa aquí. Puede ser que haya otro aspecto que no se puede exportar.
Ramón:	Seguramente el ambiente en el que se saborea la delicia influye en cómo se la percibe. No se puede por completo imitar el aire, ni los sonidos, ni la lengua que se oye al disfrutarlas en otro lugar. También se prohíbe la exportación de algunos de los ingredientes. El jamón serrano, por ejemplo, no se permite exportar a todos los lugares done se querría tenerlo. Aun cuando se puede, la frescura se pierde en el transporte. Los ingredientes más frescos siempre resultan en los sabores más deseados.
Turista:	Me ha convencido. Probaré las tapas mientras esté aquí. Pero cuando vuelva a casa, por cierto intentaré reproducir algunas de ellas. Aunque no goce de los mismos sabores, experimentaré el placer de evocar las fantásticas memorias del viaje. Podré imaginarme que estoy de vuelta. También compraré unos de estos libros de recetas para preparar tapas. Quizás trataré de inventar mis propias recetas para tapas americanas al estilo español.

INTERPERSONAL SPEAKING

Sample Script

Track 34

(El teléfono suena.)

Paco:	**Hola.**
Tú:	Salúdalo.
	Explica la razón por la llamada.
Paco:	**Ah, sí, gracias por llamarme. Querría invitarte a acompañarme a la escuela este fin de semana. Hay un drama buenísimo que se da, se llama _Sueño_.**
Tú:	Reacciona a su idea.
Paco:	**Me dijeron que nuestro compañero de clase es fantástico en el drama.**

Interpreta el papel de un rey. Como recuerdas, leímos una parte de este drama en la obra *La vida es sueño* en la clase de español hace un mes. Me gustaron esos versos de "¿Qué es la vida? Una ilusión", . . . etcétera.

Tú: Otra vez, reacciona.

Hazle una pregunta.

Paco: Sí. Los otros de la clase ya han ido y dicen que les gustó. ¿Te gustará ir conmigo? Te invito.

Tú: Contesta a la pregunta de Paco.

Paco: ¡Estupendo! Te encontraré enfrente del teatro a las siete.

Tú: Finaliza los planes.

Despídete.

Paco: De acuerdo, amigo. Nos vemos. (Paco cuelga el teléfono.)

Conversación número 1

Track 35

Dependiente: Buenas tardes, señor. ¿En qué puedo servirle?

Tú: (Respondes apropiadamente.)

(Le haces una pregunta.)

Dependiente: Bueno, no estoy seguro. Me parece familiar pero en este momento no lo recuerdo exactamente. ¿Tiene Ud. La dirección?

Tú: (Respondes que no tiene la dirección.)

Dependiente: A ver, ¿por casualidad está cerca de un lugar bien conocido? Quizás si supiera yo otro negocio o restaurante cerca, podría reconocerlo.

Tú: (Le nombras otro lugar.)

Dependiente: Tampoco reconozco ese lugar. Puede ser que sea tan nuevo que no lo conozco. Pues, ¿recuerda Ud. Otro detalle, como el color del edificio, algo en las ventanas de enfrente, unas escaleras, algo distinto?

Tú: (Le das otro detalle descriptivo.)

(Le pides la dirección.)

Dependiente: Ah, sí. ¡Ese hotel! Es pequeño, pero muy bueno. Está a una distancia de dos cuadras. Doble Ud. aquí a la izquierda, siga recto hasta llegar a la próxima esquina. Está en esa bocacalle.

Tú: (Reacción apropiada.)

(Te despides del dependiente.)

Dependiente: No hay de qué.

Conversación número 2

Track 36

Profesor Sánchez: Buenos días. Gracias por venir tan pronto. Espero que no te haya causado ninguna molestia.

Tú: (Saluda y responde apropiadamente.)

Profesor Sánchez: Bueno, empezamos entonces. Ya sabes que nuestro mundo enfrenta muchos desafíos en cuanto al medio ambiente. Si fueras de recibir la beca, ¿en qué asunto medioambiental piensas enfocarte y por qué?

Tú: (Contesta la pregunta ofreciendo detalles.)

Profesor Sánchez: Interesante. Al realizar este proyecto, queremos que fuera disponible a nuestra comunidad escolar. ¿Cómo piensas presentar los resultados de tu investigación?

Tú:	(Contesta la pregunta con detalles.)
Profesor Sánchez:	Muy bien. Parece que tienes las ideas bien claras. Para finalizar este proceso, quiero que encuentres a la Sra. Gómez, quien me ayudará con la selección de los candidatos. Desafortunadamente no está aquí ahora pero volverá esta tarde. ¿Puedes volver a las dos para hablar con ella?
Tú:	(Contesta negativamente, y ofrece una alternativa.)
Profesor Sánchez:	Perfecto. Muchas gracias por venir a verme y te veré luego.
Tú:	(Termina la conversación y despídete.)

Track 37

Conversación número 3

Cristina:	Hola, creo que no te conozco. Es tu primer día aquí, ¿no?
Tú:	(Saluda y responde apropiadamente.)
Cristina:	¿De dónde viniste?
Tú:	(Reacciona apropiadamente con detalles.)
Cristina:	Entiendo. Ya puedes ver que somos una escuela compuesta por estudiantes de todos tipos, pero son muy comprensivos. Sólo llevo dos años aquí y me hicieron sentir muy cómoda inmediatamente. Pero tienes que aprovechar toda oportunidad para conocerlos. Si tienes algún interés especial, puedes juntarte a uno de nuestros clubes. ¿Qué te gusta hacer en tu tiempo libre?
Tú:	(Contesta la pregunta con detalles.)
Cristina:	¡No me digas! A mí me encanta el boliche porque siempre hay tiempo para charlar con los amigos mientras se juega. Un grupo va a jugar este viernes. ¿Por qué no nos acompañas?
Tú:	(Contesta negativamente, y ofrece una alternativa.)
Cristina:	Me parece bien. Mira, tengo que irme pero te veré luego. Espero que te gusten tus clases y que todo vaya bien. Hasta pronto.
Tú:	(Termina la conversación y despídete.)

Track 38

Conversación número 4

Gerenta:	Muy buenos días, Sr. Díaz. ¿Cómo está Ud.?
Tú:	(Respondes apropiadamente.)
Gerenta:	Le agradezco por venir a hablar con nosotros. Tenemos un grupo de empleados muy dedicados en esta oficina y estamos muy orgullosos del trabajo que hacemos. Nuestro trabajo es un poco especializado, pero sí tenemos algunos puestos de internado para verano para estudiantes especiales. ¿Con qué motivo quiere Ud. trabajar para una compañía de telecomunicaciones?
Tú:	(Le explicas tus razones.)
Gerenta:	Um, muy interesante. Su interés en los aspectos técnicos es muy importante. Pero, ¿tiene Ud. alguna experiencia con la aplicación de esa tecnología que le interesa al trabajo que hacemos nosotros?
Tú:	(Le cuentas algo que ha hecho.)
	(Le expresas tus esperanzas.)
	(Le haces una pregunta.)

Gerenta: Por supuesto que siempre es mejor tener experiencia antes de tener un puesto de responsabilidad, pero sé que eso es muy difícil para los jóvenes cuando están empezando sus carreras. Le podemos ofrecer un puesto en la oficina si quiere empezar la semana que viene.

Tú: (Aceptas la oferta.)

Gerenta: Excelente. Estoy segura que esta esperiencia nos beneficiará a los dos. No olvide llamarme si tiene otra pregunta.

Tú: (Le das las gracias.)
(Te despides de ella.)

Track 39

Conversación número 5

Director: Buenos días. ¿Qué tal?

Tú: (Le respondes apropiadamente.)

Director: Me alegro. Uds. no me visitan mucho. ¿A qué debo el placer de tu visita hoy?

Tú: (Explicas el propósito de la visita.)
(Te haces una pregunta.)

Director: Había oído que Uds. estaban haciendo esa encuesta. Me interesa saber qué opinan los estudiantes del menú. Sabes que es un negocio muy delicado equilibrar el dinero que recibimos de los alumnos con los gastos por la comida y el mantenimiento del local.

Tú: (Le cuentas los resultados de la encuesta.)
(Le haces otra pregunta.)

Director: ¿Qué proponen los estudiantes que ofrezcamos en el menú?

Tú: (En tu respuesta comunicas los deseos de los estudiantes.)

Director: Siempre queremos satisfacer los deseos de los estudiantes. A ver si podemos formar un comité estudiantil para oír sus consejos.

Tú: (Reaccionas a la idea.)

Director: Entonces podemos dirigirnos al problema juntos para ofrecer algo que sea más saludable y algo con lo que no perdamos dinero. Muchas gracias por haber venido para hablar conmigo. Esperaré tu llamada para reunirnos otra vez.

Tú: (Te despides de él.)

Track 40

Conversación número 6

Tú: (Salúdale y pregunta por su estado de ánimo.)

Luis: Ay, estoy bastante frustrado. Todos mis amigos tienen cuentas en las redes sociales, pero mis padres no permiten que yo tenga ni una. No es justo.

Tú: (Reacciona y trata de consolarlo.)

Luis: Me dicen que meterme en las redes sociales va a interferir con mis estudios y capacidad de desarrollar amistades. Sé que tú usas las redes sociales. ¿Cuáles son las que usas más? ¿Han tenido algún impacto en tus estudios?

Tú: (Contesta la pregunta con detalles.)

Luis: ¿Y qué piensas del tema que las redes no permiten desarrollar amistades verdaderas?

Tú: (Contesta la pregunta con detalles.)

Luis: Esto es lo que yo pensaba. Tengo una idea, ¿podrías hablarles a mis padres para convencerles que tener una cuenta en una red social no perjudica tanto como ellos piensan?

Tú: (Contesta negativamente y ofrece una alternativa.)
             (Despídete.)
Luis: Pues, gracias por nada.

Conversación número 7

Track 41

Dependienta: Buenos días, señorita. ¿En qué puedo servirle hoy?
Tú: (Respondes apropiadamente.)
             (Le explicas lo que necesitas.)
Dependienta: Como ve Ud., no tenemos mucha ropa de ese tipo este mes. Cuando hace mucho frío generalmente tenemos más para la nieve que para el sol. Pero sí tengo algunos artículos en espera de las necesidades de viajeros que van a Florida. Déjeme mostrárselos.
Tú: (Le agradeces.)
             (Le dices lo que buscas en particular.)
Dependienta: Tenemos unas blusas preciosas en colores muy bonitos que le harán juego con el color del pelo. ¿Cuál es su talla?
Tú: (Contestas la pregunta.)
             (Expresas una preferencia.)
             (Le haces otra pregunta.)
Dependienta: Sí. Por supuesto. Tenemos la amarilla en un tamaño grande, si la quiere. El color amarillo le cae muy bien. ¿Quiere probársela?
Tú: (Respondes.)
Dependienta: Ha hecho una selección muy buena. Estoy segura de que estará muy satisfecha.
Tú: (Expresas gratitud.)
Dependienta: El placer es mío. Vuelva Ud. cuando necesite otra ropa de verano. Adiós.

Conversación número 8

Track 42

Tú: (Te diriges apropiadamente al cliente.)
             (Le haces una pregunta.)
Cliente: Buenas tardes. Sí, querría un vaso de agua, por favor. Me podría dar el menú?
Tú: (Respondes.)
             (Le haces otra pregunta.)
Cliente: Creo que estoy listo para pedir algo. Pero querría saber si Uds. tienen una especialidad de casa.
Tú: (Nombras unos platos.)
Cliente: Todo me parece bueno. ¿Tiene Ud. alguna sugerencia para ayudarme a decidir?
Tú: (Sugieres un plato de los que nombraste recién.)
Cliente: Sí, creo que hoy tengo hambre para pollo asado. ¿Y los vegetales del día?
Tú: (Le nombras la selección.)
Cliente: Bueno, tomaré los tomates y los pepinos. Gracias.
Tú: (Terminas la conversación.)

Conversación número 9

Track 43

	(Suena el teléfono.)
Enfermera:	Buenos días. La oficina del doctor González.
Tú:	(Respondes apropiadamente.)
	(Explica el motivo de su llamada.)
Enfermera:	¿Cuáles son los síntomas que tiene Ud.?
Tú:	(Explicas tus síntomas.)
Enfermera:	Ya oigo que no se siente bien. ¿Qué temperatura tiene Ud.? ¿Qué toma para la tos?
Tú:	(Contestas.)
	(Haces una pregunta.)
Enfermera:	Bueno, una temperatura tan alta casi siempre indica una infección. Puede ser que el doctor querrá verlo. Parece que hay posibilidad de que se mejore más rápido si lo ve pronto. Otro paciente canceló para las dos. ¿Puede venir a esa hora?
Tú:	(Explicas que sí, pero con una condición.)
Enfermera:	Dejémoslo para las dos, y si no puede, avíseme.
Tú:	(Respondes apropiadamente.)
	(Te despides.)
Enfermera:	Esperamos verlo esta tarde.

Conversación número 10

Track 44

Tú:	(Saluda y empieza la conversación.)
Carlota:	Muchas gracias por venir. Estoy un poco molesta porque mis padres me regañaron por mis gustos musicales. Dicen que no puedo tocar este tipo de música mientras que esté en su casa.
Tú:	(Reacciona y pídele más información.)
Carlota:	Me gustan todos tipos de música, pero recientemente tengo una pasión por el hip hop. El ritmo, los temas . . . todo me fascina. No sé, es como si fuera parte de mi alma y me hace sentir bien cuando lo escucho. Y tú, ¿te gusta el hip hop?
Tú:	(Contesta la pregunta con detalles.)
Carlota:	Mis padres dicen que los temas no son apropiados, pero no todos temas son malos. Hay varios sobre injusticias sociales y problemas que enfrentamos nosotros como jóvenes. Por eso creo que identifico tanto con este estilo. Pero ellos no entienden y no sé si hay manera de convencerlos. ¿Qué harías tú en mi situación?
Tú:	(Contesta la pregunta con detalles.)
Carlota:	Si solamente mis padres fueran tan comprensivos como tú . . . Desafortunadamente no creo que sea tan fácil. Oye, hay un concierto de un grupo nuevo este sábado. ¿Te gustaría acompañarme?
Tú:	(Contesta negativamente explicando por qué.)
	(Termina la conversación y despídete.)
Carlota:	Entiendo. Quizás otro día. Gracias por venir a verme. Sabía que podía contar contigo. Nos veremos luego.

PRACTICE TEST 1

Section I, Part B

INTERPRETIVE COMMUNICATION

Selección número 1

Fuente número 2

Primero tienes un minuto para leer la fuente número uno.

[1-minute pause]

Ahora pasa a la fuente número 2. Te queda un minuto pare leer la introducción y prever las preguntas.

[1-minute pause]

Ahora escucha la fuente número dos.

Un consejero y un estudiante hablan de sus alternativas.

Sr. Gómez:	Pasa, Raúl. Me alegra verte aquí esta mañana. Hace tiempo que no te veo y tenemos mucho que discutir, ¿verdad? ¿Ya has visto los materiales que te di sobre las universidades que deseas considerar para el año que viene?
Raúl:	Hola, Sr. Gómez. Sí. Muchas gracias por mandármelos. Mis padres también están interesados en verlos. Estaban contentos de oír que yo vendría a verlo esta mañana. Pero yo todavía no he tomado una decisión respecto a cual universidad planeo ingresar. Mis padres me recomendaron que solicite ingreso en por lo menos diez universidades diferentes.
Sr. Gómez:	Pues, para eso estoy, para ayudarte a aclarar la situación. Con el éxito que has gozado hasta este punto, me parece possible que tengas una gran selección. Todo depende de lo que quieras.
Raúl:	No estoy seguro. Algunos amigos me han recomendado que los acompañe a las escuelas que ya han elegido, pero éstas están muy lejos y son muy enormes, y eso me inquieta un poco.
Sr. Gómez:	Vale. Entonce, lo más útil sería pensar en tus intereses. De lo que veo en el trasunto, parece que el año pasado tuviste las notas más altas en química y las más bajas en historia. Por lo general, esto refleja un mayor interés en las ciencias y una falta del mismo en historia, o bien, que te gustaba más un profesor que otro. ¿Verdad?
Raúl:	Las lenguas siempre me han costado mucho, especialmente el inglés. En general, escribir es para mí algo muy difícil de hacer y no tengo ninguna habilidad en ese campo. Y creo que al profe yo no le gustaba tampoco.
Sr. Gómez:	Lo dudo. ¿Por qué crees eso?
Raúl:	Todo el año me regañó mucho, especialmente cuando tardaba en entregarle mis composiciones. Siempre hice mis tareas y leí todas las lecturas que nos dio y tomé buenos apuntes, pero siempre salí mal en los exámenes. Nunca alcancé más de setenta en ninguno de ellos.
Sr. Gómez:	¿Fuiste alguna vez a verlo para discutir el problema?
Raúl:	No, pero el año entrante seguramente lo haré.

Sr. Gómez:	Sería buena idea. Esto me sugiere que quizás sería mejor buscar una universidad que tenga clases más pequeñas, lo cual te permitiría hablar más a menudo con tus profesores.
Raúl:	Puede ser. Eso también le gustaría a mis padres, porque ellos se preocupan mucho al saber que siempre suelo tardar en enfocarme en las materias. Bueno, ahora me doy cuenta que hemos hablado de todo menos de estudiar . . .
Sr. Gómez:	Todavía te queda un año aquí para esforzarte en los estudios y remediar las notas. Mira esos folletos sobre universidades y hablaremos de nuevo el lunes.
Raúl:	Se lo agradezco mucho. Y lo veo el lunes.

Ahora tienes un minuto para empezar a responder a las preguntas de esta selección. Después de un minuto, vas a oír la selección una vez más.

[1-minute pause]

Ahora escucha la selección una vez más.

[audio repeats]

Ahora termina de responder a las preguntas para esta selección.

Selección número 2

Fuente número 2

Track 46

Primero tienes cuatro minutos para leer la fuente número uno.

[4-minute pause]

Ahora pasa a la fuente número 2. Te quedan dos minutos pare leer la introducción y prever las preguntas.

[2-minute pause]

Ahora escucha la fuente número dos.

El uso del suelo en América Latina
(*www.eurosur.org/medio_ambiente*)

Análisis más detallados revelan que una tendencia importante de la agricultura latinoamericana ha sido la conversión de cultivos tradicionales como frijol y maíz a "nuevos" cultivos como oleaginosas, en particular soya y sorgo. Se calcula que de la tierra incorporada al cultivo entre 1970 y 1980 cerca de 62% fue para oleaginosas, específicamente soya, y que otro 24% se destinó a trigo, arroz y sorgo. Entre 1978 y 1983 el área destinada al cultivo de soya aumentó en dos millones de hectáreas. El aumento de los cultivos de exportación ha ido asociado con la reducción del uso de la tierra para cultivos tradicionales como el frijol negro en Brasil o el maíz en México.

Se observa también una clara relación entre deforestación y aumento de pastizales para ganadería: entre 1974 y 1983 la producción ganadera en América Latina aumentó 28%. De las tierras de los Andes orientales colombianos incorporadas entre 1960 y 1980 sólo 16% fueron para cultivos, mientras que 54% se dedicaron a la producción ganadera y 31% no fueron utilizadas del todo. Más de la mitad de los nuevos ranchos ganaderos son propiedades de más de 500 hectáreas.

Desde la perspectiva espacial, no cabe duda de que las actividades agropecuarias son las que tienen mayor incidencia sobre el medio ambiente dadas sus extensions y, por lo tanto, el espacio afectado, la magnitud de las explotaciones y el hecho que América Latina es fundamentalmente una región centrada en la agricultura.

Los impactos que causan las modificaciones del suelo por la intervención humana se han ido magnificando con la creciente mecanización, la aplicación de agroquímicos, en particular fertilizantes sintéticos, plaguicidas, herbicidas y fungicidas, así como el uso de variedades genéticas mejoradas de elevado rendimiento, el aumento del riego, etcétera.

Algunas estimaciones señalan que la superficie cultivable de América Latina podría ampliarse hasta alcanzar entre 27% y 32% del total; sin embargo, esta ampliación de tierras cultivables se haría a costos crecientes. Hay que distinguir entre la incorporación propiamente dicha de nuevas tierras y la recuperación de tierras degradadas. Por ejemplo, se calcula que la incorporación de tierras en áreas desérticas costaría alrededor de 20.000 dólares por hectárea; pero la recuperación de terrazas y bancales abandonados en las zonas andinas altas de Perú y Bolivia sería del orden de los 2.000 dólares por hectárea, y un costo similar tendría la recuperación de tierras salinizadas en las áreas costeras regadas del Perú.

Ahora tienes un minuto para empezar a responder a las preguntas de esta selección. Después de un minuto, vas a oír la selección una vez más.

[1-minute pause]

Ahora escucha la selección una vez más.

[audio repeats]

Ahora termina de responder a las preguntas para esta selección.

Selección número 3

Primero tienes un minuto para leer la introducción y prever las preguntas.

[1-minute pause]

Ahora escucha la grabación.

(Música)

ER: La música hip hop puede mejorar la sociedad y promover la participación juvenil. La Oficina de la ONU contra la Droga y el Delito en Colombia, la UNODC, ha auspiciado el concurso "Tu voz cuenta", con el objetivo de encontrar las mejores líricas sobre denuncia social. Los músicos de las principales ciudades del país pueden mandar propuestas artísticas que invitan a los jóvenes a reflexionar sobre su estilo de vida, su entorno y su capacidad de liderazgo. Lisseth Ángel, de la UNODC, tiene más detalles sobre ese concurso.

LA: Es un concurso dirigido a jóvenes pertenecientes a agrupaciones musicales y culturales de hip hop de diferentes ciudades del país de Colombia, entre las cuales están Baranquilla, Calí, Cartagena, Medellín, Pereira y la idea es invitar esta agrupaciones a utilizar el rap, el break dance, el graffiti y otros componentes en la difusión de mensajes pro-positivos sobre la convivencia, sobre la cultura, la legalidad, sobre una vida libre de drogas . . .

(Música)

LC: ¿Qué difusión tendrán las propuestas musicales ganadoras?

LA: Inicialmente se va a seleccionar a través del concurso con un jurado especializado en el tema del hip hop, se va a seleccionar un tema musical por ciudad. Posteriormente se va a hacer un festival, que se llama "Tu voz cuenta", y es la intención de este festival es que sea un gran evento nacional con una gran tarima de civilización para estos temas musicales y también para los jóvenes y posteriormente después del festival vamos a hacer la grabación y las posproducción de los temas.

LC: ¿La música hip hop puede fomentar la participación juvenil y apartar a los adolescentes de las drogas y el crimen?

LA: Mira, nosotros estamos convencidísimos que la música es una herramienta muy potente, tanto al nivel preventivo como en la construcción de pensamiento, en la construcción de una expresión política genuina para los jóvenes. Esta herramienta de la música, del baile, del graffiti, son herramientas, son caminos muy bellos para los jóvenes.

ER: ¿El concurso también servirá para terminar con los prejuicios entorno a la cultura del hip hop o una cierta estética juvenil?

        Estos jóvenes como líderes de prevención, no solo del consumo de drogas, sino de estilos de vida saludables, pues tienen mucho que decir a través de sus líricas. Esto ya rompe como las barreras de las estigmatizaciones porque ojalá la gente a partir de eso se pueda dar cuenta que los jóvenes tienen mucho más que decir y son más que la ropa que usan.

(Música)

ER: Escuchamos a Lisseth Ángel de UNODC de Colombia, que nos habló del concurso de hip hop "Tu voz cuenta". Emma Reverter, Naciones Unidas, Nueva York.

[1-minute pause]

Ahora escucha la selección una vez más.

(audio repeats)

Ahora termina de responder a las preguntas para esta selección.

Selección número 4

Primero tienes un minuto para leer la introducción y prever las preguntas.

Track 48

[1-minute pause]

Ahora escucha la grabación.

El *Popol Vuh*

    El *Popol Vuh* presenta una versión mitológica de la creación del mundo, seguida por un relato de las aventuras de los dioses gemelos, Hunahpú y Xbalanqué, en tiempos primordiales, anteriores a la creación del ser humano. Los triunfos de los héroes en contra de las fuerzas primordiales y los dioses de la muerte dan lugar a la creación del hombre a partir del maíz. La segunda parte del texto se concentra en los orígenes de los linajes gobernantes del reino quiché, su migración hacia el altiplano de Guatemala, su conquista del territorio, el establecimiento de su ciudad principal y la historia de sus reyes hasta la conquista española.

El texto original del siglo XVI se ha perdido. Se sabe que estaba escrito en idioma quiché, pero utilizando el alfabeto español. Al principio y al final del libro, los autores mencionaron que lo escribían porque ya no era posible ver un libro llamado *Popol Vuh*, que existía antiguamente. Se ha especulado mucho sobre la naturaleza de este libro, que debió existir antes de la conquista española. Es probable que haya sido un manuscrito pictórico similar a los códices postclásicos que se conocen en el centro de México.

El texto más antiguo que se conserva del *Popol Vuh* es una transcripción del texto quiché hecha a principios del siglo XVIII por el fraile dominico Francisco Ximénez, que también hizo la primera traducción conocida al español. Ximénez presentó en doble columna el texto quiché junto a la versión española, y lo tituló "Empiezan las Historias del Origen de los Indios de esta Provincia de Guatemala". Este manuscrito se encuentra en la colección Ayer de la Biblioteca Newberry de la ciudad de Chicago. Fue extraído de la biblioteca de la Universidad Nacional de Guatemala por el abate francés Charles Etienne Brasseur de Bourbourg, quien lo publicó por primera vez en forma completa en 1861. Desde entonces, se han realizado númerosas ediciones y traducciones.

La palabra *Popol Vuh* significa literalmente "libro de la estera". Entre los pueblos mesoamericanos, las esteras o petates eran símbolos de la autoridad y el poder de los reyes. Eran utilizadas como asientos para los gobernantes, cortesanos de alto rango y cabezas de linajes. Por esta razón, el título del libro se ha traducido como "Libro del Consejo".

Ahora tienes un minuto para empezar a responder a las preguntas de esta selección. Después de un minuto, vas a oír la selección una vez más.

[1-minute pause]

Ahora escucha la selección una vez más.

(audio repeats)

Ahora termina de responder a las preguntas para esta selección.

Selección número 5

Primero tienes un minuto para leer la introducción y prever las preguntas.

Track 49

[1-minute pause]

Ahora escucha la grabación.

NAR 1: Tenemos el placer de hablar con José Antonio de Urbina, diplomático professional y experto en protocolo en la Corte española, quien ha escrito un libro que se titula *El arte de invitar.*

NAR 1: Este libro, ¿lo ha escrito Ud. para que lo conozcan y se lo sepan de memoria los presidentes de comunidades autónomas, los políticos, o para que nosotros, los ciudadanos de a pie, lo leamos, así, curioseemos en ese gran mundo y sus problemas?

NAR 2: Pues, no. El objetivo es que sea útil para todos, para todos. Curiosamente, cuando estaba escribiendo al principio, pues me di cuenta de que tanto personaje importante—reyes, presidentes—esto le va a asustar al lector de a pie, y por eso ya la segunda mitad la dedico más al lector común. Pero digo lo que es verdad, que, en esencia, el ban quetede estos de gala en el Palacio Real y la mesa a la cual, por ejemplo, una señora, unos señores, reúnen unos amigos, en esencia, es lo mismo.

NAR 1: ¿Y cuál es, digamos, la base, la médula de esa esencia, para que aprendamos, por lo menos, lo fundamental?

NAR 2: Pues, la médula es, sencillamente, que la gente esté confortable, que se sienta en su casa. Por supuesto, si hay que comer, que la comida sea buena, ¿verdad? Pero lo esencial es que se encuentren cómodos, porque si no están cómodos, ¿para qué sirve el invitar?

NAR 1: Pero vamos a ver, vamos a ver. Eh, lo de chico, chica, chico, chica, señora, señora . . . ¿Eso es correcto, no?

NAR 2: Sí, sí, sí, claro.

NAR 1: Eso hay que hacerlo así.

NAR 2: Eso hay que hacerlo.

NAR 1: Parejas o matrimonios juntos, nunca.

NAR 2: Claro, hay que dejarles a los pobres que descansen un poco, y para eso se separan.

NAR 1: Así que hay que sentarse hombre, mujer, hombre, mujer, nunca las parejas juntas . . . Eh, dice usted en el libro que las señoras nunca deben estar en las puntas de la mesa.

NAR 2: Claro, es una elemental, diría yo, cortesía hacia la mujer, ¿verdad? Las puntas es un poco el último sitio. No hay que dejar los últimos sitios con señoras.

NAR 1: Sí. En una casa, tal vez esta noche muchos de nuestros oyentes vayan a reunirse con ocho o nueve amigos. Eh, para que se sienten diez personas o doce, ¿hay algún truquillo especial o alguna alerta que quiera usted hacer para que no se caiga en determinado . . . ?

NAR 2: Sí, bueno, hay que tener mucho cuidado con el número trece.

NAR 1: Ah, no. ¿Trece, no?

NAR 2: Nunca.

NAR 1: Porque si son trece, ¿qué hacemos? ¿Matamos a uno o invitamos a otro?

NAR 2: Nunca. No, por una razón. La gente es mucho más supersticiosa de lo que creemos. No lo dice, por supuesto.

NAR 1: Ah, ¿pero cuenta a ver si hay trece?

NAR 2: Pero, como el número trece es mala suerte, pues trece nunca. Y entonces, ¿qué haces? Catorce. Pero si se te descuelga un invitado en el último momento quedas en trece. Y claro, pues, ahí está el cuidado. El truco es, le llamas a un íntimo amigo: —Mira, me pasa esto. ¿Quieres venirte a casa porque es que hemos quedado en trece . . . ? —Y por supuesto va, claro.

Ahora tienes un minuto para empezar a responder a las preguntas de esta selección. Después de un minuto, vas a oír la selección una vez más.

[1-minute pause]

Ahora escucha la selección una vez más.

[audio repeats]

Ahora termina de responder a las preguntas para esta selección.

Section II

PRESENTATIONAL WRITING: ARGUMENTATIVE ESSAY

Track 50

Primero tienes un minuto para leer las instrucciones.

[1-minute pause]

Ahora tienes seis minutos para leer el tema del ensayo y las fuentes número uno y dos.

[6-minute pause]

Ahora pasa a la fuente número tres. Tienes treinta segundos para leer la introducción.

[30-second pause]

Ahora escucha la grabación.

Fuente número 3

El Museo del Barrio celebra 30 años de excelencia promoviendo el arte latino en los Estados Unidos. Por Tania Saiz-Sousa

(*http://elmuseo.org/30annprs.html*)

Fundado en 1976, El Museo del Barrio ha tenido un gran impacto en la vida cultural de la ciudad de Nueva York, y es ahora una parada principal en la acreditada Milla de los Museos en Manhattan.

"Estamos orgullosos de las raíces puertorriqueñas de El Museo del Barrio, y también hemos extendido nuestra misión para así abarcar a las diversas comunidades latinas que hoy residen en la ciudad de Nueva York", comentó Susana Torruella Leval, directora ejecutiva. "Nuestro trigésimo aniversario marca un momento clave en nuestra historia. Estamos muy entusiasmados con los nuevos diálogos multiculturales y con las oportunidades para preservar y presentar la herencia cultural de los nuevos miembros de nuestra comunidad. También, aumentaremos el ámbito de nuestra colección permanente y exposiciones, y presentaremos nuevos programas educativos para la comunidad, grupos escolares y público asistente a nivel nacional e internacional", agregó Leval.

El aumento considerable en términos de las exposiciones, los programas educativos y número de visitantes—los cuales se han multiplicado en un 500% en los últimos cinco años—preparan a El Museo para los retos del nuevo milenio, y para alcanzar sus planes a corto y largo plazo. Estos planes incluyen la apertura del Teatro Heckscher en el verano del 2000, una joya arquitectónica de los años veinte con murales espectaculares y capacidad para 600 personas, el cual se encuentra localizado en el edificio que ocupa el Museo; la expansión de su tienda de souvenirs Imanosí, en la actualidad un lugar muy importante para impulsar las obras de los artistas latinos a nivel local y nacional; y la creación de ¡Las Américas Cafés!, un lugar de reunion informal donde se servirán cafés, refrescos y bocadillos caribeños y latinoamericanos.

Ahora escucha la selección una vez más.

(audio repeats)

Ahora tienes cuarenta minutos para preparar y escribir tu ensayo.

Track 51

Section II

INTERPERSONAL COMMUNICATION: CONVERSATION

Primero tienes un minuto para leer las instrucciones

[1-minute pause]

Ahora tienes un minuto para leer la introducción.

[1-minute pause]

En este momento va a comenzar la conversación. Presiona el botón de grabar y empieza tu grabación.

[Suena el teléfono.]

Eva: Hola, ¿te cuento? ¡Mis papás me dieron permiso para invitarte a acompañarnos a Florida! Iremos cuando lleguen las vacaciones de primavera, ¿qué te parece?
(20-second pause)

Eva: Vamos a ir a Disney World y después seguramente iremos a nadar y a pescar en el océano.

[20-second pause]

(Hace una pregunta.)

Eva: ¡Ay sí! Espero que nos dejen manejar el coche y así podamos salir con todos los amigos de allá.

[20-second pause]

Eva: No, no creo que podamos andar a caballo, porque el rancho de mi tío está en el norte del estado y eso está muy lejos.

[20-second pause]

Eva: ¡Pero sí podemos ir a bailar todas las noches! Los papás se acuestan temprano, pero sé que nos permitirán salir hasta las 11.

[20-second pause]

Eva: Bueno, me voy de compras. Qué buenas noticias, ¿no? Adiós, te llamo mañana.

[20-second pause]

Se ha terminado la conversación.

PRACTICE TEST 2

Section I, Part B

INTERPRETIVE COMMUNICATION

Selección número 1

Track 52

Fuente número 2

Primero tienes un minuto para leer la fuente número uno.

[1-minute pause]

Ahora pasa a la fuente número 2. Te quedan un minuto pare leer la introducción y prever las preguntas.

[1-minute pause]

Ahora escucha la fuente número dos.

El Salvador tiene una población de más de seis millones de habitantes.

Esta nación centroamericana es calificada por la Organización Internacional para las Migraciones (OIM) como un país emisor de migrantes.

Un claro ejemplo de ello es que dos millones y medio de salvadoreños viven actualmente en los Estados Unidos, según datos de la OIM.

La preocupación principal del gobierno salvadoreño es generar las condiciones de desarrollo nacional óptimas para evitar que la migración sea muchas veces la mejor opción para la gente que busca un futuro mejor, señaló en una entrevista a la Radio de la ONU el embajador de El Salvador ante Naciones Unidas, Joaquín Maza Martelli.

JMM: Es una obligación histórica de El Salvador brindar un proceso de desarrollo, un proceso social integral que permita precisamente que la emigración no sea una alternativa para los salvadoreños, sino que la emigración pueda ser, en un momento dado, un complemento que por diferentes formas pues tengamos en El Salvador que . . . que continuar en este camino

CM: Actualmente hay muchos salvadoreños viviendo afuera de su país. ¿Qué programas o iniciativas se han implementado para apoyarlos?

JMM: Actualmente el ministerio de relaciones exteriores realiza una labor de accesoria consular permanente, se colabora con los connacionales primero en la obligación de documentarlos. Si un extranjero, un inmigrante tiene la documentación apropiada frente a las exigencias del país en el cual reside, ese trauma de la indocumentación se supera, y ese es el primer paso. Segundo, yo creo que a futuro vamos a tener que establecer una serie de estrategias y de políticas bilaterales como algunos países de recepción migratoria como Canadá por ejemplo, Australia, la misma España, que permita pues bajo la filosofía de la migración ordenada, establecer convenios internacionales, bilaterales, que le den al salvadoreño un estatus migratorio permanente. Ésa es un poco la idea y ésa es la responsabilidad.

CM: Las remesas son una parte importante de la economía salvadoreña. ¿Se han visto afectadas por la crisis mundial económica?

JMM: No en gran medida, pero indudablemente no podemos pensar que las remesas van a tener la cuantía que tienen actualmente siempre. Mientras busquemos más legalización de la emigración y la emigración se va incorporando al país sede, también las remesas van disminuyendo porque el desarraigo tiene efectivamente esa consecuencia, que el inmigrante se vaya olvidando de su terruño. También hay que saberlas encauzar, yo creo que ahí estamos trabajando, y hay algunos programas ya para encauzar inversiones allí en El Salvador por parte de los salvadoreños que quieren hacerlo, la ayuda familiar, la educación de su familiares, la compra de viviendas y de terrenos en El Salvador. Esa es una nueva fase que nosotros tenemos que profundizarla para precisamente buscar un encauce productivo a esta remesa familiar y la población siempre riqueza. Nosotros queremos . . . ojalá si fuera que la mayoría de connacionales que está fuera pueda algún día también retornar a nuestro país. Y por eso es que nuestro gobierno pues tiene una preocupación fundamental que es lograr mejores niveles de desarrollo.

CM: Escuchamos al embajador de El Salvador ante la ONU, Joaquín Maza Martelli. Carlos Martínez, Naciones Unidas, Nueva York.

Ahora tienes un minuto para empezar a responder a las preguntas de esta selección.

Después de un minuto, vas a oír la selección una vez más.

[1-minute pause]

Ahora escucha la selección una vez más.

[audio repeats]

Ahora termina de responder a las preguntas para esta selección.

Selección número 2

Fuente número 2

Track 53

Primero tienes cuatro minutos para leer la fuente número uno.

[4-minute pause]

Ahora pasa a la fuente número 2. Te quedan dos minutos para leer la introducción y prever las preguntas.

[2-minute pause]

Ahora escucha la fuente número dos.

Hola, soy Mertxe Pasamontes tu psicóloga 2.0. En el día de hoy, os traigo un nuevo episodio del podcast de mi blog que se titula "¿Sabes equilibrar trabajo y descanso?"

Vivimos en una sociedad obsesionada con ser productivos, con hacer cosas, con aprovechar el tiempo. Es algo que se fomenta y que se valora en muchas empresas como una cualidad esencial e incluso se habla de que nuestro país, España, debería ser "más productivo". Queda claro pues que se habla mucho de productividad pero la mayoría de las veces no se habla lo suficiente del descanso necesario para poder ser productivos. Porque una persona absolutamente agotada no podrá ser productiva en modo alguno, cometerá errores y en según que trabajos, puede incluso suponer un riesgo. Y es que el descanso y el ocio son tan importantes como el trabajo o tiempo productivo. Y posiblemente, son mucho mejores. Ya lo decía Sócrates: Los ratos de ocio son la mejor de todas las adquisiciones. Pero no podemos negar que tenemos que trabajar, y por tanto hay que aprender equilibrar el tiempo entre trabajo y descanso. Porque hemos de tener en cuenta que el trabajo produce un desgaste, y en según las ocasiones puede llegar incluso al estrés. Por lo que es necesario, imprescindible, tener períodos de recuperación de ese esfuerzo. Y esa recuperación debe darse tanto dentro como fuera del ámbito laboral. Nadie puede rendir ocho horas seguidas a menos que seas Superman o una máquina. Diversos estudios han demostrado además que los descansos en la jornada laboral aumentan la productividad.

El segundo tipo de descansos es obviamente los que se realizan fuera del trabajo. Es en donde se produce la mayor parte de los descansos, así que listaremos más o menos las diferentes opciones, que serían: lo primero es diferenciar el tiempo libre del tiempo de ocio. Parte del tiempo de fuera del trabajo se dedica a dormir, comer, higiene personal, eso no es tiempo de ocio. El tiempo que queda después de trabajar y realizar todo el resto de las actividades citadas es el que consideraremos realmente tiempo de ocio. Las actividades domésticas o de cuidado de niños, se han encontrado que tienen una recuperación diferente de la del trabajo, más ligera. Sí bien no pueden considerarse estrictamente tiempo de ocio. Las vacaciones es uno de los grandes momentos de desconexión de la mayoría de las personas, pero hay que tener en cuenta que no podemos dejar la recuperación solo para el momento vacacional, ya que es necesario recuperarse cada día.

Ahora tienes un minuto para empezar a responder a las preguntas de esta selección. Después de un minuto, vas a oír la selección una vez más.

[1-minute pause]

Ahora escucha la selección una vez más.

[audio repeats]

Ahora termina de responder a las preguntas para esta selección.

Selección número 3

Primero tienes un minuto para leer la introducción y prever las preguntas.

Track 54

[1-minute pause]

Ahora escucha la grabación.

Un hombre adinerado, en su afán por hallar la verdadera felicidad se encaminó hacia un templo donde habitaba un sabio muy famoso por sus buenos consejos. Al entrar al templo y encontrarse cara a cara con el sabio de barba y pelo canoso, se postró ante él y le habló entre sollozos:

—O venerable sabio entre los sabios, te habla un desdichado. Te suplico que me ayudes a encontrar la verdadera felicidad. Te daré lo que me pidas.

El anciano dibujó una sonrisa de compasión en su rostro, y acto seguido, puso su mano sobre la espalda del hombre.

—Nada podrá darme mejor que la noticia de que has encontrado la felicidad. Pero he de decirte que no podrás hallar en este templo, ni obtenerla de mí—se apresuró a decir el sabio.

—Entonces ¿qué he de hacer si quiero obtenerla?

El anciano meditó la respuesta, entró en una habitación del templo y salió con algo entre sus manos—Yo no puedo darte la solución, pero conozco a quien te la dará. Se trata de un amigo que se encuentra en otro templo a diez kilómetros de aquí. Pero tendrás que llevarle esto.—Y puso en las manos del hombre el objeto envuelto en una tela.

El hombre se puso en camino con el objeto misterioso guardado en su bolsa. ¿Qué sería aquello que escondía la tela? No podía aguantar la curiosidad, y al hallarse a una distancia prudente, sacó de la bolsa el objeto y lo despojó de su envoltura. Parecía un cristal, pero más brillante. Al mirarlo más detenidamente se dio cuenta de que no era más que un pedazo de espejo que tenía grabada la palabra "Aquí". Lo envolvió nuevamente, y con un interrogante en su cabeza se puso en marcha ansioso por hallar al segundo sabio.

El templo al que llegó parecía exactamente igual que el anterior, pero con la diferencia de que este estaba abandonado. Se adentró a través de un jardín lleno de maleza y atravesó la entrada sin puerta. Al final del templo, le llamó la atención un reflejo. Se acercó para ver qué era, y se dio cuenta de que se trataba de un espejo apoyado en la pared que reflejaba toda su figura. Al espejo le faltaba un pedazo en la esquina superior que coincidía exactamente con el pedazo que llevaba en su bolsa, así que lo sacó e intentó colocarlo en su sitio. Al encajarlo, la palabra "Aquí" se unió con el resto de la frase que estaba inscrita:

"Aquí verás a quien alberga la felicidad"

—A quien alberga la felicidad—repitió mecánicamente—Lo único que veo es a mí.—Al ver sus propios ojos llenos de ilusión, cayó en la cuenta. Todo este tiempo había estado buscando la felicidad en el lugar equivocado, mientras la felicidad viajaba a todos lados con él sin saberlo.

—El anciano sabio tenía razón. En el templo he encontrado al único que podía darme la felicidad.

Ahora tienes un minuto para empezar a responder a las preguntas de esta selección. Después de un minuto, vas a oír la selección una vez más.

[1-minute pause]

Ahora escucha la selección una vez más.

(audio repeats)

Ahora termina de responder a las preguntas para esta selección.

Selección número 4

Primero tienes un minuto para leer la introducción y prever las preguntas.

Track 55

[1-minute pause]

Ahora escucha la grabación.

ER: Con Motivo del Día Internacional del Libro y del Derecho de Autor, que se celebra el 23 de abril, tres escritores de habla hispana compartieron los libros que los aficionaron a la lectura de niños. La escritora, poeta y dramaturga mexicana Carmen Boullosa, radicada en Nueva York, explicó que su padre le introdujo a la literatura a través de clásicos universales.

CB: Recuerdo en las noches cuando ya me iba a dormir mis papás se sentaron en la orilla de la cama y nos leían. Y no leían libros para niños, sino que fue la manera en que nos leyó desde *El Buscón* de Quevedo, el *Quijote*, fragmentos de obras de Lope, clásicos mexicanos, desde *El periquillo sarniento*, buscaron los pasajes que eran más atractivos, que eran cómicos, que tenían ganas de releer, y ese fue mi primer, digamos, mi primer gancho amoroso con la gran literatura al margen de los libros que yo leía, *El tesoro de los niños*, donde también había como una selección de libros que podían gustar a niños, que eran libros además atractivos, bellos, clavados de imágenes y de . . . y de tipografía muy hermosa que hacían el placer de la lectura también . . . el placer del contacto con un objeto digno.

ER: El autor nicaragüense Sergio Ramírez, autor de númerosos cuentos y novelas, reconoció que se aficionó a los libros a través de los cómics y los libros de aventuras.

SR: Yo empecé leyendo historietas cómicas, quizás no es muy digno para un buen escritor revelar este dato, ¿no? Pero el sentido de la aventura, de seguir a un personaje, a una mujer o a algún malvado me lo dieron a mí los cómics que son lo que yo leía de niño. Antes de entrar en el mundo ya sabido de Salgari y de Julio Verne, tierras extrañas, que es lo que atrae a la mente de un niño, ¿no? Que le revelen misterios, que lo lleven por territorios o mundos que no conoce. Yo diría que comencé a escribir relatos a los diecisiete años y a publicarlos porque sentí aún una necesidad de transmitir a los demás lo que yo veía como singular en el universo, y mi reflexión era, bueno, esto que estoy viendo alguien se lo está perdiendo y se lo tengo que contar.

ER: El escritor peruano Santiago Roncagliolo lo explicó que fue su padre quien le compró la primera novela, y cómo vivirá la jornada en Barcelona donde la fiesta de hoy, Sant Jordi, se celebra en la calle.

SR: Bueno, uno se hace escritor por muchos libros, pero la primera novela que leí fue *Tiburón*, de Peter Benchley. Mi padre, que era un obsesivo de la lectura y de la cultura me llevó un día a la librería y me dijo: "te compraré el libro que tú quieras pero tiene que ser diverso de los dibujitos, tiene que ser una novela". Y yo tenía ocho años, y escogí el libro que tenía un tiburón persiguiendo a una mujer desnuda en el mar, y ese era *Tiburón*, de Peter Benchley y esa fue la primera novela que yo leí.

Es que como yo vivo en Barcelona, celebraré el Sant Jordi, y eso significa que saldré a la calle, habrá libros por toda la calle, y . . . um . . . y es un día muy bonito porque vas por la calle y los libros están en la calle y los escritores están en la calle pues así es, y es un día que yo voy a disfrutar mucho.

ER: Escuchamos a los autores Carmen Boullosa, Sergio Ramírez y Santiago Roncagliolo. Emma Reverter, Naciones Unidas, Nueva York.

Ahora tienes un minuto para empezar a responder a las preguntas de esta selección. Después de un minuto, vas a oír la selección una vez más.

[1-minute pause]

Ahora escucha la selección una vez más.

[audio repeats]

Ahora termina de responder a las preguntas para esta selección.

Selección número 5

Primero tienes un minuto para leer la introducción y prever las preguntas

[1-minute pause]

Alimento y salud

Las investigaciones entorno a la dieta mediterránea son incontables, y en su mayor parte no hacen más que reforzar su prestigio y añadirle más bondades aún. La última viene desde nuestro país, se trata de un macroestudio publicado en la prestigiosa revista médica *The New England Journal of Medicine* en el que han participado diecisiete grupos distintos de investigación, que sugiere que la dieta mediterránea acompañada de aceite de oliva virgen o frutos secos, reduce la incidencia de problemas cardiovasculares graves de un 30%. El estudio comenzó en el año 2003, con el inicio de un seguimiento de pacientes que, aunque no tenían problemas cardiovasculares, sí tenían muchas probabilidades de desarrollarlos en el futuro porque presentaban al menos tres de los principales factores de riesgo: tabaquismo, hipertensión u obesidad. Se crearon tres grupos aleatorios, el primero consumía dieta mediterránea con un extra de aceite de oliva, el segundo, se le añadieron frutos secos al patrón de la dieta mediterránea, y al tercero se le redujeron las grasas. Cinco años después los investigadores comprobaron que la incidencia de problemas graves como infartos o ictus era significativamente menor en los dos primeros grupos, tanto que decidieron parar el estudio antes de tiempo para que el tercer grupo pudiera beneficiarse también de las virtudes de la dieta mediterránea enriquecida con aceite de oliva virgen y frutos secos. El ensayo, denominado Predimed, es uno de los mayores estudios clínicos de nutrición que se han hecho en el mundo y sus resultados, además de cambiar los hábitos de las personas colaboradoras, van a permitir también cambiar la política nutricional global. Entre otros puntos, y según el doctor Ramón Estruch, coordinador del estudio, se ha perdido miedo a la grasa vegetal en personas con sobrepeso, y se ha demostrado que la fama de la dieta mediterránea tiene un fundamento científico real. Alimentoysalud@RTVE.es, Radio 5 Todas Noticias.

[1-minute pause]

Ahora escucha la selección una vez más.

[audio repeats]

Ahora termina de responder a las preguntas para esta selección.

Section II

PRESENTATIONAL WRITING: ARGUMENTATIVE ESSAY

Primero tienes un minuto para leer las instrucciones.

[1-minute pause]

Ahora tienes seis minutos para leer el tema del ensayo y las fuentes número uno y dos.

[6-minute pause]

Ahora pasa a la fuente número tres. Tienes treinta segundos para leer la introducción.

[30-second pause]

Ahora escucha la grabación.

Fuente número 3

Vida moderna en Hispanoamérica

—¿Por qué no estudiaste en la universidad?

—Yo no ingresé a la universidad porque no pude aprobar el examen de admisión, los varios años que di el examen.

—A la persona que no va a la universidad, ¿qué caminos le quedan?

—Bueno, el que no ingresa a la universidad tiene que ponerse a trabajar de todas maneras, para contribuir al sostenimiento de la casa. Uno se ve obligado a trabajar porque la familia no lo considera productivo y porque la familia necesita el dinero . . . y porque uno también necesita el dinero para obligaciones sociales, salir con alguna chica, salir con los muchachos, y eso no puede hacerse si no se tiene más que un terno. Pero un muchacho de clase media no puede, sin avergonzar a la familia, no puede conseguir un trabajo de obrero. Entonces tiene que buscar trabajo de un empleado de cualquier forma, digamos un banco . . .

—O de oficinista . . .

—Exacto. Quizás en la administración pública, trabajar en un ministerio, quizás.

—Pero un muchacho de las masas puede trabajar en una fábrica o un taller, o puede tratar de establecer un comercio pequeño, quizás una tienda, puede ser chofer de ómnibus. Y lo interesante es que algunas actitudes no han cambiado. No están basadas solamente en lo económico de la persona, sino en lo que la persona hace para obtener dicho dinero. Yo por mi cuenta, cuando estaba en la secundaria, me había puesto a aprender electrónica. Las personas que se dedican a la reparación de aparatos electrónicos en el Perú son considerados obreros. Mi familia se opuso vehementemente a que yo tuviera nada que ver con la electrónica, arreglando televisores, lo cual es una profesión obrera, y lo cual a mi familia nunca le pareció bien, aunque fuera al doble de sueldo de un empleado de algún ministerio. El hecho de que un empleado de ministerio es un empleado y el señor que repara televisores es un obrero es mucho más importante que su sueldo, socialmente. A mi familia todavía no le gusta mucho que yo esté trabajando de supervisor de electricistas. Aún siempre me preguntan, "¿Y? ¿Todavía estás trabajando en lo mismo?"

Ahora escucha la selección una vez más.

[audio repeats]

Ahora tienes cuarenta minutos para preparar y escribir tu ensayo.

Section II

INTERPERSONAL COMMUNICATION: CONVERSATION

Track 58   Primero tienes un minuto para leer las instrucciones

[1-minute pause]

Ahora tienes un minuto para leer la introducción.

[1–minute pause]

En este momento va a comenzar la conversación. Presiona el botón de grabar y empieza tu grabación.

La conversación

La empleada: Buenos días, señor. ¿En qué puedo servirle?

[20-second pause]

La empleada: Qué bueno que esté para el empleo de guardavidas. Es buen trabajo para un joven porque puede pasar el tiempo al aire libre, gozando del sol. ¿Lleva Ud. experiencia con ese tipo de trabajo? ¿O puede demostrarnos que está calificado para el puesto?

[20-second pause]

La empleada: Siempre vale tener tanta experiencia. Pero sabe Ud. que siempre hay muchos niños que acuden a la frescura del agua a medida que se calienta el tiempo. Muchas veces no están acostumbrados a hacer caso a nadie. Puede ser difícil mantener el ojo en todos a la vez. ¿Tiene experiencia con el cuidado de los niños en alguna capacidad?

[20-second pause]

La empleada: Qué bueno. Al satisfacer estos requisitos del empleo, creo que sólo necesita Ud. rellenarme este formulario. Las horas serán de las nueve de la mañana a las seis de la tarde, todos los días durante junio, julio y agosto. Puede empezar el lunes.

[20-second pause]

La empleada: Creo que podremos acomodarlo y darle unos dos días para acompañar a sus padres. Muchas gracias por venir. Que lo pase bien y si hay algún problema, no deje de llamarme.

[20-second pause]

La empleada: Dicho y hecho. Bienvenido y espero que se divierta un poco también.

[20-second pause]

Se ha terminado la conversación.

Grammar Review

The following section is a brief review of the most commonly missed points of grammar. The items are divided according to the structural function of words. In some of the previous sections you are referred to this section so that you can understand why you have made inappropriate choices in the fill-in-the-blank sections or on the multiple-choice section. You need to categorize the kinds of errors you make so that you can learn to recognize the structure. If you do not understand the overall rule, then you will spend time learning specific examples, which may or may not help you on the actual exam.

TONIC STRESS AND WRITTEN ACCENTS

In Spanish the stress (an elevation of the pitch of voice) occurs normally on the second to last syllable of a word when the word ends with any vowel (**a, e, i, o, u**), or the letters **s** or **n**, and no accent is written over the syllable. For words that end with the letters **r, j, l, or z**, the stress normally falls on the last syllable. For this reason, all infinitives have a stress on the last syllable. Any deviation from this rule is indicated by writing an accent above the stressed syllable.

When an accent is needed to stress a syllable containing a diphthong (two vowels, a strong and a weak one), or a triphthong (three vowels, one strong and two weak), the accent is written over the strong vowel in the syllable. For example, in the second person plural forms an accent is written over the **ái**s and **éi**s to indicate the stress on the last syllable of that verb form as in averi**guái**s and entre**guéi**s.

At times the accent is written over a weak vowel to form two syllables out of one. For example: at**aú**d has two syllables because the two vowels are equally emphasized. Normally, in the **au** combination, the sound of the **a** dominates because it is the strong vowel.

Sometimes an accent is written over a vowel to differentiate one part of speech from another. Such is the case with the words **él** (he) and **el** (the), **si** (if) and **sí** (yes), **tú** (you) and **tu** (your), **mí** (me) and **mi** (my), **dé** (give) and **de** (from), and **sé** (be, I know) and **se** (reflexive pronoun). Accents are used to differentiate demonstrative pronouns from demonstrative adjectives, such as **ése** and **ese**, as well as interrogative pronouns from relative pronouns, such as **quién** from **quien** and **cuándo** from **cuando**.

NOUNS

Gender of Nouns

Masculine

All nouns are either masculine or feminine, with the gender of the noun usually indicated by the vowel at the end of the word. Generally, nouns that end with **-o** or **-or** are masculine. You should learn the gender of all nouns when you learn the word. It is helpful to remember that nouns that end with **-ama**, **-ema**, and **-ima** are frequently masculine in spite of the fact that they end with the vowel **-a**. Common nouns that fall into this category are:

el clima	*el planeta*	*el sistema*	*el problema*
el día	*el tema*	*el lema*	*el diploma*
el mapa	*el poema*	*el monarca*	*el Papa*
el cometa	*el idioma*	*el tranvía*	*el albacea*

Usually the names of men, male animals, jobs, and titles concerning men, seas, rivers, mountains, trees, metals, languages, days, months, colors, and infinitives used as nouns are all considered masculine nouns.

Feminine

Most words that end with the vowel **-a** are feminine, along with words that end with **-ción**, **-dad**, **-ie**, **-umbre**, **-ud**, and **-sión**. For words that end in **-dor**, a masculine ending, an **-a** is added onto the **-dor** ending, thereby making the noun feminine. You should also remember that **mano** is feminine. (*La mano, las manos.*)

Some exceptions to the rule that words that end in **-ud** are feminine are the words:

el ataúd	*el césped*	*el talmud*

There are some nouns that end with the vowel **-a** that are feminine, but require the masculine singular article because the noun begins with a stressed **a** vowel. Some of these nouns are:

el agua	*el alma*	*el ama*	*el ave*
el águila	*el hada*	*el hacha*	*el haba*

When other adjectives modify these nouns, the adjectives take the feminine form:

el *agua fría*   **el** *ave negra*

In the plural forms, these nouns take feminine articles. For example:

las aguas	*las almas*	*las amas*	*las aves*
las águilas	*las hadas*	*las hachas*	*las habas*

Masculine nouns end with the letters **-o**, **-aje**, or with **-or** (except for *la sor, la flor, la coliflor,* and *la labor)*.

Making Nouns Plural

To make nouns plural: if the noun ends with a vowel you add **-s**. If the noun ends with a consonant (anything other than -a, -e, -i, -o, -u) add **-es** to the word. If the noun ends with the letter **z**, it changes to **c** before the **-es** is added to the end.

For example:

la luz, las luces

If the noun carries a written accent on the last syllable, remove the written accent, since the stress will normally fall on the second to last syllable of any word that ends in the letter **s**.

For example:

*la civiliza****ción*** (with a written accent)

*las civiliza****ciones*** (no written accent)

Some nouns will add a written accent when they become plural forms.
For example:

el jov*en* (no written accent)

los j**ó***venes* (with a written accent)

With a few nouns the syllable that carries the tonic stress shifts when the noun is made plural, such as: r**é***gimen*—re**gí***menes*, es**pé***cimen*—espe**cí***menes*, ca**rá***cter*—carac**te***res*.

If the written accent occurs on the third to last syllable, do not change it.

Compound nouns that end in a plural form, such as the word *parabrisas*, do not add an -**es** to the end. But the number of the article changes from **el** *parabrisas*, for example, to **los** *parabrisas*. Days of the week that end with -**es** also do not take -**es**, but rather take a plural article; *el jueves, los jueves*.

Nouns that end with an accented vowel also add -**es**, such as *el rubí, los rubíes*.

Remember that if the accent is not written in the correct location, no credit is given for that item in the fill-in-the-blank section of the writing part of the exam.

PRONOUNS

Pronouns are words that function in the place of nouns. There are seven kinds of pronouns. For each person and number they are:

Personal (Subject) Pronouns

These pronouns function as the subject of verbs.

	Singular	Plural
First Person	*yo*	*nosotros, nosotras*
Second Person	*tú*	*vosotros, vosotras*
Third Person	*él*	*ellos*
	ella	*ellas*
	usted	*ustedes*

(*Usted* can be abbreviated: *Ud.* or *Vd.; ustedes* as *Uds.* or *Vds.*)

These pronouns come before the verbs in declarative sentences. They normally come after the verb in questions, but sometimes are used before.

Direct Object Pronouns

These function as the object of the verb and answer the questions who or what.

	Singular	Plural
First Person	*me*	*nos*
Second Person	*te*	*os*
Third Person	***lo***	***los***
	la	***las***

In Spain the form *le* is used in place of *lo* when the noun the pronoun replaces is masculine.

Indirect Object Pronouns

These function as indirect objects of the verb and answer the questions, *to, for, from, by who* or *whom*.

First Person	*me*	*nos*
Second Person	*te*	*os*
Third Person	*le*	*les*

Reflexive Pronouns

These pronouns show that the action of the verb reflects back on the subject.

First Person	*me*	*nos*
Second Person	*te*	*os*
Third Person	*se*	*se*

Notice in all of the above three types of pronouns, that the first and second forms are the same, and only the third person forms are different.

These pronouns are located in the following places:

Before:

1. conjugated verb forms,
2. negative commands.

After and attached to:

1. affirmative commands,
2. present participles (verb forms ending with **-ando** and **-iendo**),
3. infinitives.

When there are two object pronouns, the indirect object pronoun always comes before the direct object pronoun. When a reflexive pronoun and a direct object pronoun are used together, the reflexive object pronoun comes before the direct object pronoun.

When the double object pronouns are both third person (indirect object: *le* or *les*, and the direct object: *lo, la, los, las*), the indirect object is changed to *se*.

When one or two pronouns are added to an affirmative command, an accent is written over the syllable where the stress falls on the verb if the pronouns were not there.

For example:

Lea Ud. el libro. Léalo Ud. (*Lea* is two syllables, **e** is the stem of the verb.)

Lea Ud. el libro a su hermano. Léaselo Ud.

When one or two pronouns are added to a present participle, an accent is written over the beginning of the present participle ending.

For example:

Estoy leyendo el libro. Estoy leyéndolo.

Estoy leyendo el libro a mi hermano. Estoy leyéndoselo.

Imaginaos que estáis vistándonos cuando suena el teléfono.

Estabáis peinándoos cuando llegamos si mal no me acuerdo.

When two pronouns are added to an infinitive, an accent is written over the infinitive ending.

For example:

Voy a leer el libro a mi hermano. Voy a leérselo.

When one pronoun is added to an infinitive, no accent is written over the infinitive ending because the stress normally falls on the last syllable of infinitives since the words end with the letter **r**.

For example:

Voy a leer el libro a mi hermano. Voy a leerlo a mi hermano.

Voy a leer el libro a mi hermano. Voy a leerle el libro.

Prepositional Pronouns

These pronouns function as the object of a preposition, such as *a, de, en, por, para, sobre, sin,* and *con.* Any preposition, simple or compound, requires the use of these forms.

	Singular	Plural
First Person	*mí*	*nosotros, nosotras*
Second Person	*ti*	*vosotros, vosotras*
Third Person	*él*	*ellos*
	ella	*ellas*
	usted	*ustedes*

In the prepositional pronouns, notice that except for the first and second persons singular, these pronouns are the same forms as for the subject pronouns. In addition to the above forms, with the preposition *con* there is a special form, *conmigo, contigo,* and *consigo.*

Demonstrative Pronouns (this, that, these, those)

These forms are either masculine or feminine, depending on the gender of the nouns to which they refer.

este	*estos*	*ese*	*esos*	*aquel*	*aquellos*
esta	*estas*	*esa*	*esas*	*aquella*	*aquellas*

When the antecedent (the thing to which these pronouns refer) is a whole idea or phrase, the neuter form can be used:

esto	*eso*	*aquello*

Indefinite Pronouns

These forms have positive and negative forms.

algo	*nada*
alguien	*nadie*

Relative Pronouns

These pronouns function to introduce dependent clauses.

el que (la que, los que, las que)

el cual (la cual, los cuales, las cuales)

quien quienes

ADJECTIVES

Most of the problems you will find with adjectives are in recognizing the gender of some of the nouns. Usually on the exam there are no clues as to the gender of the nouns; the modifiers are indeterminate because they end in **e**, because they are possessive adjectives, or because there are no modifiers, such as articles. Make sure when you learn nouns that you learn the gender from the beginning so you can avoid problems with agreement of adjective endings and nouns.

All adjectives agree in gender and number with the nouns they modify. This means that if a noun is feminine, singular or plural, the ending of the adjective is feminine, singular or plural. For example:

La *mujer alt***a** *lleva* **una** *chaqueta negr***a**.

Las *mujeres alt***as** *llevan* **unas** *chaquetas negr***as**.

If the noun is masculine, singular or plural, the endings are masculine, singular or plural. For example:

El *hombre alt***o** *lleva* **un** *hermos***o** *traje negr***o**.

Los *hombres alt***os** *llevan* **unos** *hermos***os** *trajes negr***os**.

If the adjective ends in an **e**, it cannot agree in gender, only in number. For example:

El *elefante gigant***e** *es muy inteligent***e**.

Los *elefantes gigant***es** *son muy inteligent***es**.

If an adjective ends with **-or**, **-ón**, **-án**, or **-ín**, an **a** is added to form the feminine singular, and **-as** for the feminine plural. For example:

El *nuev***o** *criado es muy trabajad***or.**

La *nuev***a** *estudiante es muy trabajad***ora.**

Las *nuev***as** *estudiantes son muy trabajad***oras.**

Some adjectives are invariable; their endings do not change no matter what the gender of the noun they modify. Some of these are:

maya   azteca   marrón   rosa   alerta   hipócrita

In many cases the **past** participles (forms of the verb ending with **-ado** or **-ido**) can function as adjectives. In these cases, when the past participle always ends with **-o**, simply make the vowel on the end agree in gender and number with the nouns the past participles/adjectives modify. Remember that some past participles are irregular. In some cases there is a different form derived from the verb for the adjective, instead of the past participle. For example, *despertar* has as its past participle, *despertado*. But when used as an adjective, the form is *despierto*. The same is true of the following verbs:

concluir	*concluido*	*concluso*
elegir	*elegido*	*electo*
soltar	*soltado*	*suelto*
sujetar	*sujetado*	*sujeto*
bendecir	*bendecido*	*bendito*
convertir	*convertido*	*converso*
maldecir	*maldecido*	*maldito*

There are a few verbs for which the present participle can be used as an adjective:

hervir	*hirviendo*
arder	*ardiendo*

Position of Adjectives

In general, adjectives that refer to quantity come **in front** of the noun, such as numbers and definite articles.

In general, adjectives that refer to descriptive qualities or characteristics of nouns come **after** the noun.

When there are two or more descriptive adjectives that refer to the same nouns, sometimes one is placed before the nouns; otherwise, they both follow the nouns and are joined by a conjunction, **y**, or are separated by a comma.

There are some adjectives that can come before or after a noun, but whose meaning is determined by where they are placed. The following adjectives are the most common ones of this type:

Adjective	Meaning Before	Meaning After
cierto	some	sure, certain
grande	great, famous	large
mismo	same	only
nuevo	another	modern, just made
solo	only	lone
pobre	unfortunate	destitute, penniless
simple	uncomplicated	silly, stupid
viejo	former	elderly
diferentes	various	not the same
antiguo	former	antique

Some adjectives drop the final **-o** before masculine singular nouns. These adjectives are **bueno**, **malo**, **primero**, **tercero**, **veintiuno**, **uno**, **alguno**, and **ninguno**. The adjectives **alguno** and **ninguno** add a written accent when the final **-o** is dropped: **algún, ningún**.

The adjective **grande** drops the final **-de** before masculine and feminine nouns.
For example:

    Una **gran** *dama*   *Un* **gran** *hombre*

The number **ciento** drops the final **-to** before any nouns, masculine or feminine.
For example:

    cien *años*   **cien** *noches*

The title **santo** drops the final **-to** before all masculine names except those beginning with **Do** or **To**.
For example:

    San Amselmo   **Santo Domingo**
    San Isidro   **Santo Tomás**

Nominalization of Adjectives

Placing **lo** before an adjective means that it can be used as a noun.
For example:

Lo importante (The important thing)

Los rojos (The red ones)

Possessive Adjectives

The possessive adjectives are:

mi, mis	=	my	*nuestro, -a*	=	our
			nuestros, -as		
tu, tus	=	your	*vuestro, -a*	=	your
			vuestros, -as		
su, sus	=	his	*su, sus*	=	their
		her			your
		its			
		your			

Possessive adjectives agree in gender and number with the objects that are possessed, not with the possessor.
For example:

El chico llevó **sus** *libros.* = The boy took his books.

(**Sus** is plural because **libros** is plural.)

Demonstrative Adjectives

The demonstrative adjectives are:

este = this (masculine)	*estos* = these (masculine)	
esta = this (feminine)	*estas* = these (feminine)	
esto = this (neuter)		
ese = that (masculine)	*esos* = those (masculine)	
esa = that (feminine)	*esas* = those (feminine)	
eso = that (neuter)		
aquel = that (masculine)	*aquellos* = those (masculine)	
aquella = that (feminine)	*aquellas* = those (feminine)	

The significant point of grammar to remember about demonstrative adjectives is the difference between *ese* (*esos, esa, esas*) and *aquel* (*aquellos, aquella, aquellas*). *Ese* refers to objects or persons nearer at hand than *aquel*. This distance can be expressed in temporal or spatial dimensions. For example: *En aquellos días vivía un rey muy poderoso...* meaning *in those long ago times there lived...* (Distance in time is implicit since *aquellos* is used.)

The following suffix can be added to adjectives: *-ísimo*

When the suffix is added to an adjective that ends with **-co**, the spelling is changed to preserve the **k** sound of the **c**.

For example:

poco	*poquísimo*
rico	*riquísimo*

Comparatives of Inequality

To form the comparatives of adjectives and adverbs the following structures are used:
Place **más** or **menos** before the noun, adjective, or adverb; then follow it with **que**.
For example:

*Este estudiante tiene **más** libros **que** el otro.*

*Este estudiante tiene **menos** libros **que** el otro.*

*Este chico es **más** aplicado **que** el otro.*

*Este chico es **menos** aplicado **que** el otro.*

*Este chico trabaja **más** rápidamente **que** el otro.*

*Este chico trabaja **menos** rápidamente **que** el otro.*

The following adjectives have irregular forms in the comparative:

Adjective	Comparative
bueno (good)	**mejor** (better)
malo (bad)	**peor** (worse)
joven (young)	**menor** (younger)
viejo (old)	**mayor** (older)

These comparative forms cannot agree in gender with the nouns they modify, but they can be made plural.

For example:

Esta máquina es **mejor que** *la otra.*

Estas máquinas son **mejores que** *las otras.*

Esta máquina es **peor que** *la otra.*

Estas máquinas son **peores que** *las otras.*

Esta casa es **mayor que** *la otra.* (This house is older than the other one.)

Estas casas son **mayores que** *las otras.* (These houses are older than the other ones.)

The irregular forms for the adjectives **mucho** and **poco** are **más** and **menos**.
For example:

Hay **mucha** *gente en la cafetería.*

Hay **muchas** *personas en la cafetería.* (There are many people in the cafeteria.)

Hay **más** *personas en la cafetería.* (There are more people in the cafeteria.)

Hay **poca** *gente en la cafetería.* (There are few people in the cafeteria.)

Hay **pocas** *personas en la cafetería.* (There are a few people in the cafeteria.)

Mayor in the comparative form means greater and **menor** means lesser.
For example:

El asunto de **mayor** *importancia es la cuestión de moralidad.* (The matter of greater importance is the question of morality.)

Es de **menor** *importancia preocuparse de este asunto.* (It is of lesser importance to worry about this matter.)

Comparatives of Equality

The comparatives of equality are formed as follows:

as + adjective or adverb + as

tan + adjective or adverb + **como**

For example:

Este chico es **tan** *alto* **como** *su compañero.* (This boy is as tall as his friend.)

Este chico corre **tan** *rápido* **como** *su compañero.* (This boy runs as fast as his friend.)

as + the noun + as

tanto (a) + noun + **como**

For example:

Este chico tiene **tanto** *talento* **como** *su compañero.* (This boy has as much talent as his friend.)

Este chico tiene **tanta** *energía* **como** *su compañero.* (This boy has as much energy as his friend.)

Este chico tiene **tantos** *libros* **como** *su compañero.* (This boy has as many books as his friend.)

Este chico tiene **tantos como** *su compañero. (This boy has as many as his friend.* OR *This boy has as much as his friend.)*

Superlative Constructions

The superlatives of adjectives are formed by placing a definite article (**el, la, los, las**) before the comparative forms.

For example:

Este chico es **el más** *alto* **de** *la clase.* (This boy is the tallest in the class.)

Este chico es **el mejor** *jugador de fútbol* **de** *la clase.* (This boy is the best soccer player in the class.)

Notice that the English word *in* is rendered with **de**.

The expressions for *as soon as possible* are:

cuanto antes

lo más pronto posible

tan pronto como posible

Absolute Superlatives

When no comparison is expressed, the ending **-ísimo** (**-a, -os, -as**) is added to the adjective.

For example:

Tiene **muchísimos** *problemas.* (He has many, many problems.)

Tiene **muchísima** *tarea.* (He has a lot of work.)

Adjectives ending in a vowel drop the vowel before adding **-ísimo**. Adjectives that end in **-co** change the **co** to **qu**; endings of **-go** change the **g** to **gu**, **z** changes to **c** and **-ble** changes to **-bil**.

For example:

*Esta película es mal***a***—Esta película es malísima.*

*Este hombre es ri***co***—Este hombre es ri***qu***isímo.*

*Este libro es lar***go***—Este libro es lar***gu***ísimo.*

*Este chico está feli***z***—Este chico está feli***c***ísimo.*

*Este profesor es ama***ble***—Este profesor es ama***bil***ísimo.*

When the absolute superlative form is added to an adverb, the form is invariable; it always ends with **-ísimo**.

VERBS

Verbs have four different kinds of forms: (1) the infinitive, (2) the conjugated verb, (3) the past participle, and (4) the present participle.

Infinitives

Infinitives are somewhat different in Spanish than they are in English. In Spanish the function of an infinitive in a sentence can be as the subject of a conjugated verb, the object of a conjugated verb, or the object of a preposition. When the infinitive functions as the subject of a sentence, it is translated into English as a gerund.

For example:

El caminar le ayuda mantenerse en forma. (Walking helps you stay in shape.)
Me gusta caminar por el parque. (I like to walk through the park.)

When the infinitive functions as the object of a verb, it can also be translated as a gerund. For example:

Su padre le dejó salir en seguida. (His father let him leave immediately.)
No pudo soportar más las injurias del gentío en la calle. (He could not stand the insults of the crowd in the street.)

As the object of a preposition, the translation of the infinitive depends upon the preposition used. The preposition **a** is used after verbs of motion, beginning, inviting, helping, and exhorting.

After the preposition **a** and article **el**, the infinitive indicates that two things are happening simultaneously.

For example:

Al divisar la costa por la neblina, lloró por pura alegría. (Upon seeing the coast through the mist, he cried out of joy.)

In conversational Spanish, the preposition **a**, followed by an infinitive is sometimes used in place of a direct command.

For example:

¡A ver! (Let's just see!)

When the preposition **con** comes before the infinitive, the meaning is one of concession or manner.

For example:

Con dedicar más tiempo al trabajo, lo acabarás. (With a harder effort, you will finish it. OR If you work a little harder, you will finish it.)

When the infinitive follows the preposition **de**, some kind of condition is indicated. For example:

De haberlo pensado un poco más, no lo habría hecho. (If he had thought about it a little more, he would not have done it.)

Notice that in this case, the clause introduced by the preposition is part of an if-then statement and has replaced the clause that normally contains the past subjunctive.

The preposition **por** followed by an infinitive indicates motive for an event or situation. For example:

No le permitieron entrar por no llevar una corbata ni traje formal. (They did not let him in because he was not wearing proper attire.)

The preposition **sin** indicates a negative meaning. For example:

El asunto todavía quedó sin resolver. (The matter is still unresolved.)

The preposition **para** indicates purpose and means *in order to*. For example:

Lo invitó para hacerle sentirse bien acogido. (She invited him to make him feel very welcome.)

Conjugated Verb Forms

There are three conjugations: verbs that end with **-ar**, verbs that end with **-er**, and verbs that end with **-ir**. For each conjugation there are different endings indicating tenses and moods. The tenses are:

Indicative	Subjunctive
Present	Present
Present Progressive	Present Progressive
Present Perfect	Present Perfect
Imperfect	Past (Imperfect)

Indicative	Subjunctive
Past Progressive	Past Progressive
Pluperfect	Past Perfect
Preterite	
Pluscuamperfect	
Future	
Future Progressive	
Future Perfect	
Conditional	
Conditional Progressive	
Conditional Perfect	

Within each of these tenses there are four different categories of verbs: (1) regular conjugations, (2) irregular conjugations, (3) stem changing conjugations, and (4) orthographic or spelling change conjugations. To conjugate verbs in all of these categories, take the infinitive ending off of the stem of the verb (the **-ar**, **-er**, **-ir** ending) and add the appropriate ending (the ending that agrees with the subject of the verb). For each kind **except** regular verbs, however, there are changes that must be made in the stem of the verb in many verbal tenses. Irregular verbs have forms that do not conform to any regular pattern and these must be memorized. Stem changing verbs can be classified so that the changes are more easily remembered. Orthographic verbs have spelling changes that occur for the letters **c**, **g**, and **z** when they are followed by certain vowels.

1. REGULAR VERBS

To conjugate verbs, for the following tenses, take off the infinitive ending, (**-ar**, **-er**, or **-ir**) and add the following endings:

Simple Indicative Tenses

Present Indicative of **-ar** verbs		Present Indicative of **-er** verbs		Present Indicative of **-ir** verbs	
-o	-amos	-o	-emos	-o	-imos
-as	-áis	-es	-éis	-es	-ís
-a	-an	-e	-en	-e	-en

Preterite Indicative of **-ar** verbs		Preterite Indicative of **-er** verbs		Preterite Indicative of **-ir** verbs	
-é	-amos	-í	-imos	-í	**-imos**
-aste	-asteis	-iste	-isteis	-iste	-isteis
-ó	-aron	-ió	-ieron	-ió	-ieron

Imperfect Indicative of **-ar** verbs		Imperfect Indicative of **-er** verbs		Imperfect Indicative of **-ir** verbs	
-aba	-ábamos	-ía	-íamos	-ía	-íamos
-abas	-abais	-ías	-íais	-ías	-íais
-aba	-aban	-ía	-ían	-ía	-ían

The following endings are added to the infinitive form of all three conjugations:

Future Indicative

-é	-emos
-ás	-éis
-á	-án

Conditional Indicative

-ía	-íamos
-ías	-íais
-ía	-ían

(Notice that these endings are the same as endings for the second and third conjugation imperfect endings, except that they are only added to the end of the infinitives.)

Compound Indicative Tenses

To form the compound or perfect tenses, conjugate the verb **haber** in each of the above tenses and follow it with the past participle. The past participle is formed by removing the -**ar**, -**er**, or -**ir** endings and adding -**ado** for -**ar** verbs and -**ido** for -**er** and -**ir** verbs. The forms for the verb **haber** in each of the above tenses are:

<table>
<tr><td colspan="2">Present Indicative</td><td colspan="2">Imperfect Indicative</td></tr>
<tr><td>he</td><td>hemos</td><td>había</td><td>habíamos</td></tr>
<tr><td>has</td><td>habeis</td><td>habías</td><td>habíais</td></tr>
<tr><td>ha</td><td>han</td><td>había</td><td>habían</td></tr>
<tr><td colspan="2">Preterite Indicative</td><td colspan="2">Conditional Indicative</td></tr>
<tr><td>hube</td><td>hubimos</td><td>habría</td><td>habríamos</td></tr>
<tr><td>hubiste</td><td>hubisteis</td><td>habrías</td><td>habríais</td></tr>
<tr><td>hubo</td><td>hubieron</td><td>habría</td><td>habrían</td></tr>
<tr><td colspan="2">Future Indicative</td><td colspan="2"></td></tr>
<tr><td>habré</td><td>habremos</td><td></td><td></td></tr>
<tr><td>habrás</td><td>habrán</td><td></td><td></td></tr>
<tr><td>habrá</td><td>habrán</td><td></td><td></td></tr>
</table>

There are a number of irregular past participles that are commonly found on the Advanced Placement exam. They are as follows:

<table>
<tr><td>abrir</td><td>**abierto**</td><td>revolver</td><td>**revuelto**</td></tr>
<tr><td>cubrir</td><td>**cubierto**</td><td>deshacer</td><td>**deshecho**</td></tr>
<tr><td>descubrir</td><td>**descubierto**</td><td>satisfacer</td><td>**satisfecho**</td></tr>
<tr><td>decir</td><td>**dicho**</td><td>bendecir</td><td>**bendito**</td></tr>
<tr><td>hacer</td><td>**hecho**</td><td>maldecir</td><td>**maldito**</td></tr>
<tr><td>morir</td><td>**muerto**</td><td>imponer</td><td>**impuesto**</td></tr>
<tr><td>poner</td><td>**puesto**</td><td>oponer</td><td>**opuesto**</td></tr>
<tr><td>romper</td><td>**roto**</td><td>suponer</td><td>**supuesto**</td></tr>
<tr><td>soltar</td><td>**suelto**</td><td>sobreponer</td><td>**sobrepuesto**</td></tr>
<tr><td>volver</td><td>**vuelto**</td><td>componer</td><td>**compuesto**</td></tr>
<tr><td>envolver</td><td>**envuelto**</td><td>resolver</td><td>**resuelto**</td></tr>
<tr><td>devolver</td><td>**devuelto**</td><td></td><td></td></tr>
</table>

SIMPLE SUBJUNCTIVE

Present Subjunctive

To form the present subjunctive, notice that the endings for **-er** and **-ir** verbs are identical.

-ar		-er and -ir	
-e	-emos	-a	-amos
-es	-éis	-as	-áis
-e	-en	-a	-an

Past (Imperfect) Subjunctive

There are two sets of endings that can be used interchangeably, although there are some regional preferences for one or the other in some cases in the Spanish-speaking world.

-ar (Set 1)		-er and -ir (Set 1)	
-ara	-áramos	-iera	-iéramos
-aras	-arais	-ieras	-ierais
-ara	-aran	-iera	-ieran

-ar (Set 2)		-er and -ir (Set 2)	
-ase	-ásemos	-ese	-ésemos
-ases	-aseis	-eses	-eseis
-ase	-asen	-ese	-esen

Compound Subjunctive Tenses

To form the present perfect or the pluperfect subjunctive, conjugate the verb **haber** in either the present or the past subjunctive with a past participle (**-ado, -ido**). **(See past participles for discussion of irregular past participles.)**

haya	hayamos	hubiera OR hubiese	hubiéramos OR hubiésemos
hayas	hayais	hubieras OR hubieses	hubieseis OR hubieseis
haya	hayan	hubiera OR hubiese	hubieran OR hubiesen

2. IRREGULAR VERBS

There are only a dozen or so irregular verbs that you are likely to use on the exam. They are **caber, dar, decir, estar, hacer, ir, oír, poder, poner, querer, saber, ser, tener, traer, valer, venir, ver.**

CABER

Present Indicative		Present Subjunctive	
quepo	cabemos	quepa	quepamos
cabes	cabéis	quepas	quepáis
cabe	caben	quepa	quepan

Preterite Indicative		Past Subjunctive	
cupe	cupimos	cupiera	cupiéramos
cupiste	cupisteis	cupieras	cupierais
cupo	cupieron	cupiera	cupieran

Imperfect Indicative

cabía	cabíamos
cabías	cabíais
cabía	cabían

Future Indicative

cabré	cabremos
cabrás	cabréis
cabrá	cabrán

Conditional Indicative

cabría	cabríamos
cabrías	cabríais
cabría	cabrían

DAR

Present Indicative

doy	damos
das	dais
da	dan

Present Subjunctive

dé	demos
des	deis
dé	den

Preterite Indicative

di	dimos
diste	disteis
dio	dieron

Past Subjunctive

diera	diéramos
dieras	dierais
diera	dieran

Imperfect Indicative

daba	dábamos
dabas	dabais
daba	daban

Future Indicative

daré	daremos
darás	daréis
dará	darán

Conditional Indicative

daría	daríamos
darías	daríais
daría	darían

DECIR

Present Indicative

digo	decimos
dices	decís
dice	dicen

Present Subjunctive

diga	digamos
digas	digáis
diga	digan

Preterite Indicative

dije	dijimos
dijiste	dijisteis
dijo	dijeron

Past Subjunctive

dijera	dijéramos
dijeras	dijerais
dijera	dijeran

(The imperfect indicative is regular.)

Future Indicative

diré	diremos
dirás	diréis
dirá	dirán

Conditional Indicative

diría	diríamos
dirías	diríais
diría	dirían

ESTAR

(The verb **andar** is conjugated the same as the verb **estar** in the preterite.)

estoy	estamos	esté	estemos
estás	estáis	estés	estéis
está	están	esté	estén
estuve	estuvimos	estuviera	estuviéramos
estuviste	estuvisteis	estuvieras	estuvierais
estuvo	estuvieron	estuviera	estuvieran
estaba	estábamos		
estabas	estabais		
estaba	estabam		

HACER

hago	hacemos	haga	hagamos
haces	hacéis	hagas	hagáis
hace	hacen	haga	hagan
hice	hicimos	hiciera	hiciéramos
hiciste	hicisteis	hicieras	hicierais
hizo	hicieron	hiciera	hicieran
haré	haremos	haría	haríamos
harás	haréis	harías	haríais
hará	harán	haría	harían

IR

voy	vamos	vaya	vayamos
vas	vais	vayas	vayáis
va	van	vaya	vayan
fui	fuimos	fuera	fuéramos
fuiste	fuisteis	fueras	fuerais
fue	fueron	fuera	fueran
iba	íbamos		
ibas	ibais		
iba	iban		

OÍR

oigo	oímos	oiga	oigamos
oyes	oís	oigas	oigáis
oye	oyen	oiga	oigan
oí	oímos	oyera	oyéramos
oíste	oísteis	oyeras	oyerais
oyó	oyeron	oyera	oyeran

Whenever the verb ending contains an unstressed **i** in the ending after a vowel in the stem, as in the third person singular and plural of the second and third conjugation infinitives (**-ió**), the **i** is changed to **y**. This happens with the verbs **creer**, **poseer**, and **leer** in the preterite: **creyó**, **leyó**. Notice that this will not happen with verbs that end with **-ar** because there is no **i in the third person singular or plural preterite endings**.

(The imperfect, future, and conditional forms of this verb are regular.)

PODER

Present Indicative

puedo	podemos
puedes	podéis
puede	pueden

Present Subjunctive

pueda	podamos
puedas	podáis
pueda	puedan

Preterite Indicative

pude	pudimos
pudiste	pudisteis
pudo	pudieron

Past Subjunctive

pudiera	pudiéramos
pudieras	pudierais
pudiera	pudieran

(The imperfect forms for this verb are regular.)

Future

podré	podremos
podrás	podréis
podrá	podrán

Conditional

podría	podríamos
podrías	podríais
podría	podrían

PONER

Present Indicative

pongo	ponemos
pones	ponéis
pone	ponen

Present Subjunctive

ponga	pongamos
pongas	pongáis
ponga	pongan

Preterite Indicative

puse	pusimos
pusiste	pusisteis
puso	pusieron

Past Subjunctive

pusiera	pusiéramos
pusieras	pusierais
pusiera	pusieran

(The imperfect forms of this verb are regular.)

Future

pondré	pondremos
pondrás	pondréis
pondrá	pondrán

Conditional

pondría	pondríamos
pondrías	pondríais
pondría	pondrían

QUERER

Present Indicative

quiero	queremos
quieres	queréis
quiere	quieren

Present Subjunctive

quiera	queramos
quieras	queráis
quiera	quieran

Preterite Indicative

quise	quisimos
quisiste	quisisteis
quiso	quisieron

Past Subjunctive

quisiera	quisiéramos
quisieras	quisierais
quisiera	quisieran

(The imperfect forms of this verb are regular.)

Future Indicative		Conditional Indicative	
querré	*querremos*	*querría*	*querríamos*
querrás	*querréis*	*querrías*	*querríais*
querrá	*querrán*	*querría*	*querrían*

SABER

Present Indicative		Present Subjunctive	
sé	*sabemos*	*sepa*	*sepamos*
sabes	*sabéis*	*sepas*	*sepáis*
sabe	*saben*	*sepa*	*sepan*

Preterite Indicative		Past Subjunctive	
supe	*supimos*	*supiera*	*supiéramos*
supiste	*supisteis*	*supieras*	*supierais*
supo	*supieron*	*supiera*	*supieran*

(The imperfect indicative forms of this verb are regular.)

Future Indicative		Conditional Indicative	
sabré	*sabremos*	*sabría*	*sabríamos*
sabrás	*sabréis*	*sabrías*	*sabríais*
sabrá	*sabrán*	*sabría*	*sabran*

SER

Present Indicative		Present Subjunctive	
soy	*somos*	*sea*	*seamos*
eres	*sois*	*seas*	*seáis*
es	*son*	*sea*	*sean*

Preterite Indicative		Past Subjunctive	
fui	*fuimos*	*fuera*	*fuéramos*
fuiste	*fuisteis*	*fueras*	*fuerais*
fue	*fueron*	*fuera*	*fueran*

Imperfect Indicative	
era	*éramos*
eras	*erais*
era	*eran*

(The future and conditional forms of this verb are regular.)

TENER

Present Indicative		Present Subjunctive	
tengo	*tenemos*	*tenga*	*tengamos*
tienes	*tenéis*	*tengas*	*tengáis*
tiene	*tienen*	*tenga*	*tengan*

Preterite Indicative		Past Subjunctive	
tuve	*tuvimos*	*tuviera*	*tuviéramos*
tuviste	*tuvisteis*	*tuvieras*	*tuvierais*
tuvo	*tuvieron*	*tuviera*	*tuvieran*

(The imperfect forms of this verb are regular.)

Future Indicative		Conditional Subjunctive	
tendré	*tendremos*	*tendría*	*tendramos*
tendrás	*tendréis*	*tendrías*	*tendríais*
tendrá	*tendrán*	*tendría*	*tendrían*

TRAER

Present Indicative		Present Subjunctive	
traigo	*traemos*	*traiga*	*traigamos*
traes	*traéis*	*traigas*	*traigáis*
trae	*traen*	*traiga*	*traigan*

VALER

Present Indicative		Present Subjunctive	
valgo	*valemos*	*valga*	*valgamos*
vales	*valéis*	*valgas*	*valgáis*
vale	*valen*	*valga*	*valgan*

Preterite Indicative		Past Subjunctive	
valí	*valimos*	*valiera*	*valiéramos*
valiste	*valisteis*	*valieras*	*valierais*
valió	*valieron*	*valiera*	*valieran*

(The imperfect forms of this verb are regular.)

Future Indicative		Conditional Indicative	
valdré	*valdremos*	*valdría*	*valdríamos*
valdrás	*valdréis*	*valdrías*	*valdríais*
valdrá	*valdrán*	*valdría*	*valdrían*

VENIR

Present Indicative		Present Subjunctive	
vengo	*venimos*	*venga*	*vengamos*
vienes	*venís*	*vengas*	*vengáis*
viene	*vienen*	*venga*	*vengan*

Preterite Indicative		Past Subjunctive	
vine	*vinimos*	*viniera*	*viniéramos*
viniste	*vinisteis*	*vinieras*	*vinierais*
vino	*vinieron*	*viniera*	*vinieran*

(The imperfect forms of this verb are regular.)

Future Indicative			Conditional Indicative	
vendré	*vendremos*		*vendría*	*vendríamos*
vendrás	*vendréis*		*vendrías*	*vendríais*
vendrá	*vendrán*		*vendría*	*vendrían*

VER

Present Indicative			Present Subjunctive	
veo	*vemos*		*vea*	*veamos*
ves	*veis*		*veas*	*veáis*
ve	*ven*		*vea*	*vean*

Preterite Indicative			Past Subjunctive	
vi	*vimos*		*viera*	*viéramos*
viste	*visteis*		*vieras*	*vierais*
vio	*vieron*		*viera*	*vieran*

Imperfect Indicative	
veía	*veíamos*
veías	*veíais*
veía	*veían*

(The future and conditional indicative forms of this verb are regular.)

3. STEM CHANGING VERBS

Verbs whose conjugated forms have a change in the stem (the radical) of the verb can be classified as follows: Class I, Class II, or Class III.

CLASS I

All of the verbs in Class I are **-ar** and **-er** infinitives. These verbs have a change **only** in the **present tense**. The change is from **e** to **ie** and **o** to **ue** in the first, second, and third person singular and the third person plural. It does not have a change in the first and second person plural because the stress is on the ending of the verb form, not on the stem of the verb. An example of these two changes is:

Present Indicative

pensar (ie)			*volver (ue)*	
pienso	*pensamos*		*vuelvo*	*volvemos*
piensas	*pensáis*		*vuelves*	*volvéis*
piensa	*piensan*		*vuelve*	*vuelven*

In the subjunctive forms, all the stem changes occur exactly as they do in the indicative, in all of the same persons and numbers:

Present Subjunctive

piense	*pensemos*		*vuelva*	*volvamos*
pienses	*penséis*		*vuelvas*	*volváis*
piense	*piensen*		*vuelva*	*vuelvan*

These verbs are indicated in dictionaries with the letters of the change in parentheses after the infinitive. Other verbs of this Class I change are: *sentarse, empezar, encontrar, contar, costar, despertar, atravesar, recomendar, comenzar, entender, volver, envolver, devolver, revolver, perder, defender, rogar, negar, nevar, oler, soltar, mover, mostrar, demostrar, llover, jugar.*

The verb *oler* is irregular in the present because an **h** is added to the beginning of the verb:

Present Indicative			Present Subjunctive	
huelo	olemos		**h**uela	olamos
hueles	oléis		**h**uelas	oláis
huele	**h**uelen		**h**uela	**h**uelan

The verb is regular in all other tenses and forms.

CLASS II

These stem changing verbs are all third conjugation verbs (they end with **-ir**). These verbs change **e** to **ie** and **o** to **ue** in the same persons and numbers as the Class I verbs (first, second, and third persons) in the present tense, but also have a change in the preterite forms. The preterite changes are **e** to **i** and **o** to **u** in the third person singular and plural.

Present Indicative

sentir (ie, i)			*dormir (ue, u)*	
s**ie**nto	sentimos		d**ue**rmo	dormimos
s**ie**ntes	sentís		d**ue**rmes	dormís
s**ie**nte	s**ie**nten		d**ue**rme	d**ue**rmen

Preterite Indicative

sentir (ie, i)			*dormir (ue, u)*	
sentí	sentimos		dormí	dormimos
sentiste	sentisteis		dormiste	dormisteis
s**i**ntió	s**i**ntieron		d**u**rmió	d**u**rmieron

In the present subjunctive the **e** changes to **ie** in the first, second, and third singular and the third plural forms, and changes from **e** to **i** in the first and second person plural:

Present Subjunctive

sentir (ie, i)			*dormir (ue, u)*	
s**ie**nta	s**i**ntamos		d**ue**rma	d**u**rmamos
s**ie**ntas	s**i**ntáis		d**ue**rmas	d**u**rmáis
s**ie**nta	s**ie**ntan		d**ue**rma	d**ue**rman

In the preterite forms the change occurs in all forms in the past subjunctive:

sentir (ie, i)			*dormir (ue, u)*	
s**i**ntiera	s**i**ntiéramos		d**u**rmiera	d**u**rmiéramos
s**i**ntieras	s**i**ntierais		d**u**rmieras	d**u**rmierais
s**i**ntiera	s**i**ntieran		d**u**rmiera	d**u**rmieran

Morir is the only other Class II verb in which **o** changes to **ue**. Other verbs that are similar to the above verbs are: *divertirse* and *arrepentir.*

The present participles (-**iendo**) will have the change in the stem of the participle, from **e** to **i** and **o** to **u**. For example: *sintiendo* and *durmiendo.*

CLASS III

These stem changing verbs all end in -**ir** and change **e** to **i** in the first, second, and third person singular, and third person plural in the present tense. The change in the preterite is from **e** to **i** in the third person singular and plural. There are no **o** to **ue** changes.

Present Indicative		Present Subjunctive	
		pedir (i, i)	
pido	*pedimos*	*pida*	*pidamos*
pides	*pedís*	*pidas*	*pidáis*
pide	*piden*	*pida*	*pidan*

Notice the same stem change occurs in all forms of the present subjunctive.

Preterite Indicative		Past Subjunctive	
pedí	*pedimos*	*pidiera*	*pidiéramos*
pediste	*pedisteis*	*pidieras*	*pidierais*
pidió	*pidieron*	*pidiera*	*pidieran*

The same stem change occurs in all forms of the past subjunctive.

Other verbs that are conjugated like *pedir* are *elegir, pedir (impedir, despedir), servir, vestir, reñir,* and *reír.*

The verb *reír* has the following changes in accent marks because it is a single syllable stem:

Present Indicative		Present Subjunctive	
río	*reímos*	*ría*	*riamos*
ríes	*reís*	*rías*	*riáis*
ríe	*ríen*	*ría*	*rían*

Preterite Indicative		Past Subjunctive	
reí	*reímos*	*rieran*	*riéramos*
reíste	*reísteis*	*rieras*	*rierais*
rio	*rieron*	*riera*	*rieran*

In the above forms notice that *reír* is a stem changing verb, so the stem contains an **i** in the third person singular and plural, and the accent falls in the normal position for the preterite -**ir** conjugations.

The present participles of Class III verbs will have the stem change of **e** to **i**: *pidiendo, riendo.*

4. ORTHOGRAPHIC VERBS

Verbs that have spelling changes because of the sequence of certain consonants, **c**, **g**, and **z** when followed by certain vowels, are called orthographic verbs.

The vowels **a** and **o** are hard vowels; **e** and **i** are soft vowels. When the letter **c** is followed by a hard vowel, the sound of **c** is the same as **k** in English. (*Sacar* in Spanish is pronounced as if the **c** were a **k**.) When the **c** is followed by a soft vowel the **c** has an **s** sound. (*Conocer* is pronounced as if the **c** were an **s** in the last syllable.) Therefore, wherever the initial vowel of an ending is the opposite of what is found in the infinitive, there are the following spelling changes:

1. **-car** infinitives. Change the **c** to **qu** when the ending begins with an **e** or an **i**:

Buscar

(preterite indicative, first person singular)

busqué	*buscamos*
buscaste	*buscasteis*
buscó	*buscaron*

(Notice that only the first person singular ending begins with the letter **e**, so it is the only one that changes spelling.)

Buscar

(present subjunctive, all forms)

busque	**busquemos**
busques	**busquéis**
busque	**busquen**

(Notice that all of these endings begin with the letter **e** so there is a change in the spelling. Notice also that there is no accent on the first person singular form.)

Some other common verbs that have this change are: *practicar, explicar, tocar, comunicar, ahorcar, abarcar, embarcar, arrancar, atacar, equivocar, provocar, destacar, marcar, ubicar, evocar, sacar,* and *volcar.*

2. **-cer** infinitives. Add a **z** before the **c**:

Conocer

(present indicative, first person singular only)

conozco	*conocemos*
conoces	*conocéis*
conoce	*conocen*

(Notice that all the other endings begin with the letter **e**, which is soft, so no other change is needed.)

Conocer

(present subjunctive, all forms)

conozca	*conozcamos*
conozcas	*conozcáis*
conozca	*conozcan*

(Notice that all of the endings in the subjunctive begin with a hard vowel, so all the forms change.)

Some other common verbs that have these changes are: *parecer, perecer, fallecer, crecer, nacer, merecer, establecer, padecer, obscurecer, anochecer, amanecer, acontecer, aborrecer, apetecer, aparecer, complacer, carecer, desaparecer, empobrecer, enriquecer, embrutecer, enrojecer, entristecer, envejecer, florecer, permanecer, pertenecer, torcer,* and *yacer.*

3. -ducir infinitives:

(In the present indicative, add a **z** before the **c** in the first person singular indicative.)

Traducir
(present indicative, first person singular)

traduzco	traducimos
traduces	traducís
traduce	traducen

(Notice that the first person singular indicative is the only ending that begins with a hard vowel, so it is the only one that adds **z** before **c**.)

Traducir
(present subjunctive, all forms)

traduzca	traduzcamos
traduzcas	traduzcáis
traduzca	traduzcan

(Notice that all the endings begin with the letter **a** so all of the forms add the **z**.)
In the preterite change the **c** to **j**:

Traducir
(preterite indicative, all forms)

traduje	tradujimos
tradujiste	tradujisteis
tradujo	tradujeron

Traducir
(past subjunctive, all forms)

tradujera	tradujéramos
tradujeras	tradujerais
tradujera	tradujeran

Some other common verbs that are conjugated like *traducir* are *producir, conducir, balbucir, lucir, deducir,* and *reducir.*

The letter **g** has two sounds depending on which letter follows it. When **g** is followed by the letter **a**, **o**, or **u** (as in *pagar*), it has a hard sound like the **g** in the English word *go.*

When the letter **g** is followed by the letter **e** or **i**, then the sound is soft, as in the English word, *general.*

4. -gar infinitives. Add a **u** before the endings with soft vowels:

Pagar
(first person singular in the preterite only)

pagué	pagamos
pagaste	pagasteis
pagó	pagaron

(Notice that the first person is the only ending that begins with the letter **e** in the preterite, so it is the only form that changes in this tense.)

Pagar
(present subjunctive, all forms)

pague	paguemos
pagues	paguéis
pague	paguen

(Notice that all of the present subjunctive endings begin with the letter **e** so all the forms add the **u** before the ending.)

Some other common verbs that are conjugated like *pagar* are *jugar, llegar, rogar, negar, ahogar, investigar, indagar, obligar, abrigar, castigar, interrogar, embriagar, propagar, entregar, cegar, colgar, desasosegar, fregar,* and *desplegar.*

5. **-ger** infinitives. Change the **g** to **j** before **a** and **o**:

Escoger
(present indicative, first person singular only)

escojo	escogemos
escoges	escogéis
escoge	escogen

(Notice that the first person singular is the only ending that begins with a hard vowel (**a** or **o**) so it is the only form that changes in the indicative.)

Escoger
(present subjunctive, all forms)

escoja	escojamos
escojas	escojáis
escoja	escojan

(Notice that all forms change because the endings all begin with the letter **a**.)

6. **-gir** infinitives. Change the **g** to **j** before **a** and **o**.

Dirigir
(present indicative, first person singular only)

dirijo	dirigimos
diriges	dirigís
dirige	dirigen

(Notice that these forms are the same as for the **-ger** ending infinitives for all the same reasons.)

Dirigir
(present subjunctive, all forms)

dirija	dirijamos
dirijas	dirijáis
dirija	dirijan

(Notice that these forms are the same as for the **-ger** verbs for all the same reasons.)

Some other common verbs that are conjugated like *dirigir* are *elegir, mugir,* and *exigir.*

7. **-guir** infinitives. Drop the **u** when the ending begins with a hard vowel:

Seguir
(present indicative, first person singular only)

si**g**o	seguimos
sigues	seguís
sigue	siguen

(Notice that the first person singular is the only ending that begins with a hard vowel, **o**, so it is the only form with a change.)

Seguir
(present subjunctive, all forms)

si**g**a	si**g**amos
si**g**as	si**g**áis
si**g**a	si**g**an

(Notice that all of the subjunctive endings begin with the letter **a**, so the **u** is dropped in all six forms.)

8. **-zar** infinitives. Change the **z** to **c** before endings that begin with soft vowels:

Empezar
(preterite indicative, first person singular only)

empe**c**é	empezamos
empezaste	empezasteis
empezó	empezaron

(Notice that the first person singular is the only ending that begins with a soft vowel, **e**.)

Empezar
(present subjunctive, all forms)

empie**c**e	empe**c**emos
empie**c**es	empe**c**éis
empie**c**e	empie**c**en

(Notice that these endings all begin with a soft vowel, **e**, so these forms all change to **c**.)

Some other common verbs that are conjugated like *empezar* are *analizar, utilizar, comenzar, almorzar, rezar, gozar, avergonzar, cruzar, cazar, destrozar, sollozar, tropezar, esforzar, adelgazar, calzar,* and *reemplazar.*

9. **-uir** infinitives. Add **y** before the ending when the stem is stressed:

Construir
(present indicative, all forms)

construyo	construimos
construyes	construís
construye	construyen

(Notice that in the first and second person plural, the first letter of the ending is stressed, so the forms do not add **y**.)

Construir
(present subjunctive, all forms)

*constru**ya***	*constru**yamos***
*constru**yas***	*constru**yáis***
*constru**ya***	*constru**yan***

(Notice that all forms change because the stem for the subjunctive is the first person singular, present indicative.)

Remember that for **-uir** ending infinitives in the preterite indicative, the unstressed **i** is changed to a **y**:

Construir
(preterite indicative)

construí	*construimos*
construiste	*construisteis*
*constru**yó***	*constru**yeron***

Some other common verbs that are conjugated like *construir* are *destruir, atribuir, influir, distribuir, sustituir, concluir, disminuir, excluir, fluir,* and *instruir.*

The following verbs have changes in the written diacritical marks because of the phonetics:

10. -uar infinitives. Add written accent marks when conjugated in order to retain the stress on the stem of the verb:

Present Indicative

Graduar
(first, second, and third person singular, and third person plural)

*grad**ú**o*	*graduamos*
*grad**ú**as*	*graduáis*
*grad**ú**a*	*grad**ú**an*

(Notice that the stress in the first and second person plural forms is on the first letter of the ending, so the accent mark is omitted.)

Present Subjunctive

Graduar
(first, second, and third person singular, and third person plural)

*grad**ú**e*	*graduemos*
*grad**ú**es*	*graduéis*
*grad**ú**e*	*grad**ú**en*

(Notice that these changes are in the same persons and number as the indicative forms.)

11. **-guar** adds a dieresis over the **u** (**ü**) when the ending begins with an **e**, in order to keep the hard sound of the letter **g** that is found in the infinitive:

Preterite Indicative

Averiguar
(first person singular)

averigüé	averiguamos
averiguaste	averiguasteis
averiguó	averiguaron

(Notice that only the first person singular ending begins with **e**.)

Present Subjunctive

Averiguar

averigüe	averigüemos
averigües	averigüéis
averigüe	averigüen

(Notice that since all of these endings begin with the letter **e**, the dieresis is written on the letter **u** to preserve the hard sound of the **g**.)

Other verbs like *averiguar* are *santiguar* and *apaciguar*.

12. **-iar** infinitives add an accent on the stem.

Present Indicative

Enviar

envío	enviamos
envías	enviáis
envía	envían

(Notice that these changes occur where the stress should fall on the stem, not on the first letter of the ending.)

Present Subjunctive

Enviar

envíe	enviemos
envíes	enviéis
envíe	envíen

(Notice that the accent is added in the same forms as in the present indicative.)

Use of the Indicative Mood

The indicative mood is used in main clauses, simple declarative statements, or questions where no doubt, uncertainty, or contrary-to-fact information is expressed. With the indicative mood, the simple present corresponds to several different meanings in English. For example: *hablo* = I **talk**, I **am talking**, I **do talk**, **Do** I **talk...?** and **Am** I **talking...?** In the past there are two simple tenses: the imperfect and the preterite. The imperfect is used to describe background information about an event, to describe an action that was going on at some time in the past without regard for when it began and/or ended, an action that was going on when something else happened, habitual action, repetitive action in the past, and for telling time. The preterite tense is used to stress the fact that an event took place in a finite period of time in the past.

An action expressed using the preterite is one that is completed, a definite beginning and/or ending to the action is communicated through the selection of the preterite tense. These actions are said to be narrated instead of described. The preterite is also used to relate events or actions in a series in the past. There are five verbs whose meanings are different in the preterite, based on the meaning implied from the selection of the tense. They are:

Conocer: in the preterite *conocer* means *to meet*.
in the imperfect *conocer* means *knew*.

For example:

Yo la conocí en la fiesta. (I met her at the party.)
Yo la conocía antes de la fiesta. (I knew her before the party.)

Querer: in the affirmative preterite *querer* means *to try*.
in the negative preterite *querer* means *to refuse*.
in the imperfect *querer* means *wished* or *wanted*.

For example:

Yo quise llamarte anoche. (I tried to call you last night.)
No quise llamarte otra vez. (I refused to call you again.)
Yo quería llamarte anoche. (I wanted to call you last night.)

Poder: in the preterite *poder* means *managed*, with accomplished action implied.
in the imperfect *poder* means *could*.

For example:

El chico pudo ir a la fiesta. (The boy managed to go to the party.)
El chico podía ir a la fiesta. (The boy was able to go to the party./
The boy could go to the party.)

Saber: in the preterite *saber* means *found out*.
in the imperfect *saber* means *knew*.

For example:

Ayer supe la dirección. (Yesterday I found out the address./
Yesterday I discovered the address.)
Ayer sabía la dirección. (Yesterday I knew the address.)

Tener: in the preterite *tener* means *received*.
in the imperfect *tener* means *had*.

For example:

Ayer tuve una carta. (Yesterday I received a letter.)
Ayer tenía una carta. (Yesterday I had a letter.)

The future is used to express actions that have not yet taken place. This tense is also used to express conjecture (the probability or supposition) that something will happen. This meaning is expressed in English with phrases such as *I wonder . . . , What can be . . . ?*, and the like.

The conditional tense expresses the same meaning in the past. This tense is frequently expressed by one of the several meanings of the verb *would*. (In English *would* can indicate a variety of other time frames, such as past, or provisional actions.) For example, *He would go when he had the time.*

The conditional tense in Spanish is also used to communicate probability or conjecture in the past. Its meanings correspond to the future of probability, except in the past instead of the present tense.

For example:

¿Qué hora será? (What time can it be?/I wonder what time it is?)

¿Qué hora sería? (What time could it be?/I wonder what time it was?)

The compound tenses are used to refer to a time frame immediately prior to a specified point in time. For example, the present perfect refers to a period of time immediately before the present, as in: *He has done his homework.* The pluperfect and pluscuamperfect (the imperfect and the preterite of *haber* + a past participle, respectively) refer to a period of time occurring before a specified point in time in the past.

For example:

Había hecho la tarea cuando sus amigos llegaron. (He had done his work when his friends arrived.)

The future perfect corresponds to a time occurring before another referenced point of time in the future, but after the present.

For example:

Ellos se habrán ido cuando yo llegue. (They will have gone by the time I arrive.) (My arrival will take place in the future, and they will go after that future time when I arrive.)

The Use of the Subjunctive

The conventions for using the subjunctive are changing; they vary according to location and who is using it, so there is a lot of variety in the way the subjunctive is used. The following guidelines for using the subjunctive are generally accepted as standard, if there is such a thing in Spanish grammar outside of the *Real Academia Española* in Spain.

The subjunctive mood expresses doubt, uncertainty, hypothetical situations, contrary to fact situations, and anything not considered by the speaker to be a fact. The subjunctive mood is used in **dependent** or **subordinate** clauses and some **independent** clauses.

In **independent** clauses the subjunctive is frequently used after *quizás* or *tal vez*, which can introduce either the indicative or the subjunctive, depending on the degree of conjecture or probability the speaker wishes to communicate. After the expression *Ojalá* the present or the past subjunctive is used. Often the past subjunctive is used as a softened request, a polite way to make a request of someone, such as in *¿Quisiera usted . . . ?* or *¿Pudiera usted . . . ?* The subjunctive is used in elliptical statements, clauses that begin with *Que*. There are a variety of ways to translate these expressions.

For example:

¡Que se divierta esta noche! (I hope you have a good time tonight!)

¡Que te vaya bien! (May you have a good trip!)

¡Que duermas bien! (Sleep tight! Get a good night's sleep!)

In subordinate clauses the subjunctive usually occurs in noun, adjective, or adverb clauses. As a rule, there is a change of subject; the subject of the verb in the main clause is different from the subject of the verb in the dependent clause. When there is no change of subject, an infinitive functions as the object of the verb.

For example:

Yo quiero leer el libro. (I want to read the book.)

Yo quiero que tú leas el libro. (I want you to read the book.)

Me alegro de estar aquí. (I am glad to be here.)

Me alegro que estés aquí. (I am glad you are here.)

In noun clauses the subjunctive is used when the verb in the main clause expresses a request, a wish, desire, approval, opposition, preference, suggestion, recommendation, advisability, necessity, obligation, or a command. Some common verbs of this type are *querer, pedir, desear, prohibir, mandar, rogar, permitir, dejar, impedir, sugerir, recomendar, exigir, oponer, requerir, aconsejar, hacer,* and *preferir.*

At times *decir* indicates volition (a request), and at other times it expresses facts. When it indicates a request, then the subjunctive is used. The other times, it is followed by the indicative.

For example:

Él dice que su hermano viene mañana. (He says that his brother is coming tomorrow.)

Él le dice a su hermano que venga mañana. (He tells his brother to come tomorrow.)

Notice that when the verb indicates a request, an indirect object pronoun is often used. The English translation of the sentence often uses an infinitive construction instead of the subjunctive.

After verbs that express an emotion, the subjunctive is used in the dependent clause. Some common verbs of this type are *alegrarse de, estar contento, lamentar, molestar, parecerle extraño, sentir,* and *arrepentir.*

After verbs that express doubt or denial the subjunctive is used. Common verbs of this type are *negar, dudar, no estar seguro,* and *no estar cierto.*

For example:

Dudo que vengan. (I doubt that they are coming.)

Niego que lo escriban. (I deny that they are writing it.)

When the negative of the above verbs is used, however, a certainty is expressed and the indicative is used.

For example:

No dudo que vienen. (I do not doubt that they are coming.)

No niego que lo escriben. (I do not deny that they are writing it.)

After an impersonal expression (the verb *ser* + an adjective), the subjunctive is used. The verb *ser* can be used in any tense, but it is always in the third person singular form, meaning *it is, it was, it will be,* etc.

For example:

Será preciso que lean. (It will be necessary for them to read.)

Puede ser que lo tengan. (It could be that they have it.)

Often an infinitive construction can be used in place of a subordinate clause containing the subjunctive. When the infinitive is used, the verb *ser* is preceded by an indirect object pronoun that is the subject of the verb in the subordinate clause in English.

For example:

Les fue imposible asistir. (It was impossible for them to come.)

Fue imposible que asistieran. (It was impossible for them to come./It was impossible that they come.)

The only impersonal expressions that require the indicative mood are those that express a certainty, such as *es obvio, es evidente, es claro, es seguro, es verdad, es cierto,* and *no cabe duda.* (Remember that the verb *es* can be in any other tense also: *es, fue, era, será sería, ha sido, había sido, habrá sido,* and *habría sido,* or even the present participle *siendo necesario.*)

For example:

Es obvio que les gusta leer. (It is obvious that they like to read.)

Fue obvio que les gustaba leer. (It was obvious that they liked to read.)

When any of the above impersonal expressions of certainty are negated, then the subjunctive is used since doubt is then implied.

For example:

No es obvio que les guste leer. (It is not obvious that they like to read.)

In adjective clauses, the subjunctive is used if the antecedent (the noun that the clause modifies) is indefinite, unknown to the speaker, uncertain, hypothetical, or nonexistent.

For example:

Buscan un apartamento que sea barato. (They are looking for an apartment that is inexpensive.)

Buscan un estudiante que pueda traducirlo. (They are looking for a student who can translate it.)

No encontraron ningún estudiante que pudiera leerlo. (They did not find any student who read it.)

No hay nadie que recuerde toda esa historia. (There is no one who remembers all of that story.)

When the antecedent is indefinite, the personal *a* is often omitted. The absence of a personal *a,* then frequently indicates the subjunctive is necessary.

For example:

Buscan un estudiante que sepa de ingeniería eléctrica. (They are looking for a student who knows electrical engineering.)

Buscan al estudiante que sabe de ingeniería eléctrica. (They are looking for the student who knows electrical engineering.)

The construction *por ... que* indicates the subjunctive. The phrase is expressed several ways in English.

For example:

> *Por rico que sea, no me casaré con él.* (No matter how rich he may be, I will not marry him.)

> *Me quedaré hasta la conclusión, por tarde que sea.* (I will stay until the end, however late that may be.)

> *Por mucho que se quejaran, los estudiantes hicieron el trabajo.* (For all the complaining they did, the students still did the work.)

In adverbial clauses the kind of conjunction determines whether the subjunctive is used or not. After the following conjunctions, the subjunctive is always used, regardless of the tenses of the verbs: *para que, con tal que, a menos que, a ser que, a fin de que, antes de que, sin que, a no ser que,* and *en caso de que.* The preposition *de* in most of the above adverbial conjunctions is normally omitted. These conjunctions, except for *antes de que,* introduce clauses of concession, proviso, or purpose.

For example:

> *El chico hizo la tarea para que pudiera ir a la fiesta.* (The boy did the chores so that he could go to the park.)

> *Ella dijo que vendría con tal que viniera su compañera.* (She said she would come provided that her companion came.)

> *Salieron sin que los viéramos.* (They left without our seeing them.)

Notice the variety of ways that the subjunctive is expressed in English, especially the last example where English uses a gerund, and Spanish uses the subjunctive.

Two adverbial conjunctions that take either the subjunctive or the indicative depending on the meaning desired by the speaker are: *de manera que* and *de modo que.* The selection depends on the kind of information that is being communicated.

For example:

> *El conferenciante habló de manera que todos los delegados lo oyeron.* (The speaker spoke so that the delegates understood him./The speaker spoke in such a way that the delegates understood him.) (Whichever the meaning, the delegates understood him.)

> *El conferenciante hablo de manera que todos los delegados le oyeran.* (The speaker spoke in a way that the delegates could understand him.)
> (It is unknown whether the delegates understood him or not.)

Aunque and *a pesar de que* also can take either the subjunctive or the indicative according to what the speaker wishes to communicate. The selection of the subjunctive expresses uncertainty about the facts in the mind of the speaker, and the indicative expresses the opposite meaning.

For example:

> *Aunque lloverá mañana, iremos.* (Although it will rain tomorrow, we will go.) (The speaker is reasonably certain it will rain.)

> *Aunque llueva mañana, iremos.* (Although it may rain tomorrow, we will go.) (The speaker makes no statement about whether it will rain or not.)

In adverbial clauses of time, the sequence of tenses is especially important. After the following adverbial conjunctions, use the subjunctive if the verbs in the independent clause are in the future (the action has not yet taken place), and the subjunctive in the subordinate clause: *en cuanto, tan pronto como, cuando, después, hasta que, mientras, una vez que*. The subjunctive is used because since these events have not taken place yet, they cannot be considered factual.

For example:

> *Pídales que se queden hasta que volvamos.* (Ask them to remain until we return.)
>
> *Te veremos tan pronto como llegues.* (We will see you as soon as you get here.)
>
> *Lo agradecerá cuando venga.* (They will thank him when he comes.)

When the action or event takes place in the past, the indicative is used. When the above sentences, for example, are expressed in the past, notice that the subjunctive is not used, since once the event has occurred, it is a fact, or is perceived as fact by the speaker.

For example:

> *Les pidió que se quedaran hasta que volvimos.* (He asked them to stay until we returned. OR We did return.)

The subjunctive is still used in the dependent noun clause after *pedir*, but after the adverbial conjunction, *hasta que*, the indicative is used.

For example:

> *Te vimos tan pronto como llegaste.* (We saw you as soon as you arrived. OR We saw you return; it is a fact.)
>
> *Lo agradecí cuando vino.* (I thanked him when he came. OR He came; it is a fact.)

The use of the subjunctive after *si* depends upon the tense of the verb, also, and the construction in which it occurs. After *si*, the present subjunctive is so seldom used that it is not likely to appear on the exam. (The exception would be when *si* means *cuando*.) When the present or future indicative is used, *si* is followed by the present indicative, or future.

For example:

> *Le pago si hace el trabajo.* (I pay him if he works.) (The speaker does not know if he will work or not, but when he works he gets paid.)

Compare this sentence with:

> *Le pagaré cuando trabaje.* (I will pay him when he works.) (I will pay him when he works, but he has not worked yet. I have not paid him yet.)
>
> *Si hará el trabajo, le pagaré.* (If he will do the work, I will pay him.)

When the sentence structure indicates an *if-then* statement, then the **past** subjunctive is used in the *if* portion of the sentence, or in both clauses. The subjunctive is used in the *if* portion of the sentence because the information expressed in that kind of clause is contrary to fact, which requires the use of the subjunctive.

For example:

> *Le pagaría si trabajara.* (I would pay him if he would work.)

(This sentence structure, using the conditional implies very strongly that he will not work. The information communicated through the use of this grammar is that it is uncertain whether he will work or not. The meaning implied is *if he would work, which he probably would not do,* meaning that his working is contrary to fact.)

In the past perfect (pluperfect and pluscuamperfect), the helping verb *haber* is conjugated in the appropriate tenses.

For example:

Le habría pagado si hubiera trabajado. (I would have paid him if he had worked.)

Look at the following sequence of tenses to help fix in mind the progression from what is perceived as fact by the speaker, to hypothetical statements (*if-then* sentences.)

Si tengo dinero, voy a la fiesta. (If I have money I will go to the party.)

Si tenía dinero, iría a la fiesta. (If I had money, I would go to parties.)

Si tuviera dinero, iría a la fiesta. (If I had the money, I would go to the party.)

Si hubiera tenido dinero, habría ido a la fiesta. (If I had had money, I would have gone to the party.)

Another case where the past subjunctive is always used because it expresses contrary to fact information is after the expression *como si*, meaning *as if*. Even in English this structure uses the English equivalent of the subjunctive.

For example:

Les habló como si fueran niñitos. (He spoke to them as if they were children.)

Les habla como si fueran niñitos. (He speaks to them as if they were children.)

Les hablará como si fueran niñitos. (He will speak to them as if they were children.)

Les ha hablado como si fueran niños. (He has spoken to them as if they were children.)

Les había hablado como si hubieran sido niños. (He had spoken to them as if they had been children.)

The other instance in which the subjunctive is used is in imperative sentences—commands.

A command is really a portion of a sentence in which the speaker means *I want that . . .* or *I order that . . . .* For example, in the following cases, notice how the part of the sentence that is in parentheses actually expresses what is the main clause, followed by the dependent noun clause, with the subjunctive used after the verb that expresses volition.

(Yo quiero que usted) Diga la verdad. (I want that you) Tell the truth.

(Yo mando que usted) No revele el secreto. (I order that you) Do not reveal the secret.

(Yo exijo que ustedes) Lean el libro. (I require that you) Read the book.

(Yo pido que nosotros) Aceptemos su oferta. (I request that we) Accept their offer.

The one difference between the simple declarative sentence that uses the subjunctive in the dependent noun clause, and the imperative sentence is that the location of pronouns is different for imperative sentences.

For example:

Dígamelo. (Tell it to me.)

The pronouns are added to the end of the verb since it is a command form:

(Yo quiero que usted) me lo diga. (I want that you) tell it to me.

There is a command form for every person and number except the first person singular. The subjunctive is used for commands in all forms except for the second person singular and plural affirmative commands. The following shows which verb form to use for which command.

Second Person Singular, Tú

Affirmative form: the third person singular **present indicative**

For example:

Entrega (tú) los papeles. (Turn in the papers.)

Negative form: the second person, singular **present subjunctive**
For example:

No entregues (tú) los papeles. (Do not turn in the papers.)

Third Person Singular, Usted

Affirmative and negative forms: the third person singular, **present subjunctive**
For example:

Entregue Ud. los papeles. (Turn in the papers.)
No entregue Ud. los papeles. (Do not turn in the papers.)

First Person Plural, Nosotros, Nosotras

Affirmative and negative forms: the first person plural, **present subjunctive**
For example:

Entreguemos los papeles. (Let's turn in the papers.)

When the reflexive pronoun, **nos**, is added to affirmative forms, the final *s* of the ending is dropped.
For example:

Sentémonos. (Let's sit down.)

Frequently the expression *Vamos a + infinitive* is used in place of the subjunctive command form. The one exception to this rule for formation of the *nosotros* command is the verb *irse* in the affirmative, which is simply *Vámonos.* (The negative form conforms to the rule: *No nos vayamos.*)

Second Person Plural, Vosotros, Vosotras

Affirmative form: the infinitive with *d* in place of *r* of the infinitive ending
For example:

Entregad los papeles. (Turn in the papers.)

When the reflexive pronoun is added to the affirmative form, the *d* is not used. Simply take off the *r* from the infinitive and add the pronoun, *os*.

For example:

Acostaos. (Go to bed.)

When the infinitive is an -**ir** verb, an accent is written over the **i** of the infinitive ending when the pronoun is attached.

For example:

Servíos. (Serve yourselves.)

The exception to this rule is the verb *ir*, whose second person plural form, affirmative, is **Idos**.

Negative form: the second person plural of the **present subjunctive**
For example:
No entreguéis los papeles. (Do not turn in the papers.)

Third Person Plural, Ustedes

Affirmative and negative forms: the third person, plural, **present subjunctive**
For example:

Entreguen Uds. los papeles. (Turn in the papers.)
No entreguen Uds. los papeles. (Do not turn in the papers.)

All of the above mentioned forms are for regular, stem changing, and spelling change verbs. There are, however, different forms for some irregular verbs.

For the second person singular irregular verbs, the affirmative and negative forms are:

Infinitive	Affirmative	Negative
decir	di	no digas
hacer	haz	no hagas
ir	vé	no vayas
poner	pon	no pongas
salir	sal	no salgas
ser	sé	no seas
tener	ten	no tengas
valer	vale	no valgas
venir	ven	no vengas

For the third person singular and plural commands, the irregular forms are derived from the first person, singular, present indicative. That means that the only forms that cannot be determined from the present tense are those irregular first person singular forms that end in -**oy**. The irregular third person forms for these kinds of verbs are:

dar	doy	dé usted, den ustedes
estar	estoy	esté usted, estén ustedes
ir	voy	vaya usted, vayan ustedes
saber	sé	sepa usted, sepan ustedes
ser	soy	sea usted, sean ustedes

THE PAST PARTICIPLE

When the past participle functions verbally, the ending is invariable; it always ends in **-o.** It will always follow the verb *haber* when it functions as a part of a verbal form. When the past participle functions as an adjective, however, after the verbs *ser*, *estar*, or any other verb, then the ending must agree in gender and in number with the noun to which it refers.

Some verbs have irregular past participles. They are:

abrir	*abierto*
cubrir	*cubierto*
decir	*dicho*
escribir	*escrito*
hacer	*hecho*
imprimir	*impreso*
morir	*muerto*
poner	*puesto*
soler	*suelto*
ver	*visto*
volver	*vuelto*

Any of the compound forms of these verbs will take an irregular past participle form, such as *descubrir, desdecir, predecir, describir, deshacer, proponer, componer, satisfacer, devolver, envolver, revolver, prever*, etc.

Past participles also commonly function as absolutes. This use is found mainly in written language.

For example:

Determinada la ruta que había de seguir, salieron. (Having decided on the route they were to follow, they left.)

In conversation the past participle can follow the verb *tener* to indicate that something is done.

For example:

Tengo hecha la tarea para mañana. (I have the chores for tomorrow done.)

The Passive Voice

The structure of the passive voice is almost a formula. The agent in the true passive voice is either expressed or strongly implied. Sometimes the difference between the selection of the true passive and the substitute for the passive depends on what the speaker wishes to emphasize—either the fact that the act was done **by** someone, or some aspect of the action itself.

The structure for the true passive is:

TO BE + PAST PARTICIPLE + POR + THE AGENT

For example:

La tienda fue cerrada por el gerente. (The store was closed by the manager.)

The agent is the person acting upon the subject; the agent does the action.

Notice that in Spanish the object comes before the verb. Also notice that the past participle agrees in gender and number with the noun to which it refers: *la tienda* is the antecedent for *cerrada*.

When the agent is not emphasized, or when the subject is a nonspecific subject (often expressed as *one, they,* or *you* in English), it is possible to use the pronoun **se** and the third person singular or plural of the verb instead of the true passive construction.

For example:

> *Se cierran las tiendas a las cinco.* (The stores are closed at five o'clock. OR They close the stores at five o'clock.)

Another way to express this in Spanish is with the third person plural.
For example:

> *Dicen que el español es fácil.* (They say that Spanish is easy.)
>
> *Se dice que el español es fácil.* (They say that Spanish is easy. OR It is said that Spanish is easy.)

This construction is not to be confused with the use of the past participle with the verb *estar*, which indicates resultant action. In this case the past participle also agrees in gender and number with the noun it modifies.

For example:

> *La tienda estaba cerrada cuando llegué y tuve que volver a casa.* (The store was closed when I arrived and I had to return home.)

Present Participles

When the present participle is used as an adverb in Spanish, it is called a *gerundio*. The term has not been used in this book to avoid any confusion about what precisely is meant by a *gerundio*, or a present participle. Remember that in English a gerund is a present participle that functions as a noun. (For example: Running is good for your health.) Remember that in Spanish the present participle, or *gerundio*, can never function as a noun. In its place an infinitive is used. (*El correr es muy saludable.*) The present participle is formed by removing the infinitive ending and adding **-ando** for **-ar** verbs and **-iendo** for **-er** and **-ir** verbs. For verbs that end in **-er** or **-ir**, the **i** changes to **y** when the unstressed **i** comes between two other vowels.

For example:

leer	*leyendo*
creer	*creyendo*
construir	*construyendo*
traer	*trayendo*
ir	*yendo*

Class II and III stem changing verbs have a change in the stem in the present participle. These verbs will change the **e** or **u** to an **i** or **u**, respectively.

For example:

dormir	*du**rmiendo***
morir	*m**uriendo***
sentir	*s**intiendo***
reír	*r**iendo***
vestir	*v**istiendo***
pedir	*p**idiendo***

Verbally, the only use of the present participle is as a part of the progressive forms. *Estar* followed by the present participle is the progressive form. (See below.)

When this part of speech functions verbally, the ending in invariable; it always ends in -**o**. The present participle never functions as an adjective (it can never modify a noun). Even when the present participle is used adverbially, it is invariable.

For example:

Estábamos jugando al fútbol ayer. (We were playing soccer yesterday.)

In the adverbial usage, the present participle tells how something is being done.
For example:

El chico salió corriendo porque ya era tarde. (The boy left running because it was already late.)

The present participle frequently follows verbs of perception, such as *oír, ver, percibir, sentirse, mirar, escuchar,* etc. In these cases the word describes more about the verb.
For example:

Oí al gato maullando fuera de la puerta cerrada. (I heard the cat mewing outside the closed door.)

The verbs *continuar* and *seguir* take the present participle normally to complete their meaning.
For example:

Los chicos siguieron cantando dulcemente. (The boys continued singing sweetly.)
Continuamos divirtiéndonos toda la noche. (We continued to have a good time all night.)

At times the present participle can also provide explanatory or parenthetical information.
For example:

Temí que mi hermano, no estando yo presente, cometiera algún disparate. (I feared that my brother, I not being present, would commit some blunder.)
Pasando ayer por el mercado, encontré a mi antigua novia. (Going through the market yesterday, I met my former girlfriend.)

Progressive Forms

The progressive forms are always expressed with *estar + the present participle.*

The verb *estar* is conjugated in any desired tense and the present participle is added. These forms are not used as much in Spanish normally as they are in English because the simple tenses in Spanish are translated into the progressive as one of the meanings. The progressive forms are used to underscore the fact that something is actually in the process of taking place.

For example:

Estoy leyendo este libro en este momento. (I am reading this book at this moment.)

Estaba leyendo cuando entraron los chicos. (He was reading when the children came in.)

Estará volando a la Florida mientras tú manejarás. (He will be flying to Florida while you will be driving.)

The one instance where the Spanish will not use the progressive form where English does is in a time expression using *hacer.* What in English is the present perfect progressive becomes a simple tense in Spanish.

For example:

*Hace unos meses que **estudio** el español.* (I **have been studying** Spanish for a few months.)

***Hacía** unos meses que estudiaba el español.* (He **had been studying** Spanish for a few months.)

ADVERBS

Adverbs modify verbs, adjectives, or other adverbs. The ending **-mente** is added to the adjectives that end with **-e** or any consonant.

For example:

general—generalmente

frecuente—frecuentemente

When the adjective ends with **-o**, then the ending **-mente** is added to the feminine form of the adjective.

For example:

rápido—rápidamente

When two adverbs are used together, the first adverb in the feminine form of the word and the ending **-mente** is added to the second adverb only.

For example:

Los rayos solares del amanecer se abrieron paso lenta y brillantemente al este.

Frequently adverbs are replaced by prepositional phrases.

For example:

generalmente	*por lo general*
cuidadosamente	*con cuidado*
cortésmente	*con cortesía*

GRAMMAR PRACTICE

The AP Spanish Language and Culture exam does not test grammar individually, and therefore the following practice activities are not essential to your preparation for the examination. Therefore, they should be considered optional activities meant to reinforce your understanding of grammar and will not have a negative impact on your preparation for the examination if skipped.

On the following pages you will find some exercises to help you review grammar. The answers are explained, so you can learn from your mistakes. Keep track of the kinds of mistakes you make and then go back to a pertinent section of grammar and check it.

TIPS FOR GRAMMAR REVIEW EXERCISES

- Scan the whole passage.
- Determine what part of speech is needed.
- If a verb is needed, find the subject in the passage, then determine what tense and mood to use.
- If the word is an adjective, find the noun to which it refers and apply the noun's gender and number to the adjective.
- If the word is an adjective, find the noun to which it refers and apply the noun's gender and number to the adjective.

EXERCISES AND ANSWERS

> **DIRECTIONS:** On the numbered line corresponding to a numbered blank in the selection, write the correct form of the word needed to complete the passage logically and grammatically. All spelling and all diacritical marks must be correct. You may use more than one word. You must write the answer on the line after the number, even if you do not change the root word in any way. You have seven minutes to read and write your responses.

GROUP ONE

El caso es que la princesa, bella, brillante y sonriente no es feliz. En verdad, tiene que esforzarse para parecer tan sonriente. Y ahora tiene que soportar que ___(1)___ sus tristezas ___(2)___ que la ___(3)___ a desear la paz. Es mucha carga ___(4)___ responsabilidad, y los discursos de bienvenida, y toda la agenda que le deja poco tiempo para vivir. Pero siempre se comporta como si no ___(5)___ nada. A veces, viéndola tratar de aparecer elegante y ___(6)___ , se pregunta si tendría ___(7)___ rasgo de acidez ___(8)___ . Hay que preguntarse si, por toda la riqueza que ___(9)___ como princesa, de veras ___(10)___ la pena.

1. _____ (publicar)
2. _____ (profundo)
3. _____ (llevar)
4. _____ (tanto)
5. _____ (pasar)
6. _____ (sencillo)
7. _____ (alguno)
8. _____ (disimulado)
9. _____ (tener)
10. _____ (valer)

Answers and Answer Explanations for Group One

1. *publiquen*   *Publicar* is an orthographic verb. The subjunctive is used because this is a dependent noun clause after a verb of volition.
2. *profundas*   This adjective modifies *tristezas*, a feminine plural noun.
3. *llevan*   The subject is *tristezas*. This verb occurs in an adjective clause with a known antecedent, so the indicative is correct.
4. *tanta*   This comparative structure requires that the adjective agree in gender and number with the noun, *responsabilidad*. All words that end in *-dad* are feminine.
5. *pasara*   The past subjunctive must always be used after *como si*. The subject of *pasara* is *ella*, the same subject as for *se comporta*.
6. *sencilla*   The adjective agrees with *ella*. The referent is given in the direct object pronoun at the end of the verb form: *viéndola*.

7. *algún* This adjective is apocopated, and an accent is written over the *u* in the last syllable. No credit is given if the accent is not written on the vowel.

8. *disimulado* This adjective modifies *rasgo*, not *acidez*, so the masculine singular form is used.

9. *tenga* The subjunctive is used because this is a dependent adjective clause and the antecedent, *riqueza,* is indefinite. In the adjective clauses look for the construction *por* + (adjective) + *que . . .* to indicate to you to use the subjunctive.

10. *vale* The present indicative is used because the present subjunctive is not frequently used after *si*.

GROUP TWO

Me estuve muy quieta, ____(1)____ en la cama, mirando recelosa alrededor, asombrada del retorcido mechón de mi propio cabello que resaltaba oscuramente contra mi hombro. Habituándome a la penumbra, ____(2)____ , uno a uno, los desconchados de la pared, las grandes enzarzadas de la cama, como serpientes, dragones o misteriosas figuras que apenas me atrevía a mirar. Incliné el cuerpo cuanto ____(3)____ hacia la mesilla, para coger el vaso de agua ____(4)____ , y entonces, en el vértice de la pared, descubrí una hilera de hormigas que ____(5)____ por el muro. Solté el vaso que se ____(6)____ al caer, y me ____(7)____ de nuevo entre las sábanas, tapándome la cabeza. No me decidía a sacar ni ____(8)____ mano, y así estuve mucho rato, ____(9)____ los labios. Hice recorrer mi imaginación como por ____(10)____ bosque y jardín desconocidos hasta tranquilizarme.

1. _____ (sentado)

2. _____ (localizar)

3. _____ (poder)

4. _____ (tibio)

5. _____ (trepar)

6. _____ (romper)

7. _____ (hundir)

8. _____ (uno)

9. _____ (morderse)

10. _____ (alguno)

Answers and Answer Explanations for Group Two

1. *sentada* This past participle functions as an adjective and the antecedent is feminine, indicated by the ending of the previous adjective: *quieta.*

2. *localicé Localizar* is an orthographic verb. The preterite indicative is used because the action occurred in a defined point of time in the past. If no accent is used, no credit is given, since the verb without the accent would be a present subjunctive form.

3. *pude* The preterite indicative is used here because the action takes place in a defined point in time in the past. The meaning of the preterite of *poder* is *managed,* or *was able to.*

4. *tibia* This adjective modifies *agua*, which is a feminine noun, even though in the singular form a masculine article, *el*, is used.

5. *trepaban* The imperfect indicative is used here to describe an action. The narrator is telling what the ants *were doing*, in which case the imperfect is indicated.

6. *rompió* The preterite indicative is used because the action occurred at a specific point of time in the past. The action is narrated, not described.

7. *hundí* The preterite indicative is used because the action takes place at a specific point in time in the past. The action is narrated.

8. *una* *Mano* is a feminine noun, requiring the feminine form of the indefinite article, *una*.

9. *mordiéndome* The present participle is used as an adverb, showing the attitude or how the narrator was huddled under the sheets on the bed. Remember to use the first person singular reflexive pronoun to agree with the subject of the verb *estuve*.

10. *algún* The indefinite adjective *alguno* is shortened before masculine singular nouns, such as *bosque*. Notice that there is an accent written on the final syllable. *Algunos* is correct if the adjective refers to *jardines* and *bosques*.

GROUP THREE

Su agradable y delicado perfume, ___(1)___ a una eficacia indiscutible ___(2)___ inigualable, han sido, sin lugar a dudas, las claves del éxito de este producto y el motivo de que millones de personas ___(3)___ tanto tiempo ___(4)___ en este producto, que lejos de ser una moda o un *invento* es EL DESODORANTE. Toda una línea de higiene personal ha sido ___(5)___ al amparo de la imagen de marca más fuerte en el mundo. La ___(6)___ fidelidad de marca de que goza este producto, lo ha situado en un privilegiado ___(7)___ puesto que siempre ha intentado ___(8)___ alcanzado por las restantes marcas de la competencia. Desde su creación, hace ya más de 50 años, este producto ___(9)___ liderando el mercado nacional. ___(10)___ Ud. en nuestro producto.

1. _____
   (unido)
2. _____
   (y)
3. _____
   (llevar)
4. _____
   (confiar)
5. _____
   (crear)
6. _____
   (grande)
7. _____
   (primero)
8. _____
   (ser)
9. _____
   (venir)
10. _____
    (Confiar)

Answers and Answer Explanations for Group Three

1. *unido* The adjective agrees with the noun *perfume*, not with the noun's adjectives: *agradable* and *delicado*. The following sentence makes clear that the qualities of the perfume, combined with the effectiveness of the product, are the keys to the success of the product.

2. *e* The conjunction *y* changes because the initial letter of the following word is *i*, *inigualable*.

3. *lleven*   The present subjunctive is used because in the adverbial clause motivation, or purpose, is expressed.

4. *confiando*   The present participle is used as an adverb to describe how people are using so much time.

5. *creada*   The feminine form of the past participle is used because it is the object of *ser*. It agrees with the subject of *ha sido*, which is *línea*.

6. *gran*   The adjective, *grande*, is apocopated before singular nouns, such as *fidelidad*. Use the apocopated (shortened) form with both masculine and feminine singular nouns.

7. *primer*   The adjective, *primero*, is apocopated before masculine singular nouns, such as *puesto*.

8. *ser*   The infinitive is used because it is the object of the verb: *ha intentado*.

9. *viene*   The present indicative is used because the verb occurs in the main clause with an expression of time.

10. *Confíe*   The command form is indicated by the placement of *Ud.* after the verb. Notice the accent written on the *i*.

GROUP FOUR

Al sol, ya se sabe, hay que ____(1)____ con las espaldas bien ____(2)____. ____(3)____ imprudencia nos está ____(4)____ , pues este astro, que ____(5)____ una memoria de elefante, puede ____(6)____ factura cuando menos nos lo esperamos. Sirve que nosotros lo ____(7)____ en cuenta al comprar un bronceador. Vale que ____(8)____ uno que nos____(9)____ seguridad total de los efectos de los rayos ultravioleta. Ahora____(10)____ del sol veranal traspasa cuestiones estéticas.

1. _____
   (acercarse)

2. _____
   (cubierto)

3. _____
   (Ninguno)

4. _____
   (permitido)

5. _____
   (poseer)

6. _____
   (pasarse)

7. _____
   (tener)

8. _____
   (buscar)

9. _____
   (ofrecer)

10. _____
    (protegerse)

Answers and Answer Explanations for Group Four

1. *acercarse*   Although the verb is preceded by *que*, in this case it forms part of the expression *hay que*, which requires the infinitive.

2. *cubiertas*   The past participle is used as an adjective and refers to the noun, *espaldas*.

3. *Ninguna* The negative indefinite adjective refers to a feminine noun, *imprudencia*. The feminine form of this adjective is never shortened.

4. *permitida* The past participle is used as an adjective and refers to the subject of the verb *está*, which is *imprudencia*.

5. *posee* The present indicative is used because it occurs in an adjective clause referring to a definite antecedent, *astro*, which in turn is another name for *el sol*.

6. *pasarnos* The infinitive is used because it is the object of the verb *puede*. The first person plural indirect object pronoun is used because the first person plural subject is indicated in the following verb: *esperamos*.

7. *tengamos* The present subjunctive is used because it occurs in a dependent noun clause after an impersonal expression: *sirve que*.

8. *busquemos* The present subjunctive is used because it occurs in a dependent noun clause after an impersonal expression: *Vale que*. Notice that not all impersonal expressions begin with the verb *ser*. If you can determine that the subject of the verb is *it* and it has no specific antecedent, you can always recognize when to use the subjunctive after an impersonal expression.

9. *ofrezca* The present subjunctive is used because it occurs in a dependent adjective clause in which the antecedent is indefinite, *uno*, which in turn refers to *un bronceador*.

10. *protegernos* The infinitive is used because it is the subject of the verb *traspasa*. The first person plural object pronoun is used because *our* reactions to the power of the sun's rays has been the topic of the passage.

GROUP FIVE

Estas Olimpiadas prepárate a ganar. __(1)__ dos códigos de barras de __(2)__ producto que tú __(3)__ a Marca X al Apartado 999, 38565 Madrid, y un fantástico Lulu de Oro puede ser tuyo. O bien __(4)__ millón de pesetas. Los sorteos se __(5)__ ante notario el treinta de junio, el treinta de julio y el __(6)__ de septiembre del año próximo. ¡Anímate! Tienes mucho que ganar. Y __(7)__ que __(8)__ más cartas __(9)__, más fácil será ganar. No __(10)__ escapar tu Lulu. Es una ocasión de oro.

1. _____
   (Enviar)

2. _____
   (cualquiera)

3. _____
   (querer)

4. _____
   (uno)

5. _____
   (celebrar)

6. _____
   (primero)

7. _____
   (recordar)

8. _____
   (cuánto)

9. _____
   (mandar)

10. _____
    (dejar)

Answers and Answer Explanations for Group Five

1. *Envía*   The affirmative familiar singular command form of the verb is indicated by the use of the second person singular command in the first sentence, *prepárate*. Do not be confused because the object in the sentence comes first. This stylistic device, inverting the word order of the sentence, simply emphasizes the noun, *Olimpíadas*.

2. *cualquier*   This indefinite adjective is apocopated before nouns of both genders.

3. *quieras*   The present subjunctive is used because the verb occurs in a dependent adjective clause after an indefinite antecedent: *un producto*.

4. *un*   The apocopated form of *uno* is required before the number *millón*. Notice that *millón* takes the preposition *de* when it is followed by a noun.

5. *celebrarán*   This verb is the *se* substitute for the passive voice. *Los sorteos* is plural, so the verb is in the third person plural.

6. *primero*   The ordinal number for the first day of the month is not apocopated.

7. *recuerda*   The affirmative familiar singular command form is required because the context of the verb in the selection and the meaning of the word indicate an instruction to the reader.

8. *cuántas*   The interrogative form agrees with *cartas*.

9. *mandes*   The present subjunctive is used because it occurs in an adjective clause referring to *cuántas cartas*, an indefinite antecedent.

10. *dejes*   The verb is a negative familiar singular command, which is indicated by the context of the verb.

GROUP SIX

El Real Decreto dice: *El producto cosmético indicará la fórmula cualitativa y cuantitativa de las substancias* ____(1)____ *presencia* ____(2)____ *en la denominación del producto o en su publicidad.* ____(3)____ quiere decir que todos los productos en cuya confección ____(4)____ materias activas naturales provenientes de plantas deben especificar claramente el porcentaje de materia activa en sus etiquetas, estuches y publicidad. Consecuente con esto, y con ____(5)____ más de 75 años ____(6)____ con extractos naturales de plantas, le informamos que nuestros productos tienen un porcentaje exacto porque en nuestra opinión, ____(7)____ porcentajes son los necesarios para que ____(8)____ materias activas ____(9)____ el beneficio natural esperado de la planta. ____(10)____ la forma de averiguar la materia activa que cada producto contiene, usted debe decidir lo que más le conviene.

1. _____
   (cuyo)

2. _____
   (anunciarse)

3. _____
   (Este)

4. _____
   (intervenir)

5. _____
   (nuestro)

6. _____
   (trabajar)

7. _____
   (ese)

8. _____
   (dicho)

9. _____
   (realizar)

10. _____
   (Conocer)

Answers and Answer Explanations for Group Six

1. *cuya*   This possessive agrees with *presencia*, not *sustancias*.
2. *se anuncie*   The present subjunctive is used because it occurs in an adjective clause referring to the indefinite antecedent *presencia*.
3. *Esto*   The neuter demonstrative pronoun is used here because *This* refers to the whole idea expressed in the previous sentence.
4. *intervengan*   The present subjunctive is used because the verb occurs in a dependent adjective clause with an indefinite antecedent *confección*. The subject is *materias*.
5. *nuestros*   This possessive modifies *años* so it is masculine plural.
6. *trabajando*   This present participle tells how an action was done.
7. *esos*   The masculine plural form of the demonstrative adjective is used because it modifies *porcentajes*.
8. *dichas*   The feminine form of the past participle is used because it functions as an adjective modifying the word *materias*.
9. *realicen*   The present subjunctive is used because it occurs in a dependent adverbial clause after *para que*.
10. *Conociendo*   The present participle functions as an absolute. An absolute construction means that the present participle refers to the whole sentence that follows it.

GROUP SEVEN

La Ley Civil ____(1)____ ayuda en ____(2)____ modo a que las parejas ____(3)____ se lo ____(4)____ un poco más antes de presentar la demanda de divorcio: el matrimonio entra de nuevo en vigor si los separados vuelven a convivir. Si a pesar de todo el divorcio se presenta como la opción más ____(5)____, hay que ____(6)____ que ____(7)____ un año desde que se firmó la solicitud de separación. No es necesario que se haya ____(8)____ sentencia. También se puede acceder al divorcio sin una separación previa, aunque ____(9)____ transcurrir dos años y ____(10)____ las causas debidamente.

1. _____
   (español)

2. _____
   (cierto)

3. _____
   (separado)

4. _____
   (pensar)

5. _____
   (aconsejable)

6. _____
   (esperar)

7. _____
   (transcurrir)

8. _____
   (dictado)

9. _____
   (deber)

10. _____
   (acreditar)

Answers and Answer Explanations for Group Seven

1. *española* This adjective modifies *ley*, which is a feminine singular noun. The form *español* is the masculine singular form of the adjective of nationality, and thus does not change, but the feminine form adds an *a*.

2. *cierto* This adjective modifies *modo*, which is a masculine singular noun; therefore, there is no change in the form.

3. *separadas* This adjective modifies *parejas*, which is feminine plural. The adjective must also be feminine plural.

4. *piensen* This verb occurs in an adverbial clause introduced by the conjunction, *a que*, which indicates purpose or cause. The subjunctive is always used after this adverbial conjunction.

5. *aconsejable* Adjectives that end in *-ble* do not change the ending to make them agree in gender. But if the noun had been plural, the ending on this adjective would have been made plural by adding *-s*.

6. *esperar* Even though this verb comes after *que*, in this case it is part of a modismo. *Hay que* is always followed by the infinitive form of the verb and expresses impersonal obligation.

7. *transcurra* The present subjunctive is used because *hay que esperar* is considered an impersonal expression. *Transcurra* occurs in a dependent noun clause, introduced by *que* after an impersonal expression in the main clause.

8. *dictado* The past participle in this case functions verbally. The invariable form of the past participle is always used after *haber*; therefore, the ending is *-o*.

9. *deben* The conjunction *aunque* can take either the indicative or the subjunctive, depending on the degree of uncertainty about the veracity of the statement. In this case the context makes it rather plain that according to the spirit of the law governing divorce, couples ought to wait two years before filing. When no uncertainty is implied, the indicative is used.

10. *acreditar* The infinitive is used because the verb functions as the object of another verb. *Deben* in this case functions as a modal verb, which means that another verb is needed to complete the meaning of *deber*. The verb *transcurrir* is also used as an object of the modal verb, and the conjunction *y* indicates that the two verbs form a compound object.

GROUP EIGHT

Por fin, a ____(1)____ dos días de navegación, el buque ____(2)____ en la enseñada de Labadee, ____(3)____ isla arrendada por los armadores para diversión de su clientela que, ____(4)____ de una moneda especialmente ____(5)____ para el crucero, podía comprar caracolas marinas y corales ____(6)____ de Taiwan, sin ____(7)____ las botellas de *Coca-Cola*. Un grupo de tambores y bidones musicales recibía en fila a ____(8)____ turistas. Luego de una sesión intensa de sol, la misma charanga caribeña les ____(9)____ después de horas en idéntica formación, aunque ____(10)____ la voluntad.

1. _____
    (el)
2. _____
    (fondear)
3. _____
    (diminuto)
4. _____
    (provisto)
5. _____
    (acuñado)
6. _____
    (traído)
7. _____
    (olvidar)
8. _____
    (el)
9. _____
    (despedir)
10. _____
    (pedir)

Answers and Answer Explanations for Group Eight

1. *los*   This definite article modifies *días*, which is a masculine plural noun. Even though *día* ends in *a*, it is masculine.
2. *fondeó*   The preterite indicative is used because the action is completed in the past. It is the beginning of the narrative on what happened when the cruise ship arrived at the port of call. Even if you do not know what the verb means, the use of the preterite is obvious from the words *por fin* and *dos días*.
3. *diminuta*   This adjective modifies *isla*, which is feminine singular; therefore *diminuta* is used in the feminine singular form.
4. *provista*   This adjective refers back to *clientela*, which is a feminine singular noun.
5. *acuñada*   This adjective modifies *moneda*, which is feminine singular. Even if the meaning of *acuñada* is unknown, knowing that *moneda* is feminine singular provides enough information to arrive at the correct answer.
6. *traídos*   This past participle used as an adjective refers to both *caracolas* and to *corales*. Since one of the nouns is feminine and the other masculine, the masculine plural form of the adjective is used.
7. *olvidar*   This verb occurs after a preposition, in which case the infinitive form of the verb is always used.
8. *los*   The noun *turistas* is one of those nouns that ends with an invariable form, *-ista*, *-istas*. The rule for mixed gender groups means that the masculine plural article should be used with *turistas*.

9. *despedía*   This verb is frequently a reflexive verb. In this case, however, the subject is *charanga*, a third person singular subject, and the object pronoun, *les*, is a third person plural pronoun. The imperfect is used because the action is described and there is no reference to the beginning and/or the end of the action stated in the passage.

10. *pidiendo*   The present participle occurs as an adverb describing manner in an explanatory clause, introduced by *aunque*. The conjunction *aunque* can also be followed by a conjugated verb. In this sentence, the present participle is used to avoid repetition of sentence structure. The implied meaning of the present participle in this case is *pedía*.

GROUP NINE

Se había producido una estampida entre los burlangas, y cada _____(1)_____ de ellos encontró refugio en los rincones más insospechados mientras los ___(2)___ iban ___(3)___ el garrito patas arriba con su furor ___(4)___ de manifestarse ante Luisito, el Nabo, que estaba ___(5)___ detrás de una cortina. Parecía que lo ___(6)___ reconocido por el olfato, y hacia él se ___(7)___ ambas fieras a un tiempo, pero el joven atracador vestido de esmoquin tuvo los reflejos a punto para sacar la recortada del armario, y sin pensarlo nada ___(8)___ un par de disparos que fueron suficientes. En medio de un charco de sangre quedaron ___(9)___ dos hombres desconocidos que habían ___(10)___ los sicarios transformados en cerdos por la dama Georgina.

1. _____ (uno)
2. _____ (jabalí)
3. _____ (poner)
4. _____ (tratar)
5. _____ (esconder)
6. _____ (haber)
7. _____ (abatir)
8. _____ (soltar)
9. _____ (tumbado)
10. _____ (ser)

Answers and Answer Explanations for Group Nine

1. *uno*   The noun *burlangas* is masculine, as is indicated by the definite article, *los*. *Uno* refers to *burlanga*. The verb *encontró* is singular, which indicates that *uno* must be third person singular.

2. *jabalíes*   The plural of words that end with a stressed -í is formed by adding -es. The written accent is retained.

3. *poniendo*   The present participle (*gerundio* in Spanish) is used as an adverb in order to describe how they went. After verbs of motion and perception the present participle is frequently used adverbially.

4. *tratando*   The present participle is used here to describe further how they went, even though no conjunction is used to indicate that the structure is compound.

5. *escondido*   The past participle is used as an adjective, that is masculine singular in this case because it refers to Luisito, el Nabo.

6. *habían*   The subject of this verb is *los jabalíes*, who are pursuing Luisito, el Nabo. The imperfect form of the verb is used (the pluperfect is indicated by the past participle *reconocido*) because the action is described, not narrated.

7. *abatieron*   The verb is used in the preterite in this case because it narrates, or retells, the action when the wild boars finally located their quarry.

8. *soltó*   The subject of the verb is the young hunter, *el joven atracador*, who had the presence of mind, *tuvo los reflejos*, to shoot at the *jabalíes*. The preterite is used because the action is begun and completed at a definite moment in time in the past.

9. *tumbados*   The past participle in this case refers back to the *jabalíes*, as is indicated by the use of the third person plural of the verb *quedaron*. The past participle is masculine because *jabalíes* is a masculine plural noun.

10. *sido*   The pluperfect is used because the time frame indicated is prior to a point of time in the past, when they had been shot by the young hunter. *Sido* is the past participle that must follow the helping verb *haber*.

GROUP TEN

Del mismo modo, hoy nos _____(1)_____ por el abandono de las relaciones

_____(2)_____. El tocadiscos, la radio, la televisión y el vídeo han ido

_____(3)_____ a las gentes en sus casas y _____(4)_____ el ocio en onanismo.

Las computadoras y el fax pueden lograr que las personas ni siquiera

se _____(5)_____ que juntar para el trabajo. Cada vez se vive más en la

soledad, en la unidad aislada, en el individuo. Hoy todo _____(6)_____ nos

parece terrible, pero quizás dentro de un par de siglos los humanos

_____(7)_____ hacia atrás y se pregunten: "Y esos bárbaros del siglo XX,

¿cómo _____(8)_____ vivir así de _____(9)_____, así de mezclados? ¿Cómo

podían necesitar el contacto sucio y ancestral de los amigos? ¿Cómo

se las arreglaban para trabajar en _____(10)_____ caos invasor de una

oficina?"

1. _____
   (doler)

2. _____
   (interpersonal)

3. _____
   (encerrar)

4. _____
   (convertir)

5. _____
   (tener)

6. _____
   (este)

7. _____
   (mirar)

8. _____
   (poder)

9. _____
   (promiscuo)

10. _____
   (el)

Answers and Answer Explanations for Group Ten

1. *dolemos* The verb is used in the first person plural in this case because it is reflexive. Frequently the indirect object pronoun is used with *doler* and the subject of the verb is whatever it is that causes the hurt. But in this instance the reflexive is indicated because *doler* is followed by the prepositional phrase, *por el abandono*. Farther down in the passage, the subject, *we*, is indicated again in the phrase, *Todo esto nos parece* . . . . This is an example of a passage that needs to be read in its entirety before the fill-ins are begun; otherwise, subtleties such as the subject, or the narrative voice in this passage, would be missed.

2. *interpersonales* The adjectives that end with *-l* can only agree in number with the nouns they modify, not gender. The adjective modifies *relaciones,* not *abandono.*

3. *encerrando* The present participle is used to describe the action of the verb, which is a verb of motion, *han ido.*

4. *convirtiendo* This present participle, like *encerrando,* describes the action of the verb, which is indicated by the conjunction *y. Convertir* is a Class II stem changing verb, which accounts for the change of the *e* to *i* in the stem of the present participle.

5. *tengan* The expression *pueden lograr* indicated volition (request, will, permission) in the main clause, so the subjunctive is needed in the dependent clause.

6. *esto* The neuter form of the demonstrative pronoun is used because it refers to the preceding concept, not to any noun in particular. In the last portion of the passage, the speaker tries to put the current perception of isolation in perspective by asking rhetorically if what we consider modern will not appear as strange to people of the next century.

7. *miren* The present subjunctive is used after *quizás* to express conjecture. *Quizás* indicates the uncertainty of the speaker. Also, *pregunten* is in the subjunctive, indicating probability.

8. *podrían* The conditional is used to express probability or conjecture in the past. From the perspective of the future, the people who ask the question could not know how or why present-day people do and think the way they do, a perspective communicated by the conditional tense.

9. *promiscuos* The adjective is plural because it refers to *esos bárbaros.*

10. *el* *Caos* is a masculine singular noun.

Track Listing

Track Number   Track Title

PRACTICE EXERCISES

**Section I, Part B—Listening Comprehension:
Print and Audio Text (Combined)**

Track 1: Selección #1

Track 2: Selección #2

Track 3: Selección #3

Track 4: Selección #4

Track 5: Selección #5

Track 6: Selección #6

Track 7: Selección #7

Track 8: Selección #8

Track 9: Selección #9

Track 10: Selección #10

Section I, Part B—Listening Comprehension

Track 11: Selección #1

Track 12: Selección #2

Track 13: Selección #3

Track 14: Selección #4

Track 15: Selección #5

Track 16: Selección #6

Track 17: Selección #7

Track 18: Selección #8

Track 19: Selección #9

Track 20: Selección #10

Track 21: Selección #11

Track 22: Selección #12

**Section II, Part A2—Presentational Writing:
Argumentative Essay**

Track 23: Sample Prompt

Track 24: Ensayo #1

Track 25: Ensayo #2

Track 26: Ensayo #3

Track 27: Ensayo #4

Track 28: Ensayo #5

Track 29: Ensayo #6

Track 30: Ensayo #7

Track 31: Ensayo #8

Track 32: Ensayo #9

Track 33: Ensayo #10

Track Number   Track Title

Interpersonal Speaking

Track 34: Sample Script

Track 35: Conversación #1

Track 36: Conversación #2

Track 37: Conversación #3

Track 38: Conversación #4

Track 39: Conversación #5

Track 40: Conversación #6

Track 41: Conversación #7

Track 42: Conversación #8

Track 43: Conversación #9

Track 44: Conversación #10

PRACTICE TEST 1

**Section 1, Part B—Interpretive Communication:
Print and Audio Text (Combined)**

Track 45: Selección #1

Track 46: Selección #2

Track 47: Selección #3

Track 48: Selección #4

Track 49: Selección #5

Section II—Presentational Writing: Argumentative Essay

Track 50

Section II—Interpersonal Speaking: Conversation

Track 51

PRACTICE TEST 2

**Section 1, Part B—Interpretive Communication:
Print and Audio Text (Combined)**

Track 52: Selección #1

Track 53: Selección #2

Track 54: Selección #3

Track 55: Selección #4

Track 56: Selección #5

Section II—Presentational Writing: Argumentative Essay

Track 57

Section II—Interpersonal Speaking: Conversation

Track 58